Keep this book. You will
need it and use it throughout
your career.

Contemporary
Club Management

Educational Institute Courses

Introductory

INTRODUCTION TO THE HOSPITALITY INDUSTRY
Fourth Edition
Gerald W. Lattin

AN INTRODUCTION TO HOSPITALITY TODAY
Third Edition
Rocco M. Angelo, Andrew N. Vladimir

TOURISM AND THE HOSPITALITY INDUSTRY
Joseph D. Fridgen

Rooms Division

FRONT OFFICE PROCEDURES
Fifth Edition
Michael L. Kasavana, Richard M. Brooks

HOUSEKEEPING MANAGEMENT
Second Edition
Margaret M. Kappa, Aleta Nitschke, Patricia B. Schappert

Human Resources

HOSPITALITY SUPERVISION
Second Edition
Raphael R. Kavanaugh, Jack D. Ninemeier

HOSPITALITY INDUSTRY TRAINING
Second Edition
Lewis C. Forrest, Jr.

HUMAN RESOURCES MANAGEMENT
Second Edition
Robert H. Woods

Marketing and Sales

MARKETING OF HOSPITALITY SERVICES
William Lazer, Roger Layton

HOSPITALITY SALES AND MARKETING
Third Edition
James R. Abbey

CONVENTION MANAGEMENT AND SERVICE
Fifth Edition
Milton T. Astroff, James R. Abbey

MARKETING IN THE HOSPITALITY INDUSTRY
Third Edition
Ronald A. Nykiel

Accounting

UNDERSTANDING HOSPITALITY ACCOUNTING I
Fourth Edition
Raymond Cote

UNDERSTANDING HOSPITALITY ACCOUNTING II
Third Edition
Raymond Cote

BASIC FINANCIAL ACCOUNTING FOR THE HOSPITALITY INDUSTRY
Raymond S. Schmidgall, James W. Damitio

MANAGERIAL ACCOUNTING FOR THE HOSPITALITY INDUSTRY
Fourth Edition
Raymond S. Schmidgall

Food and Beverage

FOOD AND BEVERAGE MANAGEMENT
Second Edition
Jack D. Ninemeier

QUALITY SANITATION MANAGEMENT
Ronald F. Cichy

FOOD PRODUCTION PRINCIPLES
Jerald W. Chesser

FOOD AND BEVERAGE SERVICE
Second Edition
Ronald F. Cichy, Paul E. Wise

HOSPITALITY PURCHASING MANAGEMENT
William P. Virts

BAR AND BEVERAGE MANAGEMENT
Lendal H. Kotschevar, Mary L. Tanke

FOOD AND BEVERAGE CONTROLS
Fourth Edition
Jack D. Ninemeier

General Hospitality Management

HOTEL/MOTEL SECURITY MANAGEMENT
Raymond C. Ellis, Jr., Security Committee of AH&MA

HOSPITALITY LAW
Third Edition
Jack P. Jefferies

RESORT MANAGEMENT
Second Edition
Chuck Y. Gee

INTERNATIONAL HOTEL MANAGEMENT
Chuck Y. Gee

HOSPITALITY INDUSTRY COMPUTER SYSTEMS
Third Edition
Michael L. Kasavana, John J. Cahill

MANAGING FOR QUALITY IN THE HOSPITALITY INDUSTRY
Robert H. Woods, Judy Z. King

CONTEMPORARY CLUB MANAGEMENT
Edited by Joe Perdue for the Club Managers Association of America

Engineering and Facilities Management

FACILITIES MANAGEMENT
David M. Stipanuk, Harold Roffman

HOSPITALITY INDUSTRY ENGINEERING SYSTEMS
Michael H. Redlin, David M. Stipanuk

HOSPITALITY ENERGY AND WATER MANAGEMENT
Robert E. Aulbach

Contemporary
Club Management

**Edited by Joe Perdue, CCM, CHE
for the Club Managers Association
of America**

EDUCATIONAL INSTITUTE
American Hotel & Motel Association

Disclaimer

This publication is designed to provide accurate and authoritative information in regard to the subject matter covered. It is sold with the understanding that the publisher is not engaged in rendering legal, accounting, or other professional service. If legal advice or other expert assistance is required, the services of a competent professional person should be sought.

—*From the Declaration of Principles jointly adopted by the American Bar Association and a Committee of Publishers and Associations*

The authors are solely responsible for the contents of this publication. All views expressed herein are solely those of the authors and do not necessarily reflect the views of the Club Managers Association of America (CMAA), the Educational Institute of the American Hotel & Motel Association (the Institute), or the American Hotel & Motel Association (AH&MA).

Nothing contained in this publication shall constitute a standard, an endorsement, or a recommendation of CMAA, the Institute, or AH&MA. CMAA, the Institute, and AH&MA disclaim any liability with respect to the use of any information, procedure, or product, or reliance thereon by any member of the hospitality industry.

©Copyright 1997
By the Club Managers Association of America
1733 King Street
Alexandria, Virginia 22314
and the
Educational Institute of the
American Hotel & Motel Association
2113 N. High Street
Lansing, Michigan 48906

The Educational Institute of the American Hotel & Motel Association is a nonprofit educational foundation.

Printed in the United States of America
3 4 5 6 7 8 9 10 01 00 99 98

Library of Congress Cataloging-in-Publication Data
Contemporary club management/edited by Joe Perdue . . . [et al.].
    p. cm.
    Includes bibliographical references and index.
    ISBN 0-86612-168-4
    1. Clubs—Management. 2. Country clubs—Management. 3. Golf courses—Management. 4. Restaurant operations. 5. Total quality management. I. Perdue, Joe. II. American Hotel & Motel Association. Educational Institute.
TX911.3.M27C64 1997   97–25007
647.9473'05'068—dc21   CIP

Cover photograph courtesy of Walter R. Allen, president of Ferry, Hayes & Allen Designers, Inc., Atlanta, Georgia

Cover design by Stacy Duwe, The McNenly Group, Lansing, Michigan

Contents

Congratulations. . .

You have a running start on a fast-track career!

Developed through the input of industry and academic experts, this course gives you the know-how hospitality employers demand. Upon course completion, you will earn the respected American Hotel & Motel Association certificate that ensures instant recognition worldwide. It is your link with the global hospitality industry.

You can use your AH&MA certificate to show that your learning experiences have bridged the gap between industry and academia. You will have proof that you have met industry-driven competencies and that you know how to apply your knowledge to actual hospitality work situations.

By earning your course certificate, you also take a step toward completing the highly respected learning programs—Certificates of Specialization, the Hospitality Operations Certificate, and the Hospitality Management Diploma—that raise your professional development to a higher level. Certificates from these programs greatly enhance your credentials, and a permanent record of your course and program completion is maintained by the Educational Institute.

We commend you for taking this important step. Turn to the Educational Institute for additional resources that will help you stay ahead of your competition.

Preface

Contemporary Club Management is the product of a close partnership between club industry professionals and hospitality educators. The Club Managers Association of America's certification program for club managers guided the development of the book's content. Once the book's subject areas were identified, hospitality educators were selected to develop detailed chapter outlines and managerial competency statements. These authors were chosen for their leadership and proven experience in hospitality education in the area of club management. Then, a task force of seasoned club managers reviewed and refined each chapter's outline and competency statements, validating the content and providing authors with suggestions for making the chapters even more club specific. At that point, the approved outlines and competencies were sent back to the authors and the writing began. Once the chapters were written and sent in, editors at the Educational Institute of the American Hotel & Motel Association assisted me in working with the authors to make sure the chapters were as informative and easy to read and understand as possible. Rest assured that we kept the reader foremost in our minds as we worked to put the finishing touches on each chapter.

The text is divided into three parts. Part I introduces readers to the world of private clubs. Part II discusses what it takes for club managers to truly lead their clubs and their staff members. The chapters in Part III cover various club operational areas and topics—marketing, human resources, food and beverage outlets, computers, and so on.

Throughout the text, interviews of club industry professionals provide students with glimpses into the world of club operations. Case studies outline real-life dilemmas faced by club managers and challenge students to come up with workable and creative solutions. Definitions of key chapter terms are conveniently located at the end of each chapter, along with review questions and a review quiz to help students evaluate their knowledge of the material. An additional-reading list at the end of each chapter points readers to more information. Some chapters also include a list of Internet sites for those readers with access to the Internet.

Managing a private club requires knowledge, skills, flexibility, vision, diplomacy, stamina, empathy, patience, integrity, common sense, uncommon energy, and—above all—a never-ending dedication to providing extraordinary service to club members each and every day. The hope of everyone who worked on *Contemporary Club Management* is that readers will find much that will inform, challenge, and inspire them in its pages.

Acknowledgments

A textbook is never the work of just one person; this book is certainly no exception, and in fact is perhaps an extraordinary example of the dedication it takes from so many individuals to turn a book from an idea into a reality.

First, I would like to thank the industry professionals who were in on the planning stages of the book—the members of the CMAA Task Force: G. Mead Grady, CCM, Peachtree Golf Club, Atlanta, Georgia; Brian R. Kroh, CCM, John's Island Club, Vero Beach, Florida; Jonathan F. McCabe, CCM, Union League Club of Chicago, Chicago, Illinois; C. Douglas Postler, CCM, The Camargo Club, Cincinnati, Ohio; Sally Burns Rambo, CCM, former general manager (now retired) of the Lakewood Country Club, Dallas, Texas; and Michael Wheeler, CCM, Westmoreland Country Club, Wilmette, Illinois. These dedicated club managers critiqued the chapter outlines and competencies, provided photos and other materials for the text, and identified professionals within the industry to be interviewed for the book.

Next I would like to thank the authors of the various chapters, who wrote and polished their chapters while teaching classes, serving on committees, and handling the myriad other tasks that make up a college professor's professional life. Their hard work and openness to suggestions were greatly appreciated.

I would also like to thank the club managers and other club industry professionals who agreed to be interviewed for this book. Their insights and stories from the front lines gave the book valuable real-world perspectives.

A special thank you to the three club professionals who took time out of their busy schedules to fly to East Lansing and spend a few days at the Educational Institute developing some of the book's industry-based case studies: Cathy Gustafson, CCM, former general manager of the Faculty House, Columbia, South Carolina, and now a professor at the University of South Carolina, Columbia, South Carolina; Kurt D. Kuebler, CCM, Vice President and General Manager of The Desert Highlands Association, Scottsdale, Arizona; and William A. Schulz, MCM, General Manager, Houston Country Club, Houston, Texas, and past president of the Club Managers Association of America.

Thank you also to Walter R. Allen, president of Ferry, Hayes & Allen Designers, Inc., Atlanta, Georgia, and J. William Kessler, CCM, general manager of The Commerce Club, Atlanta, Georgia, for the picture of the Commerce Club library that appears on the cover.

A special thank you to James B. Singerling, CCM, CEC, and the staff of the Club Managers Association of America, who provided constant support for this project.

And, last but not least, thank you to three individuals at the Educational Institute for their tremendous help with this textbook: to George Glazer, Senior Vice President of Publications, for his vision and support in seeing the project through; to Bridgette Redman, for her very significant contributions to Chapter 2; and to Jim Purvis, Writer/Editor, whose dedication to quality and excellence made him a perfect choice to work on a textbook for the club industry, an industry filled with people dedicated to quality and excellence.

Joe Perdue, CCM, CHE
Club Managers Association of America
Alexandria, Virginia

Study Tips for Users of Educational Institute Courses

Learning is a skill, like many other activities. Although you may be familiar with many of the following study tips, we want to reinforce their usefulness.

Your Attitude Makes a Difference

If you want to learn, you will: it's as simple as that. Your attitude will go a long way in determining whether or not you do well in this course. We want to help you succeed.

Plan and Organize to Learn

- Set up a regular time and place for study. Make sure you won't be disturbed or distracted.

- Decide ahead of time how much you want to accomplish during each study session. Remember to keep your study sessions brief; don't try to do too much at one time.

Read the Course Text to Learn

- *Before* you read each chapter, read the chapter outline and the competencies. Notice that each competency has page numbers that indicate where you can find the concepts and issues related to it. If there is a summary at the end of the chapter, you should read it to get a feel for what the chapter is about.

- Then, go back to the beginning of the chapter and *carefully* read, focusing on the material included in the competencies and asking yourself such questions as:

  —Do I understand the material?

  —How can I use this information now or in the future?

- Make notes in margins and highlight or underline important sections to help you as you study. Read a section first, then go back over it to mark important points.

- Keep a dictionary handy. If you come across an unfamiliar word that is not included in the textbook glossary, look it up in the dictionary.

- Read as much as you can. The more you read, the better you read.

Testing Your Knowledge

- Test questions developed by the Educational Institute for this course are designed to measure your knowledge of the material.

- End-of-the-chapter Review Quizzes help you find out how well you have studied the material. They indicate where additional study may be needed. Review Quizzes are also helpful in studying for other tests.

- Prepare for tests by reviewing:

  —competencies

  —notes

  —outlines

  —questions at the end of each assignment

- Before you begin to take any test, read the test instructions *carefully* and look over the questions.

We hope your experiences in this course will prompt you to undertake other training and educational activities in a planned, career-long program of professional growth and development.

Part I

Introduction

Chapter 1 Outline

What Is a Club?
Ownership of Clubs
    Equity Clubs
    Non-Equity Clubs
Types of Clubs
    Country Clubs
    City Clubs
    Other Types of Clubs
        Military
        Athletic
        University
        Tennis
        Yacht
        Corporate
        Developer-Owned
Club Membership
    Membership Categories
        Regular
        Social
        Nonresident
        Junior
        Senior
        Other
    Reciprocity
    Selection Process
    Member Discipline
Club Organizational Structure
    Equity Clubs
        Board of Directors
        Executive Committee
        Other Club Committees
        General Manager
        Club Professionals
        Department Managers
        Employees
    Non-Equity Clubs

Competencies

1. Describe the nature and appeal of a private club, explain how private clubs are owned, and describe types of clubs. (pp. 3–11)

2. List and describe club membership categories, explain reciprocity, describe a typical member-selection process, and summarize membership discipline procedures. (pp. 11–16)

3. Describe the organizational structure for equity clubs, and summarize the work of a club's board of directors, executive committee, and other club committees. (pp. 16–23)

4. Summarize the duties of a club's general manager, club professionals, and typical department managers, explain the role of club employees, and summarize the organizational structure of non-equity clubs. (pp. 23–31)

Overview of Club Operations

This chapter was written and contributed by Joe Perdue, Vice President, Club Managers Association of America, Alexandria, Virginia.

IN 1890, APPLYING FOR A CHARTER for the Philadelphia Country Club, John C. Bullitt wrote the following:

> Most of the [club's] subscribers are heads of families, the induce-
> ment to whom is that they, as well as their wives and sons and
> daughters, can visit the club for the purpose of recreation and
> pleasure without encountering any person or anything which
> will in the least degree be inconsistent with good behavior or
> good manners.[1]

This statement contains the essence of what private clubs are all about. Clubs today, however, face challenges that did not exist 100 years ago. Life is more complex and so are clubs and club management. That is why today's clubs need well-educated, professional club managers. In this chapter we will discuss the ownership of clubs, introduce you to various types of clubs, summarize club membership options, and conclude with a section on the organizational structures of clubs and the club managers and professionals who use their expertise to make private clubs such special places for their members.

What Is a Club?

A **private club** is a place where people with a common bond of some type—similar interests, experiences, backgrounds, professions, and so on—can congregate for social and recreational purposes. By definition, a private club is a place that is not open to the public; an individual must be accepted by the rest of the membership before he or she may join. Once someone is accepted, he or she usually must pay an initiation fee and monthly membership dues. Some clubs also have minimum spending requirements for members (members must spend a certain amount of money each month or year in the club's food and beverage outlets, for example).

People join private clubs for a variety of reasons. Some like the exclusive atmosphere of some clubs and see club membership as a statement of social position. Others join clubs because of the recreational facilities, or because the club is convenient for them in some way: perhaps the club is close to their home or business, or

3

they appreciate the fact that they are not faced with long waits to be seated at the club's dining facilities or don't have as much trouble getting a golf tee time at their club as they would at a public golf course. Some people see club membership as a way to get ahead in business, because other people in their professions are also members of their clubs or because their clubs give them an impressive place to entertain business clients. Some people are given club memberships by their companies as an employment perk. Other people join clubs because their parents and grandparents were club members and club membership is a family tradition. And still others simply enjoy the personal recognition and service they receive at a private club.

Private clubs are built for many reasons. U.S. clubs that began in the nineteenth century or earlier were often started by a small group of individuals who decided to each put up a sum of money to buy a piece of land or an already-existing building and begin a club for purely social reasons. Many modern-day private clubs are built by developers as a way to help them sell homes; the club and its golf course are the centerpiece of a housing development, and individuals who buy the homes surrounding the club either are automatically members of the club or have the option to become members.

Part of the appeal of private clubs is their unique environment. Private clubs tend to have the best of furnishings and impressive, well-kept grounds. The goal of most private clubs is to provide a level of service that is rarely found in public facilities. A member's club is a place where the member is called by name and is treated as someone special; a club is the member's home-away-from-home.

All of a club's facilities face competition from public facilities. Competitors of a club's food and beverage outlets are independent gourmet restaurants, family-dining chain restaurants, and even fast-food restaurants (if a club has a fast-food type of food and beverage outlet). Public golf courses compete with a club's golf facilities. Public health clubs, including many large chain operations, compete with the fitness facilities of private clubs. Luxury resorts and hotels pamper their guests with extraordinary service and compete with private clubs for a club member's discretionary dollars. All of these competitive pressures make it essential that private clubs be led by professional managers who can provide quality club products and the extraordinary level of service members want, at a cost members perceive as giving their club membership high value.

Ownership of Clubs

Private clubs are owned in one of two ways: they are either member-owned clubs, called equity clubs, or non-member-owned clubs, called non-equity clubs. Non-equity clubs may be owned by real-estate developers, corporations, or other owners.

Equity Clubs

Equity clubs are clubs owned by their members and governed by a board of directors elected by the members. In effect, the members are not just "customers," but also shareholders (they own equity in the club). Each member has a vote when it comes to electing board members or deciding major club issues (unless the member

The Origins of Private Clubs

Although English social clubs and the golf club of St. Andrews in Scotland are the direct forerunners of city clubs and country clubs in the United States, the origins of clubs extend back to ancient times. For example, the Roman baths can be viewed as clubs, in the sense that the baths were establishments run by managers in which selected groups of people met with their peers for recreational and social purposes. In some respects, the merchant and craft guilds of medieval Europe resembled clubs.

Clubs have been an integral part of the social fabric of upper-class English society for centuries. The origins of English city clubs lie in the coffeehouses that sprang up in the mid-seventeenth century with the importation of coffee. The first coffeehouses were formed at three major English universities: Oxford, All Souls, and Cambridge. The Oxford coffeehouse was the first to be called a club.

Early London city clubs featured extensive libraries and cultivated a quiet, relaxed atmosphere where members could read the *Times* or hold quiet conversations. Venerable London clubs such as White's and the Marlborough Club are still open today, having survived economic depressions, political upheavals, radical social changes, and two world wars.

The Royal and Ancient Golf Club of St. Andrews, established in Edinburgh in 1754, is world renowned for its contributions to the game of golf; the club's committees have formulated and periodically updated the rules of golf during the more than 200 years of the club's existence. This club is considered the first country club.

Clubs in the United States

The first U.S. city clubs were established in the Colonies during the eighteenth century. These were loosely formed men-only social clubs that met in lodges or taverns, where the men drank rum and other alcoholic beverages and discussed the news of the day.

A wave of city-club building occurred in the mid-nineteenth century. The Somerset Club in Boston was founded in 1842; the San Francisco Commercial Club and Honolulu's Pacific Club were founded in 1851. The Pacific-Union Club in San Francisco dates from 1852, Delaware's Wilmington Club from 1859. The Olympic Club in San Francisco, the Union Leagues in Philadelphia and New York City, and the Rochester Club in Rochester, New York, were all organized during the Civil War. Then as now, U.S. city clubs were organized primarily to provide a place for individuals with similar interests to dine and socialize together.

The Country Club in Brookline, Massachusetts, founded in 1882 with antecedents to 1860, is generally considered the oldest U.S. country club. Until the 1940s, country clubs were reserved for the most affluent members of U.S. society; applicants were carefully screened by powerful membership committees, and merely submitting one's name for membership sometimes required tremendous influence. However, during World War II, hundreds of thousands of ordinary servicemen were exposed to the game of golf on military bases, and after the war they generated a demand for public golf courses and affordable clubs with golf facilities. This led to the vast country club construction programs of the sixties, seventies, and eighties. Today country club membership is within the reach of many more Americans than in the past.

Sources: Ted E. White and Larry C. Gerstner, *Club Operations and Management*, 2d ed. (New York: VNR, 1991), pp. 5–9; *Club Management Operations*, 4th ed. (Dubuque, Iowa: Kendall/Hunt, 1989), p. 2; and Rocco M. Angelo and Andrew N. Vladimir, *Hospitality Today: An Introduction*, 2d ed. (East Lansing, Mich.: Educational Institute of the American Hotel & Motel Association, 1994), p. 207.

Club Ownership

Equity Clubs—In equity clubs, each regular member is like a shareholder in a corporation, and the members collectively own the club. Members write the club's bylaws, make up the committees, and sit on the club's board of directors. All major policy decisions and rules are ultimately approved either by the members or their elected representatives on the board of directors. The managers of equity clubs work for the members.

Non-Equity Clubs—In non-equity clubs, an individual or a corporation—not the members—owns the club, and members generally do not have much say in the club's operations or in major policy decisions. The manager of a non-equity club works for the club's owner, not the club's members.

Source: Adapted from "Tax Planning for the Changing Economic Environment in Clubs," prepared by Condon, O'Meara, McGinty & Donnelly, LLP, for the 1997 World Conference on Club Management.

has purchased a type of membership that does not include voting rights). The managers of equity clubs work directly for the members, since the members own the club. Equity clubs are usually established as nonprofit corporations that are exempt from federal income taxes and some state and local taxes. Most private clubs are equity clubs.

Non-Equity Clubs

Non-equity clubs represent another form of ownership; the assets of the club are owned by an individual or a corporation, not the club's members, and the members' control over the club is much more limited. Members do not often participate in major policy decisions, as they do in equity clubs, and club managers in non-equity clubs work for the club's owners, not the members. Non-equity clubs typically are not tax-exempt; they are usually for-profit organizations. Most non-equity clubs are corporate clubs or developer-owned clubs.

Types of Clubs

Clubs are hard to categorize, because there can be so much variation among clubs within a category, and because so many clubs can be categorized in more than one way (an athletic club is also usually a city club, for example). Most clubs fall into one of two broad categories: country clubs or city clubs. While this is helpful, these categories refer primarily to location and only hint at the nature of the clubs. However, for purposes of discussion, it is useful to divide clubs into three categories: country clubs, city clubs, and "other" or specialty clubs. (While reading the following sections, keep in mind that the club descriptions are general in nature and that, as just mentioned, there are many variations among the clubs in each category.)

Country Clubs

A **country club** is a club that has a clubhouse and enough acreage for a golf course; most country clubs have other sports facilities as well. Country clubs are the most common type of private club in the United States, numbering somewhere between

Exhibit 1   Sample Organization Chart for a Small Country Club

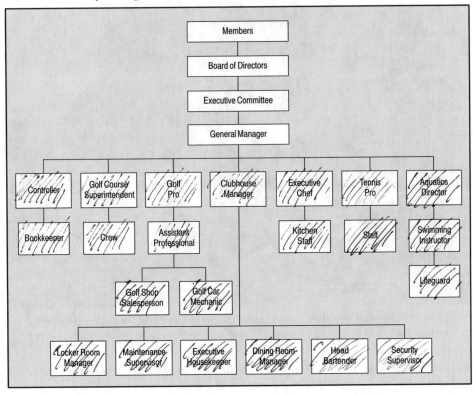

6,000 and 7,000. The average country club has 646 members, with an average initiation fee of $16,142 and average monthly dues of $266.[2] See Exhibit 1 for a sample organization chart for a small country club.

In addition to a golf course and its ancillary facilities (which typically include a driving range, chipping and putting practice areas, golf car barns, and sheds for golf course maintenance equipment), most country clubs have tennis courts and swimming pools for member use, and may also have such varied recreational facilities as the following:

- A fitness center with exercise rooms, weight-lifting areas, and courts for basketball, volleyball, squash, racquetball, and handball
- Billiard rooms
- Sauna and steam rooms
- Croquet areas and areas for other lawn games
- Stables and trails for horseback riding
- Skeet, archery, rifle, and pistol ranges
- Skating rinks
- Cross-country skiing trails

A country club's tennis pro shop sells tennis equipment, apparel, and other items related to tennis. (Courtesy of Patrick McKenna, CCM, and The Landings Club, Inc., Savannah, Georgia)

A country club's recreational facilities are limited only by what its members want and what they can afford. For example, some country clubs have what amount to golf teaching centers, with large indoor driving facilities so that members can practice their swings during the winter months. These centers may include video rooms where members can be filmed swinging a golf club; later they can sit down and watch their videos with the club's golf pro and have their swings critiqued.

In addition to recreational facilities, it is common for country clubs to offer formal and informal dining outlets and a variety of beverage facilities. Country clubs typically have one or more pro shops that sell golf and tennis equipment and apparel, and locker rooms for members who use the club's recreational facilities. Some country clubs have massage rooms in or near the locker rooms. A country club might also have rooms set aside in the clubhouse for members who play cards (bridge, gin rummy, poker, and so on). A few also offer overnight accommodations, though this is more typical for city clubs.

City Clubs

City clubs are the second most common type of private club; there are more than 2,000 city clubs in the United States. The average city club has 1,204 members, with an average initiation fee of $2,521 and average monthly dues of $114.[3] A city club is usually housed in a building or part of a building located within a city or in a suburban office complex. Some city clubs offer only food and beverage services

Exhibit 2   Sample Organization Chart for a City Club

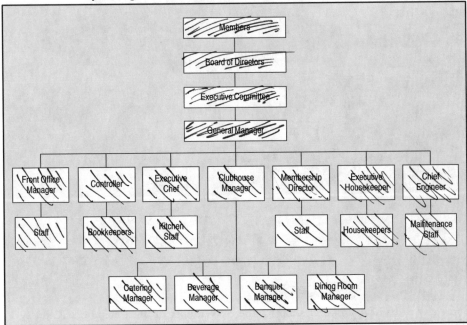

to their members and consist of little more than a restaurant and a bar or cocktail lounge. Other city clubs have multiple food and beverage facilities, meeting rooms, indoor sports facilities (billiard rooms, swimming pools, weight-lifting/fitness facilities, and so on), reading rooms/libraries, and overnight accommodations for members and guests. Very large city clubs might also have parking garages or decks, barber/beauty shops, and floral shops. The main purpose of a city club is to serve the business, entertainment, and social needs of its members in an urban setting. City clubs usually offer fine dining to members and their guests, and may cater special parties and banquets for members. See Exhibit 2 for a sample organization chart for a city club.

Other Types of Clubs

Other types of clubs include military, athletic, university, tennis, yacht, corporate, and developer-owned clubs. (There are other types of clubs as well, such as polo, rowing and paddling, shooting, and swim clubs, but they are relatively rare compared to the clubs discussed in the following sections.)

Military. All branches of the military operate **military clubs** for officers and enlisted personnel. All of these clubs used to be managed by military personnel; however, with the downsizing of the U.S. military, most military clubs are now run by civilian managers. Most of these clubs are similar to city clubs in the facilities and services they offer. Some are more elaborate, however, and offer additional

Some city clubs have a barber shop for the convenience of their members. (Courtesy of Stephen Joyce, CCM, and the Kansas City Club, Kansas City, Missouri)

facilities and services. With the loss of appropriated funding, military clubs must now operate on a profitable or break-even basis.

Athletic. Private **athletic clubs** offer members such fitness and sports facilities as gyms, swimming pools, racquetball and handball courts, weight-lifting areas, and exercise rooms. Many athletic clubs also have food and beverage facilities and operate similarly to city clubs. Like city clubs, some athletic clubs also offer hotel-style overnight rooms for members and their guests. A few athletic clubs even offer golf; these clubs closely resemble country clubs.

University. As the name implies, **university clubs** are clubs for university graduates, faculty, and certain levels of university staff. Most university clubs are for individuals from a single university; others, like the University Club in Seattle, are not affiliated with a single school; you only have to be a university graduate in order to join. Typical facilities for university clubs include dining facilities, meeting and banquet rooms, libraries, and sometimes fitness facilities and overnight accommodations.

Tennis. A **tennis club** is organized around the game of tennis and provides tennis courts and other tennis facilities and services to its members. A tennis club might also have a clubhouse with food and beverage outlets, banquet rooms for member parties, and additional athletic facilities.

Yacht. **Yacht clubs** are located on large bodies of water and are designed for people who own boats or enjoy boating. Some yacht clubs allow only sailboats, others only powerboats, and others allow both. Yacht clubs offer marina services such as wet and dry storage, refueling facilities, and dock services (electricity, sewage disposal facilities, and so on). Some yacht clubs also have a clubhouse and provide food and beverage services for members; some also have a swimming pool and other athletic facilities.

Corporate. Corporate clubs are owned by one or more individuals or a large corporation and are expected to operate at a profit. Members of corporate clubs purchase a membership in the club, not an equity share. A corporate club is usually managed by a general manager hired by and responsible to the owners. Members have little or no say in the operation of a corporate club. If there is a board of governors in a corporate club, it is strictly advisory in nature, as are a corporate club's committees.

There are more than 60 management companies that either own or manage clubs. Some management companies are very large, such as ClubCorp and American Golf, which own or manage hundreds of clubs; on the other end of the spectrum, some management companies own or manage only one club.

The most widely known corporate-club company is ClubCorp. In 1957, Robert H. Dedman started the first of several companies that eventually evolved into the Club Corporation of America (CCA) and was later renamed ClubCorp. ClubCorp owns and operates clubs as well as provides management services to equity (member-owned) clubs. ClubCorp is a multi-faceted company, operating more than 250 clubs, resorts, semi-private and daily-fee golf courses, and real-estate developments worldwide.

A corporate club can also be a single private club owned by a corporation as part of its real-estate holdings or for the purpose of providing a club for the corporation's employees. For example, the DuPont company originally built its own club—the DuPont Country Club—in Wilmington, Delaware, for DuPont employees and their families.

Developer-Owned. As mentioned earlier, many private clubs are built by developers to enhance the attractiveness of a housing development. Usually, developers do not want to retain ownership of such clubs; rather, they seek to maximize their investment by selling the clubs to a club corporation or to the surrounding homeowners through equity conversion programs, turning the clubs into equity (member-owned) clubs. With an equity conversion program, a separate nonprofit corporation is formed to sell club memberships to the development's homeowners. An equity club conversion may be implemented at the beginning of the residential development (an "up-front" conversion), after the sale of a portion of the residential units (a "midterm" conversion), or at a point when most or all of the houses are sold (a "tail-end" conversion). Once developer-owned clubs are turned over to their members, they are organized and operated like other equity clubs.

Club Membership

If someone were to tell you "I'm a member of the ABC Club," you would have to ask him or her several more questions before you would know what kind of privileges the person enjoyed at the club. That is because today many clubs offer a variety of membership options to encourage club membership.

Although clubs tend to be exclusive, they must balance their exclusivity with their need to generate revenue so that they can be operated and maintained in an efficient manner. Clubs also have to take into account the optimum capacities of their facilities, such as their golf courses. Therefore, clubs have created numerous membership categories in addition to the traditional "full membership," which entitles a member to everything the club has to offer but also obligates the member to pay the highest initiation fees and dues. Other membership categories give people an opportunity to join a club for less money, in exchange for enjoying fewer club privileges. This "unbundling" of club services allows individuals or families to join a club and pay for only those facilities and services they really want or will use.

Membership Categories

Because so many membership categories exist within private clubs, in the following sections we will confine our discussion to the most common ones: regular, social, nonresident, junior, and senior. To give you an idea of the large variety of membership categories, we will also briefly mention other, less common memberships.

Regular. A **regular membership,** also referred to as a full, resident, or stock membership, gives the member full use of all of the club's facilities as well as voting rights and the right to hold office. As mentioned earlier, this type of membership has the highest dues and initiation fees. There is also usually an age requirement attached to this type of membership; the minimum age for a regular member varies from club to club but is usually somewhere in the early thirties. This requirement makes it more likely that a regular member has attained a certain business or professional status. In most cases, a regular member's spouse and children can also enjoy all of the club's facilities at no extra cost.

Social. A **social membership,** also called a house membership, gives a member the use of the clubhouse and its facilities, but does not allow the member to use the club's other facilities (golf course, tennis courts, and so on) unless the member pays a user fee. At some clubs, social members are further restricted; they are only allowed to use the club's other facilities on specified "slow" days. Other clubs define their social membership a bit differently; social members are allowed to use the clubhouse and all recreational facilities with the exception of golf.

Nonresident. The **nonresident** membership category is for members who live a certain distance from the club (the distance is specified in the club's bylaws). This membership is usually available for lower dues than the regular membership—the assumption being that, because nonresident members live some distance from the club, they will use the club less frequently than other members. At some clubs, the nonresident category may restrict the number of times the member can use the club within a specified period of time—for example, a nonresident member may only be able to use the club two times a month.

Junior. A **junior membership** is for individuals, usually the children of regular members, who have not yet attained the age required for regular membership but are too old to be afforded membership status on the basis of their parents' membership. Junior members are entitled to use all of the club's facilities, but rarely have

Insider Insights

Albert Armstrong, CCM, General Manager
University Club of Washington, Washington, D.C.

It used to be said that all the rich guys in Washington belonged to the Metropolitan Club, all the smart guys belonged to the Cosmos Club, and all the athletes belonged here. Every club is different. We really don't compete with each other. That's part of what I love about the club business; these other clubs are three blocks away from me, yet we don't compete. Because the people who join there are different from the people who join here.

To me the clubs that are most interesting are the clubs that are multidimensional. Like one of our past presidents said, this club is fabulous because it's an interesting tapestry woven together with a lot of different people, colors, nationalities, and religious and political beliefs. Clubs whose members are all the same are one-dimensional. They're easier to manage, because everyone wants the same thing. Clubs with a diverse membership are a much more interesting challenge.

Many clubs have a tradition of commissioning a portrait of each of their presidents. We never did that, but I always thought that was cool, so one day I thought, let's redo history. Camus said that history is but the version that we have all agreed to. What I thought we should do is start with the first president of our club, William Howard Taft, so we had his portrait painted, based on what he would have looked like when he was club president. Taft is the only American to serve as a president and a chief justice of the United States. When he was club president in 1904 he was also serving as the Secretary of War, the cabinet post now called the Secretary of Defense. Four years later he was elected president of the United States, and the club members escorted him from the clubhouse down to his inaugural speech. We like to say that it was because he was president of the club that he became president of the nation.

Proctor Dougherty, born in 1873, founded the club. He sent out letters to 40 university alumni organizations, all of which were having meetings in separate Washington hotels. He said, let's come together and find a place where we can all gather. Proctor Doughterty was 31 when he founded the club, and was a member here until 1956. He had to be about 90 when he died. Proctor got the club started, but he thought it would be better for the club if Taft, somebody really famous, was the first president. Ultimately, Proctor did serve as president during a critical time for the club, the Great Depression years.

About five years ago we named the main dining room after Taft. Formerly it had the highly creative name of "Main Dining Room." We found the trowel that Taft used to lay the cornerstone of our second clubhouse, so we put that up on a dining room wall. We recreated the image of the whole room based on him.

This saying was placed over the door of the original clubhouse: "Enter all ye with a degree of good fellowship." Which alluded to the fact that a college degree was required to join the club, and that the club was looking for friendly people who wanted to get together with other people who had shared the same experience of having earned a college degree. That's what our club is really about—bringing people with some similar experiences and interests together. That's what all clubs are really about.

an equity interest in the club or the right to vote or hold office. Dues and initiation fees for this type of membership are lower than those for regular members.

Senior. A **senior membership,** sometimes called a life membership, is for club members who have been members of the club for a specified number of years and have reached a certain age. Dues for senior members are lower than for regular members. Clubs created this membership category (1) to take into account that the income of some club members goes down when they reach their senior years, and (2) to reward club members who have been members of the club for many years. However, clubs must be careful in setting requirements for this membership; otherwise, a club might have so many senior members that its revenues are substantially reduced. A club might require, for example, that a club member have a total of 90 points in order to qualify for a senior membership—the point total being some combination of the member's age and his or her years with the club (a 70-year-old member who had been a member of the club for 20 years would qualify, for example).

Other. Other memberships less common than the memberships just discussed include founder, absentee, surviving spouse, honorary, and clergy.

    Founder. Some clubs have a founder membership category that designates members who provided funds to initially build or purchase the club. Dues may be reduced for founder members.

    Absentee. An absentee membership is sometimes extended to members who will be out of the state or country for a year or more, during which time dues are suspended.

    Surviving spouse. If a club member dies, many clubs have a surviving-spouse membership category that allows the member's spouse to become a member of the club in the same membership category that the deceased member was in, or in a special category requiring lower dues but with more limited rights (for example, no voting privileges or right to hold office).

    Honorary. Some clubs elect honorary members to the club, such as politicians and other community leaders. These members usually have all the rights and privileges of regular members, except that they cannot vote or hold office. Honorary members usually do not pay initiation fees and pay lower dues or no dues at all.

    Clergy. Some clubs grant clergy memberships to members of the clergy in their local communities. These members usually have all the rights and privileges of regular members, except that they cannot vote or hold office. Clergy members generally pay no initiation fees and may pay lower dues.

Reciprocity

A discussion of club membership would not be complete without some mention of reciprocity. **Reciprocity** refers to agreements clubs make with each other so that their members who are traveling can visit other private clubs and enjoy their facilities and services while the members are away from their home clubs. For example, a city club might have reciprocity agreements with other city clubs throughout the United States as well as internationally. Members of this city club would be allowed to use these other city clubs when they travel. Charges are usually billed back to the member's home club.

A club can also have reciprocity agreements with nearby clubs, so that members can use another club when theirs must be closed for a substantial amount of time. Some clubs close down for a few weeks each year to give all of their staff members a vacation at once; others close down for two weeks for maintenance and minor renovation. Or, a club might have to close for a substantial period of time during a major renovation or after a fire or other disaster.

Selection Process

If you want to become a member of a private club, first you must be nominated for membership. Some clubs allow candidates for membership to apply directly to the club; at other clubs, a member (or more than one member) must sponsor a candidate's nomination.

The selection process for prospective members is governed by the club's bylaws. Typically, nominations are reviewed by the club's membership committee. Some members of the committee might check the references of candidates; others might interview the candidates and their spouses (if the candidates are married). The committee then notifies the club's membership of the candidates and asks for comments for or against admitting them to the club. The list of candidates and the call for comments may be published in the club's newsletter, posted in the clubhouse, or mailed directly to members. Common reasons that members have for objecting to a candidate include personal dislike, the fact that the candidate is a business competitor, or a feeling that the candidate isn't compatible with the character of the club. After taking these comments into consideration, the membership committee sends a recommendation to the club's board, and the board votes on whether to accept or reject each candidate. At some clubs, the board may arrange to meet the candidates before voting.

Member Discipline

A club's bylaws spell out rules for using the club that members must abide by. Clubs have the authority to create additional rules if necessary. A club has the right to suspend or expel any member who violates the club's bylaws or other club rules or whose conduct is otherwise improper and not in the best interests of the club. (It should be noted that suspension and expulsion are matters decided by a club's members, not its managers.)

Typical reasons for suspending or expelling a member include the following:

- Conduct unbecoming a member of the club
- Conviction for a crime
- Harassment of other members or staff
- Nonpayment of club dues or other bills
- Flagrant and repeated violation of club rules

A member facing suspension or expulsion usually receives a notification outlining why the club is considering such a drastic action and inviting the member to respond.

Suspending or expelling a club member is a very rare event, and a club must undertake such an action with great care. Proper documentation is critical, and the club's legal counsel should be consulted. In practice, when expulsion is being considered, the club's board may choose to give the member a chance to resign from the club before expulsion takes place.

Besides suspension or expulsion from the club, there are other ways that a club can discipline members. For example, a club may suspend a member's privilege to use a certain club facility. If a member becomes enraged over a bad golf shot and damages part of the golf course by whacking trees or smashing flowers, the member's golf privileges might be suspended for a period of time. Or, if members have large and growing club bills that they have neglected to pay for a significant length of time, some clubs post the names of these delinquent members on a club bulletin board or in the club newsletter, hoping to embarrass the members into paying. Because of possible legal actions by angered club members, even this action should be given careful consideration. A less drastic method of encouraging club members to pay their bills on time is for the club to impose late-payment penalties on members.

Club Organizational Structure

A club's organizational structure depends in part on whether the club is an equity club or a non-equity club.

Equity Clubs

To govern the club, provide assistance to club managers, and carry out other functions, members of equity clubs elect fellow club members to serve on the club's board of directors. The elected president of the club appoints club members to serve on the club's committees. The club's general manager actually runs the club on a day-to-day basis. The club's department managers and professionals (such as the golf professional) report to the general manager, and the general manager reports to the board.

In the following sections we will take a closer look at the organizational components and positions that make up an equity club:

- Board of directors
- Executive committee
- Other club committees
- General manager
- Club professionals
- Department managers
- Employees

Board of Directors. Generally speaking, an equity club's **board of directors** (called a board of governors at some clubs) makes club policies and governs the club. A club board is made up of directors (the number varies from club to club) and the club's officers—president, vice president, secretary, and treasurer. The club's general manager attends board meetings but is not considered a board member.

A board's specific duties and responsibilities are spelled out in each club's bylaws. Typical responsibilities include establishing general operating policies; overseeing the financial stability of the club (which includes reviewing the club's financial statements, approving its operating budget, taking action if the budget is not being followed, and so on); voting on new member candidates; and handling member discipline problems, including voting on whether to suspend or expel members.

Another very important responsibility of the board is to hire the club's general manager. The board should also evaluate the general manager at least once a year. Some boards shy away from this responsibility, but this does a disservice to the club and the manager. General managers can perform better if they have a clear understanding of what their boards expect of them. As one board president put it, "Not so long ago, our club was at a standstill. And we soon realized why: our general manager spent so much time trying to figure out what the board wanted him to concentrate on that he never had time to get his real job done."[4] A club board shouldn't micro-manage the general manager, but give overall directions, such as "We think you should give developing new member services a very high priority, since new services will help us grow and accomplish the financial goals we've set for the club."

Ideally, the club's president should conduct the general manager's evaluation, because it is very difficult for an entire board (especially if it is a large one) to hold productive evaluation sessions.

Above all, a club's board should avoid the temptation to try to actually run the club; that job belongs to the general manager. The board should restrict itself to setting policy and overseeing the club's operation, not actually giving directions to club managers and employees. (See Exhibit 3 for a summary of a club board's ideal relationship with the general manager.)

The term of office for board members varies among clubs. Whatever their length, terms should be staggered to keep new blood and new ideas flowing to the board while maintaining some measure of continuity: part of the board—one-half or one-third, for example—might be elected each year.

Executive Committee. If a club has an **executive committee,** it is usually composed of the club's officers (president, vice president, secretary, and treasurer). Sometimes the club's immediate past president is included, and the bylaws of some clubs permit the current president to appoint additional members if necessary.

An executive committee usually has duties and responsibilities similar to those of the board of directors. It essentially is a "mini-board" that acts in lieu of the club's full board between board meetings, whenever an emergency comes up, or when something minor must be handled quickly that doesn't necessitate calling the whole board together.

Other executive committee duties vary depending on the club and might include the following:

Exhibit 3   Summary of a Club Board's Ideal Relationship with the Club's General Manager

Ideally, a club's board of directors should:

1. Delegate responsibility for all of the club's operational functions to the general manager.
2. Consult with the general manager on all matters that the board is considering.
3. Share all official board communications with the general manager.
4. Make all of the club's staff responsible to the general manager.
5. Hold the general manager accountable for the supervision of all club staff members.
6. Give the general manager counsel and advice.
7. Support the general manager in all the decisions and actions he or she takes that are consistent with the policies of the board and the standards of the club.
8. Give the general manager a performance evaluation at least once a year.

- Handles matters considered too sensitive for the full board
- Monitors the performance of the full board
- Monitors the performance of club managers
- Serves as a bridge between the full board and the club's general manager on sensitive issues, taking the board's concerns to the general manager and the general manager's concerns to the board
- Receives reports in detail so as to conserve the full board's time
- Prioritizes issues to be brought before the full board for resolution
- Revisits the club's mission statement periodically to help keep club efforts in focus
- Conducts a performance appraisal of the general manager (rather than the club president alone or the board as a whole)

The executive committee usually has a regular monthly meeting but should also be prepared to meet whenever the president deems it necessary.

The club's general manager should participate in executive committee meetings, just as in meetings of the entire board, unless the committee is in executive session.

Other Club Committees. Other club committees exist to (1) perform the responsibilities assigned to them by the club's board or bylaws, (2) advise the board and help it carry out certain responsibilities and duties, (3) provide input and assistance to club managers, and (4) listen for suggestions and other feedback from members and act as liaisons between club members and the club's board and managers.

There are two types of club committees: standing and ad hoc. **Standing committees** are permanent committees that help the club conduct ongoing activities.

Ad hoc committees are formed for a special purpose, such as assisting with a bigger-than-usual golf tournament, researching the club's history and making preparations for a club's centennial celebration, or helping plan a club renovation. An ad hoc committee is usually focused on a single problem or issue and remains in existence until that problem or issue is resolved, which might take a few days, a few months, or even longer. The club's board dissolves an ad hoc committee once its purpose is served.

The club's president usually appoints the chairpersons of the various committees. Sometimes the president also appoints the committee members, sometimes this is left up to each committee's chairperson, and—in a few cases—the club's general membership elects people to committees—it all depends on the particular club. Typically, chairpersons of the club's major committees (such as finance and golf) are also members of the club's board of directors. The club president is an ex-officio (nonvoting) member of every club committee and is free to attend all committee meetings, but should not feel obligated to do so.

Club committees vary in size, depending on their responsibilities and the needs of the club. (The size of some committees might be stipulated in the club's bylaws.) Clubs should keep in mind that the ability of a committee to make decisions seems to decrease as its size increases. The length of a committee member's term varies from club to club. Two-year terms seem to work well, with 50 percent of committee members replaced annually.

Many club committees meet once a month. A few, like the insurance committee, might meet quarterly; some might meet just once a year (the strategic planning committee, for example); other committees, such as a legal/governmental affairs committee, bylaws committee, or nominating committee, might meet on an as-needed basis.

All committee actions require board approval, except in those areas where authority to act independently has been delegated (for example, the aquatics committee might have the authority to change the opening and closing hours of the club's pool, but not to change the user fee that members in certain membership categories must pay for using the pool). Just as a club's board shouldn't try to run the club, neither should its committees. Rather, committees should help shape and then support club goals and objectives. Committees basically serve in an advisory role to the board of directors.

Club committees can be very positive forces for a club. They can help generate enthusiasm among club members for club events and programs, they help the club draw on the expertise of club members, and they provide an outlet for members who want to learn more about or get more involved in their club. On the other hand, without direction and focus, committees can damage a club. At their worst, committees can violate club policies, put a club in financial difficulty by not working within their budgets, and create trouble among the club's general membership. To avoid possible problems with committees, the club's president and management team should hold an orientation meeting of all committees at the start of each year. At this meeting, the club's president and general manager can cover the role of each committee, committee objectives for the year, specific tasks, and budget constraints. The keys to effective committees are an effective chairperson, active members, and supportive club staff.

In the following sections we will take a brief look at standing committees commonly found in clubs: strategic or long-range planning, finance, bylaws, nominating, membership, house, social, athletic, and golf course. Keep in mind that all of these committees may or may not be found in a single club and that a club might have many other committees in addition to these (such as wine and food, debutante ball, and employee relations); each club decides on the committee structure that best meets its needs.

Strategic or long-range planning. A club's **strategic planning** or **long-range planning committee** is responsible for making recommendations for long-range capital improvements to the club and recommending other long-range plans for the club and its assets, including land use. It may review long-range projects suggested by the club's board of directors as well as suggest such projects to the board. Some strategic planning committees are charged with developing and maintaining a comprehensive three- to five-year plan that is consistent with the club's mission statement.

Finance. The primary responsibility of a club's **finance committee** is to keep the board of directors informed of the club's financial condition and all matters affecting the club's fiscal affairs. The finance committee sets the parameters of the club's annual operating and capital budgets (with input from the club's general manager and controller) for consideration by the board, recommends fiscal policies to protect the club's assets, and exercises control over the club's financial interests. Committee members might give advice and guidance to the club's managers and controller with respect to the club's finances. The finance committee typically reviews the club's financial statements and the annual audit, and oversees other financial matters such as capital-project funding, dues levels, delinquent accounts, cash flow projections, and cash management. This committee might also suggest capital improvements, make sure the club has adequate insurance and bonding, and recommend ways to generate additional revenue.

Bylaws. The **bylaws committee** oversees the club's bylaws and makes recommendations to the board concerning whether certain bylaws should be amended, supplemented, or repealed. The committee also must make sure the club's bylaws are legal.

Nominating. A club's **nominating committee** is charged with presenting to the club's general membership a slate of candidates for election to the board of directors. Unless otherwise directed by the club's bylaws, this committee is appointed by the club president and reports to the board. Committee deliberations are confidential, and the committee meets on an as-needed basis.

Membership. A club's **membership committee** reviews nominations for membership and makes recommendations to the board of directors regarding each new candidate. (Because this committee deals with such sensitive issues, the names of the members who are serving on it are kept secret at some clubs.) In some clubs, the membership committee also makes recommendations regarding current members who request a change in status (from a social member to a regular member, for example). As mentioned earlier, members of the membership committee might be responsible for interviewing prospective new members, posting their names on club bulletin boards or in the club's newsletter, and inviting comments from the general membership. Maintaining a waiting list of prospective members and a roster of current members might also be a duty of the membership committee.

In some clubs, the membership committee oversees the conduct of current members and supports management in maintaining the decorum of the club. Problems with current members that the membership committee might deal with include member drunkenness, abuse or harassment of employees, and past-due bills. Other clubs set up a separate rules committee to deal with these issues or let the board of directors handle them.

House. The **house committee,** sometimes called the clubhouse committee, is responsible for overseeing the maintenance of the clubhouse and the grounds that surround it. In many clubs, the house committee also oversees the operations that occur within the clubhouse, such as the food and beverage operations and clubhouse social events. (In some clubs, social events are the responsibility of a social or an entertainment committee.) The house committee also may consult with management about menus, wine lists, selling prices, and the clubhouse's hours of operation, and may assist management in preparing capital improvement budgets for the clubhouse.

The house committee does not manage clubhouse personnel, but at many clubs it does monitor clubhouse service and quality levels. If service and quality are not meeting member expectations, the committee brings this to the attention of the general manager for correction. Conversely, this committee might look for ways to congratulate staff members for a job well done. The house committee might also monitor whether members are adhering to clubhouse rules.

Social. The **social committee,** referred to in some clubs as the entertainment or special-events committee, is responsible for overseeing the entertainment activities of the club. (At clubs without social committees, this function is usually performed by the house committee.) The social committee typically sets or approves the club's entertainment calendar for the year. It might also help club managers plan special events, select entertainers, and stay within each event's budget. In some clubs, the social committee also assists with sporting events held at the club. Committee members listen to suggestions and feedback from members and might oversee advertising and promotional material for special events. Most clubs rely on the members of the social committee to personally promote the club's special events to other club members. This committee also helps managers prepare the entertainment portion of the club's annual budget.

Athletic. A club typically has several separate **athletic committees** (golf, tennis, swim or aquatics, and fitness); in rare cases, a club may choose to assign the responsibilities and duties of all of these committees to one committee called an athletic committee, recreation committee, or sports committee. Clubs may also maintain separate golf and tennis committees but lump aquatics and fitness together in one committee, or may have a separate committee for women's sports—it all depends on the club, its sports facilities, and the extent to which members participate in each sport. For example, some large country clubs with several golf courses have many separate golf-related committees, such as a golf committee, a

Insider Insights

Mariana Nork
Member of the University Club of Washington _____

The University Club is a good example of how a volunteer committee structure can work positively. The club's committees work very well with the club's staff. Even though many of our members are pretty significant people from very powerful think tanks and corporations, they are willing to share their knowledge. They like their membership in the club enough that they're willing to serve on committees to help the club's staff make the club even better. For example, last year the membership development committee put a tremendous amount of time and energy into a very strong demographic study for the club. I found the study very informative, and it was totally volunteer driven.

The University Club's committees don't try to run the club. They want to augment what the club's staff is already doing. It's a very strong committee structure and I'd like to think that the committees help the club's staff members rather than drive them crazy!

Committees can also serve as sounding boards for the general membership. Sometimes it's awkward for club members to go directly to staff persons. If they can route their concerns or suggestions through an organized committee structure, it plays out so much better in the long run.

Right now the club is considering a renovation plan that will add a lot of new facilities to the club. The renovation decisions are going through the club's committees and board, which is good for the staff and the members. Since the staff is not making the decisions, members can't accuse the staff of being self-important or making decisions that it shouldn't be making. Because the decisions are being made through the committees and the board, with input from member focus groups, members are given a chance to speak up. You're never going to please every member, but with a committee structure, the decisions the club makes are more likely to represent the majority of the members' feelings.

Another thing committees can do for clubs is bring together members from different age groups and backgrounds. The membership at our club has changed dramatically. It's no longer just 50-and-older male lawyers. The members serving on our committees are representative of the club as a whole, which helps when the committees must make difficult decisions. I've been a member of clubs with very lax or nonexistent committee structures, and when difficult decisions had to be made, the staff was unjustly accused of promoting its own interests or making decisions that should have been made by the membership. When you have good committees that represent all of the club's members, it's much easier for members to accept the decisions that are made. It runs very smoothly here.

women's golf committee, a grounds committee, a handicap committee, and a rules committee.

Athletic committees recommend operational policies to the club's board (such as tee times for golf, or hours of operation for the club's pool or tennis courts). Athletic committees work closely with their sport's pro to enforce the rules of the sport, plan tournaments or meets, maintain member golf handicaps or bowling averages, and help prepare their portion of the club's annual budget. Athletic committees also recommend equipment acquisitions to the board and may review nonroutine maintenance requested by club pros (the tennis pro might request that the club's tennis courts be resurfaced, for example). It's up to the athletic committees to publicize tournaments and other sports events held at the club.

Golf course. The **golf course committee** is concerned with the maintenance of the golf course. In some clubs, this committee is still referred to as the grounds committee or greens committee. It is an important committee at many country clubs, because members are usually very concerned about the condition of the club's golf course(s). The golf course committee oversees policies governing such maintenance issues as irrigation, weed control, fertilization, day-to-day maintenance (mowing, care of bunkers and greens, maintenance of golf car paths, and so on), and maintenance of drinking fountains and course signs/markers. Committee members might be called on to communicate with local public officials about the club's golf course irrigation policies, especially if the local area experiences a water shortage. The golf course committee reviews and recommends policies for regulating play so as to permit proper course maintenance with a minimum of inconvenience to members. This committee might also investigate vandalism of the golf course and recommend measures to prevent it.

As with other committees, it is important that golf course committee members remember that their role is advisory; they should avoid the temptation to actually manage. Committee members can make suggestions but should not give specific direction to the club's golf course superintendent, for example.

General Manager. Private equity clubs, because they are owned by the members, can operate in any way the members deem most suitable. For example, years ago it was typical for clubs to not have a general manager; the managers of the club's various departments and the club professionals reported to committee chairpersons and the club's board instead. A few clubs still operate that way. However, today the preferred organizational structure for clubs, the one outlined in this chapter and endorsed by the Club Managers Association of America, is for club professionals, department heads, and other staff members to report to a general manager. (See Exhibit 4 for the Club Managers Association of America's official position on the club general manager's role.)

A club's **general manager** is the chief operating officer of the club. Titles vary from club to club—this position is sometimes referred to as executive director, director of club operations, or chief operating executive—but in this chapter we will refer to this individual simply as the general manager. (However, it should be noted that the trend in large clubs is to use the "chief operating officer" title.) As mentioned earlier, the general manager is hired by the club's board of directors and is responsible to the entire board but usually reports to the club president. It is the general manager's duty to carry out the policies set by the board. The general manager attends board meetings to report on club operations and answer questions, but does not vote on board matters. He or she has the somewhat daunting task of providing the quality facilities and services that members demand, while at the same time generating sufficient cash reserves to ensure that the club can maintain its

Exhibit 4   The Club Managers Association of America's Position on the General Manager/Chief Operating Officer

The General Manager/Chief Operating Officer (GM/COO) is hired by the Board of Directors, reports to the President or Executive Committee, and is responsible for carrying out the Board's policies. The GM/COO will be held accountable for all areas of the club and will ensure the synergism of all club activities. He/she becomes the Board's bridge to the staff and committees and enables a Board to avoid the intricacies and short-term focus that are the staff's responsibility. This will allow the Board to work more exclusively on the holistic and long-term focus of club governance. The GM/COO will prepare such special reports as may be requested by the Board and will report back on the effectiveness of the club's policies, operations, and new programs.

The characteristics of a successful GM/COO include honesty, straightforwardness, integrity, accountability, leadership, and dedication. He/she must demonstrate interpersonal relations skills, be a good communicator, be administratively competent, and be able to communicate the club's vision.

Guidelines

The GM/COO is a partner with the Board in achieving the club's mission and discusses issues confronting the club with the Board. He or she also assists the Board in developing a format for assessing the progress of the club and reviews any issues of concern with the Board.

The GM/COO keeps the Board apprised of the organizational climate, identifies problems (either actual or anticipated), communicates with the directors, and offers consultative assistance as well as shares responsibility with the Board for the club's organizational development and organizational change programs.

The GM/COO has ALL club department heads reporting to him or her. The GM/COO will assume or delegate the duties and responsibilities of the department heads if they are absent or disabled. The GM/COO will complete all responsibilities and duties as prescribed in the bylaws of the club and perform other duties as directed by the Board of Directors.

The GM/COO monitors long- and short-term objectives, monitors financial reports, and prepares a financial plan for the club.

The GM/COO sets the standard for effective management, maintaining a high level of ethics, prudence, creativity, and productivity, and demonstrating a concern for the supervision and development of the staff.

The GM/COO helps the Board arrive at a consensus about important matters by providing pertinent information and interacting with the Board to investigate more efficient operating procedures and new club activities.

The GM/COO apprises the Board of trends, changing circumstances, and unexpected occurrences that could call for innovation or adaptation of the strategic plan.

The GM/COO helps set and maintain high standards for all facilities, services, and communications.

The GM/COO oversees all programs, services, and activities to ensure that objectives are met.

The GM/COO coordinates and edits all membership and public relations communications.

The GM/COO maintains a comprehensive knowledge of operational procedures and principles used throughout the club and takes responsibility for developing, maintaining, and documenting consistent procedures.

The GM/COO has knowledge of key situations or problems facing the club. The GM/COO monitors all activities in progress in order to achieve the Board's objectives and provides feedback to the Board on the progress being made.

Exhibit 5   Backgrounds of Club General Managers

Background Area	Percent
Food and Beverage	81
Athletics	17
Hotel	33
Military	11
Chef	11
Golf Pro	5
Superintendent	2
Tennis Pro	1
Other*	21

*Accounting, finance, sales, general business, college degree program

Source: Club Managers Association of America, *Club Operations and Financial Data Report* (Alexandria, Virginia: CMAA, 1996), p. 16.

physical plant and even expand that plant when and if the members so desire. (Major expansion or renovation may also be financed through member assessments.)

In addition to directly supervising all club professionals and department heads (and being indirectly responsible for all other club staff members), the general manager also prepares the annual budget (which is subject to the board's approval) and, after the budget is approved, is responsible for managing and controlling club operations to achieve budgeted revenue and expense targets.

Just as the board should not try to directly manage the club or get involved in day-to-day management decisions, the general manager should not try to set club policies. As mentioned earlier, the board is the policy-making body of the club; the general manager carries out the board's policies and decisions while efficiently managing the club and its staff.

Where do club general managers come from? Exhibit 5 shows the results of a survey that asked club general managers about their backgrounds. Note that the column does not add up to 100 percent because some general managers had varied backgrounds or their careers fit into more than one background area (a general manager might have previously been a food and beverage director in a hotel, for example). Exhibit 6 gives a profile of the "typical" general manager.

How many hours do club general managers work in a normal week? According to a survey of club general managers:

- 19 percent work 40 to 50 hours per week
- 47 percent work 50 to 60 hours per week
- 29 percent work 60 to 70 hours per week
- 5 percent work more than 70 hours[5]

Exhibit 6   The Typical Club General Manager

The typical club general manager:

- Is male.
- Is 30 to 40 years old.
- Is married.
- Works at a country club.
- Manages a club with more than 600 members.
- Works 50 to 60 hours per week.
- Has been in the club profession 10 to 15 years.
- Has been at his present club more than 7 years.
- Plans to stay at his present club for 1 to 3 more years.

Source: Edward A. Merritt, "Hospitality Management: A Study of Burnout in Private Club Management" (master's thesis: Pepperdine University, Malibu, California, 1995).

The general manager's salary and fringe benefits are negotiable, but usually correlate to the size of the club and the manager's experience. (The Club Managers Association of America periodically conducts a comprehensive compensation and benefits survey.) Fringe benefits for general managers might include all or some of the following:

- Vacation—usually two to four weeks per year
- Sick leave
- Insurance—health, disability, life
- Pension
- Use of the club's facilities
- Living quarters
- Auto
- Paid membership in the Club Managers Association of America
- Continuing education for professional development

See the chapter appendix for a sample job description for a club general manager.

Club Professionals. Professionals commonly found at country or city clubs are golf professionals and tennis professionals. Although a club's golf course superintendent is not considered a club professional, we will discuss the superintendent position in this section because superintendents work very closely with golf professionals and are considered to be at a similar organizational level. Because of its sports-related nature, we will also discuss the aquatic director's position in this

Club Managers and Burnout

Some jobs are difficult because of the physical labor involved. At times, club general managers and department managers must put physical effort into their work, but the physical demands are not why being a club manager is difficult. Managing at a club is challenging because of the emotional energy it consumes. It takes a lot of mental and psychological energy to treat every member as a VIP in all situations, not to mention deal with employees and other club managers under the often stressful conditions found at clubs. The constant pressure to please members and maintain very high service standards can lead to manager burnout.

A 1995 study of 152 private club managers and burnout by Edward A. Merritt, CCM, found the following:

- Male club managers are considerably more burned out than female managers.
- The youngest club managers rate far above older club managers in burnout; the oldest club managers show the least burnout.
- Married managers suffer from burnout the most.
- Managers with less than five years in the club profession are the most burned out; managers with the least amount of time at their present clubs are the most burned out.
- Managers who manage clubs with the fewest members (less than 300) are the most burned out; managers who manage clubs with the most members (more than 600) are the least burned out.
- More than 44 percent of the managers studied planned on leaving their present jobs within three years.

Why is burnout a problem for club managers? Apart from the personal toll it takes, burnout also shows up in their work. Emotionally exhausted managers don't put their heart in their work, quality begins to slip, and club members and staff personnel begin to notice and react negatively. Then the manager's job becomes even more difficult, which worsens the downward emotional spiral.

Club managers have identified two major contributors to burnout: staff turnover and what one club manager referred to as "face time." Constantly having to hire, orient, and train new staff members takes its toll. Also, inexperienced staff members don't deliver the same quality of service as veteran employees, at least in the beginning, and are not familiar with the club's members. This can lead to member complaints. Some members might even feel that a good manager wouldn't suffer so much staff turnover, so turnover can damage a manager's reputation in some members' eyes.

Because of the labor shortage in many sections of the country, sometimes it's difficult to find replacements for staff members who leave the club, and positions can go unfilled for long periods of time. This also causes management stress, as managers sometimes find themselves having to make up for departed workers by filling in as dining room captains, food servers, even dishwashers. Managers must also deal with the resentment staff members feel when they have to work harder because of the reduced staff.

"Face time" refers to the enormous amount of time club managers spend dealing with club members and other people with whom the managers must be at their best. "It's very stressful to remember that the people we serve—our members, officers, directors, and committee members—are also our owners," one club manager commented.

Continued

Another added that "contact overload is the problem. We deal with lots of individuals from varied backgrounds, each with unique expectations and demands." One club general manager lamented that "I learned a long time ago that even if I work 15 hours a day, 7 days a week, I'm still not going to be visible enough for some members. 'Where's the manager?' 'Have you been on vacation?' 'We used to see you in the dining room all the time.' I try to work smart, breezing through operations at high-profile times, but it's still very stressful."

Another factor that club managers must contend with when interacting with club members is alcohol. One club manager put it this way: "Any job is full of stress, but mix alcohol in with the normal situations that come up and you can count on a magnified version of the gory details when something goes wrong. And that's the problem. Most of our dealings with members occur around a setting of alcohol."

The labor shortage is not going to go away in the near future, and there's no getting around the fact that if you are a club manager, you must learn to deal with club members, even the ungracious ones or the ones who have had one too many. So how can club managers reduce job stress? The bookstores are filled with self-help books, and a stressed-out club manager might do well to browse the shelves and find a good book on relaxation or stress management. Apart from that, there are several common stress-reducing techniques that club managers can try:

- *Check off tasks.* Club managers should make a prioritized task list every day so they can stay organized and enjoy checking off their accomplishments.

- *Make time for fun.* Play is important for well-being at work; if at all possible, club managers should plan a fun break from the daily routine.

- *Use humor.* Finding the humor in trying situations can help a manager put them in perspective.

- *Create a quiet scene.* Club managers can create a sense of tranquility by taking a few minutes each day to concentrate on peaceful images, meditate, or just deep-breathe.

- *Share the load.* Talking to a friend can help a manager cope with worries and concerns.

- *Get physical.* Exercise can help club managers release stress and anxiety. People who exercise tend to be less stressed, more self-confident, and more optimistic than those who don't exercise.

- *Take care of themselves.* Club managers should try to eat right and get enough rest.

Source: Edward A. Merritt, "Hospitality Management: A Study of Burnout in Private Club Management" (master's thesis, Pepperdine University, Malibu, California, 1995).

section, even though the person who fills this position is not usually considered a club professional.

Golf professional. A club's golf professional, also referred to as a golf pro or director of golf, is in charge of all activities related to the club's golf program, such as working with the general manager to prepare the golf budget, teaching golf to members and supervising other teaching pros on staff, conducting club golf tournaments, overseeing the club's handicap system, overseeing the tee-time reservation system, arranging a tee-time schedule, supervising the use and maintenance of the club's golf cars, and running the golf pro shop. The golf pro may or may not own the pro shop merchandise, depending on the club.

The golf professional does not supervise the maintenance of the golf course; that is the job of the golf course superintendent. However, the golf professional and superintendent work closely together to keep the golf course in optimum playing condition for the club's members. See the chapter appendix for a sample job description for a golf professional.

Tennis professional. A club's tennis professional manages the club's tennis program. He or she gives individual lessons to members, establishes clinics for members of all ages, oversees the maintenance of the tennis courts, actively works with the club's tennis committee to keep tennis-playing members happy with the club's tennis program, and works with the general manager to prepare a budget for the program. At some clubs this is a part-time, seasonal position. See the chapter appendix for a sample job description for a tennis professional.

Golf course superintendent. A club's golf course superintendent is in charge of maintaining the club's golf course(s) in ideal playing condition. Without the golf course superintendent's expertise, a golf course's fairways and greens would deteriorate in a matter of days. A golf course superintendent typically has a degree in turf grass management or agronomy and works to mold the natural elements of grass, trees, hills, streams, and ponds (or, in a dry climate, rock formations, cacti, and so on) into a beautiful golf course. The superintendent must constantly monitor the environment to protect the course. It's a constant battle with insects, adverse weather conditions, and other environmental factors that threaten to undo all of the hard work of the superintendent and his or her staff. The golf course superintendent also works with the club's general manager and golf course committee to develop the golf course budget. See the chapter appendix for a sample job description for a golf course superintendent.

Aquatics director. A club's aquatics director, also known as the swim professional in some clubs, should be selected with great care. An aquatic director's responsibility is enormous, because he or she is constantly dealing with members in situations where bad judgment or lack of training might end in tragedy. The aquatics director should be a mature person, professionally trained in physical education and possessing superior administrative abilities and aquatics skills. An aquatics director should be friendly but at the same time command respect so that he or she can effectively enforce the club's safety rules.

At some clubs this is a part-time, seasonal position (traditionally late May through early September). Rather than hire a part-time aquatics director, some clubs with a fitness center hire someone full-time who can run the club's aquatics program as well as the fitness center. Clubs that do not have fitness centers but do have indoor swimming pools also have an aquatics director on staff year-round. See the chapter appendix for a sample job description for an aquatics director.

Department Managers. The number and type of department managers a club has depends on the type and size of the club. For example, a very small city club might have only an executive chef and a catering or banquet manager in addition to the general manager. At the other extreme, a very large country club might have a food and beverage director, an executive chef, a banquet manager, a beverage

Club general managers must work closely with their department managers. (Courtesy of Patricia Calder, CCM, and the Charleston Country Club, Charleston, South Carolina)

manager, a clubhouse manager, a director of security, an executive housekeeper, a controller, a membership director, a director of human resources, and a director of purchasing. A yacht club has a department head—harbor master—who appears in no other type of club.

In this section we will discuss department managers found at most country or city clubs: clubhouse manager, controller, executive chef, and banquet manager.

Clubhouse manager. The clubhouse manager is usually the general manager's second in command. He or she is in charge of managing the clubhouse and its personnel and enforcing clubhouse policies and operating procedures. (At some clubs, an assistant manager might assume the second-in-command role and have more extensive duties.) See the chapter appendix for a sample job description for a clubhouse manager.

Controller. A club's controller develops and oversees policies to control and coordinate accounting, auditing, budgeting, and related duties; prepares or oversees the preparation of the club's financial statements; and forecasts and analyzes financial information for the club's managers, board of directors, and committees. See the chapter appendix for a sample job description for a club controller.

Executive chef. The executive chef is responsible for all food production in a club's food and beverage outlets. Executive chefs develop menus, food purchase specifications, and recipes; supervise food-production staff members; and develop and monitor food and labor budgets for the club's food and beverage department. A club's executive chef must maintain the highest food quality and sanitation standards. At some clubs, a food and beverage director oversees the executive chef and other food and beverage department managers, in which case the executive chef's role is more restricted. See the chapter appendix for a sample job description for an executive chef.

Banquet manager. A club's banquet manager promotes the club's dining facilities for private banquets, business and social meetings, and other activities. He or she oversees all administrative and operational aspects of preparing and serving food at banquets, and works with the executive chef to put together banquet menus. See the chapter appendix for a sample job description for a club banquet manager.

Employees. A club's employees report to department managers (or intermediate supervisors) and create products and services for club members. As with a club's managers and professionals, the number and types of employees a club has depends on the type and size of the club. For example, at a small city club, the kitchen might only have a few cooks in addition to the executive chef. A large country club might employ an executive chef, a sous chef, a sauce cook, fry cooks, line prep persons, breakfast cooks, a garde manger, a butcher, broiler cooks, sauté cooks, and salad prep persons.

Club employees often enjoy wages and benefits competitive with or even higher than the wages and benefits of other employees in the hospitality industry. Many club employees stay with their clubs for a long time; it's not unusual to find club employees who have worked at their clubs for decades. These employees appreciate the unique nature of the club environment and the job security that working in a club affords them, as well as the family atmosphere and upscale facilities that are typical of clubs.

Non-Equity Clubs

The organizational structure of a non-equity club differs from an equity club's structure because non-equity clubs are not owned by their members, but rather by an individual or corporation. There is no board of directors made up of club members; the club is directed by the club's general manager, who follows the owner's policies, not policies established by the club's members.

Although there is no board of directors with policy-making authority, there might be an advisory board (sometimes called a board of governors) and other member committees for the more important club areas (such as the clubhouse, golf course, and tennis facilities). However, these bodies have no power or authority; they are strictly advisory, making their recommendations to the club's general manager. Depending on the scope of a committee recommendation, the general manager might act on it or pass it along to the corporate office for review. The general manager is usually given complete authority to operate the club and accept new members, subject to the owner's oversight.

Endnotes

1. Club Managers Association of America, *Club Management Operations*, Fourth Edition (Dubuque, Iowa: Kendall/Hunt Publishing Company, 1989), p. ix. The introductory

paragraph of this chapter was adapted from the fourth edition's preface by Donald R. Beever, CCM.

2. Club Managers Association of America, *Club Operations and Financial Data Report* (Alexandria, Virginia: CMAA, 1996), pp. 1–3, 11.

3. *Club Operations and Financial Data Report,* pp. 1–3, 11.

4. *Administrator Evaluation Manual: A Complete Guide for Board Members* (Frederick, Maryland: Aspen Publishers, Inc., 1991), p. 4.

5. Edward A. Merritt, "Hospitality Management: A Study of Burnout in Private Club Management" (master's thesis, Pepperdine University, Malibu, California, 1995), Appendix C, p. 10.

Key Terms

ad hoc committee—A club committee formed for a special purpose. An ad hoc committee is usually focused on a single problem or issue and remains in existence until that problem or issue is resolved.

athletic club—A private club that offers its members such fitness and sports facilities as gyms, swimming pools, racquetball and handball courts, weight-lifting areas, and exercise rooms. Many athletic clubs also have food and beverage facilities and operate similarly to city clubs. Some athletic clubs may also offer golf.

athletic committee—A club committee that recommends operational policies for club sports programs to the board. Most clubs have several separate athletic committees (such as golf, tennis, swim or aquatics, and fitness); a few clubs choose to assign the responsibilities and duties of all of these committees to one committee called an athletic committee, recreation committee, or sports committee.

board of directors—An equity club's governing body, made up of club members elected by club members.

bylaws committee—An equity club committee that oversees the club's bylaws and makes recommendations to the board of directors concerning whether certain bylaws should be amended, supplemented, or repealed. The committee also must make sure the club's bylaws are legal.

city club—A private club usually housed in a building or part of a building located within a city or in a suburban office complex; a city club serves the business, entertainment, and social needs of its members in an urban setting.

country club—A private club that has a clubhouse and enough acreage for one or more golf courses; most country clubs have other recreational facilities as well.

equity club—A private club owned by its members and governed by a board of directors elected by the members.

executive committee—An equity club committee that is usually composed of the club's officers (president, vice president, secretary, and treasurer); this committee has duties and responsibilities similar to those of the board of directors and is essentially a "mini-board" that acts in lieu of the club's full board.

finance committee—An equity club committee whose primary responsibility is to keep the board of directors informed of the club's financial condition and all matters affecting the club's fiscal affairs; it also recommends fiscal policies for protection of the club's assets, exercises control over the club's financial interests, and gives financial advice and guidance to the club's general manager.

general manager—A club's chief operating officer, in charge of all club staff members and operations.

golf course committee—A club committee concerned with the maintenance of the golf course. Also referred to as the grounds committee or greens committee.

house committee—A club committee responsible for overseeing the maintenance of the clubhouse and the grounds that surround it; in many clubs, the committee also oversees the clubhouse operations and events that occur within the clubhouse. Also called the clubhouse committee.

junior membership—A private-club membership category for individuals—usually the children of regular members—who have not yet attained the age required for regular membership.

membership committee—An equity club committee that reviews nominations for membership, interviews membership candidates, and makes recommendations to the board of directors regarding each new candidate; the committee also makes recommendations regarding current members who request a change in status, and might be responsible for maintaining a waiting list of prospective members and a roster of current members.

military club—A private club for military officers and enlisted personnel.

nominating committee—An equity club committee charged with presenting to the general membership a slate of candidates for election to the board of directors.

non-equity club—A private club that is owned by an individual or a corporation, not its members; with this type of club, the members' control over the club is limited.

nonresident membership—A private-club membership category for members who live a specified distance from the club.

private club—A place where people with a common bond of some type—similar interests, experiences, backgrounds, professions, and so on—can congregate for social and recreational purposes.

reciprocity—Refers to agreements clubs make with each other so that members who are traveling can visit another club and enjoy that club's facilities and services while the members are away from their home clubs. A club can also have reciprocity agreements with nearby clubs, so that members can use another club when theirs must be closed for a substantial amount of time (for major renovations or some other reason).

regular membership—A private-club membership category that gives members the full use of all of the club's facilities, along with voting rights and the right to hold office. Also referred to as a full, resident, or stock membership.

senior membership—A private-club membership category for club members who have been members of the club for a specified number of years and have reached a certain age. May be called a life membership in some clubs.

social committee—A club committee responsible for overseeing the entertainment activities of the club. Also called the entertainment committee.

social membership—A private-club membership category that gives members the use of the clubhouse and its facilities but restricts their use of the club's recreational facilities.

standing committee—A permanent club committee that helps the club conduct ongoing activities.

strategic planning committee—A club committee responsible for making recommendations for long-range capital improvements to the club and recommending other long-range plans for the club. Also called a long-range planning committee.

tennis club—A private club organized around the game of tennis, providing tennis courts and other tennis facilities and services to its members.

university club—A private club for university graduates, faculty, and certain levels of university staff.

yacht club—A private club for people who own boats or enjoy boating; such clubs offer marina services and usually have a clubhouse that provides food and beverage and other services to members.

Review Questions

1. What is a private club?
2. Who owns an equity club? Who might own a non-equity club?
3. What types of facilities might be found at a country club? a city club?
4. What are some common private-club membership categories?
5. How is an equity club organized?
6. A board of directors performs what types of duties for an equity club?
7. What are some standing committees commonly found in equity clubs?
8. A club's general manager performs what types of duties?
9. What are some club professional and department manager positions commonly found in clubs?

Additional Reading

Brewer, James H. "Developing a Club's History Book," in *Master Club Manager Monographs*, Volume I, Numbers 1–6. Alexandria, Virginia: Club Managers Association of America, 1995.

Club Managers Association of America. *Club Bylaws.* Alexandria, Virginia: Club Managers Association of America, 1996.

———. *Job Descriptions in the Private Club Industry,* Fourth Edition. Dubuque, Iowa: Kendall/Hunt, 1993.

Hall, Laurice T. "New Member Orientation for Private Clubs." *Master Club Manager Monograph,* Volume II, Number 1. Alexandria, Virginia: Club Managers Association of America, 1996.

Henderson, Edward. "Lions Among Us," in *Master Club Manager Monographs,* Volume I, Numbers 1–6. Alexandria, Virginia: Club Managers Association of America, 1995.

McCoy, Jerry. "The Value of Contract Documents in Club Construction and Renovation Programs," in *Master Club Manager Monographs,* Volume I, Numbers 1–6. Alexandria, Virginia: Club Managers Association of America, 1995.

McDeson, A. Graham. "Implementing Total Quality Management as an Integral Part of Strategic Management," in *Master Club Manager Monographs,* Volume I, Numbers 1–6. Alexandria, Virginia: Club Managers Association of America, 1995.

Redman, Bridgette M. *Topical Reference Series: White Papers on Club Management, Issues 1–6.* East Lansing, Mich.: Educational Institute of the American Hotel & Motel Association, 1997.

Schulz, William A. "Club Management Opportunities: Assistant Manager Development Program." *Master Club Manager Monograph,* Volume III, Number 1. Alexandria, Virginia: Club Managers Association of America, 1997.

Spitzig, Norman J., Jr. "Is It Time to Move?" in *Master Club Manager Monographs,* Volume I, Numbers 1–6. Alexandria, Virginia: Club Managers Association of America, 1995.

Winker, Mac. "Innovativeness/Entrepreneurship in Clubs: A Systematic Approach," in *Master Club Manager Monographs,* Volume I, Numbers 1–6. Alexandria, Virginia: Club Managers Association of America, 1995.

Internet Sites

For more information, visit the following Internet site. Remember that Internet addresses can change without notice. If the site is no longer there, use a browser to look for additional sites.

http://www.cmaa.org [the online member-service of the Club Managers Association of America (CMAA), linking club managers around the world with each other and with CMAA]

Case Studies

Case Study 1

Charlie Davis is the manager of the Blue Creek Club. As he walks through the grill area one afternoon, someone from a nearby table calls his name. It's John Martinez, vice president of the club board. He has a guest with him.

Charlie approaches the table. "Hello there, Mr. Martinez," he says. "How are you?"

"I'm fine, thanks," Mr. Martinez responds. He pauses, then motions toward his guest, "Charlie, let me introduce you to my friend, Sam Jacobs. He's a board member of the Cherrywood Club, the most prestigious club in this area. And Sam, this is Charlie, the manager here at Blue Creek."

Sam and Charlie exchange hellos and shake hands. John continues. "You know, Sam, Charlie is quite a successful manager. He's been here several years, and the club runs like clockwork under his direction. He keeps costs down and keeps the place looking good."

Sam turns to Charlie. "Glad to hear it, Charlie," he says. "Boy, I wish we could have a manager like you at the Cherrywood Club. Sometimes the management there can't seem to get its act together. For example, last Saturday, two wedding receptions were scheduled at the club. From what I heard, it was quite chaotic. The second wedding was delayed and the dinner was late."

"I was at the second wedding," John says. "The guests had to wait in a holding room while the reception room was being set up. The holding room was too small for the number of people there, and we had to wait an hour for dinner to begin."

"And that's not the only thing that has happened recently," Sam says. "One member who owns a liquor store asked if he could bring his own champagne for his daughter's wedding reception, and the management wouldn't allow it. This man is a good friend of mine. He was pretty upset when he was told that he couldn't bring in his own champagne. He had to pay regular club prices to have champagne served at the wedding. In addition to those incidents," Sam continues, "the club operated with a $20,000 loss last month. And to top that off, ol' Ben Pilote was fired. He's been a favorite employee at Cherrywood for years. Lots of members are angry about that."

Charlie is silent. He doesn't mention that he and Henry Reed, the manager of the Cherrywood Club, have worked together in the past. On a few occasions, Charlie and Henry have shared staff and combined purchases. In addition, Charlie and Henry have been good friends for several years. They have dinner together with their wives every other month. Although Charlie would rather not say anything to Sam, he feels he must respond—especially since he is in the presence of John Martinez, who will be his board president next year—and so he makes a few remarks.

A week later, Charlie receives a phone call from Sam Jacobs.

"Say, Charlie," he says. "Here at the Cherrywood Club, the manager position may be opening up soon. I was wondering if you'd be interested in coming over and talking to us about the position. A couple of board members and I would like to meet with you to discuss this further. I'm sure we could offer you twice the salary you're making now. But, don't mention anything about it to John Martinez. Again, we can discuss details later."

Charlie is surprised by the offer. The Cherrywood management job is an attractive one. The club is the most prestigious in the area, and the pay raise certainly would be nice. Charlie's thoughts are interrupted by another phone call just a few minutes later. This time, the caller is Henry Reed, Charlie's good friend and the manager of the Cherrywood Club.

"Hi, Charlie. It's Henry. I've got some great news! Susan and I are expecting a baby in December! We're very excited. And we've finally settled into our new house. Everything at the club's going great, too. Our revenue is up from two weddings last month, and I finally got rid of Pilote—remember me telling you about him? He's the server that couldn't get an order right to save his life. Things are really looking up. Whaddya say—how about you and Patty joining Susan and me for dinner this Friday? We've got lots to celebrate!"

(To provide you with an additional factor to consider in this case, we are including the Club Managers Association of America's code of ethics, a code that club general managers are encouraged to live by.)

CMAA Code of Ethics

We believe the management of clubs is an honorable calling. It shall be incumbent upon club managers to be knowledgeable in the application of sound principles in the management of clubs, with ample opportunity to keep abreast of current practices and procedures. We are convinced that the Club Managers Association of America best represents these interests, and as members thereof, subscribe to the following CODE OF ETHICS.

We will consistently promote the recognition and esteem of club management as a profession and conduct our personal and business affairs in a manner to reflect capability and integrity. We will always honor our contractual employment obligations.

We shall promote community and civic affairs by maintaining good relations with the public sector to the extent possible within the limits of our club's demands.

We will strive to advance our knowledge and abilities as club managers, and willingly share with other Association members the lessons of our experience and knowledge gained by supporting and participating in our local chapter and the National Association's educational meetings and seminars. We will not permit ourselves to be subsidized or compromised by any interest doing business with our clubs.

We will refrain from initiating, directly or through an agent, any communications with a director, member or employee of another club regarding its affairs without the prior knowledge of the manager thereof, if it has a manager.

We will advise the National Headquarters, whenever possible, regarding managerial openings at clubs that come to our attention. We will do all within our power to assist our fellow club managers in pursuit of their professional goals.

We shall not be deterred from compliance with the law, as it applies to our clubs. We shall provide our club officers and trustees with specifics of Federal, State and Local laws, statutes and regulations, to avoid punitive action and costly litigation.

We deem it our duty to report to local or national officers any willful violations of the CMAA CODE OF ETHICS.

Discussion Questions

1. Given the fact that John Martinez will soon be the president of the club board, Charlie felt he had to respond when Sam described the conditions of the

Cherrywood Club. What should Charlie have said in response to the situations that Sam described?

2. How should Charlie respond to Sam Jacobs' telephone call about the management position that might be open soon?

3. What should Charlie say to Henry? Does Charlie have any obligation (according to CMAA's code of ethics) to do anything?

The following industry experts helped develop this case: Cathy Gustafson, CCM, University of South Carolina, Columbia, South Carolina; Kurt D. Kuebler, CCM, Vice President, General Manager, The Desert Highlands Association, Scottsdale, Arizona; and William A. Schulz, MCM, General Manager, Houston Country Club, Houston, Texas.

Case Study 2

Tom Westerman recently became the general manager at the Overlook Country Club, a small club that's been going through some growing pains in the past few years. Tom formerly worked at a number of successful clubs and has a reputation for turning clubs around.

Since coming to the Overlook a few months ago, Tom has noticed very little consistency or control in the levels and types of responsibilities held by committee members and chairpersons. No written guidelines outlining specific responsibilities for committee members exist for any of the club's committees. Tom has learned that various committee chairpersons, under the previous general manager, frequently took actions that impeded the work of the club's managers. In fact, some committee chairpersons were still overstepping their authority by trying at times to manage parts of the club. All in all, things just weren't working the way Tom believed they should. Tom has made an appointment to talk with Mr. Carpenter, the club's president, about some of the problems he's seen.

"Mr. Carpenter, I realize the previous general manager had a strong relationship with the committee chairpersons and allowed them a lot of latitude in the decisions they made. Did anyone ever outline actual roles and responsibilities, as well as limitations, for each chairperson?"

Mr. Carpenter chuckled. "Are you kidding? The last general manager was around for so long, everyone just understood what their responsibilities were after awhile. Why? Is there a problem?"

"Well, Mr. Carpenter," Tom said, "actually there does seem to be a problem. A lot of the committee chairs are making decisions without getting input or approval from me. In some cases they're authorizing expenditures without notifying me. It's starting to affect the club's operations and our bottom line. And there are times when they are trying to actually run the club."

"Give me specifics," Mr. Carpenter said. "And please don't beat around the bush."

"Okay, here's an example of what I'm talking about. The chairperson of the golf committee, Fred Jarvis, has started to micro-manage the golf staff and Brian, our golf pro. Mr. Jarvis seems to think he's Brian's boss, and he doesn't like the way

Brian is managing the golf staff. Mr. Jarvis wants to change tee times and has actually started giving directions to the golf staff that contradict Brian's. Mr. Jarvis has also decided that slow play shouldn't be tolerated and has demanded that Brian penalize golfers who take more than four hours to play a round by restricting their access to the course. Brian is really upset with the entire situation."

"Well, slow play *is* an issue, Tom," Mr. Carpenter said.

Tom nodded. "Of course it is, but we shouldn't be so heavy-handed in how we deal with it. All we'll do is upset our members."

"Good point. We want to maximize course usage, but our members won't be very happy if they feel they're being herded through the course like cattle." Mr. Carpenter paused. "Are Fred's complaints about Brian mismanaging the golf staff valid?"

"Not really. Most of Mr. Jarvis's concerns are his own opinions and don't take into account the big picture." Now it was Tom's turn to pause. "I know it's Mr. Jarvis's responsibility to be concerned with Brian's performance," Tom continued. "However, he should bring those concerns to me and let me decide how best to handle them, not go directly to Brian."

Mr. Carpenter frowned. "Are we in any danger of losing Brian?"

"I think it's a possibility if the situation continues," Tom said, "and we were lucky to get him in the first place."

"Yes, we can't afford to lose our golf pro, especially at this time of year," Mr. Carpenter agreed. "But Fred Jarvis is a longtime and well-respected board member. We can't just ignore his concerns." Mr. Carpenter was interested in hearing how the new general manager would handle this problem. He asked Tom, "So what do you plan to do about the situation with Fred?"

"I'm going to meet with Mr. Jarvis to discuss his concerns about Brian's management of the golf staff and tell him I'll communicate his concerns to Brian at the right time," outlined Tom. "If I approach Mr. Jarvis tactfully, I think he'll let me handle the situation. I'm also going to speak with Brian and tell him I understand his frustrations and I'm working on resolving the problem. That should help him be more patient with Mr. Jarvis."

Mr. Carpenter smiled. "Sounds good. You don't want to make an enemy of Fred, but you've got a point about committee chairpersons overstepping their bounds."

"I'm glad you agree, Mr. Carpenter, and you could really help in this situation. Would you be willing to speak with Mr. Jarvis and set the stage for me?"

"I'd be glad to, Tom," Mr. Carpenter said. He leaned back in his chair. "What I'll do is hand out an organization chart and make a blanket statement to the entire board at our next board meeting. If I reinforce the idea that part of your job is to mediate between board or committee members and the club's staff, they should get the picture." Mr. Carpenter laughed. "I'll appeal to their egos and remind them that they are all too busy to waste their valuable time on trying to manage the club. Then, if the situation with Fred hasn't changed, I'll speak to Fred directly and prepare him for a meeting with you. If we handle it that way, maybe we won't have to step on any toes or hurt anyone's feelings."

Discussion Questions

1. What could Tom do to prevent committee chairpersons from overstepping their authority?

2. What obstacles might Tom encounter when he implements his plan to create written guidelines for committee members? What actions should Tom take to overcome those obstacles?

3. What process should Tom follow to establish written guidelines for committee members?

The following industry experts helped develop this case: Cathy Gustafson, CCM, University of South Carolina, Columbia, South Carolina; Kurt D. Kuebler, CCM, Vice President, General Manager, The Desert Highlands Association, Scottsdale, Arizona; and William A. Schulz, MCM, General Manager, Houston Country Club, Houston, Texas.

Chapter Appendix

The following are sample job descriptions adapted from the Club Managers Association of America's *Job Descriptions in the Private Club Industry,* Fourth Edition, published by Kendall/Hunt. These job descriptions will give you an idea of the typical duties, responsibilities, and reporting relationships of the positions listed, although it is important to note that these will vary from club to club.

Position: General Manager or Chief Operating Officer (COO)

Related Titles: Club Manager

Job Summary: Serves as chief operating officer of the club; manages all aspects of the club, including its activities and the relationships between the club and its board of directors, members, guests, employees, community, government, and industry. Coordinates and administers the club's policies as defined by its board of directors. Develops operating policies and procedures and directs the work of all department managers. Implements and monitors the budget, monitors the quality of the club's products and services, and ensures maximum member and guest satisfaction. Secures and protects the club's assets, including its facilities and equipment.

Job Tasks (Duties):

1. Implements general policies established by the board of directors; directs their administration and execution.

2. Plans, develops, and approves specific operational policies, programs, procedures, and methods in concert with general policies.

3. Coordinates the development of the club's long-range and annual (business) plans.

4. Develops, maintains, and administers a sound organizational plan; initiates improvements as necessary.

5. Establishes a basic personnel policy; initiates and monitors policies relating to personnel actions and training and professional development programs.

6. Maintains membership with the Club Managers Association of America and other professional associations. Attends conferences, workshops, and meetings to keep abreast of current information and developments in the field.

7. Coordinates development of operating and capital budgets according to the budget calendar; monitors monthly and other financial statements for the club; takes effective corrective action as required.

8. Coordinates and serves as ex-officio member of appropriate club committees.

9. Welcomes new club members; "meets and greets" all club members as practical during their visits to the club.

10. Provides advice and recommendations to the club president and committees about construction, alterations, maintenance, materials, supplies, equipment, and services not provided in approved plans and/or budgets.

11. Consistently ensures that the club is operated in accordance with all applicable local, state, and federal laws.

12. Oversees the care and maintenance of all the club's physical assets and facilities.

13. Coordinates the marketing and membership relations programs to promote the club's services and facilities to potential and present members.

14. Ensures the highest standards for food, beverage, sports and recreation, entertainment, and other club services.

15. Establishes and monitors compliance with purchasing policies and procedures.

16. Reviews and initiates programs to provide members with a variety of popular events.

17. Analyzes financial statements, manages cash flow, and establishes controls to safeguard funds. Reviews income and costs relative to goals; takes corrective action as necessary.

18. Works with department heads to schedule, supervise, and direct the work of all employees.

19. Attends meetings of the club's executive committee and board of directors.

20. Participates in outside activities that are judged as appropriate and approved by the board of directors to enhance the prestige of the club; broadens the scope of the club's operation by fulfilling the public obligations of the club as a participating member of the community.

Reports to: Club President and Board of Directors

Supervises: Assistant General Manager (Clubhouse Manager), Food and Beverage Director, Controller, Membership Director, Director of Human Resources, Director of Purchasing, Golf Professional (Director of Golf), Golf Course Superintendent, Tennis Professional, Athletic Director, Executive Secretary

Position: Golf Professional

Related Titles: Director of Golf, Golf Pro

Job Summary: Manages all golf and golf-related activities and business.

Job Tasks (Duties):

1. Designs, promotes, and directs all golf activities.

2. Prepares annual and monthly budgets for golf operations.

3. Orders merchandise for the golf shop.

4. Orders supplies associated with golf activities.

5. Maintains an attractive, orderly appearance in the pro shop.
6. Supervises the maintenance of golf cars and golf car maintenance personnel.
7. Supervises pro shop personnel.
8. Provides golf lessons to members and guests.
9. Plays golf with members of all skill levels to encourage enthusiasm.
10. Designs and conducts golf clinics.
11. Supervises assistant golf professionals.
12. Designs and conducts junior golf clinics and training programs.
13. Supervises locker room staff.
14. Supervises golf range staff.
15. Supervises golf bag and golf-club storage facilities and staff.
16. Supervises on-course personnel.
17. Collects charges and fees for all golf-related activities.
18. Organizes and conducts club golf tournaments.
19. Interprets and enforces golf rules and regulations.
20. Interprets and enforces club golf policies, rules, and regulations.

Reports to: General Manager

Supervises: Assistant Golf Professional

Position: Tennis Professional

Related Titles: Director of Tennis, Tennis Pro

Job Summary: Organizes and directs all club tennis activities, events, exhibitions, tournaments, and lessons.

Job Tasks (Duties):
1. Plans and directs instructional programs.
2. Gives lessons and clinics on the techniques and strategies of tennis to members and guests.
3. Organizes, administers, and officiates at tennis tournaments, exhibitions, and inter-club and intra-club social events.
4. Administers and enforces club tennis policies and procedures regarding play on club courts.
5. Strings rackets and performs other light equipment repairs.
6. Purchases and maintains adequate beverage inventory.
7. Sells beverages to members and guests.

8. Coordinates the maintenance, repair, and cleaning of tennis courts with the grounds and maintenance departments.

9. Writes and edits all tennis-related news for the club newsletter.

10. Supervises assistant tennis professionals and other tennis staff members.

11. Manages the tennis pro shop.

12. Establishes and implements an accurate inventory-control system and reports results accordingly.

13. Provides all charge tickets generated in the tennis shop to the accounting department.

14. Budgets for the tennis profit center.

15. Ensures that all club members and guests receive courteous, prompt, and professional attention to all their tennis needs.

16. Markets tennis facilities to members and guests.

Reports to: General Manager

Supervises: Assistant Tennis Professional

Position: Golf Course Superintendent

Related Titles: Greenskeeper

Job Summary: Maintains the club's golf course(s) and related golf equipment.

Job Tasks (Duties):

1. Maintains all grounds.

2. Maintains golf course maintenance equipment.

3. Schedules, trains, supervises, and evaluates personnel assigned to the department.

4. Supervises all planting, fertilizing, and care of turf, plants, shrubs, trees, and other facilities on the golf course.

5. Supervises operations of and the personnel in the equipment repair shop.

6. Records all work activities of personnel in the department.

7. Records all maintenance of the course.

8. Prepares an annual budget for the department.

9. Selects and prepares proper fertilizers and nutrients for all flora.

10. Develops and maintains drainage, irrigation, and watering systems.

11. Maintains the course in proper playing condition.

12. Provides necessary input for all required personnel records.

13. Implements and enforces a comprehensive safety program for employees, members, and guests on the course, in compliance with local, state, and federal laws.

14. Maintains accurate work records for all personnel in the department.

Reports to: General Manager

Supervises: Maintenance Supervisor, Pesticides Application Specialist, Irrigation Specialist, Equipment Operator, Equipment Mechanic

Position: Aquatics Director

Related Titles: Swim Professional, Swimming Pool Manager

Job Summary: Supervises safe, clean, and appealing club swimming facilities.

Job Tasks (Duties):

1. Supervises aquatics staff, including assistant pool manager, swimming instructors, and lifeguards.
2. Formulates weekly work schedules and rotation schedules for all pool employees.
3. Purchases pool chemicals.
4. Maintains proper chemical balance in pools and maintains mechanical equipment in coordination with the club's maintenance department.
5. Maintains correct payroll records.
6. Registers members at the pool and charges for all guests, lessons, etc.
7. Provides necessary orientation and training for pool staff.
8. Enforces club safety and conduct rules.
9. Plans and directs special events.
10. Arranges a program of private and group swim and diving lessons.
11. Represents the club in activities as required.
12. Develops an annual operating and staffing budget, subject to approval by the general manager or athletic director.
13. Orders and sells swim suits, suntan oil, sunglasses, and other pool accessories; keeps accurate accounting records of sales.
14. Maintains and keeps all necessary records concerning pool attendance, pool chemicals, accident reports, problem-member reports, lifeguard and instructor schedules, time cards, etc.
15. Develops and implements the pool safety program.
16. Hires, trains, and supervises all lifeguards.

Reports to: General Manager or (at some clubs) the Athletic Director

Supervises: Lifeguard, Swim Team Coach (at some clubs)

Position: Clubhouse Manager

Related Titles: Assistant General Manager, Assistant Manager, Assistant Club Manager

Job Summary: Works closely with the general manager. Responsible for the general operation of staff functions relating to rooms, housekeeping, maintenance/repair, and security. (Supervises the work of the directors of these departments.) Responsible for operation of all aspects of the club in the absence of the general manager and performs specific tasks as requested by him or her.

Job Tasks (Duties):

1. Manages all aspects of the club in the absence of the general manager.
2. Approves plans, budgets, staffing, and general operating procedures for the rooms, housekeeping, maintenance/repair, and security departments.
3. Monitors the budget and directs the taking of corrective action as necessary to ensure that budget goals are attained.
4. Functions as an administrative link between departments.
5. Monitors internal cost-control procedures.
6. Coordinates training programs.
7. Assists the general manager in developing and implementing long-range and annual plans, operating reports, forecasts, and budgets.
8. Monitors safety conditions and employees' conformance with safety procedures; updates emergency plans and procedures; and assures that effective training for these programs is conducted in all departments.
9. Maintains contact with members and helps ensure maximum membership satisfaction.
10. Receives, investigates, and acts upon complaints from club members, guests, and employees.
11. Ensures that the club's preventive maintenance and energy management programs are in use.
12. Participates in ongoing facility inspections throughout the club to ensure that cleanliness, safety, and other standards are consistently attained.
13. Serves as an ad-hoc member of appropriate club committees.

Reports to: General Manager

Supervises: Executive Housekeeper, Chief Engineer, Director of Security, Valet, Coat Checker

Position: Controller

Related Titles: Accountant, Office Manager, Director of Finance

Job Summary: Develops policies to control and coordinate accounting, auditing, budgets, taxes, and related activities and records; develops, establishes, and administers procedures and systems pertaining to financial matters; prepares financial statements, forecasts, and analyses for all administrative and managerial functions.

Maintains all accounting records and is responsible for the development, analysis, and interpretation of statistical and accounting information. Evaluates operating results in terms of costs, budgets, policies of operation, trends, and increased profit possibilities.

Supervises the staffing, scheduling, training, and professional development of department members.

Job Tasks (Duties):

1. Directs financial operations of the club.

2. Formulates, receives, and recommends policy proposals for approval relating to accounting and auditing, the budget and cost control, preparation and payment of payrolls, tax matters, compilation of statistics, and office methods and procedures.

3. Prepares monthly trial balances and resulting financial statements for the club, along with required supporting schedules and other data necessary for financial reports and records.

4. Manages and conducts internal-auditing programs to ensure that records are accurately maintained and that established policies and practices are satisfactorily and consistently followed.

5. Prepares budgets and financial forecasts in coordination with various club committees and departments and the general manager; analyzes financial information, monitors budgeted versus actual expenditures, and advises management about variances and their potential causes.

6. Works with the club's external auditors to ensure that accounting procedures are consistent with club policies.

7. Prepares and verifies reports made to agencies and trade and professional organizations for which dissemination is consistent with club policies.

8. Directs, participates in, and verifies the taking of various inventories for beverages, food, supplies, equipment, furnishings, etc.

9. Verifies that all insurance records for club property are maintained.

10. Supervises accounting staff.

11. Informs and advises other department heads regarding the financial aspects of their areas.

12. Prepares and supervises preparation of applicable federal, state, and local tax returns.

13. Prepares accounting reports as necessary and appropriate for dissemination to the board of directors, executive committee, and other club committees.

14. Ensures that procedures for effective receiving and storeroom control are in place and consistently used.

Reports to: General Manager

Supervises: Bookkeeper, Accounts Receivable Clerk, Accounts Payable Clerk, Cashier, Payroll Clerk, Receiving/Storeroom Clerk

Position: Executive Chef

Related Titles: Chef, Food Production Manager, Culinary Director/Manager

Job Summary: Responsible for all food and pastry production, including that used for food and beverage outlets and banquet functions. Develops menus, food purchase specifications, and recipes. Supervises production and pastry management staff. Develops and monitors the food and labor budget for the department. Maintains the highest professional food quality and sanitation standards.

Job Tasks (Duties):

1. Hires, trains, and supervises the work of management staff in the food and pastry production departments.

2. Plans menus (with the food and beverage manager, if the club has one) for all club food and beverage outlets, taking into consideration guests, marketing conditions, popularity of various dishes, holidays, costs, and a wide variety of other factors.

3. Schedules and coordinates the work of chefs, cooks, and other kitchen employees to ensure that food preparation is economical and technically correct.

4. Approves the requisition of food supplies.

5. Ensures that high standards of sanitation and cleanliness are maintained throughout the kitchen areas at all times.

6. Establishes controls to minimize food and supply waste and theft.

7. Safeguards all food preparation employees by implementing training to increase their knowledge about safety, sanitation, and accident prevention principles.

8. Develops recipes and techniques for food preparation and presentation that help ensure consistent high quality and minimize food costs; exercises portion control over all items served; assists in establishing menu selling prices.

9. Prepares all necessary data for the budget in his or her areas of responsibility; projects annual food and labor costs and monitors actual financial results; takes corrective action when necessary to help ensure that financial goals are met.

10. Attends general manager's food and beverage meetings.

11. Consults with the banquet function committee about the food production aspects of special events being planned.

12. Cooks or directly supervises the cooking of items that require skillful preparation.

13. Evaluates food products to ensure that quality standards are consistently attained.

14. Interacts with the managers of the club's food and beverage outlets and banquet manager to ensure that food production consistently exceeds the expectations of members and guests.

15. Plans and manages the employee meal program.

Reports to: General Manager or (at some clubs) the Food and Beverage Director or Clubhouse Manager

Supervises: Executive Steward, Banquet Chef, Sous Chef, Garde Manger, Pastry Chef

Position: Banquet Manager

Related Titles: Catering Manager, Catering Coordinator

Job Summary: In charge of the banquet service function in the club. Supervises banquet service personnel to ensure member and guest satisfaction through proper food and beverage service and presentation. Maximizes the club's profits from the catering function.

Job Tasks (Duties):

1. Works with the catering manager, banquet chef, and others to schedule and coordinate personnel requirements for private functions.

2. Develops detailed plans for each banquet event in conjunction with the club's function committee (members of this committee might be the club's food and beverage director, executive chef, banquet chef, catering manager, and executive housekeeper).

3. Serves as a liaison between banquet service personnel and other club staff members.

4. Diagrams buffet tables, guest tables, and other function-room setup needs for special events.

5. Holds pre-function meetings with servers to ensure smooth, efficient service; assigns server stations and coordinates the timing of courses.

6. Ensures that all banquet staff members are well-groomed and in proper uniform (including nametags).

7. Assists with ongoing sales efforts for banquet business.

8. Assists in the preparation of the marketing plan and annual budget to increase the profitability of the banquet operation; monitors performance against budgets; recommends advertising.

9. Ensures proper inventory of all banquet server equipment and supplies.

10. Acts as head server at special, private functions and may greet and seat guests as necessary.

11. Handles complaints and comments.

12. Hires, trains, and supervises banquet service staff.

13. Regularly inspects all front- and back-of-the-house service areas and equipment to ensure that sanitation, safety, energy management, preventive maintenance, and other standards for the department are met.

Reports to: Food and Beverage Director

Supervises: Banquet Captain

REVIEW QUIZ

When you feel you have covered all of the material in this chapter, answer these questions. Choose the *best* answer.

1. A private club that has a clubhouse, a golf course, tennis courts, a swimming pool, and fitness facilities is a _____ club.

   a. city
   b. yacht
   c. country
   d. tennis

2. A membership that gives a member the use of the clubhouse but does not allow the member to use the club's other facilities (golf course, tennis courts, and so on) unless the member pays a user fee is called a(n) _____ membership.

   a. house
   b. associate
   c. junior
   d. nonresident

3. An equity club's board of directors:

   a. manages the club.
   b. makes club policies.
   c. governs the club.
   d. b and c.

4. Which of the following is the general manager's second in command?

   a. executive chef
   b. clubhouse manager
   c. banquet manager
   d. golf professional

Answer Key: 1-c-C1, 2-a-C2, 3-d-C3, 4-b-C4

Note: In the answer key, the number of the question is given first, then the letter of the correct answer, then the number of the competency that the question relates to. For example, "1-c-C1" means that for question 1, "c" is the right answer, and the question is drawn from chapter material that relates to Competency 1 (competencies are listed next to the outline on the chapter's first page). There is a page range given after each competency, so if you missed a question that relates to Competency 2, for example, you can turn to the first page of the chapter, look at the end of Competency 2, and find out where in the chapter the material that relates to Competency 2 is located.

Chapter 2 Outline

Competencies

1. Explain the board of directors' role in a private club, describe its size and makeup, and summarize issues connected with board member tenure, selection, and orientation. (pp. 53–61)

2. Describe the basic written records associated with clubs and club boards. (pp. 61–69)

3. Describe issues of importance to club general managers, such as starting new jobs and working with club boards, and summarize professional development opportunities for club general managers. (pp. 69–74)

2

A Club's Board and Its General Manager

This chapter was written and contributed by Joe Perdue, Vice President, Club Managers Association of America, Alexandria, Virginia.

TWO CRITICAL PIECES of a club's puzzle are the club's board and its general manager. They must work together for a club to be successful. For that reason, in the first part of this chapter we will take a close look at club boards—who serves on them, how they function, their duties, and so on. The second part of the chapter looks at club general managers—how to start a job at a club, how to work with boards, and other tips for success. The chapter concludes with a look at educational opportunities for club general managers.

The Board of Directors

A private club's **board of directors** is the club's governing body, made up of club members elected by club members.[1] A club depends on its board of directors for long-term guidance, leadership, and policy-making. Each member of the board plays an important role in ensuring that the club continues to thrive and meet the needs of its members.

While the specific duties of board members vary among clubs, there are three primary legal duties that all board members assume:

- *Duty of care.* Board members must take the same precautions in governing the club that an "ordinarily prudent" person would take.

- *Duty of loyalty (or good faith):* Board members must put the interests of the club ahead of their own personal interests.

- *Duty of obedience:* Board members must remain faithful to the mission of the club.

Some clubs have a written position description for board members. A position description can help educate a board member about his or her board duties by spelling out the roles and responsibilities a board member is expected to fulfill and outlining the structure of the club, club policies, and the club's strategic goals. Exhibit 1 gives a list of typical board member duties (of course, these vary somewhat from club to club).

Exhibit 1   Board Member Duties

1. Establish club policies.
2. Oversee the fiscal management of the club.
3. Enact regulations (bylaws, rules, resolutions).
4. Adopt budget plans.
5. Approve membership applications.
6. Hire the general manager.
7. Meet prospective new members.
8. Oversee the administration of policies.
9. Fill vacancies on the board.
10. Supervise the administration and enforcement of club regulations.
11. Discipline, suspend, or expel a member when necessary.
12. Review and approve programs submitted by club committees.
13. Oversee transfers of memberships.
14. Attend special meetings.
15. Supervise club elections.
16. Set an example by abiding by all club rules.

Board Structure

Every club struggles to find the ideal structure for its board. How many people should serve on it? How long should each person serve? How should club members be chosen for the board? There are no standard answers that fit every club. Each club has its own challenges and needs, and the way a board is put together and operated depends on the structure and purpose of each club.

Size. The size of most boards is determined more by their histories than by studies of what would be most effective. Some club experts say that a club board's ideal size is between 9 and 12 directors; others put the ideal range at 8 to 15. However, some clubs operate very effectively with a board whose size falls outside of these recommended ranges. The key for each club is to find a board that is small enough to make timely decisions but large enough to effectively handle its duties.

A large board that serves one club extremely well could be a disaster at another club. A board that is too large for a club can cause several problems. For one thing, once a board gets too large, it is no longer able to make decisions effectively. Other potential disadvantages of an oversized board include the following:

- Board discussions/debates tend to be of lower quality
- Board members become less personally involved in the board
- Board members fail to assume responsibilities
- Less frequent board meetings
- Increased apathy among board members

A board that is too small carries its own set of challenges. If a board is too small, there may not be enough directors to do the work that needs to be done, making the board weak and ineffective. Some other problems a too-small board might cause include the following:

- Not enough policy guidance for the club's general manager
- Failure to represent some segments of the club's membership
- A tendency for board members to become clannish
- Difficulties in achieving a quorum
- Lack of discussion on important issues

Whatever the board's size, board experts encourage clubs to have an uneven number of people on their boards to eliminate the problem of deadlock.

Makeup. A club board of directors is presided over by a president (the board's president is also referred to as the club's president). The president may be elected by the general club membership or, in some cases, the members of each new board may elect the president and the board's other officers (vice president, secretary, and treasurer) from among themselves.

Even though a club's bylaws may spell out many specific duties and responsibilities for its board president, the president's most important role is to lead the club. As the board of directors' guidelines for one club put it:

> The president's role, even as defined in the bylaws, is specifically non-specific. He is, in fact, "responsible for everything" at the club. His job is leadership. Ideally he should have qualities of wisdom, understanding, concern for everybody (staff as well as members), statesmanship, salesmanship, patience (and, when the time is right, impatience), and availability. He should have a love affair with the club because, for a full year, he must care more deeply than any other member, and spend more time, sweat, and perhaps tears, than will ever be appreciated.

At most clubs, the president's term is one year; at others, it might be two. Rarely is it more than two years.

The board's vice president presides at board meetings in the absence of the president. He or she should be the president's advisor, principal confidant, aide, and supporter. The vice president should learn the president's job and be prepared to assume and perform the duties of president if needed.

The club's secretary keeps the minutes of all board meetings (or sees that they are kept by someone) and is in charge of the club's records. He or she notifies board members of meetings and conducts board correspondence. At some clubs, the secretary is in charge of maintaining a correct roll of members and coordinating the election of board officers and directors.

The club's treasurer reports to the board each month on the club's financial status, and in fulfilling that role must meet periodically with the club's managers to go over financial reports. The treasurer must be the financial watchdog for the board, since most other board members rely on him or her (and the club's general manager) regarding financial matters.

What do the other members of the board of directors do? Ideally, a director's role is to be a representative of the membership, a policy maker, an overseer, a planner, and a supporter of the club's management. According to one industry expert, directors should exercise their responsibilities primarily by asking good and timely questions rather than by trying to actually run club programs or implement their own policies.[2]

The club's general manager attends board meetings as well, to report on the club's status and answer any questions board members might have. The general manager does not vote on board matters, however.

Board Member Tenure. Like a board's size, a board member's tenure or term of service is usually established by history and tradition rather than by careful analysis. Depending on the club, tenures of club board members range anywhere from one year to a lifetime appointment.

Samuel Adams, a hero of the American Revolution, voiced his distrust of anyone who governs for too long, saying "Where annual elections end, tyranny begins." A similar fear that long-serving board members might abuse their power led some clubs to establish short terms for board members. More frequently, a short term was chosen for the sake of the board members; becoming a board member typically means taking on a lot of work and responsibility. Some advantages to short terms include the following:

- More club members are able to serve on the board because positions open more frequently.

- A board member's typically heavy workload need be carried for only a short time.

- The board is constantly infused with new ideas and viewpoints.

- "Problem" board members do not have as much time to do damage as they would with longer terms.

These advantages haven't convinced everyone that board member terms should be short. Cyril O. Houle, a member of several boards and author of many books and papers on board governorship, says that "a short period of service does not provide enough time for the individual member to absorb what he needs to know, to make a substantial contribution, or to be prepared through experience for later major responsibilities."[3]

Frequent board turnover also has its drawbacks from a club general manager's point of view. New presidents and board members bring their own ideas and agendas to the table, sometimes making it hard for a club to stick to a consistent direction. As one general manager put it: "Board members, committees, and presidents change annually at my club. It's very frustrating to find the emphasis and thinking changes each time they do. Direction becomes confusing—in fact, quite often there is no direction or fundamental plan for the year."[4]

As these criticisms imply, there are advantages to long terms of service for board members (especially in clubs where there are many departments and activities):

- Board members have more time to master the club's complexities and challenges.

- The commitment of board members is at a higher level.

- The board has greater stability.

- The board has a greater commitment to long-term and strategic planning.

The major disadvantages to a long term are that fewer people get a chance to serve on the board, thus limiting the infusion of new ideas, and that the club may not develop enough new leaders.

A question related to term length is: how many terms should someone be permitted to serve on the board? In some clubs, there are no term limitations for board members; it is left to the personal judgment of the individual as to how many terms to serve (if he or she continues to be nominated). If a board does choose to enact term limitations, it should spell out how those limits apply to half-terms, and whether a person can serve on the board again after a period of absence.

Most board experts encourage the staggering of terms. A club that replaces all of its board members at once loses all of its experienced board leadership and sacrifices continuity. The most common way to stagger terms is to have one-third of the board members begin their term of service each year; with this plan, a board loses only one-third of its members in any given year. Houle cites two advantages to staggered terms:

- Staggered terms allow for both continuity and a change in membership.

- Staggered terms make it easier to plan for diversity and maintain a board that is representational of the membership.

Board Member Selection. Short board tenures and term limits can help rotate an ineffective board member out of service, but it is far better for a club that an ineffective member never occupy a board seat in the first place. This places great importance on the selection of board members. At most clubs, the general membership elects board members from among club members who have been nominated for board service either by a nominating committee or the current board.

A club should consider several factors when selecting board members. One of the most important is to make sure the diversity of the general membership is represented on the board. Some clubs address this by requiring that there be board members from each of the club's membership categories. This prevents a board from being made up of all golfing members or all social members, for example.

Ralph F. Lewis, editor and publisher of the *Harvard Business Review,* talked at a board conference about several potential hazards in selecting board members. They were:

- *Tokenism.* Clubs should not bring unqualified people onto the board just because they represent particular club groups. A club should take the time to find qualified people from those groups.

- *Conflict of interest.* Clubs should carefully consider whether potential board members have any current or potential conflicts between their business or personal lives and the needs of the club.

Exhibit 2   Guidelines for Nominating Board Members

A board member candidate should:

- Have outstanding business, administrative, or other valuable experience, proven ability, and significant accomplishments.

- Either hold a position of high responsibility or have recognized expertise in one or more areas.

- Have no present or visible potential for conflict of interest and should not be an officer or director of any major club supplier or competitor of the club.

- Be able to show some connection with organizations that serve the community in civic, social, or charitable activities.

- Possess self-confidence and be at ease with individuals of distinguished attainment.

- Be articulate and command respect from peers.

- Possess maturity, but also display youthful initiative and a progressive attitude.

- Be enthusiastic about the prospect of serving and be able to devote the necessary time.

- Be neither chosen nor excluded solely because of race, color, or sex.

Source: Adapted from Arthur D. Little, Inc., *The Corporate Director: A Report of the Corporate Directors Conference* (Boston, Mass.: Cahners Books).

- *Too many directorships.* If a person is already on a number of boards, he or she will probably not be able to devote as much time to the club's board as needed.[5]

However a club selects its board members, there are certain traits that it should look for in a potential board member. Exhibit 2 lists some of the qualities that nominating committees or boards should look for when nominating club members for board service.

It should be noted that club managers have no official responsibilities or input regarding the selection of board members. This is strictly a decision for the club's members, and wise club managers stay out of the process.

Board Member Orientation. Considering the crucial role that board members play in guiding their club, it is important that new board members fully understand their new responsibilities. A well-planned orientation can help a new board member make a successful transition from neophyte to contributor. Orientations:

- Set a clear role for new board members.

- Provide new board members with the materials they need to govern effectively.

- Shorten the learning curve of new members and help them become productive more quickly.

- Help new members understand what is and (just as important) what is not expected of them.

- Give current board members and the general manager a chance to welcome the new members.

In 1996, the Club Managers Association of America found that 45 percent of the clubs it surveyed had orientation programs for new board members. The likelihood that a club would have an orientation program increased as the number of total club members increased. While 30 percent of clubs with less than 400 members had board orientation programs, this number increased to 55 percent among those clubs with more than 900 members. The club's general manager is the facilitator in at least half of these orientation programs. In nearly half of the programs, the club president is involved as well.

The bulk of the work involved with planning and conducting new-board-member orientation programs usually falls to the club's general manager, since he or she is frequently the person with the fullest knowledge of how the club works. Many general managers like being in charge of the orientation, since it is in their best interest to have board members properly oriented to their roles and responsibilities. Although the general manager may plan, coordinate, and even facilitate the new board member orientation, it is often the role of the club president to set the stage in the actual orientation session and emphasize the importance of serving on the club's board.

Exhibit 3 is a sample checklist general managers might use when planning an orientation. A key decision that must be made early on is whether the orientation session should be held on- or off-site. The general manager and board president usually make this decision. Holding the orientation at the club allows for a tour of club facilities that new board members may not have seen before (such as the clubhouse kitchen or other back-of-the-house areas); it also allows the general manager and board president easy access to additional resource materials if any are necessary. However, holding the orientation session off-premises may provide a more comfortable environment for new board members. At a different site, everyone is usually more relaxed and there should be fewer interruptions for the general manager to deal with.

A general manager can orient new board members individually or hold a group session. If holding a group session, the general manager should check everyone's schedule and choose a time convenient for everyone. The general manager will also need to make sure that all materials and equipment needed for the orientation are in place for the meeting. Exhibit 4 is a list of materials that are commonly used in orientations.

An orientation typically includes the following activities:

- A tour of the club (if the orientation is held on-site), including back-of-the-house areas
- Distribution of printed material
- A discussion/overview session
- A meal
- A slide or media presentation

Exhibit 3   Sample New-Board-Member Orientation Checklist

Setting Orientation Objectives

_____   Write clear, measurable objectives for the orientation session.

_____   Compare objectives to previous years' objectives.

_____   Review orientation materials to make sure they meet objectives.

_____   Update orientation materials to reflect objectives (if necessary).

Delivering Materials

_____   Send a welcoming letter to each new member.

_____   Compile all necessary orientation materials.

_____   Mail or hand-deliver orientation materials to new board members.

Planning the Agenda

_____   Set a date or dates for the orientation session or sessions.

_____   List each orientation activity:

    _____   Tour of club

    _____   Distribution of printed orientation material

    _____   Discussion/overview session

    _____   Meal

    _____   Slides or media presentation

    _____   Panel discussions

    _____   Question/answer session

    _____   Board meeting

    _____   Other:

_____   Assign a time to each activity.

_____   Prepare agenda and make copies.

Informing the Involved Parties

_____   Call or write individuals making presentations during the orientation(s):

    _____   Board president

    _____   Committee chairpersons

    _____   Experienced board member(s)

    _____   Club attorney

    _____   Club controller

    _____   Other:

_____   Call or write all new board members.

_____   If necessary, reserve the room where the orientation will be conducted.

(continued)

Exhibit 3 *(continued)*

Conducting the Orientation

_____ Arrive at the orientation site early.

_____ Bring all necessary materials.

_____ Distribute the agenda.

_____ Begin on time.

Following Up with New Members

_____ Call every new member after the first orientation session.

_____ Call every new member after the first board meeting.

_____ Call every new member a few months into the new members' terms.

- Panel discussions
- A question/answer session

All new board members should receive a manual containing a board-member position description and other written materials they might wish to consult as they carry out their board duties. General managers can use computers to help them produce these manuals each year. Information stored on the computer can be updated as club rules and procedures change.

General managers who take the time to put together fun and informative orientation sessions are making an investment that will greatly benefit the new members, the board, and the entire club.

Written Records

Every board relies on a wide range of written records. Although these records vary depending on the club and its board and general manager, there are a few basics that no club can do without:

- Articles of incorporation
- Bylaws
- Rules
- Financial records
- Meeting minutes
- Agendas

Articles of Incorporation. Articles of incorporation establish the club's legal existence (in some clubs, this document is referred to as the club's constitution). The articles of incorporation establish that the organization is a club and state the name, location, and purpose of the club (see Exhibit 5). Articles of incorporation typically are very short and extremely difficult to change.

Exhibit 4   Materials Commonly Used in New Board Member Orientations

- Position descriptions for board members
- Club organization chart
- Club mission statement
- Definition of responsibilities
- Club articles of incorporation and bylaws
- Club rules
- Club policies and procedures
- Club financial information
- Minutes of previous year's board meetings
- Pending issues before the board
- Calendar of events and meetings
- Names and biographies of board members
- Names of all club committees and their chairpersons
- Director's and officer's insurance information
- Board meeting procedures and customs
- Club history
- Applicable state laws
- List of resources (Club Managers Association of America, Professional Golfers' Association of America, and so on)
- The club general manager's responsibilities
- Guidelines for effective board meetings
- Sample club forms
- Current club news releases
- The club's long-range plans
- The club's conflict of interest policy

Bylaws. A club's **bylaws** govern its board and set the foundation for club rules. Bylaws are the backbone of a club. The following topics are typically covered in a club's bylaws:

- Membership requirements
- Membership classes (regular, social, junior, and so on)
- Admission policies and procedures
- Member assessments and minimum charges
- Policies for reprimands, suspensions, and expulsions of members
- Guidelines for the board of directors and its officers, the general manager, and club committees
- Election procedures

Exhibit 5 Sample Articles of Incorporation

Articles of Incorporation issued February 11, 1889; amended October 17, 1900; May 26, 1908; and May 23, 1935; to read as follows:

1. The name of such corporation is the XYZ Club.

2. The object for which it is formed is the promotion of literature and art, by establishing and maintaining a library, reading-room and gallery of art, and by such other means as shall be expedient and proper for such purposes.

3. The governance of the aforesaid XYZ Club shall be vested in a board of eighteen directors to be elected by the members as provided by its bylaws.

4. The location is in [city], in the County of [county name], and State of [state name].

- Membership meeting guidelines
- Use of the club by members, spouses, other family members, and guests of members
- Bylaw amendment procedures

Most club general managers advise against having items subject to frequent change in the bylaws, because bylaws are usually difficult to change. Matters such as member dress codes and how much the membership dues should be are better placed in club rules or policy statements.

Before it is adopted, every bylaw should be subjected to rigorous analysis by the board and its legal advisors. A club's general manager can be very useful during this process because of his or her knowledge of club operations. Each bylaw should be:

- Consistent with federal, state, and local laws
- Consistent with the club charter
- Consistent with reason (the bylaw should make sense)
- Capable of being complied with
- Consistent with ownership or contractual rights
- Consistent with the club's tax status

Although it is not uncommon for bylaws to be written in "legalese," such language frequently obscures the meaning of the bylaws. A club's bylaw committee should delete all ambiguities that might cloud a bylaw's intent. E. B. White's oft-quoted statement "It is easier for a man to be loyal to his club than to his planet; the bylaws are shorter and he is personally acquainted with the members" might be taken as an admonition. The shorter and easier to understand the bylaws are, the more loyalty and obedience the club is likely to engender.

It is important that a club have bylaws that are responsive to the club's members. Clubs that never review their bylaws sometimes end up burdened with antiquated bylaws that no longer reflect the club's mission, direction, or needs. (For example, one club formed during the Great Depression had a bylaw that stated that the club's board could not approve any capital loan greater than $10,000 without getting a vote of approval from the club's full membership; needless to say, this made it more difficult for the club to make improvements.) Some clubs are facing membership shortages for the first time. For this and other reasons, many clubs are seeing the need to revise their bylaws.

Rules. Private clubs have always had rules to cement the expectations of the majority of their members. Rules in a club are important because they facilitate:

- Efficient operation of the club
- Maximum enjoyment of the club
- Better member relations
- Problem resolution
- Equitable access to facilities
- Better service

A club's rules answer questions about how members should dress, how they should use the club's facilities, where they can go within the club, who has access to which services, and so on. Without rules, club members would be adrift in a sea of undefined expectations. Rules establish what club members can expect from each other, the board, and the club's staff. A club's rules are meant to establish expected behavior, not limit or restrict the members' enjoyment of the club.

Financial Documents. There are many financial documents that boards use on a regular basis. It is important for board members to become familiar with these documents so they can use them to check on the club's current financial status. Financial documents commonly reviewed by boards include operating budgets, capital appropriation requests, capital budgets, statements of income and expense, and balance sheets.

Meeting Minutes. Keeping **minutes** can aid the effectiveness of board meetings. Minutes, in their simplest form, can help keep board members informed of prior decisions, pending issues, and repeating agenda items. At a slightly more complex level, the minutes can be used as a living document to help facilitate the current meeting. Minutes may be kept on a flip chart or chalkboard. As board discussions progress, the person recording the minutes writes down key words or main points. When necessary, he or she can ask "Is this what you're saying?" or "Is this OK?" If a flip chart is used, pages can be hung around the room as they fill up and used as references to help keep the discussion moving. Since the club's general manager might be called on to keep the minutes, Exhibit 6 has some tips for keeping minutes during a board meeting. It should be noted that board meeting minutes serve as a permanent record of the actions and discussions of the board, so they must be accurate and concise.

Agendas. The bane of every general manager is the board meeting that lasts for many hours but accomplishes little. While some general managers have resigned

Exhibit 6   Tips for Minute Taking

When recording minutes, keep the following tips in mind:

- Don't worry about spelling while recording information.
- Listen for key words and phrases to capture basic ideas.
- Interrupt the discussion and ask for clarification if you get behind.
- Focus on ideas rather than names. The board speaks as "one," so it is not necessary to record the names of who said what. (Use names in the minutes to indicate assignments given to board members. Names may also be used when thanking a person or group.)
- Read back your notes to the board at the end of the meeting to make sure there aren't any additions or corrections.
- Finish your notes by outlining the agenda for the next meeting.
- Write clearly.

If using a chalkboard or flip chart:

- Underline for clarity.
- Change colors for visual relief or organizational purposes.
- Star, box, or circle for emphasis.

themselves to sitting silently while board meetings go on and on, other general managers have identified and implemented ways to make board meetings more efficient for the participants and the club. Consistently, club general managers and meeting experts cite the **meeting agenda** as the single most important tool for successful meetings. Every meeting should have an agenda that serves as a "road map" showing board members what route the meeting should take. Without an agenda, participants are likely to turn off at every interesting side street, which might be entertaining but rarely makes for a successful meeting.

At many clubs, it is the general manager who puts board meeting agendas together, subject to the approval of the board president. (Exhibit 7 contains tips offered by club general managers for preparing a board meeting agenda.) Although putting an agenda together every month can be time consuming, many general managers welcome this responsibility because it gives them a measure of control over board meetings and helps them keep board members focused on policy and governance issues and away from the temptation to manage the club.

Many general managers recommend that board meeting agendas be as detailed as possible. For example, instead of simply listing "Treasurer's Report," ideally an agenda should list something like the following:

Treasurer's Report—15 minutes

> *Financial Review.* (See the attached statement.)

> *Capital Requests.* The grounds committee is requesting a supplemental air conditioner for the Kaiser Building.

> *Information Item.* The accounting department has just completed a self-audit. (See the attached report.)

Exhibit 7   Checklist for Preparing a Board Meeting Agenda

When preparing a written agenda for a board meeting, a club general manager should check to be sure that:

- The agenda contains a clear indication of why the meeting is being called.

- The agenda is sent out in advance to everyone expected at the meeting.

- Relevant supplementary material is attached (reports, statistical information, proposals).

- Time is reserved for announcements.

- It says who is running the meeting.

- Time is reserved for breaks during long or unusually difficult meetings.

- Time is budgeted for each agenda item.

- There is an explanatory line or two after each agenda item to set the tone of the discussion.

- The agenda follows a consistent format for each meeting.

- The agenda identifies the type of action that must be taken on a given agenda item when necessary (a recommendation, an assignment, a decision, and so on).

- The agenda clearly identifies the location, starting time, and ending time of the meeting.

- The names of individuals making reports are clearly noted.

- The agenda avoids technical terms that might not be understood by all board members (or explains any technical terms used).

- Guests making presentations are placed early on the agenda so that they can leave when their presentations are complete.

> *Delinquent Accounts.* This month we have four delinquent accounts. (See the attached report.)

Just putting down "Treasurer's Report" is too vague. It doesn't outline what the board members are expected to concentrate on, which tempts some board members to wander and unnecessarily prolong the meeting. If agendas indicate the expected length of the meeting with a starting and an ending time, board members will have an idea of how much time they should devote to a given topic. Sometimes every agenda item is given an estimated time, as with the example just given ("Treasurer's Report—15 minutes").

Another tip from club general managers: only list committees on the agenda that actually have something to report. (The general manager can check with committee chairpersons before putting the agenda together.) Traditionally, the board meeting agendas at many clubs listed every club committee, month after month. With that format, all committee chairpersons felt they had to give some sort of report, even if they didn't have anything to say, which put some of the chairpersons on the spot and slowed the meetings down.

Determining in what order to place items can also present general managers with a challenge. There are many ways to arrange an agenda. In the past, board meeting agendas typically started with the approval of minutes, then moved on to committee reports, old business, then new business. Some club general managers have suggested a new agenda model that facilitates the flow of discussion and schedules difficult items for when board members are freshest. This "action" agenda model is structured like this:

- *Announcements (15 minutes or less).* These are quick items that require no debate. Announcements could include everything on the consent agenda (an agenda listing everything that will be voted on without discussion). By quickly dealing with these items, the board meeting's facilitator (typically the board president) helps board members start to focus their attention on board matters and away from their outside concerns.

- *Easily discussed items (15 minutes).* These are black and white issues that can be addressed quickly. Dealing with these items early in the meeting helps the board feel that progress is being made and can establish a sense of momentum and teamwork.

- *Most difficult item* (25 to 40 minutes). This is the hardest or most controversial item on the agenda. It's usually something that needs a lot of discussion or relates to a long-term need of the club. The facilitator should first state what is expected of the members—discussion only or a decision. Board members should then be given a chance to air their viewpoints.

- *Break (10 minutes).* This is a chance for everyone to take a breather and think about the current discussion. It also allows for some behind-the-scenes persuasion or politicking. Board members might also take this time to smooth over any controversies raised during the debate.

- *Most difficult item, continued (20 minutes).* After the break, the discussion of the most difficult item is continued. Important points can be repeated and written down. If the board's goal is to make a decision, the facilitator can call for a vote after this discussion period.

- *Discussion-only items (30 to 40 minutes).* This is the time to introduce new topics or present committee and other reports. Placing committee reports near the end of the meeting, when people are getting eager to wrap things up, can help keep the reports short.

- *Least difficult items (10 minutes).* These items are ones that can be quickly voted on. Putting least difficult items at the end of the meeting can leave board members with the feeling that they can decide things efficiently and quickly. It ends the board meeting on a high note.

Many general managers feel strongly that a board meeting's agenda should be mailed out to board members before the meeting. This gives board members a chance to review the agenda and do any research they feel is necessary. Mailing the

Insider Insights

William Schulz, CCM, General Manager
Houston Country Club, Houston, Texas

Probably the biggest key to a general manager's success is good communication with the club's board and committees. What's a general manager's best strategy for communicating with board and committee members? I can sum it up in two words: "No surprises." The worst thing you can do is surprise them. Anticipate problems and keep your board and committee members informed—that's the best way to work with boards and committees. You also must be honest. If there's a problem, don't try to hide it, bring it out in the open. If the building inspector says you've got to do something to come into compliance with the building codes and it's going to cost the club X amount of dollars, don't hide it, bring it to the forefront right away and talk about it.

A communication tool I use here at the Houston Country Club is an effective board-meeting agenda. You don't want to waste board and committee members' time. If a club manager creates an agenda with the board president and gets it to the board members before the meeting, they'll have a lot of information up-front so they can come to the meeting prepared. That's really the best way to do things. If a board member doesn't understand something on the agenda, he or she has time to find out about it before the meeting.

I produce the board-meeting agendas at my club. That helps me make sure that the meeting agendas and supporting documents are complete. For example, rather than merely listing "Treasurer's Report" on an agenda, I'll also list as subheads the things that the treasurer is going to cover during the meeting. One month the subheads might be "Financial Review," "Capital Request," "Information Item—Self Audit," and "Delinquent Accounts." To help board members with the financial review, we'll send out with the agenda a financial statement as an exhibit. Under "Capital Request," perhaps for that particular month we'll note that we're requesting a supplemental air conditioner for one of our remote buildings on the property. The "Information Item—Self Audit" subhead will remind the treasurer to tell the board that we just completed a self-audit in our accounting department, and the treasurer can elaborate on some of the things we do to keep things in line financially at the club. The fourth item, "Delinquent Accounts," is pretty self explanatory. The subheads help us zero in on specific subjects, get right to the point and keep things on track. Just listing "Treasurer's Report" on the agenda leaves it too open-ended. If it's too open-ended, you never know what questions will come up.

One of my board presidents and I developed this new agenda together. We introduced it on an experimental basis, after telling the board why we wanted to make changes. The board was very pleased with it. We used to use a very basic, old-fashioned type of meeting agenda. It listed every committee on every agenda, whether the committee had a report or not. A committee chairperson would see the committee listed on the agenda and feel obligated to say something, even if there was nothing to report. We stopped that practice with our new agendas. The chairpersons really liked the new agendas when they saw that they didn't have to report at every meeting.

(continued)

Insider Insights *(continued)*

We create an annual schedule for committee reports, set up according to the needs of the club. For example, if we know our employees' health insurance plan is up for renewal on June 1, on the agenda for the April board meeting we'll ask for a report from the insurance committee. The annual schedule isn't etched in stone, however; if there's a need, a committee can report at an unscheduled time. Before a board meeting I contact the committee chairpersons scheduled to report at the meeting to see if they need anything to help them with their reports, or whether they're still going to make a report—they might decide to defer it to another month. I'll also confirm with the committee chairpersons just prior to the meeting. At the meeting, any committee chairperson can make a report, it's not limited to just those listed on the agenda. However, for several years now on each month's agenda we've scheduled just the committees we think we need to hear from for that month, and the discipline has been very good.

General managers should take a look at when board meetings are held, too. Are they starting at eight o'clock at night? Four o'clock in the afternoon? Twelve noon? People tend to be fresher earlier in the day. Do you want board meetings to be finished prior to dinner? Before dinner, you're less likely to have to deal with someone who might have had a little too much to drink. A general manager might also want to reexamine whether to provide dinner at the club for board members. If you hold late afternoon or early evening meetings and don't provide dinner for the board, board members will have to make their own plans for dinner; consequently, they'll probably end the meeting on time.

At the beginning of the year I assign a staff liaison to each club committee. For example, the golf pro is the staff liaison for the golf committee. The staff liaison is the staff contact person for the committee chairperson. If the chairperson needs something, he or she usually goes to the committee's staff liaison first rather than to me. The liaisons always attend their committees' meetings. I do, too, whenever I can, but we have 19 committees at our club and it's hard for me to attend every meeting.

Some general managers view committees negatively. I feel very strongly that, in a nonprofit organization, working through and with committees is much more effective than trying to work around them. Club general managers will be a lot better off if they use committees correctly. General managers can't do everything themselves. The collective wisdom of many people is greater than the wisdom of just one.

agenda out ahead of time can save a lot of meeting time when the board gets together. Clubs that follow this practice have discovered that their boards act more quickly and table fewer issues because board members arrive informed and ready to tackle the challenges they face.

The General Manager

A club's board governs the club, establishing policy; the club's **general manager** manages it. In today's club world, it usually takes formal education and some practical

Exhibit 8   Getting Started at a Club

The following list is certainly not exhaustive, but gives some examples of actions a new general manager can take to get off to a good start at a club:

- Get to know your staff members as quickly as possible. It might be a good idea to have a private "get acquainted" meeting with each staff member.

- Be visible. Circulate through the club each day for at least an hour, chatting informally with club members and staff members.

- Hold well-organized weekly staff meetings.

- Communicate with your board. A weekly written status report might be a good idea.

- Inspect the club each day.

- Familiarize yourself with upcoming club events.

- Learn about the club's traditions.

- Don't rush to implement change.

Source: Adapted from "A Manager's Staying Power," *Executive Career Services Kit: For Member Use in Selecting a Club* (Alexandria, Virginia: Club Managers Association of America).

experience to attain even an entry-level management position. Today, one of the first steps to becoming a club general manager is to get a degree at an accredited school with a hospitality curriculum; some colleges offer specialized training in club management. Many club general managers began getting practical club experience while still in college—often as dishwashers, cooks, or food servers. From these line-level positions, club management students can be promoted into supervisory positions, with promotions to assistant manager positions possible after graduation.

Club management is a service profession. To excel, a club general manager must genuinely like people and enjoy serving others. Other characteristics of a successful general manager include integrity, creativity, and dedication. He or she must possess social and leadership skills, be a good communicator and administrator, and be able to communicate a club's vision.

Starting a New Job

The first six months on the job are critical to a general manager's success. This period is the general manager's "honeymoon" with the club's board, and is also the time during which the general manager establishes relationships with the club's department managers, club professionals, and employees. Exhibit 8 is a checklist of things a club general manager can do to get off to a good start at a club.

It's important for a new general manager to establish his or her credibility as soon as possible. For the first three months, it may be a good idea for the general manager to be the first to arrive at the club and the last to leave. Successful general managers say this is important because it shows the club's staff members that you care as much as they do.

Unless they encounter a drastic situation, new general managers should not rush to make changes. New managers usually will quickly see things that they want to change, but it is wise to go slowly at first. Changes made too fast, or simply for the sake of change, can upset the routine and rhythm of a club.

Some club general managers recommend that new general managers write weekly status reports and fax them to their board members. They also suggest that new general managers visit with board members individually to get their input. Establishing good lines of communication with the board is a top priority and will help keep transition problems to a minimum. It is also important for new general managers to find out if there are any groups of unhappy members at the club. Difficult situations can often be defused if the general manager talks to members of these unhappy groups to uncover the source of their discontent.

Club tradition is important to many club members, even though some traditions may seem unimportant or even comical to outsiders. For example, one private club has a rule that states that the club will serve vegetable soup every Wednesday and, according to the general manager, "there's never been a Wednesday in the past 120 years that the club has not served vegetable soup." Members usually feel a sense of ownership in their club and the history and traditions that they have helped build and sustain. That's why a new general manager will not make friends (or keep a job long) if he or she comes in, denounces the club's traditions as silly or impractical, and proceeds to "update" them or eliminate them entirely.

Because traditions are rarely written down, it can be difficult for a general manager to know when he or she is treading on sacred ground. New general managers should take the time to talk to staff members, board members, and others to find out what the club's traditions are. It's also a good idea for new general managers to write the traditions down; this will give the managers something to refer to until they've learned the traditions.

If a club tradition has a negative effect on the club, the general manager may eventually be able to propose starting a new tradition to replace it. This is often a more effective strategy than trying to simply eliminate the tradition.

Working with the Board

There are many groups and individuals at a club with which the club general manager must work—club professionals, department managers, and club committee members are some obvious examples. But, above all, a club general manager must work harmoniously with the club's board of directors. A club's board provides the strategic direction for the club that the general manager must carry out. The board is also responsible for hiring and firing the general manager and providing him or her with regular performance evaluations. Because a general manager reports to the board, his or her relationship with the board is extremely important.

One of the most delicate issues club general managers face in working with boards is keeping board members from overstepping their roles and trying to actually manage the club. How can a general manager discreetly encourage his or her board to stick to governing the club and not interfere with daily operational decisions? According to Richard Chait's *How to Help Your Board Govern More and Manage Less*, there are several things a club general manager can do. The general manager can:

- Structure written materials for the board, such as club status reports and board meeting agendas, to direct the attention of board members to issues of policy and strategy.

- Equip board members with the capacity to monitor the club's performance and progress.

- Create clear expectations for the board.[6]

Other Tips for Long-Term Success

There are no rules club general managers can follow that will guarantee that they will keep their jobs or be happy managing their club. But there are a few principles veteran general managers cite that might help a club general manager achieve long-term success with a club:

- *Be yourself when interviewing.* The best thing a general manager can do during the hiring process is to let the board know exactly who he or she is so that there is a better chance that the right match between club manager and club will be made.

- *Ask for an employment contract.* A general manager should have an employment contract, or at least a letter of agreement, from the club's board. It is always wise to have employment terms and conditions in writing, especially if the club's board changes annually. The general manager should make sure this document is updated and signed each time he or she goes through a benefit or compensation review.

- *Work with the club's committees.* Club committees are resources that general managers should tap into. General managers should make an effort to know what's going on with the club's committees and attend as many of their meetings as possible. A general manager who works closely with club committees often has greater membership support.

- *Continue your education.* It becomes more important every year for club general managers to continue their educations. Some general managers are able to put aside funds in the club's annual budget for professional development. Educational opportunities give general managers a chance to pick up money-saving ideas and other ways to improve their clubs. (We will discuss continuing-education opportunities for general managers in the next section.)

- *Communicate, communicate, communicate.* Communication is a general manager's lifeline. He or she must keep in touch with the membership. General managers should listen to the vocal minority, but not forget to communicate with the silent majority. A great way to keep in touch is by writing a monthly article in the club newsletter. Also, the general manager must communicate with the board about everything going on at the club. The general manager should never spring any last-minute surprises on the board.

- *Don't forget the basics.* Do communicate. Do be visible to the membership. Do dress the part. Do continue to improve the club for the members, making sure that you know what they really want. Do continue your education—keep moving ahead in your career.

- *Don't use the club.* This may sound surprising, but many experienced club general managers maintain that a general manager shouldn't use his or her club—ever.[7] General managers who frequently play on their club's golf course or use other club facilities may regret it because, inevitably, at least a few of the club's members will frown on it, or make remarks such as the following: "Gee, I couldn't get a tee time this morning, but I noticed the club manager didn't have any trouble getting on the course."

Professional Development

Because of the constantly changing nature of the club industry, a club general manager's education should be ongoing. Fortunately, there are many professional development opportunities available.

Club Managers Association of America. The Club Managers Association of America (CMAA) is a major source of professional development opportunities for club managers.[8] CMAA offers a variety of educational programs designed for club managers at all career levels, including:

- Business Management Institute
- World Conference on Club Management
- Leadership/Legislative Conference
- Chapter Education

   Business Management Institute. CMAA's Business Management Institute (BMI) is a series of intensive university-based one-week courses ranging from the first level, designed for the entry-level club manager, through the fifth level, designed for advanced senior-level managers. These competency-based courses are offered at major U.S. hospitality schools and are taught by university faculty and industry professionals. The five BMI programs are:

- BMI I: The Basic Club Management School
- BMI II: The Leadership Edge
- BMI III: The Chief Operating Officer Concept
- BMI IV: Managerial Excellence: Tactics for Today
- BMI V: Strategies for Tomorrow ... Realities of Today

   Elective courses in the BMI program include one-week programs in the following areas:

- Sports Management
- Food and Beverage Management
- Culinary Orientation for Club Managers
- Culinary Update for Club Managers

- Certified Hospitality Education Workshop

- Certified Club Manager Review Course

World Conference on Club Management. Held in a major U.S. city each year, CMAA's World Conference on Club Management serves as the centerpiece of the association's annual functions. Educational opportunities abound at this conference, including approximately 100 educational programs on club management that range from 90-minute sessions to full-day pre- and post-conference workshops. The 90-minute sessions allow club managers to receive updates on such topics as government regulatory issues and environmental concerns. The workshops provide an in-depth look at topics ranging from golf course management for club managers to technology and computer applications in private clubs. Day-long case studies provide participants with an opportunity to analyze real club problems and come up with creative solutions. In addition, the World Conference hosts the club industry's largest exposition of products and services and an Idea Fair of creative club programs.

Leadership/Legislative Conference. CMAA's Leadership/Legislative Conference is designed for CMAA chapter leaders, offering extensive information on leadership techniques for use in chapter management as well as information on legislative issues affecting the club industry.

Chapter Education. A variety of educational programs are offered on a monthly or quarterly basis by the more than 50 CMAA chapters located throughout the United States and around the world.

Other Associations. Educational opportunities for club general managers are also available from a number of other associations that serve the club and hospitality industries. The Educational Institute of the American Hotel & Motel Association has a wide range of textbooks, seminars, and certifications that are of value to club managers.[9] The Educational Foundation of the National Restaurant Association offers educational seminars and workshops dealing with food and beverage operations.[10] The American Management Association is an excellent source of materials on management and offers hundreds of courses and seminars in such general management categories as purchasing, research and development, human resources, technology, and finance and accounting.[11] The National Club Association represents the mutual business interests of social, recreational, and athletic clubs; it provides a variety of club-related publications and other services.[12]

Endnotes

1. Much of the information in this chapter was adapted from Bridgette M. Redman, *Topical Reference Series: White Papers on Club Management, Issues 1–6* (East Lansing, Mich.: Educational Institute of the American Hotel & Motel Association, 1997). Copies of this book can be obtained by contacting the Club Managers Association of America, 1733 King Street, Alexandria, VA 22314; tel. (703) 739-9500.

2. Gerald F. Hurley, *The Private Club Leadership Guide* (Washington, D.C.: National Club Association, 1991), p. 7.

3. Cyril O. Houle, *Governing Boards* (San Francisco, Calif.: Jossey-Bass Publishers, 1990), p. 72.

4. Edward A. Merritt, "Hospitality Management: A Study of Burnout in Private Club Management" (master's thesis, Pepperdine University, Malibu, California, 1995), Appendix C, p. 10.

5. Ralph F. Lewis, "The Art of Choosing Board Members," in *The Corporate Director: New Roles, New Responsibilities* (Boston, Mass.: Cahners Books, 1975).

6. Richard P. Chait, *How to Help Your Board Govern More and Manage Less* (Washington, D.C.: National Center for Nonprofit Boards, 1993).

7. George P. Carroll, "Here Today, Here Tomorrow: Improving a Manager's Staying Power," *Club Management*, June 1990.

8. For more information about the Club Managers Association of America's programs for club managers, call (703) 739-9500; or write CMAA, 1733 King Street, Alexandria, VA 22314; or fax (703) 739-0124; or contact CMAA via the Internet at http://www.cmaa.org; or email them at cmaa@cmaa.org.

9. Information on services and products provided by the Educational Institute of the American Hotel & Motel Association can be obtained by calling (800) 752-4567; or writing the Educational Institute, 800 N. Magnolia Ave., Suite 1800, Orlando, FL 32803; or faxing (517) 372-5727; or using EI's Internet address: http://www.ei-ahma.org.

10. Information on courses as well as other professional services offered by the Educational Foundation of the National Restaurant Association can be obtained by calling (800) 765-2122; or writing the Educational Foundation, 250 S. Wacker Dr., No. 1400, Chicago, IL 60606; or using EF's Internet address: http://www.restaurant.org/educate/educate.htm.

11. A complete description of the American Management Association's courses can be obtained by writing the association at 1601 Broadway, New York, NY 10019-7420; or calling (800) 225-3215; or emailing at cust_serv@amanet.org.

12. Information on National Club Association seminars and educational programs can be obtained by calling (800) 625-6221; or writing NCA at 1120 20th Street NW, Suite 725, Washington, DC 20036; or faxing (202) 822-9808; or emailing at ncaclubdir@aol.com.

🔑 Key Terms

articles of incorporation—The document that establishes a club's legal existence. Also called a constitution.

board of directors—An equity club's governing body, made up of club members elected by club members.

bylaws—Rules adopted by a club to govern the club.

general manager—A club's chief operating officer, in charge of all club staff members and operations; he or she reports to the club's board of directors and carries out club policies set by the board.

meeting agenda—A tool used to help make meetings more effective; it lists all topics to be covered in a meeting.

minutes—A document recording what takes place at a board or committee meeting.

Review Questions

1. What are some problems that might occur if a club's board of directors is too big? too small?

2. What are some of the advantages a club enjoys by having long terms of service for board members?

3. Why is it a good idea to give new board members an orientation to their new roles as board members?

4. What are some topics typically covered by a club's bylaws?

5. Why is it important for a board meeting to have a written agenda?

6. What are some ways a new general manager can get started on the right foot with his or her club?

7. How can a club general manager discreetly encourage his or her board to govern the club, not try to manage it?

8. What are some of the professional development opportunities available to club general managers?

Additional Reading

Carroll, George P. "Here Today, Here Tomorrow: Improving a Manager's Staying Power." *Club Management*, June 1990.

Chait, Richard P. *How to Help Your Board Govern More and Manage Less.* Washington, D.C.: National Center for Nonprofit Boards, 1993.

Henderson, Edward. "Lions Among Us," in *Master Club Manager Monographs,* Volume 1, Numbers 1–6. Alexandria, Virginia: Club Managers Association of America, 1995.

Houle, Cyril O. *Governing Boards.* San Francisco, Calif.: Jossey-Bass Publishers, 1990.

Hurley, Gerald F. *The Private Club Leadership Guide.* Washington, D.C.: National Club Association, 1991.

Lewis, Ralph F. "The Art of Choosing Board Members," in *The Corporate Director: New Roles, New Responsibilities.* Boston, Mass.: Cahners Books, 1975.

Merritt, Edward A. "Hospitality Management: A Study of Burnout in Private Club Management." Master's thesis, Pepperdine University, Malibu, California, 1995.

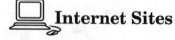Internet Sites

For more information, visit the following Internet sites. Remember that Internet addresses can change without notice. If the site is no longer there, use a browser to look for additional sites.

American Management Association
http://www.amanet.org

Club Managers Association of America
http://www.cmaa.org

Educational Foundation of the National Restaurant Association
http://www.restaurant.org/educate/educate.htm

Educational Institute of the American Hotel & Motel Association
http://www.ei-ahma.org

Virtual Clubhouse Home Page
http://www.club-mgmt.com

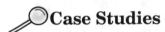

Case Studies

Case Study 1

Chris Miller is the new general manager of the Mountainview Country Club, a 1,000-member club just ten years old. The club's board fired the previous general manager because it was unhappy with the way the club was run. When Chris interviewed for the job, several board members mentioned that club operations seemed "chaotic" and that the club was bogged down with one problem after another. They wanted Chris to "turn things around." Despite some misgivings (Chris knew that he would be the club's fourth general manager in ten years), Chris took the position because he felt the club's potential was worth the risk.

It didn't take Chris long to realize that one of the biggest problems with the club was the board itself. At Chris's first monthly board meeting, he had been surprised at how Ted Fisher, the board's president, ran things. First, there was a generic agenda that consisted of an extremely simple outline: "Call meeting to order; Read previous minutes; Finance committee reports; House committee reports; Greens committee reports"; and so on. There were three new board members at the meeting, but they were not formally welcomed and they obviously had not been given any orientation because they looked lost throughout the meeting. The meeting itself wandered from subject to subject and took three hours to accomplish almost nothing. It was obvious that many of the committee chairs had nothing to report, but felt obligated to say something anyway. After the meeting, Chris had asked President Fisher about the generic agenda. "We always go in the same order," Fisher said, "so that's all we really need." What about the new board members—had they been given any orientation? "We've never bothered with that," Fisher replied. "What is there to learn, really? They've been members for years."

After that first board meeting, Chris had asked his assistant manager, Linda, for some background information about the board and how it operated. Unfortunately, his worst suspicions were confirmed. Some of the board members are retired, Linda said, and have a lot of time on their hands, so they want to micromanage everything. On the other hand, many of the board members are very busy executives and they present an opposite problem: they are so pressed for time they hardly give the matters that come before the board any attention. Julia, the club's only female board member, had promised her friends that if she was elected to the board she would do something about the men-only Saturday-morning tee times. Her proposal to open the Saturday-morning tee times to women was defeated early in her term and she'd had a poor attitude ever since; she took scant interest in other club business and appeared to be just going through the motions until her term ended. Other board members, too, tended to focus on their pet projects to the exclusion of everything else.

Chris also learned that board members had a history of abusing their power in matters both large and small—not because they were deliberately trying to disrupt the club, but because they didn't know any better. Many board members habitually gave direct orders to club employees, for example. This bad habit had gotten started after the first general manager left the club and the club struggled without one for six months. Apparently the members didn't realize the havoc they caused when they contradicted a club manager's directives, or asked valets on duty to take them to the airport, or told a banquet server to drop what he was doing and drive by their house to pick up the wedding gift they forgot.

Some board members asked to be seated in the main dining room during busy periods without making reservations. Last year the club's dining room manager quit because she received a tongue-lashing and then a very harsh letter of reprimand from a board member. Her crime? She had refused to seat his party because some of his guests were wearing blue jeans and the club has a firm policy against blue jeans in the main dining room.

One of the board members tends to drink a little too much, Linda went on, and sometimes discusses with club bartenders things like the previous general manager's bonus plan and why the club fired its last golf pro. Around Christmas time an outbreak of food poisoning had occurred at the club, and a board member thought it would be helpful if he went to the media and explained the situation. Without the board's or anyone else's knowledge, he went to the local newspaper and told such a confused and contradictory tale that the newspaper launched a full-blown investigation and turned an unfortunate but minor incident into a front-page story. And last but not least, the board's vice president had almost gotten the club involved in a lawsuit because he repeatedly made inappropriate advances toward one of the club's female servers. Because this was another period when the club was between general managers, the server went directly to the board with her complaints, but the board ignored the problem. Soon afterwards the server graduated from college and landed another job, and it looked like she would not be pressing charges, but one never knew if the problem would reoccur more seriously.

All in all, it was a picture of an undisciplined board that was doing more harm than good to the club. Chris knew that if he was going to make positive changes at the club, he would have to start with the board, and he had his work cut out for him. Chris also knew from working at other clubs that timing was a critical factor. Since he had just been hired, he had the board's attention and a brief window of opportunity in which to address the issues that needed immediate action.

Discussion Questions

1. What challenges does Chris face with the club's board?

2. Which of these challenges should Chris address immediately (Priority A challenges), and which are not so critical and can be addressed over time (Priority B challenges)?

3. How should Chris address the immediate, Priority A challenges?

4. What can Chris do immediately to encourage the board president to run more effective meetings?

5. How can Chris help the board president see the need for an orientation program for new board members?

6. What elements should a new-board-member orientation program contain?

The following industry experts helped generate and develop this case: Cathy Gustafson, CCM, University of South Carolina, Columbia, South Carolina; Kurt D. Kuebler, CCM, Vice President, General Manager, The Desert Highlands Association; Scottdale, Arizona; and William A. Schulz, MCM, General Manager, Houston Country Club, Houston, Texas.

Case Study 2

Tom Frost has recently become the general manager of the Leisure Resort Club, a private, residential, golf course community at which the average age of members is 65. Most of its members are retirees. Many members used to be CEOs or in the upper management of large corporations. They previously led very hectic lifestyles and are now learning to unwind.

Tom used to be the general manager of the Vertigo Club, a large downtown club. The average age of members there was 45—many members were hardworking professionals. Board meetings for the club were typically held for no more than an hour over breakfast one day a month. The president of the Vertigo Club was known for his efficient meeting-time management with the board; he would mail out agendas in advance that included timeframes for each item, and he knew how to diplomatically keep discussions on schedule.

In the course of his orientation, Tom learned from the Leisure Resort Club president that monthly board meetings typically start at 3:00 P.M. and vary in length. Sometimes they finish by the dinner hour, sometimes they do not. Tom has met with each of the board members and he has been impressed with the warmth and cooperative attitudes they exhibit. His understanding from the president is that he is to conduct a review of club operations, so he reviews human resources records and gathers reports from the accounting division, the food and beverage outlets, the golf and greens operations—all the branches of the club's operation. He puts tremendous effort into reading minutes from previous board meetings, internalizing the club's goals and organizational structure, and reviewing, analyzing, and reformatting reports. His goal is to give a "State of the Club" address at the upcoming board meeting, which will be his first, and receive feedback on his observations from board members.

The day arrives for Tom's first board meeting. He learns at 10:00 A.M. that there is a schedule conflict for the boardroom, so he has the board meeting moved to the Smith Room, a private room off the main dining room. Tom has his staff spread the word to the board members while he calls to inform the club president. When Tom asks whether the board members will be badly distracted by the unusual setting of the meeting, the president tells him not to worry about it. Tom arrives at the Smith Room at 2:30 P.M. and arranges his presentation materials. Tom hands the president a copy of the meeting agenda, complete with time frames for each agenda item. The president comments, "Wow, we've never had anything this detailed before. This should really help us stay focused." Tom places copies of the agenda and of his report summaries at each place around the table. At 3:00, as members start to arrive and look at the materials before them, Tom hears many comments about how organized his handouts are and how helpful they are sure to be.

The president opens the meeting with a welcome to Tom. The board members offer a hearty round of applause, and Tom beams, thinking to himself, "This bunch of people makes it worth all the effort I put in last week." The president continues with his own report: "One of the most pressing issues we are facing here, Tom, is the renovation of the main clubhouse. All of you know how it has been a mixed blessing for us in the past months. I feel that it is important that Tom know the depth of this board's struggles and feelings over our extensive but necessary reno-vation enterprise. Wouldn't you say so, Bill?"

Bill jumps in. "You're right, Reynold. Why just the other day a member came to me and said she had seen what she feared was asbestos hanging down from a section of ceiling..." As they talk, two servers come in, looking for a contact lens a member might have lost in that room earlier.

Three hours later...

Tom has been taking notes from time to time, but has been getting more and more anxious. The board has discussed the renovations, slow play on the golf course, the renovations, their most recent golf games, the renovations, cigar smoking, the ren-ovations, soft spikes, and the renovations. Two board members spent part of the time on their hands and knees, helping the servers look for the contact lens. The president is just summing up the discussion on the renovations when a dining room employee enters and whispers in Tom's ear. As the president takes his seat, Tom says, "I'm terribly sorry, everyone, but there's another group scheduled to meet here in fifteen minutes, so we need to wrap things up."

Tom eagerly begins to cover agenda item 3 of 11, the general manager's report. He quickly outlines the results of his analysis. A board member interrupts and says her copy of a particular page is too light to read. Two other members start talking about how shameful it is that they are the most important decision-making body in the organization and they can't even have a meeting room for an adequate period of time. The president steps in and says, "I think Tom has done an excellent job at tak-ing the pulse of our club, and I encourage all of you to take these report summaries home and read them. It's just about time to go. Tom, do you have any more com-ments to share?"

Tom says, "I thank you in advance for the effort you will put into reading these materials."

Floyd, a committee chair whose report is always last on the agenda, asks the president for a chance to speak. The president gives him the floor, and Floyd begins: "Tom has obviously put a lot of work into these summaries. He will need to hear our feedback and to begin to know what actions to take on his conclusions. If we leave him to muddle through the next month, we'll have only ourselves to blame if he takes actions we don't like. Let's all be timely in reading these reports and giving Tom our feedback." The president agrees and hears a motion to adjourn the meeting. After a quick vote, the board members file out. Bill finds the contact lens on his seat cushion, and the board members nearby hail him as a hero.

By the time Tom has gathered his belongings and vacated the conference room, the next group is almost ready to start their meeting. On the way out, Tom sees a copy of his report on the bar counter. He grabs it and hopes the bartender hasn't read anything, especially the section about poor liquor control on the part of the bar staff.

"What a disaster," Tom thinks to himself as he shuffles back to his office. He feels too exhausted to think, but he makes himself call the general manager of the Schenkles Club, a sister club to the Vertigo Club. The manager listens carefully to his story and then offers to give Tom some suggestions.

Questions for Discussion

1. What more does Tom need to know to conduct an effective board meeting? What skills does he need to exercise and develop if future board meetings are to be effective?

2. In terms of the setting, interaction with board members, and the agenda, what went wrong at Tom's first board meeting?

3. In terms of the setting, interaction with board members, and the agenda, what should the Schenkles Club general manager suggest that Tom do differently at the next board meeting?

The following industry experts helped generate and develop this case: Cathy Gustafson, CCM, University of South Carolina, Columbia, South Carolina; Kurt D. Kuebler, CCM, Vice President, General Manager, The Desert Highlands Association; Scottdale, Arizona; and William A. Schulz, MCM, General Manager, Houston Country Club, Houston, Texas.

Chapter Appendix

A Typical Day in the Life of a Club Manager

What follows are daily-activity diaries that four club general managers kept during one recent holiday season. All four managers said that these were "typical" days—if you can call any club general manager's day typical!

G. Mead Grady, CCM, General Manager
Tuesday, November 18

8:00 A.M.

Arrived at the office and looked through the business section of the morning paper. Visited the kitchen and spoke with the cooks about today's Leadership luncheon. Spoke with the marketing director about functions in progress. Also spoke with the club's utility man about repair work in progress.

8:20 A.M.

Returned to my desk to read the mail from the past three days (this was my first day back from a business trip).

8:25 A.M.

Visited the accounting office.

8:30 A.M.

Returned to my desk to review sales reports. Interrupted by the clubhouse manager, who briefed me on happenings that occurred in my absence.

8:50 A.M.

Brief meeting with the utility man.

8:55 A.M.

Desk work continues; brief meeting with the marketing director.

9:10 A.M.

Unscheduled walk-in meeting with the president of the chamber of commerce to discuss membership matters.

9:20 A.M.

Back to my desk to continue reading the mail. Received and placed several phone calls.

10:00 A.M.

Visited the Lane Room to inspect it in preparation for the Leadership luncheon.

10:15 A.M.

Returned to my desk, approved the weekly payroll, and approved the head-table luncheon reservations with the clubhouse manager. Called the membership director to discuss the new membership-matriculation campaign.

11:00 A.M.

Visited the accounting office; on the way there inspected the re-roofing work in progress.

11:15 A.M.

Returned to my desk; wrote two letters and a memo.

11:30 A.M.

Inspected the parking entryway and spoke with the valets before the luncheon crowd began to arrive; visited private dining rooms and member areas as members arrived.

11:50 A.M.

Returned to the office to check my voice mail and other messages from the receptionist before the luncheon activities began.

11:55 A.M.

Greeted members and attended the Leadership luncheon; enjoyed the speech; monitored member reaction.

1:45 P.M.

Returned to my desk; returned a phone call; read mail.

1:55 P.M.

Left to attend a city function off-site.

3:45 P.M.

Returned to the club. Checked my voice mail, then visited with the director of communications.

4:15 P.M.

Returned to my desk for "normal duties."

4:50 P.M.

Unscheduled walk-in meeting with the clubhouse manager; the meeting ended at 5:20 P.M. I began clearing my desk.

5:30 P.M.

Visited the main kitchen to check details for this evening's wine dinner.

5:45 P.M.

Back at my desk, making notes for tomorrow's agenda of phone calls. Called an employee who is on sick leave, then called my wife (a relaxing moment). Completed tomorrow's agenda.

6:40 P.M.

Freshened up, then went to the wine dinner reception to introduce the guest of honor to arriving members; observed the dinner service; had dinner in the kitchen.

9:20 P.M.

Back to my office to check for messages and tidy up my desk for tomorrow.

10:05 P.M.

I'm outta here.

C. Douglas Postler, CCM, General Manager
Friday, December 2

8:30 A.M.

Arrived at work. (Depending on the season and the activities of the day, I usually arrive at the club between 8:00 and 8:30.) Took a quick walk through the clubhouse. Poured a cup of coffee. Said hello to the cook. Headed for my office on the second floor. Checked phone messages from the previous day.

9:00 A.M.

Continued my preparation for an orientation meeting designed for the incoming club secretary. The purpose of the meeting is to review responsibilities and coordinate communication between the secretary and the membership chairperson. I drafted a few last-minute changes to some memos and made copies of each memo to complete three orientation binders for the secretary, club president, and membership chairperson.

10:00 A.M.

Met the plumbing contractor and the club superintendent at our swimming pool to discuss options to resolve a suspected leak in the lines between the pool and the pump room.

10:30 A.M.

Left the club for a half-hour drive downtown for the orientation meeting.

11:00 A.M.

Met with three club board officers and their administrative assistants to discuss responsibilities and transfer records. During the meeting I agreed to an expanded role in notifying club directors of each board meeting and recording the minutes of the meetings.

Noon

The orientation meeting ended. Drove back to the club.

12:30 P.M.

Entered the club and touched bases with the clubhouse manager regarding the buffet the previous evening, the Christmas decoration schedule, and a few other small items. Made a quick pass through the clubhouse and spoke to various members having lunch. Returned to the kitchen and spoke to the chef and his staff, who were taking inventory. Had a "small-talk" lunch with the accounts receivable secretary and clubhouse manager.

1:15 P.M.

Back in my office to look at the day's mail. Called the golf pro concerning his perception of a need for an updated course rating for the club's women golfers. Reviewed a request for information about the club. Skimmed the latest issue of *Outlook*. Reviewed a letter of agreement for reciprocity with another club during our club's shutdown time.

2:00 P.M.

Reviewed two bills for parties that members had booked at the club the previous weekend and drafted thank-you notes to accompany each. Began writing notes for this log.

2:30 P.M.

Reviewed a quote for a new employee health-insurance plan, which I requested due to a substantial increase in our current plan's premium. Completed a questionnaire as part of an application for other health insurance options.

3:00 P.M.

Responding to an inquiry by a member earlier in the week, I called the manager of the stables (an operation located on our property, but leased to an independent contractor) to make a second inquiry into the circumstances of an IRS tax lien against the stables, noted in a local paper. I followed up with a call to the manager's lawyer and the club's legal counsel. They agreed to send a letter to me outlining the situation and detailing the resolution. I will pass this along to our board.

3:45 P.M.

Received a call from a member who said she had not been billed for a party she held at the club last month. I asked the clubhouse manager and the accounts receivable secretary to follow through on this inquiry. They reported back that the bill had been addressed to the wrong member, but the mistake was now resolved.

4:00 P.M.

Walked through the clubhouse and spoke to a few members who had just finished playing bridge, then wished one of our bartenders "Happy 40th!" From the bar area, I proceeded to the golf shop to get a golf car for a drive out to our 12th hole. We are having an outside contractor install a multi-row irrigation system on the golf course and I just wanted to drive by and see the progress. I spoke briefly to the foreman, who expressed frustration with the multitude of equipment failures he had been experiencing and the fact that more trenching was required than originally anticipated.

4:30 P.M.

Upon my return to the clubhouse, I received a call from an angry member who expressed her displeasure at being charged for a glass of wine during our annual-meeting dinner the week before Thanksgiving. Since she never drinks alcoholic beverages, she did not want to pay for alcohol consumed by others. I told her we would gladly credit her account and try not to let this happen in the future. After I got off the phone, I spoke to the clubhouse manager and the accounts receivable secretary, asking them to make sure that alcohol charges are not billed to this particular member's account.

4:45 P.M.

Engaged in some non-club work during the next half hour. This included calls to two fellow CMAA chapter members and a touch-up of a policy I'm planning to propose at a savings and loan association board meeting tomorrow morning.

5:15 P.M.

Made a final pass through the clubhouse. I checked on dinner reservations for that evening, said goodnight to staff members, and headed home. As a rule, I tend to work from 8:00 or 8:30 in the morning until about 5:00 in the evening. If we have a large evening function, I stay later, until at least the entrée is served and I'm sure all is running smoothly. Since I manage a relatively small club, functions tend to be somewhat seasonal, and we don't have one every night even during the busiest of times.

I really enjoy and look forward to going to work, but I also try to balance this with responsibilities at home.

Sally Burns Rambo, CCM
Early in December

7:15 A.M.

Arrived at work. Went over the day's worksheets for parties. Talked to setup employees about how to set up one of the parties; the host had changed his mind.

8:00 A.M.

Started to write up all the party sheets for the week of December 13 through 18. (It ended up taking many hours because of all the interruptions.)

9:00 A.M.

Ordered 50 chairs for a wedding party. Answered the phone four times in a row.

9:30 A.M.

Signed payroll checks (92 of them!). Talked for 15 minutes to the membership chairperson about our membership drive. We have 20 new members. Set up a membership meeting for Tuesday, December 13, at 6 P.M.

10:30 A.M.

Changed the count on three parties for Wednesday. Ordered 200 chairs and 20 8-foot tables for a party of 450 on Thursday.

11:00 A.M.

Ordered two cakes for Sunday—one for 300 for a 50th wedding anniversary and one for 100 for a birthday party.

11:30 A.M.

I was called to the bar—a member wanted to know what day the January wine-tasting will be held. On my way back to my office I was stopped by another member, who ordered turkey dinner to go for 20 (Christmas dinner). I wrote the order on a bar napkin; when I got back to my office I transferred the order to a party sheet. Called and got a piano player for a book signing for 250 on Sunday, December 11.

Noon

Talked to the clubhouse manager at another local club about Christmas parties. He also wanted me to book the North Texas club managers party at my club on January 8, which I did.

12:15 P.M.

Talked to a member about a party (he has three parties planned for Christmas). He wanted to change the count on one of them.

1:00 P.M.

Returned a member's call about a party change—the party's date was moved from November 1 to November 4 next year.

1:15 P.M.

Booked a party for next December for a member.

1:20 P.M.

The band called about the setup for a company party on December 17. Returned the call of a general manager of a local club.

1:30 P.M.

Booked a Christmas party for 20 for December 20 at noon. Signed 6 checks.

1:45 P.M.

Two members came in to pay for their luncheon party. (Every party at the club is sponsored by a member.)

1:55 P.M.

Talked for 15 minutes to a gentleman about joining our club.

2:10 P.M.

Stopped for 20 minutes and had a bowl of soup for lunch.

2:30 P.M.

Went to the kitchen to change the count from 350 to 340 for a party on Wednesday.

2:35 P.M.

Returned a call from a member who has a party on December 12. Talked about her party for 10 minutes and wrote up what she wanted. Xeroxed her party sheet and took it to eight stations around the club.

Took another birthday cake order for 7 people for Sunday, December 11.

2:50 P.M.

Talked to a member. (My office is near the club's entrance and members stop in to say hello all day. I love that.)

I was called to the members' card room to talk to a member about his membership (15 minutes).

3:10 P.M.

Began working on the list of employees who will receive Christmas bonuses this year. Bonuses will be passed out on Friday, December 9th. Some bonuses are larger than others because of number of years of service, salaries, and merit.

3:20 P.M.

Talked to my daughter-in-law (10 minutes).

Signed check for a new broiler for $29,562.

Put some more Christmas decorations in the members' card room. I've decorated it Western: I put three small wagons in there filled with poinsettias, plus put in some lights—real cute. The men loved them. (Ladies are not allowed in the card room—except me.)

3:30 P.M.

Talked to a lady about a party for 340 tomorrow. She told me she had changed her mind about the setup. We had already set up for 200, but she wanted the napkins put in wine glasses—she is bringing in napkin rings. We had to redo the arrangements. The setup people will be here at 6:30 to set up for all parties. Wednesday we have 452 for lunch, plus members coming in for à la carte dining.

3:40 P.M.

Someone called about joining our club; I sent a prospective-member package to him. A fellow club manager called and asked if I would contact a potential speaker for our North Texas CMAA chapter meeting (we invite the officers of each club in the area to attend).

4:00 P.M.

Went over all the changes to parties for the rest of the week with my clubhouse manager—he will make the changes.

Got two more calls from people wanting to become members.

I have five phone calls from members to return (some talk forever).

4:50 P.M.

Started working on the Christmas bonus list again.

4:55 P.M.

A member called and reduced her party tonight from 60 to 48.

5:10 P.M.

The manager of another local club called to ask me to come to a meeting of club managers working in the Dallas/Fort Worth area; it's about an issue that is important to all of us. The meeting is scheduled for January 19 at his club—a luncheon. We also talked about his retirement from the club business coming up soon.

6:30 P.M.

Just finished the Christmas bonus list for employees.

We have three parties tonight—one for 48, one for 40, and one for 110. My clubhouse manager and I will work these parties.

7:00 P.M.

Worked on the party sheets for the week of December 13 through 18 again; I want to finish all the details.

Scheduled car parkers for each day and night of this week.

7:15 P.M.

A member of our board called and wanted me to write a letter to all junior members explaining the upgrade on the new membership program. (Junior members have to upgrade to a stock membership when they reach age 36.)

7:20 P.M.

Called a member and told her we were moving her party to another room tomorrow. Had two tables removed from one party; had to put one back. Checked on all the parties again—counts go up and down like see-saws.

8:00 P.M.

Back to working on the December 13–18 party sheets. Stopped at 8:30 because most members weren't home to answer my questions.

I average 50 phone calls a day. The members just won't talk to anyone but me about parties—or anything else it seems. I'm going on my 19th year at the club and I spoil my members. That is probably bad for me but I love them dearly and would never hurt their feelings. I'm from the old school—"Hard Knocks College."

8:30 P.M.

I went to where we put dirty linen and, just as I feared, the staff had mixed green and red napkins with the white tablecloths, which ruins the tablecloths. Unfortunately, I threw a fit, which doesn't help a bit. I told my clubhouse manager and assistant manager in charge of part-time help that one more time and they are in deep trouble. (It might not help, but it made me feel better.)

I have almost 500 in for lunch tomorrow—parties of 340, 50, 22, 47, and 11, in different rooms, plus all the à la carte diners.

9:30 P.M.

Left club.

Michael Wheeler, CCM, General Manager
Wednesday, December 14

8:00 A.M.

Arrived at the club.

Visited with the housekeeper regarding a problem a member brought to my attention the day before.

Got a cup of coffee.

Visited with the chef regarding the previous night's menu specials.

Walked the club.

Emptied the suggestion boxes in the exercise room and men's locker room.

Planned the rest of the day using my Day-Timer.

Reviewed daily special-event sheets for parties and to-go orders.

Called the maintenance engineer to make sure the clubhouse manager had made him aware of the problem with the Christmas lights in front of the clubhouse.

Reviewed the security report from the previous night.

Left a message for the greens superintendent regarding a meeting next Tuesday with some people from the standards committee.

9:00 A.M.

Decorating committee meeting.

10:00 A.M.

Staff meeting.

11:00 A.M.

Ate lunch while standing in the kitchen talking with the clubhouse manager about this evening's party and the catering meeting later in the afternoon.

11:30 A.M.

Back to my office and returned phone calls from the morning.

One call was from an angry member, who wondered how the club could possibly charge anything more than cost plus $15 for two tenderloins to go? Called the house committee chairperson, warning him of a call he may receive from a hostile lady who cannot understand our pricing policies for to-go items.

Spoke with the controller regarding the receptionist and accounts-receivable positions that are open at the club. Asked her if she needed some assistance due to the shortage of help at this time.

Noon

Greeted the "men of the round table" in the Grill. Received various comments regarding how the club could be run better. Received various comments about how well the club was running. Someone asked if we had a new chef, because the food has been great lately. (The chef has been with the club for almost two years.) Received several comments on how beautiful the club looks for the Christmas holiday season.

12:30 P.M.

Made the rounds in the other dining rooms.

1:00 P.M.

Returned to my office and went through the mail.

1:30 P.M.

Attended a catering meeting with the chef and clubhouse manager about a February wedding.

2:30 P.M.

Dictated a letter for the board of directors, preparing them for the following week's board meeting.

3:00 P.M.

Called applicants for the swim-professional position for interviews. Confirmed the interviews and called appropriate committee members to inform them of the date of the interviews. Had the résumés of the applicants mailed to the committee members.

3:30 P.M.

Reviewed the proposed new employee handbook, which was received from the club's attorney the day before. Sent a copy of the handbook and a memo to the management staff regarding a meeting to go over the handbook. At the meeting I will be looking for suggestions to improve the handbook and for possible problems with the new policies being implemented.

4:30 P.M.

Standards committee meeting.

6:00 P.M.

Walked through the club, checking the party rooms for proper setup and follow-through by the staff. Consulted with the chef and clubhouse manager regarding the party for the evening.

6:30 P.M.

Returned to my office and returned phone calls from the afternoon.

7:00 P.M.

Made the rounds of the dining rooms.
Greeted the member having the party in the ballroom.

7:30 P.M.

Wrote the general manager's column for the January newsletter.
Spoke to the editor of the newsletter committee regarding January's newsletter.

8:30 P.M.

Walked through the dining room to ensure everything was all right.
Talked with the host of the party again.
Spoke to the clubhouse manager about an employee dispute over vacation time during the Christmas holidays.
Grabbed a few bites of what the party was having for dinner.

9:30 P.M.

Organized my calendar for tomorrow, cleaned off my desk, and went home.

REVIEW QUIZ

When you feel you have covered all of the material in this chapter, answer these questions. Choose the *best* answer.

1. "Board members must take the same precautions in governing the club that an 'ordinarily prudent' person would take." This is which of a board member's three legal duties?

   a. duty of loyalty (or good faith)
   b. duty of obedience
   c. duty of trust
   d. none of the above

2. Which of the following is an advantage clubs enjoy when they establish short terms of service for board members?

   a. New people are constantly joining the club's board, bringing with them new ideas and viewpoints.
   b. More club members are able to serve on the board.
   c. A board member has to carry the usually heavy board-member workload for only a short time.
   d. All of the above.

3. The document that establishes the club as a club and states its name, location, and purpose is called a club's:

   a. bylaws.
   b. articles of incorporation.
   c. meeting minutes.
   d. agendas.

4. A general manager who is new to a club should *not:*

   a. attend club committee meetings.
   b. ask for an employment contract.
   c. rush to make changes.
   d. communicate with the club's board.

Answer Key: 1-d-C1, 2-d-C1, 3-b-C2, 4-c-C3

Each question is linked to a competency. Competencies are listed on the first page of the chapter. An answer reading 3-b-C4 translates to:

   3: the question number
   b: the correct answer
   C4: the competency number

Part II

Leading Club Operations

Chapter 3 Outline

Understanding the Role of Service
    Moments of Truth
    The Service Encounter
Identifying Member Needs and
    Expectations
    Suggestion Boxes/Comment Cards
    Focus Groups
    Member-Needs Surveys
    The Lost Art of Listening
    Developing Member-Driven Service
    Standards
Creating a Service Culture
    Service Gaps
    Service Recovery
Service Ethics
Conclusion

Competencies

1. Describe the role of service in private clubs, define "moments of truth," and summarize strategies for controlling service encounters. (pp. 95–101)

2. Explain methods for identifying member needs and expectations, summarize techniques club managers can use to create a positive and dynamic service culture at the club, and list ten steps that can help club managers make ethical decisions. (pp. 102–114)

3

Service Excellence in Clubs

This chapter was written and contributed by Rhonda J. Montgomery, Associate Professor, William F. Harrah College of Hotel Administration, University of Nevada-Las Vegas, Las Vegas, Nevada.

THE PRIMARY JOB of club managers is to provide club members with a positive experience every time they come to the club. If managers fail to do this, over time some members will visit the club less frequently and might eventually even resign their membership. In the extremely competitive world of hospitality, there are many other facilities ready, willing, and able to provide the amenities and services club members desire.

What differentiates private clubs from public restaurants, golf courses, and fitness clubs? Extraordinary service. Extraordinary service is more than just smiling and remembering the member's name (although that's a good start). It's an attitude that should permeate every aspect of a private club. This attitude must start at the top, for without a dedicated, almost fervent commitment to quality service from the general manager, a club's service plan, regardless of how well it is put together, will probably fail. Extraordinary service is the point of distinction for today's private clubs; successful general managers understand this and set their sights on delivering such service to members.

Understanding the Role of Service

What is **service?** Unfortunately, service defies a clear and concise definition. In their book *Total Customer Service: The Ultimate Weapon,* Davidow and Uttal define "service" as "all features, acts, and information that augment the customer's ability to realize the potential value of a core product or service."[1] Any definition of service that leaves out the perception of the recipient is incomplete, because excellent service, like beauty, is in the eye of the beholder.

Understanding that providing outstanding service to club members is at the very core of their mission does not necessarily mean that all general managers understand *how* to provide it. Exhibit 1 lists seven characteristics people need in order to provide outstanding service. Successful general managers must embody these characteristics. They must be committed to studying service and striving always to improve service within their clubs. If a general manager understands service but does not have some of the personality characteristics outlined in Exhibit 1, he or she should hire key service personnel who do have them. This is commonly referred to as "hiring your weaknesses." Although a private-club general manager needs to be something of a "Renaissance person," it is unrealistic to

95

Exhibit 1   Seven Qualities of Service

S-ociable:	being genuinely and honestly interested in people and actually paying attention to your members.
E-ffervescent:	being excited about life, about the possibilities you have, about the people you meet, and about the things you do.
R-egard:	treating each person you meet with respect; treating them the way they want to be treated, with courtesy, dignity, politeness, and consideration.
V-alues:	being honest, following through, and being reliable.
I-nvolvement:	being connected with the people you work with, caring about them and how they are doing; being part of the team.
C-reative:	seeing beyond the surface and the obvious; seeing the big picture and what needs to be done without being told to do so.
E-nergetic:	bringing energy and enthusiasm to every task and relationship.

Source: Adapted from Susan Clark of Motivation Unlimited, "Providing Superior, Motivated Service" (presentation).

expect him or her to be all things to all people. It is important that general managers understand their own strengths and weaknesses and hire people who are strong in the areas where they are weak.

Providing extraordinary service to members is not something that just happens; it must be carefully planned. Albrecht and Bradford, in their book, *The Service Advantage*, state three features outstanding service organizations have in common:

- A well-conceived strategy for service
- Customer-oriented frontline people
- Customer-friendly systems

Hiring, training, and supporting member-oriented employees in a member-friendly environment should be at the heart of every general manager's service vision. Everything in the vision should center on the member.

Moments of Truth

Because a club is an extension of the member's home, the club's staff should strive to make members feel cared for when they are at the club. The goal of a club's staff should be to raise members' spirits by providing them with great food or recreation in a soothing atmosphere. If a member's spirits are not lifted by the time he or she leaves the club, the staff has failed. Every time a member enters the club, whether it is to play golf, have a meal, book a party, or attend a meeting, there will be many opportunities for the staff to provide excellent service. Each time a member comes into contact with a staff member, there occurs a **moment of truth.** A moment of truth can be defined as the moment when a member comes into contact

Insider Insights

Cathy Gustafson, CCM
Professor, University of South Carolina
Former General Manager of The Faculty House of Carolina,
Columbia, South Carolina

The unique appeal of private clubs is founded on service. Many things that clubs offer—fine-dining, catering, golf, tennis, fitness facilities, and so on—people can get elsewhere. What they can't find in a public facility is the level of service they can expect from a private club. Most private clubs are willing to absorb the labor costs and hire the staff members it takes to provide extraordinary service.

A "moment of truth" happens with every encounter a member has with the club. It can be an encounter with a staff person, a product, or some aspect of the club's physical facilities. Did the server greet me courteously? Are the golf cars charged, clean, and ready to go? Are the restrooms clean? Did the employee in the pro shop answer the phone right away? Service is about details, so club managers must train the club's staff to take care of the details. An attendant at the club's pool, for example, must be trained to go get a towel for a member who forgets to bring one, rather than just tell the member where the towels are located.

The service goal is to make the members say "Wow." A club should try to exceed member expectations. This is harder to do in a club than in a hotel or restaurant. Hotels and restaurants have different people in every day. A club member might be at the club several times a week year after year. This makes it harder to provide "wow" service. The club has to constantly work to keep the service level high.

One of a club manager's primary tasks is to make sure staff members have what they need to do the job properly. If you're not directly serving members, you should be serving the people who are. Club managers should talk to staff members frequently to find out about obstacles that are hindering them from providing great service. An obstacle can be a flawed process or something physical—it can be as simple as a piece of furniture that's in the way. Club managers should make the work environment as efficient as possible so employees are not frustrated, because employee frustration can get taken out on the members.

A club's management team is small relative to the number of employees. Because of that, it's important that club managers give each employee the proper training. Training is an ongoing management function; it's a cycle. Club managers set the standards, communicate the standards to the staff, provide the tools and training, and then gather feedback from members to make sure the standards are right and the training is working. Of course, the most important measure of staff performance is member satisfaction. Taking a membership-satisfaction survey on an annual basis provides wonderful feedback. A manager should work to constantly raise the level of satisfaction.

A feature of private clubs, one that makes providing great service both easier and at times more challenging, is that there is a finite number of members. Over time, club managers are able to get to know members and their families and can

(continued)

Insider Insights *(continued)*

provide very personalized service. Not only can club managers smile, say hello, and call members by name, they can also ask them about the grandchildren, the new house, or the bank merger. Members like to talk about themselves, but not on a superficial level. They don't want a generic "How are you?" from a club manager.

Weddings are perhaps the biggest opportunity for a club to provide superior service. There are a lot of extras a club can do to help the big day go smoothly. For example, when I worked at the Faculty Club, many members would get married at a chapel across campus. We would invite the bride to get dressed at the club instead of in a small room at the chapel. The club would provide beverages and assorted items that a bride would be likely to forget but would need, like safety pins. This took some of the pressure off of her. We'd also do other things to help, like move the flowers from the chapel to the reception so that the wedding party didn't have to worry about it.

A chance to taste banquet items before ordering them is another service that clubs provide but most catering businesses do not. A member who is planning a large banquet can taste sample hors d'oeuvres and entrées before making a decision. At the Faculty Club we showed members pictures of banquet items and helped them narrow the choices down, then scheduled a tasting if necessary—usually at no additional cost. The club wanted to make sure that members made informed choices and ended up with items that best met their needs.

One of the biggest service challenges clubs face is the basic fact that clubs deal with people. Communication is not always perfect. You've got to meet or exceed what members expect again and again. It is very difficult to maintain standards so high that members are impressed every time they walk in. That's the service challenge that club managers face every day.

with any aspect of the club and, on the basis of that contact, forms an opinion about the quality of the club and its products and services.[2] Properly handling each moment of truth is critical to a club's success.

The Service Encounter

Successful club managers understand how to control service encounters to ensure that members are satisfied. In the past, controlling the service encounter primarily meant making sure that the club had the best physical facilities in town. Today, service-oriented clubs realize that member satisfaction is not guaranteed by just providing outstanding facilities. Member satisfaction is more closely tied to the way the members are treated by the club's staff. Controlling the service environment means that everything—from the club's physical facilities to the way the dishes get washed—should be focused on helping employees and other club staff meet the needs of members.

> ### Service Quiz for Staff Members
>
> According to one source, many club staff members would answer two of the following three questions incorrectly:
>
> 1. What is your name?
> 2. Who do you work for?
> 3. Who pays your salary?
>
> **Answer Key:**   1. (Staff member's name.)
>
>   2. The club's members.
>
>   3. The club's members.

Source: *TQM in Golf & Country Clubs,* Sample Issue, 1995.

Strategies for Controlling Service Encounters. Andrew Szpekman, in his article *Quality Service Sets You Apart,* gives an overview of how a service-driven organization can control the service environment to ensure outstanding customer service:

- Empower employees
- Delegate authority
- Provide appropriate technology and equipment
- Treat employees like important customers and reward employee efforts

These principles can be applied to private clubs as well.

Empower employees. In recent years, it has been difficult to pick up a management magazine, read a management book, or attend a management-related conference without hearing something about empowering employees. What is **employee empowerment?** Employee empowerment is when "power, or responsibility, is distributed or shared throughout an organization. It fosters the inclusion of all employees in the decisions that affect their job functions and performance.... The results can be measured in terms of employee dedication to both maximum productivity and superior quality."[3] Simply put, employee empowerment, in a club environment, means allowing employees to take the initiative in serving club members.

Since it is physically impossible for club managers to be present at every service encounter, they must recruit, select, and hire employees who will be able to make good decisions when their managers are not around. Once applicants are hired, managers should give careful thought to their training. It is vital for the trainer to share not only the mechanics of the new job with trainees, but also the club's mission statement and service philosophy. The next step in training should be to educate trainees on how their jobs fit into the bigger picture. It is imperative for new employees to understand how their jobs affect members and ultimately the success or failure of the club. After giving new employees a complete overview of the club's service philosophy, club managers should provide training in how to handle service encounters and make responsible decisions.

Exhibit 2   Service-Oriented Organization Chart

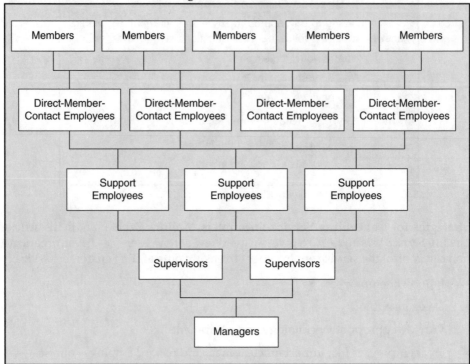

Delegate authority. Empowering employees means delegating authority to them. Delegating authority enables employees to go the extra mile to immediately handle out-of-the-ordinary service encounters with members, without having to seek permission from a superior.

If it is handled correctly, delegating authority can have many positive effects. The employee/employer relationship will generally be strengthened because of the implied trust and respect that comes when authority is delegated. Club managers will have more time to do their own work. The most important outcome, however, is the improved member satisfaction that occurs when employees can take care of member needs immediately.

Many clubs have adopted an empowerment strategy and have actually redesigned their organization charts (see Exhibit 2). If a club's number-one priority is providing outstanding service to its members, the members should be at the top of its organization chart; next should come the employees who have direct contact with members, then should come the staff members who support these employees. Club managers should strive to do what they can to make it easy for employees to provide extraordinary service to members.

Provide appropriate technology and equipment. Training employees, empowering them, and delegating authority to them will not be as effective as managers expect unless employees are also provided with the technology and equipment

The Faculty House, Columbia, South Carolina. (Courtesy of Cathy Gustafson and the Faculty House of Carolina, Inc.)

necessary to do their jobs efficiently. Many clubs have recognized the importance of technology and have invested in computers, software, and training to help improve member service.

Updating equipment doesn't only mean buying more or newer computers, however. Clubs face many equipment issues. For example, the Faculty House, a city club near the University of South Carolina, is in a 182-year-old building that was originally a duplex for faculty members. Although the historical building has charm and elegance, it leaves much to be desired as a functional city club. The kitchen is located on the first floor and services all three floors of the club. Staff members must carry trays from the main kitchen to all floors using a very narrow and steep staircase. This provides constant challenges for the staff. The general manager is continually looking at ways to improve the delivery system, because a poor delivery system can lower a staff's morale and negatively affect the service members receive.

Treat employees like important customers and reward employee efforts. Treating employees like important customers is a concept that many clubs have adopted. In an economy where the labor pool for service personnel is dwindling and personnel costs are escalating, club managers need to develop policies that will improve employee retention rates. For many clubs, the strategy that has been most successful is that of treating employees like important customers or club members. The premise of this strategy is that if club managers treat their employees well, the employees will in turn treat club members well, and both the employees and the members will stay around longer. This strategy should include a generous reward system designed to communicate to employees just how valuable they are to the club.

To the Members of

Lakewood Country Club

OUR MEMBERS are the most important people around here—in person, by phone, or by letter.

OUR MEMBERS can get along without us, but we cannot get along without our members.

OUR MEMBERS are not interfering with our work—they are the reason for it.

OUR MEMBERS are not numbers on a list. They are people, entitled to likes and dislikes and human feelings, just like you and I.

OUR MEMBERS are not people to try to outsmart or out-argue. Winning an argument means losing a member.

OUR MEMBERS are people we ask to bring us their needs. It is our responsibility to take care of them.

Sincerely,

Sally and Staff

Our Pledge to You

The general manager of the Lakewood Country Club took a full page in the club newsletter to communicate to members the staff's service philosophy. (Source: Adapted from *The Lakewooder: Lakewood Country Club News*, Dallas, Texas: Lakewood Country Club.)

Identifying Member Needs and Expectations

Ask club managers what their first priority is, and they will almost unanimously reply "to provide excellent service to my membership." If you ask them how they are doing this, their answers will vary greatly, because what is considered excellent service differs from club to club. As mentioned earlier, excellent service is defined by the recipient of the service; each club's membership defines service excellence in its own way. This is perhaps the most challenging part of a manager's job—finding out what the membership wants or expects in terms of service. The average club member does not spend much time talking to managers or employees. Most members tend to keep their opinions and service expectations to themselves. Many managers use spending trends at the club as barometers for member satisfaction, because members vote on what they like or dislike at the cash register. Declining sales will alert managers to the fact that there is a problem, but it will not help them identify the problem. Therefore, club managers should give members many opportunities to provide feedback on existing services and to suggest the services they would like in the future.

There are a variety of ways club managers can learn about the needs and expectations of members and the members' opinions about the club's services. Some managers use suggestion boxes or comment cards, while others hire research firms to design and administer elaborate member-needs surveys. In the following sections, we will briefly address some of the ways club managers can ask for member input regarding service. Remember, there are almost as many ways to solicit member opinions as there are clubs. The key is not so much how you do it, but that you do it.

Suggestion Boxes/Comment Cards

If they are used correctly, suggestion boxes and comment cards can be excellent sources of member feedback. For suggestion boxes or comment cards to be most effective, club managers should follow a few guidelines:

1. Educate members about what the comment cards are for and how the information will be used. This could be done through the club newsletter.

2. Place the suggestion boxes or comment cards in highly visible locations throughout the club—in locker rooms, outside the main dining room, in the pro shop, and so on.

3. Check suggestion boxes frequently.

4. Periodically report to the board and the general membership on the issues raised by members and what management's response has been.

As with any form of feedback, club managers should not ask the question if they do not want to hear the answer. If managers are not committed to acting on the suggestions and concerns members bring up, they should not use suggestion boxes or comment cards. Members become frustrated and angry if their suggestions are ignored.

Focus Groups

Focus groups can be excellent sources of feedback. A focus group is a group of members who are brought together by the club to discuss specific issues. There are typically five to eight club members in a focus group, which is led by a facilitator (usually someone who is not a member of the club's staff) who asks questions and directs the discussion. Usually the focus group is videotaped or audiotaped. If not, the group's comments should be written down.

A focus group is a powerful source of feedback because it can give club managers an indication of what the membership thinks and how it feels about the club. It is important to note, however, that the information gathered from focus groups cannot necessarily be generalized to the overall club, so managers should proceed with caution. For example, just because six out of eight members of a particular focus group think the clubhouse should be painted pink does not mean that club managers should rush out and buy some pink paint. Club managers should not

---

Why Service Is So Important

A researcher several years ago conducted a survey on why customers quit a business. Although it surveyed businesses in the public sector and speaks of "customers," this study may also have applicability to many private clubs.

According to the survey, the percentages of people quitting a particular business broke down as follows:

- 1 percent die
- 3 percent move away
- 5 percent go to other friends
- 9 percent leave for competitive reasons
- 14 percent are dissatisfied with the product
- 68 percent leave because of an attitude of indifference by the owner, manager, or employees

---

Source: Michael LeBoeuf, *How to Win Customers and Keep Them For Life* (New York: Berkley Books, 1987), p. 52.

take any actions based on the opinions of a single focus group; rather, they should always do more investigating to make sure that a focus group's major concerns are indeed major concerns of the overall membership.

The following are guidelines that might be helpful to club managers who are considering conducting focus-group research:

1. *Identify the issues.* Identify the issues you wish to have the focus group address. This can be accomplished by having staff members come up with issues they think should be addressed by club members. Or, managers could form a focus group whose purpose is to identify important membership issues that other focus groups will explore further.

2. *Determine the number of focus groups.* It is important to have a good representation of your membership; therefore, perhaps several focus groups should be formed, representing several membership categories (full members, social members, and so on) or such major interest groups as golfers and tennis players.

3. *Develop a format.* Club managers should develop a standard format and train the facilitator on how to use it (if the club hasn't hired an outside consultant). The format should be consistent from group to group. The facilitator should understand that his or her job is to ask questions, move the discussion forward, and keep the group on task.

4. *Choose a recording method.* Next, club managers should determine how the focus-group's discussion will be recorded. The most comprehensive form of recording is to use a video camera, because it records not only the words participants say but visual clues about the way participants feel about the issues discussed. However, a drawback to videotaping is that many people are uncomfortable with being videotaped and therefore may be somewhat guarded.

The second-most comprehensive form of recording is to audiotape the group. This provides a word-for-word record of the participants' responses and tends to be less threatening than videotaping.

The least-threatening form of recording is to have someone take notes throughout the focus group's meeting. The person responsible for taking notes should *not* be the facilitator; the facilitator must be free to concentrate on guiding the discussion and keeping the group on track.

5. *Recruit participants.* There are many ways to recruit members to participate in focus groups. The two most common are to ask for volunteers or randomly select members from your membership directory. If you ask for volunteers, you risk hearing only from the "squeaky wheels," whereas if you randomly select members from the membership directory, you are more likely to get a good representation of the club's membership.

6. *Conduct the focus groups.* As mentioned earlier, the facilitator should be sure to keep the format consistent for each focus group. That said, the facilitator should also be prepared to explore unexpected issues that come up if they appear to be worth pursuing.

7. *Debrief the facilitator.* Club managers should meet with the facilitator immediately after each focus group to make note of any especially important or unusual information that came up during the meeting.

8. *Report on the findings.* Club managers should report on their findings to interested parties such as the club's board of directors. In these reports, club managers should make it clear that focus-group information should be viewed not as gospel but merely as helpful information in pinpointing what may be key issues to the members.

Focus groups are not only valuable in helping club managers learn about members' perceptions of specific issues or problems; focus groups can also be of great help in developing member-needs surveys.

Member-Needs Surveys

Member-needs surveys have become extremely popular in recent years, perhaps because clubs have become more focused on service than ever before. Unfortunately, developing a good member-needs survey can be very difficult and time-consuming. It is not the intent of this section to turn club managers into survey experts, but to provide managers with a brief overview of a good process to follow if they want to design a survey.

Club managers conduct a member-needs survey for three common reasons: (1) the managers want to determine how club members perceive the club's current facilities, products, and services; (2) the club is proposing changes in current facilities, products, or services and club managers want to find out how members feel about the proposals; or (3) club managers want to influence or persuade club members regarding a particular issue.

There are five steps to putting together a member-needs survey. Step one is planning the survey. The planning stage consists of identifying what information

---

Steps in Putting Together a Member-Needs Survey

1. Plan the survey
2. Create the survey instrument
3. Collect data
4. Process the data
5. Report survey results

---

you need or want. What is your objective and how can the survey help you reach it? If a club wants to use an outside research firm, it should bring it in during the planning stage. Research firms conduct surveys for various types of companies. Because clubs are different from other types of businesses, and because no two clubs are identical, you should be cautious about hiring a firm that wants to provide you with a standardized assessment tool. Some of the questions on such a standardized survey may be pertinent, but the majority of a club's member-needs survey should be customized so that it meets the specific needs of the club.

Step two is to create the survey instrument itself, based on your goals and objectives for the survey. If your club is doing its own survey, there are probably texts and how-to books in the local library that can provide you with valuable information on survey design. Information on member surveys is also available through the Club Managers Association of America.

Step three involves the collection of data. This is the most critical stage. No matter how good your survey is, it won't serve any purpose if you can't get your members to fill it out and return it. Many clubs offer incentives to members to encourage them to complete their surveys.

Once the results are in, you must process the data (step four). Processing the data is the most intimidating step of all to club managers doing a survey for the first time. However, in most cases, using basic statistics such as percentiles, rank scoring, and means will give managers all the data they need.

Once you have collected and analyzed your data, you should report the results to interested parties (step 5). It is common courtesy for researchers to offer copies of their findings to the survey participants. Some clubs might also want to print a synopsis of survey results in the club newsletter.

Once the results have been analyzed, club managers should use the findings as a basis for developing action plans to address the problems, needs, concerns, or other issues uncovered by the survey. Club managers can then send out follow-up surveys to learn whether members think the club responded appropriately to these issues.

The Lost Art of Listening

Club managers don't have to do a formal survey to find out what members are thinking. Club managers and employees who simply listen carefully to members might be able to discover patterns or trends in member comments that warrant management attention. In today's fast-paced world, where everything is becoming high-tech and low-touch, one of the nicest things club staff members can do for members is to really listen to what they have to say.

Since listening is becoming a lost art, club managers should educate staff members on how to listen better. The following are some basic guidelines for listening to members:

- Stop talking.

- Don't give up—if you don't understand, ask clarifying questions.

- Concentrate on what the members are saying.

- Leave your emotions out.

- Control your anger (if a member is complaining angrily, it does no good to get angry in return).

- Try to relate to the ideas members are communicating.

- Listen "between the lines."

- Avoid jumping to conclusions.

Empathizing with members is also very important. This can be accomplished by not only listening to what is being said, but paying attention to body language and tone of voice. Often, if a member is voicing a complaint, he or she just wants to be heard and understood. Many member complaints center on the fact that no one on the club's staff responded or seemed to care when a problem first came up. One of the best ways managers can train employees to empathize with members is for the managers to do a good job of empathizing with employees. Employees who are listened to with empathy are much more likely to treat club members in the same fashion.

Developing Member-Driven Service Standards

Once club managers have identified member needs, they should take those needs into consideration when they develop service standards for the club. Developing member-driven service standards involves the following steps:

1. Identifying specific member needs, desires, and expectations through a comprehensive member-needs assessment

2. Developing specific goals and objectives that will help the club meet the needs, desires, and expectations of members

3. Developing standard operating procedures that will enable the club's staff to meet the needs, desires, and expectations of members

4. Providing comprehensive and ongoing training to prepare the staff to meet the needs, desires, and expectations of members

5. Measuring the staff's performance by continually soliciting feedback from members

Exhibit 3   Sample Club Mission Statement

"The Oakbrook Country Club is committed to being the premiere club in the Southeast through the provision of outstanding facilities and services designed to make the club every member's place of choice for dining, social activities, and recreation."

Even though a club has identified the needs, desires, and expectations of its membership, translated them into service standards, and trained its staff to deliver quality service, its task is not complete. Club managers must then develop a system for soliciting constant evaluation and feedback from club members, so that the club can continually modify its service standards to meet the ever changing needs of the club's members.

Creating a Service Culture

Creating a positive and dynamic service culture for your club is a time-consuming endeavor that must include the most important groups that are affected by the club's service culture. In a private club, these groups are members, employees, and managers.

There are four basic steps club managers can take to create a service culture:

1. Identify the foundational values of all club groups.

2. Develop an overall mission statement based on these foundational values.

3. Communicate the mission statement to all club groups.

4. Develop a service delivery system that serves both external customers (club members) and internal customers (staff members).

Although the process is simple to describe, actually working through the process can be difficult.

A service culture is founded on the common values of the organization's constituents (in the case of a club, its constituents are its members, employees, and managers). If the stated values of the club are not in line with the values of the club's constituents, especially its members, there will be constant conflict. Therefore, it is very important that club managers assess the values of the club's constituents. Common values held by the constituents in many clubs include, but are not limited to, honesty, trust, hard work, quality, value, personal accountability and responsibility, family, pride, professionalism, service excellence, and empowerment. Developing exercises to get club members, employees, and managers to list and review their core values can provide club managers with priceless opportunities to discuss and share issues that are critically important for the survival and success of the club. From the common values that are uncovered, club managers can then develop a management philosophy that will meet the needs of all the club's constituents.

After common values have been identified, a club can develop a mission statement (see Exhibit 3). A club's mission statement should address who the club is, its core values, and its purpose. A mission statement is not worth the paper is it written on if it has not been developed by an inclusive process that allows everyone at the club to take ownership of the statement. If the mission statement is developed and believed-in by members, employees, and managers, then the goals and objectives that flow from the mission statement will directly address the areas that club members value.

The next step in creating a service culture is to communicate the mission statement clearly and concisely to everyone at the club. This can be accomplished by printing it in membership material, staff handbooks, and the club's newsletter. Some clubs print their mission statement on posters or plaques and hang them around the club; some put their mission statement on their business cards and stationery. Communicating the mission statement to all concerned will help the club's managers and employees continually focus on the club's purpose.

Another important factor in creating a service culture is the development of a service delivery system that truly addresses the needs of club members and employees. A club's service delivery system should specify policies and procedures for delivering quality service to guests, along with identifying service quality standards and dealing with equipment, layout, and physical-facility issues that have an impact on service delivery. The external focus of the delivery system looks at how the needs, desires, and expectations of club members can be met and exceeded through providing them with excellent physical facilities, outstanding service, and quality products. The internal focus of the delivery system looks at (1) how staff members should go about providing exceptional service to members, (2) professional and personal growth opportunities for staff members, and (3) how staff members can derive personal and professional satisfaction from their jobs.

Service Gaps

So far in this chapter, we have spent a great deal of time discussing how club managers can determine what excellent service means to the members of their particular clubs. Understanding what your members want and then delivering it to them is obviously the goal of any competent club manager. Unfortunately, all too often there is a difference between member expectations and staff performance. This difference is called a **service gap.** A service gap develops when there is a shortfall between the quality of service provided by staff members and the quality of service expected by club members. When service gaps occur, the goal of club managers and staff should be to bridge them as quickly as possible.

There are four typical reasons for service gaps[4]:

1. *The club does not take a proactive stance in meeting the needs of its members.* Due to the relaxed and familiar relationships club staff members often have with club members, the staff can become complacent about providing excellent service. If club managers and employees begin to take members for granted and relax their standards of service excellence, this can lead to service gaps.

2. *The club has mistakenly developed the wrong service-quality standards.* Often, service quality standards are developed and then never reviewed or updated as the club and its membership grows and changes. This can turn formerly good standards into outdated and unnecessary ones.

3. *There is a difference between service specifications and the actual service delivery.* When clubs are implementing new service standards, there is often a reluctance or inability on the part of the staff to implement the proposed changes. Management may not have provided enough training or sought appropriate input from the staff members affected by the changes, therefore the changes are not owned by the staff and follow-through is not what was expected by the managers. To avoid this problem, club managers should involve employees in the development of new service standards and then provide extensive training for all employees on how to meet the new standards.

4. *The club fails to deliver on its promises.* Private clubs are intricately involved in very important events for their members. For example, members celebrate meaningful holidays and significant events such as baptisms, bar and bas mitzvahs, baby showers, and wedding receptions at the club. Each of these events is a milestone in the member's family and therefore holds special significance. If a member has been promised a very special event and the club fails to follow through on its promise, not only has the member not gotten the quality of service he or she expected, but a special event in the family's history has been damaged. When a club fails to deliver good service at such events, the negative fallout is tremendous.

Service Recovery

No matter how outstanding a club's employees are or how competent its managers, there will always be service problems, simply because people are not perfect and misunderstandings or miscommunication can occur despite everyone's best intentions. Club managers should constantly solicit member feedback on the club's services. A club can't recover from poor service if it doesn't know the member thinks he or she received poor service.

Club managers who are committed to providing extraordinary service must be committed to getting to know their members. This will help managers anticipate potential problems and head them off before they occur. For example, if the dining room manager knows that Mr. Jones always orders a particular menu item every Saturday night and gets very upset if it isn't available, then the manager should make sure that the club is never out of that item on Saturday night.

Managers often make the mistake of underestimating the future revenue that is lost when a member leaves the club unhappy. Many club managers, if they arrive at work in the morning and discover that a problem occurred the night before and that members left unhappy, will set aside whatever they had planned to do that morning and immediately start calling club members to find out more about the situation and apologize to the members. Unfortunately, as well-intended as these calls are, the public-relations damage is probably already done; some of the unhappy members may have already told ten people about their bad experience at the club. Therefore, it is important for club managers to empower their staffs to handle service problems immediately. Having an established system for handling service challenges or mistakes, training your staff in how to use the system, and then empowering your staff to go the extra mile to recover from service gaps will go a long way toward ensuring that club members never leave the club unhappy.

Good Service Gets Noticed—and So Does Bad Service

What follows are some observations a shopping service made at one club during a secret audit. Several shoppers posed as new club members and recorded their experiences over several days. This picture of a club as "members" see it points out how important it is to always provide good service. (These observations are not typical of clubs, but they show what can happen when staff members are not continually on guard to provide excellent service to members at every service encounter.)

- The two times that I called the club to make dinner reservations, the phone was answered on the fourth ring. The woman answering did not identify herself or thank me for calling. On both occasions I informed her that I was a new member. Neither time was I welcomed as such. After reservations were made I was not thanked or asked to enjoy my dinner.

- When our order was taken, our server neglected to ask if we would like another beverage.

- I entered the pro shop and spent five minutes walking around looking at merchandise before an employee behind the counter said anything to me. She had a plateful of Danish on the counter and was busy eating. I walked around the shop for another ten minutes. She never welcomed me or offered assistance.

- Our server passed our table nine times without acknowledging our presence. After our dinner was served, she did not come to our table to ask how everything was.

- The bartender looked at us when we walked into the room and looked away. When members walked up to the bar to order their beverages, he did not make eye contact with them or interact with them at all.

- The maitre d' failed to introduce himself to us or acknowledge us as new members. He did not refer to us by name or introduce us to our waitperson.

- It took five minutes after we were seated for our server to arrive. She did not refer to us by name, welcome us, ask us how we were doing this evening, or introduce herself. It took eight minutes to receive our beverages.

- There were two employees behind the counter in the pro shop, neither of whom looked up or said anything to me. There was a gentleman in what appeared to be the pro shop manager's office. He looked right at me but did not say anything.

- Our server was not very attentive. After we informed her that we needed a few minutes before we were ready to order, she didn't come back for 15 minutes. Our water glasses were never refreshed.

- We noticed that it took 25 minutes for two vacated tables to be bussed.

- The maitre d' had little or no eye contact or conversation with members; he gave the impression that he didn't know or recognize anyone.

- After we finished our dinner, our server did not ask us if we would like coffee or dessert and did not thank us for coming.

Source: Adapted from David M. Schreiber, "How Would Your Members Rate Your Service ... Really?" (Club Managers Association of America 70th Annual Conference, January 1997, Orlando, Florida), and the Customer Relations Group, Inc., Atlanta, Georgia.

What most members want when a service gap occurs is for someone to listen to them, offer a sincere apology, understand and empathize with them, and offer some form of compensation for their troubles. Every problem a club member experiences is an opportunity for the club to prove its commitment to service. A properly designed and carried-out service-recovery system can cement member loyalty forever.

Many service-recovery systems focus on taking care of the "squeaky wheels," but a comprehensive service-recovery system will also empower staff members to go the extra mile when a staff member perceives merely a lack of complete satisfaction on the part of a member. Staff members should be trained to look for subtle clues to determine whether a member is 100-percent satisfied with the club's service. If a member appears to be even slightly dissatisfied, employees should be empowered to handle the situation in a manner that pleases the member.

Willingness to help a member even when the problem is not the club's fault also goes a long way toward building member loyalty. Being prepared to help a member who has forgotten to schedule a tee time for golf or helping members who locked their keys in their cars are just two examples of opportunities to provide extraordinary service by helping members out of sticky situations of their own making.

The key to successfully bridging a service gap is to quickly identify the problem and respond before the club member's dissatisfaction reaches a flash point. Service problems have a way of growing in intensity very quickly and spreading throughout the membership if not handled in a timely manner. The time a club's staff has to recover from a service mistake is fleeting at best, so the staff must be ever ready to respond to service problems quickly. This can only be done if staff members have been trained to react in a service-oriented manner when faced with a challenge. Not only must the staff be trained, but it must be empowered to meet the needs of members immediately. Only then will the club be able to recover the service edge.

Service Ethics

No discussion of service excellence would be complete without a section on ethics. The link between quality service and ethics is very strong. When members enter their club, they have the right to expect fair treatment in a professional setting that is designed to provide outstanding service. Staff members have a right to expect fair and ethical treatment in employment practices. Training managers and employees to meet the goals and objectives of the club while maintaining a strong ethical code is critical to a club's success. Club managers understand the importance of ethics and have developed a code designed to communicate their commitment to ethical behavior (see Exhibit 4).

In their book *It's Good Business*, Robert Solomon and Kristine Hanson outline ten steps that can assist club managers faced with ethical decisions or dilemmas:

1. What, really, is the problem?

2. How did the problem arise?

3. What is the antagonist's position? (Play devil's advocate.)

4. Whom are you serving? Where is your loyalty?

Exhibit 4   The Club Managers Association of America's Code of Ethics

CMAA Code of Ethics

We believe the management of clubs is an honorable calling. It shall be incumbent upon club managers to be knowledgeable in the application of sound principles in the management of clubs, with ample opportunity to keep abreast of current practices and procedures. We are convinced that the Club Managers Association of America best represents these interests, and as members thereof, subscribe to the following CODE OF ETHICS.

We will uphold the best traditions of club management through adherence to sound business principles. By our behavior and demeanor, we shall set an example for our employees and will assist our club officers to secure the utmost in efficient and successful club operations.

We will consistently promote the recognition and esteem of club management as a profession and conduct our personal and business affairs in a manner to reflect capability and integrity. We will always honor our contractual employment obligations.

We shall promote community and civic affairs by maintaining good relations with the public sector to the extent possible within the limits of our club's demands.

We will strive to advance our knowledge and abilities as club managers, and willingly share with other Association members the lessons of our experience and knowledge gained by supporting and participating in our local chapter and the National Association's educational meetings and seminars.

We will not permit ourselves to be subsidized or compromised by any interest doing business with our clubs.

We will refrain from initiating, directly or through an agent, any communications with a director, member or employee of another club regarding its affairs without the prior knowledge of the manager thereof, if it has a manager.

We will advise the National Headquarters, whenever possible, regarding managerial openings at clubs that come to our attention. We will do all within our power to assist our fellow club managers in pursuit of their professional goals.

We shall not be deterred from compliance with the law, as it applies to our clubs. We shall provide our club officers and trustees with specifics of Federal, State and Local laws, statutes and regulations, to avoid punitive action and costly litigation.

We deem it our duty to report to local or national officers any willful violations of the CMAA CODE OF ETHICS.

5. Whom does your action injure? How? How badly?

6. Can you negotiate? Is there a compromise? With whom should you talk?

7. Will this decision seem like the right one a year from now? five years from now?

8. Could you describe your actions and intentions to your supervisor, your CEO (club president), the stockholders (members), the board of directors? Would you have to distort or seriously edit your description? If so, what's wrong?

9. Could you tell your family about your action? Could your children use your action as a model? Could you describe it, without qualms, to the media?

10. What self-interested motives guide your action? What altruistic motives are guiding or could guide the same actions? How could your motives be misinterpreted or misunderstood?

Thinking through these steps when faced with an ethical dilemma can help club managers avoid many poor ethical decisions that can result in poor service.

Conclusion

Providing extraordinary service is the highest call to which a club manager can respond. It is not an easy call to answer, however, because extraordinary service is not easily defined and is ever changing and evolving. Successful club managers must constantly be in pursuit of service excellence. They can do this through a fervent approach to their own education to ensure that their clubs are receiving the best the managers have to offer. They can also diligently strive to know their memberships and to understand their members' needs, desires, and expectations. They can educate their staffs about the needs, desires, and expectations of club members and train staff members to provide exceptional service. Club managers should also realize that even a "perfect" service system will fail at times, and they should have a comprehensive service-recovery system ready to help their clubs regain the service edge.

Finally, in their response to the call for quality service, club managers must understand one of the greatest truths of all: people, both club members and staff members, want to be treated with respect and dignity. If club managers create an atmosphere founded on this principle, their club members will experience exceptional service.

Endnotes

1. W. Davidow and B. Uttal, *Total Customer Service: The Ultimate Weapon* (New York: Harper & Row, 1989).

2. K. Albrecht, *Service Within* (Homewood, Ill.: Dow Jones-Irwin, 1990), p. 30.

3. Goski and Belfry, 1991.

4. Adapted from V. Zeithml, A. Parasuraman, and L. Berry, *Delivering Quality Service: Balancing Customer Perceptions and Expectations* (New York: The Free Press, 1990).

Key Terms

employee empowerment—Power or responsibility is distributed or shared throughout an organization; employee empowerment fosters the inclusion of all employees in the decisions that affect their job functions and performance.

focus group—A group of individuals brought together to discuss specific issues; the group is led by a facilitator whose role is to ask questions and direct the discussion.

member-needs survey—A research technique that involves collecting information from club members by using carefully designed questionnaires and other survey forms.

moment of truth—Anytime a club member comes into contact with any aspect of the club and, on the basis of that contact, forms an opinion about the quality of the club and its products and services.

service—All features, acts, and information that augment a club member's ability to realize the potential value of the club's products and services.

service gap—The shortfall between the quality of service provided by staff members and the quality of service expected by club members.

Review Questions

1. What is service?

2. What is a moment of truth?

3. What is employee empowerment?

4. How can a club manager identify member needs and expectations?

5. What are some of the ways a club manager can create a positive and dynamic service culture at the club?

6. What are four typical reasons for service gaps?

7. What are ten steps that can assist club managers faced with ethical dilemmas?

Additional Reading

Albrecht, K. *At America's Service*. Homewood, Ill.: Dow Jones-Irwin, 1988.

———. *Service Within*. Homewood, Ill.: Dow Jones-Irwin, 1990.

Albrecht, K., and L. Bradford. *The Service Advantage: How to Identify and Fulfill Customer Needs*. Homewood, Ill.: Dow Jones-Irwin, 1990.

Albrecht, K., and R. Zemke. *Service America*. Homewood, Ill.: Dow Jones-Irwin, 1985.

Bitner, M. "Evaluating Service Encounters: The Effects of Physical Surroundings and Employee Responses." *Journal of Marketing:* 54, 1990.

Davidow, W., and B. Uttal. *Total Customer Service: The Ultimate Weapon*. New York: Harper & Row, 1989.

Gross, T.S. *Leading Your Positively Outrageous Service Team*. New York: Mastermedia Limited, 1994.

Hard, R. *The Customer Service Manager's Handbook of People Power Strategies*. Englewood Cliffs, N.J.: Prentice-Hall, 1989.

Johnson, M., and G. Zinkham. "Emotional Responses to a Professional Service Encounter." *Journal of Marketing Research:* 5, 1991.

Lockwood, A., and P. Jones. "Creating Positive Service Encounters." *Cornell Quarterly,* February 1989.

Lowes, R. "The Strawberry Strategy: Club Corporation Translates Happy Employees into Happy Members, Using Programs, Perks ... and Strawberries." *Club Management*, August 1991.

Murdick, R., B. Render, and R. Russell. *Service Operations*. Needham Heights, Mass.: Allyn and Bacon, 1990.

Schuster, J. "Member Satisfaction: Learning What They Want Is the First Step." *Club Management*, August 1990.

Szpekman, Andrew. "Quality Service Sets You Apart."

"What Do Members Want?" *Club Management*, October 1989.

Zeithml, V., A. Parasuraman, and L. Berry. *Delivering Quality Service: Balancing Customer Perceptions and Expectations*. New York: The Free Press, 1990.

Zemke, R., and D. Schaaf. *The Service Edge: 101 Companies That Profit from Customer Care*. New York: Penguin Press, 1989.

Case Study

One of the first challenges facing Paige Reynolds, the new general manager at the Clarendon Hills Country Club, is improving service in the dining room. A stickler for service excellence, Paige is determined to enhance member satisfaction, which slipped gradually during the previous general manager's transition to retirement.

During her brief tenure at Clarendon Hills, Paige has received a disturbing number of complaints, particularly from younger members, about what they consider to be the overly familiar demeanor of two longtime servers, Richard and Lucille. Richard and Lucille have been with the club for 32 and 29 years, respectively, and are considered fixtures in the club dining room. They have watched many of the younger members grow up and, inappropriately now, still take the liberty of calling these adult members by their first names. Also, Lucille can be very "touchy" with members. She'll greet them with hugs or squeeze their shoulders. While some members casually discount this breach of etiquette, others find it disconcerting, especially when they host business functions at the club.

Paige has other issues to address with Richard and Lucille in addition to their overfamiliarity with members. Richard has a tendency to sidestep club policy and overindulge his longtime dining guests by serving them extra desserts or additional portions. Of course, they love this and particularly appreciate Richard's ability to keep track of their standing orders. Amused by his stories about the old days, senior members enjoy chatting with Richard, unaware of how this reduces his productivity. Lucille, long a favorite with older members, never forgets their drink preferences or how they like their meals prepared. She acknowledges member birthdays and anniversaries with a hug or a pat on the back, and never forgets to inquire about their grandchildren. However, she spends too much time on her preferred members, sometimes neglecting other parties and creating more work for other servers.

In addition, both Richard and Lucille avoid using the club's new point-of-sale system, because, as they tell everyone, "the old way always worked." Some of the club's newer servers have complained to Paige about Richard and Lucille because they feel they have to shoulder an unfair workload at a lower rate of pay. Recently, Paige has noticed that reservations for business lunches have fallen off, possibly due to slow service.

In an initial meeting with the house committee, Paige expressed her concern over Richard's and Lucille's declining productivity. While most of the committee members are fond of Richard and Lucille, they have to put business first and requested that Paige report her possible solutions to the problem at their next meeting.

Alec Brooker, the house committee chairperson, kicked off the meeting. "Well, Paige," he began, "we're ready to hear your recommendations regarding Richard and Lucille. While we all have a soft spot in our hearts for them, we can't just wait for this problem to go away. The club has no retirement plan, so Richard and Lucille will probably be around for many more years. How can we get the dining room productivity back on track?"

"I'm afraid the reality is we're going to have to ease these two into less critical positions," suggested another committee member. "The bottom line clearly indicates that more efficient servers would reduce our dining room labor costs."

"One option I'm considering is to move Richard and Lucille into other areas of the club, where we'll still get the benefit of their goodwill toward members but their performance won't hurt the club," responded Paige.

Mr. Brooker sighed. "Your predecessor already tried that. He told them he wanted to give them an opportunity to take it easy, since they were getting older and had been with the club for so long, and offered Richard a locker-room attendant position and Lucille a switchboard operator position. They both refused the offers and acted insulted and hurt."

"That was a dangerous brush with age discrimination, wasn't it?" interjected an attorney on the committee. "You're asking for serious legal trouble if you even mention age in this situation."

"That's for sure," agreed Paige. "We had a big lawsuit at my last club involving a valet, so I realize I've got to be careful. I'm convinced that this is a training issue. Richard's and Lucille's devotion to the club and its members deserves our respect. I think we need to return their loyalty and demonstrate our regard for their dedication by being honest with them about the situation."

Discussion Questions

1. What kinds of challenges await Paige as she attempts to resolve this situation?

2. How can Paige increase server efficiency and productivity while accommodating the needs and preferences of all club members?

3. What is Paige's most pressing training issue?

The following industry experts helped develop this case: Cathy Gustafson, CCM, University of South Carolina, Columbia, South Carolina; Kurt D. Kuebler, CCM, Vice President, General Manager, The Desert Highlands Association, Scottsdale, Arizona; and William A. Schulz, MCM, General Manager, Houston Country Club, Houston, Texas.

REVIEW QUIZ

When you feel you have covered all of the material in this chapter, answer these questions. Choose the *best* answer.

1. The primary job of club managers is to:

   a. make a lot of money for the club.
   b. provide club members with a wonderful experience each time they visit the club.
   c. form focus groups and conduct member-needs surveys.
   d. work efficiently with club-committee chairpersons.

2. Which of the following is a moment of truth?

   a. a club member is greeted by an employee in the pro shop
   b. a club manager smiles as she passes a member in the hallway
   c. a club member in the club's grill picks up a sandwich and takes the first bite
   d. all of the above

3. A group of members who are brought together by the club to discuss specific issues is called a(n):

   a. focus group.
   b. member-needs team.
   c. empowerment group.
   d. data-collection team.

4. A service gap occurs when:

   a. manager and employee expectations about service do not match.
   b. club employees are empowered to make service decisions without consulting club managers.
   c. there is a shortfall between the quality of service a club provides and the quality of service members expect.
   d. focus groups are given too much power at the club.

Answer Key: 1-b-C1, 2-d-C1, 3-a-C2, 4-c-C2

Each question is linked to a competency. Competencies are listed on the first page of the chapter. An answer reading 3-b-C4 translates to:

  3: the question number
  b: the correct answer
 C4: the competency number

Chapter 4 Outline

The New Management Paradigm
    Open-Book Management
Managers and Power
    Types of Management Power
    Building a Power Base
    Putting Politics into Action
Empowerment
    Obstacles to Empowerment
    Sharing Power with Employees
Communication
    Nonverbal Communication
    Oral Communication
    Written Communication
Goal Setting
    Characteristics of Effective Goals
    Employee Performance Goals
Coaching
    Managers as Coaches
Conflict Management
    Causes of Conflict
    Conflict Management Strategies
    Tips for Handling Staff Conflict

Competencies

1. Describe open-book management, list sources of management power, and explain how club managers can build a power base and put organizational politics into action. (pp. 121–126)

2. Explain employee empowerment, identify obstacles to empowerment, and describe how club managers can share power with employees. (pp. 126–130)

3. Summarize nonverbal, oral, and written communication skills club managers should possess. (pp. 130–136)

4. Summarize characteristics of effective goals, describe how club managers can set employee performance goals and get employees to accept goals, summarize coaching issues club managers face, and describe conflict management issues in clubs. (pp. 136–146)

Leadership in Club Operations

This chapter was written and contributed by Robert H. Woods, Associate Professor, *The* School of Hospitality Business, Michigan State University, East Lansing, Michigan.

IN ORDER TO GET THE BEST out of their employees and make their clubs as good as they can be, club managers must be leaders as well as managers. After discussing the new management paradigm and how it has changed the way managers manage organizations, we will discuss the following leadership issues in this chapter: power, employee empowerment, communication, goal setting, coaching, and conflict management.

The New Management Paradigm

A paradigm is a model or example that others follow. Historically, the term has been used to describe the predominant theme of an era. The new management paradigm is considerably different from the old. The old management paradigm focused on ensuring order and predictability in the workplace; the new management paradigm is focused on creating change, initiating strategies, empowering people, and launching processes. The new management paradigm values those managers who can influence and encourage, not force, others to attain organizational goals. In other words, the new management paradigm places a premium on leadership.

The emerging new management paradigm is an amalgam of many management styles and approaches. It is inherently different than any previous management theory. A key element in the emerging paradigm is the radical change in the relationship between managers and employees. Some have called this paradigm **open-book management.** The title seems appropriate because it emphasizes that revealing previously hidden information to employees is an important step in the process.

Open-Book Management

Open-book management eliminates the us-versus-them relationship between managers and employees by turning employees into participants in the management of the organization. Ralph Stayer, the CEO of Johnsonville Foods, Inc., used the analogy of a flock of geese to illustrate why he thinks that the open-book management approach that he implemented in his top-performing company is best:

Personal Attributes of Leaders

Club managers who are good leaders tend to have most or all of the following personal attributes:

- Passion for giving of oneself
- Common sense
- Vision
- Trust
- Nurturing of others
- Consistency
- Organization
- Ethics
- Perseverance
- Expecting the best of themselves and others

Source: Ronald A. Yudd, "Focus 2000: Reaching the Horizon of Personal and Professional Success," Ron Yudd Seminars, 1995.

> I didn't want an organizational chart with traditional lines and a bunch of boxes, but a "V" of individuals, like a flock of geese on the wing, who knew the common goal, took turns leading, and adjusted their structure to the task at hand.[1]

According to Stayer, most U.S. organizations are more like a herd of buffalo. That's a problem, because:

> buffalo follow their leader blindly. That kind of leadership almost made the buffalo extinct. Buffalo hunters used to slaughter the herd by finding and killing the leader. Once the leader was dead, the rest of the herd stood around waiting for instructions that never came, and the hunters could (and did) exterminate them one by one.[2]

To help turn employees into leaders, Stayer flattened the Johnsonville organization and created work teams, each with almost total control over its work. The teams made their own decisions about work schedules, performance standards, assignments, budgets, quality measures, capital improvements, and quality control—the whole range of managerial decisions. The control Stayer gave these teams was so complete that when it was necessary for a team to hire a new employee, the team established the job description and criteria for the job and interviewed applicants. Hiring a new employee happens infrequently at Johnsonville Foods because turnover is very low.

Open-book management is used by many other high-performing U.S. companies. At Wal-Mart, for example, all employees receive weekly and monthly data on store performance, how their store performed compared to others in the company, copies of invoices showing profit margins on the merchandise sold in the store, and a complete financial statement for the store. Wal-Mart has also made employees shareholders. Wal-Mart employees receive a percentage of their compensation in company stock; the better the company does, the more employees make. Wal-Mart is rewarded by being the most profitable company in its industry.

Managers and Power

Managers in today's clubs must be effective leaders. To be an effective leader, a club manager must learn how to build a power base and use power effectively.

What is **power?** Power is the ability to get someone else to do something that you want them to do, or the ability to make things happen in a way that you want them to happen, or the ability to get people to do something that they might not do otherwise.

Power works differently from organization to organization. In that sense, power is situational in nature. What works well in one organization may not work well in another. Empowerment, for example, works well in organizations whose managers believe that they actually increase their power through empowering others; it usually fails in organizations whose managers believe that power is synonymous with control.

Types of Management Power

Managerial power originates from a variety of sources. The earliest explanation of where management power came from was provided by authors J. R. P. French and B. Raven, who identified five types of management power: coercive, reward, expert, legitimate, and referent.[3] This classification has been modified by research findings. Today, most organizational theorists believe that there are four principal types of management power: coercive, reward, persuasive, and knowledge.

Coercive power is management power that stems from the employees' fear of punishment. Club managers use coercive power when they demote or fire an employee, withhold a raise, refuse to let an employee train for a new position, and so on. **Reward power** stems from rewards given out by managers (pay raises, good schedules, training, career opportunities, and so on). **Persuasive power** is the ability to use facts or logic to persuade others. **Knowledge power** comes from knowledge the manager possesses—"inside" knowledge about the club, knowledge of how to solve problems, knowledge of how to use equipment, and so on.

Some theorists have identified other types of power.[4] *Position power,* sometimes known as legitimate power, stems from a manager's position within the organization. *Personal power,* sometimes called charismatic power, stems from a manager's personal characteristics such as attractiveness and personality. *Opportunity power* stems from being in the right place at the right time. *Referent power* stems from people wanting to affiliate with a manager whom they perceive to be powerful or whom they like or admire.

Building a Power Base

Organizational politics are a way of life for managers in virtually every organization. This is not to suggest that all politics are bad, merely that managers often use coalitions with others to accomplish goals for themselves or their departments. One of the keys to success as an organizational politician is to build a power base from which to operate.

Whetten and Cameron, two scholars who have extensively researched power and its use in organizations, believe that managers can build a power base by creating and maintaining high levels of both position power and personal power. They offer several guidelines for enhancing position power:

1. *Increase your centrality and criticality in the organization.* Centrality is the extent to which information flows through your position; criticality is the extent to which you have control over that information. Increasing the flow of information to you and increasing your command of that information makes the work you do more important to others. One way a club manager can increase his or her criticality and centrality is by thoroughly reviewing and becoming knowledgeable about all areas of the member database and using that knowledge to communicate the needs of the membership to the board, various club committees, and staff members.

2. *Increase the personal discretion and flexibility of your job.* Being tied down to routine activities diminishes power because it limits the extent to which a manager can become involved in other issues. Initiating new projects and participating in decisions outside the normal routine build position power.

3. *Increase the visibility of your job performance.* Many people perform admirably yet are never rewarded because their superiors do not know about their work. Managers who interact with senior management personnel or the club's board, make formal presentations, and participate in problem-solving task forces often gain more position power.

4. *Increase the relevance of your work.* Providing relevant information to the club's board, committees, and staff members; being involved in important club decisions; and being a trainer or mentor for new employees all add to the relevance of your work and increase your position power.[5]

Whetten and Cameron also point out three characteristics that are especially relevant to increasing personal power:

1. *Knowledge and information.* A club manager's personal power is enhanced when he or she possesses special knowledge gained through training, education, or experience; or when he or she possesses important club information gained through access to data or people.

2. *Personal attractiveness.* How well a manager is liked by others, how pleasant a manager's personality is, how agreeable his or her behaviors are, and the manager's physical attractiveness all influence a manager's personal power.

3. *Effort.* Managers who try hard are often perceived to either know more or to deserve a break simply because of their efforts.[6]

Club managers can also gain power through influencing superiors, peers, or employees. Exhibit 1 provides guidelines for influencing each of these groups.

Exhibit 1   Guidelines for Gaining Power through Influencing Others

Influencing Superiors

- Look for ways to help them solve their problems.
- Show appreciation for things they do to help you.
- Encourage superiors to discuss their problems. Listen carefully and empathetically, and provide feedback when appropriate.
- Point out new ways in which superiors can use your skills.
- Provide constructive feedback whenever possible.
- Be loyal.

Influencing Peers

- Find ways to help peers reach their personal goals.
- Try to understand their problems and share useful information.
- Look for common goals you can mutually pursue.
- Form informal problem-solving groups with peers.
- Be supportive.
- Provide constructive feedback.
- Be loyal.

Influencing Employees

- Work to increase their trust in you.
- Give recognition for a job well done.
- Give credit when credit is due.
- Provide coaching to help them solve their workplace problems.
- Provide current and useful information.
- Provide training and guidance.
- Champion their causes.
- Point out how you depend on one another.
- Be clear about your responsibilities and theirs.

Putting Politics into Action

Merely building a power base will not be enough for most managers. Managers also need to know how to put politics into action. The following is a list of power tactics club managers can use:

- *Develop the right image.* Every club has cultural norms that dictate which behaviors are acceptable and which are not. In most clubs, dress is very important. In others, being either risk aversive or risk taking is important, and in others, getting along with co-workers is considered very important. Successful club managers learn the norms of their clubs and practice them overtly. Some managers may call this simply "knowing the ropes."

- *Gain control of scarce or important organizational resources.* Organizational resources, especially scarce or important ones, are a source of power. Club managers who control such resources typically are considered more powerful and valuable to the club.

- *Make yourself appear indispensable.* Appearance is sometimes more important than fact. Appearing to have expertise, knowledge, contacts, experience, secret techniques, or natural talents can often convince others that you actually have these attributes. The result is that club managers who appear to have these attributes are often afforded more responsibility and power. Of course, it is critical to actually develop expertise, knowledge, contacts, and so on as you become more experienced in your position.

- *Be visible.* As mentioned earlier, laboring in secret is not a successful way to gain power; being noticed for your efforts is.

- *Get a mentor.* The fact that you have a mentor is often seen as a reason for affording you more power, simply because you have allied yourself with someone who is more powerful. Mentors help managers make the right decisions, avoid unnecessary conflicts, and get noticed. Managers gain mentors through social contacts; networking; exchanging information or knowledge; belonging to the same social, religious, or professional organizations; or taking on projects for the mentor.

- *Develop powerful allies.* Many club managers will face serious problems sometime during their careers. Having mentors or other powerful allies (sometimes the allies of your mentor) can help a manager get through rough times. Allies also provide a coalition of support when needed for more routine matters.

- *Avoid close affiliations with difficult club members or staff members.* Most organizations have individuals who are considered difficult or negative. Managers who make close alliances with these individuals are often themselves seen as difficult or negative. Club managers should carefully choose with whom to form coalitions and should maintain a safe distance from club or staff members who are considered difficult or negative.

- *Support your boss.* A club manager's boss controls his or her immediate future; being loyal to this person is a big factor in a manager's success. In the case of a club's general manager, his or her boss is usually the club's president. Giving loyalty and support to the club's president is very important for a general manager, because the club president is typically a very influential person within the club membership.

Empowerment

Empowerment has become one of the most popular topics in business today, but what empowerment actually means and how it is effectively used is still a mystery to many managers. One of the reasons for this is that not all people mean the same thing when they talk about empowerment. In many cases, people mean "power-sharing" when they talk about empowerment. This is only one type of empowerment, characterized primarily by more powerful people sharing their power with less powerful people within an organization.[7] But this is not the only meaning of the word.

Empowerment can also refer to management efforts to help employees develop a sense of personal power. This definition of empowerment focuses on an employee's beliefs about his or her own self-efficacy, or sense of self. Club managers attempting to empower their employees through power sharing must also pay attention to this form of empowerment. Many empowerment programs fail because they only pass decision-making down through the organization to employees who have never had power before. Many of these employees have learned over time to wait for the directives of others rather than take the initiative themselves. Few things are more threatening to employees who have never experienced responsibility than to suddenly be told that they must now make important workplace decisions. Before attempting to give decision-making authority to employees, club managers should teach their employees to empower themselves.

Employee empowerment begins by transforming an employee's sense of self, then moves to encouraging employees to try new experiences and behaviors, helping them accept a continuous-learning mind-set, and helping them further increase their own self-confidence.

Some club managers distrust empowerment because they believe it is synonymous with abdication of authority. This is not true. Effective empowerment is synonymous with the concept of "managed participation," which calls for managers to teach, coach, and counsel employees to take active roles in decisions impacting their jobs. Managers actually gain power through developing employees who are more self-confident and energized. Employees who have more self-confidence typically feel better about themselves and their work and they reward (through loyalty and improved performance) the managers who gave them power in the first place. Empowered employees also free their managers from many routine decisions, giving managers more time to perform higher-level management tasks.

Obstacles to Empowerment

Club managers interested in implementing empowerment programs in their clubs should first learn about two important social phenomena that influence the behaviors of some of their employees and erect obstacles to empowerment. These phenomena are locus of control and learned helplessness.

Locus of Control. While some people believe that they control their own destiny, others believe that they have little or no control over what happens to them. The beliefs people hold about the amount of control they have over their lives are known as their **locus of control.** Those who believe that they control their destiny are known as "internals." "Externals" are those people who believe that their lives are controlled by fate, luck, or other outside forces (see Exhibit 2).

Considerable differences exist between internals and externals. Externals tend to be less satisfied with their jobs, have high turnover rates, have high absenteeism rates, and be less involved with their work than internals. Internals usually believe

Exhibit 2   Internal vs. External Locus of Control

Information Processing

Internals acquire information better and are better at using it than externals.

Job Satisfaction

Internals are more satisfied with work, less alienated, and believe that there is a relationship between job satisfaction and their own performance. Externals see little relationship between their performance and their work satisfaction.

Performance

Internals perform better than externals when performance is tied to valued rewards.

Self-Control

Internals exhibit greater self-control than externals.

Risk

Internals engage in less risky behaviors than externals.

Motivation

Internals are more easily motivated than externals and expect that hard work will lead to rewards.

Response to Others

Internals are more independent and rely on their own judgment more than externals. Externals are more reliant on the judgment of others and are more likely to accept what others tell them.

---

that they have a great deal of control over what happens to them at work.[8] Employees with an external locus of control probably will not be comfortable with empowerment programs and will need more help than internals before they can assume decision-making responsibilities.

Learned Helplessness. Learned helplessness is a feeling that you lack control over your life. It occurs most often to people from low-income and other socio-economic groups who have experienced few opportunities to take charge of their lives.[9] Employees can develop learned helplessness by being subjected over a period of time to circumstances in which they feel powerless. When this occurs, employees often feel a variety of emotions, including depression, apathy, fatigue, anger, and shame. The more capricious life seems, the more likely it is that an individual will develop learned helplessness. In a club in which there seems to be little relationship between rewards or punishments and performance, for example, employees can quickly develop learned helplessness traits. The same can occur in clubs where managers only sometimes punish bad behavior or only punish certain employees for bad behavior. The negative feelings that this inconsistency can evoke are sometimes referred to as "organizationally induced helplessness."[10]

Learned helplessness can even occur among individuals who have an internal locus of control. These individuals are accustomed to making decisions and feeling that they control their own fate. However, when circumstances occur that eliminate the ability of internals to control their destiny, it is not uncommon for internals to suddenly and dramatically develop a sense of learned helplessness. Internals who have lost their jobs or businesses, for example, often have more difficulty coping with this loss of control over their lives than externals, who are used to being in positions where they have little control over their destinies. In effect, externals have a sort of built-in shock absorber that helps them deal with severe adversity, while internals do not.

Learned helplessness has a significant impact on the ability of club managers to empower their employees. It is unlikely that club employees will be able to accept the responsibilities that come with empowerment if they have lived their lives in an economically disadvantaged neighborhood, for example, because such an environment of perpetual economic disenfranchisement is likely to foster both learned helplessness and an external locus of control. As a result, many employees from this type of environment simply cannot accept responsibility for making workplace decisions without first undergoing self-empowerment training so that they can learn a sense of personal power.

Sharing Power with Employees

Sharing power with employees is a process, not a single act. It begins with helping employees develop feelings of self-worth and continues with sharing work responsibilities with employees. What follows is a list of actions club managers can take to begin sharing power with their employees:

- Explain to each employee how he or she contributes to the club. It is important that employees know how their performance relates to the performance of the club as a whole.

- Don't micro-manage employees. Constantly telling employees what to do and when to do it trains employees to stand around and wait for you to tell them what to do.

- Give employees the resources to do their work. Ask them what they need to do the job.

- Give employees recognition and praise for their work. Study after study has shown that employees want what managers want: praise for a job well done and the potential for more responsibility and rewards through future good work.

- Inform employees that their job security is in their own hands. This is the concept of shared risk. Let employees know that their jobs depend on their performance, not just your performance.

- Encourage employees to work in teams. A group of employees working together to solve a problem almost always produces better solutions than employees working independently.

- Celebrate employee success.

- Tolerate failure. All employees will fail at some time, so it is important that club managers not punish failure.

- Welcome surprises. Employees may come up with workable solutions to problems that you did not anticipate. You should accept these solutions and look for their benefits.[11]

Club managers can increase the likelihood that their employees will do well with an empowerment program by following these five steps:

1. *Set expectations* with employees regarding desired output or results. Carefully spell out the goals of the organization or the unit and how employees can contribute to them. Be sure to verify that all employees fully understand and agree with the goals and responsibilities.

2. *Communicate how performance will be measured*—it is very important that employees understand exactly how they will be evaluated and how the reporting system will work. If necessary, rewrite the reporting system with the employees' participation.

3. *Tell employees whom they can count on for help.* Providing resources is very important for successful empowerment.

4. *Agree to interim checkpoints.* Periodic evaluations are very important in empowerment programs, especially at the start, when employees are most likely to need direction or assistance. Corrections made in periodic updates help to produce the desired results.

5. *Follow up* by listening to employee recommendations for further improvements in both the club and the empowerment process.

Communication

Club managers who can't communicate can't lead. Managers spend as much as 80 percent of their day communicating with others; communication skills are used in virtually every important managerial activity.[12] Managing employees (recruiting, interviewing, training, motivating, appraising, and so on), interacting with club members (service, problem resolution, sales), dealing with suppliers (negotiating, purchasing), and many other managerial responsibilities require good communication skills.

In spite of the importance of communication skills, managers often are not as good at communicating as they should be. While most managers believe that they communicate well, in many cases they do not. One study found that 95 percent of high-ranking managers believed that they had good communication skills, but only 30 percent of their employees agreed.[13]

In the following sections we will discuss nonverbal, oral, and written communication.

Nonverbal Communication

"Nonverbal communication" refers to the nonverbal cues people send along with oral messages, including body language, gestures, facial expressions, posture, and so on. We are discussing nonverbal communication before oral communication because only a small portion of spoken communication is expressed in words.[14] The way a message is sent is just as important as what is said; in fact, in most cases it may be more important. According to one expert, only about 7 percent of a spoken message is expressed in words. Facial expressions and posture account for about 55 percent, while vocal intonation and inflection account for about 38 percent.[15] When there appears to be a discrepancy between verbal and nonverbal communication, people believe the nonverbal communication in most cases.[16]

While it is relatively easy to understand that nonverbal cues play important roles in oral communication, it is much more difficult to determine exactly which nonverbal behavior is most important or effective. Eye contact is a good example of how confusing this can be. Maintaining eye contact is generally considered to be a positive nonverbal cue. However, too much eye contact can make people nervous and send a negative message.[17]

Positive body language that club managers should try to use as often as possible includes the following:

- Maintain eye contact (but don't stare).

- Use an open, relaxed body posture.

- Minimize gestures and random movement.

- Reinforce the speaker (use head nods, smiles, and so on to indicate active listening).[18]

Club managers can find out how effective their nonverbal communication skills are through a sensitivity audit. This amounts to watching the people you are communicating with to determine how they are reacting to you while you speak. If they are nodding their heads in apparent interest or approval, then you are likely sending positive nonverbal cues.

Another good way for club managers to learn the importance of nonverbal cues is to conduct their own study of how others communicate nonverbally. To do this, managers should observe others talking and make mental notes (later transferred to written notes) of the positive body-language techniques they are using. A simple form for this activity is provided in Exhibit 3.

Personal Space. The amount of space we maintain from others is also a form of nonverbal communication. There are four types of space people typically maintain from one another, depending on the circumstances and the people involved: public space, social space, personal space, and intimate space.[19]

Public space is 12 or more feet (3.7 or more meters) between you and the person or persons you are communicating with. Speakers often maintain this space during group presentations, for example. Most business communication takes place within the **social space,** which ranges from 4 to 12 feet (1.2 to 3.7 meters). In comparison, **personal space** ranges from 2 to 4 feet (.6 to 1.2 meters), and **intimate space** is 2 feet (.6 meters) or less. Club managers must maintain the proper distance when communicating or risk sending an unintended message. For example, if a club manager delivers a mild reprimand while standing within two feet of an employee, the employee might think that the reprimand is a severe one and feel

Exhibit 3   Body Language Audit

	Observations	Examples	Notes for Improvement
Physically alert			
Eye contact			
Open, relaxed posture			
Gestures			
Speaker reinforcement			

devastated, which was not the message the manager intended to send or the reaction the manager was looking for.

Oral Communication

In the following sections on oral communication, we will discuss two of the most important types of oral-communication skills for club managers: feedback skills and listening skills.

Feedback Skills. Feedback in the workplace can be defined as any communication to a staff member that gives him or her information about some aspect of his or her work behavior.[20] Positive feedback is readily accepted by most employees; negative feedback is not. People like to hear good news but tend to block out bad news.[21] This does not mean that club managers should avoid giving negative feedback. Negative feedback is required in some cases to point out inadequacies in current employee performance. For example, a food server who is offending club members has to be told about it.

The extent to which employees will accept negative feedback is often determined by the credibility of the source. A club manager who is respected by an employee is more likely to successfully communicate constructive negative feedback, for example, than a club manager who is not respected. Credibility may also be based on position power (position on the club's organization chart) or friendship. An employee is more likely to listen to negative feedback from his or her boss, for example, than from a co-worker. Negative feedback also carries more impact if it comes from a friend.

There are several techniques club managers can use to make sure the feedback they provide to employees is understood and accepted. The best feedback is feedback that:

- *Is immediate or well-timed.* Feedback is most effective if there is a short interval between the employee's behavior and the receipt of feedback. Waiting until the next day, next week, or next performance review lessens the value of the feedback considerably.

- *Is specific.* Specific feedback helps the employee understand exactly what behaviors are required. General feedback makes it more likely that an employee will not understand what is expected. Good feedback: "Jan, I'm concerned about your behavior during lunch today. Twice you let a table sit way too long before you introduced yourself. Remember, it's important to greet members promptly after they are seated." Poor feedback: "Bill, I'm just not impressed with your work."

- *Considers the needs of the receiver.* Some employees need constant feedback, others require only occasional feedback. Managers have to decide which approach is best for each employee. Attempting to provide every employee with feedback all of the time is not effective for a variety of reasons, including the fact that most managers do not have the time for such an approach and the fact that many employees can successfully improve their skills or behaviors on their own. Generally speaking, poor performers or new employees require frequent feedback, good performers and experienced employees require less.

- *Focuses on behaviors rather than personality.* Feedback based on personality generally leads to problems for managers because it appears to employees to be judgmental. On the other hand, feedback that is impersonal, descriptive, and job-related generally leads to desired employee reactions.

- *Is unemotional.* It is tempting for managers who observe an employee performing poorly to give in to feelings of irritation or anger and immediately say something that they may regret later on. While timeliness is an important concept in feedback, if a manager is angry or upset, it is usually better for the manager to take time to calm down before providing feedback.

- *Is two-sided.* Asking an employee how he or she feels about the feedback can improve the feedback provided to them. In fact, when a manager fails to establish two-way communication and does all the talking, feedback can backfire, because the employee may perceive the feedback as a tongue-lashing and become ashamed or angry and stop listening.

- *Is understood.* This should go without saying, but it is worth mentioning because it is not unusual for one person to completely misunderstand what another person is trying to communicate. No matter how clear feedback may sound to a manager, an employee may not understand it at all. An excellent technique to ensure that feedback is understood is for a manager to ask an employee to restate in his or her own words what the manager said.[22]

Listening Skills. Good listening skills are some of the most important communication skills a club manager can have. Many managers think they are good listeners, but studies have shown that many are not.[23] Fortunately, listening is something that can be learned. In fact, learning how to become a better listener is relatively easy if one follows the guidelines provided in the following sections.

Active versus passive listening. Passive listening requires only hearing. The passive listener hears the sounds and may even superficially understand some of what the speaker is saying. In contrast, active listening requires the receiver to participate in the message by working to completely understand all of the speaker's message. There are four requirements of active listening:

- Intensity—concentrating intently on what is being said and how it is being delivered.

- Empathy—putting yourself in the speaker's shoes to understand what the speaker wants to communicate, not just what is being said.

- Acceptance—concentrating on understanding the message and reserving evaluation of it for later.

- Responsibility—taking the responsibility to get the full message from the speaker.

Techniques to improve listening skills. Active listening skills can be learned through some widely used and proven techniques. Using the following techniques can help club managers fully understand what other people are saying to them:

- *Be motivated.* Listeners unwilling to hear and understand cannot be communicated with. Work to hear and understand what is being said.

- *Make eye contact.* Research shows that while people listen with their ears, they indicate they are listening with their eyes.[24] Make appropriate eye contact to focus your attention.

- *Show interest.* Nonverbal signals such as head-nodding and appropriate facial expressions show the speaker that you are interested.

- *Avoid distracting actions.* Shuffling papers, looking at your watch, yawning, and so on show a lack of interest.

- *Look for nonverbal cues.* Look for nonverbal cues and other signals that will help you understand the entire message.

- *Ask questions.* Asking questions shows interest and allows for message clarification. Probing questions such as "What happened next?" and "How did you feel about that?" send the message that you are really listening.

- *Paraphrase.* Restating comments made by the speaker helps the listener avoid potential misunderstandings. Using phrases such as "So your position is that—" and "Let me see if I understand—" are useful ways to begin paraphrasing.

- *Don't interrupt.* Interrupting disrupts the speaker's thoughts and is disrespectful.

- *Confront your biases.* Most of us tend to stereotype others to some extent. Good listeners do not allow biases to interfere with the message they are hearing.

- *Make a smooth transition between what the speaker said and your comments.* Effective listeners make smooth transitions between what the speaker has said and what they want to say. Introducing a new topic before responding to the speaker's topic is a sure sign that you did not hear what was just said or did not care about it.

- *Be natural.* Don't exaggerate the actions of a good listener. Too much eye contact, too much intensity, too much empathy, and so on all appear unreal and send the message to speakers that you are either mocking them or that you are trying to conceal disinterest.[25]

Written Communication

Writing is a difficult form of communication for many club managers. However, everyone in business must be able to communicate in writing. Because written communications are more permanent than oral ones, they may represent you for some time to come. Therefore, it is important to learn how to express yourself effectively in writing.

Good writing clearly and succinctly communicates information or ideas to readers. Good writing also obeys certain rules of grammar, spelling, sentence structure, and punctuation.

Guidelines for Better Business Writing. Writing is easier when it is well planned. What follows are four guidelines that can help you plan your writing:

- *Have a specific reader or audience in mind.* Writing will take on different tones and forms for different audiences. A memo to your staff can be more informal than a memo to the club president. A column for the club newsletter has a different tone than a formal report to the board.

- *Know your objective.* Why are you writing this memo, letter, or report? Establishing your purpose in advance—and sticking to it—helps focus your writing.

- *Decide which information is essential to include.* Good writing sticks to the point.

- *Create an outline or list.* Many club managers have trouble organizing their thoughts on paper. Preparing an outline or a list of significant points can help managers write more effectively.

A trilevel outline like the following one is usually sufficient for most business writing:

    A. Major Point
        1. Minor supporting point
            a. subpoint
            b. subpoint
            c. subpoint

    B. Major Point
        1. Minor supporting point
            a. subpoint
        2. Minor supporting point

    Etc.

If you begin by creating a trilevel outline, you will probably find that writing is easier.

Once you have a plan for writing, you can begin. It is best to use plain English and simple sentences. Club managers who want to become effective writers should use words that are familiar to their readers. Some writers try to impress others by using complicated words and sentences, but such writers usually accomplish the opposite.

Most people at work have little time for reading. Therefore, club managers should use the **inverted-pyramid** style of writing—the style newspaper reporters use—in most of their business communications. The inverted-pyramid style places the most important information at the beginning and leaves less significant information for later paragraphs. Newspaper reporters know that their final paragraphs may be deleted in order to make their stories fit into the newspaper's available space. Club managers should assume that their readers will be too busy to read all the way through their report or memo. Putting your most important points in the first paragraph or two will make it more likely that readers will get your message.

Club managers should avoid jargon when they write. Jargon may be easily understood within a particular area of the club, but it often means little to outside readers. If your writing will be read by someone who won't understand your jargon, don't use it.

Something else club managers should avoid when writing is sexist language. There are many more women in business today than in the past. Because of this, and because of changing social values, sexism has no place in business writing.

Goal Setting

Leaders are usually good at setting goals and inspiring others to attain them. Goals help managers stay focused and keep the club on track. Club managers should have a clear idea at all times of what they are trying to accomplish. Those managers who do are more likely to accomplish their objectives than those who do not.

For club managers to be good at setting goals, they must understand the characteristics of effective goals.

Characteristics of Effective Goals

Gary Yukl, author of *Skills for Managers and Leaders: Text, Cases and Exercises*, said that effective goals share certain characteristics.[26] According to Yukl, goals must:

- Be clear and specific
- Be measurable
- Be verifiable
- Have time limits
- Be challenging
- Be relevant
- Be cost-effective
- Balance needs
- Be measured over time

Each of these characteristics must be present for a goal to work effectively. Let's take a closer look at them.

Clear and Specific. Goals should be clear and specific. Goals such as "Do your best" or "Improve service in the pro shop" are not clear or specific enough. An example of a specific goal is "Increase lunchtime dessert sales in the main dining room by 5 percent next month."

Measurable. Whenever possible, goals should be stated in terms that are easy to measure. "Reduce the number of member complaints on comment cards by 10 percent in the next six months" is more measurable than "improve member service."

Verifiable. If a goal cannot be stated in measurable terms, it should be stated in verifiable terms. For example, a goal of "rearrange the golf-car storage barn satisfactorily by 5:00 P.M." is not measurable, but it is verifiable if both parties agree in advance on exactly what must be done to rearrange the storage barn satisfactorily.

Time Limits. Many goals are neglected or completed unsatisfactorily simply because the manager and employee did not agree on a time limit in advance. "As soon as possible" or "right away" is not specific enough. Goals should include specific time limits such as "by 2 P.M.," "don't take more than a half hour," "by tomorrow at noon," "the deadline is June 1," and so on.

Challenging. Goals should stretch a person's abilities, but not too far. Easy goals do not motivate because they seem unchallenging or childish; goals that are too high frustrate staff members.

Relevant. Some club managers set goals that employees consider irrelevant or trivial. For example, some managers set goals just to keep employees busy. This makes it harder for employees to attain meaningful goals, since employees may become unable to distinguish the meaningful goals from the trivial ones. Therefore, goals should always be relevant to all concerned.

Cost-Effective. Given enough time, money, and people, almost any goal can be accomplished. However, some goals cost the club too much to accomplish. Club managers must consider how important a particular goal is and devote the appropriate resources to achieving it. The more important the goal, the more resources can be devoted to it.

Balance Needs. When setting goals, club managers should keep the big picture in mind. For example, a club's general manager is responsible for all of the club's departments and should not set a goal for one department that might have a seriously detrimental effect on another.

Measure over Time. It is almost always better to measure goals over time than to measure them at a single point in time, because measurement over time gives a more accurate reading.

Employee Performance Goals

The number of performance goals a club manager sets for or with an employee is important. Most research indicates that employees can work toward no more than five to nine goals at one time.[27] This range has proven most effective because there are enough goals to capture the complexity of a work task, but not so many that employees become confused or think that they are being asked to accomplish too much.

What follows is an eight-step process for setting performance goals with employees:

1. *Specify the objective or tasks to be completed.* Goal completion depends on establishing specific objectives or tasks. Objectives that are too general, such as "You must do a better job" are not specific enough.

2. *Establish difficult but attainable goals.* Be sure to establish goals that will require effort, yet be attainable.

3. *Specify how the employee's performance will be measured.* Be specific about whether the measures will include productivity statistics, observations of changed behavior, or other measures.

4. *Specify the outcome to be reached.* Establish and discuss with the employee exactly what outcome you expect.

5. *Specify the deadline.* It's best for a goal to have a deadline, but remember to be realistic.

6. *Set priorities if there are multiple goals.* In the case of multiple goals, be sure to discuss and agree on which goal or goals are the most important.

7. *Determine coordination efforts.* If the employee needs the cooperation of others to attain a goal, be sure to arrange for this cooperation and explain to the employee how it will work. This is an especially important consideration when you set goals for work teams at the club.

8. *Establish a plan of action.* A step-by-step action plan makes goal attainment much easier. Since the steps of an action plan often represent "mini-goals," accomplishing them can encourage employees to keep progressing toward the ultimate goal.[28]

Getting Employees to Accept Goals. There is a great deal of difference between goal creation and goal acceptance. It's easy to get employees to accept some goals; for other goals, it may take all of a club manager's leadership ability. The following are some suggestions that might help persuade employees to accept goals:

- *Provide support for goal completion.* Club managers must support their employees' attempts to reach goals. Sometimes employees view goals set by management as threatening or intimidating. Providing the necessary equipment, supplies, and other club resources sends a strong message to employees that you will help them attain the goals you assign to them.

- *Encourage employees to participate in the goal-setting process.* Whenever possible, club managers should encourage employees to participate in the goal-setting process. Too often, managers pay scant attention to employee suggestions about which goals should be set or how goals can be accomplished.

- *Pay attention to each employee's capabilities.* Employees are individuals; club managers should make sure each employee has goals that are appropriate for him or her.

- *Reward those who complete their goals.* Perhaps the most important step in the goal-setting process is to reward those who successfully complete their goals. Rewards—including promotions, recognition, time off, and salary increases—given to employees who reach their goals send a strong message that the club considers goal completion a very important accomplishment.[29]

Coaching

Coaching is a leadership skill that has been defined as "a directive process used by a manager to train and orient an employee to the realities of the workplace and to help the employee remove barriers to optimum work performance."[30] A club manager's objective when coaching an employee is to help the employee become better at his or her job.

Managers as Coaches

Generally speaking, most employees are one of three types: (1) those who have no problems completing their work in an acceptable fashion, (2) those who have trouble completing their work but come to their manager for help with problems, or (3) those who have problems performing their work but do not tell their man-

...inately, many club managers think they have too few of the first type, ...f the second type, and too many of the third type.

...b managers might wish for employees who never come to them with ...t this should not be their goal. In fact, this is perhaps the opposite of ...rs should want. Why? Because employees who identify problems for ...s actually make a manager's job easier in the long run. Some of the ...ht reveal mistakes in a service process that the club uses, for example; ...d and corrected, the problem will help the manager improve service ...rs. Helping employees solve problems they have in performing their ...s the manager's reputation as a leader. It can increase opportunities

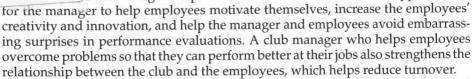

for the manager to help employees motivate themselves, increase the employees' creativity and innovation, and help the manager and employees avoid embarrassing surprises in performance evaluations. A club manager who helps employees overcome problems so that they can perform better at their jobs also strengthens the relationship between the club and the employees, which helps reduce turnover.

Not All Employees Ask for Help. Creating an environment in which employees feel that they can ask for help with work problems is a major step in building a quality club operation. However, no matter how often a club manager emphasizes that he or she has an open-door policy, some employees will not ask for help. There are many possible reasons for this. Some employees may believe that asking for help will make their manager think that they are incapable of doing their work. Other employees may feel that it is better to figure things out for themselves. Some employees may fear that asking their manager for help may make co-workers believe that they are trying to "get in good with the boss." Some employees think that managers don't have the time to help them with their problems. And some employees may not come to their managers with problems because their cultural background discourages such action.

Club managers sometimes, through their words or actions, inadvertently discourage their employees from coming to them with problems. For example, managers who praise employees who consistently solve problems on their own may be sending the message to other employees that this is expected of all employees.

Because employees often will not ask for help, club managers must become proficient at identifying employees who need help. Declining work performance or productivity; disinterest; lack of cooperativeness; disorganization; absenteeism; irritability; lack of enthusiasm; increased complaining; and defensiveness with members, co-workers, or managers are all signs that an employee needs coaching.

Why Managers Don't Want to Become Coaches. Club managers have a lot of reasons for not wanting to coach their employees. Some managers believe that they simply do not have the time. Others believe that if they take the time to coach one employee, they will end up having to coach all of them. Some managers believe that employees will feel threatened by the attention a manager gives their problems. Other managers think it is better for employees to figure things out on their own. Club managers who hold these beliefs are missing golden opportunities to improve their relationships with employees and improve the club's performance.

Coaching for High Performance. When coaching, the aim of club managers is not to solve every problem their employees bring to them. This approach has been used in the past and has failed. Instead, a club manager should help employees grow so they can better cope with current and future challenges. A club manager's objective when coaching is to build self-sufficiency in his or her employees.

Exhibit 4 provides tips for conducting coaching sessions. These are general guidelines only. Unexpected events may occur during a coaching session that a club manager must adapt to at the time. Therefore, club managers should remain flexible when coaching.

Employees may react positively or negatively to the coaching session. One employee may welcome advice and immediately consider ways in which he or she can put the advice to use; another may become argumentative or emotional. Club managers must remember that the purpose of coaching is to provide advice and assistance that will improve the employee's performance. If an employee becomes argumentative or emotional, many of the potentially positive benefits of the session will probably be lost. In such cases, it is best for the manager to terminate the coaching session, ask the employee to consider why he or she is responding in a negative manner, and plan a second session to discuss this topic.

Conflict Management

Conflict at clubs can occur among club members, between club members and staff members, and among staff members. In this section we will concentrate on conflicts that occur among staff members.

Exhibit 4   Guidelines for Coaching Sessions

Prior to the session:

1. Establish a clear agenda in advance.
2. Make sure the employee knows about and understands the agenda.
3. Clear your calendar to allow ample time for the coaching session.
4. Find a quiet place to conduct the session.
5. Ensure that there will be no interruptions during the session.

At the session:

1. Greet the employee promptly and warmly.
2. Put the employee at ease by using receptive body language and lots of eye contact.
3. Allow the employee to become comfortable by beginning with small talk.
4. Describe the performance problem or issue to be addressed.
5. Ask open-ended questions about the employee's feelings or thoughts on the issue.
6. Encourage the employee to discuss the issue.
7. Encourage the employee to identify solutions to the issue.
8. Offer suggestions to improve on the employee's solutions. If the employee's solutions are unacceptable, propose some of your own.
9. Agree on appropriate goals.
10. Agree on appropriate action plans to accomplish the goals.
11. Schedule a follow-up session to review progress.
12. Thank the employee for his or her interest, suggestions, and attention.

Staff conflict occurs in all clubs from time to time. Not all of it is based on ill feeling by one party for another. Conflict among staff members sometimes occurs simply because one person or group wants resources that another person or group also wants. For example, food and beverage managers may want to use the club's training funds to train food and beverage employees to use the department's point-of-sale computer system more effectively, while the golf course superintendent may want to use the funds for training the grounds crew in advanced golf course maintenance.

Business theorists used to say that all staff conflict was negative. This is not true, however. When managed properly, conflict can enhance creativity and innovation.[31] It can increase the likelihood that club resources are used most efficiently. Conflict has also ultimately encouraged parties with divergent options to work together more closely.[32]

While some conflict is positive, conflict can also become a negative force in a club. Negative impacts of conflict include stress, frustration, anxiety, diversion

Insider Insights

Willmoore "Bill" Kendall, CCM, General Manager
Woodmont Country Club, Rockville, Maryland

There are all kinds of situations that can create conflict at a club. For example, you get conflict when the board makes unpopular rules. A recent example at our club came up when boys started wearing baseball caps into the dining room. A lot of old-timers felt that was rude, and our board responded by making a blanket rule that you couldn't wear a hat indoors anywhere in the club. That created conflict, because some of the younger people on the board thought there were times when there was nothing wrong with wearing a hat indoors. They said that they often wear a hat when they play a round of golf, and when they stop by the grill room afterward to eat a hamburger they want to leave their hat on because their hair is a mess. Eventually the board decided to revise the rule so that in the grill you could wear a hat during the day, but you still couldn't wear one at night, and the ban on hat wearing in the formal dining room remained.

Smoking is another area of conflict. Early on, our club decided not to allow smoking in most indoor spaces. Today we don't allow smoking anywhere indoors. Recently some board members were even talking about banning smoking once you pass through the club gates and enter the grounds surrounding the club. That didn't get passed, but there was a small minority that wanted such a rule. That's the kind of thing that causes problems, because smokers are as passionate about smoking as nonsmokers are about their right to clean air. When those kinds of issues get involved, you can really get some conflict going.

The conflicts that stand out in your mind are the ones that members have with the board, or the board with members. At all the clubs I've worked, I've always tried to establish a committee to handle member-board problems or member-member problems. Members in conflict can then go to a committee of their peers. From my perspective, it's much better to form a member committee and let the committee handle it. That way I don't get in the middle and become the bad guy.

Of course, there is always the potential for conflict between you and a member. For example, if Mr. Smith gets bad service, he will probably get angry and complain. If you react by trying to give him good service, the conflict usually evaporates quickly. If you don't react, every time he comes in he's reminded of that bad service. Pretty soon he's exerting a great deal of energy to have the dining room manager replaced, the server replaced, or you replaced because you didn't react to his complaint.

When an upset member approaches, I try to remain as calm as possible. If you stay calm, usually you can get the member to calm down, too. If you get upset, you make the situation worse. So even though it's very tough sometimes, I try to hold my temper, keep a smile on my face, and talk to the member in a gentle, nice way. Because I know that if things degenerate into a fight, it will be harder to solve the problem. Members can complain to me all they want as long as they don't call me names. If they give me an opportunity to resolve their problems without getting personal with me or telling me I'm not doing my job properly, I have a

(continued)

Insider Insights *(continued)*

much easier time dealing with them. When a member starts getting personal, I cut it off immediately. I say, "Let's not talk about this now, let's get the president or the rules committee involved. I don't want us to get personal, because then we'll probably say things we'll both regret and I'd rather not let this get out of hand."

Club managers also have to deal with conflicts among employees. Those are the conflicts that I handle myself right away—that's one of the things I get paid for. Any time a staff conflict is reported to me, I feel an obligation to intervene and get it resolved as quickly as possible, because letting problems among staff members get out of hand is one of the things that can get you in the most trouble. I think club managers make a big mistake if they try to ignore a staff conflict. They should address it before it gets so big it has to be resolved through other means. That is especially true for major issues like sexual harassment. If a staff conflict comes to your attention and you don't do something about it, it certainly becomes a lot worse for the club later if you are sued. So any time a staff conflict comes to my attention, I drop what I'm doing and attend to it.

If I think it will work, I sit both parties down together, since most conflicts are due to a lack of communication. I usually ask one of my assistant managers to go along with me to these meetings because I think the assistant can learn from them—plus I have a witness in case someone tries to misquote me later. If I can get the chef and the dining room manager at the same table and I can get them to tell their story in front of each other, the stories aren't quite as exaggerated as they would be if I talked with each person separately. I do, however, try to talk to both parties individually beforehand, just to make sure this approach will work. You don't want to get people together and have them end up in a fistfight. I've seen chefs get angry and pour pots of boiling water on dining room managers, and I've seen dining room managers throw knives at chefs. You don't see it as much anymore, but it used to be the norm in this business that the chef was king in his kitchen and nobody trampled on his territory without getting into serious trouble. The best way to deal with violent responses is to call the police. I've intervened in fistfights and shoving-and-pushing matches, but when weapons are involved I usually run the other way and let the police handle it.

After the meeting you should follow up with everyone to see if the conflict was resolved by the remedies everyone agreed on at the meeting. Make sure the conflict's not just sitting there festering. The best way to follow up is to call the people involved and make sure they're getting along and things are working out. Following up makes everyone feel better because it shows you care.

from club goals, job dissatisfaction, absenteeism, and turnover. The key for club managers is to know how to manage conflict so that the positive impacts are emphasized while the negative impacts are minimized.

Causes of Conflict

The first step in knowing how to manage staff conflict is understanding why conflict occurs. Conflict within clubs usually occurs because of one or more of the following reasons:

- *Competition for resources.* Resources in organizations are always limited. As a general rule, the more scarce the resources, the more likely there will be conflict.

- *Task interdependence.* Conflict is most likely to occur among individuals or groups dependent on one another to do their jobs. For example, food servers rely on cooks to prepare food properly and on time. In some ways, the cooks also rely on the servers (for correct orders, for example).

- *Jurisdictional ambiguity.* Overlapping responsibilities often lead to conflict. This occurs when one party either gives or takes responsibility that another can also claim. Examples of this type of conflict include one party taking credit for work done at least partially by others, or refusing to take any responsibility for mistakes that the party was partially responsible for.

- *Status struggles.* Status struggles can result from perceived inequities. Conflict related to status can also occur when one person or group believes that it should be giving recommendations or instructions to another person or group instead of receiving them. This can happen between managers of different club departments. It can also occur among employees—for example, when bartenders believe that they should be giving directions to servers, not vice versa.

- *Communication barriers.* Conflicts regularly occur because two people or groups do not speak the same "language." Technical language used by one group but not understood by another can lead to misunderstandings and conflict. Conflict can also occur simply because someone does not fully understand the communication (oral or written) of another.

- *Differences in backgrounds or values.* Conflict is more likely between people with differing social, ethnic, or racial backgrounds, or differing cultural values or beliefs.[33]

Conflict Management Strategies

Twenty years ago, authors T. L. Ruble and K. W. Thomas identified five conflict management strategies: avoidance, accommodation, compromise, collaboration, and competitiveness.[34] These strategies are still appropriate today. Exhibit 5 shows the Ruble and Thomas model.

According to Exhibit 5, it would appear that collaboration is always the best approach to use because it is high in both assertiveness and cooperativeness. However, this is only the case when several conditions exist: namely, that both parties are willing to ignore political or power issues, both parties are open-minded, and both parties are aware of the potential for conflict with the other.[35]

In certain circumstances, accommodation and avoidance are effective when collaboration is not. Both accommodation and avoidance work when you have to handle a temporary situation. For example, avoidance is useful in temporarily handling conflicts in which the parties have become emotional, because this approach allows people time to regain their composure.

The competitive strategy for managing conflict may be useful when something important is at stake. For example, it may be necessary to assert yourself more and accommodate less when conflict occurs over an issue that is particularly important

Exhibit 5   Conflict Management Strategies

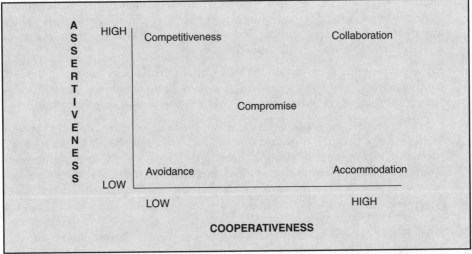

Source: T. L. Ruble and K. W. Thomas, "Support for a Two-Dimensional Model of Conflict Behavior," *Organizational Behavior and Human Performance,* Vol. 16 (1976).

to you or your club. Club managers who use this approach too often, however, might get a reputation for being hard-nosed or disagreeable. The competitive approach should be reserved for truly important issues.

Compromise may be the best approach in many situations—especially in situations in which it is necessary to work with the other party in the future and therefore it is important to maintain good relations.

Tips for Handling Staff Conflict

The following are some tips that might help club managers successfully deal with a conflict among staff members:

- *Use good listening skills.* Active listening can help managers understand what the party or parties involved in the conflict are really saying. Sometimes conflict can be resolved simply by listening carefully and achieving a better understanding of the situation.

- *Use good feedback skills.* Knowing how to provide constructive feedback to those in conflict can help soothe the confrontation.

- *Be selective about the conflicts you get involved in.* Not every staff conflict requires your intervention. Sometimes the best thing you can do to help resolve a minor conflict is to leave it alone. Letting employees resolve their own minor conflicts can be a growing experience for them. Picking the battles you want to fight is especially important in personal conflicts.

- *Evaluate the participants in a conflict.* Knowing who is involved, why they are involved, what their interests and positions are, and what they hope to gain from a conflict will help you understand and resolve the conflict.

- *Assess the source of the conflict.* Earlier we discussed some common reasons for conflicts. Competition for resources, task interdependence, jurisdictional ambiguity, status struggles, communication barriers, and differences in values and beliefs can all cause conflict. Knowing a conflict's cause can help a manager evaluate the facts and resolve the conflict.

- *Know your conflict management options.* Club managers can use any of the five conflict management strategies discussed earlier—avoidance, accommodation, compromise, collaboration, and competitiveness—to resolve a conflict.

- *Select the best strategy.* Managers tend to use their favorite conflict management strategy all of the time, but that strategy may not always be the best approach. Club managers should select a particular conflict management strategy based on the situation at hand, not on their personal preferences.

Endnotes

1. Ralph Stayer, "How I Learned to Let My Workers Lead," *Harvard Business Review,* November–December, 1990, pp. 66–83.

2. Stayer.

3. J. R. P. French, Jr., and B. Raven, "The Bases of Social Power," in D. Cartwright (ed.), *Studies in Social Power* (Ann Arbor, Mich.: University of Michigan Institute for Social Research, 1959), pp. 150–167.

4. R. M. Cyert and J. G. March, *A Behavioral Theory of the Firm* (Englewood Cliffs, New Jersey: Prentice-Hall, 1963), as cited in Stephen P. Robbins, *Organizational Behavior: Concepts, Controversies and Applications* (Englewood Cliffs, New Jersey: Prentice-Hall, 1991), p. 395.

5. David A. Whetten and Kim S. Cameron, *Developing Managerial Skills* (Glenview, Ill.: Scott-Foresman, 1984), pp. 250–259.

6. Whetten and Cameron, pp. 260–266.

7. Joseph A. Conger and R. N. Kanungo, "The Empowerment Process: Integrating Theory and Practice," *Academy of Management Review,* Vol. 13, 1988, p. 473.

8. G. J. Blau, "Locus of Control as a Potential Moderator of the Turnover Process," *Journal of Occupational Psychology,* Fall 1987, pp. 21–29. See also P. E. Spector, "Behavior in Organizations as a Function of Employee's Locus of Control," *Psychological Bulletin,* May 1982, pp. 482–497.

9. L. Y. Abrahamson, M. E. Seligman, and J. D. Teasdale, "Learned Helplessness in Humans: Critique and Reformulation," *Journal of Abnormal Psychology,* 87 (1978), pp. 19–74.

10. M. E. P. Seligman, in M. J. Martinko and W. L. Gardner, "Learned Helplessness: An Alternative Explanation for Performance Deficits," *Academy of Management Review,* Vol. 7, No. 2 (1982), pp. 195–204.

11. Ken Smith, "Hospitality and Empowerment: Trusting Employees," *Hospitality and Tourism Educator,* February, 1993, pp. 19–20.

12. Henry Mintzberg, *The Nature of Managerial Work* (New York: Harper & Row, 1973).

13. C. A. Conrad, *Strategic Organizational Communication* (New York: Holt, Rinehart and Winston, 1985).

14. Chad T. Lewis, Joseph P. Garcia, and Sarah M. Jobs, *Managerial Skills in Organizations* (Boston: Allyn and Bacon, 1990), p. 27.

15. A. Mehrabian, *Tactics of Social Influence* (Englewood Cliffs, New Jersey: Prentice-Hall, 1972).

16. P. Ekman, *Telling Lies: Clues to Deceit in the Marketplace, Politics and Marriage* (New York: Norton, 1985).

17. Lewis, et. al., p. 27.

18. Judi Brownell, *Building Active Listening Skills* (Englewood Cliffs, New Jersey: Prentice-Hall, 1986), p. 249.

19. Edward T. Hall, *The Hidden Dimension* (New York: Doubleday, 1966).

20. Cyril R. Mill, "Feedback: The Art of Giving and Receiving Help," in Larry Porter and Cyril R. Mill (eds.) *The Reading Book for Human Relations Training* (Bethel, Maine: NTL Institute for Applied Behavioral Science, 1976), pp. 18–19.

21. Daniel Iigen, Cynthia D. Fisher, and M. Susan Taylor, "Consequences of Individual Feedback on Behavior in Organizations," *Journal of Applied Psychology,* August, 1979, pp. 349–371.

22. Stephen P. Robbins, *Training in Inter-Personal Skills: TIPS for Managing People at Work* (Englewood Cliffs, New Jersey: Prentice-Hall, 1989), p. 68.

23. Stephen P. Robbins, *Training in Inter-Personal Skills*, p. 29.

24. Phillip P. Hunsaker and Anthony J. Alessandra, *The Art of Managing People* (Englewood Cliffs, New Jersey: Prentice-Hall, 1980), p. 33.

25. Hunsaker and Alessandra, pp. 32–34.

26. Gary Yukl, *Skills for Managers and Leaders: Text, Cases and Exercises* (Englewood Cliffs, New Jersey: Prentice-Hall, 1990), pp. 131–134.

27. Yukl, p. 131.

28. Edwin A. Locke and Gary P. Latham, *Goal-Setting: A Motivational Technique That Works!* (Englewood Cliffs, New Jersey: Prentice-Hall, 1984).

29. Adapted from Stephen P. Robbins, *Training in Inter-Personal Skills*, pp. 51–52.

30. Marianne Minor, *Coaching and Counseling: A Practical Guide for Managers* (New York: Crisp Publications, Inc., 1989), p. 2.

31. Stephen P. Robbins, "Conflict Management and Conflict Resolution Are Not Synonymous Terms," *California Management Review,* Winter 1978, pp. 75–76.

32. R. A. Baron, *Behavior in Organizations* (Boston: Allyn and Bacon, 1986), pp. 245–246.

33. Yukl, pp. 283–286.

34. T. L. Ruble and K. W. Thomas, "Support for a Two-Dimensional Model of Conflict Behavior," *Organizational Behavior and Human Performance,* Vol. 16 (1976), pp. 143–155.

35. Charles B. Derr, "Managing Organizational Conflict: Collaboration, Bargaining and Power Approaches," *California Management Review,* Vol. 21, No. 3 (1978), pp. 76–90.

🔑 Key Terms

coaching—A directive process used by a manager to train and orient an employee to the realities of the workplace and to help the employee remove barriers to optimum work performance.

coercive power—Management power that stems from the employees' fear of punishment; managers use coercive power when they demote or fire an employee, withhold a raise, refuse to let an employee train for a new position, and so on.

empowerment—The redistribution of power within an organization that enables managers, supervisors, and employees to perform their jobs more efficiently and effectively, with the overall goal of enhancing service to members and improving the financial position of the club by releasing decision-making responsibility, authority, and accountability to every level within the organization.

intimate space—Space that is 2 feet (.6 meters) or less between you and the person or persons you are communicating with.

inverted pyramid—A style of writing in which the most important points are placed at the beginning of the work, with less important points following in descending order of importance.

knowledge power—Management power that stems from information the manager possesses.

learned helplessness—A feeling that you lack control over your life; learned helplessness occurs most often to people from low-income and other socio-economic groups who have experienced few opportunities to take charge of their lives.

locus of control—The beliefs people hold about the amount of control they have over their lives.

open-book management—A management philosophy that involves teaching employees how they fit into the big picture of the whole company. Typically, it involves "opening the books" to employees so they can see exactly where the company gets revenues and how it spends money.

personal space—Ranges from 2 to 4 feet (.6 to 1.2 meters) between you and the person or persons you are communicating with.

persuasive power—The ability to use facts or logic to persuade others.

power—The ability to get someone else to do something that you want them to do, or the ability to make things happen in a way that you want them to happen, or the ability to get people to do something that they might not do otherwise.

public space—Twelve or more feet (3.7 or more meters) between you and the person or persons you are communicating with.

reward power—Management power that stems from rewards given out by managers (pay raises, good schedules, training, career opportunities, and so on).

social space—Ranges from 4 to 12 feet (1.2 to 3.7 meters); most business communication takes place within this space.

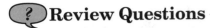 **Review Questions**

1. What is open-book management?

2. How can club managers build a power base?

3. What are some obstacles to empowering employees?

4. What are some techniques club managers can use to make sure the feedback they provide to employees is understood and accepted?

5. What are some guidelines club managers can follow to improve their business writing?

6. Effective goals possess what types of characteristics?

7. Why do employees hesitate to ask club managers for help with work problems?

8. What are some typical causes of conflict among club staff members?

 Additional Reading

Abrahamson, L. Y., M. E. Seligman, and J. D. Teasdale. "Learned Helplessness in Humans: Critique and Reformulation." *Journal of Abnormal Psychology*, 87 (1978).

Baron, R. A. *Behavior in Organizations.* Boston: Allyn and Bacon, 1986.

Berger, Florence, Dennis H. Ferguson, and Robert H. Woods. "How Restaurateurs Make Decisions." *Cornell Quarterly,* Vol. 27, No. 4 (February) 1987.

Berger, Florence, and Dennis H. Ferguson. "Myriad Management Methods: Restaurant Managers Tell All." *Cornell Quarterly,* Vol. 26, No. 4 (February) 1986.

Blau, G. J. "Locus of Control as a Potential Moderator of the Turnover Process." *Journal of Occupational Psychology*, Fall 1987.

Blitzer, Roy J., Colleen Petersen, and Linda Rogers. "How to Build Self-Esteem." *Training and Development*, February 1993.

Brownell, Judi. *Building Active Listening Skills.* Englewood Cliffs, New Jersey: Prentice-Hall, 1986.

Brymer, Robert A. "Employee Empowerment: A Guest-Driven Leadership Strategy." *Cornell Quarterly*, Vol. 31, No. 1, 1991.

Case, John. "A Company of Businesspeople." *Inc.*, April 1993.

Case, T., L. Dosier, G. Murkison, and B. Keys. "How Managers Influence Superiors: A Study of Upward Influence Tactics." *Leadership and Organization Development Journal*, Vol. 9, No. 4 (1988).

Conger, Joseph A., and R. N. Kanungo. "The Empowerment Process: Integrating Theory and Practice." *Academy of Management Review*, Vol. 13, 1988.

Conrad, C. A. *Strategic Organizational Communication.* New York: Holt, Rinehart and Winston, 1985.

Derr, Charles B. "Managing Organizational Conflict: Collaboration, Bargaining and Power Approaches." *California Management Review,* Vol. 21, No. 3 (1978).

French, J. R. P., Jr., and B. Rave. "The Bases of Social Power," in D. Cartwright (ed.), *Studies in Social Power.* Ann Arbor, Mich.: University of Michigan Institute for Social Research, 1959.

Frohman, Mark. "The Aimless Empowered." *Industry Week,* April 20, 1992.

Garcia, Joseph E. "Reflections on Teaching Diversity." *Journal of Management Education,* Vol. 18, No. 4 (November) 1994.

Hall, Edward T. *The Hidden Dimension.* New York: Doubleday, 1966.

Hunsaker, Phillip P., and Anthony J. Alessandra. *The Art of Managing People.* Englewood Cliffs, New Jersey: Prentice-Hall, 1980.

Iigen, Daniel, Cynthia D. Fisher, and M. Susan Taylor. "Consequences of Individual Feedback on Behavior in Organizations." *Journal of Applied Psychology,* August 1979.

Katz, Robert L. "Skills of an Effective Administrator." *Harvard Business Review,* Vol. 52 (September–October) 1974.

Kotter, John P. "What Effective General Managers Really Do." *Harvard Business Review,* Vol. 60 (November–December) 1982.

Lewis, Chad T., Joseph P. Garcia, and Sarah M. Jobs. *Managerial Skills in Organizations.* Boston: Allyn and Bacon, 1990.

Locke, Edwin A., and Gary P. Latham. *Goal-Setting: A Motivational Technique That Works!* Englewood Cliffs, New Jersey: Prentice-Hall, 1984.

McGregor, Douglas. *The Human Side of Enterprise.* New York: McGraw-Hill, 1960.

Mehrabian, A. *Tactics of Social Influence.* Englewood Cliffs, New Jersey: Prentice-Hall, 1972.

Mill, Cyril R. "Feedback: The Art of Giving and Receiving Help," in Larry Porter and Cyril R. Mill (eds.), *The Reading Book for Human Relations Training.* Bethel, Maine: NTL Institute for Applied Behavioral Science, 1976.

Minor, Marianne. *Coaching and Counseling: A Practical Guide for Managers.* New York: Crisp Publications, Inc., 1989.

Mintzberg, Henry. *The Nature of Managerial Work.* New York: Harper & Row, 1973.

———. "The Manager's Job: Folklore and Fact." *Harvard Business Review,* Vol. 53 (July–August) 1975.

Mirvis, P. H. *Work in the 20th Century: America's Trends and Tracts, Visions and Values, Economic and Human Developments.* Cambridge, Mass.: Rudi Press, 1985.

Quinn, Robert E., Sue R. Faerman, Michael P. Thompson, and Michael R. McGrath. *Becoming a Master Manager: A Competency Framework.* New York: Wiley, 1990.

Robbins, Stephen P. *Training in Inter-Personal Skills: TIPS for Managing People at Work.* Englewood Cliffs, New Jersey: Prentice-Hall, 1989.

————. *Organizational Behavior: Concepts, Controversies and Applications.* Englewood Cliffs, New Jersey: Prentice-Hall, 1991.

————. "Conflict Management and Conflict Resolution Are Not Synonymous Terms." *California Management Review,* Winter 1978.

Ruble, T. L., and K. W. Thomas. "Support for a Two-Dimensional Model of Conflict Behavior." *Organizational Behavior and Human Performance,* Vol. 16 (1976).

Seligman, M. E. P., in M. J. Martinko and W. L. Gardner, "Learned Helplessness: An Alternative Explanation for Performance Deficits." *Academy of Management Review,* Vol. 7, No. 2 (1982).

Smith, Ken. "Hospitality and Empowerment: Trusting Employees." *Hospitality and Tourism Educator,* February 1993.

Sparrowe, Raymond T. "Empowerment in the Hospitality Industry: An Exploration of Antecedents and Outcomes." *Hospitality Research Journal,* 17, 3 (1994).

Spector, P. E. "Behavior in Organizations as a Function of Employee's Locus of Control." *Psychological Bulletin,* May 1982.

Stayer, Ralph. "How I Learned to Let My Workers Lead." *Harvard Business Review,* November–December, 1990.

Whetten, David A., and Kim S. Cameron. *Developing Managerial Skills.* Glenview, Ill.: Scott-Foresman, 1984.

Williman, Hans. "One Day in the Life of Hans Williman," *Hotels,* August 1992.

Yukl, Gary, and Cecilia M. Falbe. "Influence Tactics and Objectives in Upward, Downward and Lateral Influence Attempts." *Journal of Applied Psychology,* Vol. 75, No. 2 (1990).

Yukl, Gary. *Skills for Managers and Leaders: Text, Cases and Exercises.* Englewood Cliffs, New Jersey: Prentice-Hall, 1990.

Internet Sites

For more information, visit the following Internet sites. Remember that Internet addresses can change without notice. If the site is no longer there, use a browser to look for additional sites.

http://www.ahrm.org/ [associations for human resources management; listings of and links to human resources organizations throughout the United States]

http://www.dol.gov [homepage for the U.S. Department of Labor; valuable searchable site]

http://www.hospitalitynet.bl [homepage for the International Hotel Association; shows interesting international HR developments]

http://www.yahoo.com/governmenthow/employment_law/ [links to government agencies' legal interpretations]

REVIEW QUIZ

When you feel you have covered all of the material in this chapter, answer these questions. Choose the *best* answer.

1. A club manager who withholds a raise from an employee is using _____ power.

   a. coercive
   b. reward
   c. persuasive
   d. knowledge

2. Which of the following is an action club managers can take to share power with employees?

   a. Explain how each employee contributes to the club.
   b. Refrain from micro-managing the employees.
   c. Give employees recognition and praise for their work.
   d. All of the above.

3. You manage the club's main dining room. During the dinner shift one Tuesday night, you notice that Tim was very late in greeting three of his tables. You are not angry—Tim is a good employee and you know that a calm reminder from you will be sufficient to keep Tim from starting a bad work habit. Which of the following is the best time to give Tim feedback about the need to greet members promptly after they are seated?

   a. that night, at the end of the dinner shift
   b. at the beginning of Tim's next dinner shift, which will be Thursday night
   c. at the Friday-morning staff meeting
   d. at Tim's next performance review (in three months)

4. Julia, a food server with your club, is angry at Frank, one of the cooks in the kitchen, because Frank is habitually late in preparing the food for Julia's tables and Julia has to deal with member complaints and decreased tips. The cause of this conflict is best described as:

   a. competition for resources.
   b. differences in values and beliefs.
   c. task interdependence.
   d. jurisdictional ambiguity.

Answer Key: 1-a-C1, 2-d-C2, 3-a-C3, 4-c-C4

Each question is linked to a competency. Competencies are listed on the first page of the chapter. An answer reading 3-b-C4 translates to:

   3: the question number
   b: the correct answer
   C4: the competency number

Chapter 5 Outline

The Quality Movement
Deming's 14 Points for Quality
Juran and Process Improvement
Principles of Quality Management
Empowerment
Fact-Based Decision-Making
Prevention vs. Inspection
Incremental and Breakthrough
Improvement
Benchmarking
Change Management
Continuous-Improvement Teams
A Continuous-Improvement Process
Target an Opportunity for
Improvement
Gather and Analyze Information
Generate Potential Improvements
Evaluate Alternative Improvements
Implement the Improvement
Evaluate the Improved Process
Implementing Quality Management
The Malcolm Baldrige National Quality
Award
Baldrige Award Criteria
The Baldrige Award Core Values and
Concepts

Competencies

1. Explain how the quality movement got started in the United States, and describe Deming's 14 points for quality and Juran's contributions to the quality movement. (pp. 155–160)

2. Summarize the following principles of quality management: empowerment, fact-based decision-making, prevention vs. inspection, incremental and breakthrough improvement, benchmarking, and change management. (pp. 160–165)

3. Explain how club managers can put together continuous-improvement teams at their clubs, summarize six steps typical of many continuous-improvement processes, and describe how club managers can implement quality management at their clubs. (pp. 166–174)

4. Describe the Malcolm Baldrige National Quality Award's contributions to the U.S. quality movement, and summarize the award's core values and concepts. (pp. 174–181)

5

Quality Management Systems for Clubs

This chapter was written and contributed by Professor Tarun Kapoor, Director of the Professional Development Institute, and Lea D. Wikoff, Associate Professor, School of Hotel & Restaurant Management, California State Polytechnic University, Pomona, California.

QUALITY MANAGEMENT SYSTEMS THAT SUCCEED in the manufacturing environment take on a very different focus when applied to clubs. The principles of quality management are the same, but the unique characteristics of clubs create a new context for managing quality through continuous-improvement efforts.

For the most part, clubs (and other components of the hospitality industry such as restaurants and hotels) do not manufacture physical products—they create and deliver intangible service experiences. While there are physical and tangible aspects to a service experience (such as the food served in the dining room or golf items sold in the pro shop), the value perceived by members in the delivery of club services cannot be held in their hands, returned for better service, or placed on a shelf for consumption at a later point in time. Production, delivery, and consumption all take place in the moment of the service experience itself. Poor service has no value because it is simply a bad experience. If club members experience poor service in the club's grill room, club managers can apologize, pick up the members' checks, and invite them back at the club's expense, but the bad experience does not go away. Compounding the difficulty of providing quality service is the fact that the total service experience a member has with a club is often made up of many service encounters, any one of which could go badly and sour the whole experience. Every service encounter is critical to producing an overall experience at the club that is valued by the member.

From an operations point of view, services are perishable. You can't inventory services in a storeroom and sell them at a later point in time. Unsold tee times at the club's golf course on Monday cannot be saved so they can be sold on Tuesday. The urgency to sell as many of each day's available services as possible is magnified for clubs because clubs have a limited number of consumers—the club's membership. Clubs must not only create valued, intangible service experiences and sell them; they must do so with a limited consumer base in a highly competitive and fast-changing business environment. New clubs are opening at a faster pace than ever before, many public-sector businesses compete with clubs, and many club markets are reaching the saturation point.

Exhibit 1   Deming's 14 Points

> 1. Create constancy of purpose.
> 2. Adopt the new philosophy.
> 3. Cease dependence on inspection to achieve quality.
> 4. End the practice of awarding business on the basis of price tag.
> 5. Improve constantly and forever the system of production and service.
> 6. Institute job training.
> 7. Institute leadership.
> 8. Drive out fear.
> 9. Break down barriers between departments.
> 10. Eliminate slogans.
> 11. Eliminate work standards (quotas).
> 12. Remove barriers that rob employees of pride of workmanship.
> 13. Institute a vigorous program of education and self-improvement.
> 14. Put everybody in the company to work to accomplish the transformation.

Source: W. Edwards Deming, *Out of the Crisis* (Cambridge, Mass.: Massachusetts Institute of Technology, Center for Advanced Engineering Study, 1982), pp. 23–24.

Service experiences at clubs must be delivered better, faster, and at less cost than ever before. Quality management systems can help club managers meet these challenges. In this chapter we will focus on fundamentals of quality management systems. From the work of Deming and Juran, to continuous-improvement teams and processes, to the Malcolm Baldrige Quality Award Criteria—the aim of the chapter is to demonstrate how club managers can meet the needs and exceed the expectations of their members by changing the way work is performed by the club's staff.[1]

The Quality Movement

In the United States, global competitive pressures gave rise to a quality movement in manufacturing industries. Many of today's quality management systems are rooted in the early work of William Edwards Deming and Joseph M. Juran. These two pioneers in quality systems are credited with playing a large role in the recovery of Japanese industries after World War II and for that country's subsequent success in world markets. Their once-radical ideas about quality are now part of the everyday language of business throughout the world.

Deming's 14 Points for Quality

The contributions of William Edwards Deming, a mathematician and physicist by training, range from detailed applications of statistical quality techniques to unrelenting criticism of traditional management methods. Perhaps the most widely known feature of his work is his list of 14 points (see Exhibit 1). The short sections that follow focus on these points, summarizing core features of Deming's approach to quality in relation to club operations.

Point 1: Create Constancy of Purpose. Deming finds that, all too often, the future of an organization is at risk when leaders and managers direct too much time and energy toward achieving immediate financial goals. He suggests that the future success of a business depends on whether it has a clear purpose and a core set of values that do not change over time. A club with constancy of purpose is likely to innovate, invest in research and education, and continuously search for ways to improve.

Point 2: Adopt the New Philosophy. Deming argues that companies must respond to the new challenges of dramatically changed domestic and world markets. In the expanding markets of the 1950s and 1960s, Western management practices couldn't fail—any management practice would have succeeded. In today's competitive club industry, new management practices have emerged from the realization that long-term success is only achieved by producing value for members through consistently meeting or exceeding their expectations.

Point 3: Cease Dependence on Inspection to Achieve Quality. As a practical matter, Deming acknowledges that a certain amount of inspection is always needed, if only to monitor progress toward a club's goals. What he wholeheartedly rejects is the notion that inspection of the result of a process creates a quality product or service. For example, inspecting prepared menu items before servers deliver them to waiting members may catch errors and defects in orders, but this type of inspection will do nothing to improve the process so that errors are not made in the first place.

Point 4: End the Practice of Awarding Business on the Basis of Price Tag. While competition may lead to lower prices, it doesn't necessarily ensure quality. Deming suggests that purchasing agents and controllers need to redefine their responsibilities in relation to quality improvement efforts. A long-term relationship of loyalty and trust with a single vendor may benefit a club more than the immediate savings derived from continually calling for supplier bids and buying from the lowest bidder.

Point 5: Improve Constantly and Forever the System of Production and Service. Deming points out that quality improvement is not a one-time effort and is not limited to simply solving problems. Problem solving "puts out fires" but usually results in putting a process back to where it was in the first place. Deming asserts that the real task of club managers is to look for ways to improve the process itself. Perhaps workflow can be redesigned or some parts of the process can be automated, thus eliminating some opportunities for errors.

Point 6: Institute Job Training. The foundation and prerequisite for any quality improvement effort is job training. Variations in club products and services are often the result of incomplete or improper training of club managers and employees.

Point 7: Institute Leadership. A club manager's job is to lead. Most important, club managers must act on the information they gather and remove the obstacles that prevent their employees from performing at their best. Leaders who know the work they supervise can identify those employees in need of individual attention, training, and coaching.

Point 8: Drive Out Fear. When managers within a club lack leadership ability and the employees are poorly trained, fear rules the workplace. The fear Deming describes leads everyone to strive to maintain the status quo: no one takes risks, no one asks questions, and no one rocks the boat because people are hoping to hide what they don't know from everyone else. Fear disappears only as management improves. More open and less threatening work environments arise as managers take their leadership responsibilities seriously and as employees develop confidence in management's ability to lead the organization.

Point 9: Break Down Barriers between Departments. In some cases, barriers between departments within a club are erected because managers are more concerned with building empires than with fostering cooperation. Barriers also arise between club departments when managers and employees focus on the success of their own areas without considering what's best for the club as a whole. Problems arise when departments:

- Have conflicting goals

- Fail to work together to solve problems

- Fail to improve processes that create value for members

To prevent these kinds of problems, each department must know not only how its work produces value for members, but also how its activities affect other departments or areas within the club.

Point 10: Eliminate Slogans. Too often, quality-improvement slogans are byproducts of the poor management practice of setting goals without describing how they will be accomplished. These empty slogans usually suggest that performance would improve if employees just tried harder. Slogans, banners, buttons, or balloons cannot sustain a quality-improvement effort. They usually try to motivate people to work faster and produce more, but, according to Deming, slogans actually have a negative impact on productivity and quality. Many employees perceive slogans as signs that managers don't understand the work problems employees face and don't care enough to try to understand them.

Point 11: Eliminate Work Standards (Quotas). Deming's argument against work standards focuses on managers who ignore quality issues (such as member expectations) and base productivity rates on what they believe to be the average performance necessary to achieve predetermined goals. For example, consider the case of a club's dining room manager who sets service quotas (number of members served or tables turned) for servers based on a predetermined "average" performance rather than on the individual talents of each server and the needs and expectations of members. Deming suggests that the key to productivity and quality improvement is for managers to identify the various levels of skill and talent among their staff members and then plan the work to make the most of these differences, thus improving overall performance.

Point 12: Remove Barriers that Rob Employees of Pride of Workmanship. Deming suggests that employees are often evaluated on outcomes over which they have little control. The desire and ability of an employee are not enough to overcome problems and barriers caused by inadequate systems, poor training, and improper tools. It's management's job to create the systems, provide the training, and furnish the tools so that employees can perform at their best and produce work they can take pride in.

Point 13: Institute a Vigorous Program of Education and Self-Improvement. As quality improvements increase, levels of productivity rise throughout an organization. As productivity rises, fewer employees are needed to produce the same results. However, Deming insists that quality must not cost jobs. If employees are to play an effective role in a continuous-improvement process, no one should lose a job because of productivity gains. Otherwise, why would employees suggest improvements that might cost them their livelihood? Deming argues that the extra labor time created by improvements should be filled with lifelong learning so that managers and employees will be ready to face new challenges and implement further improvements in the future.

Point 14: Put Everybody in the Company to Work to Accomplish the Transformation. Deming does not offer a blueprint for change. Each club must work out its own adaptation of the previous thirteen points—an adaptation suitable to its own particular mission, culture, and membership. People within the club must work together in developing a mutual understanding of the previous thirteen points, then set appropriate goals and action plans for putting these points into action at the club. Without this clubwide understanding, club departments and staff members may spin their wheels, travel in different directions, or work at cross-purposes and undercut each other's efforts.

Juran and Process Improvement

Joseph M. Juran's approach to quality agrees with many of the fundamental ideas and concepts of Deming. In Juran's framework, a **process** is defined as a set of club activities that produces value for members. A process may not be confined to the work of a single department. A process that creates value for members may well span several departments and areas within a club. Consider the process of purchase-to-payment in the club's main dining room. Members generally expect this process to be hassle-free and seamless. When errors occur in the dining room portion of a member's monthly club bill, it's usually the accounting department that gets the blame and must field the complaints, even though the discrepancies or errors may not be accounting's fault. This is because the purchase-to-payment process is not simply an accounting function. Cooks, servers, and cashiers are also involved when members make purchases in the club's main dining room. Errors discovered "downstream" at the billing stage of the process may have been made "upstream" in the purchase stage of the process.

Juran defines quality in terms of "fitness for use." This definition focuses on the perspective of the end-user of a product or service—the customer. A customer is anyone affected by a process that creates a product or service. In a club, **external customers** are the members. **Internal customers** are staff members from departments and club areas affected by processes that contribute to the making of a product or the delivery of a service. For example, consider the process of food preparation. In this case, the external customers are the members who ordered the food; the primary internal customers are the restaurant servers.

The natural flow of work within and across departments in the course of daily operations creates a network of internal customers and suppliers within a club. Everyone employed by the club is an internal customer whom someone else in the club is supplying through their work. Each internal customer, in turn, performs work (adds value) and becomes a supplier for the next internal customer in the chain of work activities that eventually ends with creating value for external customers—the club members. Each work process has an **internal customer-supplier chain** of value-creating activities. Therefore, process improvement for clubs involves breaking down barriers between club departments and personnel and opening up opportunities for club managers and employees to focus on continuous-improvement efforts.

Principles of Quality Management

Quality management's enduring principles have survived the many buzzwords and fads of the past decade. This section explores the following quality management principles and applies them directly to club operations:

- Empowerment
- Fact-based decision-making
- Prevention vs. inspection
- Incremental and breakthrough improvement
- Benchmarking
- Change management

Empowerment

A central principle of all quality management systems is the concept of empowerment. This term is one of the most used and abused buzzwords of the past 15 years. Simply stated, **empowerment** is a redistribution of decision-making within a club that enables managers, supervisors, and employees to perform their jobs more efficiently and effectively. The overall goal of empowerment is to improve service to members and increase staff productivity by releasing decision-making responsibility, authority, and accountability to every level within the club.

Member satisfaction with club services is often directly related to the level of job satisfaction among the club's employees. Empowering a staff can increase productivity and raise job satisfaction. Employees who are not empowered often feel trapped and frustrated by systems and procedures that affect their work but are beyond their control. This leads to feelings of helplessness and contributes to low job satisfaction and low morale. Empowered employees take ownership of their jobs and exercise control over their work areas and functions. Empowered employees also can be better contributors to their club's continuous-improvement efforts.

Empowering employees does not lead to anarchy, nor does it mean that managers abdicate important responsibilities. It simply means that most decisions related to work areas and functions are best made by those actually performing the work. Empowering a club's staff does not happen overnight. It takes effort and requires the leadership skills of managers. To successfully empower club employees, managers must first enable the staff to make sound decisions and then support their decisions and actions.

Managers enable their employees by providing the skills training necessary to help them become competent in their jobs. Skills training is absolutely fundamental to quality service and is most effective when it provides employees with the "why" behind the "how-to" of their jobs. Employees need to know why they perform their work tasks and how they create value for members. In the enabling process, managers share club financial information with employees and explain the important ways their performance helps the club succeed.

The enabling and empowering responsibilities of managers are interconnected. Empowering others starts with enabling them and gaining their commitment to the fundamental values, mission, and goals of the club. For empowerment to work, managers must act as coaches and persuade individual employees to accept greater personal responsibility and exercise more control over the way they perform their jobs. However, before exercising more control over their jobs, employees will want assurances from their managers that the club values their ideas, has confidence in their judgment, and will support their efforts.

For employees to be truly empowered, they must be given the resources to carry out their new responsibilities—resources such as skills training, training in decision-making, and access to information. Consider the resources needed by a dishwasher in one of the club's food and beverage outlets. In the area of skills training, the dishwasher needs to learn how to perform fundamental job tasks related to operating the dishwashing machine. These include using chemicals properly, maintaining correct temperatures, and performing minor repairs. In addition, the dishwasher needs to learn the systems and procedures that affect the dishwashing process. This includes current procedures for sorting, racking, and washing as well as tracking and reporting breakage.

Before employees are given decision-making authority in their areas, they must also be trained in how to make sound decisions. This enables them to improve current systems and processes. To continue with our example, the dishwasher needs to know what kinds of decisions are appropriate to make as well as how to identify problems and form solutions. As employees become more experienced, their responsibilities can increase. For example, an experienced and trained dishwasher might make decisions about dishwashing supplies and implement cost reduction procedures. In many clubs, dishwashers have very little access to information about the kitchen or even about how their jobs affect day-to-day operations. At the very least, club managers should provide them with information such as forecasted covers for the day so that the dishwashers can organize their time and prepare for the volume of business. In addition, simple information such as the cost per cycle of running the dishwashing machine helps dishwashers plan their work efficiently to reduce total cycle costs. Without relevant information, employees will not be able to improve work processes.

Successfully empowering a club's staff also entails designing relevant performance measures and implementing appropriate reward and recognition systems. Relevant performance measures should span only those areas in which the employee is empowered and has responsibility. The golf professional, for example, should have performance measures only in areas relevant to golf. While this seems obvious, club managers and employees are sometimes held accountable for areas over which they have little or no responsibility. For example, a chef might be reprimanded for low sales in the club dining room when, in reality, the chef is primarily responsible for food quality and food costs and has no control over the way the dining room is marketed to members.

Club managers should create reward systems that provide incentives for a club's employees to accept the increased responsibilities that accompany empowerment.

Fact-Based Decision-Making

Fact-based decision-making is critical to the success of any quality management system. Without it, decisions are made in an atmosphere of chaotic opinions, guesses, hunches, and intuitions. Empowered managers, supervisors, and employees need access to information so that their decisions and actions are based on facts. The type and detail of information needed will depend on the size and scope of the continuous-improvement efforts. For example, a trained and experienced continuous-improvement team within a club might tackle a complex area for improvement—like renovating the club's lounge. This team would need information from the club's operations budget, cash budget, and capital budget. If club managers are unwilling to share this kind of information with team members, then the team should not be given the lounge renovation project. Giving the team the project but withholding needed information would be counterproductive. Imagine how a team would feel when, after spending many weeks researching the project and recommending a renovation plan, the general manager squashes the project because it exceeds available cash resources. Not only has the team wasted time and energy, but the general manager probably has lost the trust and respect of the team.

When needed information and facts do not exist, the club's staff will need the freedom to collect data and conduct fact-finding efforts. Exhibit 2 shows a sample fact-finding planning sheet that a club continuous-improvement team might use to collect data when tackling the problem of dirty silverware turning up at service stations in the club's main dining room.

Prevention vs. Inspection

The prevention of errors and defects is more vital to the success of quality management systems than the inspection of products and services. Inspection does not add value or quality; it simply determines if errors or defects exist. Managers often spend too much time developing elaborate inspection systems and not enough time improving processes so that errors and mistakes are prevented from occurring in the first place. Empowered staff members with the resources to improve processes in their areas of responsibility will usually discover ways to prevent problems before they occur. As club employees develop the ability to

Exhibit 2 Sample Fact-Finding Planning Sheet

Problem: Dirty silverware at service stations

What do we want to know?	How and where do we get the facts?	Who will get the facts?	When do we need the facts?
1. How many racks of silverware are returned for rewashing each week?	Use a check sheet to keep track	Entire team	1 month
2. How often does the dishwashing machine break down?	Check with Engineering Records	John	1 week
3. a. Does the water pressure fluctuate? b. How much? How often?	a. Check with Engineering b. Have a check sheet	a. George and Ann b. Entire team	1 week 1 month
4. Where do we buy our soap and chemicals? Who else uses them?	Interview Manager Interview Vendor	Invite to team meeting	2 weeks
5. a. What is the rated capacity of the dishwashing machine? b. How often do we exceed it?	a. Ask managers or engineers b. Use a check sheet to keep track	a. Ralph b. Entire team	3 weeks 3 weeks
6. What is the proper procedure for using the dishwashing machine? Does everyone understand and use it?	Survey other Stewards	Susan, Tommie, Eddie, Gina	6 weeks

analyze and improve their work areas, they need less inspection and direct supervision, but more coaching and support from their managers.

Ultimately, club managers are more effective when they focus on ways to eliminate the need for inspection systems altogether. Consider the case of a club's banquet manager who discovers that alcohol inventory items are missing from the storeroom. Focusing wholly on inspection, for the next week the manager personally takes a physical count of beverage inventory at the beginning and end of each shift. The manager also stays late every night to check bar staff members and their belongings as they leave the club. The problem with this approach is that there is no guarantee that the problem will be solved when the manager stops inspecting. Also, respect and trust do not flourish in an atmosphere of inspection.

A prevention approach to the same problem would be to involve the bar's staff members in improving storeroom security as well as improving the issuing and inventory processes. Improved processes are stronger deterrents to theft than are endless inspections.

Incremental and Breakthrough Improvement

"Continuous improvement" refers to both incremental improvement and break-through improvement. The differences between the two are marked mainly by the scale of change and the magnitude of results. **Incremental improvement** activities enhance or streamline current work processes within a club. Limited but steady gains in quality, speed, and savings are usually the end results of incremental improvement activities. **Breakthrough improvement** activities (also referred to as re-engineering) radically redesign work processes and result in unprecedented levels of quality, speed, and savings.

For example, consider the case of a club that regularly draws upon its line of credit with the bank because of cash flow shortages caused by slow collection of accounts receivable. The current process at the club is one in which accounting staff members compile billings at the end of each month and mail them to members. Current policy asks members to pay their bills within 30 days. The entire process, from purchase to payment, spans a 60-day period.

An incremental improvement would be to simply change the billing policy and require members to pay within 15 days upon receiving their bills. This would speed up cash flow by 15 days, but might meet with heavy resistance from members. A breakthrough improvement would be to reengineer the entire billing and collection process by implementing a debit card system for member purchases. With a debit card system, the money for member purchases is immediately deducted from the members' bank accounts and added to the club's bank account. This breakthrough approach not only solves the cash flow problem, it also reduces labor costs in accounting and greatly simplifies a previously complex process for the club and its members. While this kind of solution may be appropriate only for some clubs, it illustrates how breakthrough improvements result from radically redesigning processes.

Benchmarking

Benchmarking is the process of establishing standards to drive continuous-improvement efforts. It often involves adapting and applying within a club the best practices from other clubs or from other industries. The key words are "adapt" and "apply." Benchmarking is not merely copying process improvements success-fully implemented by another club or industry. Each club is a unique organization, and care should be taken when introducing change within a club's culture.

Club managers benchmark to examine trends, innovations, and best practices within the club industry for new ideas to improve processes. Best-in-class bench-marking tries to find ways to improve a club's operations by focusing on the best practices across various industries. Best-in-class benchmarking can provide opportunities for breakthrough improvements and revolutionary change in the way a club conducts business.

Change Management

Implementing a continuous-improvement process can be a large-scale change for some clubs. Continuous-improvement efforts, by their very nature, change the way

Exhibit 3   **A Model for Organizational Change**

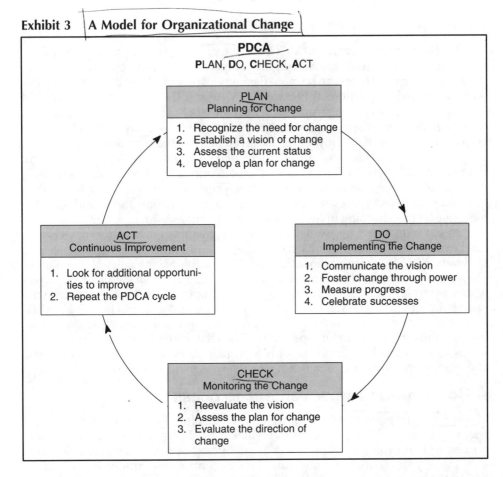

that work is done within a club. Therefore, managing change is a critical element in any quality management system. Exhibit 3 presents a model for managing change based on the PDCA cycle. "PDCA" stands for Plan, Do, Check, and Act. This model is often adapted and used to manage changes prompted by continuous-improvement efforts. Originally developed by Dr. Walter Shewhart, a pioneer in statistical process control, the model was adapted by Deming and many others as a guide for managing change within organizations.

While a model can help club managers understand the change process, club managers must keep in mind that change is dynamic. There are multiple activities in any change process. Breaking up the change process into steps suggests that the steps have clear boundaries and that the change process has a definite ending point. This is not the case in the real world of club operations. In fact, if change is viewed purely as a set of consecutive, well-defined activities, change will probably not be successful, because such an approach ignores the complexity of the change process and the interrelationships among its components.

Continuous-Improvement Teams

Continuous-improvement teams are vital to the success of quality management systems. Faced with a complex and changing competitive environment, club managers are discovering that teams can be more flexible and responsive to change than work units organized as traditional hierarchies. With the flattening of organizational structures, clubs are creating teams to identify and solve problems in the workplace. Club managers are recognizing that rapid changes are more likely to be embraced by employees if teams of employees are involved early in the planning process.

Successful continuous-improvement teams do not develop in a vacuum. Putting five or seven club employees in a room once a week to identify and solve work problems does not make a team. Employees and managers alike need direction and parameters for team activities, access to information and facilities, and—most important—training in how to work effectively as team members.

As individuals learn new skills and roles as members of teams, managers also need to develop leadership skills in coaching individuals in their departments and facilitating teamwork throughout the club. The traditional managerial functions of planning, organizing, directing, and controlling are not sufficient for managers who want to lead successful team-oriented club operations. Club managers who want to improve quality at their clubs must become teachers, coaches, and facilitators who help employees learn to solve problems and make sound decisions that increase the efficiency of club operations. The characteristics of an effective team leader listed in Exhibit 4 apply not only to team leaders, but also to club managers and employees who want to perform effectively as members of teams.

A Continuous-Improvement Process

"Continuous improvement" refers to the ongoing efforts within a club to meet the needs and exceed the expectations of members by changing the way work is performed so that products and services are delivered better, faster, and at less cost than in the past. There are many variations of continuous improvement in clubs and in the larger hospitality industry. Exhibit 5 outlines six steps typical of many continuous-improvement processes and identifies tools useful in each step. The six steps are:

1. Target an opportunity for improvement.
2. Gather and analyze information.
3. Generate potential improvements.
4. Evaluate alternative improvements.
5. Implement the improvement.
6. Evaluate the improved process.

We will take a look at each step in the following sections.

Target an Opportunity for Improvement

Club managers can identify opportunities for improvement through feedback from members and employees as well as from the efforts of continuous-improvement

Exhibit 4 [**Characteristics of Team Leaders and Facilitators**]

Effective team leaders and facilitators:

- Listen actively.
- Ask questions and listen to the answers in their entirety.
- Reserve judgment and keep open minds.
- Encourage a diversity of viewpoints.
- Teach others how to solve problems without solving the problems for them.
- Teach and coach others, without telling them what to do.
- Organize information so others can understand and act on it.
- Model the behaviors they would like to see in others.
- Know how to bring the right people together for a task.
- Know their own limitations and defer to others who are better qualified to make a decision or to complete a task.
- Help people reach consensus and strive for win-win agreements.
- Ensure that credit goes where credit is due.
- Understand that diversity can affect teamwork in positive ways.
- Know that different people are motivated by different things, so they (the team leaders and facilitators) are willing to work hard to address the needs of individuals.
- Share power and authority with others.
- Encourage team members to take responsibility for issues, problems, actions, and projects.
- Look for ways to help a team achieve its goals.
- Find opportunities to reward appropriate behavior.
- Are firm about goals but flexible about processes used to reach goals.

teams. Member feedback sources include comment cards, surveys, formal and informal interviews, and structured focus groups. Club teams can contribute ideas for improvement through group brainstorming.

Brainstorming uses group interaction to generate as many ideas as possible. It taps the collective brainpower of the group and yields greater results than could be achieved if each individual in the group worked alone. Brainstorming stimulates creativity, promotes participation, and develops a team spirit among group members, which can heighten their commitment to the continuous-improvement process. There are many brainstorming methods; one method is presented in Exhibit 6.

Once opportunities for improvement are identified, the team writes problem statements for each improvement area. A problem statement describes an area for improvement as clearly and objectively as possible. The statement should not include or imply causes or solutions; it should simply state the problem. A problem statement might read: "Too much time elapses from when members finish their meals to when they are presented with their checks."

Exhibit 5   Steps in a Continuous-Improvement Process for Clubs

PROCESS STEP	TOOLS USED
1. Target an opportunity for improvement.	Brainstorming Selection Matrix
2. Gather and analyze information.	Check Sheets Flow Charts Brainstorming Cause-and-Effect Diagrams
3. Generate potential improvements.	Flow Charts Cause-and-Effect Diagrams
4. Evaluate alternative improvements.	Selection Matrix
5. Implement the improvement.	Action Plan Worksheets Flow Charts
6. Evaluate the improved process.	Check Sheets Line Graphs, Bar Charts, Pie Charts

The team then selects a target of opportunity by applying a defined set of selection criteria to each of the problem statements. **Selection criteria** are factors the team uses to assess and rank a list of choices—in this case, the choices are problems for the team to solve. Examples of selection criteria a group might use include the following:

- Importance to members

- Importance to management

- Importance to staff

- Stability of the area targeted for improvement

- Availability of resources

- Probability of timely success

Teams should not select an area for improvement that is unstable—that is, one which is currently changing (or is scheduled to change) due to new equipment, training, renovation, and so on.

Gather and Analyze Information

Once an area for improvement has been selected, the team gathers and analyzes information related to the area. This activity includes establishing baseline measurements, analyzing processes, identifying potential causes, and determining root causes.

Exhibit 6   Steps for Conducting a Brainstorming Session

Brainstorming sessions allow a group to come up with many possible problem statements, solutions to problems, or other ideas in a short amount of time.

1. Appoint a session leader. This person will write down the group's ideas and facilitate the session.

2. The session leader should write (on a chalkboard or flip chart, for easier viewing by the group) the purpose of the brainstorming session and make sure that everyone in the group understands it.

3. The session leader should encourage group members to be creative and unconventional in their thinking, and emphasize that the goal is to come up with as many ideas as possible.

4. The group should take a few minutes to silently think about the question or problem.

5. The session leader should inform group members that at first the goal is to simply list ideas. There should be no discussion of ideas, and group members should not express approval or disapproval of any ideas, although it is okay to build on the ideas of others.

6. To begin the first round, the session leader should ask each member of the group in turn to share one idea only. The group member should simply state his or her idea, not explain it. The session leader should record each idea exactly as it is stated by the group member.

7. If a group member does not have an idea, he or she should simply say, "Pass" and let the next member state an idea.

8. The brainstorming session ends when all the group members pass during one go-round of the group.

9. The session leader should go over each idea and ask group members to clarify those ideas that are not understood by everyone in the group. The session leader can then group and combine similar ideas.

Baseline measurements are taken during fact-finding efforts to help the team analyze the area targeted for improvement. In the case of our example, the club team might gather information over a week and refine the problem statement to include their measurements: "On average, 15 minutes elapse from the time members finish their meals to the time they are presented with their checks." The baseline measurement (15 minutes) specifies how much is too much time. The baseline becomes the standard against which to gauge the effectiveness of solutions developed and implemented by the team in later steps of the continuous-improvement process.

Process analysis begins when the team documents exactly what happens in the process responsible for producing the problem. The team uses check sheets and **flow charts** to document the sequence of steps and decisions that are made in the process. (Exhibit 7 shows commonly used flow chart symbols.) For example, the club team would observe servers during a number of meal periods and document exactly what servers do during the 15-minute period under question. Let's assume they find that servers typically do the following:

Exhibit 7   Commonly Used Flow Chart Symbols

The most commonly used flow chart symbols have fairly standard meanings and are as follows:

An oval, or "terminal symbol," signifies the beginning or end of a process. Inside the oval, the instruction "Start" or "End" is written.

———▶ **Arrow**

An arrow shows the direction of the process flow. Arrows signify that something—information, a person, paper, supplies, etc.—is traveling from one point to another.

Rectangle

A rectangle is the symbol for an activity. A brief description of the activity should be written in the rectangle. A rectangle may have more than one arrow flowing into it, but only one arrow flowing out.

Major process steps should be written inside a double rectangle. A double rectangle should have one arrow flowing into it and one arrow flowing out.

A diamond is used for those steps in a process where a decision must be made. A diamond will usually have one arrow flowing in, but two or more arrows flowing out. A question is written in the diamond, and the number of "out" arrows will depend on the question. Usually, groups try to use only questions that can be answered "yes" or "no," so that there are no more than two arrows leading out of a diamond. This simplifies the flow chart.

- Servers take 6 minutes to make two trips to the kitchen getting meals for other tables in their sections.

- Servers take 8 minutes to bus one table in their section, freeing space for waiting members. Bussing includes retrieving a tray stand, tray, and clean table-settings at a server station; walking to the table; bussing the table; resetting the table; and taking the dirty dishes to the dishroom where the server sorts the silverware, dishes, cups, and glasses into the proper racks.

- Servers spend at least 1 minute presenting a check to a table in their section, collecting the signed check, and thanking the members for dining at the club.

After documenting the current process, the team uses brainstorming techniques and may complete a **cause-and-effect diagram** to identify potential causes of the problem. Categories generally used with cause-and-effect diagrams are:

Exhibit 8   Sample Cause-and-Effect Diagram

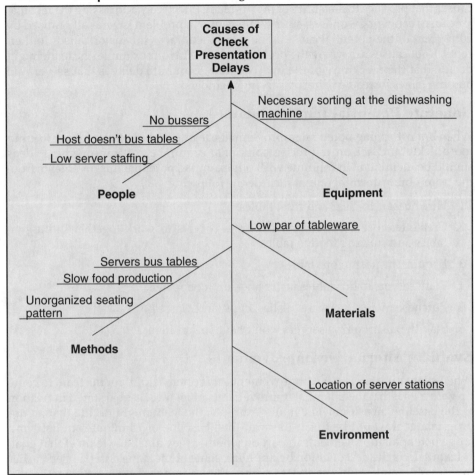

- People—members, staff, and others (if applicable) who interact within the process
- Methods—current procedures governing relevant tasks, activities, or relationships
- Equipment—machines, tools, computers, and other items that are used in the process
- Materials—supplies or things used in the process
- Environment—the workplace or area in which the process occurs

The purpose of these main categories is to help make the task of brainstorming potential causes manageable. Also, the categories help team members more completely analyze a problem by prompting them to consider potential causes they might otherwise have missed. Exhibit 8 presents a sample cause-and-effect diagram that could have been created by the team in our example.

The team pares down the number of potential causes to a vital few major causes that produce the majority of the problem. Effectively addressing the few major causes can work wonders, since 80 percent of a problem is generally caused by 20 percent of the potential causes. The team then traces the major causes to their roots. **Root causes** are where the problem starts. With our example, the team might decide that the root cause of the unacceptable 15-minute delay is that servers are bussing tables instead of directly serving members.

Generate Potential Improvements

When brainstorming potential improvements, teams should be careful not to jump too quickly and act on imprecise solutions. A number of improvement ideas should be identified. To continue with our example, potential improvements from the team's brainstorming might include the following:

1. Hire bussers to clear and reset tables.

2. Create team service sections and train servers to work together in bussing tables and running food to tables.

3. Require the host to bus tables.

4. Train servers to bus tables faster and run food faster.

5. Purchase more silverware, dishes, cups, and glasses.

6. Staff the dishroom so servers won't have to sort items.

Evaluate Alternative Improvements

When evaluating alternative improvements, it is often helpful for the team to come up with a goal that the potential improvements must meet, a goal stated in relation to the baseline measurements. In our example, the team might decide that an appropriate goal would be to cut the wait-time baseline of 15 minutes in half, and judge potential improvements in part on whether they are likely to meet that goal. A team selects the best solution by applying some of the same criteria used earlier to assess and rank problems and, as appropriate, adding new criteria as well. Solutions that substantially increase the costs of service usually do not work because they create a new problem—increased costs. Let's assume that the team decided that idea 2 was the best solution on its list of improvement ideas: "Create team service sections and train servers to work together in bussing tables and running food to tables."

Implement the Improvement

When possible, a club team should test a solution on a limited, trial basis before implementing it. During the test period, the team observes the new process and continues its fact-finding efforts by determining if the new process actually solves the problem and achieves the goal of halving the baseline measurement. During a test period, teams often find additional items that need to be included in the final implementation of the solution. At this point, it may be helpful for the team to develop a revised flow chart of the new process to ensure that the process gets

Exhibit 9   Quality Management Implementation Model

Step 1—Obtain leadership commitment

Step 2—Guarantee member satisfaction

Step 3—Create continuous-improvement teams

Step 4—Conduct the continuous-improvement process

Step 5—Align job responsibilities

Step 6—Implement continuous staff training and development

Step 7—Provide direction and support

implemented as planned. In the case of our example, the team would develop a flow chart for a process that requires teams of servers working together to bus sections and run food to tables.

Evaluate the Improved Process

Once the solution becomes part of day-to-day operations, the team follows up by evaluating the effectiveness of the improvement. The team may find that the new process needs to be modified to ensure continued improvement. The first part of the evaluation is quantitative in nature: the team measures the improved process and compares these measurements to the baseline measurements of the old process. In the case of our example, does the new process cut the 15-minute waiting time in half? Line graphs, bar charts, and pie charts are tools used for visually displaying information gathered during the evaluation of the process. **Line graphs** are used to show patterns or trends, **bar charts** illustrate relationships between two or more variables, and **pie charts** are useful for showing how a whole is broken down into parts. The main purpose of each of these tools is to display significant data in a format that is quickly and easily understood.

The second part of the evaluation is more qualitative in nature. The new process will not be effective if club members, managers, or staff members are unhappy with the results. As with defining the target of opportunity, feedback is important for determining overall levels of member, manager, and employee satisfaction with the implemented improvement.

Implementing Quality Management

Exhibit 9 outlines steps for implementing a quality management system for clubs. No single model will work for every club. Differences related to membership characteristics, staff expertise, and organizational culture require that each club adapt any model to its own unique circumstances. The following material is meant to illustrate in general terms a sample process for implementing a quality management system in clubs.

The success of any quality management system is based on leadership commitment. There are two levels of leadership in a club. The first level is the club's governance structure, which includes the board of directors and member committees. Clearly, if a quality management system is to persist through time, the commitment of the board, the current president, and the incoming president must be assured because the process may entail reallocation of financial resources, reorganization of the club, and realignment of management and employee responsibilities. Because the president and other members of the board may change from year to year, leadership commitment to quality management is not guaranteed. Ongoing communications as well as detailed orientations for new board members are vital to sustaining a commitment to quality management from the club's board. The club's general manager is critical to keeping the board enthusiastic about and supportive of the club's quality management efforts.

The second level of leadership is the club's management team. The club's general manager must be fully committed to implementing a successful quality-management system. People, time, and money must be allocated to the process. Large clubs might hire a director of quality to guide their continuous-improvement efforts. The responsibilities of a director of quality include targeting opportunities for improvement, analyzing and interpreting information, implementing new processes, evaluating the effectiveness of each new process, and training staff members in teamwork and quality tools. A director of quality also facilitates continuous-improvement teams and guides department managers in quality-management processes. At a small club, typically the general manager assumes some of these duties and delegates others to talented members of the management team.

Commitment to the quality management system must be driven by the need to guarantee club member satisfaction. Members are the reason for the club's existence. To guarantee member satisfaction, the club's staff must find ways to channel feedback from members into immediate operational improvements. Sometimes this also means finding ways for members to feel comfortable in providing feedback. If members know that they are part of a continuous-improvement process, they might be more willing to offer feedback than if they think their comments will be taken as simply "more member complaints."

One outcome of an effective continuous-improvement process will likely be a realignment of management and staff responsibilities. Managers and supervisors will need to learn new roles as coaches and facilitators to enable their staffs to assume new decision-making responsibilities. None of this will happen overnight or on its own. A club must provide training and development opportunities to managers as well as employees, and supply direction and support on a daily basis.

The Malcolm Baldrige National Quality Award

On August 20, 1987, President Ronald Reagan signed the Malcolm Baldrige National Quality Improvement Act. This act emphasized the importance of continuous quality improvement as a strategy for U.S. companies competing in a fast-changing, global marketplace. This act also established the Malcolm Baldrige National Quality Award. The award is named for Malcolm Baldrige, who served as Secretary of Commerce from 1981 until his death in 1987, and whose managerial excellence contributed to long-term improvement in the efficiency and effectiveness of the federal government.

In the years since Congress created the Baldrige Award, the award has become the standard of excellence for U.S. businesses, and the award's criteria have become a widely accepted guide for running a successful company. More than any other public or private quality-improvement initiative, the Baldrige Award has reshaped the behavior and thinking of U.S. managers, creating a common vocabulary and quality philosophy that bridges companies and entire industries. The following sections frame many of the topics and issues presented earlier in this chapter in the wider contexts of contemporary business practices encouraged by the Baldrige Award criteria.[2] Club managers should be able to use some of the information in the following sections to help them evaluate and improve operations in their clubs.

Baldrige Award Criteria

The Baldrige Award criteria are designed not only to serve as a reliable basis for making awards, but also to permit a diagnosis of any company's overall management system. The award criteria play important roles in strengthening U.S. competitiveness and aim to:

- Help improve performance practices and capabilities
- Facilitate communication and sharing of best-practices information among U.S. organizations of all types
- Serve as a working tool for understanding and managing performance, planning, training, and assessment

Also, the award criteria focus on two results-oriented goals: (1) to deliver ever-improving value to customers, resulting in marketplace success, and (2) to improve overall company performance and capabilities. As shown in Exhibit 10, the 1997 award criteria fall into the following seven categories:

1. Leadership
2. Strategic Planning
3. Customer and Market Focus
4. Information and Analysis
5. Human Resource Development and Management
6. Process Management
7. Business Results

There are no hard-and-fast rules for interpreting these categories. Since quality efforts vary tremendously from one industry to another (and from company to company within the same industry), the award process gives companies some freedom in interpreting these categories.

Comparing the 1997 award criteria to the 1995 award criteria reveals how the Baldrige Award criteria responds to changes in contemporary business practices. "Business Results" jumped from 25 percent of the total point values in 1995 to 45

Exhibit 10   1997 Baldrige Award Criteria

CATEGORIES	POINT VALUES
1. Leadership	**110**
1.1 Leadership System	80
1.2 Company Responsibility and Citizenship	30
2. Strategic Planning	**80**
2.1 Strategy Development Process	40
2.2 Company Strategy	40
3. Customer and Market Focus	**80**
3.1 Customer and Market Knowledge	40
3.2 Customer Satisfaction and Relationship Enhancement	40
4. Information and Analysis	**80**
4.1 Selection and Use of Information and Data	25
4.2 Selection and Use of Comparative Information and Data	15
4.3 Analysis and Review of Company Performance	40
5. Human Resource Development and Management	**100**
5.1 Work Systems	40
5.2 Employee Education, Training, and Development	30
5.3 Employee Well-Being and Satisfaction	30
6. Process Management	**100**
6.1 Management of Product and Service Processes	60
6.2 Management of Support Processes	20
6.3 Management of Supplier and Partnering Processes	20
7. Business Results	**450**
7.1 Customer Satisfaction Results	130
7.2 Financial and Market Results	130
7.3 Human Resource Results	35
7.4 Supplier and Partner Results	25
7.5 Company-Specific Results	130
TOTAL POINTS	**1,000**

Source: Malcolm Baldrige National Quality Award 1997 Award Criteria.

percent in 1997. The categories of "Leadership," "Strategic Planning," and "Information and Analysis" increased slightly from 1995 to 1997, while "Customer and Market Focus," "Human Resource Development and Management," and "Process Management" decreased significantly in point values from 1995 to 1997.

The Baldrige Award Core Values and Concepts

The award criteria are built upon a set of core values and concepts (see Exhibit 11). These values and concepts can be helpful to quality-conscious club managers and are briefly addressed in the following sections.

Exhibit 11   Core Values and Concepts of the Baldrige Award Criteria

- Customer-driven quality
- Leadership
- Continuous improvement and learning
- Employee participation and development
- Fast response
- Design quality and problem and waste prevention
- Long-range view of the future
- Management by fact
- Partnership development
- Company responsibility and citizenship
- Results focus

Customer-Driven Quality. A core value of the Baldrige award is that quality is judged by customers (or, in the case of clubs, judged by members). Thus, quality must take into account all product and service features and characteristics that contribute value to customers and lead to customer satisfaction and retention.

Value and satisfaction may be influenced by many factors throughout the customer's overall purchase, ownership, and service experiences. These factors include the company's relationship with customers that helps build trust, confidence, and loyalty.

Customer-driven quality not only addresses the product and service characteristics that meet basic customer requirements; it also includes those features and characteristics that differentiate a company's products and services from competing offerings. Such differentiation may be based upon new or modified offerings, combinations of product and service offerings, customization of offerings, more rapid responses, or special relationships.

Customer-driven quality is thus a strategic concept. It is directed toward customer retention, market share gain, and growth. It demands constant sensitivity to changing customer and market requirements and the factors that drive customer satisfaction and retention. It also demands an awareness of developments in technology and of competitors' offerings, and rapid and flexible responses to customer and market requirements.

Customer-driven quality means much more than defect and error reduction, meeting specifications, or reducing complaints. Nevertheless, defect and error reduction and elimination of causes of dissatisfaction contribute to the customers' view of quality and are thus also important parts of customer-driven quality. In addition, correcting mistakes—"making things right for the customer"—is crucial to building customer relationships and retaining customers. This is certainly true for clubs and their members.

Leadership. A company's senior leaders must set directions, create a customer orientation among their company's personnel, create clear and visible company values, and set high expectations. (In a club, the club's board and general manager would be considered its senior leaders. The board must set directions, foster or reinforce club values, and set high expectations for the club's managers; the general manager must create a member orientation among the club's staff members and set high performance expectations for them.) The company's values, directions, and expectations should address all stakeholders. A company's senior leaders should commit to the development of the entire work force and should encourage participation, learning, and creativity by all employees. Through their personal roles in planning, communications, review of company performance, and employee recognition, the senior leaders serve as role models, reinforcing a company's values and expectations and building leadership and initiative throughout the company.

Continuous Improvement and Learning. Achieving the highest levels of performance requires a well-executed approach to continuous improvement and learning. The term "continuous improvement" refers to both incremental and breakthrough improvement. Improvement and learning should be embedded in the way a company operates. "Embedded" means that improvement and learning (1) are a regular part of daily work; (2) seek to eliminate problems at their sources; and (3) are driven by opportunities to do better, as well as by problems that must be corrected. Sources of improvement and learning for companies include employee ideas, research and development, customer input, and benchmarking. Improvement and learning should be directed not only toward better products and services but also toward being more responsive, adaptive, and efficient—giving the company additional marketplace and performance advantages.

Employee Participation and Development. A company's success depends increasingly on the knowledge, skills, and motivation of its work force. (The club industry has long emphasized staff training as a way of ensuring that club members receive superior service.) Employee success depends increasingly on having opportunities to learn and practice new skills. A company should invest in the development of its work force through education, training, and opportunities for continuing growth. Opportunities might include classroom and on-the-job training, job rotation, and pay for demonstrated knowledge and skills. On-the-job training offers a cost-effective way to train and directly links training to work processes. Work force education and training programs may need to use advanced technologies, such as computer-based learning and satellite broadcasts.

Fast Response. Success in competitive markets demands ever-shorter cycles for new or improved product and service introduction. Also, faster and more flexible responses to customers are now more critical than before. A major improvement in response time often requires simplification of work units and processes. To accomplish this, the time performance of work processes should be among the key process measures. There are other important benefits derived from this time focus: time improvements often drive simultaneous improvements in organization, quality, and productivity. Hence it is beneficial to integrate response time, quality, and productivity objectives.

Design Quality and Problem and Waste Prevention. Companies should emphasize design quality. Problems and waste can be prevented through (1) building quality into products and services, and (2) building efficiency into production and delivery processes. Costs of preventing problems at the design stage are usually much lower than costs of correcting problems that occur "downstream." Design quality includes the creation of fault-tolerant (robust) or failure-resistant processes and products.

A major success factor in competition is the design-to-introduction ("product generation") cycle time. To meet the demands of rapidly changing markets, companies need to carry out state-to-stage integration ("concurrent engineering") of activities from basic research to commercialization. Increasingly, design quality also depends on the ability to use information from diverse sources and databases so that designers can take into account customer preferences, competitive offerings, price, marketplace changes, and other external research findings. More emphasis should also be placed on capturing learning from other design projects within the company.

From the point of view of public responsibility, the design stage is critical. In manufacturing, design decisions determine the type of industrial wastes a company will produce. The growing number of environmental protection regulations means that design strategies need to anticipate possible impacts on the environment.

Long-Range View of the Future. Pursuit of market leadership requires a strong future orientation and a willingness to make long-term commitments to key stakeholders—customers, employees, suppliers, stockholders, the general public, and the local community. Company planners (the equivalent in clubs would be their boards, general managers, and strategic or long-range planning committees) need to anticipate many changes, such as evolving customer expectations, new business opportunities, technological developments, new customer segments, changing regulatory requirements, changing community/societal expectations, and challenges by competitors. A major part of a company's long-term commitment is developing employees and suppliers and fulfilling public responsibilities.

Management by Fact. A modern business depends on the measurement and analysis of its performance. Many types of information are needed to measure and improve company performance—information about customers, product and service performance, operations, markets, competitors, suppliers, employees, and costs and other financial information. Analysis refers to extracting larger meaning from data and information to support evaluation and decision-making at all levels within a company. Analysis entails using data to determine trends, projections, and cause-and-effect situations that might not be evident without analysis. Data and analysis support a variety of company purposes, such as planning, reviewing company performance, improving operations, and comparing company performance with competitors' or with "best practices" benchmarks.

A major consideration in performance improvement involves the creation and use of performance measures or indicators. Performance measures or indicators are measurable characteristics of products, services, processes, and operations a company uses to track and improve performance. The measures or indicators should be selected to best represent the factors that lead to improved customer, operational, and financial performance.

Partnership Development. Companies should build internal and external partnerships to better accomplish their overall goals. Internal partnerships might include labor-management cooperation, such as agreements with unions. Agreements might entail employee development, cross-training, or new work organizations, such as high-performance work teams. (Some clubs are experimenting with the work-team concept in an effort to improve quality.) Internal partnerships might also involve creating network relationships among company units to improve flexibility, responsiveness, and knowledge sharing.

External partnerships can be developed with customers, suppliers, and educational organizations. An increasingly important kind of external partnership is the strategic partnership or alliance. Such partnerships might offer a company entry into new markets or a basis for new products or services. An external partnership might also permit the blending of a company's core competencies or leadership capabilities with complementary strengths and capabilities of partners, thereby enhancing the company's speed, flexibility, and overall capability. Issues partners should address together include key requirements for success, means of regular communication, approaches to evaluating progress, and means for adapting to changing conditions. In some cases, joint education and training could be cost-effective.

Company Responsibility and Citizenship. A company's leadership should stress the company's responsibilities to the public and make sure the company practices good citizenship. This responsibility refers to basic expectations that the public has of the company—that the company will conduct business ethically and protect the public's health and safety as well as the environment. Companies should emphasize resource conservation and waste reduction at their source. Company planning should anticipate adverse environmental impacts from its facilities and the production, distribution, transportation, use, and disposal of its products. (One obvious club example in this area is that the public might have some concerns about the pesticides and other chemicals used to maintain club golf courses. Many clubs are already looking for environmentally friendly ways to keep their courses in shape.) Companies should seek to prevent environmental problems and provide a forthright company response if environmental problems occur. Companies should not merely meet all local, state, and federal environmental laws; they should treat these and related requirements as areas for continuous improvement "beyond mere compliance."

Practicing good citizenship also refers to supporting—within the limits of a company's resources—initiatives that address education, health care, environmental excellence, resource conservation, and other areas of concern to the public. (The Club Managers Association of America's Club Foundation helps clubs set up foundations in order to support charities, hospitals, and other worthwhile organizations in their local communities.)

Results Focus. A company's performance measurements must focus on key results. These results should be guided and balanced by the interests of all stakeholders—customers, employees, stockholders, suppliers and partners, the public at large, and the local community. In the world of clubs, the most important key result is member satisfaction.

Endnotes

1. Some of the information in this chapter was adapted from Robert H. Woods and Judy Z. King, *Quality Leadership and Management in the Hospitality Industry* (East Lansing, Mich.: Educational Institute of the American Hotel & Motel Association, 1996).

2. Much of the following material on the Baldrige Award was taken from *The Malcolm Baldrige National Quality Award 1997: Criteria for Performance Excellence,* a public domain document. Copies of this document can be obtained each year free of charge by writing to:

    Malcolm Baldrige National Quality Award
    Technology Administration
    National Institute of Standards and Technology
    Route 270 and Quince Orchard Road
    Administration Building, Room A537
    Gaithersburg, MD 20899-0001

    or by telephoning (301) 975-2036, or by faxing (301) 948-3716, or by email: oqp@nist.gov, or by Web site: http://www.quality.nist.gov.

Key Terms

bar chart—A graphic display illustrating relationships between two or more variables.

baseline measurement—A measurement used as a basis for comparisons or for control purposes; a baseline measurement is a beginning point in an evaluation of output observed over a period of time. A baseline measurement represents how a process performs prior to any improvement effort.

benchmarking—The process of establishing standards to drive continuous-improvement efforts. This often involves adapting and applying within a club the best practices from other clubs or industries.

brainstorming—An idea-gathering technique that uses group interaction to generate as many ideas as possible within a given time period.

breakthrough improvement—Continuous-improvement activities that radically re-design work processes and result in unprecedented levels of quality, speed, and savings. Also called reengineering.

cause-and-effect diagram—An analytical tool used to structure brainstorming and to organize potential causes of a problem. Also called a fishbone diagram (because of its appearance).

continuous improvement—The ongoing efforts within a club to meet the needs and exceed the expectations of members by changing the way work is performed so that products and services are delivered better, faster, and at less cost than in the past.

empowerment—The redistribution of decision-making within a club that enables managers, supervisors, and employees to perform their jobs more efficiently and effectively.

external customer—Someone who purchases a product or service produced by an organization; in the case of clubs, their external customers are their members.

flow chart—A pictorial representation of steps in a process.

incremental improvement—Continuous-improvement activities that enhance or streamline current work processes within a club, resulting in limited but steady gains in quality, speed, and savings.

internal customer—Someone on the club's staff who is affected by processes that contribute to the making of a product or delivery of a service.

internal customer-supplier chain—A network of internal customers and suppliers within a club that produces value for members.

line graph—A graphic display used to show patterns or trends.

PDCA cycle—A model for managing change within a club; "PDCA" stands for Plan-Do-Check-Act.

process—A set of club activities that produces value for members.

pie chart—A graphic display useful for showing how a whole is broken down into parts.

root cause—A primary contributor to a problem.

selection criteria—Factors used to assess and rank a list of choices.

Review Questions

1. What are Deming's 14 points for quality?

2. How does Juran define "quality"?

3. How does employee empowerment contribute to quality management?

4. What are the differences between incremental improvement and breakthrough improvement?

5. What are six steps typical of many continuous-improvement processes?

6. How does the Malcolm Baldrige National Quality Award contribute to the quality management movement?

Additional Reading

Belasco, James A., and Ralph C. Stayer. *Flight of the Buffalo: Soaring to Excellence, Learning to Let Employees Lead.* New York: Warner Books, Inc., 1993.

Butterfield, Ronald W. "Deming's 14 Points Applied to Service." *Training,* March 1991.

Deming, W. Edwards. *Out of the Crisis.* Cambridge, Massachusetts: Massachusetts Institute of Technology, Center for Advanced Engineering Study, 1982.

Dobbs, John H. "The Empowerment Environment." *Training & Development*, February 1993.

Duck, Jeanie D. "Managing Change: The Art of Balancing." *Harvard Business Review.* November–December 1993.

Hall, G., J. Rosenthal, and J. Wade. "How to Make Reengineering Really Work." *Harvard Business Review.* November–December 1993.

Juran, J. M. *Juran on Planning for Quality.* New York: The Free Press, 1988.

———. *Juran on Quality by Design.* New York: The Free Press, 1992.

———. *Managerial Breakthrough,* Revised Edition. New York: McGraw-Hill Inc., 1995.

Partlow, Charles G. "How Ritz-Carlton Applies 'TQM.'" *Cornell Quarterly,* August 1993.

Reichheld, Frederick F., and Earl W. Sasser, Jr. "Zero Defections: Quality Comes to Services." *Harvard Business Review.* September–October 1990.

Rienzo, Thomas F. "Planning Deming Management for Service Organizations." *Business Horizons,* May–June 1993.

Scherkenback, William W. *Deming's Road to Continual Improvement.* Knoxville: SPC Press, Inc., 1991.

Internet Sites

For more information, visit the following Internet site. Remember that Internet addresses can change without notice. If the site is no longer there, use a browser to look for additional sites.

http://www.quality.nist.gov/

REVIEW QUIZ

When you feel you have covered all of the material in this chapter, answer these questions. Choose the *best* answer.

1. The quality movement began in the United States because:

   a. President Ronald Reagan signed an executive order.
   b. service industries felt a need for a more systematic approach to improving services to customers.
   c. manufacturing industries in the United States began to feel greater competitive pressures from global competitors.
   d. Malcolm Baldrige instituted a nationwide quality-improvement effort when he was Secretary of Commerce.

2. Joseph M. Juran defines quality in terms of:

   a. zero defects.
   b. fitness for use—that is, from the customer's perspective.
   c. how well internal customer-supplier chains function within an organization.
   d. none of the above.

3. Activities that enhance or streamline current work processes and lead to limited but steady gains in quality, speed, and savings are referred to as _____ activities.

   a. incremental improvement
   b. benchmarking
   c. breakthrough improvement
   d. reengineering

4. Why is the Malcolm Baldrige National Quality Award important to the quality movement in the United States?

   a. It has become the standard of excellence for U.S. businesses.
   b. The award's criteria have become a widely accepted guide for running a successful company.
   c. It has reshaped the behavior and thinking of U.S. managers more than any other public or private quality-improvement initiative.
   d. All of the above.

Answer Key: 1-c-C1, 2-b-C1, 3-a-C2, 4-d-C4

Each question is linked to a competency. Competencies are listed on the first page of the chapter. An answer reading 3-b-C4 translates to:

   3: the question number
   b: the correct answer
   C4: the competency number

Chapter 6 Outline

Strategic Management
    Benefits of Strategic Management
    Club Challenges in Strategic
      Management
Strategic Planning—The Foundation
    Strategic Planning Sessions
    Values Statement
    Mission Statement
    Vision Statement
    Key Result Areas and Strategic Goals
Operational Planning—The Implementation
    Human Resources Example
    Food and Beverage Example
Strategy Evaluation

Competencies

1. Summarize the three components of a strategic management system, explain how a club benefits from strategic management, and explain how the governance structure of clubs can make strategic planning difficult. (pp. 187–191)

2. List and describe the steps in a strategic planning process for clubs, summarize decision-making models a club's strategic planning group might adopt, and explain how internal and external scans can help a club's strategic planners. (pp. 191–203)

3. Explain how a club's short-term operational planning builds on the goals listed in the club's strategic plan, and describe how strategies are evaluated at clubs. (pp. 203–207)

Strategic Management in Clubs

This chapter was written and contributed by Tarun Kapoor, Professor and Director of the Professional Development Institute, and Lea D. Wikoff, Associate Professor, School of Hotel & Restaurant Management, California State Polytechnic University, Pomona, California.

CLUB MANAGERS ARE INVOLVED in a dizzying array of planning activities: long-range planning, strategic planning, business planning, operational planning, marketing planning, financial planning, budget planning, and more. For each planning activity there are usually several viable approaches, and for each approach there may be dozens of unique methods, each with its own vocabulary of terms and definitions. As planning activities increase and as planning methods become more complex, it's possible for club managers to lose sight of the fact that the purpose of planning is not to produce a plan—it's to produce results.

This chapter focuses on strategic management as a system for coordinating a club's basic planning activities. A strategic management system can help ensure that club departments and functional areas achieve short-term, operational results that will help the club achieve its long-term, strategic goals.

Strategic Management

All clubs plan, although the number and types of planning activities can vary tremendously from one club to another. A strategic management system can help a club by coordinating the club's planning activities into three distinct but related processes:

- Strategic planning
- Operational planning
- Strategy evaluation

All three planning components are necessary if a club wants to achieve consistent organizational results. However, each of the three components serves a distinctly different purpose. Strategic planning focuses on the fundamental future direction of the club. Operational planning concentrates on how to implement the club's strategic plan and produce short-term results. Strategy evaluation is concerned with monitoring results and periodically comparing what the club planned to accomplish with what the club actually accomplished.

Strategic planning is broad-based and conceptual in nature and requires long-range, visionary thinking. The primary participants in strategic planning activities should include the club's president, board of directors, and some club committees (such as the strategic committee or finance committee), as well as the club's general manager and selected representatives from the management team. In some clubs, supervisors and line employees may also play a role in strategic planning efforts. The best time for strategic planning is early in a club's fiscal year. This allows ample time for completion of the strategic plan before the club must develop its operational plan. In the strategic planning process, a well-developed values statement, mission statement, and vision statement form the basis for developing long-range directions for a club. From these directions, strategic planners create broad goals for a club's departments and other functional areas, goals to be achieved over a period of three to five years. The general manager's role in the strategic planning process is critical. The general manager needs to spearhead the strategic planning effort and make sure that the club's strategic planning activities result in a plan that will serve as the foundation for effective operational planning.

Exhibit 1 diagrams a planning model useful for club operations. The triangular shape of planning activities depicts strategic planning as the broadest level of activity and as the foundation for developing and implementing specific strategies and actions of the operational plan. The inverted triangle of planning participants illustrates how planning activities involve every operational level within a club. Later sections of the chapter describe each planning activity in greater detail. The important point here is to note that the building block approach of this planning model strives to create a direct connection between the strategies and actions of the club's management and staff and the values, mission, and vision of the club's governance structure.

Operational planning requires short-term, practical thinking. The primary participants in operational planning activities are the club's general manager, management team, supervisors, and appropriate line staff. The club's president, board of directors, and appropriate club committees review and approve the operational plan in light of directions set by the overall strategic plan. Simply put, the operational plan implements the strategic plan (or at least the first phase of it) over an upcoming twelve-month period. Each department and functional area within the club translates the long-range directions and goals outlined in the strategic plan into short-term strategies and actions that will advance the club through the upcoming year toward the club's desired future. Operational planning activities typically begin during the latter part of the current fiscal year and end in the preparation of the club's budget for the upcoming year. Each department contributes to achieving the broad goals outlined in the strategic plan by developing specific action plans detailing what will be done next year, who will be responsible for doing it, when it will be completed, and resources needed. Departmental plans are rolled together and finalized during the club's budgeting process.

Strategy evaluation is the ongoing monitoring and assessment of the strategic plan and the operational plan in relation to the actual results of club operations. Periodic evaluations enable the club's leadership to modify goals, revise strategies, and initiate new actions in light of changing circumstances and conditions.

Exhibit 1   A Strategic Planning Model

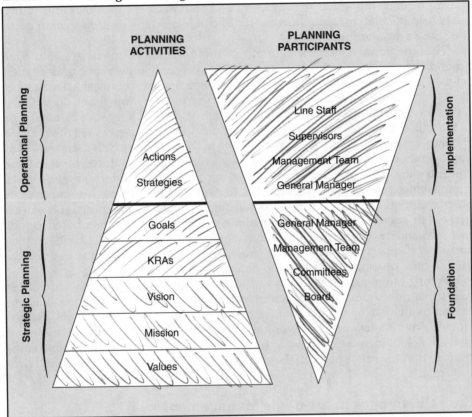

The club's board and committees are interested in seeing progress toward achieving the goals outlined in the strategic plan. Department heads are primarily interested in the success of their action plans. The club's general manager is the organizational link between strategy development and strategy implementation. As such, the general manager focuses on the effectiveness of operational action plans in achieving the goals set by the overall strategic plan. As you can see, strategy evaluation is concerned with both the strategic plan and the operational plan and is conducted at all leadership levels within the club.

Benefits of Strategic Management

A strategic management system enables a club to objectively examine its current status, define future directions, and measure progress toward specific goals. Examining the current status of the club establishes baselines against which progress toward future goals can be measured. A long-term strategic plan, a one-year operational plan, and periodic evaluations of these plans enable a club to create a road map to its desired future. The strategic plan keeps the club moving in a specific direction and keeps the club's future destination fully in view of the club's board, membership, management team, and staff. Current baselines and future goals help the club measure how far it has come and how far it has yet to go to arrive at its desired future.

A strategic management system can unite members, managers, and staff around common goals. However, this will happen only if everyone understands why the goals are important and how they can be achieved. This means that a club's strategic plan and operational plan cannot be treated as top secret documents, locked away in board rooms and managers' offices. To feel a sense of commitment to the club's future, club members and staff members must see where they fit into the club's plans and how they can contribute to them. While a club's strategic plan and operational plan are bound to have some confidential features, most of their contents should be communicated to all of the club's stakeholders. Progress in accomplishing club goals can be reported to club members through summaries of board meetings, minutes of committee meetings, management reports, and articles in the club's newsletter. The operational plan should be widely distributed to staff members and discussed to ensure understanding and commitment. Charts, graphs, and other displays of measurable progress can be posted in departments throughout the club, keeping everyone up-to-date on accomplishments.

A long-range strategic plan and a short-term operational plan that supports it can help a club secure financial resources; financial institutions are more likely to extend credit to a club if it can demonstrate a firm sense of direction as well as measurable progress toward clearly defined goals. Members of a club are also more likely to accept increases in dues or fees when they understand how the increases relate to the immediate needs of the club as well as how they fit into the overall strategic plan.

Club Challenges in Strategic Management

The governance structure of a club often presents unique challenges in planning and executing strategic management activities. Unlike the leadership structures of many for-profit businesses, the composition of a club's board of directors and member committees can change dramatically from year to year. New presidents and new board members naturally want to make a difference during their terms of office. They may feel that leading the club in new directions is one of their primary responsibilities.

Complicating the situation is the fact that the club president, board members, and members of club committees are often experienced business executives who lead strategic efforts within their own companies. It is only natural for them to want to implement the same planning systems that have proven successful for their own organizations. However, if strategic directions and planning processes change radically from year to year, the result could be a confused membership, a frustrated management team, and wasted resources.

For clubs, the challenge is to adopt a strategic management system that promotes ongoing commitments to future directions while making full use of the talents and experience of current board and committee members. One way to promote ongoing commitments is to establish the duration of a strategic plan so that it exceeds the terms of office for the presidency and membership on the board of directors. For many clubs, this means that a strategic plan should span a five-year period. While the plan can be reviewed and evaluated before the beginning of each year, the fundamental future directions for the club usually should roll over from one year to the next. An annual evaluation of the strategic plan gives the presiding club president and board a chance to fine-tune it, but the roll-over nature of the plan should discourage them from dramatically changing the overall direction of the club. This ensures the stability and continuity necessary to sustain progress toward fundamental strategic goals.

Orientation programs for the incoming president and other new board members should clearly define their roles and responsibilities in planning the club's future. Orientations should also outline the planning processes used at the club, how decisions are made, the roles and responsibilities of the club's management team and staff, and the staff's timetables for completing action plans and goals.

Strategic Planning—The Foundation

The following sections explore basic components of a strategic planning process by which clubs can set and achieve long-range goals. A values statement, mission statement, and vision statement can provide continuity to the strategic management effort, enabling everyone to see progress toward creating a desired future for the club. These statements form the rationale for the future allocation of the club's financial and human resources and also defend the overall strategic direction of the club against the whims or agendas of individuals. When a club's values, mission, and vision are clearly articulated, there should be no confusion on direction or disagreement on priorities. However, in most clubs there is a great deal of latitude and flexibility in how the club moves in strategic directions and how priorities are addressed along the way.

Strategic Planning Sessions

Ideally, clubs should organize strategic planning sessions as retreats held away from the club, with the sessions conducted by an outside facilitator. Depending on the size of the club and the complexity of the issues to be addressed, the retreat could be as short as one day or as long as three days. Strategic planning sessions are convened away from the club to minimize distractions for participants. A neutral environment also helps create an atmosphere in which participants feel on equal footing as they discuss the club's future direction. As mentioned earlier, the usual participants in a club's strategic planning sessions are the club's president and board, chairpersons and perhaps others from the club's committees, and the general manager and other members of the club's management team.

Sessions are best facilitated by an experienced consultant. A consultant can help direct the planning process and assist the strategic planning group in arriving at decisions. As an "outsider," the consultant can objectively guide the group without favoring one idea over another or one participant over another. The consultant's job is to ensure that all participants feel that they can safely share ideas in a non-threatening environment. This can be accomplished by:

- Encouraging all participants to become actively involved
- Encouraging different points of view
- Probing issues by posing questions to the group
- Mediating conflict

An important initial responsibility of the facilitator is to help the group decide how it will make decisions during the planning sessions. At the very start, the group should agree on a systematic process for dealing with issues and arriving at decisions. This ensures the most productive use of everyone's time. Decision-making models include:

- Decision by authority
- Decision by minority
- Decision by majority
- Decision by unanimity
- Decision by consensus

Decision by authority occurs when a single participant, usually the club president, has the final say on all issues or matters under consideration. Although the president may ask for input and discussion, under the decision-by-authority model he or she has the power to make decisions that run counter to the suggestions and recommendations of the group. This approach to decision-making may be appropriate for situations in which only the president is held accountable for the decisions made by the group. However, these situations are rare, especially in clubs where member committees have defined responsibilities and authority commensurate with those responsibilities. A major drawback to this decision-making model is that it discourages active participation by group members. Also, stifling the group's involvement in the decision-making process usually decreases the group's acceptance of final decisions and reduces its commitment to the strategic plan.

Decision by minority occurs when agreement from less than half of the participants is all that is needed to make a decision. This decision-making model might be used when a minority of participants has expert knowledge in relation to the matters under consideration. For example, some participants at a strategic planning session may have special expertise about the club's restaurant and banquet facilities. This minority group may be granted the authority to override suggestions from the majority of the group and make decisions affecting the future direction of these operations. A major disadvantage of this decision-making model is that representatives from club departments or other functional areas may act to protect their own "territories," which can mean that decisions will not be made in the best interests of the club as a whole. Also, decisions by minority can become divisive and provoke conflict, even hostility, among participants.

Decision by majority occurs when votes from more than half of the participants are needed to approve a decision. This model works best when time is limited and participants who are in the minority are not negatively affected by the consequences of the majority's decision. However, sometimes this form of decision-making creates a "win-lose" atmosphere at strategic planning sessions, because participants in the minority must concede to the wishes of the majority in order for the planning session to move forward.

Decision by unanimity occurs when every participant at the strategic planning session agrees to a decision. This model is only useful when the matter at hand is so important that it is critical to gain everyone's support and commitment. If this form of decision-making is used for every action taken by the group, probably little will actually get done.

Decision by consensus is usually the most effective model to use in strategic planning sessions. A consensus decision is not a unanimous decision. A unanimous decision is one that everyone in the group agrees with; there is no conflict. A consensus decision, on the other hand, may involve conflict within the group. In fact, group members with conflicting ideas should be encouraged to speak up, so that all sides of an issue are acknowledged and discussed before the group makes a decision. Consensus means that, while all participants may not believe that an idea or decision is the best one, no one has major reservations about it.

Cooperation and constructive discussion are the keys to consensus decision-making. Ideally, consensus decision-making grows out of a clash of ideas (not a clash of personalities) and the serious consideration that participants give to different alternatives. Conflict, or disagreement, is a natural and essential part of this process. The very idea of discussion presupposes different points of view about the best way to resolve a situation or address a concern. If the strategic planning group stifles discussion by discouraging disagreement, it is more likely to make superficial or unwise decisions.

Values Statement

The first step in the strategic planning process is to identify the core values that should shape the culture of the club and guide the behavior of individuals (see Exhibit 2). Values are not empty mottoes, snappy slogans, or vague ideals. A **values statement** embodies shared beliefs, common convictions, and acknowledged principles that unite a club's membership, management, and staff as they create the club's future.

A long list of values does not create a shared foundation upon which to build a future. Too many values complicate what should be simple and confuse what should be clear. A club's values statement could be as short and to the point as the following for the fictional Highroad Country Club:

At the Highroad Country Club, we believe in and are committed to:

- *Member satisfaction*
- *Employee satisfaction*
- *Ethical business practices*
- *Service to our community*
- *Environmentally safe practices*

Exhibit 2   Step One: Develop a Values Statement

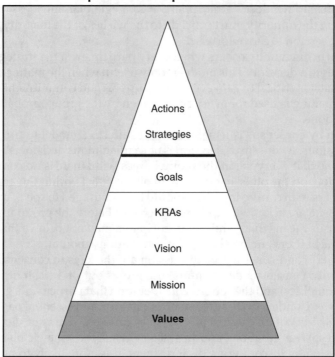

A more detailed values statement might provide brief explanations of each of the club's core values; American Telephone and Telegraph Corporation's values statement takes this approach (see Exhibit 3). The key for a club is to identify, communicate, and reinforce a limited number of values that are simply stated, easily remembered, and can be adopted without reservation by the club's members, managers, and employees.

The most effective way to identify a club's core values is through the input and consensus of the club's stakeholders. Typically, several groups of representatives from the club's board and general membership meet with the general manager and selected staff prior to the strategic planning session to identify the fundamental beliefs that the club's strategic planning group will turn into the club's values statement. Involving the club's stakeholders promotes understanding and acceptance of the club's core values. After the core values have been identified and written up in a values statement, the club's board, managers, and staff should communicate throughout the club how these values drive activities and day-to-day work processes. However, simply identifying and communicating core values is not enough. Individuals throughout the club need to "live the values" as they interact with one another in carrying out their responsibilities. Over time, the culture of the club changes as the core values become second nature, guiding individual behavior.

Exhibit 3   Sample Values Statement

AT&T
Our Common Bond

We commit to these values to guide our decisions and behavior:

Respect for Individuals

We treat each other with respect and dignity, valuing individual differences. We communicate frequently and with candor, listening to each other regardless of level or position. Recognizing that exceptional quality begins with people, we give individuals the authority to use their capabilities to the fullest to satisfy their customers. Our environment supports personal growth and continuous learning for all AT&T people.

Dedication to Helping Customers

We truly care for each customer. We build enduring relationships by understanding and anticipating our customers' needs and by serving them better each time than the time before. AT&T customers can count on us to consistently deliver superior products and services that help them achieve their personal or business goals.

Highest Standards of Integrity

We are honest and ethical in all our business dealings, starting with how we treat each other. We keep our promises and admit our mistakes. Our personal conduct ensures that AT&T's name is always worthy of trust.

Innovation

We believe innovation is the engine that will keep us vital and growing. Our culture embraces creativity, seeks different perspectives, and risks pursuing new opportunities. We create and rapidly convert technology into products and services, constantly searching for new ways to make technology more useful to customers.

Teamwork

We encourage and reward both individual and team achievements. We freely join with colleagues across organizational boundaries to advance the interests of customers and shareowners. Our team spirit extends to being responsible and caring partners in the communities where we live and work.

By living these values, AT&T aspires to set a standard of excellence worldwide that will reward our shareowners, our customers, and all AT&T people.

Source: P. Jones and L. Kahaner, *Say It and Live It: The 50 Corporate Mission Statements that Hit the Mark* (New York: Currency Doubleday, 1995), pp. 1–2.

(For ease of discussion, it should be noted that this section and the following sections assume that a club is going through the strategic planning process for the first time. Once a club has gone through this process initially, in succeeding years the steps will remain the same but some of the activities will be slightly different. For example, instead of creating a values statement, the strategic planning group will review the already existing values statement to make sure it still reflects the

Exhibit 4   Step Two: Develop a Mission Statement

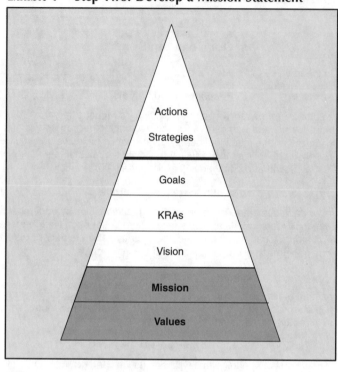

club's values. Depending on the review, the group may decide to leave the values statement as it is, slightly revise it, or completely revise it.)

Mission Statement

Step two of the strategic planning process is creating a mission statement (see Exhibit 4). A **mission statement** is a broad description of a club's reason to exist. It outlines the fundamental purpose of the club and focuses members, managers, and employees in a single direction. In times of fast change and potential confusion, people within a club can turn back to the club's mission statement for clarity and stability.

While mission statements vary from club to club, common features of well-written mission statements include general descriptions of all or some of the following:

- Club products and services
- Club markets and customers
- Core values
- Broad goals
- Competitive position
- Desired public image

Depending on the desires and needs of the club, a mission statement can be short and simple or long and complex. Consider the following mission statement for our fictional Highroad Country Club, a 400-member club with two 18-hole golf courses and a 10-court tennis facility:

> *The mission of the Highroad Country Club is to provide the best recreational facilities in golf and tennis in southern California.*

This brief statement presents the nature of the club (a country club) and why it exists (to provide the best recreational facilities). It also defines its major products (golf and tennis) and projects its desired public image (to be the best in southern California). This short mission statement provides a clear focus for everyone in the organization. For example, if one of the golf courses needs repair, the club's mission statement would help decision-makers decide on what types of repairs to make and how much to spend. The Highroad Country Club's mission statement would encourage members, managers, and employees to make the kinds of repairs that would contribute to making the golf course the best in southern California.

But how would the food and beverage manager at the Highroad Country Club feel about the mission statement? While the club's restaurants and banquet facilities are not alluded to in the club's mission statement, these areas cannot be ignored. A club's food and beverage outlets as well as its banquet services are important support functions that indirectly affect the ability of the club to achieve its mission. As we will see in later sections of the chapter, the strategic management process includes several opportunities for the club's food and beverage areas to significantly help the club achieve its mission.

If a club redefines its mission or repositions itself in the marketplace, a more complex mission statement than the Highroad Country Club's may be appropriate. Also, if a club decides to move in a new direction or simply needs to further explain its reason for existence, more detail may be required. To take an example from another industry, Delta Air Lines suffered substantial losses in the early nineties due to changes in the airline industry. To refocus the company, Delta created the mission statement that appears in Exhibit 5. This mission statement defines the company's product, describes its customers, and broadly explains its objectives, organizational values, position in regard to competitors, and desired public image. It also incorporates an easily remembered short version of its mission—"Worldwide Airline of Choice."

Delta Air Lines could not have designed its mission and set its direction without first identifying challenges both inside and outside the company. A club can do this by conducting an internal and an external scan. Whether a club is developing its mission statement for the first time or reviewing its current one during its strategic planning sessions, it needs to put its deliberations in context. An internal scan of operations can identify a club's strengths and weaknesses, while an external scan can identify opportunities and threats arising from the wider environment in which the club conducts business. Obviously, these scans must be performed before the strategic planning group meets. The club's general manager should bring the results of these scans to the strategic planning session so that group members can analyze and discuss the findings of the scans before creating or reviewing the club's mission and vision statements.

Exhibit 5   Sample Mission Statement

Delta Air Lines
Worldwide Airline of Choice

Worldwide   We provide our customers access to the world, and we will be an innovative, aggressive, ethical, and successful competitor committed to profitability and superior customer service. Looking ahead, we will consider opportunities to expand through new routes and alliances.

Airline   We will stay in the business we know best and where we are leaders—air transportation and related services. We believe air transportation will grow worldwide, and we will focus our time, attention, and investment in building on our leadership position.

of Choice   We will be the airline of choice for customers, investors, and Delta people. For experienced business and leisure travelers, we will provide value and a superior travel experience from the time a reservation is made to when baggage is claimed. For air shippers, we will provide service and value. For our stockholders, we will earn a consistent, superior financial return. For Delta people, we will offer challenging, rewarding, results-oriented work in an environment that respects and values their contributions.

Source: P. Jones and L. Kahaner, *Say It and Live It: The 50 Corporate Mission Statements that Hit the Mark* (New York: Currency Doubleday, 1995), pp. 69, 75.

Internal and External Scans. The results of an **internal scan** profile the strengths and weaknesses of a club in relation to its organizational structure, work systems, and human resources. The findings are often compared to a similar scan and analysis of competitors. The main purposes of an internal scan are to (1) identify unique strengths that the club can build upon throughout the strategic planning process, and (2) identify areas that the club must improve to meet future challenges.

For example, a strong governing board and a stable management team might be viewed as important strengths of a club. On the other hand, that same club might have an overly bureaucratic organizational structure, with short spans of control and many layers of reporting. This could be seen as a weakness, impeding the club's ability to respond quickly to new challenges.

An internal scan should also analyze gaps and redundancies across club operations. Gaps are areas in which a club lacks the resources necessary to respond to future changes in operations. For example, the strategic planning group may project a future increase in the use of computer technology throughout club operations. This could identify a gap in human resources, equipment needs, and cash. For example, it might reveal that the club will soon need to hire a computer systems manager. Redundancies represent areas in which the club currently wastes resources due to duplication of efforts. The internal scan reviews current work systems with an eye toward increasing efficiency.

The results of an **external scan** identify opportunities and threats outside the club that may positively or negatively affect a club's success over the next five years. An external scan looks into how each of the following may impact future club operations:

- Projected demographic shifts in the local area (for example, a city club may find that the number of professional women in its metropolitan area is growing, which may mean that the club should consider offering athletic facilities for women)

- Anticipated changes in the products and services of suppliers

- Sources of labor and anticipated changes in the local unemployment rate

- Proposed legislation and regulations by local and state governments

- Strengths and weaknesses of primary competitors

Scanning the competition includes identifying new clubs opening in the area as well as businesses in the public sector that could discourage people from joining the strategic planning group's club.

An external scan also addresses factors in the wider environment that impact society as a whole, such as:

- Economic factors—inflation rates, interest rates, unemployment rates, and changes in the amount of disposable income of families

- Socio-cultural factors—population growth and shifts, consumer activism, and cultural attitudes

- Political and regulatory factors—anticipated changes in taxation, the minimum wage, health care, and social legislation

- Technological factors—computer upgrades and interfaces, changes in telecommunications, and new Internet possibilities

- Ecological factors—indoor and outdoor air quality, water quality, solid waste management, and recycling issues

Strategic planning participants should not hurry through their analysis of the club's internal and external scans. It takes time and focused attention to identify important details that could give a club a significant edge in creating its future.

Vision Statement

Step three of the strategic planning process is creating a vision statement (see Exhibit 6). While a club's mission statement describes the fundamental purpose of the club, its **vision statement** projects the club's future—where it wants to be and what it wants to look like at a specific point in the future. Building on the club's mission statement, the vision statement projects a standard of future success. Consider the following vision statement for the Highroad Country Club:

> *Our vision of the Highroad Country Club is to be the premier country club in southern California within 5 years, with 800 members enjoying 4 championship golf courses and 25 tennis courts.*

Exhibit 6   Step Three: Develop a Vision Statement

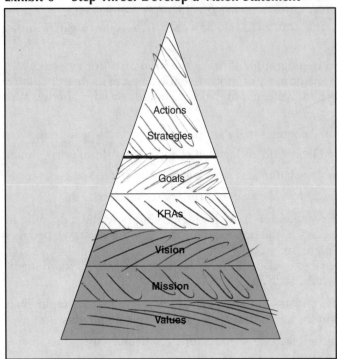

The future direction and priorities of the club are clear. By contrasting where the club is today with where it wants to be in five years, club members, managers, and staff members are able to focus their strategic planning and implementation efforts. As the vision statement makes clear, the Highroad Country Club wants to double its membership from 400 to 800 members, expand its current 36-hole golf facility to 72-holes of championship quality, and expand its present 10-court tennis facility to 25 courts.

Key Result Areas and Strategic Goals

Taking direction from the values, mission, and vision statements, the strategic planning group should now identify **key result areas (KRAs)**—major club areas whose performances will be measured in relation to how well they are contributing to the club's desired future (see Exhibit 7). KRAs can be functional areas, such as human resources, or operated departments, such as the club's food and beverage department. The Highroad Country Club's strategic planning group might decide that the club's KRAs are as follows:

KRA #1   Membership

KRA #2   Golf facilities

KRA #3   Tennis facilities

Exhibit 7   Step Four: Identify Key Result Areas (KRAs)

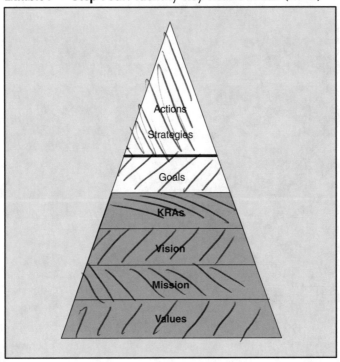

KRA #4	Financial resources
KRA #5	Human resources
KRA #6	Food and beverage facilities

The strategic planning group has latitude in identifying KRAs. For example, note that financial resources, human resources, and food and beverage facilities were not specifically mentioned in the club's mission or vision statements. However, they represent areas that affect the success of the club in creating its future.

After identifying the club's KRAs, the strategic planning group creates goals for each KRA (see Exhibit 8). Generally, the group should develop no more than seven or eight goals for each KRA and should prioritize them according to the club's needs and available resources. This helps provide direction for later budgeting activities. The goals in each KRA should be *SMART*:

- *S*pecific

- *M*easurable

- *A*chievable

- *R*ealistic

- *T*ime-dated

Exhibit 8   Step Five: Set Goals for Each Key Result Area

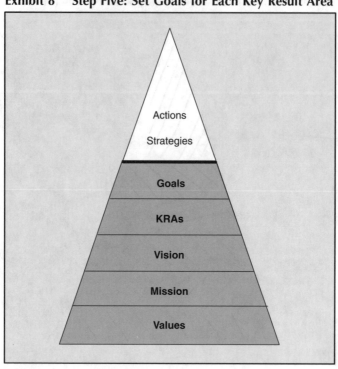

Consider the case of the Highroad Country Club. Employee satisfaction was identified as important in the club's values statement. The club's mission is to offer the best recreational facilities, and its vision is to become the premier country club in southern California. Employees who feel good about working at the club will help the club achieve its mission and vision. Therefore, the following goals might be set for the human resources KRA:

KRA #5   Human resources

  Goal #1   Achieve 90 percent employee satisfaction ratings by the end of year one.

  Goal #2   Achieve 95 percent employee satisfaction ratings by the end of year two.

  Goal #3   Maintain 95 to 100 percent employee satisfaction ratings from year three to year five.

After the strategic planning group develops goals for each KRA, responsibility and accountability are assigned to specific members of the management team, who can begin to create operational plans. In the case of our example, although the KRA is human resources, the human resources goals span every department in the club. Department managers will, of course, need the expertise and support of the human resources director, but responsibility and accountability lay squarely on the

Exhibit 9   Step Six: Develop Strategies and Action Plans

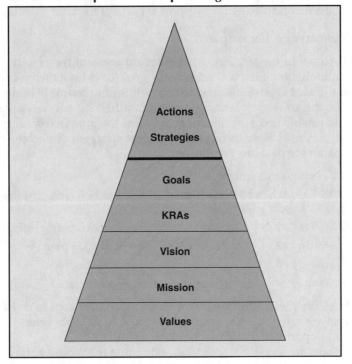

shoulders of the department managers to develop strategies and action plans that will produce the desired results.

Operational Planning—The Implementation

Operational planning builds on the goals listed in the club's strategic plan. Each department and functional area within the club translates the long-range directions and goals outlined in the club's strategic plan into short-term strategies and actions that will advance the club through the upcoming year toward the club's desired future (see Exhibit 9). The following sections present two examples of how club functional areas and departments could proceed.

The first example involves the Highroad Country Club's human resources KRA and its number one goal (presented in the previous section). In this example, the human resources area of the club as well as individual departments develop strategies and action plans that follow directly from the goals listed in the club's strategic plan.

The second example demonstrates how some of the planning activities performed by a club's strategic planning group may be replicated within individual club departments. In this example, the Highroad Country Club's food and beverage department reaffirms the club's values statement and goes on to develop its own departmental mission statement and identify KRAs specific to the food and beverage operation. Department goals are then developed, along with strategies and action plans that implement or support aspects of the club's strategic plan.

Human Resources Example

For each KRA goal of the strategic plan, relevant areas of the club must develop **strategies** outlining how they will achieve the goal (or at least the first phase of the goal) within the next twelve months. In our continuing example of the Highroad Country Club, the strategic planning group identified human resources as a key result area and established a number of goals. Now the human resources area must develop strategies to achieve those goals. Possible strategies for achieving Goal #1 of the club's strategic plan are as follows:

KRA #5   Human resources

    Goal #1   Achieve 90 percent employee satisfaction ratings by the end of year one.

        Strategy #1   Conduct a survey to measure employee satisfaction.

        Strategy #2   Implement departmental training programs.

        Strategy #3   Conduct team building workshops.

        Strategy #4   Empower supervisors and line staff.

All four of the strategies address what the club as a whole needs to do to achieve 90 percent employee satisfaction. Action plans must now be developed that detail how the club's departments will carry out each strategy.

Action plans are step-by-step activities defining the who, what, where, when, and how of implementing a strategy. For example, action plans for Strategy #1 from the human resources area might be as follows:

KRA #5   Human resources

    Goal #1   Achieve 90 percent employee satisfaction ratings by the end of year one.

        Strategy #1   Conduct a survey to measure employee satisfaction.

            Action #1   The human resources department will develop an employee-satisfaction survey instrument by January 1 of year one.

            Action #2   The human resources department will distribute the surveys to employees on the first payday of each quarter.

            Action #3   The human resources department will report all findings to the club's departments by the second week of each quarter.

            Action #4   Departments will implement changes to their operations to improve employee satisfaction by the fourth week of each quarter.

The club's board and general manager might monitor and review these action plans on a quarterly basis as part of the strategy evaluation component of strategic management. In addition, individual departments throughout the club would develop and implement their own action plans for improving employee satisfaction within their areas.

Food and Beverage Example

For some clubs, particularly large clubs with several major departments, the operational planning activities within departments mirror the activities of the strategic planning group. The general manager, or each department's department manager, might facilitate off-site planning sessions for the department that are conducted according to the same guidelines as the strategic planning meetings. Participants should include key department managers and staff and, in some cases, a board member or the chairperson of the appropriate club committee. The following example centers on the operational planning activities of the food and beverage department of our fictional Highroad Country Club.

The departmental planning group begins with an affirmation of the club's values statement. This serves as the foundation upon which to build the department's operational plan. Next, the group reviews and discusses the club's strategic plan, noting aspects that relate directly to the food and beverage operation. This review provides parameters for the group as it develops its short-term operational plan to support the strategic plan.

The departmental planning group then focuses on the club's food and beverage operation and examines the strengths and weaknesses of current F&B operations. For example, a strong food and beverage management team might be recognized as a strength, while high food costs would be identified as a weakness. The group might then review the club's external scan report to examine opportunities and threats outside the club and analyze their effects on the food and beverage operation. For example, an opportunity might be identified in relation to a sociocultural trend of increased dining out by various demographic groups. Similarly, a threat might be recognized in connection with information from the external scan that projects a reduction in household disposable income over the next few years.

After this analysis of strengths, weaknesses, opportunities, and threats, the departmental planning group can develop a mission statement for the food and beverage operation, such as the following:

> *The mission of the food and beverage department of the Highroad Country Club is to provide high-value food and beverage products and services that meet or exceed member expectations.*

The departmental planning group can then project where the food and beverage department wants to be at the end of the upcoming year. Here, the departmental planning group turns to directions outlined by the club's strategic plan and determines what the food and beverage department can do over the upcoming twelve months to further the club's overall strategic goals. The KRAs and goals established by the strategic plan of the Highroad Country Club focus on expansion of the club's recreational facilities. The food and beverage planning group might determine that the best way for the department to support these efforts is to increase the profitability of its products and services so that adequate funds are available for expansion. Therefore, the short-term operational plan of the department might specify that the department increase its profitability by four percent in the upcoming year. The KRAs to focus on would become the food and beverage outlets throughout the club:

KRA #1	Club dining room
KRA #2	Banquets
KRA #3	Member lounge

Goals for each of these areas would specify the level of profitability needed so that the entire department will be four percent more profitable next year than in the current year. Department managers, supervisors, and selected employees from each outlet would then develop strategies for achieving the goals, and action plans for carrying out the strategies. A portion of the operational plan for KRA #2—Banquets—might take the following form:

KRA #2   Banquets

   Goal #1   Increase revenue by 20 percent and profitability by 4 percent in the upcoming year.

      Strategy #1   Develop and promote special packages for wedding receptions.

         Action #1   The chef will prepare special wedding-reception menus with graduated pricing based on food costs by early January.

         Action #2   The bar manager will develop special pricing packages for hosted and non-hosted beverage functions by early January.

         Action #3   The food and beverage director will develop promotional materials by the end of January and establish a distribution schedule for the year; the director will also advertise the special wedding-reception packages in the club newsletter and through direct mailings to members.

The food and beverage department's operational plans (as well as the operational plans from the club's other departments and functional areas) will be reviewed and adjusted during the club's budgeting process to ensure that priorities are consistent with the club's strategic plan and that adequate financial resources exist to fund departmental action plans.

Strategy Evaluation

As mentioned earlier, throughout the year a club's board, general manager, and appropriate committees should monitor the club's operational results to make sure that all of the club's departments and functional areas are on track, and what they are accomplishing is really moving the club toward the desired long-range goals outlined in the club's strategic plan. This evaluation can be done as often as the club deems it necessary; quarterly or semiannually are two common options. If any club areas are falling short, or if circumstances or conditions have changed since the strategic plan was put together, the club might decide to modify goals, revise strategies, or initiate new action plans.

Key Terms

action plans—Step-by-step activities defining the who, what, where, when, and how of implementing a strategy.

external scan—A strategic planning tool that identifies opportunities and threats outside the club that may affect a club's future success.

internal scan—A strategic planning tool that profiles the strengths and weaknesses of a club in relation to organizational structure, work systems, and human resources.

key result areas (KRAs)—Club departments or other functional areas in which performance results are measured in relation to directions outlined by the club's strategic plan.

mission statement—A broad description of a club's reason to exist, forming a basis for developing goals and objectives and guiding the allocation of resources within the club.

strategies—Statements outlining how goals will be achieved.

values statement—Embodies the shared beliefs, common convictions, and acknowledged principles that unite a club's membership, management, and staff as they create the club's future.

vision statement—Projects a standard of future success, describing where the club wants to be and what the club wants to look like at a specific point in the future.

Review Questions

1. How does strategic planning differ from operational planning?

2. What are the benefits of strategic management?

3. How does the governance structure of clubs present a challenge to a club's strategic management efforts?

4. What are some decision-making models available to a club's strategic planning group?

5. What is a values statement? a mission statement? a vision statement?

6. How do internal and external scans help a club's strategic planners?

7. What is a key result area?

8. How does a club's operational planning build on the goals listed in a club's strategic plan?

9. Who is typically involved in evaluating how well a club is progressing toward its strategic goals?

REVIEW QUIZ

When you feel you have covered all of the material in this chapter, answer these questions. Choose the *best* answer.

1. How does a club benefit from a strategic management system?

   a. A strategic management system enables a club to objectively examine its current status, define future directions, and measure progress toward specific goals.
   b. A strategic management system can unite club members, managers, and staff around common goals.
   c. The strategic and operational plans that arise from a strategic management system can help a club secure financing.
   d. All of the above.

2. The Riverdale Country Club has decided to hold some off-site strategic planning sessions. The strategic planning group has decided to reach decisions by consensus. This means that the group:

   a. will let the club president make all of the decisions.
   b. will go with a decision only if everyone in the group agrees with it.
   c. will go with a decision if it seems to be the best one and no one has major reservations about it.
   d. will let a minority of the group decide everything because the members of this minority have special expertise.

3. A statement that embodies shared beliefs, common convictions, and acknowledged principles that unite a club's membership, management, and staff is called a _____ statement.

   a. mission
   b. values
   c. vision
   d. purpose

4. Typically, strategies are evaluated at clubs by:

   a. the club's board.
   b. the club's general manager.
   c. appropriate club committees.
   d. all of the above.

Answer Key: 1-d-C1, 2-c-C2, 3-b-C2, 4-d-C3

Each question is linked to a competency. Competencies are listed on the first page of the chapter. An answer reading 3-b-C4 translates to:

   3: the question number
   b: the correct answer
   C4: the competency number

Part III

Managing Club Operations

Chapter 7 Outline

Understanding the Role of Marketing
    Marketing Strategy
    Situation Analysis
    Service Marketing
    Internal Marketing
Understanding Buyer Behavior
    Consumer-Buyer Behavior
    Organizational-Buyer Behavior
The Marketing Mix
    Product Concepts
    Promotion Concepts
    Place or Distribution Concepts
    Pricing Concepts
Marketing Research
    Types of Research
    Sources of Data
Toward an Ethical Approach to Club
    Marketing

Competencies

1. Define the terms "marketing" and "markets," describe five marketing orientations, describe a situation analysis, identify four marketing growth strategies, and explain service marketing and internal marketing. (pp. 211–217)

2. Summarize two consumer-buyer behavior models and describe organizational-buyer behavior. (pp. 217–223)

3. List the Four Ps of marketing and describe product, promotion, place or distribution, and pricing concepts. (pp. 223–239)

4. Define "marketing research," describe types of marketing research and sources of marketing data, and explain the role of ethics in marketing. (pp. 239–241)

7

Marketing Clubs

This chapter was written and contributed by Lawrence E. Ross,
Assistant Professor, Department of Business and Economics,
Florida Southern College, Lakeland, Florida.

INVENTING A BETTER MOUSETRAP has long been touted as a way to get the world to beat a path to your door. In reality, you probably won't enjoy much success with your mousetrap unless the world *needs* a better mousetrap, is made *aware* of the new mousetrap, sees the price of the new mousetrap as being worthy of the *benefits* that derive from its use, and is able to purchase the mousetrap at a time and place that is convenient and consistent with the world's needs. Since the world isn't likely to beat a path to your door, you will probably have to turn to marketing to help you sell your wonderful new invention.

What do mousetraps have to do with the club industry? They serve to illustrate one of the misconceptions about the definition and role of marketing in operating a hospitality enterprise such as a private club. Marketing was rarely a topic for discussion in the club industry until the competitive, legislative, sociocultural, and economic pressures of the recent past began to erode club memberships and revenues. When an otherwise successful product, company, or industry is faced with the prospect of disappointing revenues, marketing nearly always becomes a topic of great interest among owners and managers. What is marketing, and what role can marketing play in a successful club operating in the current environment? That's the question this chapter will attempt to answer.

Understanding the Role of Marketing

What does the term "marketing" mean to you? Many people equate marketing with selling or advertising. **Marketing** is a word that is often misused in business and society to describe the merchandising and distribution of products in a capitalistic, free economy. The American Marketing Association defines marketing this way:

> Marketing is the process of planning and executing the conception, pricing, promotion, and distribution of ideas, goods, and services to create exchanges that satisfy individual and organizational objectives.[1]

The most basic function of marketing is to bring buyers and sellers together to make an exchange. In clubs, members exchange money—membership fees, bills for food and beverages, greens fees, and so on—for goods and services from the club. What the members receive must be of greater perceived value than the amount of money the members pay or else the club will soon find itself with dissatisfied members. In time, the failure to satisfy its members will lead to the demise of the club.

A **market** is defined as the set of all actual and potential buyers of a product. In any market there will typically exist groups of buyers with similar needs and marketing response characteristics. These homogeneous groups are called **market segments.** Market segments are important to understand because they help define specific marketing objectives, strategies, and tactics for a club to pursue. Club managers have long recognized that not all residents of a community are potential club members. They have learned to divide community members into market segments based on income, lifestyles, and so on, and to pursue only those market segments that are the most likely to contain potential club members.

There are many ways to segment a market: geographically (where potential members live or work), demographically (who they are in terms of gender, age, income, and family life cycle), psychographically (who they are in terms of personality, lifestyles, attitudes, and beliefs), or some combination of these, such as geodemographically (who they are *and* where they live or work). A market can also be segmented in terms of the benefits people in the market are seeking (such as health or business-related benefits). Once a basis for segmentation is selected, data can be gathered to help club managers prioritize market segments into target markets. Target markets can be categorized as primary markets, secondary markets, and tertiary (insignificant or peripheral) markets. Those residents of the community who are most likely to be interested in club membership are considered to be a club's **primary target market.**

Marketing Strategy

A well-formulated marketing strategy makes it easier for a club to allocate its resources to achieve a unique and workable market position. This market position is influenced by the club's internal strengths and weaknesses, anticipated changes in the environment, and the competitive moves of its rivals.

A club's marketing strategy should be long-term and should guide its short-term marketing activities. All elements of a well-developed marketing strategy should be interrelated. A club without a well-thought-out marketing strategy can easily drift in the execution of its short-term marketing action plans. This does not mean that once a club develops a marketing strategy it is cast in stone. On the contrary, as a club's internal and external environment changes, so too must its marketing strategy.

Most marketing strategies can be classified according to the marketing orientation or concept that serves as the strategy's focal point. Over time five such orientations have been identified in business marketing:

- Production orientation

- Product orientation

- Selling orientation

- Marketing orientation

- Societal orientation

While a club's marketing efforts may incorporate elements of more than one of these concepts, one concept will usually dominate.

Production Orientation. Marketing that is production-oriented is based on delivering the product to the customer at the lowest-possible unit cost. McDonald's exemplifies this approach in the quick-service restaurant industry. McDonald's products are standardized, and the emphasis is on producing them quickly and at maximum cost efficiency. If the customer wants even a slight variation to a menu item, it requires extra waiting time while the item is custom-produced. If McDonald's encouraged its customers to custom-order every sandwich on its menu, the production system would be brought to a screeching halt. Being the lowest-cost-per-unit producer does not mean that McDonald's products are priced lowest in the market. Rather, it means that McDonald's is able to take the extra profit it earns on each item, use it to market its products more effectively, and thereby increase its market share.

Product Orientation. Not every customer wants the same standardized product. Some customers want options and are willing to pay for them. This is the basis for product-oriented marketing. Wendy's, to continue with quick-service examples, offers its basic hamburger product 256 different ways. This broad selection of choices, available to the customer on demand, is made possible by an efficient production system, but that is not the emphasis of Wendy's marketing strategy. Instead, Wendy's offers its customers a seemingly endless array of choices from a very limited menu.

Selling Orientation. An organization with a selling-oriented marketing approach sends salespeople into the marketplace to stimulate demand for its products. The goals of the salespeople are to (1) make potential customers aware of the organization's products and services, and (2) persuade some of them to buy. Unfortunately, many customers view this marketing approach negatively, since it sometimes leads to high-pressure sales tactics and unethical approaches. For many people, the stigma attached to personal selling overshadows their entire view of marketing. There need not be such a stigma. Most successful organizations that use a sales force are very ethical and do not use high-pressure tactics. Most clubs have a very professional sales staff. A club's "salespersons" are its staff members, especially those in such sales-oriented positions as food server, bartender, and golf pro.

Marketing Orientation. After World War II, there was tremendous economic expansion in the United States and it was fairly easy to sell anything you could produce, because, after years of rationing and low production of consumer goods due to the war effort, everyone needed everything. By the mid-1950s, however, as the economy began to stabilize and demand slowed, a new approach to marketing was developed. This approach, which dominates businesses today, is known as marketing-oriented marketing. This concept is based on the premise that it is best to first determine what the market *needs* and then develop products and services—in fact, the entire organization—around meeting those needs. This is the most profitable way to do business. Few resources are wasted, very little selling is necessary to stimulate demand, and customers get exactly what they want.

Societal Orientation. The fifth approach to marketing grew out of the marketing-oriented approach. Examples of societal-oriented marketing include the promotion of products that are "good for the environment" or are "low in fat" and touted as being good for the customer's health. Under the societal orientation, if the benefits to customers outweigh the costs to society in general, then the product is marketable. Disposable diapers were introduced under the marketing orientation as a product that clearly met the needs of consumers. However, if the marketers had used a societal orientation, disposable diapers might never have been introduced to the market, since they stack up in landfills and are costly to society in terms of the environment and prematurely closed landfills.

Originally, societal-oriented marketing was treated with some suspicion by marketers. Eventually it was embraced, and now it is in danger of being abused, with biodegradable plastics and anything that is recyclable being perceived as having a market advantage. The customer is becoming confused and seeks to understand which products are or are not good for society and at the same time are or are not good for the customer.

Situation Analysis

Whether a club chooses a production, product, selling, marketing, or societal orientation as its primary marketing strategy will depend on the competencies of the club's staff and the opportunities and threats that the club faces. These factors can be identified by conducting a **situation analysis** for the club. Exhibit 1 includes the common elements of a comprehensive situation analysis. A situation analysis defines the circumstances that the club's general manager confronts as he or she prepares to develop a marketing strategy and ultimately a marketing plan. A situation analysis is often referred to as a SWOT analysis. The SWOT acronym refers to the idea that what is to be identified and analyzed are the club's Strengths, Weaknesses, Opportunities, and Threats. Once the club's current situation has been assessed, an effective marketing strategy can be developed.

Assuming that the situation analysis indicates that it is feasible, most clubs would choose a marketing strategy focused on growth. Such a strategy is not always feasible, however, and internal constraints may dictate a strategy of retrenchment or even a "harvesting" strategy where the club may eventually be closed or merged with another organization.

If a club wants to grow and the situation analysis indicates that the club has the potential to grow, one of several growth strategies may be selected to guide the development of the club's marketing plan. Exhibit 2 presents a classification scheme for growth strategies. There are four growth strategies that depend on either product-related decisions, market-related decisions, or some combination of both. Product-related decisions pertain to either staying with the current product offerings or developing new products. Market-related decisions pertain to either continuing to focus on the current markets being served or attempting to identify and reach new, unserved markets. The four growth strategies in Exhibit 2 are defined as:

1. *Market penetration*—increasing revenue by increasing market share with current products in current markets. Examples include providing more

Exhibit 1   Components of a Situation Analysis

Internal Constraints	
Strengths	**Weaknesses**
Breadth and depth of product lines	Narrow or outdated product lines
Degree of market coverage	Limited market coverage
Production competencies	Increasing or inefficient cost trends
Marketing skills	Poor marketing plan
Information systems competencies	Inadequate information systems
Human resource competencies	Inadequate human resources
Brand name reputation	Loss of brand name equity
Cost/financial advantages	Financial instability
Depth of management skills	Inadequate management skills
Efficient control systems	Lack of control
Well-developed strategy	Inappropriate organizational structure
Location advantages	Location disadvantage
External Constraints	
Opportunities	**Threats**
Expansion of core business	Attacks on core business
Exploit new market segments	Increase in direct competition
Widen the breadth of product lines	Increase in indirect competition
Extend cost/financial advantage	Change in consumer preferences
Diversify into new business	Rise in new or substitute products
Vertical integration (forward/backward)	Shifts in demographic factors
Reduce rivalry among competitors	Changes in economic conditions
Make profitable acquisitions	Increased regulation
Apply brand name in new areas	Legal challenges to existing structure
Seek fast market growth	Rising labor costs
Incorporate new technologies	Slower market growth (decline)

Source: Adapted from Arthur A. Thompson, Jr., and A. J. Strickland, III, *Strategic Management*, 8th ed. (Chicago: Richard D. Irwin, Inc., 1995), p. 94.

opportunities for tennis court time or additional golf tee times for the current membership base.

2. *Market development*—increasing revenue by taking present products to new markets. An example of a market development strategy would be to offer a new golf-only membership category or open the golf course to nonmembers.

3. *Product development*—increasing revenue by introducing new products to current markets. A club that builds a new skeet-shooting range that current members will pay a fee to use is an example of product development.

4. *Diversification*—increasing revenue by introducing new products or services to new markets. For example, a club might diversify by hiring an in-house travel planner and offering tour packages to members for a fee. This new service might

Exhibit 2   Alternative Growth Strategies

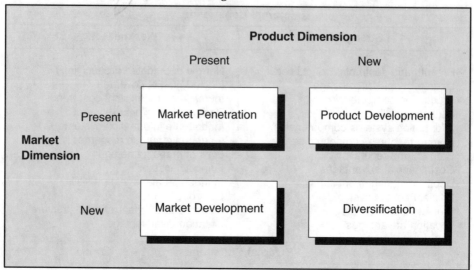

Source: Thomas C. Kinnear, Kenneth L. Bernhardt, and Kathleen A. Krentler, *Principles of Marketing,* 4th ed. (New York: HarperCollins, 1995), p. 95.

appeal to club members who never used any of the club's other products or services, thereby creating a new market for the club.

Whichever growth strategy is chosen, when combined with one of the five marketing orientations, it will serve as the basic approach the club intends to use to compete for members and their discretionary spending.

Service Marketing

Marketing services, such as those services that clubs provide to their members, is quite different from marketing manufactured goods. What is being marketed—service—is intangible; very perishable (services can't be manufactured and stockpiled); not often identical from day to day, employee to employee, or member to member; and usually produced (by club employees) while it is being simultaneously consumed (by members).

With tangible products, there is often an emphasis on advertising and moving a static inventory off the shelves. Service marketing, on the other hand, attempts to maximize the frequency of purchase, the average amount of the purchase, and the satisfaction of the customer/member—all at the same time. Little traditional external marketing (such as advertising) is used, and there is a greater emphasis on the people-oriented dimensions of marketing, such as personal selling and excellent service.

Internal Marketing

Because clubs market their services, and club employees are the providers of those services, employees often become the focus of a unique marketing effort on the part of club managers. Instead of thinking of employees as functionaries, management recognizes the need to sell employees on the importance of their jobs and the value of their contributions to the members' level of satisfaction with the club. This emphasis on the employee as a "customer" and his or her job as a product can be termed **internal marketing.**

Club managers should communicate to employees that their contributions are important to meeting member needs and making the club successful. If this is not accomplished, management often ends up with dissatisfied employees who may sometimes communicate their dissatisfaction to members in the form of poor service or poor attitudes. This can result in dissatisfied members who may take their business elsewhere.

Understanding Buyer Behavior

To better market their club, club managers should have an understanding of buyer behavior. Buyer behavior can be defined as the processes consumers use to (1) make purchase decisions, and (2) use and dispose of the purchased goods and services.[2]

In addition to dealing with individuals who buy club products and services for themselves ("consumer buyers"), clubs deal with individuals who buy for a group or organization that they represent ("organizational buyers"). In this section we will first look at two models of consumer-buyer behavior, then look at organizational-buyer behavior.

Consumer-Buyer Behavior

The two consumer-buyer behavior models we will examine are the family life cycle and the consumer-purchase-decision process. These two models can help a club manager understand what forces are affecting a club member's purchase behavior.

The Family Life Cycle. Knowing the gender and age of a member is not enough to explain the member's buying behavior. Often, differences in purchase and consumption patterns among members of the same sex and age result from being in different stages of the family life cycle. The **family life cycle (FLC)** is a series of stages within a family determined by a combination of age, marital status, and the presence or absence of children in the home. In the club business, it may be the most valuable tool for understanding the buying behavior of members.

Exhibit 3 illustrates FLC stages. The FLC provides club managers with insight about how a family's needs, incomes, resources, and expenditures differ at each stage. For example, people in the "young married with children" stage are most likely to be candidates for a developer-owned club membership, since they are in the peak period for buying a home. However, young marrieds with children typically have very little discretionary cash and may not be able to support an aggressive food and beverage budget for the club. They are likely to make great demands on the club's amenities, such as the pool and other sporting facilities. Conversely, people in the "middle-aged married without dependent children" stage have the extra cash and financial stability to be frequent customers of the club's food and beverage outlets and other revenue centers. This group will not

Exhibit 3   Sample Family Life Cycle (FLC) Model

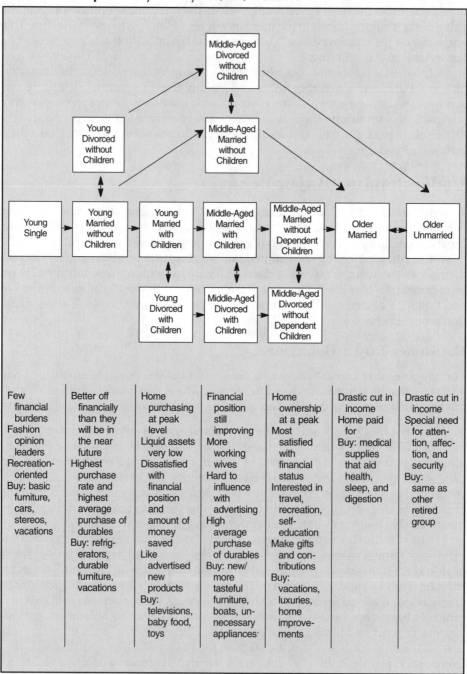

Source: Patrick E. Murphy and William A. Staples, "A Modernized Family Life Cycle," *Journal of Consumer Research,* June 1979, pp. 16–17.

Exhibit 4   Simplified Model of the Consumer-Purchase-Decision Process

```
┌──────────────┐      ┌──────────────┐      ┌──────────────┐      ┌──────────────┐      ┌──────────────┐
│   Problem    │  ⇨   │ Information  │  ⇨   │  Evaluation  │  ⇨   │   Purchase   │  ⇨   │    Post-     │
│ Recognition  │      │   Seeking    │      │     of       │      │   Decision   │      │  Purchase    │
│              │      │              │      │ Alternatives │      │              │      │  Evaluation  │
└──────────────┘      └──────────────┘      └──────────────┘      └──────────────┘      └──────────────┘
```

Source: Thomas C. Kinnear, Kenneth L. Bernhardt, and Kathleen A. Krentler, *Principles of Marketing*, 4th ed. (New York: HarperCollins, 1995), p. 180.

place as much demand on the sporting facilities (other than the golf course) as the young marrieds with children.

The Consumer-Purchase-Decision Process. Exhibit 4 illustrates a simplified model of the consumer-purchase-decision process. This model shows that a buyer's purchase decision is a dynamic process. A potential new member of the club will go through a complex decision-making procedure before choosing a club. He or she will seek out information from various sources to help evaluate the alternatives that are available. The simplified model shown in Exhibit 4 contains five stages. Each of these stages is influenced by a multitude of either inferred or directly observable factors. These factors are summarized in Exhibit 5 in an expanded model of the consumer-purchase-decision process.[3]

Inferred influences. The top third of Exhibit 5 shows that there are three influences on consumer behavior that are indirect or inferred influences: psychological factors, external/social factors, and situational factors. Let's take a brief look at a few of these factors in the following paragraphs.

"Motivation," one of the psychological factors, can be defined as "activity directed toward a goal." A motivated state is the result of tension, which arises out of an unfilled need. People try to reduce the tension by satisfying the need. The need is therefore a critical element in the motivation process. When a need is aroused, it becomes a motive or drive that stimulates behavior. Buying motives are often classified as being either a primary buying motive or a selective buying motive. Primary buying motives are associated with general categories of products/services such as whether to join a club or buy a sport-utility vehicle. Selective buying motives are associated with specific brands within a category—for example, whether to join the Pleasantview Country Club or the Green Meadow Golf Club, or whether to buy a Jeep Grand Cherokee or a Ford Explorer.

Needs, which form the basis for motives, are most often classified on the basis of the work done by Abraham Maslow in the 1930s and 1940s. In Maslow's model, the lowest level of needs must be met before an individual is motivated to satisfy a higher-level need. Maslow classified needs from the most basic physical needs to the highest psychological need—the need for self-actualization or self-fulfillment. In between are the needs for safety and security, social or affection needs, and esteem

Exhibit 5   Expanded Model of the Consumer-Purchase-Decision Process

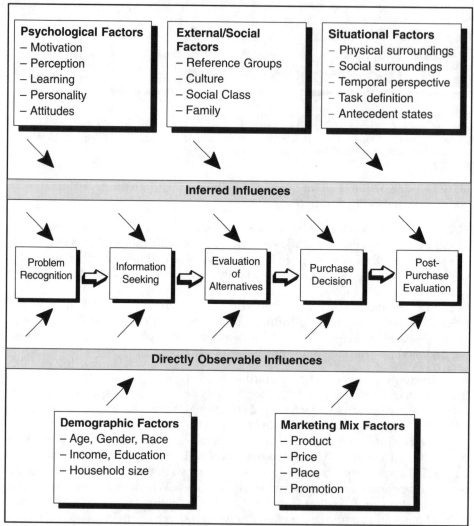

Source: Thomas C. Kinnear, Kenneth L. Bernhardt, and Kathleen A. Krentler, *Principles of Marketing,* 4th ed. (New York: HarperCollins, 1995), p. 187.

needs. Every person has at least one level of need to be met at all times. Through its products and services, a club attempts to meet its members' needs at every level in Maslow's model.

The attitudes factor is closely related to the concept of personality. An attitude is a learned tendency to respond consistently toward a given object, such as a brand. Attitudes also encompass a person's value system, which represents personal standards of good and bad or right and wrong. A club member may have the attitude that racquet clubs are a waste of money. This same member may also have a stronger attitude that only activities that get you out and involved with nature (such as golf) are worthwhile. Attitudes change over time. Typically the changes are gradual and are influenced by a person's age, education, and economic or social standing. Sometimes, however, an attitudinal change occurs suddenly, such as the shift that might occur in a person's feelings about drinking alcohol after a loved one is injured in a drunk-driving accident.

A third factor that deserves a closer look is culture. Culture refers to the set of values, norms, attitudes, and other meaningful factors that shape human behavior and the artifacts or products of that behavior as they are transmitted from one generation to the next. Culture is a relatively permanent, but dynamic, influence on behavior. What we eat and how we eat it are two examples of how culture affects our lives. While grits may be an acceptable side dish in the South, it would be largely ignored by members of a club located in the North. Even club membership is largely related to culture. In a culture that encourages club membership we would expect to find a greater propensity to join clubs than we would in a culture that does not.

Directly observable influences. The lower third of the Exhibit 5 model lists those directly observable factors that also influence the consumer-purchase-decision process. These factors include demographics (discussed earlier in the chapter) and the marketing mix (discussed in the next section of the chapter). Club managers and marketers should thoroughly understand the influences that both inferred and direct forces have on consumer behavior and what impact those influences have on the final choices that club members make. Demographic factors are outside the control of club managers, but understanding the relationship of these factors to member-purchase behavior will help managers develop and market products and services that better satisfy member needs.

Organizational-Buyer Behavior

Organizational-buyer behavior is different from consumer-buyer behavior because the nature of the purchase is different and the "buyer" is often a group of individuals, some of whom may not even consume the product. An **organizational buyer** is defined as the purchaser of hospitality products for a group of people with a common purpose.[4] Examples of organizational buyers include members of business organizations, social clubs, or associations; people buying products and services for special occasions (such as weddings and anniversaries); and other representatives of groups who may need hospitality products and services. Although all of the basic factors—inferred and observable influences—are the same for an organizational buyer as for a consumer buyer, organizational buyers are buying for other people. The organizational buyer seeks to satisfy the needs and wants of others.

Buying Centers. Club managers should understand that often an "organizational buyer" is not an individual, but a group of individuals known as a **buying center.** Each of the persons who make up a buying center has a specific role to carry out. Several persons may occupy the same role, and one person can undertake several roles simultaneously. What follows are the five roles in a typical buying center:

1. *User.* This individual actually will consume or use the product or service. In many cases, the user initiates the buying process. Often, the user will also be involved in the post-purchase evaluation.

2. *Influencer.* This buying-center member may develop purchase criteria or provide information that is used to evaluate alternatives. His or her influence on the purchase process may be direct or indirect.

3. *Buyer.* This individual has formal authority for actually selecting the company to purchase from, and usually arranges the actual terms of the purchase. Although the buyer is responsible for negotiating, the buyer is subject to the constraints placed on him or her by the other members of the buying center.

4. *Decider.* This person controls the purse strings and is termed the decider because he or she is the person with the authority to "decide" to spend the money on the product or service, although often the decision he or she makes is to go along with what the buyer recommends. This member of the buying center is often referred to as the fund provider. In his or her role as the fund provider, the decider permits the buyer to complete the purchase. In large, formally structured organizations, the buyer and the decider are two distinct members of the buying center; in small, informal organizations, these two roles are often performed by the same person.

5. *Gatekeeper.* This individual controls the flow of information into the buying center. A gatekeeper may have a formal position such as secretary or purchasing agent, but often his or her role is largely informal.

The buying-center concept can be best understood through a simple illustration. Consider Mr. and Mrs. Smith, whose daughter is planning a wedding in the spring. The Smiths will attend the wedding reception at the club, consume the food and beverages, and enjoy the other services that the club provides, so they qualify as users. Mrs. Smith's mother has some definite ideas about the theme and specifics of the reception—she takes on the role of influencer. The Smiths' daughter, Lauren, will be the person who actually negotiates with the club manager about the specifics for the reception, and as such she plays the role of the buyer. She is also, clearly, a user and an influencer. Mr. Smith ultimately has to sign the contract and pay the club; this designates his role as decider. The information Mr. Smith is given will be tightly controlled by his daughter, his wife, and the club manager. Each of these individuals takes on the role of gatekeeper.

Buy Classes. Not all organizational purchases are subject to the same complex interplay of buying-center members. One factor that moderates a purchase's complexity is the type of buying decision that must be made. The various types of buying decisions made by organizations are called **buy classes.** Buy classes are based on the newness of the problem to the group, the amount of information needed to make an informed purchase decision, and the degree to which alternatives are considered. Exhibit 6 illustrates three types of buy classes: new task, modified rebuy, and straight rebuy.[5]

In a new-task situation, the group faces a requirement or problem that has not occurred before. The group has little or no relevant previous buying experience, so

Exhibit 6   Buy Classes in the Organizational-Purchase Process

	New Task		Modified Rebuy		Straight Rebuy
Buying Situation (Buy Class)		⇨		⇨	
	↑↑↑ ↓↓↓		↑↑↑ ↓↓↓		↑↑↑ ↓↓↓
Newness of the Problem	High		Medium		Low
Information Requirements	Extensive		Moderate		Minimal
Importance of New Alternatives	Very Important		Limited		None

Source: Adapted from Patrick Robinson, Charles Faris, and Yoram Wind, *Industrial Buying and Creative Marketing* (Boston: Allyn and Bacon, 1967), p. 28. This is the original buy-class model upon which subsequent models have been based.

a great deal of information is needed, and alternative suppliers are carefully considered. Lauren Smith's wedding would be a new-task situation if the Smiths had never planned a wedding before.

In a modified-rebuy situation, the purchase is common or recurring, but the suppliers might change. An example of a modified-rebuy situation would be if the Smiths had the wedding receptions for their first three daughters at their club, but Lauren has asked them to consider a new hotel that just opened in the last year. The Smiths must solicit a bid from the hotel and meet with the catering sales staff so they can compare the hotel's proposal to the club's.

A straight-rebuy situation involves a very common or recurring purchase and is usually handled on a routine basis. A list of acceptable product/service sources exists, and no new suppliers are considered; buyers have a great deal of relevant buying experience and need little or no additional information. An example of a straight-rebuy situation might be the bridge club planning its next weekly luncheon at the club. The specific menu, the price, or the date and time may change somewhat from purchase to purchase, but a new supplier isn't considered and the purchase process is routine.

The Marketing Mix

Marketing becomes much more down-to-earth when a club manager moves from concepts and strategies to the more pragmatic aspects of a detailed marketing plan. The marketing plan affects club members directly. It represents the implementation of the club's marketing strategy through specific tactics taken in each of four areas: product, promotion, place, and price—the Four Ps of marketing. These four areas together are called the **marketing mix.**

Product Concepts

The first and most important element of the marketing mix is the product itself. Club marketing decisions in this area may be concerned with the number and types of recreational activities that the club should offer, the depth and breadth of the menu in the dining room or grill, the physical appearance of the club, and the policies and procedures for taking dining room reservations or tee times. It is helpful to explore product concepts when trying to understand club products and the impact that product-related marketing decisions will have on the satisfaction of club members and the club's financial performance. Product concepts include:

- Product classifications
- Product positioning
- Product differentiation
- Product life cycles

Product Classifications. A product can be defined, for marketing purposes, as a bundle of benefits, both physical and psychological, that satisfies the needs and wants of the purchaser. There are various types of products, and a product-classification scheme is beneficial when trying to understand how the club's products may best be marketed. One of the most common methods for classifying products is to define them as convenience goods, shopping goods, or specialty goods.[6]

Convenience goods are those products bought with a minimum of time and effort. A soft drink purchased at the snack bar by a club member is an example of a convenience good. The price is typically quite low and does not justify an extensive shopping effort. In addition, the purchaser usually has a high level of knowledge about the product and its benefits. Purchasers of convenience goods typically have little brand loyalty; if they are thirsty, they will usually buy a soft drink regardless of the brand name. The key to marketing convenience goods is convenience; the product must be readily available when the person wants it. This implies that the level of distribution is of critical importance. In other words, to successfully market soft drinks, a club should plan to have soft drinks available wherever members are likely to be thirsty—on the fairways, near the tennis courts, beside the pool, and even in locker rooms.

Shopping goods are products that require some comparison shopping on the part of the purchaser. Consumers may compare price, quality, and style before making a purchase decision. Extensive information-seeking is necessary because the purchaser has incomplete knowledge. Shopping goods are not purchased as often as convenience goods and generally are higher-priced. The bottle of wine that a club member buys from the club's wine list is an example of a shopping good. For this type of product, promotional efforts take on added importance. It takes more personal selling to sell a shopping good than to sell a convenience good, and price is often used as a device to help guide purchase decisions. Unlike soft drinks, for which price matters little, wine should be priced in a way that indicates its quality. The price of a fine Bordeaux wine should be higher than that of a domestic blended wine, for example.

A product for which no reasonable substitute exists is called a **specialty good**. The purchaser is willing to spend a considerable amount of time and effort to locate and purchase this type of product. The purchaser is typically very brand-loyal and willing to pay a premium price for a specialty good. An example of a specialty good would be a signature seafood dish prepared by an acclaimed chef, or an exclusive club. Being able to market a club product or the club itself as a specialty good gives the club an advantage in the marketplace.

Product Positioning. Product positioning refers to the process of developing a strategy for designing a club's product and service offerings and the image of the club so that the club's target markets understand and appreciate what the club stands for in relation to its competition. There may be several competing clubs in a given market. If a club manager wants to position the club as the premier club in the market, the best club in relation to all the others, then efforts must be made to create and maintain a premier image in the members' minds and in the minds of the market in general.

Product Differentiation. Product differentiation refers to the efforts or action steps club managers perform to carry out the product-positioning strategy. Product packaging and physical changes to the club can help differentiate a club from its competition. If the products and features chosen to differentiate the club are important and believable to people in the market, then this strategy will help increase revenues.

Market research techniques can yield product position maps that show the positions occupied by competing club products. Product position maps similar to the one in Exhibit 7 can help managers position new club products or reposition current ones. If a club manager wants to position the club as the premier club in the market, and he or she determines that the market thinks that very challenging golf courses with high greens fees are the mark of a premier club, then the manager must make sure the club's golf course is positioned high in the top left quadrant of the product position map. That might entail redesigning the golf course to make it more challenging, and raising greens fees.

Product differentiation is often used along with market segmentation for maximum results. A club that has identified a large market of retirees and targets their need for value by featuring extensive golf opportunities at prices lower than what competing clubs are charging can be said to be following a product differentiation strategy. In this case, the club manager is positioning the club for the retiree market as the club to join because it offers rounds of golf at low prices.

Product Life Cycles. Products pass through well-defined life-cycle stages. The life of a product is measured in terms of its revenues and rate of revenue growth. When a club is first built and introduced to the market, revenues may be relatively low and costs relatively high, resulting in operating deficits. This is referred to as the introductory stage of the product's life cycle (PLC). The same scenario may be true for a new menu item or activity program at the club. As a product is accepted and

Exhibit 7   Product Position Map—Golf Course Attributes

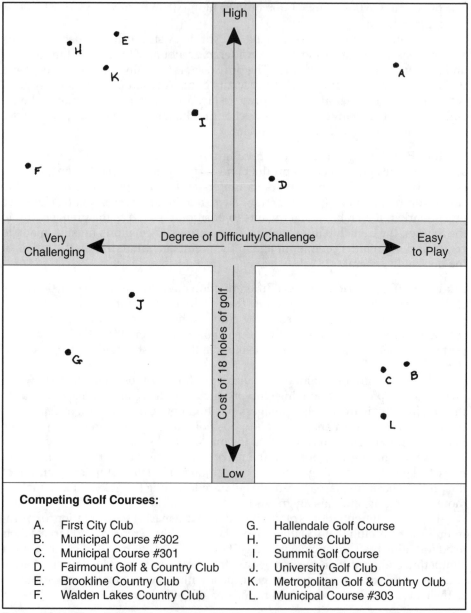

Competing Golf Courses:

A.   First City Club
B.   Municipal Course #302
C.   Municipal Course #301
D.   Fairmount Golf & Country Club
E.   Brookline Country Club
F.   Walden Lakes Country Club

G.   Hallendale Golf Course
H.   Founders Club
 I.   Summit Golf Course
J.   University Golf Club
K.   Metropolitan Golf & Country Club
L.   Municipal Course #303

Source: Adapted from Robert C. Lewis, Richard E. Chambers, and Harsha E. Chacko, *Marketing Leadership in Hospitality*, 2d ed. (New York: Van Nostrand Reinhold, 1995), p. 364.

becomes more popular, the product enters the growth stage of the PLC. Revenues go up rapidly and costs are moderate, and the club is able to charge a premium price for the product because of its popularity. The combination of increasing revenues and moderate costs results in a generous operating profit margin on this product. This is a very desirable stage in the PLC. The extra profit margin may be used to support products that are in the introductory stage or in later stages of the PLC.

As the club enjoys the increasing revenues that accompany the product's increasing popularity, the product may attract the attention of competitors. When competitors enter the market and the product's revenue growth slows down, this indicates that the product has entered the mature stage of the PLC. During maturity, profit margins begin to fall. Competitors begin to copy the successful aspects of the product, so that the products of competing clubs become more similar and less differentiated. At this stage, price competition becomes common and total revenues level off while product profit margins move to lower levels yet.

The decline stage is the final stage in the product life cycle. Examples of declining club products are high-fat menu items. Technological progress, shifts in member tastes and lifestyles, and competitive attacks from rival operations are among the reasons products enter the decline stage. Sales and profits fall off rapidly, and cost concerns become paramount. Declining products drain the club's resources and efforts away from healthy (growth stage) products.

Sometimes declining products are simply dropped. Another option for dealing with a declining product is to reformulate it so that a new life cycle is generated and decline is avoided. A third option is to dramatically reduce costs through improved operating procedures that allow the club to keep offering the product and still generate profits from its sale. For example, a club might offer high-fat items only one night a week so that the needs of the members who want such products can still be met, but the costs associated with offering those products can be isolated to one night for greater cost efficiency.

The product life cycle is primarily useful as a planning tool. Strategies based strictly on the PLC should not be followed blindly. One danger of using the PLC is the self-fulfilling prophecy. A club manager who suspects that a product is entering the decline stage might drastically reduce the amount of resources committed to the product. The product might not actually be in the decline stage, but if the manager pulls promotion and other resources away from it, he or she can cause the product's premature decline.

Promotion Concepts

Decisions affecting how a club communicates information about its product offerings to members are known generally in marketing as promotional decisions. Promotional elements of a club's marketing mix may include personal selling, publicity, sales promotions, and—in some cases—advertising. These elements or activities serve to remind and inform members about the club and its offerings. Promotional efforts in clubs are somewhat constrained by the limited market for the club—its membership.

The Promotional Mix. The combination of promotional elements used to communicate with members is called the club's promotional mix. There is no one correct promotional mix for a club, because all of the promotional elements are essentially substitutes or reinforcements for each other. For instance, a coupon in the club newsletter for a discount on dinner may be more or less effective than a personal recommendation from the staff of the pro shop regarding the Friday-night seafood buffet. Both are examples of promoting dinner, and either one or a combination of both techniques might be used to build member participation and revenues. An effective promotional mix is one that accomplishes the club's promotion or communication objectives.

Creating an effective promotional mix is more art than science and will typically require trial and error, with managers carefully comparing actual results to the desired objectives. Factors that guide a club manager in developing a good promotional mix include: (1) the resources available, (2) characteristics of the club, (3) characteristics of the club's membership, (4) the product-life-cycle stage that the club is in, and (5) club policy. For most club operations, advertising will take a minor role in the mix, while personal selling, direct mail, and the club newsletter will get the greatest share of resources and deliver the best results. Any decisions regarding the promotional tactics to pursue must be made with the image of the club in mind and be consistent with the club's overall marketing strategy.

The following sections discuss common marketing activities that may be considered for inclusion in a club's promotional mix:

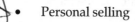

- Personal selling
- Direct mail
- Newsletters
- Merchandising the menu
- Sales promotions
- Advertising
- Public relations

Personal selling. Probably no other element of marketing communication has as important a role in promoting a club's products as personal selling. In clubs, personal selling is most often done by the service staff. Good service usually involves determining a member's needs and then satisfying those needs with some aspect of the club's product offering. Good service, then, can be said to be synonymous with personal selling. Personal selling is the most dynamic, flexible, and efficient form of two-way marketing communication available to club managers and staff.

Direct mail. One of the most common techniques clubs use to market to members is direct mail. Direct mail is popular in clubs for many reasons. One important reason is the availability and low cost of computer hardware and software, which has enhanced management's ability to aim direct mailings more precisely. For example, a club can reach members who infrequently eat at the club with an offer designed to entice them to the club's dining room. The idea behind this direct-mail promotion is that the dining experience will be so positive that the infrequent diner will begin to visit the club's dining room more often and purchase more regularly. Using the club's billing data base, the club manager could target only those members with a food and beverage purchase history below a certain minimum. Conversely, frequent diners might be mailed a free meal coupon as a reward for their loyalty and their contribution to the club's operating revenues.

Exhibit 8 Sample Club Newsletters

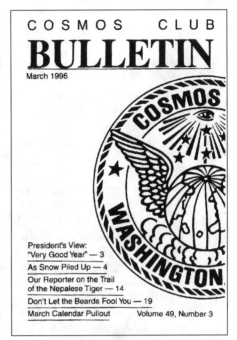

Courtesy of The University Club, Washington, D.C., and The Cosmos Club, Washington, D.C.

The heart of any direct-mail marketing system is the mailing list. A club's membership roster and billing data base provide a ready-made, up-to-date, low-cost mailing list that club managers can use to send marketing messages to selected club members or the entire membership.

Newsletters. Nearly every club uses a newsletter to communicate with its members (see Exhibit 8). A newsletter can tell members about upcoming special events, changes in the hours of operation in the dining room, renovation plans, and so on. A club newsletter should also have a column or section that showcases members and their accomplishments. Member recognition is one of the most effective ways to ensure member satisfaction. A letter-to-the-editor section that solicits feedback from members is an excellent two-way communication device.

Additional sections can include staff highlights (any staff changes or accomplishments that have taken place since the previous newsletter), food and beverage information such as recipes or new wines offered in the dining room, general information about the community that may affect club members, and promotional offers designed to encourage club use and increase product sales. Other points to consider when developing a newsletter are shown in Exhibit 9.

Merchandising the menu. The principal marketing communication tools available to club managers for improving food and beverage revenues are the club's menus. In much the same way that a clothing company uses catalogues to

Exhibit 9   Tips for Effective Club Newsletters

- Set goals for your publication and know the audience you are trying to reach. Don't try to be everything to everybody.

- Make sure a professional communicator is responsible for producing the newsletter.

- Do not use the newsletter to preach to club members. It should be more than just a tool to promote the club or sell products. It should enlighten, entertain, and stimulate a genuine dialogue between the club and its members.

- Provide a forum in which readers may respond. Give members a chance to feel a sense of ownership of the publication by soliciting priceless feedback from them.

- Write to express, not impress. Use words that communicate your message clearly and concretely. Use short sentences and paragraphs, and avoid jargon that will not be easily understood by your entire audience.

- Establish a recognizable format so that readers can become comfortable with the publication and quickly find information.

- Publish on a consistent schedule with firm deadlines. The members should be able to anticipate the arrival of the newsletter and plan to use the information in a timely fashion.

- Use well-planned photography and artwork. Don't wait until the design stage to begin thinking of graphics to use. Readers typically look at interesting photos first.

- Keep your readers in mind when choosing a typeface. They generally want large, easy-to-read type. Avoid the urge to cram too much into each edition. By saying less you may communicate more.

Source: Carolyn Walkup, "Newsletters Prove to be Effective Marketing Tools," *Nation's Restaurant News*, February 25, 1991, p. 12; Chris Brennan-Martin, "Food-Focused Newsletters Pique Curiosity," *Restaurants & Institutions*, March 27, 1991, pp. 125–130; Steve Friedman, "Keep Needs of Readers in Mind When Publishing Newsletter," *Marketing News*, January 1992, p. 5.

show what it has to offer, a club uses its menus to guide club members in making food and beverage purchases.

A menu is not just a list of food and beverage products offered for sale. It is a marketing tool that can be used to merchandise specific items that are good for members (in terms of need satisfaction) and good for the club (in terms of profitability). Identifying the most eye-catching areas on a club menu can help club managers place house specialties and high-profit menu items (see Exhibit 10). For example, with a two-page menu, the right page gets the most attention; with a three-panel menu, the middle panel gets the most attention. Club managers can also draw member attention to high-profit menu items by placing them at the head of lists, putting them in boxes, or using graphic elements such as line drawings or decorative borders to set them apart. Regularly conducting a thorough analysis of the popularity and profitability of each menu item can help in the development, design, and pricing of subsequent menus.

Exhibit 10   Menus and Eye Movement

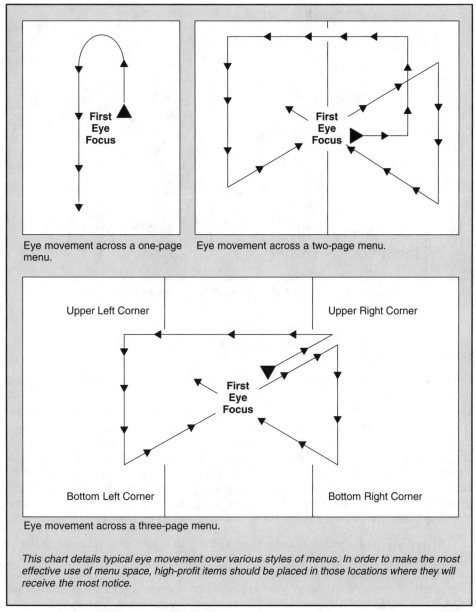

Eye movement across a one-page menu.

Eye movement across a two-page menu.

Upper Left Corner

Upper Right Corner

First Eye Focus

Bottom Left Corner

Bottom Right Corner

Eye movement across a three-page menu.

This chart details typical eye movement over various styles of menus. In order to make the most effective use of menu space, high-profit items should be placed in those locations where they will receive the most notice.

Other menu considerations besides layout, content, and pricing include decisions about the type style to use, the weight and quality of the paper stock, the style of the menu cover, and the use of artwork. The menu should reflect the club's marketing strategy and be consistent with the expectations of club members. For

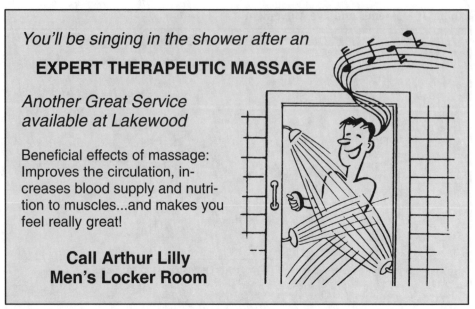

You'll be singing in the shower after an

EXPERT THERAPEUTIC MASSAGE

Another Great Service available at Lakewood

Beneficial effects of massage: Improves the circulation, increases blood supply and nutrition to muscles...and makes you feel really great!

Call Arthur Lilly Men's Locker Room

This "advertisement" appeared in a club newsletter. (Courtesy of Lakewood Country Club, Dallas, Texas)

example, a photocopied menu on typing paper does not belong in a white-table-cloth gourmet dining room.

Sales promotions. A club sales promotion is any activity or incentive designed to induce an immediate response from (1) targeted members, or (2) employees responsible for selling the promoted product. Sales promotions include offering members free samples of a product; sponsoring a sweepstakes or other contest offering price incentives, rebates, or giveaway items to members; demonstrating products; and offering employees incentives (cash, lottery tickets, time off, etc.) for selling the promoted product. Sales promotions aimed at club members are called "pull techniques" because they give members incentives for requesting the product. Sales promotions directed at club staff members are called "push techniques" because they encourage the staff to more actively sell the product to members.

Advertising. Many club managers would say that advertising has no place in a club's promotional mix, but there are other ways to advertise besides buying a display ad in the local newspaper or a 30-second spot on the local radio or television station. Club advertising may be as simple as a poster at the club entrance that promotes the club's Valentine's Day dinner and dance, or a page in the club's newsletter encouraging club members to take advantage of the club's prime-rib special every Wednesday night. Promotional pieces can also be stuffed in the envelope along with each member's monthly bill.

Public relations. Publicity refers to the unpaid mention of a product or organization by the media. Publicity is often the product of a club's public-relations decisions and efforts. Public-relations activities can be characterized as positive or negative. Positive public-relations activities are usually done on a proactive basis. For example, the club might send out a press release regarding the hiring of a new golf pro or the first-place ribbon the executive chef won in a culinary competition. The key aspects of good-news publicity are to know how to write an effective press release and know to whom to send it. The club may want to engage the services of a public relations firm to ensure maximum exposure and efficiency in all of the club's publicity efforts.

Negative public-relations activities are typically reactive and deal with erroneous impressions or damaging reports about the club. A news story about a sexual-harassment lawsuit being brought by a former employee against a club member would be an example of this type of public-relations challenge. The best way to prepare for negative publicity is to develop a set of public relations contingency plans for dealing with bad news. Most importantly, avoid the temptation to stonewall. If you refuse to explain what happened, usually a multitude of unofficial information sources will spring up.[7] The best policy is to get the news out quickly, accurately, and completely. A designated club spokesperson should become the media's best source for all information related to the incident. A second aspect of handling bad publicity is to try to turn the negative into a positive. Members and potential members will watch how the club's spokesperson performs during the crisis. If the spokesperson appears to have the situation under control, it will reflect well on the club.

Place or Distribution Concepts

Place or distribution in marketing parlance refers to the tactics and techniques used to get products and customers together. Distribution issues are concerned with matching the supply and demand for a product in a timely fashion while meeting the financial objective of pricing for a profit. Specifically, marketing distribution decisions involve coordinating the firms or individuals who participate in the flow of goods and services from producers to consumers.

Goods versus Services. When the manufacturer of a typical tangible product makes decisions about how to get the product into the end-user's hands, the decisions are focused on the channels of distribution to be used. How many and what type of intermediaries should be used between the point of production and the point of consumption? Types of intermediaries include agents or brokers, wholesalers, and retail outlets. Not every tangible product is distributed in the same way. There are an almost infinite variety of options available.

In the case of intangible or service-based products, such as are found in a club, there are many distribution options as well. However, because of the unique nature of service-based products, there is a fundamental difference between tangible-goods distribution plans and service-based plans. In order to purchase and consume a service, the buyer must be in the presence of the service-provider. For example, club revenue from the services provided by the club's golf professional are only realized when the pro is working with a member. If no one is scheduled for golf lessons Thursday morning, then the revenue the club could have realized, had someone taken golf lessons Thursday morning, is gone forever. Because services are highly perishable and involve simultaneous production and consumption, distribution plans for organizations that provide services are usually focused on getting purchasers (in the case of clubs, the members) to come to the point of production (the club).

Hospitality distribution channels rarely involve a separate wholesaler or retailer taking physical possession of the product and selling it to the end-consumer at a later date. A club is not only the retailer, but the manufacturer of its products as well. The problem, then, is not how to distribute the club's products to retailers, but how to get members to the retail outlet of the club's products—which is the club itself. This problem gives rise to the need for a special kind of distribution system. In a business where the product is very perishable and where production and consumption are simultaneous, it is imperative for a club to consider distribution options that allow its members to more easily visit the club and purchase club products and services. For single or independent club operations, distribution options or decisions are limited to the selection of the physical location of the club and issues such as accessibility, operating hours, and offering various levels of membership. For multi-unit clubs, however, distribution options are more complex.

Distribution Options for Multi-Unit Clubs. While many clubs are single-entity operations, there is a growing trend toward establishing groups of clubs, or "chains," as they are called in other areas of hospitality such as restaurants and hotels. For multi-unit club operations, decisions regarding distribution might include how to expand the reach of the club chain and facilitate member usage through increased visibility and recognition of the clubs in the chain. This goal is similar to the goal McDonald's has of wanting the Golden Arches on all of the best street corners in the market. Distribution options for a multi-unit club chain, or a single club considering expansion into a multi-unit chain, include forming a "mini-chain" of independent clubs, franchising the clubs, or affiliating with other clubs.

Independent "mini-chains." Most private clubs today are independently owned and operated, and most prize their independence and do not want to be seen as franchised properties. However, some independent clubs that have a common bond of some type—they are in the same city, for example, or are owned by the same developer—decide to band together and in some ways act as a chain in order to gain certain purchasing and accounting advantages. These "mini-chains" of from two to five clubs reap some economies of scale by banding together, but not as much as clubs that belong to bigger franchise-type organizations such as the Club Corporation of America, which has more than 200 clubs under its umbrella. Also, these mini-chains add little value to the clubs within the chain from a distribution point of view; since each club maintains its appearance of independence, there is no "brand-recognition value" to the mini-chain, so belonging to the chain does little to bring more new members to any of the clubs within the chain. It also does not encourage members of clubs within the chain to visit the other clubs in the chain.

Franchised operations. In the case of a non-equity (profit-oriented) club, managers may represent or work for a franchisor-based organization. The owners, or shareholders, of the club will choose this option when they want immediate member recognition of the reputation and image that accompanies the franchising parent's name. In addition, this option provides a club with greater access to capital funds for expanding or improving the club's facilities and, in some cases, may make available better-trained managers. A popular benefit of being a franchised operation is the professional marketing support that the parent organization can provide. Other benefits of a franchise relationship include support services that act as safeguards in areas of legal matters, safety regulations, and insurance issues.

There are also some significant disadvantages to operating a club under a franchise. The operating objectives of the franchise organization and the club's members may differ. For example, the members may want moderate pricing and restricted access, but the franchisee may want higher prices and a liberal membership policy in order to maximize membership and revenue numbers. Another disadvantage arises because the financial risk of the club is borne by the club's owners and not by the franchisor. When the return on investment is below the owners' expectations, they may want to take steps to reduce their risk (or increase their return) that are not permitted under the franchise agreement. This in turn leads to conflict and may interfere with management's ability to meet the needs of club members.

Affiliations. Many club members travel frequently and extensively or belong to a club with limited facilities in a market with many competitors. Some clubs affiliate with other clubs to share facilities, engage in joint-marketing efforts, and achieve economies of scale in purchasing. Affiliated clubs extend privileges to nonmembers at little or no cost in exchange for reciprocating privileges. This is a relatively limited approach to distribution and provides very few financial advantages. It does, however, increase the value of a club membership and can help entice prospective members to join a club.

Pricing Concepts

"Price" is not as simple a concept as it first appears. Generally, "price" can be defined as "the monetary value that the producer of a good or service puts on the utility that the purchaser will receive from the good or service."

From a purely economic viewpoint, pricing products and services in monetary terms is important because price facilitates the establishment of relative value and makes complex transactions possible. On a more practical level, price is important to a club because it affects the quantity of product the club can sell and the amount of revenue it can generate to cover the costs of doing business. If prices are too low, there may be too much demand for the club's services and insufficient revenue to cover operating costs. This scenario will result in such great popularity for the club that it will quickly go out of business unless prices are adjusted upward to a profitable level. Price is important to members as well, who use it as a measure of their cost of living. Members might get angry if the price of a club product is too high and may choose not to purchase it, which results in a need going unsatisfied. If members see a product's price as reasonable, they will be happier to pay it and should purchase the product more frequently than they would if they felt the product was overpriced. In addition to increasing the club's operating revenues, satisfied members will place a higher value on their club membership and will be more likely to renew their memberships in the future.

The importance of pricing to a club dictates that club managers develop a set of pricing strategies before attempting to implement either a rational or an emotional pricing approach. Pricing strategies are typically based on a combination of demand, cost, and competitive and promotional factors. Pricing strategies can range from relatively low pricing (i.e., introductory pricing designed to encourage first-time buyers) to relatively high or prestige pricing designed to indicate that the club or club product has a high degree of exclusivity and quality.

One of the most important aspects of pricing is the concept of elasticity of demand. **Elasticity of demand** is a means of measuring how sensitive demand is to changes in price. In general, as the selling price of a product decreases, the quantity demanded will increase; when the price of a product is increased, the quantity demanded will decrease. When the demand for a product is highly sensitive to price changes, such that an increase in price leads to a decrease in total revenue, the demand is said to be elastic. When the demand for a product is not very sensitive to changes in price, such that an increase in price leads to an overall increase in the revenue from that product, the demand is said to be inelastic. It is possible to mathematically calculate the demand elasticity for any product if the exact demand characteristics are known for a full range of possible prices. Knowing a product's demand elasticity can be helpful to a club manager in guiding price decisions. If the demand for a club product is elastic (that is, price-sensitive), then a conservative pricing strategy is called for.

Rational Approaches to Pricing. Setting price levels can be done with techniques ranging from simple to complex. Because setting prices is arguably a rational, objective, and quantifiable process, it is easy to overlook the subjective and emotional implications that should be addressed. Whichever pricing strategy or method is employed, the resultant price should then be submitted to a subjective test of reasonableness before the price is implemented. Rational pricing approaches include the following:

- Full-cost pricing

- Mark-up pricing

- Gross-profit pricing

- Integrated pricing

Full-cost pricing. Full-cost pricing, also referred to as cost-plus pricing, is product pricing that covers all variable costs of production, administrative costs, allocated fixed costs, and a desired level of profit. Full-cost pricing has long been an appealing method for setting prices because it is relatively straightforward and relies on the fundamental premise that if all product costs and a profit are accounted for before setting prices on club products, the club will prosper. However, this approach assumes that the decision-maker can accurately identify all costs associated with each product and that the products can be sold at the resultant prices.

In order to use the full-cost pricing method, a club manager must be able to identify all production costs and understand the relationship between fixed and variable costs. In addition, knowing the elasticity of demand for the product is essential to successfully using this pricing method.

While full-cost pricing is arguably the best method of rationally setting prices, it is also the most difficult and complex method because it requires the decision-maker to know the nature of all the costs of the operation and be able to incorporate them into a single set of pricing guidelines. This difficulty is often overcome by establishing a pricing ratio, or factor, that estimates the relationship between the costs and the forecasted demand and makes the actual setting of prices a simple mathematical exercise. This alternative to full-cost pricing is called mark-up pricing. One area where mark-up pricing is often used is food and beverages.

Mark-up pricing. Food and beverages constitute a significant portion of a club's revenues, but may constitute a disproportionately small amount of the club's operating costs. In such a case, it may be more practical to use a mark-up factor to establish the selling price of a menu item whenever the direct costs of producing the item are easily identified. The mark-up factor is designed to cover all non-product costs, such as labor, utilities, supplies, interest costs, taxes, and other elements of the club's operating overhead.

Under the mark-up approach, the first step is to determine the menu item's ingredient costs. Second, the club manager must calculate the appropriate mark-up factor to use in multiplying the ingredient costs. The third step is to multiply the ingredient costs by the mark-up factor to determine the desired selling price. Finally, the club manager must assess the price in terms of its reasonableness to the members. The multiple, or mark-up factor, is usually based on a desired level of food cost (or beverage cost) and is calculated by dividing the number 1 by the desired product-cost percentage. A desired cost of 40% would result in a factor of 2.5 $(1 \div .40 = 2.5)$ or a price that is two and a half times the ingredient costs.

Gross-profit pricing. Gross-profit pricing is a variation of full-cost pricing. With this method, all of the non-product costs are estimated for a given period of time in the future. These costs include the fixed and variable costs of operating the club, but do not include the cost of providing the specific product. Second, an estimate of the number of products or transactions to be completed during the same period of time is calculated. The total non-product costs reflect the amount of total gross profit that is necessary to successfully operate the club. The gross margin is then divided by the expected number of transactions (sales) and the result is the necessary amount of gross profit the club needs to recover from each transaction. This amount is then added to the cost of producing the product to arrive at the desired selling price.

The disadvantages of the gross-profit pricing method are the same as those for full-cost pricing. These disadvantages include the need for the decision-maker to know all production costs and be able to identify the relationship between fixed and variable costs, as well as knowing the elasticity of demand for the product in question. In addition, the accuracy of the forecasted number of transactions is critical to the successful implementation of this method. Failure to properly allocate costs or an underestimation of the number of transactions could result in an operating deficit.

Integrated pricing. Many clubs have several revenue-producing departments. If each department were allowed to price its products independently, the club might fail to realize its profit goals and operate at a deficit. For instance, setting greens fees very high might result in maximizing golf revenues at the expense of the food and beverage department, because the higher greens fees would probably mean that fewer members would use the course and there would be fewer customers for the grill room or snack bar. If the profit potential from food and beverage outlets is not realized, other operating costs may go unmet.

Prices for all operated departments should therefore be established in such a way that they maximize the club's overall revenue. This requires an integrated pricing policy set by the club's board and the general manager and coordinated among all of the club's department managers. While integrated pricing benefits the club as a whole, it can mean that some departments will not maximize their revenues or departmental profit.

Emotional Approaches to Pricing. Rational approaches to setting prices may need to be tempered by subjective factors. Subjective or emotional pricing approaches should be given consideration, but should never be the primary basis for setting prices. It is more appropriate to set prices using a rational or objective approach and then submit the prices to subjective tests for reasonableness.

One subjective approach to pricing is to base a club's prices on what the competition is charging. In the club environment this will usually mean pricing below the competition. Unfortunately, this does not take into account the price sensitivity of club members or such factors as the club's location, the unique capabilities of the club's staff, member goodwill, and the exclusivity of the club. Pricing above the market may yield high gross profits, but reduce demand so much that overall revenues and departmental profits are below expectations.

Another emotional approach to pricing is to base the selling price on the club manager's intuition. Typically, a manager who uses this approach bases the selling price on what he or she "feels" that members are willing to pay. The manager relies on his or her experience regarding member reactions to prices. Unfortunately, intuition suffers from the same disadvantages as competitive pricing; the intuitive method ignores costs and may decrease demand so much that the club fails to recoup its operating costs.

Psychological pricing methods are often employed by club managers trying to tune in to the emotional impact of pricing. Odd-numbered pricing is an example of a psychological pricing method. Prices are set so that the last digit is always an odd number, usually 9. This is done to create a consistent impression among buyers that the prices are lower than they actually are. For example, managers who set the price of a menu item at $8.99 hope that members will think to themselves "That's less than $9" and therefore the item is a "good value"; these thoughts would not be encouraged if the price were set just a penny higher at $9.00. Other psychological considerations include not listing prices in either ascending or descending order. With such lists, members are able to match prices to their "mental budget line" too easily, and low-priced items will have an unnecessary advantage.

The last emotional pricing approach is simply trial and error. Under this method, the price is set and then member reactions are monitored to determine whether the price should be adjusted up or down. Problems with this approach include the failure to consider costs and the time lag between when the price is set and when member reactions are recorded and analyzed. A long time lag could result in irreparable damage being done before corrections can be made. Also, frequent price changes may confuse or anger members. Another disadvantage of the trial-and-error method is that it fails to isolate the cause of the member reaction. A member's negative reaction to a price may be the result of a bad day at the office or even the weather and may have no relation to the actual price being charged.

Marketing Research

Most private clubs have conducted informal marketing research for many decades. In an effort to better understand the needs and wants of members, club managers periodically ask for member opinions. Often, this solicitation of opinions takes the form of a member comment card or an annual membership survey. Managers may also meet with servers from the dining room on a weekly basis to ask them how members reacted to the daily or weekly specials offered by the club. Training servers to effectively solicit such feedback is one element of a well-designed marketing information system. In addition, managers may read articles that appear in the business press or in club-industry trade publications about trends affecting the club. All of these efforts to collect and process data about the market and the club's products are associated with marketing research. Most, however, are done informally and with little concern for the importance or "fit" of the data with the overall forces affecting the club's operation.

A formal marketing research effort is distinguished from informal approaches by the fact that it is systematic and follows an orderly sequence of steps designed to provide reliable information for decision-making. **Marketing research** is defined as the process of identifying and defining a marketing problem or opportunity, specifying and collecting the data required to address the problem or opportunity, analyzing the results, and communicating information to decision-makers.[8]

Club managers, facing a challenging and dynamic marketplace, are responding to the need for up-to-date and reliable marketing information by creating what are referred to as marketing information systems. A **marketing information system** is a structured, interacting complex of people and equipment designed to generate pertinent marketing information from sources within and outside the club. The information is generated for use in both current decision-making and future planning in regard to formulating marketing strategy, identifying buyer behaviors, and developing an effective marketing mix.

Types of Research

There are two broad marketing-research categories. Subjective methods of collecting marketing data are typically referred to as qualitative research; objective methods are referred to as quantitative research.

Qualitative Research. **Qualitative research** is concerned with exploring the attitudes and behaviors of specific club members. The most common form of qualitative research is called focus group research. A typical club focus-group comprises six to ten members familiar with the club and its products and services. These club members are brought together with a trained moderator to discuss some aspect of the club's product offerings.

A focus group is often used when a club develops a new menu. The focus group may be the club's house or food and beverage committee or may be selected from the general membership. The club manager may produce a draft of the proposed menu and then invite the focus group to discuss the menu over a one- to two-hour period. To avoid interjecting his or her own biases, the manager should hire a skilled moderator to lead the focus group and explore the members' opinions fully. Skilled moderators build rapport with group members so that they are more likely to share their true feelings, attitudes, and beliefs. The group's discussion can be recorded (either on audio- or videotape) and then subsequently analyzed by decision-makers.

Qualitative research is useful because it allows the moderator to get information from the direct consumers of the product, which can lead to the development of new ideas and concepts. The major drawback to this type of research is that managers can only be certain that the findings apply to the focus group and not to the club's general membership. Some clubs overcome this difficulty by convening more than one focus group to get a better sampling of the membership.

Quantitative Research. Quantitative research deals with numbers. One type of quantitative research is called descriptive research. **Descriptive research** describes the number of members who like or dislike something and includes the members' ages and other demographic characteristics represented as averages, frequencies, or other percentages. While descriptive research can tell managers how many members feel or act a certain way, it cannot tell them *why* the members feel or act a certain way.

An example of a descriptive study is the annual membership survey. A membership survey asks club members to respond to a printed survey form containing a list of questions with possible answers. Questions could request demographic data such as age, income, or gender of family members. Additional questions might ask for opinions about the quality of club services offered, the availability of services, and the prices of specific products or services. This data is then tabulated into a statistical summary and presented to club staff for further analysis. Techniques exist for examining two or more of these variables simultaneously to establish how they correlate. For instance, the members who responded favorably to the availability of lowfat menu choices could be correlated with the gender or age of the respondents. The results of this analysis could suggest when and where lowfat food should be offered and how many lowfat offerings to make available on future menus.

Sources of Data

There are two basic sources of data used in marketing research: primary and secondary. Secondary data is the most common type of marketing data. **Secondary data** is information that has already been collected for another purpose. Because it has already been collected, secondary data can be obtained more quickly and less expensively than primary data. The unique nature of secondary data—that it already exists—is the principal advantage, and principal disadvantage, of using this type of data. Since secondary data was collected for some other purpose, it may not provide a manager with exactly the information he or she needs for the marketing decision at hand. In addition, the data may be out of date or in a form that is of little use to the manager. The major sources of secondary data are internal records, syndicated data, and government data. Syndicated data refers to information that has been collected, analyzed, or archived by private sources or "syndicators" and subsequently made available for a fee. Sources for this type of secondary data include credit-reporting bureaus and companies such as Claritas, which compiles marketing data on neighborhoods (as defined by postal zip codes) with its PRIZM system (Potential Rating Index for Zip Markets). Government data is often available at little or no cost to users because tax revenues were spent to generate it. Unfortunately, government data is often not in a form that is immediately useful. Some syndicators specialize in reformatting government data to a more "user-friendly" form and selling it.

Primary data, on the other hand, is information that is collected specifically for the current use. Because it is almost always expensive and time-consuming to collect primary data, primary-data collection should be considered only after secondary sources are exhausted. Primary-data sources include surveys, telephone interviews, and in-person interviews. Focus group research is an example of collecting qualitative primary data.

Toward an Ethical Approach to Club Marketing

Club managers must be concerned not only with successfully marketing their clubs, but marketing them within the range of what is considered ethical and appropriate behavior. **Ethics represent a set of beliefs about what is right or wrong.** Ethics may be determined by an individual or by a group. What is proper and ethical in one setting may not be so in another.

There is increasing awareness by the public of the ethical aspects of business decisions.[9] Club managers constantly face ethical dilemmas. For example, should one member always be given the best table in the dining room? Should club managers promote the consumption of alcohol when overconsumption can lead to health or legal problems for members? Even marketing research raises ethical questions: how much information should managers know about club members, and what means are acceptable in gathering that information?

One way club managers can resolve ethical dilemmas in marketing is to submit a marketing decision to three ethical tests:

1. Does the decision violate someone's rights or the law?

2. Is everyone who is affected by the decision treated fairly?

3. Would you mind reading about your decision and its consequences in the newspaper or club newsletter?

Ethical marketing is not only important for club managers to practice, monitor, and improve, it is also important for all of the club's employees. The example set by the management of the club, in terms of ethical behavior, influences employee behavior and in turn affects the members' perceptions of and satisfaction with the club itself.

Endnotes

1. Peter D. Bennett, *Dictionary of Marketing Terms* (American Marketing Association, 1988), p. 115.

2. Charles W. Lamb, Jr., Joseph F. Hair, Jr., and Carl McDaniel, *Principles of Marketing,* 2d ed. (Southwestern Publishing, 1994), p. 102.

3. Thomas C. Kinnear, Kenneth L. Bernhardt, and Kathleen A. Krentler, *Principles of Marketing,* 4th ed. (San Francisco: HarperCollins, 1995), p. 187.

4. Robert C. Lewis, Richard E. Chambers, and Harsha E. Chacko, *Marketing Leadership in Hospitality,* 2d ed. (New York: VNR, 1995), p. 243.

5. Patrick Robinson, Charles Faris, and Yoram Wind, *Industrial Buying and Creative Marketing,* (Boston: Allyn and Bacon, 1967), p. 28.

6. Melvin T. Copeland, "The Relationship of Consumer Buying Habits to Marketing Methods," *Harvard Business Review,* April 1923, pp. 282–289. This article from 1923 is a seminal piece and truly a classic in marketing thought. It is still cited in consumer-buying texts because it serves as the foundation upon which subsequent theory has been built.

7. Stephen M. Agins, "How to Survive Bad Publicity," *Lodging,* January 1991, pp. 33–34.

8. William F. Schoell and Joseph P. Guiltinan, *Marketing: Contemporary Concepts and Practices,* 6th ed. (Englewood Cliffs, N.J.: Prentice-Hall, 1995), p. 106.

9. Stephen S.J. Hall, "Ethics in Hospitality: How to Draw Your Line," *Lodging,* September 1989, pp. 59–61.

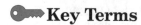 # Key Terms

buy class—A type of buying decision based on the newness of the problem to the organization, the type of information required, and the consideration of new alternatives.

buying center—A group of individuals functioning as an organizational buyer.

convenience good—A product that is purchased with a minimum of time and effort.

descriptive research—A type of quantitative marketing research that counts the number of members who like or dislike something and includes the members' ages and other demographic characteristics represented as averages, frequencies, or other percentages. An example of descriptive research in the club industry is the annual membership survey.

elasticity of demand—A term economists use to describe the change in the quantity demanded by consumers as a result of a given change in the price charged.

ethics—A set of moral principles and values that we use to answer questions regarding the right or wrong action to take.

family life cycle (FLC)—A series of stages within a family, determined by a combination of age, marital status, and the presence or absence of children in the home.

internal marketing—A marketing effort managers direct toward employees, in which managers sell employees on the importance of their jobs and the value of their contributions to the success of the business.

market—A population group that has purchasing power and is currently, or could be, a purchaser of an organization's products or services.

market segment—A group of consumers with similar needs, wants, backgrounds, incomes, buying habits, or other attributes.

marketing—The process of planning and executing the conception, pricing, promotion, and distribution of ideas, goods, and services to create exchanges that satisfy individual and organizational objectives.

marketing information system—A structured, interacting complex of people and equipment designed to generate marketing information from sources within and outside an organization.

marketing mix—The combination of the Four Ps of marketing—product, price, place, and promotion—used to achieve marketing objectives.

marketing research—The process of identifying and defining a marketing problem or opportunity, specifying and collecting the data required to address the problem or opportunity, analyzing the results, and communicating the information to decision-makers.

organizational buyer—A purchaser of products for a group of people within an organization.

primary data—Research information that is collected specifically for the current use.

primary target market—The market segment whose members are most likely to want a business's product or service.

product differentiation strategy—A marketing strategy that involves creating a difference in consumers' minds between a particular product and competing products.

product positioning—A marketing strategy aimed at creating and maintaining a desired image for a product relative to the image of competing products.

publicity—The gratuitous mention in the media of an organization's people, products, or services.

qualitative research—The collection of verbal marketing data, usually to analyze the attitudes and behaviors of buyers.

quantitative research—Marketing research that deals with numbers.

secondary data—Research data that has been previously gathered for a purpose other than the one at hand.

shopping good—A product that requires shoppers to do some comparison shopping before making a purchase.

situation analysis—An analysis of an organization's strengths, weaknesses, opportunities, and threats.

specialty good—A product for which no reasonable substitute exists.

Review Questions

1. How is a market defined and segmented?

2. What are five marketing concepts that can serve as the focal points for marketing strategy?

3. What is a situation analysis?

4. What is service marketing? internal marketing?

5. How can understanding the concept of the family life cycle help club managers market their club?

6. What is the consumer-purchase-decision process?

7. What are buying centers? buy classes?

8. What are some common product concepts that can help club managers understand the products they offer to members?

9. A typical club's promotional mix consists of what elements?

10. What are some common place or distribution concepts that can help club managers better understand how to market their clubs?

11. What are some typical approaches to pricing club products and services?

12. What are the differences between qualitative research and quantitative research?

13. Ethics play what role in club marketing?

Additional Reading

Agins, Stephen M. "How to Survive Bad Publicity." *Lodging,* January 1991.

Bennett, Peter D. *Dictionary of Marketing Terms.* American Marketing Association, 1988.

Copeland, Melvin T. "The Relationship of Consumer Buying Habits to Marketing Methods." *Harvard Business Review,* April 1923.

Hall, Stephen S.J. "Ethics in Hospitality: How to Draw Your Line." *Lodging,* September 1989.

Kinnear, Thomas C., Kenneth L. Bernhardt, and Kathleen A. Krentler. *Principles of Marketing,* Fourth Edition. San Francisco: HarperCollins, 1995.

Lamb, Charles W., Jr., Joseph F. Hair, Jr., and Carl McDaniel. *Principles of Marketing,* Second Edition. Southwestern Publishing, 1994.

Lewis, Robert C., Richard E. Chambers, and Harsha E. Chacko. *Marketing Leadership in Hospitality,* Second Edition. New York: VNR, 1995.

Robinson, Patrick, Charles Faris, and Yoram Wind. *Industrial Buying and Creative Marketing.* Boston: Allyn and Bacon, 1967.

Schoell, William F., and Joseph P. Guiltinan. *Marketing, Contemporary Concepts and Practices*, Sixth Edition. Englewood Cliffs, N.J.: Prentice-Hall, 1995.

Case Study

As hard as he tried, Fred Lee couldn't get his clubhouse manager's comment out of his head. "You know, it's funny that the drop in club membership started just after the new country club on the south side of the city opened." The clubhouse manager wasn't trying to be critical, but the comment bothered Fred for several reasons. First, his club had been the premier club in the city for several decades. The membership roster was a virtual who's who of the city's leaders: the top executives, doctors, and business owners all belonged to his club. Second, the south side of the city was just beginning to attract some development. The better neighborhoods and established residential areas were all located on the north side. Third, the conservative nature of the club's board had ensured that little changed from year to year and the current members seemed to like that.

The most disturbing aspect of the declining membership was that the food and beverage revenues were falling at a faster rate than the membership revenues. It seemed that the older and more loyal members were not spending as much time in the club's dining room or grill room, and the snack bar revenues were down almost 50% from just 10 years ago. As Fred considered the revenue problems, he thought back to when he had first joined the club as an assistant manager nearly 15 years earlier. The pool and tennis courts had always been crowded, especially in the summer months when school was out. The club had been the site of all the most important wedding receptions back then, but lately wedding business had been down significantly.

The club's facilities were in great repair—the reserves for replacements and renovation had been one of the strengths of the club since Fred had joined the management team. The city was growing, and local businesses were attracting more and more young professionals with young families. Fred was concerned that if the club continued on its current course, there would be operating deficits before the end of the decade.

Discussion Questions

1. Why do you think the club on the south side of the city has affected membership in Fred's club? What can Fred do about it?

2. Develop an outline for a marketing research project for Fred's club that would provide him with information about the underlying demographic trends and other buyer issues that are affecting the marketplace in which his club is located.

3. List some of the important marketing issues that Fred should consider in developing a marketing plan to increase current member usage of the food and beverage facilities. Also list those marketing issues that Fred should consider in attracting new members to the club.

REVIEW QUIZ

When you feel you have covered all of the material in this chapter, answer these questions. Choose the *best* answer.

1. If an organization decides to concentrate on manufacturing its products in a super-efficient way in order to produce them at the lowest possible unit cost and pass on savings to the consumer, it is following the _____ marketing orientation.

   a. production
   b. product
   c. selling
   d. societal

2. A "buying center" is:

   a. a marketing term for any retail outlet.
   b. that point on a continuum at which consumer price resistance and product appeal are perfectly balanced.
   c. a group of individuals who make purchases for an organization.
   d. the price point at which optimum sales can be achieved for a product.

3. If each department in a club prices its products independently without regard to the impact those prices might have on other club departments, the club is *not* following a(n) _____ pricing strategy.

   a. integrated
   b. gross-profit
   c. mark-up
   d. full-cost

4. Information that has been gathered for some other purpose but can be used by marketers for market-research purposes is called:

   a. qualitative research.
   b. secondary data.
   c. principal research.
   d. primary data.

Answer Key: 1-a-C1, 2-c-C2, 3-a-C3, 4-b-C4

Each question is linked to a competency. Competencies are listed on the first page of the chapter. An answer reading 3-b-C4 translates to:

   3: the question number
   b: the correct answer
   C4: the competency number

Chapter 8 Outline

Workplace Antidiscrimination Laws
    Major U.S. Employment
        Antidiscrimination Laws
Recruitment
    The Recruitment Process
    Recruitment Advertising
Selection
    Elements of the Selection Process
Orientation
    Orientation Kits
Training
    The Training Cycle
Evaluation
    Functions of Performance Appraisals
    Common Appraisal Errors
    Who Should Evaluate Performance?
    How Often Should Appraisals Be
        Conducted?
    Performance Appraisal Methods
Discipline
    Approaches to Discipline
    Appeal Mechanisms
    Discharge: The Last Resort

Competencies

1. Summarize major U.S. employment antidiscrimination laws that affect clubs. (pp. 249–254)

2. Describe recruitment, selection, and orientation tasks. (pp. 255–268)

3. List and summarize the elements of the training cycle, and describe off-the-job and on-the-job training methods. (pp. 268–276)

4. Explain the issues and tasks club managers should be familiar with regarding employee performance appraisals. (pp. 276–282)

5. Describe approaches to employee discipline, summarize common appeal mechanisms of discipline programs, explain why and how club managers should discharge employees, and explain employment at will. (pp. 282–289)

Managing Human Resources in Clubs

This chapter was written and contributed by Robert H. Woods,
Associate Professor, *The* School of Hospitality Business,
Michigan State University, East Lansing, Michigan.

MUCH HAS CHANGED in human resources management in recent years. Not too long ago, most organizations paid little attention to human resources management. At one time, clubs and other service organizations found it easy to find employees to work. That isn't true today. Many clubs now find it difficult to fill vacant positions. As a result, clubs have needed to become more sophisticated in their approaches to hiring, training, and retaining employees. Since most clubs are not large enough to employ a human resources specialist, every club manager should become familiar with human resources issues.

Human resources issues in clubs are similar to the human resources issues in other service organizations such as hotels and restaurants. However, there is one major difference between clubs and other hospitality organizations: club managers serve a more or less permanent population of "customers"—the club's members. In many clubs, the club members own the club, so they are in a sense the managers' bosses. This fact, coupled with the fact that some club members give club managers advice on how they should deal with employees, puts an added pressure on club managers that managers in other hospitality organizations don't have to deal with.

In this chapter we will look at workplace antidiscrimination laws that club managers should be aware of, then explore the human resources issues involved in recruiting, selecting, orienting, training, evaluating, and disciplining employees.

Workplace Antidiscrimination Laws

Prior to the 1960s, workplace discrimination in the United States was widespread. This led to the passage of the Civil Rights Act of 1964, the first major employment antidiscrimination act, which prohibited discrimination on the basis of race, color, religion, sex, or national origin. Since then, other antidiscrimination laws have been enacted that affect club managers.

Club managers discriminate among employees all the time. Hiring, training, promoting, and many other human resources functions all involve discrimination—that is, they all involve choosing one or more individuals over others. Discrimination practices that follow the guidelines of equal employment opportunity

249

laws are legal; however, discrimination practices that fail to follow these guidelines are illegal.

Clubs incorporated under 501(c) regulations must follow the provisions of the major employment antidiscrimination laws or risk losing their tax-exempt status.[1] Passages in the Internal Revenue Service (IRS) Code that relate to 501(c) clubs set forth five general criteria for tax exemption; the fifth criterion states: "At no time can the charter, bylaws, or other governing instrument of the club contain a provision that discriminates against any person on the basis of race, color, or religion." In recent years this passage has been assumed to also include discrimination on the basis of disability.

Some clubs have tried to get around employment antidiscrimination laws (and Social Security and unemployment taxes) by contending that some of their employees are independent contractors rather than employees. The IRS test for whether a worker is an employee or an independent contractor contains 20 questions. If the club answers positively to any of these questions, the worker is considered an employee of the club and therefore subject to antidiscrimination laws. The first two questions: "Does the worker comply with the employer's instructions about work?" and "Does the worker receive training from or at the direction of the employer?" should be enough to convince most club managers that their workers are employees. Other questions, such as "Can the worker be fired?" should confirm this relationship. Therefore, club managers should obey the employment antidiscrimination laws listed in the following sections. To do otherwise may place their clubs and their careers in jeopardy.

Major U.S. Employment Antidiscrimination Laws

What follows are brief descriptions of the major U.S. employment antidiscrimination laws.

Wage and Hour Laws. Private clubs must follow both federal and state wage and hour laws unless they can prove that their workers are independent contractors rather than employees.

Equal Pay Act of 1963. The Equal Pay Act of 1963, passed as an amendment of the Fair Labor Standards Act of 1938, requires that men and women working for the same organization be paid the same rate of pay for work that is substantially equal.

Title VII of the Civil Rights Act of 1964. Title VII of the Civil Rights Act of 1964 prohibits employment discrimination based on race, color, sex, religion, and national origin. Title VII also provided for six exemptions to this law:

1. Bona fide occupational qualifications

2. Seniority systems

3. Pre-employment inquiries

4. Testing

5. Veterans preference rights

6. National security

The most important of these for clubs is the **bona fide occupational qualifications (BFOQs)** exceptions that permit some legal discrimination based on the need to hire certain types of people for specific jobs. Under this provision, some discrimination based on sex, religion, and national origin is acceptable if there is a BFOQ that makes it necessary. An example of a BFOQ in the club industry would be female attendants in a women's locker room.

Age Discrimination in Employment Act of 1967. The Age Discrimination in Employment Act of 1967 (ADEA) prohibits employers from discriminating against persons aged 40 or older on the basis of age. All employment actions—hiring, recruiting, appraising, promoting, advertising, and so on—that affect employees 40 or older are subject to the provisions of this act. The ADEA stipulates that employers cannot discriminate on the basis of age (for persons over 40) in any way.

Occupational Safety and Health Act of 1970. While not really an employment discrimination law, the Occupational Safety and Health Act of 1970 (OSHA) does materially affect the relationship between employees and clubs. The essential provisions of OSHA make employers responsible for providing a safe and "sufficiently risk-free" workplace for employees. OSHA requires that employers post notices advising employees of various aspects of the OSHA law.

OSHA compliance officers may enter clubs and inspect the premises to determine compliance. Compliance officers can issue citations in eight categories:

1. Imminent danger
2. Willful or repeated violations
3. Serious danger
4. Nonserious danger
5. Failure to correct a violation
6. Willful violation that causes the death of an employee
7. Posting requirements
8. De minimis (or minimal) violations

Minimum penalties of $5,000 for each willful violation and penalties of up to $70,000 for repeated violations are possible. Most citations range from $400 to $500. Each workplace must also maintain a file on each employee detailing occupational illnesses or injuries. Most businesses report as many accidents as possible as "minor first-aid" to minimize recordkeeping requirements.

Vocational Rehabilitation Act of 1973. The Vocational Rehabilitation Act of 1973 requires all employers holding federal contracts of $25,000 or more to employ "qualified handicapped individuals" when "reasonable accommodations" can be made for them. This does not apply to most private clubs. However, it does apply to those private clubs that come under federal government supervision, such as military clubs.

Pregnancy Discrimination Act of 1978. Prior to enactment of the Pregnancy Discrimination Act of 1978, an employer could require an employee to take a pregnancy leave for a stipulated period or at a specific time in her pregnancy. This is no longer the case. In addition, this act prohibits employers from refusing to hire a pregnant applicant, so long as the applicant is able to perform the major functions of the job. Employers also cannot provide health coverage to employees that does not include pregnancy coverage or that imposes high costs for this type of coverage.

Immigration Reform and Control Act of 1986. The Immigration Reform and Control Act of 1986 (IRCA) was designed to regulate the employment of non-U.S. citizens in the United States. Employers with four or more employees are prohibited from discriminating against applicants on the basis of citizenship or nationality. This act also prohibits illegal aliens from working lawfully in the United States; employers, no matter how small, must verify that applicants are authorized to work in the United States within three days after their hire. Employers must do this by completing the Employment Eligibility Verification Form (Form I-9).

While IRCA does not allow for illegal discrimination, it does allow employers to show preference to U.S. citizens or nationals over aliens when hiring. For example, a club manager can legally discriminate by choosing an applicant who is a U.S. citizen over one who is not. Discharges and layoffs cannot be based on U.S. citizenship, however.

Employee Polygraph Protection Act of 1988. The Employee Polygraph Protection Act of 1988 prohibited the use of polygraphs in about 85% of the employment situations in which they previously had been used. Under this law, employees are protected from dismissal, discipline, or discrimination solely on the basis of their refusals to submit to a polygraph exam. An employer can still require polygraph tests if he or she is willing to state in writing that an employee is guilty of some wrongdoing. However, it is rarely wise for club managers to subject themselves or their clubs to the lawsuits that can arise from accusing employees of wrongdoing in writing. As experienced club managers know, it is often more difficult for a club to prove wrongdoing than it is for an accused employee to win a wrongful discharge lawsuit.

Drug Free Workplace Act of 1988. According to the U.S. Chamber of Commerce, drug and alcohol abuse cost the United States approximately $140 billion per year in lost productivity. Research has shown that this problem affects almost 95 percent of American companies.[2]

The Drug Free Workplace Act of 1988 does not require a drug-free work environment among all private employers; however, it does require federal contractors to establish policies and procedures that ensure that their organizations are free of drug abuse and to make a good-faith effort to sustain a drug-free working environment. Given the mood of the country regarding drug abuse and the employer awareness of the cost of such abuse, it seems probable that federal and state legislation providing for drug-free work environments among all businesses will be passed in the future.

Americans with Disabilities Act. On July 26, 1992, the Americans with Disabilities Act (ADA) became law. The ADA, known to its sponsors as the "Emancipation

Proclamation for the Disabled," forbids workplace discrimination against people with disabilities. The result of this legislation is that "protected group" legal status was created for approximately 43 million disabled U.S. citizens, two-thirds of whom are in the 16 to 64 age bracket and are regarded as chronically unemployed.[3]

Stringent penalties are outlined for employers who fail to comply with ADA provisions. For example, it is within a court's power to assess civil penalties against any employer to a maximum of $50,000 for a first violation, and up to $100,000 for subsequent violations. The ADA also provides for equitable remedies in job discrimination lawsuits, including job reinstatement, back pay, and even front pay for disabled applicants who were discriminated against by their potential employers.

An employer will be considered in violation of the law if employment practices are used that discriminate against the disabled—even if the discrimination was unintended. This is much like the adverse-impact provision of Title VII of the Civil Rights Act, upon which so many discrimination lawsuits have been filed since the act was passed in 1964. According to this provision, even employment practices that appear neutral yet have the result of adversely impacting the disabled will be considered discriminatory.

Defining disabilities under the ADA. According to the ADA, an individual is considered disabled who (1) has a physical or mental impairment that substantially limits one or more major life activities, (2) has a record of such an impairment, or (3) is regarded as having such an impairment. Therefore, the ADA does not apply only to those who use wheelchairs. For example, speech, visual, and hearing impairments as well as mental retardation and emotional illnesses are considered disabilities. In addition, people with cancer, heart disease, palsy, epilepsy, multiple sclerosis, arthritis, asthma, and diabetes are considered disabled, as are those with infections such as HIV (AIDS). Some learning disabilities are also considered disabilities. Drug or alcohol addiction is considered a disability if the person is participating in a supervised rehabilitation program or has undergone rehabilitation and is not currently using drugs or alcohol.

Qualifying for work under the ADA. Persons with disabilities are considered qualified if they can perform the **essential functions of a job** with or without **reasonable accommodation.** These two issues are critical ones for club managers to understand. "Essential functions" refers to job tasks that are fundamental to a job. For instance, "cooking skills" would be considered fundamental for a cook. However, the ability to hear spoken food orders would not be considered a fundamental skill. As a result, in a club kitchen in which servers inform cooks of food orders by speaking to the cooks, reasonable accommodation might be required to make cooking positions open to someone with a hearing disability.

"Reasonable accommodation" refers to what employers must do in order to make the workplace accessible to people with disabilities. As a general rule, employers are required to provide accommodations for the disabled unless it would impose an *undue hardship* on the employer. The issue of undue hardship is still being defined by the courts and will likely depend on the specific circumstances. According to the Equal Employment Opportunity Commission (EEOC), approximately 50 percent of people with disabilities require no reasonable accommodation. Of the remaining 50 percent, the EEOC believes that approximately 20 percent need accommodations that cost less than $50.[4]

According to the EEOC, the following would be considered reasonable accommodations (unless particular issues in a specific case made them unreasonable):

1. Making facilities accessible (constructing wheelchair ramps, widening isles, raising a cashier station on blocks for a person in a wheelchair, and so on).

2. Restructuring jobs (eliminating nonessential functions in a job).

3. Reassigning someone to a vacant job (moving employees to other jobs if they become unable to perform their present jobs).

4. Modifying work schedules (to allow for medical appointments, for example).

5. Modifying equipment or acquiring special equipment necessary for disabled individuals to perform essential job functions.

6. Providing readers or interpreters (for those who cannot read or are visually impaired).

What these "reasonable accommodations" mean is that clubs must make their work areas accessible and barrier-free so that disabled employees can be hired and can reach their work areas. Physical barriers—stairs, curbs, narrow doorways, and so on—must be modified to accommodate disabled employees, elevators must have audio cues or braille buttons for people who are visually impaired, and so on.

Family and Medical Leave Act. Passed in 1993, the Family and Medical Leave Act (FMLA) applies to employers with 50 or more employees and allows employees to take unpaid time off from work (up to 12 weeks per year) for certain medical and parental reasons. For example, the FMLA provides that employees, male or female, may take time off from work to care for a newborn child or a sick immediate-family member. Employers must allow this time off and "hold" the employee's position for a stipulated period of time. It's possible for state laws to allow employees more time off than the FMLA, in which case the state laws would supersede the federal laws. Therefore, club managers should consult with state equal-employment-opportunity officials to determine the amount of time an employee can take unpaid leave for family or medical reasons without penalty.

State and Local Laws. Nearly all states, and many localities, have equal-employment-opportunity laws. In many cases, these laws provide much broader protection than federal EEOC legislation. For example, while federal laws often provide protection for employees in companies with specific-sized payrolls, state laws often do not include this restriction. As a result, employers of all sizes, including most clubs, are generally required to follow state EEOC regulations. In addition, many states and municipalities have enacted laws that protect groups not included in federal protection plans. For example, some states and localities have passed "sexual preference" laws protecting gay men and women from discrimination. Because these provisions vary from state to state and city to city, club managers should not assume that compliance with federal laws is enough.

Recruitment

The fact that the U.S. population is growing at only about one percent annually while job growth is much higher has made recruitment a very difficult task. The inability of many hospitality organizations, including clubs, to convince employees that positions in their organizations represent good lifelong career opportunities contributes to the problem. The job of recruiting will also become harder because of the aging work force. Many clubs already realize that it often takes extra effort these days to recruit, hire, and retain the right employees. As a result, these clubs are quickly gaining an edge over the clubs that they compete with for employees.

The Recruitment Process

Recruitment should be thought of as a process. Much of the work in recruiting is done prior to actually placing any recruitment advertising. The recruitment process begins by reviewing the information contained in job analyses, job descriptions, and job specifications. After reviewing the information on these forms (and updating them if necessary), the process continues until desirable candidates are identified and encouraged to apply. The last step in the process is to evaluate the club's recruiting methods. Overall recruitment costs, costs per hire, the number of contacts made, and acceptance-offer ratios are all ways to measure the effectiveness of a club's recruitment process.

Club managers can recruit either from external sources (sources outside the club) or internal sources (from employees already working for the club). There are advantages and disadvantages to both approaches (see Exhibit 1). If club managers maintain adequate skills inventories, replacement charts, and succession charts, internal recruiting is easier because the managers have a better idea of which current employees can perform the needed skills of an open position and who might be interested in such a position. Many clubs use job postings on bulletin boards to let current employees know about job openings. Typically these postings include a complete job description and specification so that interested employees can read about the job's responsibilities and the skills needed.

Some club managers ask current employees for leads on external recruits. This helps managers locate friends and acquaintances of current employees; these potential recruits often have more realistic views about the advantages and disadvantages of working at the club than do other candidates. Another advantage to this method is that current employees typically refer only those friends whom they believe would make good employees. Some clubs have even offered bonuses to current employees who can help persuade friends or acquaintances to work at the club.

While sources for external recruiting differ depending on the local circumstances, those listed in Exhibit 2 represent good sources for many clubs.

Recruitment Advertising

Many hospitality organizations, including clubs, are guilty of breaking antidiscrimination laws in their employment advertising. A study published in *Personnel,*

Exhibit 1   Advantages and Disadvantages of Internal and External Recruiting

Internal Recruiting

Advantages

- Improves the morale of the promoted employee.
- Improves the morale of other employees who see future opportunities for themselves.
- Managers can better assess the abilities of internal recruits, since their performances have been observed over time.
- Internal recruiting for supervisory and management positions results in a succession of promotions (one to fill each vacated job), which reinforces the "internal career ladder."
- The cost of internal recruitment is lower than the cost of external recruitment.

Disadvantages

- Internal recruiting promotes "inbreeding."
- Internal recruiting can cause morale problems among those employees who were skipped over for promotion.
- Internal recruiting can have political overtones; some employees attribute internal promotions to friendships with managers and supervisors.
- Filling a gap in one department through internal recruiting may create an even more critical gap in another department.

External Recruiting

Advantages

- External recruiting brings new blood and new ideas into the company.
- Recruits from the outside can often provide not only new ideas but news about how and what competitors are doing.
- External recruits can provide a fresh look at your club, which sometimes reinforces the reasons current employees work for you. Consider, for example, the value of an external recruit saying such things as "You keep your kitchen much cleaner than they do at XYZ club where I used to work" or "The helpful attitude of employees here certainly makes this a more pleasant place to work than my old job."
- External recruiting sometimes avoids many of the political problems associated with internal recruiting.
- External recruiting serves as a form of advertising for the club (newspaper ads, posters, bulletin board notices, and so on remind the public of your products and services).

(Continued)

Exhibit 1   *(continued)*

Disadvantages

- It is more difficult to find a good fit with the club's culture and management philosophy when recruiting externally.

- Internal morale problems can develop if current employees feel that they have no opportunity to move up in the organization.

- It takes longer to orient external recruits than it does internal recruits.

- External recruiting can lower productivity over the short run because external recruits usually cannot produce as quickly or effectively as internal recruits.

- When employees believe that they could have done the job as well as the external recruit who was hired, political problems and personality conflicts can result.

---

based on evidence gleaned from nearly 40,000 newspaper ads, found that the hospitality industry accounted for approximately 19 percent of the illegal and questionable recruitment ads, even though the industry only posted about 4 percent of the total ads.[5] (No similar study has been conducted about the club industry specifically.) Specifying gender and age are still the most common abuses. Gender discrimination occurs in advertising most frequently when sex-specific terms such as "girl," "man," "woman," "maid," "waiter," "waitress," or "hostess" are used instead of generic terms such as "server" or "busperson" or even "waiter/waitress." Another form of discrimination is found in ads that specify certain age groups, such as "excellent opportunity for college student" or "part-time position for retiree." These are discriminatory because they discourage equally qualified applicants from other age groups.

Selection

Selecting the right person for the job is one of the most important functions a club manager performs. Conducted properly, selection will provide a club with the personnel the club needs to excel. However, selection that is conducted haphazardly or improperly will usually lead to wasted management time and effort, misuse of employee time and effort, and member discontent with the employees hired. It is important that managers take the selection process seriously. Managers shouldn't take shortcuts with the selection process or delegate selection to untrained managers or employees.

Elements of the Selection Process

Exhibit 3 illustrates basic steps in the selection process. The number of steps can vary. For example, materials produced by Training House, Inc., identify as many as 20 steps in the selection process. While clubs, by law, must accept and dutifully consider each application, it is also legal to establish club policies (based on BFOQs

Exhibit 2   External Recruiting Sources

- Employment agencies—state and private
- Schools—high school job fairs, club managers as guest speakers in classes, notices with guidance counselors, personal contact with teachers and coaches, participation in work-study programs
- Student organizations—Future Homemakers Association, Future Farmers of America, Distributive Education Clubs of America, and so on
- Colleges—job fairs, contact with placement counselors, club managers as classroom guest speakers, contact with teachers and coaches, participation in work-study programs, contact with campus social and professional clubs, hospitality management programs, dormitory counselors
- Churches and synagogues
- Youth groups
- Apartment complexes—laundry-room bulletins, doorknob brochures
- Apartment newsletters
- Local sports teams (sponsorship)
- Women's groups
- Child-care centers
- Professional and trade journals
- Libraries
- Craft centers
- Exercise centers
- Sales, supply, and machinery representatives
- Participation in community events
- Senior-citizen groups
- Governmental division-on-aging unit
- Agencies for the disabled
- Urban League and other agencies that provide skills training and job placement—Vietnam Refugee Fund, Mexican-American Opportunity Foundation, and so on
- Government rehabilitation agencies
- Government veterans agencies
- Chamber of Commerce
- Social/health organizations such as YMCA or YWCA
- Social service organizations such as the American Red Cross or the Salvation Army
- Volunteer groups—League of Women Voters, homeless shelters, health agencies, and so on

(Continued)

Exhibit 2   *(continued)*

- Welcome organizations—Welcome Wagon, Hello Club, Newcomers, and so on
- Military agencies—reserve and active units of the local National Guard
- Open job fairs
- Employees at other hospitality companies or service-oriented organizations that you meet while dining out, shopping, or doing other day-to-day activities
- State American Hotel & Motel Association
- State restaurant associations
- Local chapters of the Club Managers Association of America
- Local and state assistance programs—for example, clothing and food drives for the needy
- Ads in local "pennysaver" and other low- and no-cost papers

and job descriptions that specify skills required of applicants) that eliminate applicants early in the process if they are deemed unsatisfactory.

While selection methods vary from club to club, most selection programs contain common elements. In the following sections we will discuss selection elements that most club managers address when selecting employees: application blanks, pre-employment tests, employment interviews, and reference checks.

Application Blanks. The purpose of **application blanks** is to learn what applicants have done in the past. An application blank typically asks an applicant to report on his or her employment history, educational background, work references, personal references, and other personal data.

Application blanks should not be too long. Excessively long or complex applications can discourage potential applicants and cause concern over whether all of the questions on the form are truly job-related. On the other hand, application blanks that are too short can fail to collect the information needed to assess the ability of an applicant to perform the job.

Questions on application blanks must relate to bona fide occupational qualifications. Therefore, questions that require applicants to reveal their gender, age, birthplace, race, marital or family status, sexual preferences, religion, military record, or convictions or arrests not related directly to the job at hand are all illegal. Asking applicants for photographs and specific types of references (religious, military, and so on) are also potentially illegal.

Many application blanks in the past included questions such as "Do you suffer from any permanent ailment or disease?" and "Have you ever suffered a serious accident while on the job?" Some application blanks included sections that asked applicants to identify any disabilities that they had (hearing, visual, and so on). While some organizations still use application blanks with these types of questions on them, such questions are illegal under provisions of the Americans with

Exhibit 3 Basic Steps in the Selection Process

1. Confirm that an opening exists
2. Review the job description for the position for clarity and responsibilities
3. Review the job specification to identify qualifications applicants should possess
4. Identify sources of applicants
5. Review applications
6. Select an interviewing environment
7. Select an interviewing strategy
8. Develop questions to ask during interviews
9. Conduct interviews
10. Close interviews
11. Evaluate candidates
12. Check the candidates' references
13. Select a candidate

Disabilities Act unless they are proven to be specifically job-related. Since in most cases this is very hard to prove, as a general rule clubs should eliminate such questions from their applications.

Pre-Employment Tests. Pre-employment tests represent an attractive selection method to managers because they are an easy way to compare candidates. A candidate who scored 90 on a test would appear to be a more attractive candidate than one who scored 80 on the same test. However, using tests to evaluate candidates can often lead to charges of discrimination.

Tests, especially general intelligence and mechanical-comprehension tests, were used widely in the 1950s and 1960s as selection devices. However, after the passage of Title VII of the Civil Rights Act of 1964, tests became the focus of many discrimination suits. The first testing issue was to demonstrate the job-relatedness of the tests. In many cases, tests used prior to the Civil Rights Act were not job-related. The second issue that came under fire was the validity of the tests. In many court cases, companies using tests as selection devices were unable to prove that the results were valid predictors of job success. Pre-employment tests may only be used if the employer can prove that they are accurate predictors of job performance. While most clubs may never be forced to prove this, it is safer to avoid this problem by not using tests that do not relate directly to work issues.

Another potential problem with pre-employment tests is unintentional discrimination. Employment tests cannot discriminate against certain protected groups even if there is no intention for this to happen.

Employment Interviews. There are several problems associated with interviewing applicants. The one that receives the most attention is the inability of an interviewer to determine in a single interview whether an applicant can perform all of the functions of a job and fit in well with the organization's culture. This problem can sometimes be overcome through using a system of two separate interviews with a different interviewer each time; this system allows a club to get two opinions of an applicant. Unfortunately, this system also has problems. The principal problem with two interviews is related to the issue of inter-rater reliability. If two interviewers interview the same candidate, it is unlikely that they will arrive at the same conclusions. While both might agree on general issues, it is unlikely that they will agree on the more subjective issues such as the likelihood of the applicant's success in the posted job. Some of the other problems associated with interviewing reliability are outlined in Exhibit 4.

Preparing for interviews. A club manager's likelihood of collecting useful information during an interview can be substantially enhanced by following a few simple rules:

1. Do your homework before the interview. Completely read the applicant's application or résumé prior to the meeting.

2. Establish an appropriate setting.

3. Ensure that you will not be interrupted during the interview.

4. Establish a rapport and put the applicant at ease by asking the applicant to tell you about his or her accomplishments.

5. Prepare questions in advance (including follow-up questions).

6. Know the job and its specifications.

Reading from a candidate's résumé during the interview signals to the candidate that you either did not care enough to prepare in advance or that you are unorganized. Establishing an appropriate setting is critical; a private spot is usually best. Generally, a club manager should block out whatever time is needed to conduct the interview and focus solely on the candidate (no phone calls or other interruptions). Establishing a rapport is important in order to get the applicant talking; you can learn much more from an applicant by putting him or her at ease. Knowing the job in advance can be achieved by thoroughly reviewing the position's job analysis and job description prior to conducting an interview.

Types of interviews. Interviews fall into three categories, depending on the degree of latitude allowed the interviewer: unstructured interviews, semistructured interviews, and structured interviews. These are also known as nondirective, mixed, and patterned interviews, respectively.

Unstructured interviews are probably the most commonly used. In unstructured interviews, questions are not planned in advance. Instead, the interviewer directs the interview down whatever path seems appropriate at the time. Some experts believe that unstructured interviews are likely to skip over important job-related issues; others believe that skilled interviewers can use this method to achieve a better understanding of the candidate, since areas can be explored that both semistructured and structured interviews might miss.

When using a **semistructured interview,** a club manager plans out what issues will be explored, but allows for flexibility during the interview. Typically the

Exhibit 4   Common Problems Associated with Interviewing

Similarity Error

Many interviewers are predisposed to react positively to candidates who are similar to themselves (in outside interests, personal background, and even appearance) and react negatively to candidates very different from themselves.

Contrast Error

Candidates should be compared to the standards that the club has established for the position, not to each other. Comparing candidates to one another, whether consciously or subconsciously, is particularly troublesome when two poor candidates are followed by a merely average candidate. Because of the contrast between candidates, the average candidate may be viewed as excellent, resulting in a contrast error.

Overweighting Negative Information

It is human nature to notice negative information more than positive information. When we examine a résumé or an application, we tend to look for the negative, not the positive. This also happens in interviews.

First-Impression Error

Many interviewers tend to form a strong first impression of a candidate that they maintain throughout the interview.

Halo Effect

Sometimes an interviewer's favorable impression of a single dimension about a candidate—appearance, background, and so on—can substantially color his or her overall impression. The halo effect occurs when an interviewer views everything that a candidate says or does in this favorable light.

Devil's Horns

The opposite of the halo effect. This phenomenon can often cause interviewers to see everything a candidate says or does in an unfavorable light.

Faulty Listening and Memory

Interviewers do not always hear what is said in the way it was intended, nor do they remember everything that was said.

Recency Errors

An interviewer is likely to remember a candidate's most recent behaviors or responses, rather than behaviors or responses that occurred earlier in the interview.

Nonverbal Factors

Nonverbal factors such as clothing, smiles, speech patterns, and eye contact substantially influence an interviewer's impression of candidates. Some interviewers make up their minds about whom to hire based almost solely on the candidate's attire and demeanor.

manager will prepare very broad or open-ended questions about the topics he or she wants to cover and allow the candidate to speak freely about each topic.

In **structured interviews,** questions are fully prepared in advance and are asked in the same way at the same time during each interview. Very little flexibility is allowed. This makes it easier for club managers to compare the answers the job

Insider Insights

John Jordan, CCM, General Manager
Cherokee Town & Country Club, Atlanta, Georgia

When we need to recruit someone, we start with what we call a profile. We use a profile for every skilled position. If you could invent the world's greatest chef, or golf pro, or whatever position you're considering, what attributes and qualities would that person have? We put that in a profile. The profile will say that the sort of individual we're looking for has certain qualities, certain work experiences, and other criteria. We then put the profile into a set format.

Now you've got a description of the world's most perfect "whomever you're looking for." Let's say it's a chef. Then, from the chef profile, we develop questions. The questions help us discover how well an applicant matches up with the world's greatest chef.

Then we devise a rating scale. I have a big thing about integrity and honesty, so let's say on a 100-point scale, integrity and honesty get 40 points. Then, I'd make experience worth 30 points, education 20 points, and give 10 points for culinary shows or competitions. That's not one of the scales we use at the club, I'm just making this up to illustrate a point. Now we develop questions to get information on these topics from applicants. Using the answers to these questions, we make certain determinations about the individuals we're considering for the chef position. We find out that candidate A has had three jobs in three months. Why? We delve into it and find out she was caught stealing a case of 109 prime ribs and on and on and on. Well, perhaps we might give her a zero in integrity. Candidate B borrowed a knife as an apprentice and somehow the knife got lost in his tool kit. Twelve years later he found it and flew from where he was working—New Orleans—to Seattle, Washington, where he served his apprenticeship, to return the knife to its rightful owner. He would get the full 40 integrity points. If you have lots of candidates to choose from, these scores help you compare them and make a decision.

Some people who are really into wines wouldn't think of drinking a wine that didn't score at least 90 or above on a scale of 100. Well, the truth is, very few wines rate that kind of score. And very few people can afford to be that picky. I've found that when I'm interviewing candidates for an assistant manager job, very few rate in the 90s. Generally they score in the 80s, usually because they're just getting out of school and they don't have a lot of experience yet. So we don't say that until we get a perfect 100 we won't hire anyone. That's not practical. No applicant is ever going to achieve 100 points on a 100-point scale. You're going to be hard-pressed to even find people in the 90s. You're probably going to hire, using my methodology, people in the 80s. What you try to do after they're on the job is grow them into the 90s.

You've got to be careful with your hiring profiles, though, because time marches on. Take a maintenance engineer: what was important 20 or 30 years ago, I don't know that I'd use those same hiring criteria today. Today I'd want an engineering applicant to have some computer skills and know how to use a computerized maintenance program that tells him that every quarter he should

(continued)

Insider Insights *(continued)*

put grease in the grease-fittings on the air-handling units, and so on. Thirty years ago, an applicant would have had zero computer skills. All I'm suggesting is that periodically you need to look at your profiles and update them. Then, once you update them, obviously you've got to change your questions and point scales accordingly.

I believe in promoting from within as much as possible. I also believe in not putting someone in a supervisory position without giving him or her supervisory training. We make sure new supervisors get supervisory training, and we try to make sure they get something out of the training. We might ask them, "What five things did you learn from the seminar you just attended and how are you going to apply them to your position?" We hold them accountable for staying awake, paying attention, and participating in the training.

Certainly it's a big morale boost if you know that if you work hard and do well and know the position, there's a distinct possibility you can advance. On the other hand, there are employees who do a marvelous job, are very happy doing it, and don't want to be a supervisor. Not everyone wants to advance. You have to be careful—just because John is a great food server doesn't mean he'll be a great supervisor. Sometimes managers get caught up in taking the very best workers and making them supervisors without giving them the training. That's frustrating for the people promoted and frustrating for the people being supervised.

Today's management theories emphasize self-managed teams. I believe very strongly in self-directed work teams and we're working toward establishing them here at the club. If we're going to survive the cost of operating a club, we've got to get more efficient and more effective. Eventually we're going to get to the point that our work teams will do the interviewing and hiring. We'll give them guidelines to follow, but they're going to interview and hire their co-workers. We haven't gotten there yet, but we will. People who are hired by their teammates probably won't let the team down. Very few people ever have the opportunity to be part of a first-class team, and once people get that opportunity, they usually cling to it for dear life.

I have an analogy that illustrates a theory I have about employees. You can get a good radial tire for $75; you can get a recap for $20. Certainly $20 is a lot less expensive than $75. But the radial will take you 60,000 miles; with the recap you'll be lucky to go 5,000 miles. So when you compare cost per mile, the cost of the radial tire is a great deal less than the cost of the recap. Therefore, even though the initial expense is more, you're much better off with the radial. I feel the same way about employees. The very best employees you can hire will also be much more cost-effective for the organization in the long run because they'll do better work, they're more highly motivated, and so on. I look for the very best and pay them accordingly. I believe in finding out what the market prices are for the skill levels and in paying just above those prices. Whatever percentage above the market I am, I get it back many times over because I get top-quality people who do fantastic work and are self-motivated.

For high-skill jobs, I would say networking is the best way to recruit. For lower-skill jobs, you start with newspaper ads. But there are times when you have

(continued)

Insider Insights *(continued)*

to get creative. For example, we've had difficulty finding teenagers to work the pool and snack bars in the summer. One day it struck me that what we ought to do is recruit workers from the school lunch programs. We have a member at the club who sells institutional food service equipment and knows all the school lunch people. And I thought, why don't we go to these workers and find a few who would like some extra income during the summer? The school system probably doesn't pay them a whole lot more than minimum wage, which certainly we could beat. Maybe we hire three of them so they still have some summertime off as well. If you need 60 hours, you hire three of them at 20 hours each, that sort of thing. Sometimes finding people is a question of being creative. You've got to sit down and think of all the things you can do to find good people.

candidates gave to the questions. However, this approach tends to produce information that is narrower or shallower; issues are typically not explored in depth with this approach.

Legal do's and don'ts in interviews. Club managers must be careful not to break any laws during interviews. Important points for club managers to remember include the following:

- Only ask questions that relate directly to the job.

- Do not ask applicants questions that could be construed as discriminatory, such as questions about race, national origin, or religion.

- Do not ask applicants about their family lives. Their family life has no bearing on whether they qualify for the job.

- Do not promise terms of employment. Even pointing out examples of employees who have worked at the club for long periods could be considered an indirect promise of long-term employment.

- Do not, under any circumstances, inquire about personal relationships. Such questions can be construed as sexual harassment.

Reference Checks. Checking references should be an integral part of the selection process. As many as 30 percent of the résumés in the United States contain at least one major fabrication. Many of these fabrications relate to either educational accomplishments or past work experience. According to the FBI, there are as many as 100 diploma factories in the United States that issue up to 15,000 phony educational diplomas each year.[6] One company reported that up to 25 percent of the MBAs it has checked on over the years were fraudulent.[7]

Failing to conduct a thorough reference check can leave a club open to negligent-hiring lawsuits. "Negligent hiring" is commonly defined as an employer's failure to exercise reasonable care in the selection of its employees. It is becoming more common for employers to be sued for not taking reasonable precautions to protect their customers or guests from the actions of employees. Restaurant delivery companies have been successfully sued, for example, for criminal acts committed by delivery drivers, and hotels have been successfully sued for criminal acts by maintenance people and other employees with access to guestrooms or opportunities for confronting guests in secluded settings.[8]

When checking references, club managers should maintain a genuine concern for the privacy of the applicant. In fact, a number of states have passed laws to protect an employee's or potential employee's right to privacy. Therefore, as a general rule, club managers should review the appropriate state legislation regarding this issue prior to undertaking any action.

Credit reference checks. Many companies have begun using credit references to evaluate the character of job applicants.[9] However, club managers should be forewarned that this practice has come under close scrutiny for its potential to violate individual-privacy provisions of the Fair Credit Reporting Act.

Third-party reference checks. Club managers can hire a third party to check the references of an applicant. Pre-employment background checks can cost as little as $75, depending on the depth of information required. Perhaps as many as 25 percent of U.S. firms now use such agencies.[10] Using these agencies can save managers a lot of time.

How should club managers respond when asked for a reference? A survey by the Society of Human Resource Managers revealed that most of the information released on reference checks relate to either employment dates (96 percent of respondents released such information) or position/responsibility issues (89 percent of respondents released information on these issues).[11] Issues that could be of more value in making employment selection decisions have much lower response rates, such as salary information (43 percent responded), reason for leaving (30 percent), performance evaluation information (6 percent), rehire eligibility (3 percent), and medical history (1 percent). The reason for this is that ours is a litigious society. As a result, many employers are reluctant to report on the past performance of employees for fear of someday ending up in court. Club managers who want to play it safe should only report a person's job title and dates of employment. The best rule of thumb for club managers is to secure written permission from employees before releasing any other information about them.

Orientation

Employee turnover in hospitality companies often averages as much as 200 to 300 percent per year. This does not mean that the entire staff turns over from 2 to 3 times every year. Instead, turnover of this magnitude is usually characterized by very high rates of turnover in the first 30 days on the job for certain positions and by diminishing rates after that. Much of the turnover that occurs within the first 30 days can be attributed to employees getting poor starts on their new jobs.

On the first day of a new job, a new employee is faced with new surroundings, work rules, responsibilities, bosses, and co-workers. At best, all this newness will make a new employee feel somewhat insecure. At worst, it will provoke a feeling of anxiety that the employee cannot get over that will eventually drive the employee to quit. When turnover of this type occurs, all the time and money spent in locating, recruiting, selecting, and hiring the employee is wasted.

Exhibit 5   Checklist for Orientation Planning

- Determine orientation goals
- Identify the range of topics that should be covered
- Determine the time and duration of orientation sessions
- Divide orientation topics into club, departmental, and job topics
- Build enough flexibility into the orientation to allow for differences in education and work experience among new employees
- Identify the new-employee training that will be done by the club's human resources department (if applicable)
- Identify the new-employee training that managers and supervisors will conduct
- Provide any training that managers and supervisors might need in order to conduct an effective orientation program and train new employees
- Ensure that the social aspects of orientation are covered as well as the technical
- Brainstorm methods for encouraging employee discussion and feedback during the orientation
- Review and update (if necessary) the employee handbook before giving it to new employees

Source: Adapted from Wayne F. Cascio, *Managing Human Resources: Productivity, Quality of Work Life, Profits* (New York: McGraw-Hill, 1989), p. 228.

Orientation programs are intended to reduce the stress that employees feel when beginning a new job. However, ineffectively conducted orientations can actually increase the pressure new employees feel. Exhibit 5 is a checklist club managers can use to help them create an orientation program. Effective orientation programs are typically divided into two sections: general property orientation and specific job orientation.

Employees should first be oriented to the club as a whole. During the **general property orientation,** issues such as insurance, benefits, personnel forms, general policies and procedures, club member and employee relations, the club's mission statement and management philosophy, and the role of employees in helping the club meet club goals are the focus of the orientation.[12]

During the **specific job orientation,** the focus shifts from organizational and departmental issues to subjects that relate directly to the performance of specific job responsibilities. During this stage, employees should be introduced to the specific responsibilities outlined in the job description, the location of their work area(s) in relation to other club areas, the location of equipment, performance appraisal forms used within the department for the specific job, and specific portions of the employee handbook that relate to job responsibilities. During this orientation phase, new employees also should be taken on a tour of the property and introduced to personnel with whom they will work and come in contact.

Orientation Kits

Many club managers prepare orientation kits that new employees can take home with them to study (see Exhibit 6). This enables employees to review the material

Exhibit 6   Sample Items in an Orientation Kit

- Current organization chart
- Projected organization chart (illustrating succession)
- Map of the club
- Key terms unique to the club industry, the club, and the job
- Copy of the club's employee or policy handbook
- Copy of the club's union contract (if applicable)
- Copy of specific job goals and descriptions
- List of holidays and other days off given to club employees
- List of employee fringe benefits
- Copies of performance appraisal forms
- Copies of other club forms (requisitions, expense forms, and so on)

and share the information with their families. While going through their orientation kits, employees may think of questions to ask on the following day.

Although Exhibit 6's list is a good start, clubs should consider adding the following items to their orientation kits:

- Copies of EEOC notices, and company policies regarding compliance

- Recent club newsletters

- Names and telephone numbers of other employees in the department

- A schedule of remaining orientation sessions

- Information regarding family activities associated with the club (a summer picnic for employees and their families, for example)

Training

Training magazine conducted a survey of more than 2,500 U.S. organizations to evaluate the amount of money spent on training in the United States. According to the study, roughly $40 billion is spent each year on formal off-the-job training.[13] While no estimate of the money spent for on-the-job training is available, costs are undoubtedly just as high.

The Training Cycle

Effective training does not happen by accident; it takes careful planning. Training should be viewed as a continuous cycle rather than a single event. This cycle is depicted in Exhibit 7 and consists of the following steps:

- Develop and conduct needs assessment

- Identify training objectives

Exhibit 7   The Training Cycle

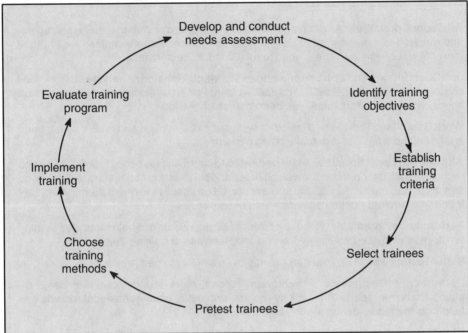

- Establish training criteria
- Select trainees
- Pretest trainees
- Choose training methods
- Implement training
- Evaluate the training program

Develop and Conduct Needs Assessment. The training cycle "begins" when club managers conduct a needs assessment—essentially an identification of a problem or a discrepancy between a desired outcome at the club and what is really occurring. A variety of needs-assessment techniques are available to club managers; some common techniques are presented in Exhibit 8. No single method can be recommended for all circumstances or environments; club managers should choose the methods that best suit their objectives and their clubs.

Identify Training Objectives. In the second step of the training cycle, club managers develop training objectives. Objectives vary, of course, depending on many circumstances. Some objectives will lead directly to improved service for club members, while others may lead to better productivity or reduced costs.

It's important for club managers to state training objectives in clear and measurable terms. Objectives such as "increase employee job satisfaction" and "improve member service" are too vague. However, "reduce employee turnover

Exhibit 8   Methods of Conducting a Needs Analysis

Advisory Committee: A committee—typically composed of club members, managers, and employees—reviews job skills and behavior demands and compares these to the current level of employee performance relative to those demands.

Job Descriptions and Job Specifications Task-and-Behavior Analysis: This method compares the knowledge, skills, and abilities identified in current job descriptions and job specifications to current employee performance on the job.

Work Sampling: This method includes systematic observation and review by a trained analyst of the work that is actually being performed.

Attitude Surveys: Not all training is dedicated to improving task completion. Most clubs recognize that appropriate employee attitudes and behaviors are critical to providing good service to club members. Attitude surveys can be an effective way to determine whether training is required on the behavioral side of service.

Performance Appraisals: Regular performance appraisals can help managers identify employees who need additional training and the types of training they need.

Skills Tests: Skills tests measure an employee's ability to perform tasks.

Performance Documents: Absenteeism reports, sales reports, club-member complaints, turnover reports, productivity reports, and many other operational records can help club managers determine training needs.

Club Member Feedback: Member feedback can help managers determine areas where additional training is needed.

Questionnaires: Questionnaires are a useful means of collecting training-needs information because of the large amount of data that can be easily and cheaply collected.

Exit Interviews: Employees or managers leaving the club are often willing to provide information that can help club managers determine where training needs exist.

Critical Incidents: This method requires observers (managers or outsiders) to notice and record specific incidents that are examples of either good or poor performance. These examples can point to areas where employees need additional training.

---

by 10 percent this year as a measure of increased job satisfaction" would be a recognizable and measurable objective.

Establish Training Criteria. The third step in the training cycle is the establishment of training criteria. Objectives refer to what training is supposed to accomplish; criteria are benchmarks that allow managers to measure whether the training objectives were accomplished. Specific knowledge learned, behaviors displayed, ability to perform specific tasks, and many other benchmarks or goals all represent effective training criteria.

Select Trainees. The fourth step consists of selecting trainees. Trainees can be either new or veteran employees. Club managers should take care to select employees for whom the training will be worthwhile. Too often, training programs

Club Policies and Programs for Employees	
Program	**Percent of Clubs**
Safety Program	68%
Employee Manual	87%
Formal Training Program	61%
Employee Orientation	63%
Formal, Written Employee Evaluations	77%
Formal Grievance Procedure	53%
Cafeteria Plan of Employee Benefits	37%
Training Program on the HIV Virus	10%
Employee Assistance Program	17%
Carpooling Program	3%
Handicapped Parking	54%
Daycare/Daycare Assistance	4%
Anti-Harassment Policy	72%
Substance Abuse Policy	56%

Source: Club Managers Association of America, Club Operations and Financial Data Report (Alexandria, Virginia: CMAA, 1996), p. 20.

are either too simple or too complex for the trainees selected. Both errors will result in an ineffective training program.

Pretest Trainees. The training cycle's fifth step is pretesting employees to establish the "baseline" or "before-training" knowledge, skills, or abilities that the employees possess. Club managers can evaluate the effectiveness of the training program by comparing post-training test results with pretraining test results. If no baseline of knowledge, skills, or abilities is identified prior to the training, it is difficult, if not impossible, to judge how effective the training was.

Choose Training Methods. The sixth step in the training cycle is selecting the proper training methods to use. Training methods vary substantially, depending on the training program, the criteria developed for evaluating learning, and the current level of employee performance.

To be effective, a training method should enable a trainer to:

- Motivate trainees to improve their performance
- Clearly demonstrate desired skills

- Provide for active participation by trainees
- Provide an opportunity for trainees to practice
- Provide timely feedback on trainee performance
- Provide some means for reinforcement while trainees learn
- Move from simple to complex tasks
- Be adaptable to specific problems
- Encourage transfer of learning from the training environment to the job[14]

There are a variety of training methods available to club managers. Generally, these methods can be divided into two groups: off-the-job training methods and on-the-job training methods.

Off-the-job training methods. Training that takes place in an environment other than the actual workplace is called off-the-job training. Common off-the-job training methods include the following:

- Lectures
- Vestibule training
- Programmed instruction
- Case-study training
- In-basket training
- Role playing
- Behavioral modeling
- Business games
- Conference training

Lectures. Perhaps the most common form of off-the-job training is **lectures.** This method is appropriate when information must be passed on to a large audience. Advantages of this approach are that a great deal of information can be delivered in a relatively short time to a large group. The lecture method is also very cost-effective.

Disadvantages of lectures include the lack of two-way communication in most lectures and the fact that there is no allowance for varying levels of understanding among participants. Because of this second problem, some participants may find a lecture boring and slow while others in the same audience may have trouble keeping up.

Vestibule training. Also called simulation training, **vestibule training** involves the duplication of parts of the work environment in an off-site location. The advantage of using this environment rather than the actual workplace is that training can take place without interrupting the normal flow of business. While this method usually results in a fairly high level of learning, it also can be expensive. Some training done in clubs is well-suited for this method. For instance, club managers can train employees to use a club restaurants' electronic point-of-sale terminal by simply setting up a similar terminal in an empty room.

Programmed instruction. **Programmed instruction** is designed to allow trainees to learn at their own pace. Originally, programmed instruction was accomplished through instruction booklets or manuals. Paper-and-pencil tests were used to evaluate whether trainees had learned enough to proceed to the next booklet/manual. Today, in many cases, these paper-based instructional materials have been replaced by computers. Computerized training programs are sometimes referred to as computer-assisted instruction. The principal disadvantage of computerized programmed instruction is the start-up cost.

Case-study training. Typically, **case studies** detail a series of events, either real or hypothetical, that take place in a business environment. Participants are asked to sort through data provided in the case to identify the principal issues and then propose solutions to the dilemmas these issues pose. An example of a case study can be found at the end of this chapter.

Case studies can be particularly useful in developing the problem-solving skills of trainees. One disadvantage to this approach is that the cases take place in a vacuum—that is, the trainees are in a classroom or some other training setting and are allowed to concentrate on one case at a time, while managers and employees often have to make decisions while facing many other problems or dilemmas simultaneously.

In-basket training. With **in-basket training,** trainees usually confront a wide array of problems, such as those they might find in their in-baskets at work. When used as a training tool, the in-basket method is designed to train participants in how to identify which issues require an immediate response, how to delegate authority to others to solve problems that do not require personal attention, and how to work on several problems simultaneously. When used as a selection tool, the in-basket method is often used to see which problems managerial candidates choose to deal with first and how well they delegate authority to others. Research has shown that this method is effective in predicting future job behavior.[15]

Role playing. **Role plays** typically are either portrayals of real work situations or exaggerations of such situations. The purpose of role playing is to allow participants to experience real-world situations in a controlled setting. For example, in a training session designed to teach participants how to deal with angry club members appropriately, one participant might play the role of the angry club member while another plays the role of an employee.

The principal advantage of role playing is that real emotions and feelings are generally evoked by this type of training. Because four principles of learning are involved (active participation, modeling, feedback, and practice), learning is usually quite high when the role play is done properly.[16] Since it is important that participants get thoroughly into their roles in order for learning to take place, a major task of the training facilitator is to encourage involvement.

Behavioral modeling. Most human behavior is learned by observing others. **Behavioral modeling** provides participants with the opportunity to actually see how someone acts in a certain situation, rather than simply being told how to act.

Several steps must be taken in sequence for behavioral modeling to be effective:

1. A specific interpersonal skill is introduced (usually via lecture).
2. A model acts the skill (either on video or in real life).
3. Key points in the acting are highlighted by the trainer.
4. Trainees practice the skill by role-playing with other trainees.
5. Feedback on the role playing is provided by the trainer and other participants.

The advantage of this type of training is the emphasis on doing rather than telling. Using this approach, for example, club managers can be *shown* how to delegate authority, conduct a meeting, or discipline an employee. The role of the facilitator in this process is to encourage the participants to closely imitate the behaviors seen in the model.[17] Most research has shown that this form of training is an effective way to teach supervisors and others to develop more effective interpersonal skills.[18]

The disadvantages of this approach are that the training method is limited to behavioral issues and that the training facilitator must be adept at conducting sessions. However, since so much of club management is related to interpersonal-skill issues, this method often represents an excellent form of training for club managers and supervisors.

Business games. **Business games** allow participants to learn how to deal with a variety of issues in a simulated business environment. Commercial forms of this type of training (board games, computer simulations, and so on) are available from a wide variety of sources. The advantages of business games are that the games are fun, they provide a setting that simulates reality, and many issues can be introduced using the same game. Disadvantages include the cost and the fact that some participants sometimes become engrossed in winning the games and forget the learning intended.[19]

Conference training. **Conference training** consists of one-on-one discussions between the trainer and a trainee. In such a setting, virtually any issue can be explored in depth. The obvious advantage is the close contact between trainer and trainee. Disadvantages include the time and cost of such training.

On-the-job training methods. While on-the-job training can be a very effective method of learning, unfortunately it is often done incorrectly. Typically, when this method is used, one employee is simply asked to teach another some desired skill. In far too many cases, the employees doing the training are assigned to do so not because of their ability to teach, but simply because they perform the tasks or behaviors well themselves. However, being good at a job does not necessarily make someone an effective trainer. On the other hand, when done correctly, this training can be very cost-efficient (because the training can be conducted during business operations), and effective (because of the resemblance this method has to behavioral modeling). In addition, since training is done on the job, trainees typically learn the things they really need to know.

However, there are disadvantages to this approach. In addition to the mishandling of training assignments discussed earlier, this type of training sometimes interferes with normal business. Also, because the pace is usually fast, there's little

Exhibit 9   Steps in Job-Instruction Training

Step 1: Prepare the Employee
- Put the employee at ease
- Arouse interest in training

Step 2: Present the Task or Skill
- Tell
- Show
- Explain
- Demonstrate
- Allow time for questions and repeat steps if necessary

Step 3: Try Out the Performance
- Allow the employee to try on his or her own
- Have the employee explain key points
- Correct errors
- Re-instruct if necessary

Step 4: Follow Up
- Allow the employee to perform on his or her own
- Check on the employee frequently
- Gradually reduce assistance

time for feedback or reiteration of important steps. This type of training tends to perpetuate the status quo, too. Trainees are very likely to copy the mistakes their trainers make as well as their good qualities.

Job-instruction training. **Job-instruction training (JIT)** is a structured approach to training that requires trainees to proceed through a series of steps in a sequential pattern (see Exhibit 9). This type of training is good for task-oriented jobs, such as operating equipment or preparing food. However, job-instruction training is not a good method for behavioral training.

Job rotation. **Job rotation** moves trainees from one job to another. This method is widely used in training club managers, many of whom spend a certain number of weeks in various club jobs prior to assuming their managerial duties. Advantages of this approach are that trainees are able to see how work is performed in many jobs and they get to know a lot of employees as they progress from position to position. In addition, when used to train employees, the method can provide a club with employees who are cross-trained. However, how much learning takes place with this type of training depends on how training is conducted at each stop along the rotation. If on-the-job training is used in each assignment, oftentimes the trainee doesn't learn very much.

Implement Training. The seventh step of the training cycle is the implementation of the training program itself. This is the stage where the trainees actually receive the training. Proper implementation is just as important to the success of a training program as the proper selection of methods, trainers, and trainees. Even managers who plan their training programs thoroughly sometimes fumble the ball when it comes to actually implementing their plans. Careful follow-through on all details is critical in the implementation stage.

Evaluate the Training Program. The eighth and final step in the training cycle is training evaluation. Unfortunately, many managers—even those who are good at identifying training needs, selecting the proper approach to training, and conducting training—fail to effectively evaluate whether the training goals they established earlier were achieved.

There are several reasons for this. The first is that managers often see some change in the trained employees and simply assume that the training has had an effect. Managers also tend to assume that training works, with or without observing any changes. In addition, in many cases managers take ownership of a training program because they were the force behind promoting the program; because of this, the managers simply do not want to go through an objective evaluation for fear that this might reveal that the training program was not worthwhile. Some managers don't conduct training evaluations simply because they don't know how to do them.

Effective training evaluation consists primarily of re-visiting the training objectives and criteria to find out whether the goals of the training program were met. This can be accomplished through managerial evaluations, employee feedback, post-training tests, member evaluations, third-party evaluations, or a combination of these methods.

Evaluation

More than 90 percent of all U.S. organizations use some sort of employee evaluation or appraisal system.[20] However, because so many managers don't use performance appraisals correctly, appraisals often fail to achieve their intended purpose.

Evaluating someone's performance is often difficult. One expert described the difficulties associated with performance appraisals by likening them to telling someone, "Here's what I think of your baby."[21] No matter what you say, the employee receiving the appraisal may think of you as a heel.

Performance appraisals are subject to human emotions, human judgments, and, therefore, human errors. They are never likely to be completely objective. It should not be surprising, therefore, to learn that in one survey, 70 percent of employees indicated that their performance appraisals failed to provide them with a clear picture of what was expected of them.[22] But does this mean that club managers should junk the system and not evaluate employees? The answer is clearly no—one of the primary management roles is to get the most out of employees, and to do this, club managers need some system of performance appraisal.

Functions of Performance Appraisals

If you were to ask club managers why their clubs use a performance appraisal system, you would likely get a lot of different answers. This is because performance appraisals can be used for many purposes:

- *Performance feedback.* Appraisals are primarily used to provide feedback to employees. It is imperative that managers tell employees how they are doing on a regular basis. If managers don't do this, employees might believe anything along a spectrum between "I must be doing very badly" to "My performance must be perfect." Employees typically believe that silence means everything is okay. By providing feedback during a regularly scheduled performance appraisal, managers can prevent a lot of employee guessing and misunderstanding.

- *Training and development.* Managers can use appraisals to determine which employees require additional training and which may be ready to be promoted. Appraisals can also be used to determine training needs on a departmental basis. For example, if the appraisals of several department employees show that all of them need to work on member relations, that tells the department head that he or she probably should provide training in this area to everyone in the department.

- *Personnel decisions.* Appraisals can also be used to help managers reach personnel decisions. When used in this way, performance appraisals provide a good way to separate poor performers from good ones, and often figure into promotion, discipline, training, and merit-increase decisions. In discharge and grievance cases, performance appraisals give managers documentation that might be useful in grievance proceedings or lawsuits.

- *Selection validation.* Sometimes appraisals are used in ways that don't directly affect the employees at all. The goal during a club's selection process is to predict which candidates will perform the best and which will fit in the best. These predictions should be tested to determine whether the selection system is working properly. Performance appraisals are excellent yardsticks with which to measure the selection process. For example, if most of the recently hired employees are rated as poor performers during their performance appraisals, this might be evidence that the selection process is flawed.

Common Appraisal Errors

Club managers can make many errors when trying to evaluate an employee; the following list briefly describes some of the most common errors:

- *Recency errors.* People tend to remember best those events that happened most recently. A club manager is more likely to remember what employees did a few weeks before their performance appraisals than what they did six or eight months ago. Unless club managers keep a record throughout the year, it is likely that employees will only be judged on recent performance.

- *Past-anchoring errors.* Managers tend to rate an employee's performance close to what it was rated in the past. If an employee's ratings in the past were high, managers tend to rate the employee high again even if the ratings should be lower this time; the reverse is true for employees who have been rated low in the past.

- *Halo errors.* Halo errors occur when managers judge employees positively based primarily on the basis of a single trait, behavior, or action. A typical employee will perform some tasks well, others poorly, and others about average, but the halo effect causes a manager to rate an employee high in all areas if the employee does well in one area that is important to the manager.

- *Leniency errors.* Some managers give more lenient ratings to employees than they deserve. If a large enough sample were taken, we would expect that employee ratings would approximate the shape of a bell curve, but this is not the case with all managers. For example, if ratings of 1 to 5 were given to all employees (1 = poor, 5 = excellent), we would expect that the majority of employees would be rated near the midpoint on the scale. Managers who are more lenient than others would likely give more ratings near 5 than near 1. As a result, the ratings overall would be higher than normal.

- *Severity errors.* Severity errors are the reverse of leniency errors. As a result of severity errors, more employees would be rated nearer the lowest point on the scale (1) than near the high point.

- *Central-tendency errors.* Some managers tend to rate all employees, regardless of their performances, near the midpoint on a scale. Therefore, in this case many more employees would be rated near the midpoint than would be normal.

The problems caused by leniency, severity, and central-tendency errors are magnified in the club industry because club managers tend to change jobs frequently. As a result, club employees are often rated by a new manager. If the first manager tended to be lenient and the second severe, it would look like employee performance was going down when in fact no change had occurred. On the other hand, too-severe ratings from the first manager and too-lenient ratings from the second manager could result in the erroneous conclusion that employees were getting much better (and possibly deserved raises and promotions) when the employees had not actually improved their performances. Central-tendency errors make employee appraisals subject to the same distortions: if the old manager tended to rate all employees in the middle of the scale, and the new manager tends to be more lenient, then improvement would be noted when none occurred; the reverse would be true if the new manager tended to be severe.

Another problem with leniency, severity, and central-tendency errors is that an employee's rating may depend more on who rates him or her than on his or her actual performance. This can lead to injustices. Employees in one department, for example, may be passed over for promotions or career-development assignments because their manager tends to be severe, while employees in another department may receive raises and plum assignments simply because their manager is more lenient.

Who Should Evaluate Performance?

According to research, an employee's immediate supervisor is responsible for an employee's performance appraisal 93 percent of the time.[23] Sometimes, however, even immediate supervisors don't spend much time with their employees. Researchers have found that some managers spend as little as 5 to 10 percent of their time with any given employee during a given week.[24] Club managers who don't spend much time with an employee might ask themselves if they can adequately evaluate the employee's performance.

A case can be made that for many club employees, peers are best-suited to evaluate employee performance because of the high amount of contact employees have with each other, as well as the important role teamwork plays on the job. However, it is probably better to include peer appraisals as supplements to appraisals by immediate supervisors rather than leave the appraisals completely up to peers.

Some clubs allow employees to evaluate their manager's performance. Employees know from experience how well-developed a manager's interpersonal skills are, how well he or she delegates authority, and how well the manager leads. Using this type of appraisal calls for managers to trust their employees. Unless the appraisal is strictly quantitative in nature (and therefore protects the anonymity of the employees), it may not be advisable to ask employees to evaluate their managers in some situations, because managers (who ultimately hold reward and punishment power over employees) might find out who said what.

The old adage that we are always harder on ourselves than on others is not true when it comes to performance appraisals; self-appraisals tend to be more lenient than appraisals by others.[25] Nevertheless, when used with other appraisal methods, self-evaluations can help managers establish goals and objectives for employees.

Club employees and managers could also be evaluated by club members. This seems to be a logical appraisal method, since the ultimate goal of any club is member satisfaction. Unfortunately, collecting accurate information from members is difficult. Many members do not fill out such items as comment cards unless they are either extremely pleased or extremely displeased. Members also usually do not want the responsibility of evaluation. Therefore, while this approach looks good in theory, it is often difficult to do in practice.

How Often Should Appraisals Be Conducted?

While research has consistently shown that performance appraisals should be conducted more than once or twice a year, this is the norm. The problems associated with annual or biannual performance appraisals relate to the appraiser's difficulty in remembering events that transpired as long as twelve months ago. This problem can be helped somewhat by thorough note-keeping throughout the year, but this will not entirely correct the problem. Unless club managers take the time to make very exhaustive notes—and few have the time or inclination to do so—they still must rely on their memory for the details associated with behaviors and actions on dates long past.

If at all possible, club managers should try to conduct performance appraisals quarterly or even more often in cases in which managerial turnover is high. An alternative to this is to conduct appraisals immediately after the completion of specific assignments or special projects.

Exhibit 10   Example of Paired Comparisons Ranking

Employees to be ranked: Macaulay, Simpson, Taylor, Nathan

Macaulay is better than Simpson
Simpson is better than Taylor
Nathan is better than Simpson
Macaulay is better than Taylor
Macaulay is better than Nathan
Nathan is better than Taylor

Macaulay is ranked #1
Nathan is ranked #2
Simpson is ranked #3
Taylor is ranked #4

Performance Appraisal Methods

Ranking Methods. Three ranking methods are commonly used. Each eventually results in ranking employees from best to worst or from first to last. The three methods are: (1) simple or straight ranking, (2) alternative ranking, and (3) paired comparisons.

In **straight ranking,** a manager simply uses his or her best judgment to rank all employees from best to worst. **Alternative ranking** closely resembles straight ranking; the difference between the two is in how the ranking is determined. In alternative ranking, the manager lists each of the employees on a separate sheet of paper and then chooses the best and puts him or her at the top, then chooses the worst and puts him or her at the bottom, chooses the second-best and places him or her second from the top, then chooses the second-worst and places him or her second from the bottom, and so on until the list is exhausted. **Paired comparison** involves comparing each employee to each other employee directly on *each* job criterion. An example of this method is presented in Exhibit 10. The simplest way to compute final rankings in this method is to count the number of times an employee's name appears on the left side of the chart. The employee whose name appears most often is ranked best and the one whose name appears least often is ranked worst.

Forced Distribution. The **forced distribution** method of appraisal relies on the assumption that, under normal circumstances, the final rankings of all employees would conform statistically to a bell-shaped curve. Therefore, it assumes that about 5 percent of employees are exceptional, 5 percent are very poor, 10 percent are outstanding, 10 percent are poor, 15 percent are above average, 15 percent are below average, and the remaining 40 percent are average. An example of employees ranked using this method is presented in Exhibit 11.

Graphic Rating Scale. The most widely used method of performance appraisal is the **graphic rating scale.** When using this method, club managers typically rank employees on from 10 to 15 criteria. The criteria used in the ratings usually contain

Exhibit 11   Forced Distribution Scale

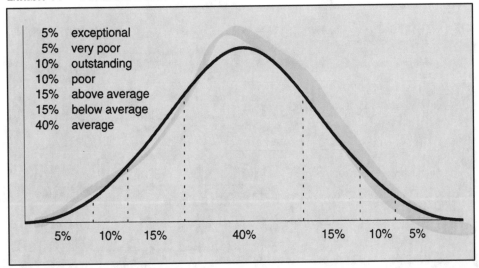

5%	exceptional
5%	very poor
10%	outstanding
10%	poor
15%	above average
15%	below average
40%	average

5%   10%   15%   40%   15%   10%   5%

such items as work characteristics, quality of work, quantity of work, dependability, attendance, job knowledge, and so on (see Exhibit 12). The criteria ratings can then be added together to compile a score for each employee.

Behaviorally Anchored Rating Scale. Like the graphic rating scale, the **behaviorally anchored rating scale (BARS)** requires raters to rate employees on a scaled continuum—from poor to excellent, for example (see Exhibit 13). However, in this case, the scale defines dimensions to be rated in behavioral terms, and critical incidents are used to describe the various levels of performance. As a result, raters rate specific actions of employees.[26] Therefore, there is less reliance on raters' opinions of what is good and bad or high and low performance. The critical incidents found on a BARS appraisal provide exact examples of what is assumed to be good and bad behaviors.

Narrative Essays. When using the **narrative-essays** method, club managers simply write essays that describe the employees they are rating. If a rater takes care to write essays that present a good picture of employee performance, they are very useful in filling gaps left by more quantitatively oriented methods.

Critical Incidents. When using the **critical-incidents** method, club managers keep a log of critical incidents in which each employee was involved. Typically, the incidents focus on behaviors instead of skills, and usually on behaviors that are either exceptionally desirable or exceptionally undesirable.

Management by Objectives. Unlike the other appraisal methods we've described, **management by objectives (MBO)** uses a system of establishing goals jointly in a meeting between employees and managers (or, since it is frequently used to evaluate managers, between a manager and his or her superior). Also during this meeting, specific plans for attaining each goal are established. Finally, measurements are agreed on between the manager and employee. Typically, MBO requires regular

Exhibit 12   Sample Graphic Rating Scale

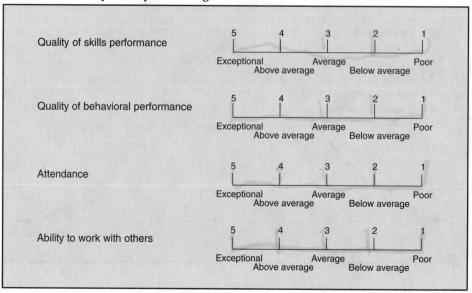

meetings to assess progress on the goals established in the initial meeting. Ulti-mately, employees are graded on their attainment of the goals. See Exhibit 14 for steps in establishing an MBO-based appraisal.

Discipline

Most employees want to do a good job and want to keep their jobs. However, prob-lems invariably arise that require managers to discipline and, in some cases, dis-charge some employees. In that sense, discipline is an indispensable management tool. However, it is also one of the hardest tools for managers to use. Too many managers view discipline simply as a way to punish bad behavior. Discipline should be much more than that. In fact, when used properly, discipline is a very effective management tool for encouraging desired behaviors.

The goal of a discipline program should be the promotion of positive em-ployee behaviors. To effectively lay the groundwork for a discipline system that promotes positive behaviors, club managers must first clearly establish the club's rules and then communicate to employees how those rules should be carried out. This communication can occur via general orientation, training, job descriptions, performance standards, performance appraisals, posted notices, and employee handbooks.

Approaches to Discipline

Club managers must choose between two substantially different types of disci-pline systems. One type of system, normally referred to as the traditional approach to discipline, emphasizes administering punishment after an employee fails to

Exhibit 13   Sample Behaviorally Anchored Rating Scale

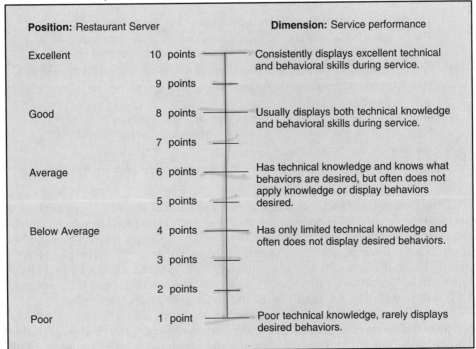

Position: Restaurant Server		Dimension: Service performance
Excellent	10 points	Consistently displays excellent technical and behavioral skills during service.
	9 points	
Good	8 points	Usually displays both technical knowledge and behavioral skills during service.
	7 points	
Average	6 points	Has technical knowledge and knows what behaviors are desired, but often does not apply knowledge or display behaviors desired.
	5 points	
Below Average	4 points	Has only limited technical knowledge and often does not display desired behaviors.
	3 points	
	2 points	
Poor	1 point	Poor technical knowledge, rarely displays desired behaviors.

follow the club's norms and standards. The other type of system, normally referred to as positive or preventive discipline, attempts to direct employee behavior by emphasizing correct behavior rather than punishing incorrect behavior.

Traditional Discipline. There are two common approaches to traditional discipline: the hot-stove approach and the progressive-discipline approach.

If you touch a hot stove, you immediately get burned. With the hot-stove approach to discipline, if someone breaks a rule, he or she is immediately disciplined. This approach has five foundations:

- Immediacy—corrective action must be taken immediately after the infraction occurs. This links punishment with the unwanted behavior.

- Consistency—corrective action must be consistent; that is, a hot stove will burn everyone to the same degree and for the same type of infraction.

- Warning—managers must clearly state company rules and the consequences for breaking those rules; in other words, employees must be warned that "hot stoves will burn."

- Impersonality—the behavior is punished, not the person.

- Appropriateness—the degree of punishment must equal the extent of the infraction.

Exhibit 14   Steps in Establishing an MBO-Based Appraisal

1. The employee proposes goals for the upcoming evaluation period.
2. The employee and manager discuss goals, modify them as necessary, and reach an agreement on specific goals; this agreement is recorded in writing.
3. The employee and manager agree on specific action plans to attain the goals.
4. The manager informally encourages goal attainment during the evaluation period.
5. At the end of the period, the employee and manager meet again to discuss accomplishments and agree on the extent to which the goals were attained.
6. The process is repeated.

This system makes a lot of sense to many managers, because it appears to be fair to all employees, and because it establishes which rules result in which punishments. However, there are problems with this system. Oddly, the fact that the hot stove does not discriminate is the biggest problem. For example, an employee who joined the club last week and may not fully understand all the rules will be "burned" for breaking a rule as badly as an employee who breaks the same rule but has been with the club for 15 years and has a clear grasp of the rules.

Like the hot-stove approach, progressive discipline also relies on a clear and complete definition of behaviors that will be punished and the type of punishment that will be meted out for each infraction. A progressive-discipline program might include, for example, a rule that an employee who is late for work twice will receive an oral warning, an employee who is late three times will receive a written warning, an employee who is late four times will be suspended, and so on.

Most progressive-discipline programs include four steps:

1. Oral warning—either formal or informal

2. Written warning—formal warning in which a copy is placed in the employee's file

3. Suspension—usually without pay

4. Discharge

One of the reasons many club managers like the hot-stove approach and the progressive-discipline approach is that both approaches bring order to the discipline process. Both clearly establish ground rules and both emphasize consistent and non-discriminatory treatment of rule breakers. As managers know, however, it is a lot easier to describe these systems on paper than to carry them out. Managers want to discriminate in their discipline programs because some employees are better performers than others, some deserve a break, and some are more likely to succeed than others. Neither the hot-stove approach nor the progressive-discipline approach allows this type of discrimination, however. Any manager who discriminates when using either of these systems risks grievances, discrimination charges, or lawsuits. In addition, both traditional approaches focus on symptoms rather than causes for poor performance. Rule-breaking is usually a symptom of an underlying problem, not the cause of the problem.

Positive Discipline. Proponents of positive or preventive discipline point out that the difference between this approach and traditional approaches is that the focus is on the cause of dysfunctional behavior rather than on the behavior itself. Unlike the traditional discipline approaches, in which "don't do anything wrong" is emphasized, this approach emphasizes that employees should "do the right thing."[27] U.S. companies that use the positive discipline approach include some of the largest and most successful: General Electric, Union Carbide, AT&T, Martin Marietta, Procter & Gamble, and Pennzoil.[28]

Positive discipline places disciplinary emphasis on recognizing and reinforcing good performance, rather than recognizing and punishing bad performance. Club managers who believe that today's employee is more likely to respond to positive encouragement than negative punishment are more likely to use positive discipline than the more traditional approaches.[29]

Critical steps in a positive disciplinary system, very similar to those used in progressive discipline, include the following:

1. Oral reminders

2. Written reminders

3. Decision-making leave—usually paid

4. Discharge

In each stage of this process, except discharge, the emphasis is on positively encouraging good behavior. An oral reminder, for example, would emphasize what should have been done in the situation in question—not what was done wrong. Step 3, decision-making leave, differs from progressive discipline's step 3, suspension, in that a suspension is usually designed merely to punish employees and remove them from the premises. Decision-making leave requires employees to think about their actions during their day off and, when they report back for work, tell their managers how they (the employees) can improve their performance.

Critics of positive discipline contend that the "decision-making day off" encourages employees to perform poorly to get a paid day off. However, research indicates that employees view even a paid day off as a severe punishment and often shape up as a result of this form of discipline.[30]

Appeal Mechanisms

A discipline program should have built into it a system for appeals by employees. A well-communicated appeal process allows employees to present their side of an issue; this gives employees a voice in how issues are settled. Additionally, appeal mechanisms provide evidence in court cases of managerial efforts to give employees due process. There are four commonly used types of appeal mechanisms:

- Hierarchical system

- Open-door policy

- Peer review

- Ombudsman

Hierarchical System. The hierarchical system emphasizes an organization's chain of command. According to this system, employees who believe they were unfairly disciplined appeal first to their immediate supervisor. If unsatisfied, employees appeal to one level higher in the organization. If still unsatisfied, employees can appeal to the next highest level, and to each succeeding level until the employees are satisfied or all levels are exhausted. Appeals are generally made in writing.

Open-Door Policy. Unlike the hierarchical system, which emphasizes the chain of command, an open-door policy allows employees to appeal to any manager in the organization, regardless of the manager's position. While this works in many cases, in some it fails because managers are reluctant to overrule lower-level managers or managers in other departments. As a result, appeals are often simply referred back to the employee's immediate supervisor. Another disadvantage of an open-door policy is that treatment is sometimes inconsistent. For example, one manager might work diligently to ensure that the appeal process is fair and that employees have a chance to be heard, while other managers may take this responsibility lightly.

Peer Review. Peer-review appeal systems typically require the formation of a committee of employees and managers. This committee or appeal board hears appeals and rules on issues brought before it. Employees are usually elected to serve on the board, while managers are usually appointed. An advantage of this system is that it allows employees to participate directly in the appeal process. As a result, employees often believe that, regardless of the outcome, their appeals were conducted fairly.

Ombudsman. The ombudsman system is widely used in governments, colleges, and universities but has not, as yet, been widely accepted in industry. This system involves the use of mediators or ombudsmen who listen to both sides of a case and attempt to mediate an acceptable solution. Ombudsmen typically have no authority to issue judgments in the event that the two sides cannot agree.

Discharge: The Last Resort

The same managers who use discipline strictly as a punishment probably also view discharge as the ultimate punishment for employees who fail to perform. Many experts believe that this is an incorrect view of discharge. When an employee is discharged, who really is punished the most? Is it the employee who must find a new job, or is it the manager who must find a replacement for the discharged employee? Each discharged employee can cost an organization as much as $3,500 to replace. At that rate, who is punished the most by a discharge?

Who really is at fault when a discharge is required? Is it the employee being discharged, or is it the manager? In Japanese companies, managers who discharge employees are viewed as failures because they were unable to help their employees become productive members of the organization. An increasing number of U.S. companies are beginning to hold similar views.

Club managers should use discharge only as a last resort. The employee can be severely affected by the loss of the job, and the employer can end up in court if the discharge is not properly handled. Therefore, discharging an employee should be taken extremely seriously and approached with great caution.

Before a club manager exercises this final option, he or she should ask the following questions. If the answer is yes to each of these questions, the manager can safely proceed with the discharge. If the answer is no to any of them, the manager should correct the situation described by the question prior to discharging the employee; otherwise the manager can be held liable for **wrongful discharge** in court:

- Were the rules that were broken reasonable and important to the club? Did management explain to the employee why the rules were important?

- Were the rules clearly and fairly communicated to the employee? Was the employee advised clearly *in advance* that certain behaviors would result in discharge?

- Did management make a sincere effort to identify poor performers and correct their behaviors or actions?

- Was the appraisal process fair, complete, and equitable?

- Was the evidence that precipitated the discharge substantial and reliable?

- Is the punishment for breaking rules applied consistently to all employees?

- Is the discipline (in this case, discharge) equal to the seriousness of the offense?

To repeat, a "no" response to any of these questions can mean a club manager is vulnerable to a wrongful-discharge lawsuit. Wrongful-discharge suits can be extremely serious to a club. Employees can successfully sue their employers for back pay, front pay, and punitive damages in wrongful-discharge cases. In 1986, plaintiffs won 78 percent of the wrongful-discharge cases filed in California, with an average award of over $424,000.[31] In 1988 the average award in a wrongful-discharge case was over $861,000.[32]

Some managers know it is hard to discharge employees, so they attempt to "get rid of them" by transferring or demoting them, hoping that the employees will simply quit. However, such actions also may be the basis for wrongful-discharge suits. A transfer can be viewed by the courts as a wrongful discharge if it is used as a method of avoiding a termination or layoff, and a demotion that involves no record of wrongdoing on the employee's part can be viewed as a wrongful discharge. Courts typically view transfers and demotions as wrongful discharges if the pay, benefits, responsibilities, travel, and so on of the new jobs are substantially different from that of the old jobs. Employers are even held liable for voluntary resignations in cases where management makes working conditions so bad that employees resign. In such cases, deliberate intent is the key element in court. To win such cases, employers typically have to prove that they could not have foreseen that the employee would resign as a result of a transfer or other personnel decision that resulted in the resignation.

While many companies have gone to great lengths to establish sophisticated systems to avoid wrongful discharge suits (complete documentation, progressive-discipline systems, and so on), they often forget to ensure that managers don't actually discharge wrongly. The easiest wrongful-discharge case for an employee to win is one in which the rules are unfairly enforced.[33] Unfortunately, this is the single area in which managers make the most mistakes. While it is difficult to tell managers that they must fairly enforce the same rules and penalties at all times, managers must do this if companies wish to avoid or win wrongful-discharge cases. To illustrate how hard it is to always be fair and consistent, consider the following simple example: Employee A is an outstanding performer who is well liked by members, management, and fellow employees. However, Employee A has a habit of tardiness. Employee B is a poor performer who is not well liked by members, managers, or fellow employees. This employee also has a habit of tardiness. A manager who "solves" the problem with Employee B by discharging him for habitual tardiness but does not discharge Employee A is opening the door for a wrongful-discharge suit.

The Discharge Interview. If a discharge becomes necessary, and a manager is sure that everything has been done properly so that the employee is not being wrongfully discharged, then the manager should schedule a discharge interview with the employee. The purpose of a discharge interview is to communicate to the employee the history that has led up to the discharge, to explain the reasons the manager must take such severe disciplinary action, and to complete the discharge. Discharging an employee is never easy or pleasant; most discharge interviews are emotionally charged, and managers sometimes are even physically attacked by enraged employees. However, there are some simple guidelines club managers can follow that should make the task less difficult (see Exhibit 15).

Discharge and Employment-at-Will. The doctrine of **employment at will** means essentially that management has the right to terminate an employee at any time for any reason. Throughout the history of the United States, this doctrine has been the predominant rule that guided employer-employee relations. However, in some cases in recent years, U.S. courts have moved decidedly away from this doctrine to one that assumes there is a contract between employers and employees.[34]

These two versions of the relationship between employers and employees—"employment at will" versus "contracts"—have been the grounds for a great deal of controversy recently. Managers typically want to claim that they have the right to employ whom they want, when they want. In the past, this right usually was upheld in court. However, the pendulum has swung in favor of employees in recent years. As a result, many employee-relations experts now believe that managers no longer have the right to enforce employment-at-will arrangements with their employees.

Some experts have contended that managers can retain the employment-at-will right by simply notifying their employees that this is their policy. For example, managers can include a clause in the employee handbook that states that the employer has the right to employ at will and is not bound by any other contract, and even require each employee to sign this clause prior to employment. Many

Exhibit 15   Guidelines for Discharge Interviews

- Make sure all supporting evidence is carefully read to the employee and is available during the discharge. This documentation should include records of all disciplinary action against the employee and past conditions and terms of such action.
- Explain specific reasons for the discharge. Managers cannot get by with simply telling an employee that "it didn't work out."
- Respect the dignity of the employee during the interview. The fact that the employee did not work out in this case does not mean that he or she will not find suitable employment elsewhere.
- Avoid a personal confrontation with the employee.
- Reasons for the discharge should remain confidential at all times; this policy should be clearly stated to the employee during the interview.
- Use the meeting to find out what went wrong (if applicable; if the employee is being discharged for stealing, for example, this would not apply). Someone in the organization thought enough of the employee to hire him or her in the first place. This is the final opportunity to learn the employee's side of the story.
- As a general rule, have a witness attend the interview.
- Most states require that discharged employees be paid in full at the time of discharge. This and other required paperwork should be completed well in advance of the interview.
- Make the employee aware of any grievance mechanisms available within the club.

companies have included such clauses in their handbooks. However, in the 1983 U.S. Supreme Court case *Pine River State Bank* v. *Matille,* the court ruled that the mere existence of an employee handbook constituted evidence of an implied contract between employee and employer.[35] Thirty state courts have also ruled that the existence and use of employee manuals imply a contract between employer and employee.[36] These rulings were made primarily on the basis of language in the employee manuals that described benefits, grounds for discipline, or affirmative action statements—all considered evidence of implied employment contracts.

Although recently some states have passed new "at-will" employment laws, in effect condoning at-will employment, the bottom line for club managers is that employment at will is very difficult to sustain. State laws differ, so what may be considered evidence of employment at will in one state may be considered evidence of a contract in another. In addition, as one expert has noted, U.S. society has become so litigious that even cases that employers will clearly win may end up in court and cost thousands of dollars to resolve.[37]

Some human-resources experts believe that managers should abandon employment at will. According to these experts, such relationships often lead to reduced risk-taking and lower levels of innovation by employees who merely do what they have to do in order to survive in the organization. Other experts see employment at will as a keystone prerequisite to ensuring employee loyalty and productivity.[38]

Endnotes

1. There are a few exceptions to this rule. For example, many clubs do not have to follow the provisions of the Vocational Rehabilitation Act of 1973, and most do not have to follow the Drug Free Workplace Act of 1988. Some lawyers also contend that clubs do not have to follow all of the provisions of the "facilities use" portion of the Americans with Disabilities Act, although this is debatable.

2. Dale Masi, "Company Responses to Drug Abuse from AMA's Nationwide Survey," *Personnel*, March 1987, p. 41.

3. J. Freedley Hunsicker, "Ready or Not: The ADA," *Personnel*, Vol. 69, No. 8, August 1990, pp. 80–86, and Richard Thompson, "Equal Access," *Successful Meetings*, May 1991, p. 44.

4. Evelyn Gilbert, "Clarity Seen Needed in Disability Act," *National Underwriter*, Vol. 95, No. 15 (April 15, 1991), p. 41.

5. Robert H. Woods, "Dubious Distinction: #1 in Discriminatory Advertising," *Cornell Quarterly*, Vol. 30, No. 1 (1989), p. 92.

6. Ellie McGrath, "Sending Degrees to the Dogs," *Time*, (April 2, 1984), p. 90.

7. Robert B. Best, "Don't Forget Those Reference Checks," *Public Personnel Journal* (November–December, 1977), pp. 422–426.

8. Robert Alan Palmer, "Crimes Against Customers: Could You Be Held Responsible?" *Restaurants USA*, January 1991, pp. 13–16.

9. Gilbert Fuschsberg, "More Employers Check Credit Histories of Job Seekers to Judge Their Character," *Wall Street Journal*, May 30, 1990, pp. B1 and B3.

10. Kathryn Hudson, "Reference Checking? Hire a Hand," *Insight*, February 1, 1988, p. 45.

11. David Steir, "Many Ask, But Don't Give References," *HR News*, Vol. 8, No. 2 (February 1990), p. 2.

12. Much of the information in this section is drawn from Raphael R. Kavanaugh and Jack D. Ninemeier, *Supervision in the Hospitality Industry*, 2d ed. (East Lansing, Mich.: Educational Institute of the American Hotel & Motel Association, 1991).

13. Chris Lee, "Training Budgets: Neither Boom nor Bust," *Training*, October 1988, pp. 41–46.

14. Wayne F. Cascio, *Managing Human Resources: Productivity, Quality of Work Life, Profits* (New York: McGraw-Hill, 1989), p. 251.

15. A. Tziner and S. Dolan, "Validity of an Assessment Center for Identifying Future Female Officers in the Military," *Journal of Applied Psychology*, Vol. 67, pp. 728–736.

16. M. E. Shaw, "Role Playing," in R. L. Craig and L. R. Bittel (eds.), *Training and Development Handbook* (New York: McGraw-Hill, 1989), pp. 206–224.

17. Gary P. Latham and L. N. Saari, "The Application of Social Learning Theory to Training Supervisors Through Behavioral Modeling," *Journal of Applied Psychology* (1979), Vol. 64, pp. 239–246.

18. Steven J. Mayer and James S. Russell, "Behavior Modeling Training in Organizations: Concerns and Conclusions," *Journal of Management*, Spring 1987, pp. 21–40.

19. Kenneth N. Wexley and Gary P. Latham, *Developing and Training Human Resources in Organizations* (Glenview, Ill.: Scott-Foresman, 1981).

20. A. H. Locher and K. S. Teel, "Appraisal Trends," *Personnel Journal*, September 1988, p. 139.

21. Berkley Rice, "Performance Ratings—Are They Worth the Trouble?" *Psychology Today,* September 1985, p. 30.

22. C. Hymowitz, "Bosses: Don't Be Hasty (and Other Tips for Reviewing a Worker's Performance)," *Wall Street Journal,* January 17, 1985, p. 28.

23. D. L. DeVries, A. M. Morrison, S. L. Shullman, and M. L. Berlach, *Performance Appraisal on the Line* (New York: Wiley, 1981).

24. DeVries, et al.

25. L. M. Shore and G. C. Thornton, "Effects of Gender on Self- and Supervisory Ratings," *Academy of Management Journal* (1986), Vol. 29, pp. 115–129.

26. W. Terry Umbreit, Robert W. Eder, and Jon P. McConnell, "Performance Appraisals: Making Them Fair and Making Them Work," *Cornell Quarterly* (1986), Vol. 26, No. 4, p. 65.

27. This analogy adapted from an unpublished paper by Daniel Smith, an MBA student at Michigan State University, December 1991.

28. Laurie Baum, "Punishing Workers with a Day Off," *Business Week,* June 16, 1990, p. 80.

29. Another description of positive discipline can be found in Ken Blanchard, *Putting the One Minute Manager to Work* (New York: Morrow, 1984). Blanchard emphasizes "catching someone doing something good" and rewarding him or her as a means of acknowledging to others that positive performance is desirable.

30. Mark Singer, *Human Resources Management* (Boston: PWS Kent Publishing, 1990), p. 244.

31. William E. Fullmer and Ann Wallace Casey, "Employment at Will: Options for Managers," *Academy of Management Executive,* 4, 2 (1990), p. 102.

32. Caleb Atwood, "Discharge Now, Pay Later," *Personnel Administrator,* 34.8 (1989), p. 92.

33. Atwood, p. 93.

34. Jeffrey L. Pellissier, "Avoiding the Wrongful Discharge Pitfall," *Cornell Quarterly,* 31, 1 (1990), p. 120.

35. Fullmer and Casey, p. 105.

36. Gerard Panaro, "Don't Let Your Personnel Manual Become a Contract," *Association Management,* 40, 8 (1991), p. 82.

37. Fullmer and Casey, p. 104.

38. Paul G. Wilhelm and Timothy R. Roth, "Employment at Will: Productivity Does Not Suffer," *HR Magazine,* 35, 9 (1990), p. 88.

🗝 Key Terms

alternative ranking—A method of ranking employees in which a manager lists each of the employees on a separate sheet of paper and then chooses the best and puts him or her at the top, then chooses the worst and puts him or her at the bottom, chooses the second-best and places him or her second from the top, then chooses the second-worst and places him or her second from the bottom, and so on until the list is exhausted.

application blank—A form used by companies to solicit background and other information from prospective employees.

behaviorally anchored rating scale (BARS)—A method of evaluating employees in which managers rate employees on specific behaviors displayed.

behavioral modeling—An off-the-job training method designed to encourage employees to behave as role models behave.

bona fide occupational qualifications (BFOQs)—Qualifications on the basis of which employers are allowed to legally discriminate during selection and promotion.

business game—An off-the-job training method in which trainees learn how to deal with a variety of issues in a simulated business environment.

case study—An off-the-job training method in which employees read about a series of events—hypothetical or real—and are asked to solve the problems or dilemmas that are presented.

central-tendency error—An error that occurs when managers tend to rate all employees, regardless of their performance, near the midpoint on a scale.

conference training—An off-the-job training method that consists of one-on-one discussions between a trainer and a trainee.

critical incidents—A method of evaluating employees in which a manager keeps a log of significant incidents in which each employee was involved; employees are rated on how well they performed during these incidents.

employment at will—An employment policy stipulating that employers can discharge employees at any time for any reason.

essential functions of a job—Language in the Americans with Disabilities Act that specifies that the disabled must not be barred from a job if they can perform the functions that are fundamental to performing the job.

forced distribution—An evaluation method in which a manager ranks employees on a bell-shaped curve.

general property orientation—A formal program presented by an employer to introduce to a new employee the organization's mission and values and to cover such issues as insurance and benefits; usually conducted shortly after hiring.

graphic rating scale—A method of evaluating employees in which managers rate employees on specific, measurable criteria.

halo error—An error that occurs when a manager rates an individual highly in all categories just because the individual possesses one or two positive traits or behaviors that the manager values.

in-basket training—An off-the-job training method in which employees confront a wide array of problems, similar to what they might find in their in-basket when they come to work.

job-instruction training (JIT)—A structured, on-the-job training method that requires trainees to proceed through a series of sequential steps.

job rotation—An on-the-job training method that involves moving employees from one job to another in order to enhance job interest or to cross-train. Also used to familiarize management trainees with various jobs.

lecture—An off-the-job training method used to impart information to a large audience.

leniency error—An error in a performance appraisal that results when managers rate employees too positively.

management by objectives (MBO)—A method of evaluating employees in which a manager meets with an employee and, with the employee's input, sets specific goals for the employee to attain; the manager and the employee meet later to assess the extent to which these goals were achieved.

narrative essay—A method of evaluating employees in which managers write, on each employee, an essay that describes the strengths and weaknesses of the employee.

paired comparison—A method of ranking employees in which each employee is compared on a one-to-one basis with each other employee to determine an overall ranking. The employee who "wins" the most comparisons is ranked first, the employee who has the second highest number of wins is ranked second, and so on.

past-anchoring error—An error in a performance appraisal that results when managers rate employees on the basis of previous ratings.

programmed instruction—An off-the-job training method in which employees learn at their own pace. Originally a paper-and-pencil method; now commonly computer-based.

reasonable accommodation—What employers must do to make their workplaces accessible to people with disabilities. Examples of reasonable accommodations include widening work aisles, lowering countertops, and installing ramps.

recency error—An error that results when managers or interviewers base someone's evaluation primarily on their most recent behaviors or responses.

role playing—An off-the-job training method that allows trainees to assume roles and act out parts in a realistic situation or setting.

semistructured interview—An interview in which an interviewer asks both planned and unplanned questions. Typically, the unplanned questions allow interviewers to ask for specific information about broad issues raised by the structured questions.

severity error—An error in a performance appraisal or job interview that results when managers rate employees or job applicants too severely.

specific job orientation—The process of introducing new employees to the specific tasks and behaviors of their jobs.

straight ranking—A ranking method in which a manager simply uses his or her best judgment to rank all employees from best to worst.

structured interview—An interview in which all questions are prepared in advance and are asked in a specific order.

unstructured interview—An interviewing style in which no questions are planned in advance. Instead, an interviewer directs the interview down whatever path seems appropriate at the time.

vestibule training—An off-the-job training method that simulates the workplace and trains employees to perform or display knowledge, skills, or abilities similar to those required at work.

wrongful discharge—A charge brought against an employer for terminating employees without due process or without substantial efforts to first call an employee's attention to improper work habits and to help the employee change; terminating an employee's employment without sufficient reason.

Review Questions

1. What does Title VII of the Civil Rights Act of 1964 prohibit?

2. How are disabilities defined under the Americans with Disabilities Act?

3. What are some of the advantages and disadvantages of external recruiting? internal recruiting?

4. What are some potential problems with pre-employment tests?

5. What items should be included in a club's orientation kit for new employees?

6. What are the steps in the training cycle?

7. What are some common employee-appraisal errors club managers should avoid?

8. What are some of the questions club managers should ask themselves before discharging an employee, in order to make sure they will not be guilty of wrongfully discharging the employee?

Additional Reading

Allen, Rex J. "The Role of CBT (Computer-Based Training)." *CD-Rom Professional,* 9, 10 (October) 1996.

Best, Robert B. "Don't Forget Those Reference Checks." *Public Personnel Journal,* November–December, 1977.

Blanchard, Ken. *Putting the One Minute Manager to Work.* New York: Morrow, 1984.

Carlson, Eugene. "The Business of Background Checking Comes to the Fore." *Wall Street Journal,* August 31, 1993.

Cascio, Wayne F. *Managing Human Resources: Productivity, Quality of Work Life, Profits.* New York: McGraw-Hill, 1989.

Chaudron, David. "Avoid the Training Waste." *HR Focus,* 72, 12 (July) 1995.

DeVries, D. L., A. M. Morrison, S. L. Shullman, and M. L. Berlach. *Performance Appraisal on the Line.* New York: Wiley, 1981.

Fuschsberg, Gilbert. "More Employers Check Credit Histories of Job Seekers to Judge Their Character." *Wall Street Journal,* May 30, 1990.

Gilbert, Evelyn. "Clarity Seen Needed in Disability Act." *National Underwriter,* Vol. 95, No. 15 (April 15, 1991).

Goodale, James. "Improving Performance Appraisals." *Business Quarterly,* 57, 2 (Fall) 1992.

Hudson, Kathryn. "Reference Checking? Hire a Hand." *Insight,* February 1, 1988.

Hunsicker, J. Freedley. "Ready or Not: The ADA." *Personnel,* Vol. 69, No. 8, August 1990.

Hymowitz, C. "Bosses: Don't Be Hasty (and Other Tips for Reviewing a Worker's Performance)." *Wall Street Journal,* January 17, 1985.

Jeffries, Rosalind. "Recapping the Rewards of Recognition." *HR Focus,* 74, 1 (January) 1997.

Kavanaugh, Raphael R., and Jack D. Ninemeier. *Supervision in the Hospitality Industry,* 2d ed. (East Lansing, Mich.: Educational Institute of the American Hotel & Motel Association, 1991).

Latham, Gary P., and L. N. Saari. "The Application of Social Learning Theory to Training Supervisors Through Behavioral Modeling." *Journal of Applied Psychology* (1979), Vol. 64.

Lee, Chris. "Training Budgets: Neither Boom nor Bust." *Training,* October 1988.

Locher, A. H., and K. S. Teel. "Appraisal Trends." *Personnel Journal,* September 1988.

Manaca, Regina. "Looking for Better Productivity: Don't Forget the 3 R's." *Harvard Business Review,* 74, 4 (August) 1996.

Masi, Dale. "Company Responses to Drug Abuse from AMA's Nationwide Survey." *Personnel,* March 1987.

Mayer, Steven J., and James S. Russell. "Behavior Modeling Training in Organizations: Concerns and Conclusions." *Journal of Management,* Spring 1987.

McGrath, Ellie. "Sending Degrees to the Dogs." *Time,* (April 2, 1984).

Mondy, R. Wayne, and Robert M. Noe. *Human Resources Management.* Englewood Cliffs, New Jersey: Prentice-Hall, 1996.

Palmer, Robert Alan. "Crimes Against Customers: Could You Be Held Responsible?" *Restaurants USA,* January 1991.

"Research Shows Training Pays." *Journal of Career and Employment,* 56, No. 2 (January) 1996.

Rice, Berkley. "Performance Ratings—Are They Worth the Trouble?" *Psychology Today,* September 1985.

Shaw, Bill. "Employee Appraisals, Discrimination Cases, and Objective Evidence." *Business Horizons,* 33, 5 (September–October) 1990.

Shaw, M. E. "Role Playing," in R. L. Craig and L. R. Bittel (eds.), *Training and Development Handbook.* New York: McGraw-Hill.

Shore, L. M., and G. C. Thornton. "Effects of Gender on Self- and Supervisory Ratings." *Academy of Management Journal* (1986), Vol. 29.

Steir, David. "Many Ask, But Don't Give References." *HR News,* Vol. 8, No. 2 (February 1990).

Talbott, Shannon Peters. "Peer Review Drives Compensation at Johnsonville." *Personnel Journal,* 73, 10 (October) 1994.

Thompson, Richard. "Equal Access." *Successful Meetings,* May 1991.

Tziner, A., and S. Dolan. "Validity of an Assessment Center for Identifying Future Female Officers in the Military." *Journal of Applied Psychology,* Vol. 67.

Umbreit, W. Terry, Robert W. Eder, and Jon P. McConnell. "Performance Appraisals: Making Them Fair and Making Them Work." *Cornell Quarterly* (1986), Vol. 26.

Vinson, Mary N. "The Pros and Cons of 360-Degree Feedback: Making It Work." *Training & Development,* 50, 4 (April) 1996.

Vodanovin, Stephen J., and Rosemary H. Lowe. "They Ought to Know Better: The Incidence of Inappropriate Application Blanks." *Public Personnel Management,* 21 (Fall) 1992.

Wexley, Kenneth N., and Gary P. Latham. *Developing and Training Human Resources in Organizations.* Glenview, Ill.: Scott-Foresman, 1981.

"What Employees Can Ask." *HR Focus,* June 1995.

Woods, Robert H. "Dubious Distinction: #1 in Discriminatory Advertising." *Cornell Quarterly,* Vol. 30, No. 1 (1989).

Internet Sites

For more information, visit the following Internet sites. Remember that Internet addresses can change without notice. If the site is no longer there, use a browser to look for additional sites.

http://www.all-biz.com/atwill.htm [wording in at-will employment policies]

http://www.astd.org/. [homepage for the American Society of Training and Development]

http://www.dol.gov/dol. [a listing of Department of Labor contacts for questions regarding application blanks]

http://www.ed.gov/ [U.S. Department of Education homepage, searchable site, provides examples of 360-degree feedback systems]

http://www.fpmi.com/index.html [Fednews online: information on recent U.S. antidiscrimination cases] http://www.hi-tech.twc.state.tx.us/medical/family.htm. [covers basics of the Family and Medical Leave Act]

http://www.law.cornell.edu [Legal Information Institute, Cornell University, provides links to government performance appraisals, advice, and case studies]

http://www.state.fl.us:80/dms/pms/sms-perf.html [state of Florida performance-appraisal-system guidelines and training advice]

http://206.54.11.3:80 training/computer network. [information on computer-based training resources]

Case Study

It was a sweltering August evening, the hottest night of the hottest summer in recent memory. It was a night when those who ventured far from air-conditioning paid a heavy price in discomfort, and it was certainly a night when no one wanted to cook. Perhaps that was why it was the busiest Saturday night of the year at the Sandstone Country Club's main dining room. Servers and cooks wilted in their uniforms as they struggled to keep up the frantic pace.

Roberto, a server who had been with the club just nine months, was having more than his share of problems. The dining room manager had already corrected him twice for improperly serving two tables. Tips had not been generous, and he'd taken a lot of grief from the cooks. Most of the diners were impatient—"Where's our food?" "Tell the chef to pick up the pace in there!"—and when Roberto dutifully went to the kitchen to check the status of orders, the cooks would brandish knives in their sweaty hands and tell him to go away.

The party that just sat down in his section was one group he didn't dare make a mistake with. Dr. Steele, his wife, and three other couples were all dressed up for a night on the town. Roberto knew that Dr. Steele was a big tipper, but he also knew the doctor was hard to please. Roberto put forth his best effort, took the order, and got it to the kitchen quickly. About ten minutes after the appetizers had been cleared, Dr. Steele stopped Roberto on his way to another table and asked him to please check on his table's order. "Yes sir," Roberto replied, and hurried to the kitchen.

When he opened the kitchen door he had to dodge two servers charging out with loaded trays. A wave of heat enveloped him and the noise was deafening: shouted orders, dishes clattering, oven doors slamming, the hissing of steam from the warewashing station. He located Steve through the maze of rushing bodies and yelled, "How we coming on the order for table 10?"

Steve, the club's assistant executive chef, looked up from stirring a boiling pot and wiped his glistening forehead with a white coat sleeve. "We've got a problem," Steve yelled back, "we've eighty-sixed that special."

"You're kidding!" Roberto wailed. Wouldn't you know it—the other seven diners had ordered something else, but Dr. Steele had ordered the whitefish special. "It's not on the board! Why didn't you tell me when I placed the order?" The cooks were supposed to write on the board any items the kitchen was out of, so the servers could stop promoting those items. If they were too busy to write it on the board, they should have said something. The stupid cooks always forget, Roberto thought, and the servers always get the grief.

"Hey, look around!" Steve jerked his head at the cooks bustling all around him. "We don't have time to baby-sit every order back here. Just go tell 'em to choose something else."

I ought to make *you* tell him, Roberto thought grimly as he left the kitchen. The other seven orders at Dr. Steele's table would be ready in five or ten minutes, but Dr. Steele's meal wasn't even started. The orders for the rest of the table would have to sit under heat lamps while Dr. Steele's order was prepared. No one was going to be happy at table 10; Roberto could see his big tip disappearing.

Roberto was right; no one in the Steele party looked very happy when he broke the news. Through thinly pressed lips, Dr. Steele ordered his second choice—a rack of lamb, medium-well. Roberto knew that would take a long time to cook, but he didn't want to give Dr. Steele any more bad news. Roberto practically ran back to the kitchen to get the order in as quickly as he could.

Twenty minutes later Roberto was filling the water glasses for guests at another table when out of the corner of his eye he saw Dr. Steele impatiently waving him over.

"Yes sir?"

"Listen, we've got tickets for the play tonight. How much longer is it going to be?"

"Well, Dr. Steele, it will probably be another fifteen minutes at least. It takes time to properly prepare a rack of lamb. I'm very sorry, I would have told you before, but I didn't know you needed to leave so soon."

"Well, we certainly can't wait another fifteen minutes. Do you have anything you can serve quickly?"

"I'm sure we have something you'd like, sir, let me check for you. I'm terribly sorry." As he left the table he saw Dr. Steele sarcastically muttering something to his guests.

Back into the chaos of the kitchen, weaving through servers, cooks, and buspersons, Roberto found Steve and told him that Dr. Steele wanted to change his order again. "Damn it!" Steve turned harassed eyes to Roberto. "The lamb's already half-cooked—who's going to pay for it?"

"I don't care!" Roberto said angrily. "What can you give me in five minutes?"

"I know what I'd like to give you," Steve said under his breath while he wiped his brow. "It'll have to be pasta," Steve said aloud. "Tell him the pasta primavara is good tonight."

Roberto went back to the Steele table with this news. "Oh, forget it!" Dr. Steele threw his napkin on the floor. "We're running late, and everyone else's meal is probably ruined by now anyway. We're leaving." Everybody gave Roberto dirty looks as they pushed back their chairs and left in a huff.

Roberto stalked angrily back to the kitchen, found the seven orders for table 10 under the heat lamps, and started scraping them into the garbage with savage strokes. "I hope you're happy!" he yelled at Steve's back. "Dr. Steele just left, madder than hell! Forty dollars in tips just walked out the door because you couldn't get it right!"

Steve turned suddenly and lunged across a countertop at Roberto, clutching at him. "You think it's so easy back here?!" he bellowed, his face mottled with rage. "We never get tips, just a lot of crap from jerks like you! I'm sick of your attitude!"

"Keep your hands off me!" Roberto pulled away and made what witnesses later said was "some sort of racial remark" in Spanish to Steve. Steve ran around the end of the counter, grabbed Roberto, and hurled him against a wire storage rack; pots, pans, and kitchen utensils rained down with a metallic crash. Steve was moving in to throw a punch when bystanders restrained him.

• • •

Lloyd Marlowe, Sandstone's general manager, sat at his desk Tuesday morning with two employee files in front of him and two decisions to make. Last Saturday's incident had surprised him; at least he was surprised that Steve was involved. Tension between cooks and servers was an age-old problem present in every food service operation since the world began, but he never expected it to erupt into violence at his club.

Lloyd had been out in the dining room that Saturday night, chatting with club members, when he had heard the big metallic crash in the kitchen. When he arrived on the scene, Steve and Roberto were yelling insults at each other, held apart by what appeared to be half the staff. Lloyd called the manager from the mixed grill and had him report to the kitchen to help restore order and resume production, then took Steve and Roberto, one at a time, to his office. He kept the interviews brief. He suspended both of them without pay for three days and told them he would take that time to review the incident. He would get in touch with them after he had made a decision on what disciplinary action to take. After escorting each of them separately to their cars and watching them drive away, he had returned to the dining room and pitched in to help the staff get through the rest of the evening.

The three-day suspensions gave Lloyd time to question witnesses and review Steve's and Roberto's employee files. Steve had been employed at the club for three years and had an excellent record. He was never late, always volunteered to work extra hours, and had been employee of the month four times. There were two letters in his file from club members praising him for his work at special events they had hosted at the club. All three of his annual performance appraisals were excellent and he had received a substantial raise each time. He was well-liked by his co-workers in the kitchen; indeed, Lloyd liked him too. Steve was a key member of the staff and it would be hard to be without him, even for a short time, because the rest of August and all of September were absolutely jammed with banquets, weddings, and other special events, not to mention the regular dining-room workload Steve carried.

Roberto, on the other hand, had been something of a problem ever since his hire last December. He was habitually late for work and had already passed from the oral-warning to the written-warning stage on the tardiness issue. The club had high standards and strict service procedures that Roberto was having trouble mastering. He was also something of a loner and didn't really fit in with the rest of the service staff. At times he tended to be rude to other staff members; his supervisor had noted in his file that she had met with him informally to discuss this problem.

All of these issues were reviewed with him at his six-month performance appraisal (new club employees received two appraisals their first year), but instead of inspiring Roberto to try harder, the appraisal seemed to embarrass and anger him. After his appraisal, his attitude took a noticeable dive. He was still careful to be polite with club members, but with his co-workers he was usually sullen and uncooperative. His supervisor had kept him on, however, in part because she thought Roberto had the potential to become a good employee despite his problems, in part because the labor market was tight and servers were very hard to find.

Witnesses to the incident Saturday night emphasized how incredibly hot it had been in the kitchen and how much pressure everyone felt because of the unusually large dinner crowd. Roberto had "had an attitude" with the cooks throughout the evening, they all agreed. On the other hand, everyone agreed that Steve had grabbed and shoved Roberto and seemed ready to throw punches. "Sure, Roberto was out of line," was the consensus, "but no more than usual, except for that last racial remark after Steve went for him." The heat and the pressure, coupled with Roberto's attitude, apparently had just made Steve lose his head momentarily.

Lloyd drummed his hands nervously on the employee files and sighed. He didn't need to review the files yet again; he needed to make some decisions. He reached for the phone and called his secretary. "Call Steve and Roberto and tell them I'd like to see them tomorrow morning. Be sure to set up separate appointments—eight o'clock and ten o'clock would be best. Let me know if there's any problem." He hung up the phone and shoved the files in a desk drawer. He was pretty sure what he was going to do, but this gave him one more night to sleep on it.

Discussion Questions

1. Should Lloyd fire Steve? Why or why not? If he shouldn't fire Steve, what disciplinary action should he take?

2. Should Lloyd fire Roberto? Why or why not? If he shouldn't fire Roberto, what disciplinary action should he take?

3. What messages will Lloyd send to the rest of the staff by the disciplinary actions he takes with Steve and Roberto?

The following industry experts helped develop this case: Cathy Gustafson, CCM, University of South Carolina, Columbia, South Carolina; Kurt D. Kuebler, CCM, Vice President, General Manager, The Desert Highlands Association, Scottsdale, Arizona; and William A. Schulz, MCM, General Manager, Houston Country Club, Houston, Texas.

REVIEW QUIZ

When you feel you have covered all of the material in this chapter, answer these questions. Choose the *best* answer.

Alternate/Multiple Choice

1. Title VII of the Civil Rights Act of 1964:

   a. prohibits employment discrimination based on race, color, sex, religion, and national origin.
   b. regulates employment of non-U.S. citizens in the United States.
   c. allows employees to take unpaid time off from work for certain medical and parental reasons.
   d. is the "Emancipation Proclamation for the Disabled."

2. You are the dining room manager of the Breezewood Country Club. You need to hire servers for the club's restaurant. You place the following advertisement in the local paper:

   > **Waitresses Wanted!** Seeking young women for full- and part-time shifts. No experience necessary—will train. Call Mr. Smith, 555-1234, weekdays.

   What is wrong with this ad?

   a. The ad names a specific person to call.
   b. The ad should not have included references to shifts.
   c. This ad discriminates on the basis of gender.
   d. There is nothing wrong with this ad.

3. Robert Jones is the pro shop manager of the Riverside Country Club. Robert gave Inez, an employee who works the counter for him, an overall excellent rating on her performance appraisal, even though much of her performance is merely satisfactory. Robert did this because Inez is always upbeat and positive, always smiling, and those are traits that he really likes to see in an employee. Robert is guilty of the _____ error.

   a. past-anchoring
   b. halo
   c. recency
   d. central-tendency

4. If an employee can go to any manager within the club to appeal a disciplinary action, the club operates a(n):

   a. ombudsman system.
   b. hierarchical system.
   c. open-door policy.
   d. peer-review board.

Answer Key: 1-a-C1, 2-c-C2, 3-b-C4, 4-c-C5

Each question is linked to a competency. Competencies are listed on the first page of the chapter. An answer reading 3-b-C4 translates to:

   3: the question number
   b: the correct answer
   C4: the competency number

Chapter 9 Outline

Unique Aspects of Private-Club Food and
Beverage Operations
    Operational Components
    The Club's Clientele
    Special Food and Beverage Services
    The Club's Food and Beverage Service
        Providers
The Role of Food and Beverage
    Departments in Clubs
    Attract New Members
    Meet Member Expectations
    Achieve a Healthy Bottom Line
        Banquets and Catering
Organizational Structure of Club Food and
    Beverage Operations
    Management Levels and
        Responsibilities
    The Role of the Club's House
        Committee and Board
The Menu
    Menu Development
        Banquet and Catering Menus
    Menu Item Pricing
    Menu Evaluation
Food and Beverage Finances
    Creating Budgets
    Establishing Payment Policies and
        Procedures
        Food and Beverage Minimums
    Analyzing Financial Results
Food and Beverage Employees
    Recruiting Employees
    Staffing
    Training and Development
    Compensation
    Recognizing Good Employees
Trends in Club Dining

Competencies

1. Summarize some of the unique aspects of private-club food and beverage operations. (pp. 303–306)

2. Explain the role of food and beverage departments in clubs. (pp. 306–310)

3. Outline the organizational structure of club food and beverage operations. (pp. 310–313)

4. Describe the importance of menus in club food and beverage operations, and summarize menu development, menu pricing, and menu evaluation strategies employed by clubs. (pp. 313–317)

5. Summarize the financial aspects of managing a club's food and beverage department, including the budget, payment policies and procedures, and the analysis of financial results. (pp. 317–323)

6. Outline human resources issues in clubs, including recruiting, staffing, training, compensating, and recognizing employees. (pp. 324–326)

7. Describe trends in club dining. (pp. 326–330)

Food and Beverage
Operations in Clubs

This chapter was written and contributed by Clayton W. Barrows,
Associate Professor; School of Hotel, Restaurant & Tourism Administration;
University of New Orleans, New Orleans, Louisiana.
The author would like to thank Mr. Bobby Crifasi, General Manager of
New Orleans Country Club, for his thoughts and insights.

IT WOULD BE IMPOSSIBLE for a single chapter to cover every aspect of food and beverage operations in clubs, or to describe all of the food and beverage activities at the many types of clubs. The major emphasis in this chapter will be on explaining how and why food and beverage operations in clubs are different from nonclub food and beverage operations.

The chapter begins with a discussion of some of the unique aspects of private-club food and beverage operations. It continues by looking at food and beverage department organizational structures in clubs. Discussions of the menu and food and beverage finances follow. The chapter concludes with sections on food and beverage employees and trends in club dining.

Unique Aspects of Private-Club Food and Beverage Operations

There is no single element of a club's food and beverage program that sets it apart from nonclub food and beverage operations. Rather, it is a combination of many elements, elements that include the club's many operational components, the club's clientele, special food and beverage services, and the club's food and beverage service providers.

Operational Components

In some clubs—city clubs, for example—the food and beverage department is the primary source of club revenue, while in other clubs it serves as a secondary revenue generator. Food and beverage service may even be a relatively minor part of a club's overall operations, as in many athletic or yacht clubs. Depending on the individual club, the food and beverage department may make money, break even, or even lose money.

Perhaps the most obvious characteristic that sets club food and beverage operations apart from other food and beverage operations is the number of outlets—and the range of products they offer—that are often housed under one roof. For example, a 1,000-member country club may have three separate à la carte outlets in its clubhouse. As one club manager put it, most clubs must serve everything from snow cones to gourmet dinners. Not many nonclub food-service operations attempt to offer such a wide variety of food. Perhaps only large convention hotels face similar food and beverage challenges.

Suppose that the three outlets of a 1,000-member country club are a formal dining room, a men's grill room (for men only), and a mixed grill room (open to both sexes and to children). All three facilities would be located in the same clubhouse and serviced by the same kitchen, but they would probably have little else in common. The formal dining room would have the most prominent location, typically with a view of the golf course or some other picturesque backdrop. Formal attire would be required, the menu would be sophisticated, and the room would exhibit all the characteristics of a fine-dining restaurant, from the table settings to the servers' uniforms. Club members would use the formal dining room primarily for special occasions, evening dining on the weekend, and business entertainment. Given the dining trend toward casualization—an increasing preference on the part of diners for informal dining—hours of operation would likely be limited.

The grill rooms, on the other hand, would offer inexpensive menu items, allow more casual dress, stay open longer, and provide a more relaxed environment. The men's grill would probably have the simplest menu of the three outlets. Due to the increasing tendency toward casual dining, grill rooms will probably become more prominent in clubs in the years to come.

These three outlets represent the bare minimum that a 1,000-member club would likely have. In addition, there might be catering facilities, smaller food and beverage outlets associated with the pool and the golf course, and outlets that target specific member groups. For example, a club in New Orleans opened a "Teen Room" that caters to the teenagers of those members who spend a lot of weekend time at the club. While parents enjoy a meal in the formal dining room or attend a special function, teens can congregate in their own facility. "Teen rooms" can be designed to offer foods that typically appeal to teenagers, such as pizza and hamburgers, and may be limited to weekend operating hours. Such specialized food and beverage outlets are a creative way clubs can appeal to their many types of members.

The number of food and beverage outlets that a club provides has operational implications that affect staffing, menu offerings, and food and beverage service. For example, most clubs do not find it cost-effective to employ separate managers for each outlet; rather, a single manager oversees all food and beverage operations, with line supervisors/hosts or senior servers in charge in the manager's absence.

Although service levels vary from outlet to outlet, it is in a club's best interest to cross-train service employees to work in every outlet. When one outlet is quiet, another will often experience a rush. If employees have been trained to work in all outlets, they can easily be moved to accommodate fluctuations in usage.

While the different types of food and beverage outlets in clubs serve varying functions and cater to different member needs, they are all part of the club, so they all must maintain the club's standards. Members and their guests should feel like guests of the club, regardless of which food and beverage outlet they patronize. A club should operate as a truly seamless organization in this respect.

The Club's Clientele

Another characteristic that differentiates a club's food service from that of a non-club restaurant is the extent to which clubs cater to their members' needs and desires. Something as simple as referring to a guest by name is considered very special treatment in most nonclub restaurants, but in a club environment such treatment is expected. And that's just the beginning. Club members have many needs that require attention, from the moment they drive up to the door to the time they settle their checks. Such needs may include a special table, a particular chair, or being seated by a specific staff member. At many clubs, if a member wants something to eat that is not listed on the menu, the member is allowed to order it anyway, and the kitchen is expected to prepare it. The needs of club members vary widely, and in most clubs there is no such thing as an unreasonable request from a club member. The club is an extension of the member's home, and in no operational area is this more true than in the food and beverage area.

Special Food and Beverage Services

Clubs offer a variety of food and beverage services that are typically not found in public restaurants. For example, club members often celebrate special occasions at their clubs, and at such times they may want a special menu, perhaps even a "one-time-only" or "single-occasion" menu for the event. This is a perfect opportunity for the club's chef to custom-design a menu. Sometimes, simple variations on existing menu items will suffice; at other times, a bit more effort will be required. However, special-event requests represent great opportunities for food and beverage staff members to showcase their talents and gain the long-term allegiance of a club member. This is precisely the type of opportunity that rarely presents itself outside the club environment.

Other special food and beverage services may include preparing takeout food or delivering prepared food to members, creating boxed lunches for outings, providing beverage cart service on the golf course, and catering pool parties for members' children.

The Club's Food and Beverage Service Providers

Because the employee turnover rate in clubs is lower than in other segments of the hospitality industry, clubs tend to have more long-term employees than hotels or public restaurants. Few hotels or restaurants these days can boast of having an employee with more than 25 years of service, but that is not uncommon in private clubs, particularly in the food and beverage area.

In general, a high number of long-term employees speaks well of a club, its management, and its members. As with all things, however, there are both advantages and disadvantages to having long-term employees. A long-term employee's familiarity with the club, its policies, and its members is one advantage; the cost savings associated with retaining rather than replacing an employee is another. However, these advantages may in some cases be outweighed by the disadvantages.

To believe that a long-term employee's experience necessarily translates into superior work habits is naive. Too often, it is just as likely that such employees have developed bad work habits that, over time, have become difficult to correct. In addition, they are often the most difficult employees to retrain; because they have been on the job so long, they may be less open to retraining or to changes in procedures.

If raises are awarded on the basis of seniority, a large salary discrepancy may exist between older and newer staff members, a situation that can cause resentment among the latter. To compound the problem, many clubs do not offer retirement packages to their employees, which leads some employees to keep working even though they may no longer be as productive as they once were. When these older, inefficient employees work side by side with new staff members who are paid much less, morale problems can result. One way to address such salary discrepancies is to award raises not just on tenure but on a combination of tenure and merit. And while most clubs cannot offer full retirement packages, they might at least offer retirement incentives to their longtime employees.

While familiarity with the members is usually an advantage of having long-term employees, it can also be a disadvantage. Club workers typically get to know many of the club's members in a relatively short period of time, as their contact with members can be quite frequent. However, there must be a clear distinction between club members and club employees. Long-term employees might be tempted to let this distinction crumble and begin to relate to certain members too personally or show favoritism toward particular members at the expense of others. Club managers should be alert for the beginnings of such situations and address them immediately.

The Role of Food and Beverage Departments in Clubs

A private club's food and beverage department plays an important role in helping the club (1) attract new members, (2) meet member expectations, and (3) achieve a healthy bottom line. While the department's exact role is determined by the club's board of directors, these three goals are the primary objectives of most club food and beverage departments.

Attract New Members

The importance of the role a club's food service operation plays in attracting new members cannot be stressed enough. Attracting new members is especially important today, as many clubs struggle to maintain their membership base. Several factors have affected the potential pool of new members—corporation downsizing, changes in tax laws, and the continued aging of the population, to name a few. As a result, every interaction with a nonmember should be viewed as an opportunity to make a positive impression, and a nonmember's first exposure to a club is often as a guest in the dining room or at a special food and beverage function. For this reason alone, a club's food and beverage department should put its best foot forward every time a meal is served.

According to a study published by the McMahon Group (an organization that provides consulting services to private clubs), dining is second only to golf among the reasons people join country clubs.[1] Club managers who understand the impact

Club managers sometimes use imaginative promotions to boost food and beverage sales. One club used a live camel to add atmosphere to a promotion built around an "Arabian Nights" theme; club members were encouraged to dine in costume. (Courtesy of Sally Burns Rambo, CCM, and the Lakewood Country Club, Dallas, Texas)

that dining at the club can have on a person's overall impression of the club know that food and beverage service is a valuable marketing tool.

Meet Member Expectations

Once a club manager accepts the fact that the number of potential club members is limited, he or she will understand the importance of member retention and seek to identify the primary reasons why members maintain their memberships at a particular club. For most clubs, food and beverage service is one of the most important reasons.

In order to plan a club's food and beverage services effectively, a manager must first understand the role of member expectations. A member's *expectations* of the club's dining services help determine the member's *satisfaction* with those services. Private club members' food service expectations tend to be very high; therefore, club managers should establish high standards for the club's dining services. If expectations are not met, members will be dissatisfied.

Meeting member expectations can be particularly challenging if the club is located in a major metropolitan area where fine dining is widely available. While all members may not expect the club to serve the best meal in town, they all do expect the club to set high standards and consistently meet them.

A club's reputation is determined in large part by the consistency of its food and service quality. Consistently high quality is achieved by establishing strict

Clubs often plan food and beverage promotions around major holidays. (Courtesy of Lakewood Country Club, Dallas, Texas)

standards, following proven policies, training and retaining staff members, and providing ongoing training. Consistency of performance is the mark of a superior operation and is what will keep members coming back year after year.

Achieve a Healthy Bottom Line

The financial contribution that a food and beverage department makes to a club's bottom line varies greatly among clubs. Food and beverage service is profitable in some clubs, while others must subsidize their food and beverage service with revenue from other areas. Some food and beverage outlets—such as the snack bar/halfway house facility commonly found in clubs that offer golf—do not come close to paying for themselves; they exist solely to serve the membership. However, even food and beverage outlets that do not make money help a club achieve a healthy bottom line by providing a service that encourages members to use other club services.

As with any food service operation, the profitability of a club's food and beverage department is a function of pricing, the product/service mix, usage, and the cost structure of the operation. For example, since club members are already paying dues, clubs might maintain a 50 to 60 percent food cost percentage in their restaurants in an effort to keep à la carte prices down. This can result in the restaurants losing money. However, clubs usually more than make up for this loss with banquets (private parties), where a 20 to 30 percent food cost percentage is common.

Food and beverage labor costs tend to be higher in clubs than in public restaurants. High service standards are one reason; more and better-trained servers cost more money. Members may also request that food and beverage outlets stay open even during slow periods. Maintaining service quality while keeping costs down is an ongoing challenge for private clubs, a challenge that increases with the number of food service outlets they have. While service is of the utmost importance in a private club, few club managers are given carte blanche when it comes to payroll. Good management is characterized by the ability to achieve a balance between costs and service quality.

Food and beverage sales represent a large percentage of club revenue for most clubs. According to one study of private clubs in the United States, over one-third of total per-member income in country clubs is generated by food and beverage sales—more than one-half when dues are excluded. The same study indicates that food and beverage sales are increasing at a greater rate than are membership dues, suggesting that sales of food and beverages are becoming a more important revenue source for clubs.[2] Clearly, the revenue generated through the sale of food and beverages impacts a club's bottom line, and the food and beverage department's importance to clubs will only increase in the future.

Banquets and Catering. At most clubs the majority of banquet dollars goes directly to the bottom line, making banquets a very important source of revenue. Because they are so profitable, banquets may be viewed by the food and beverage department's management and staff as more important than the club's daily à la carte service. The clubhouse manager must remind the service and kitchen staffs of the importance of the club's regular food and beverage operations. After all, as mentioned earlier, most clubs rely on their à la carte service to establish their reputations for quality.

Although banquets are profitable, some clubs limit the number of banquets they sell to outside groups because they feel that hosting too many such events compromises the image of a private club. Some clubs allow banquets involving outside groups only if the group is sponsored by a club member. In addition, a private club may lose tax-exempt status if its sales from nonmember functions exceed 15 percent of gross revenues.

Organizational Structure of Club Food and Beverage Operations

As with other aspects of clubs, food and beverage organizational structures vary a great deal from club to club. In a small club, each food and beverage staff person has a wide range of responsibilities; in a large club, responsibilities are spread among more people and are more narrowly defined. This holds true for both back-of-the-house and front-of-the-house positions. For example, a small club might not even have an executive chef, but rather a head cook who would be a "working chef"; a large club might have an executive chef, a sous chef, a garde-manger, and a pastry chef.

Nonetheless, there are some common organizational elements among the food and beverage departments of most private clubs, and these will be presented here. The best organizational structure for a particular club's food and beverage department is the one that most efficiently meets the needs of that club's members.

Management Levels and Responsibilities

The person ultimately in charge of the entire food and beverage operation is generally the same person who is in charge of the clubhouse—in most cases, the clubhouse manager. The number of management levels below the clubhouse manager varies, depending on the size and scope of the club. In a 1,000-member country club, the clubhouse manager would typically oversee two levels of food and beverage management: an assistant clubhouse manager and lower-level supervisors (see Exhibit 1).

In addition to being the person ultimately responsible for the club's food and beverage outlets, the clubhouse manager in a 1,000-member club oversees housekeeping, maintenance and engineering, sales, and member services, including the pool and the tennis courts at some clubs. He or she reports directly to the club's general manager.

The assistant clubhouse manager directly oversees all food and beverage activities, including banquets. While the clubhouse manager probably is involved in sales and long-range planning for the food and beverage department, the assistant clubhouse manager is more involved in day-to-day activities, such as working with food and beverage line supervisors.

Each clubhouse food and beverage outlet is under the direction of its own line supervisor. In a club with four food service areas—a formal dining room, two grill rooms, and banquet service, for example—there would be four line supervisors.

Exhibit 1   Sample Organization Chart—Club Food and Beverage Department

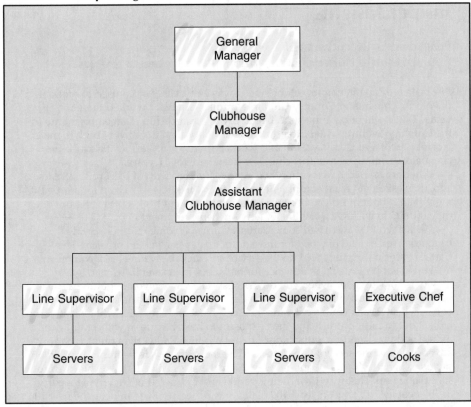

Line supervisors report to the assistant clubhouse manager. The club's executive chef, in most cases, reports to the clubhouse manager. Line supervisors and the executive chef directly supervise line employees.

The Role of the Club's House Committee and Board

Some management decision-making in clubs is centralized, some is decentralized. For example, a decision regarding which food and beverage vendors to use would be made by the assistant clubhouse manager or clubhouse manager (centralized), while a decision regarding the staffing and scheduling of line employees is more likely to be made by line supervisors (decentralized). Where and how management decisions are made is ultimately determined by the club's organizational culture, which also drives the club's policies. If the primary objective of the club and its staff is to satisfy members, then the staff will be empowered to do so, which represents a more decentralized orientation. Even so, staff members must understand that much of what they do and many of the decisions that they make are governed by the policies recommended by the club's **house committee** and established by the club's board of directors.

Insider Insights

Pete Bowden, Executive Chef
Country Club of Fairfax, Fairfax, Virginia ——————————————————————

I've been working in country clubs since I was 14 $^1/_2$ years old. I used to work at
the Norfolk Yacht and Country Club in Norfolk, Virginia. I worked there for 11 $^1/_2$
years. That's where I got my start, began my apprenticeship. That club sent me to
the Culinary Institute. After attending the Culinary Institute, I went back to the
Norfolk Yacht and Country Club and worked there for 5 years as the executive
chef before coming over to this club. I've been here for 11 years.

When we started a renovation here at the Country Club of Fairfax 3 $^1/_2$ years
ago, they asked me what equipment I wanted in the kitchen. I asked for a little bit
more than I thought I'd get, because I figured they'd cut back a little later on, but
they didn't. So we have a full line of new kitchen equipment here.

We just recently purchased some Carter-Hoffman holding units for serving
banquets. We can send out food for three or four banquets with no problem. The
Carter-Hoffmans help us speed up the service and they're great pieces of equipment.

We do not preplate far in advance for banquets. I've never liked that. Food
quality is not very good when you do that. Especially when you're putting a sauce
on the entrées, like a shittake mushroom demi-sauce. A demi-sauce is made of veal
bones, which means you've got a lot of marrow in it and the sauce will crust if you
ladle it over a meat product and then expose it to heat, because it will continue to
reduce and you'll end up with a poor-quality product. Rather than preplate far in
advance, I have the servers come back and let me know where people are with their
salads. When they're just about halfway done, that's when I tell the kitchen staff to
start plating up. That way, the holding period is very brief. If we're serving a party
of 300 people, I try to get at least 100 plates ahead, because we can plate the next 100
while the servers are taking out the first 100. And when they take out the second
100 we can plate the last 100. That way, it's a constant, ongoing process.

With large banquets, you never know quite where you stand. That's one reason
why I'm careful about preplating, because of the unexpected things that can occur.
We've had wedding receptions here at the club where the bride is late, or you can't
find the groom, or something like that holds things up. So you've got to work with
the banquet manager and you've got to communicate. Communication is very
important. If I'm back in the kitchen looking at the clock and thinking, "Whoa,
they should be sitting down now, I'd better start plating" and I'm just guessing,
that's not going to work. It takes communication.

Because of the house committee and board, decision-making in a club is quite
different from decision-making in other types of hospitality organizations. Although not a part of the management team, a club's house committee, composed of
club members, is charged with monitoring the clubhouse and its services. The
house committee's responsibilities are usually clearly spelled out in the club's bylaws. The committee typically recommends club policies, makes recommendations
for capital budgeting, and makes recommendations regarding price increases to the
board of directors. House committee members usually assist the general manager

and clubhouse manager in monitoring the quality of the club's food and service. For example, the house committee would probably be consulted if club managers decided to conduct a membership survey to gauge member satisfaction with the club's food and beverage operation.

The role of club managers is to make day-to-day decisions within the framework recommended by the house committee and established by the board of directors. Since the role of the house committee is to recommend club policies, the role of the board is to establish club policies, and the role of club managers is to implement club policies, the responsibilities of each group should rarely overlap.

The Menu

The menu is the heart of any food and beverage operation. Menus, however, are especially important to a club, because they can influence member participation throughout the club. If the members are satisfied with the food, they will not only visit the club's restaurants more often, but probably will also use other club services to a greater degree.

Most clubs have more than one menu, and every menu is important. Each should be evaluated not just on its own merits, but also on how it fits into the overall presentation of the club. While a club's menus will vary from outlet to outlet, they should all reflect the club's overall mission and goals.

There are three objectives club managers should keep in mind when planning club menus. Each menu should: (1) offer affordable items that will please members and entice members to return, (2) support other club activities, and (3) contribute significantly to the club's image.[3]

Menu Development

Since a club menu's primary purpose is to list items that members want, a club's formal-dining menu is likely to have more menu items than a typical public restaurant menu. While the trend in public restaurants in recent years has been to reduce the number of menu items offered, this has not been the trend in clubs. In fact, as clubs have diversified by offering more food service outlets to serve various groups of members, the number of menu items clubs prepare has probably increased.

Once an item appears on a club menu, it is difficult to remove it; members often "take ownership" of particular menu items and take it personally if those items are eliminated. While a changing menu may be attractive to patrons of a nonclub restaurant, the same is not necessarily true in a club. Club members often like to know what to expect, and they like a familiar menu. This in itself can make the menu development process challenging.

Menu development in a club can be handled in a variety of ways. In some clubs, menu decisions are left up to the head chef and a single club manager. Many successful operations, on the other hand, let food and beverage employees and club members help develop menus. There are advantages to this approach. Helping with menu development can add some excitement to the jobs of food and beverage employees traditionally involved only in sales and service. And if servers help decide what appears on the menu, they will probably be more committed to the menu

---

Menu-Making Software

Computers make it easier for club managers to design their own menus. There are several menu-making software programs club managers can turn to for help:

MenuPro by SoftCafe
Silver Spring, Maryland (800-747-3690)

Menu Maker by Symbiotic Systems Corp.
Ward, Colorado (800-459-8848)

Menusbyou by Menu Promotions/Ideas
Clifton, New Jersey (800-989-0556)

Source: Paul Moomaw, "Computers Help Create Menus Du Jour," *Restaurants USA*, May 1996.

and find it easier to sell. If members help develop the menu, it encourages them to "buy into" its offerings. One way to get members involved is to invite the club's board of directors and house committee members to special "previews" of potential new menu items. Soliciting feedback at this point goes a lot further than asking for opinions after the item is already on the menu; members feel like consultants and are more likely to support new menu items if they've helped select them.

In summary, menu development in clubs usually should be approached conservatively and involve more than one or two people. An unchanging core menu is appropriate for most clubs; the chef can show off his or her creative talents through weekly or daily specials and special-occasion menus.

Banquet and Catering Menus. A club's banquet and catering menus are often handled quite differently from the menus of the club's food and beverage outlets. If a club does a lot of banquet business, there may be a separate department to handle banquet sales and service that functions much like the catering department in a hotel, with a line supervisor who oversees all banquet activities, including identifying prospective clients (members and possibly nonmembers), selling the banquet space, and managing the banquets. In order to boost banquet sales, some clubs create informational packages that include banquet-room rental fees, banquet menus, and information about any other services or amenities that the club provides to banquet groups.

Once again, the menu is the heart of what the club offers banquet customers. Banquet menus must be developed for every type of function that the club might cater, such as wedding receptions, awards dinners, and such annual events as Mardi Gras balls and Fourth of July cookouts. Exhibit 2 presents some pages from a sample banquet menu.

Banquet menu items and prices vary dramatically from club to club, depending on the club's banquet facilities, the quality of service provided, the club's prestige, and the demand for banquet space. Competition and demand are more important in pricing banquet menu items than in pricing items on the club's à la carte menus, as clubs may target an entirely different clientele for banquets. The

Exhibit 2   Sample Banquet Menu

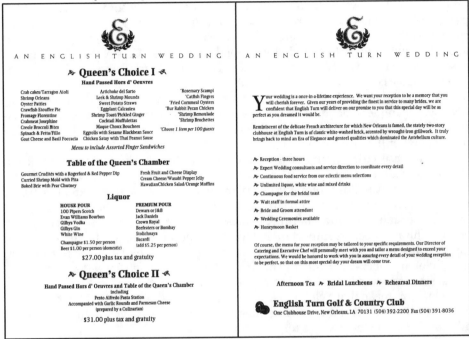

AN ENGLISH TURN WEDDING

❧ Queen's Choice I ❧
Hand Passed Hors d' Oeuvres

Crab cakes/Tarragon Aioli
Shrimp Orleans
Oyster Patties
Crawfish Etouffee Pie
Fromage Florentine
Crabmeat Josephine
Creole Broccoli Bites
Spinach & Fetta/Fillo
Goat Cheese and Basil Foccacia

Artichoke del Sarto
Leek & Shrimp Mounds
Sweet Potato Straws
Eggplant Calcasieu
Shrimp Toast/Pickled Ginger
Cocktail Muffulettas
Maque Choux Bouchees
Eggrolls with Sesame Blackbean Sauce
Chicken Satay with Thai Peanut Sauce

*Rosemary Scampi
*Catfish Fingers
*Fried Cornmeal Oysters
*Bur Rabbit Pecan Chicken
*Shrimp Remoulade
*Shrimp Brochettes

Choose 1 Item per 100 guests

Menu to include Assorted Finger Sandwiches

Table of the Queen's Chamber

Gourmet Crudités with a Rogerford & Red Pepper Dip
Curried Shrimp Mold with Pita
Baked Brie with Pear Chutney

Fresh Fruit and Cheese Display
Cream Cheese/Wasabi Pepper Jelly
Hawaiian Chicken Salad/Orange Muffins

Liquor

HOUSE POUR
100 Pipers Scotch
Evan Williams Bourbon
Gilbys Vodka
Gilbys Gin
White Wine

Champagne $1.50 per person
Beer $1.00 per person (domestic)

PREMIUM POUR
Dewars or J&B
Jack Daniels
Crown Royal
Beefeaters or Bombay
Stolichnaya
Bacardi
(add $5.25 per person)

$27.00 plus tax and gratuity

❧ Queen's Choice II ❧
Hand Passed Hors d' Oeuvres and Table of the Queen's Chamber
including
Pesto Alfredo Pasta Station
Accompanied with Garlic Rounds and Parmesan Cheese
(prepared by a Culinarian)

$31.00 plus tax and gratuity

AN ENGLISH TURN WEDDING

Your wedding is a once-in-a-lifetime experience. We want your reception to be a memory that you will cherish forever. Given our years of providing the finest in service to many brides, we are confident that English Turn will deliver on our promise to you that this special day will be as perfect as you dreamed it would be.

Reminiscent of the delicate French architecture for which New Orleans is famed, the stately two-story clubhouse at English Turn is of classic white-washed brick, accented by wrought-iron grillwork. It truly brings back to mind an Era of Elegance and genteel qualities which dominated the Antebellum culture.

❧ Reception - three hours
❧ Expert Wedding consultants and service direction to coordinate every detail
❧ Continuous food service from our eclectic menu selections
❧ Unlimited liquor, white wine and mixed drinks
❧ Champagne for the bridal toast
❧ Wait staff in formal attire
❧ Bride and Groom attendant
❧ Wedding Ceremonies available
❧ Honeymoon Basket

Of course, the menu for your reception may be tailored to your specific requirements. Our Director of Catering and Executive Chef will personally meet with you and tailor a menu designed to exceed your expectations. We would be honored to work with you in assuring every detail of your wedding reception to be perfect, so that on this most special day your dream will come true.

Afternoon Tea   ❧   Bridal Luncheons   ❧   Rehearsal Dinners

English Turn Golf & Country Club
One Clubhouse Drive, New Orleans, LA 70131 (504) 392-2200 Fax (504) 391-8036

Source: English Turn Golf & Country Club, New Orleans, Louisiana.

more banquet packages (reflecting a wide range of prices) a club offers, the more groups it will appeal to and the more revenue it can generate.

Menu Item Pricing

Most club managers must accept the fact that they will not be able to achieve a low food cost percentage in the club's à la carte operations. Many clubs will have to offer menu items at a rate around two times raw food cost, or 50 percent cost. If markup is much higher, the club runs the risk of losing a certain percentage of diners. However, if prices are much lower, revenue will be forfeited and members will become accustomed to very low prices, making future price increases difficult to implement. Many clubs can charge lower prices for their food and beverages than their public competition, since they are able to make up for lost food and beverage revenue by increasing club membership dues.

There are three primary factors to consider when pricing menu items: cost, competition, and demand. Many managers base their menu prices only on food cost, typically by targeting a desired food cost percentage and then applying the appropriate multiplier to the raw food cost to determine the selling price. The problems associated with this approach have been the subject of much industry discussion, and several recommendations have been set forth to improve the use of cost in the pricing decision. One recommendation is the use of **prime costing**, which includes both food and labor costs.[4] This strategy might be particularly appropriate for clubs, where food costs and labor costs together sometimes exceed 100 percent of food and beverage revenue. One industry report shows that the average country club spends over 95 percent of its restaurant revenue on the cost of food and labor, with the cost of food alone representing over 42 percent.[5] Thus, prices based only on the cost of food may not even cover all of a food and beverage operation's variable costs.

As pointed out earlier, many clubs subsidize their à la carte food service operations with banquets. Banquet prices are usually established so that profits are assured. If nonmember banquets are allowed at the club, prices for these banquets are usually higher than for member banquets.

In any case, costs should be used to determine the absolute minimum prices a club must charge. After this threshold is set, competition should be considered. While a club may not use competitive pricing strategies to the same extent as public restaurants, it is important for a clubhouse manager to know what prices competing clubs, restaurants, and catering businesses are charging for their food and beverages. This is especially important in today's economy, as many club members are limiting themselves to one club, foregoing multiple club memberships. In addition, many club members are probably aware of the prices being charged at competing clubs, since they are likely to visit them as guests.

Does this mean that a club must charge less than its competition? Certainly not. However, it does mean that pricing must focus on the perceived value of the food and services members receive for the price they pay.

The final pricing consideration is demand for a particular product. It would be helpful if club managers could establish the highest price that club members are willing to pay for certain menu items by raising prices until members stop buying, then adjusting prices accordingly. However, because a club's menu prices are subject to board approval, it is unlikely that club managers will ever be given permission to pursue such a strategy to determine what the market will bear.

Menu Evaluation

Menu evaluation refers to the process of reviewing the strengths and weaknesses of a menu on a regular basis. Many public restaurants should evaluate their menus annually. In clubs, however, it may not be necessary to evaluate menus so frequently. As discussed earlier, most club members prefer a menu that rarely changes; in fact, they may react negatively to change. This is not to say that club menus should never be evaluated; some periodic evaluation is necessary to keep up with the changing composition and tastes of the membership.

At some point the clubhouse manager will decide to make some menu changes, probably due to member or board feedback or a change in kitchen personnel. One method of menu evaluation that has proven successful in clubs is **menu engineering.**[6] The essence of menu engineering is to evaluate each menu item with respect to both profitability and popularity—not on the sole basis of food cost percentage. Because it takes diner preferences into account, menu engineering is an especially appropriate method of menu evaluation for clubs. Again, club managers should keep in mind that the decision to remove a menu item should not be made lightly; taking an item off the menu might raise the ire of those few members who do order the item—members who may have been with the club much longer than the current manager.

Food and Beverage Finances

The financial operation of a club's food and beverage department includes creating budgets, establishing payment policies and procedures, and analyzing financial results.

Creating Budgets

Because the food and beverage department is a revenue-generating department, it requires its own budget. Exhibit 3, sample food and beverage schedules from the *Uniform System of Financial Reporting for Clubs*, shows the types of items that managers must address in a food and beverage budget.

A properly detailed food and beverage department budget establishes realistic forecasts of revenues and expenses in all food and beverage areas. For example, a country club with three full-service food and beverage outlets, a banquet department, and various satellite food and beverage operations would prepare a separate sales forecast for each outlet. These sales forecasts would be based on several factors, including—but not limited to—the previous year's sales, the current level of member participation, special events planned, anticipated changes in the economy, price changes, and the degree to which the outlet will be attempting to increase business.

Food and beverage expenses are forecast in a similar fashion, also taking into account impending changes. In most cases, a forecasted increase in departmental revenues will be accompanied by an increase in certain variable expenses, such as food, beverage, and labor costs. Another factor to consider when forecasting food and beverage expenses is the foreseeable need for additional equipment and supplies. (Very expensive food and beverage equipment is usually included in the club's capital budget rather than the food and beverage department's operational budget.)

Forecasting is an imprecise science, and forecasted budget figures serve only as guidelines for an upcoming period of time. Variances from budgeted revenues and expenses occur for a variety of reasons. However, even though variances are inevitable, club managers should still make every effort to develop realistic budgets and meet them.

The food and beverage department budget is generally reviewed at several club levels and adjusted, if necessary, before final approval. After initial review by the general manager, the food and beverage department budget of most clubs is reviewed by the club's finance committee, which then makes its recommendation to the club's board of directors. The board grants final budget approval. The budget review process may take as long as three months, and the budget may require several revisions.

One trend in budgeting is the **zero-base** approach. With this approach, food and beverage department managers cannot simply carry over budgets from year to year, but must start from zero each year and justify their budget figures by providing adequate reasoning for their forecasts. This has generally been viewed as a

Exhibit 3   Sample Club Food and Beverage Department Budget

```
                              City or Country Club          Schedule 1-A
                                     Food

Food sales (list revenue by location)              $_____
Cost of food sold
  Cost of food consumed
  Less credit for employees' meals
           Cost of food sold                        _____

           Gross profit on food sales              _____

Other income
  Unused minimum (See page 8)
  Service charge
  Dining room rental
           Total other income                      _____
           Total gross profit and other income     _____

Departmental expenses
  Payroll and related expenses
    Salaries and wages
      Payroll taxes and employee benefits
      Employees' meals
           Total payroll and related expenses      _____
  Other expenses
    China, glassware, and silver
    Contract cleaning
    Equipment rental
    Kitchen fuel
    Laundry and dry cleaning
    Licenses and permits
    Linen
    Music and entertainment
    Operating supplies
    Other operating expenses
    Printing and stationery
    Refuse removal
    Repairs and maintenance
    Uniforms
           Total other expenses                    _____

           Total departmental expenses             _____

Departmental net income (loss)                    $_____
```

```
                              City or Country Club          Schedule 1-B
                                   Beverage

Beverage sales (list revenue by location)          $_____
Cost of beverage sold
           Gross profit on beverage sales          _____

Other income
  Unused minimum (See page 8)
  Service charge
           Total other income                      _____
           Total gross profit and other income     _____

Departmental expenses
  Payroll and related expenses
    Salaries and wages
      Payroll taxes and employee benefits
      Employees' meals
           Total payroll and related expenses      _____
  Other expenses
    China, glassware, and silver
    Contract cleaning
    Equipment rental
    Laundry and dry cleaning
    Licenses and permits
    Linen
    Music and entertainment
    Operating supplies
    Other operating expenses
    Printing and stationery
    Repairs and maintenance
    Uniforms
           Total other expenses                    _____

           Total departmental expenses             _____

Departmental net income (loss)                    $_____
```

Source: *Uniform System of Financial Reporting for Clubs.*

positive change in budget formulation and in most cases has resulted in more accurate budget forecasts.

Establishing Payment Policies and Procedures

A club's food and beverage payment policies and procedures are designed to accomplish three primary objectives: (1) encourage the use of the club's food and beverage facilities by members, (2) ensure expedient payment for services rendered, and (3) maintain control over payments.

The most important food and beverage policies and procedures concern the forms of payment members can use to settle their bills. Members in most clubs have traditionally been allowed to pay for food and beverage services by signing their guest checks, thereby agreeing to pay the charges at a later time. Most clubs—at least until recently—would not accept payment by cash, check, or credit card.

When members sign their guest checks, the club is essentially issuing credit. This easy payment method is not only convenient for members, but is also a way for the club to encourage more food and beverage sales. This method also eliminates the need for cash control, since no cash changes hands. Finally, this payment system is streamlined: food and beverage charges are billed, along with other club service charges and membership dues, at the end of the billing cycle, reducing internal paperwork. This method of payment has been successful for clubs and has been in continuous use in many clubs for a very long time.

Recently, however, some clubs have begun to change this tradition. An increasing number of clubs will accept credit cards, for example. This change has occurred for three reasons. First, it offers the same "buy now, pay later" service to members as signing guest checks, while allowing the club faster access to payment. Second, as more clubs become semiprivate, they need to offer nonmembers a convenient way to pay for food and beverage services. Third, it offers the same level of control as in-house charges.

The process and timing of member billing affects the flow of cash through the food and beverage department. Once a guest check is signed in the dining room, it is forwarded to the club's controller. The controller compiles all guest charges and posts them to individual member accounts. Most clubs bill their members for services and dues on a monthly basis.

Food and Beverage Minimums. A **food and beverage minimum** is a monthly food and beverage charge imposed on club members whether or not they use the club's food and beverage facilities. The amount is usually nominal ($25 per month is typical) and entitles the member each month to food and beverages equal to that amount; he or she pays for food and beverages beyond the minimum.

There is probably no area of club food and beverage operations that generates as much debate as food and beverage minimums. In general, most members do not like them, since they represent a charge for services that they feel they have the right to use at their own discretion; obviously, those members who always spend more than the minimum do not object as strongly. Club managers are also divided on the issue. Some see minimums as a way of "assessing" nonusers for having certain food and beverage services available to them, while others see minimums as a way of

Exhibit 4 Common Food and Beverage Operating Ratios

$$\text{Food Cost Percentage} = \frac{\text{Cost of Food}}{\text{Food Sales}}$$

$$\text{Beverage Cost Percentage} = \frac{\text{Cost of Beverages}}{\text{Beverage Sales}}$$

$$\text{Labor Cost Percentage} = \frac{\text{Cost of Labor}}{\text{Sales}}$$

$$\text{Average Check} = \frac{\text{Sales}}{\text{Number of Covers}}$$

$$\text{Food to Beverage Ratio} = \frac{\text{Food Sales}}{\text{Beverage Sales}}$$

encouraging members to spend at least a little on the club's food and beverages. Still others think that minimums are not worth the member resentment they generate.

Most clubs that do not currently impose a minimum are hesitant to institute the practice for fear of alienating the membership. The clubs that do have minimums are generally thankful for and somewhat protective of them. Food and beverage minimums are especially advantageous in clubs that offer many membership categories, as they can generate revenue from members who might not frequent the clubhouse. Some clubs vary the minimum according to membership category and, for example, may charge a $40 minimum for members with limited club privileges, a $25 minimum for members with full club privileges, and no minimum for long-time or senior members.

Analyzing Financial Results

Operating ratios are formulas used to analyze the financial results of a club; different operating ratios are used to calculate different things. Most club food and beverage operations use the same operating ratios that are used in public restaurants; some of the most common ratios are presented in Exhibit 4.

Food cost percentage (cost of food divided by food sales) and **beverage cost percentage** (cost of beverages divided by beverage sales) are calculated in order to compare actual costs with targeted costs. These percentages may be calculated for any meal period or per day, week, month, or year. In most cases, a variance of two percent or more from budgeted targets is cause for concern and should be investigated. **Labor**

Insider Insights

Bob Babyok, CCM, General Manager
Army Navy Club, Arlington, Virginia ⎯⎯⎯⎯⎯⎯⎯⎯⎯⎯⎯⎯⎯⎯⎯⎯

One of the differences between a restaurant and a country club is that members at a club pay dues and expect a certain level of service at the club's food and beverage outlets. So a club has to have enough employees on hand to sustain that level of service, even if the club loses money because of excess labor costs. That's regrettable, and a club has to try to control those costs, but a club also has to live with those costs.

Most restaurants fall in the category of fine dining, family dining, or fast food. There are other categories, but those are the basic three. After a restaurant chooses a category, it creates its menus, organizes its equipment, and trains its staff based on whatever category it picked. A country club, on the other hand, provides all three types of food service. So clubs must have a versatile kitchen as far as equipment goes. They've also got to have a versatile menu and a versatile staff. Because on a Saturday night you might find Mr. Jones and his wife at the club for a romantic dinner in the formal dining room, but the next time you see Mr. Jones he might have his entire family with him enjoying an informal meal on a week night, and the next time you see Mr. Jones he's in the grill having a quick hamburger between golf rounds. So a club doesn't have the luxury of concentrating on providing just one type of dining experience.

Plus you have banquets and functions at a club. When you have a wedding, you need an extra 20 employees to handle it. But what do you do with those 20 employees when you don't have the wedding? You've got to integrate them into the staff somehow. So there are always going to be expenses involved in keeping extra staff on hand, expenses that a club must try to minimize as best it can. But all those employees need a livable wage. You've got to pay them enough to make it worth their while to stay with you. Otherwise you'll train them and they'll go somewhere else.

The cost of these "extra" employees contributes to high overhead, and that's where the club dues come in, to pay for that overhead. We have to provide our members with the activities and facilities and services they want, even if they only want them once in a while. When I was a kid, I worked at one club restaurant where we prepared six ducks every night, and almost every night we'd throw those six ducks into the trash. But the members wanted to pay for it. They wanted to have those ducks ready for when they chose to have them.

Most country clubs want long-term employees. Members want to have that home-away-from-home feeling at their club; they want name recognition from employees and familiar faces and all that. But there's a cost attached. For example, old Harry gets on in years and starts serving meals to the wrong tables and has trouble figuring out the guest checks, but you can't get rid of old Harry, he's become an institution. He's become an ineffective employee, but he's also an institution. The manager doesn't dare fire old Harry. At several clubs I've had to create new jobs for employees, move them to different areas without having them lose face, because senior employees have a lot of credibility—maybe not as top-notch employees

(continued)

Insider Insights *(continued)*

anymore, but with the membership and with other employees. Somehow, you have to protect the club's members by putting the longtime-but-no-longer-effective employees into positions that are going to showcase their experience and their worth but not negatively impact club operations.

Many clubs require members to spend a minimum amount on food at the club each month. Personally, I have a lot of problems with food and beverage minimums. Generally speaking, they're a bad idea, because members resent them. Minimums don't make a lot of sense either. Clubs typically operate their food and beverage facilities at a loss, so the more people you encourage to use the facilities by imposing minimums, the more it costs you. If your food production is marginally profitable, you might make $1.50 for every $50 that a member spends. For such a small amount, you're better-off raising club dues $5 and not dealing with the contention.

A positive aspect of minimums, I guess—looking at it purely from a club manager's standpoint—is the unspent minimum. But I look at that with a jaundiced eye, too, because if a member pays, say, a $50 minimum for four months in a row, but for whatever reason doesn't choose to get any food or beverages for it, slowly but surely that member gets to thinking that the club owes him $200. It starts to bug him. Food and beverage minimums are very controversial with members.

With club food and beverage operations there's also the problem of food waste, since usually you're playing a guessing game as to when members are going to eat at the club. Although they're supposed to make reservations at the club, members are just not in the habit of doing it. They make them at restaurants; at restaurants they know they can't get in unless they make reservations. But clubs try to be a home away from home, so although we ask for reservations, they're not mandatory, and members know that. So, what you end up doing is guessing, hoping you'll have enough food and enough staff to serve the meals properly.

There are no food and beverage service charges at the Army Navy Club, except for special functions. That means the club has to foot the day-to-day food and beverage labor bill totally on its own, but it's a great gimmick for the members. It makes eating at the club a less expensive alternative than if they went someplace else and paid that 15 percent gratuity.

Most club managers don't want tipping at their clubs anyway. Cash tips are deadly in a country club, because the employees start complaining about service assignments and fighting about who they get to serve. And they may start giving different levels of service based on the tips they expect. Suppose the party at one table orders four lobsters and the party at another table orders four hamburgers. The tip at the lobster table is going to be much greater. So how much attention does the server give the members at the lobster table versus the members at the hamburger table? Another server may be thinking, Why did Jane get the lobster table instead of me? I only got this table over here with the two club sandwiches. So now the host who assigned the tables gets pulled into it. It goes on and on. Who gets to work on Friday nights? Who works the window seats, which tend to have higher traffic and higher turnover? Who gets the large tables, in dining rooms where table sizes vary? At the larger tables, you'll be serving more people and the tips should be larger.

(continued)

Insider Insights *(continued)*

Let's say I want to try to make it fair, so I give out service assignments using a lottery system or make the servers take turns, so the servers don't work in the same sections all the time. Even that doesn't solve the problem. Suppose one night Mrs. Smith comes to the club for dinner. Mrs. Smith is known to be a big tipper. Alphonse knows that every time she comes to the club, it's $20 for him. No doubt about it. All he has to do is do his thing, and he's going to get 20 bucks. But tonight she doesn't sit in his section. He's ticked off because he can see his 20 bucks flying out the window, right? Mary gets to serve Mrs. Smith instead. Mary thinks she's just as good as Alphonse, but for some reason Mrs. Smith doesn't like Mary's service style as much, so she only gives $10 to Mary. Mary knows that Alphonse gets $20 every time. So now she's mad at Mrs. Smith. Alphonse is mad at Mary because he lost $20, and maybe he starts feeling superior to Mary because he knows she only got $10 from Mrs. Smith. So it sets up competition among the staff members. Yikes! It's like a disease.

Good food servers are crazy to work in clubs, unless they're in it for the long haul, because they can usually make more in tips at a restaurant. Bartenders especially can make much more in tips at restaurants. So we have to get our food and beverage employees to stay with the club for different reasons. We have to push a family concept, set things up so Alphonse and Mary don't have to compete with each other. We have to let our employees know we want them for the long term, get them to stay based on the club's work environment and the fact that the atmosphere at a club is different from a restaurant's, because the people they serve are generally going to be a little nicer to deal with than the typical restaurant crowd. We have to sell them on those aspects, not the dollars.

---

cost percentage (cost of labor divided by sales) is also calculated to compare actual costs with budgeted costs. Labor cost data is most useful when it is calculated for each functional area.

Determining the **average check** (sales divided by number of covers) yields very useful information; the overall check average can be compared from meal period to meal period or across meal periods, for example, and can be used to analyze the sales efforts of food servers.

Some club managers attempt to maintain a certain **food to beverage ratio** (food sales divided by beverage sales). However, because clubs vary so widely, there is no industry standard: some clubs do quite well with a 1:1 ratio, while others may be equally successful with a 3:1 ratio. Private clubs in general operate with a lower food to beverage ratio than nonclub restaurants serving alcoholic beverages—in other words, clubs tend to serve a higher percentage of drinks.

Food and beverage department managers should understand that to use any one ratio exclusively can be misleading. It is always safest to use several ratios to analyze operations, thereby gaining a more complete and accurate picture of the effectiveness of the department.

Food and Beverage Employees

The importance of employees to the success of a food service operation is seldom a subject of debate; it has long been understood that a food service operation's employees can make or break a manager. While this is as true in clubs as in any other type of hospitality organization, a club's food and beverage managers face several unique challenges in the area of human resources.

Recruiting Employees

For the most part, clubs go about recruiting new employees in much the same way as other hospitality organizations, with one significant exception: most clubs prohibit the hiring of a current member's relative. Clubs use this rule to avoid the conflict of interest that might arise if an employee is also a club member by way of being related to a member. In addition, obvious problems could occur if a member's employed relative—for example, a son or daughter—had to be fired. Since this policy eliminates a good number of potential employees, clubs must be more creative than other organizations in their recruiting efforts. Many clubs rely heavily on internal recruiting methods, including recommendations from current employees.

In many job markets, the people who might enjoy working in a club's food and beverage department are the same people being recruited by hotels, restaurants, and casinos. Because of this, clubs must rely heavily on the appeal of a quality work environment to attract new employees.

As mentioned earlier, many clubs experience significantly lower employee turnover rates than other segments of the hospitality industry. Nevertheless, as the hospitality labor market gets even more competitive, club managers may be forced to reevaluate their hiring practices and policies—including the policy against hiring the relatives of members.

Staffing

As stated earlier, a club's labor costs can be quite high when compared to other hospitality firms'. For this reason, club managers must keep a careful eye on the schedule and the number of hours that each employee works.

One useful tool for maintaining control of the labor budget is a **staffing chart**. A staffing chart is simply a chart that shows how many employees should be scheduled, given various levels of business. It can be used to schedule both front-of-the-house and back-of-the-house employees.

Employees should be scheduled to maximize efficiency while still meeting the needs of members. For example, rarely should the entire service staff be scheduled to come in at the beginning of a meal period; rather, service employees should report to work on a staggered basis, based on reservations and forecasting. Also, as pointed out earlier, cross-training employees to work in various food service outlets allows greater scheduling flexibility, which can result in cost savings.

Training and Development

The gap that exists between what employee-training theorists propose and what actually takes place in the hospitality industry is wide indeed. Trainers constantly espouse the need for increased training, but many segments of the hospitality industry cut training budgets during tough economic times. Private clubs differ in this respect from other hospitality segments; in good times and bad, they spend time and money on training and developing their food and beverage employees.

The long-term goals of a private club usually include maintaining a high level of member satisfaction. In the long run, an effective employee-training program contributes significantly to a club's ability to realize this goal. Employee training should also reduce service- or product-related costs and employee turnover and absenteeism. Of course, employee training should also contribute to the overall professional development of employees. While training is not a cure-all, a well-organized training program should be able to achieve these goals.

The benefits that a properly implemented training program can bring to an operation are well-known. Among the most significant are an improvement in guest services, a reduction of interdepartmental and interpersonal conflicts, decreased employee stress, and a general improvement in the organization's efficiency. From the employee perspective, a strong training program can better acclimate new employees to the club and its unique culture, improve employees' competence in their job tasks, and increase feelings of job security.

Before these and other positive results can be realized, an organization must clearly identify the objectives of its training program. The primary objective of training should be to help employees at all levels improve their job performance. This in turn leads to increased job satisfaction, as well as the other benefits just described. The time and money a club spends training employees is usually paid back many times over.

Food and beverage training programs might include service seminars, role playing, or food and wine tastings. Training need not be elaborate to be successful; in fact, some of the most effective training techniques are the simplest. Club managers may also send staff members, particularly food production or culinary personnel, to outside training programs.

Compensation

In general, compensation in clubs is competitive with—if not superior to—compensation in other segments of the hospitality industry. With the exception of servers, food and beverage employees in clubs are compensated in much the same way as food and beverage employees in other types of food service operations. Generally, line-level employees, in both back-of-the-house and front-of-the-house areas, are paid a flat hourly wage, while management employees are paid a salary. (In addition, some clubs attach monetary incentives to management salaries.) Line-level supervisors (those positions between upper management and line-level employees) may be compensated differently from club to club—sometimes they are considered hourly employees and sometimes salaried, depending on their range of responsibilities.

Food servers are compensated in one of two ways: minimum wage plus tips, or a higher hourly wage with no tips (tipping is not allowed and the club adds a service charge to every food and beverage purchase). There may be variations on these two basic compensation methods, but these are the most common. The primary advantage of the first form of server compensation, which includes voluntary member tipping, is that it helps motivate servers to provide the best service they can. The second form of compensation, under which a service charge is included on member checks, has two advantages: it eliminates member tipping, a convenience for members (especially in clubs where members sign their checks), and it eliminates time-consuming tip reporting for the club.

While either of these compensation methods works, most club members probably would rather pay the service charge, because it eliminates the need for members to come up with cash tips. And while tipping can motivate employees to provide good service, it can also result in inconsistent service: employees might provide better service to members who have reputations as good tippers. For these reasons, a mandatory service charge, coupled with a higher hourly rate and a ban on tipping, may be the most desirable form of server compensation in most clubs.

Recognizing Good Employees

Club food and beverage outlets are no different than nonclub restaurants in their need to recognize good employees. Some recognition methods that clubs use include employee-of-the-month programs (see Exhibit 5), awards for longevity (such as service medals), bonuses, and sales incentives (for example, one club uses lottery tickets as a reward for servers selling the most items in various product categories, such as appetizers or desserts). Private clubs have excellent facilities for hosting picnics or parties for employees on days when the club is closed to members. Annual or biannual employee gatherings can also be an effective way to develop a cohesive work team and a positive culture.

Trends in Club Dining

Trends in club dining are almost too numerous to mention; this section will focus on some of the most important. Many of these trends are the result of the need for private clubs to keep up with changing member tastes, cope with competition from the nonclub food and beverage sector, or just provide change from the daily routine.

Increased competition has fueled many changes in club food and beverage practices, and in many instances clubs have borrowed good ideas from the nonclub food and beverage sector. Because new restaurants can represent potential competitors, clubs must pay special attention to the restaurant industry.

Casualization—the increasing preference among diners for relaxed, inexpensive dining—is perhaps the most prevalent dining trend, and it has spread to club dining. One club industry report suggests that member preferences are moving away from the formal dining room, and that grill rooms now generate 75 percent of all private-club dining sales.[7] This trend is expected to continue into the foreseeable future, due in part to tax laws that lower entertainment exemptions (casualization translates into lower check averages). In keeping with the casualization trend, many clubs have shortened the operating hours of their formal dining rooms; some clubs open their formal dining rooms only on Friday and Saturday nights, for example. Some clubs have eliminated formal dining altogether, converting their formal dining rooms into less formal food and beverage outlets.

Exhibit 5   Employee Recognition

"Employee of The Month" For December . . .

Juan Rivera

Juan started to work March 29, 1976 as our head set up person. He is married to Sophia and they have four children – John 11, Raul 8, Saul 5, and Juan, Jr. 3. He worked from 6:00 a.m. to whatever time it took to have the Christmas parties ready on time. We had the biggest Christmas month we have ever had!

Every month we will have an "Employee of The Month" award. A prize will be awarded.

CONGRATULATIONS JUAN!

You deserved the award
AND
thanks for all the hard work!

Source: *The Lakewooder: Lakewood Country Club News* (Dallas, Texas: Lakewood Country Club).

Another food and beverage trend in clubs is the increasing popularity of theme nights (see Exhibit 6). Theme nights have long been a good way to generate member interest in a club's dining room and keep the food and beverage staff thinking creatively, and they are currently enjoying a revival. Examples of theme nights include steak nights, special buffets, shrimp peels, spaghetti nights, and clambakes. Some clubs have theme nights weekly, while others may offer them on a monthly or even seasonal basis.

Closely related to theme nights, special dinners designed to complement distinctive wines or beers have become very popular and profitable for clubs. Some clubs bring in a winemaker or brewmaster for the evening and design a menu around his or her products; others simply select a variety of wines or beers and

Exhibit 6   Theme Nights

These ads for club theme nights appeared in a club newsletter. (Courtesy of Lakewood Country Club, Dallas, Texas)

build an appropriate menu. The increasing interest in boutique wines and micro-brews has fueled a corresponding interest in special club dinners featuring these products, so much so that members will pay $100 or more per person to attend. Cigars have seen a resurgence in popularity in recent years, and some clubs have planned special dinners around cigar smoking that are similar to the wine or beer dinners (see Exhibit 7). Clubs that have offered special dinners have found that they help regenerate an interest in the club's fine-dining outlet.

Private club members are not immune to the general tendency among Americans to want a healthier cuisine, and some clubs have completely revamped their menus to accommodate this trend. However, this trend is not universal, and whole-sale menu changes should be approached with caution; as mentioned earlier, it is especially difficult to change a private club's menu, and even those club members trying to eat in a healthier way want a "reward" now and then. The clubs that have capitalized on the healthy-eating trend most effectively are those that have supplemented their existing menus with healthy dishes. Providing servers with

Exhibit 7   Sample Special Dinner Menu

Cigar Lover's Dinner

Thursday, March 4th
7:00 p.m.

Cigar:
Aliados "Petite Corona"

*Messina Hof 1989 Reserve
Pappa Paulo Port*

*Cream Sherry Gonzales
Diamond Jubilee*

*Hout Médoc
Château Latour du Roc 1975*

*Château Poutet Canet
Pauillac 1982*

RECEPTION:
Assorted Hot and Cold Hors D'oeuvres

DINNER MENU:
Onion Soup au Gratin
Served in Rye Bread Bowl

California Salad
Wild Boar Pâte, Wild Mushrooms
Smoked Gouda Cheese
Balsamic Vinaigrette Dressing

Sorbet

Black Angus Steak au Poivre Flambée
Rissolé Potatoes, Fresh Asparagus
Broiled Tomato with Fresh Herbs

Chocolate Surprise "Madame Butterfly"

Cognac and Coffee

After Dinner Cigar Selection
Aliados "Toro Cetros"
Aliados "Lonsdale"
La Gloria Cubana "Churchill"
*La Gloria Cubana "Wavell"
H. Upmann Churchill, Corona "Lonsdale"
*Given a "90" Rating by "Cigar Aficionado"
Recent Issue

Michael A. Butera
Cigar and Tobacco Importer will introduce
and present the selection of fine blended
Honduran Aliados Cigars

$48.50 Per Person Plus Tax and Service Charge

Please call for reservations.
Accounts will be charged for cancellations received less than 24 hours before event.

Source: *Market-Driven Menus* (Alexandria, Virginia: Club Managers Association of America, 1996), p. 324.

nutritional information that they can communicate to members is another way clubs are addressing this trend.

Three other trends worth mentioning that affect club dining—all of which are a result of shifting American attitudes and lifestyles—are changes in the role of men's grills, changes in alcohol-consumption patterns, and changes in food and beverage spending.

The equal-rights movement has contributed to a negative perception among some people of men's grills. Despite this, men's grills are still common. While the pressure to open all club facilities to both sexes will doubtless continue, some clubs are unlikely to eliminate their men-only facilities. In addition to upholding a very long club tradition of offering men a separate area in which to congregate, the men's grill is a profitable part of the product/service mix in most clubs.

The nation as a whole has been shifting toward lower alcohol consumption for some time now. The beginning of the trend saw a sharp decline in alcohol consumption, particularly outside the home. However, some club managers have observed that alcohol consumption is on the rise in their clubs, and some clubs that had converted their bar areas to serve other purposes are restoring them to their original function. Consumer tastes continue to evolve; currently wines, specialty beers, and premium spirits are in favor.

Finally, decreased spending in a significant number of club food and beverage outlets is having a dramatic effect on the way clubs manage their food and beverage operations. The percentage of meals eaten away from home continues to increase, but only nominally, while food and beverage spending in some clubs is on the decline. Therefore it is critical that club managers seek innovative ways to attract members to the club's food and beverage outlets and provide members with the services they want. While maintaining an awareness of nonclub restaurant operations and adapting some of their successful ideas to the club world, club managers must continue to do whatever they can to differentiate their food and beverage operations from their nonclub competition if they are to regain a larger share of the food dollar spent outside the home.

Endnotes

1. McMahon Report, "Club News for Club Leaders," McMahon Group, Inc., Volume 7, Winter 1996, pp. 4, 5.

2. *Clubs in Town & Country* (New York: Pannell Kerr Forster Worldwide, 1995).

3. C. W. Barrows, "Menu Planning and Development in Club Operations," *Club Management,* 1991, Vol. 70, pp. 10, 15.

4. R. Patterson, "How Prime Costing Can Maximize Profits," *Food Service Marketing,* 1980, Vol. 42, pp. 80–82.

5. *Clubs in Town & Country* (New York: Pannell Kerr Forster Worldwide, 1992).

6. M. Kasavana and D. Smith, *Menu Engineering: A Practical Guide to Menu Analysis* (East Lansing, Mich.: Hospitality Publications, 1982).

7. McMahon Report, "Club News for Club Leaders."

Key Terms

average check—A ratio comparing the revenue generated during a meal period with the number of guests served during the period, calculated by dividing total food revenue by the number of covers sold during a period.

beverage cost percentage—A ratio that shows beverage cost as a percentage of beverage sales. Beverage cost percentage is calculated by dividing the cost of beverages sold by beverage sales.

casualization—The trend among Americans to prefer a relaxed and inexpensive dining experience.

food and beverage minimum—A monthly food and beverage charge that club members must pay.

food cost percentage—A ratio that shows food cost as a percentage of food sales. Food cost percentage is calculated by dividing the cost of food sold during a given period by food sales during the same period.

food to beverage ratio—A ratio comparing food sales to beverage sales, calculated by dividing food sales by beverage sales.

house committee—A committee made up of club members whose job it is to monitor the maintenance and operation of the clubhouse and its services, and to serve in an advisory capacity to the board of directors.

labor cost percentage—The percentage of sales that is used to pay labor, including salaries, wages, bonuses, payroll taxes, and fringe benefits. Labor cost percentage is calculated by dividing total labor costs by total revenue. Also referred to as the labor cost to sales ratio.

operating ratio—Any of a group of ratios used to analyze a business's operations.

menu engineering—A menu-management technique for evaluating decisions regarding current and future menu pricing, design, and content that requires managers to focus on the amount each menu item contributes to profit rather than simply monitoring the item's cost percentage.

menu evaluation—The process of reviewing the strengths and weaknesses of a menu on a regular basis.

prime costing—A cost-based pricing method that considers both food and labor costs.

staffing chart—A chart that shows how many employees should be scheduled, given various levels of business.

zero-base budgeting—An approach to preparing budgets that requires the justification of all expenses; this approach assumes that each department or area of a business starts with zero dollars and must justify all budgeted amounts.

? Review Questions

1. What are some of the unique problems that managers of a club's food and beverage operations face?

2. What are some of the ways that the food and beverage department meets the varied needs of club members?

3. How important is the food and beverage program in attracting new members and meeting the needs of current members?

4. What is the overall contribution that the food and beverage department makes to the club's bottom line?

5. Who should be involved in the menu development process?

6. How is the menu evaluation process in clubs different from the process used in nonclub restaurants?

7. What typically causes a club's labor costs, expressed as a percentage of sales, to be high?

8. What are some of the advantages of assessing members a service charge on their food and beverage bills?

9. What are some of the ways in which restaurant dining habits overall are affecting member dining habits in clubs?

 Additional Reading

Barrows, C. W. "Pricing and Profits: Marketing for Maximization." *Journal of Restaurant and Foodservice Marketing,* 1994, Vol. 1.

Clubs in Town & Country. New York: Pannell Kerr Forster Worldwide, 1996.

Computers, Foodservice and You (newsletter). C, F&Y, P.O. Box 338, Raton, New Mexico, 87740.

Dittmer, P., and G. Griffin. *Principles of Food, Beverage, and Labor Cost Control.* New York: VNR, 1994.

Hillman, M. "Bean Counter's Delights." *Club Management,* 1994, Vol. 73.

Hoke, L. "Member Surplus: A Concept for the 1990's." *Club Management,* 1995, Vol. 74.

———. "Economic Pricing Concepts Can Boost the Bottom Line." *Club Management,* 1992, Vol. 71.

MacDougall, R. "Playing the Numbers Game: Planning, Preparation, Control of Operational Budgeting." *Club Management,* 1985, Vol. 64.

 Case Study

The 300-member Wellview Country Club is finding it increasingly difficult to sustain its member participation at the level required to meet operating expenses. Based on the history of the club, the general manager attributes much of the problem to the food and beverage area.

When the current general manager arrived in 1993, the food and beverage department was a major strain on the club's ability to cover expenses, incurring a $41,000 loss in member food and beverage sales during that year. The revenues and associated costs for 1993 break down as follows:

	Sales	Cost of Goods Sold as a % of Sales	Labor Cost %
Food	$56,000	80.0%	94.0%
Beverage	$60,000	52.0%	44.5%

In addition to member food and beverage sales, the club generates revenue by catering special events in the ballroom for both members and nonmembers. The 1993 net income from these events (food, beverage, and room-rental sales) was $25,000 on sales of $63,446. The club currently hosts such functions about once a week. Special-event revenues almost equal the dining room and bar revenues. The manager realizes that special events are profitable, but lacks the time to solicit new business.

Since 1993, the club has improved dramatically in controlling food and beverage costs and in generating additional revenue. Food and beverage revenues from the last fiscal year were $200,000, yet the club still incurred a net food and beverage loss of $10,000. In addition, food and beverage sales have been down for two straight years. And while management is aware that food and beverage spending is down nationally in clubs, they also know that, because of the club's size and dues structure, the members should be spending more on food and beverages.

Wellview is the only club in the area that does not have a food and beverage minimum. Other local clubs charge minimums ranging from $25 to $35 per month. The "minimum issue" is addressed about every other year during board meetings. The board believes that a nominal minimum, while it would cause a few members to complain, would not have any long-term negative effect on the membership and would increase revenues by about 25 percent, putting the food and beverage area in the black. But it has not yet imposed a minimum food and beverage charge on club members.

The manager is also rethinking his pricing strategy; prices are quite low, and some of the members even volunteer that they would be willing to pay more for what they get. Food cost percentage is currently running 50 percent, and the average check is $5.50. The board has authorized price increases, but the manager is unsure about how to implement them.

About a year ago, the manager recommended to the board that the dining room stop serving dinner due to lack of patronage. The manager felt that the club would save money, because on most nights, direct variable costs exceeded dining room revenues. The manager also proposed that, in lieu of nightly dinner hours, the club host one special theme dinner each month, promoted through the club's newsletter. Past events of this kind inspired participation three times that of normal à la carte dining, at a food cost percentage of about 40 percent. The manager is still awaiting the board's decision, which is likely to be favorable.

Discussion Questions

1. Should the club focus on cost cutting or revenue enhancement as a short-term strategy for making the food and beverage department profitable?

2. List three long-term changes that will improve the financial position of the club.

REVIEW QUIZ

When you feel you have covered all of the material in this chapter, answer these questions. Choose the *best* answer.

1. What is the role of food and beverage departments in clubs?

    a. attract new members
    b. meet member expectations
    c. help the club achieve a healthy bottom line
    d. all of the above

2. The role of a club's house committee is to:

    a. recommend club policies.
    b. make day-to-day operational decisions.
    c. set club policies.
    d. hire and fire food and beverage employees.

3. Traditionally, the way the members of most private clubs have paid for their food and beverages is to:

    a. pay cash.
    b. sign their guest checks.
    c. use a credit card.
    d. write personal checks.

4. What is a food and beverage minimum?

    a. A food and beverage minimum is a service charge imposed on club guests (nonmembers) who dine at the club.
    b. A food and beverage minimum is the lowest inventory level a food and beverage item can reach in storage before it must be reordered.
    c. A food and beverage minimum is a monthly food and beverage charge imposed on club members whether or not they use the club's food and beverage facilities.
    d. A food and beverage minimum is the minimum amount a club's food and beverage department charges nonclub members for booking private parties at the club.

Answer Key: 1-d-C2, 2-a-C3, 3-b-C5, 4-c-C5

Each question is linked to a competency. Competencies are listed on the first page of the chapter. An answer reading 3-b-C4 translates to:

  3: the question number
  b: the correct answer
  C4: the competency number

Chapter 10 Outline

Competencies

1. Explain how financial statements are used by clubs, list the major financial statements, and describe the *Uniform System of Financial Reporting for Clubs*. (pp. 337–338)

2. Describe the statement of financial position, the statement of activities, and the statement of cash flows. (pp. 338–352)

3. Summarize three approaches to analyzing financial statements and describe ratios used to analyze a club's performance. (pp. 352–358)

4. Describe an operations budget, and summarize the budgeting process. (pp. 358–361)

5. Describe a capital budget (including two capital budgeting approaches), summarize options for financing capital projects in clubs, describe a cash budget, and summarize ways in which a club's general manager can ensure that a club complies with federal income tax laws. (pp. 361–367)

10

Club Financial Management

This chapter was written and contributed by Raymond S. Schmidgall, Hilton Hotels Professor, *The* School of Hospitality Business, Michigan State University, East Lansing, Michigan.

$\mathbf{A}$ CLUB GENERAL MANAGER'S main focus each day is working with the club's staff, especially the management team, to provide services to meet the needs of club members. In other words, a general manager's job is intensely "people-oriented." Yet, in dealing with the club's board and department heads, there are times when the general manager cannot rely on his or her people skills alone and must use financial statements prepared by the club's financial personnel. While these financial experts can be of great assistance to a general manager, usually it is the general manager who answers to the club's board for the financial performance of the club. Therefore it is critical that the general manager understand not only how the club operates but also how to read and interpret financial statements.

The focus of this chapter is the financial knowledge a general manager needs in order to interact with the club's board, controller, and department heads. The major topics covered include (1) the major financial statements, (2) analysis of financial statements, (3) budgeting, and (4) federal income taxes.

Financial Statements

Financial statements are used to communicate a club's financial position and results of operations. These statements should be viewed as the club's scorecards. When you compare them to the operations budget for the same accounting period, you can determine the club's degree of financial success.

The major financial statements include the statement of financial position (formerly called the balance sheet), the statement of activities (formerly called the income statement), and the statement of cash flows. (Until the new names for these statements catch on in the industry, be aware that many club managers will continue to refer to balance sheets and income statements when they are talking about statements of financial position and statements of activities.) The statement of financial position is prepared as of the final day of the accounting period and reflects the financial position of the club on that particular day. This statement shows the club's assets, liabilities, and members' equity. The statement of activities is prepared to reflect the results of operations for the accounting period. It includes revenues and expenses; you subtract expenses from revenues to get results from operations. The third financial statement is the statement of cash flows, which reveals the inflows and outflows of cash.

The statement of activities is prepared on an accounting accrual basis—that is, revenues are recorded at the time that sales are made (even though cash will often be received much later) and expenses are recorded as they are incurred. The operating performance of the club is the focus of the statement of activities. However, the club's bills are paid with cash, and in order for a club to prosper, the liabilities of the club must be paid on a timely basis. Therefore, the statement of cash flows is prepared to help club managers effectively manage the cash receipts and cash disbursements of the club.

The statement of financial position, statement of activities, and statement of cash flows are interrelated, and, in the words of financial executives, they must "articulate"—that is, they must agree with each other and fit together like gears do. For example, the difference in cash on two successive statements of financial position is reflected on the statement of cash flows; the club's operating performance, as reflected on the statement of activities, is transferred to the appropriate members' equity account on the statement of financial position.

Several sectors of the hospitality industry have a uniform system of accounts that serves as a guide for preparing financial statements. The *Uniform System of Financial Reporting for Clubs* (hereafter referred to simply as USFRC) was last revised in 1996. It is useful for several reasons:

- It is a turnkey system.

- It is a time-tested system (it was first created in 1954).

- It is organized on a responsibility-accounting basis.

- It can be adapted by clubs of any size.

The USFRC provides recommended formats for the major financial statements as well as numerous supplementary financial schedules for both city and country clubs. (Selected sample schedules will be provided later in the chapter for both types of clubs.) A large club may use every recommended schedule, while a small club will simply ignore schedules that do not apply. A new club could simply adopt, without any major changes, the recommended statement formats, and it would be reporting its financial results on a basis similar to that of clubs over a century old that use the USFRC.

The USFRC has been revised several times. With each revision, changes have been made to provide for more accurate and meaningful financial reporting. As the major accounting rule-making organizations have dictated changes in accounting, the USFRC has been updated to keep pace.

Now let's take a closer look at the major financial statements—the statement of financial position, statement of activities, and statement of cash flows.

Statement of Financial Position

The statement of financial position reveals a club's financial position at the end of an accounting period. Specifically, it is a "snapshot" that reflects a club's assets, liabilities, and members' equity on that particular day. Assets are items of value owned by the club; liabilities and members' equity represent claims to the assets. The liabilities are the claims of outsiders such as suppliers and financial institutions. Those to whom the club owes money have the first claim to assets. The residual claim to the assets belongs to the club's members and is shown as members' equity on the statement of financial position. Exhibit 1 is the USFRC's recommended format for a club statement of financial position. The asset section is divided into five parts: (1) current assets; (2) noncurrent receivables, net of current portion; (3) designated funds; (4) property and equipment; and (5) other assets. Generally, the largest percentage of a club's assets are property and equipment.

The liability section consists of current liabilities; long-term debt, net of current portion; and other noncurrent liabilities. Current liabilities represent club obligations that must be paid within the next 12 months. Long-term debt includes notes, mortgages, and other long-term debt not due in the next 12 months. Other noncurrent liabilities include deferred income taxes and refundable member deposits.

Finally, the members' equity section reflects the members' investment and the results of other activities (primarily operations) shown on the statement of activities. Past earnings and capital assessments are shown first on the statement of activities and then in this section of the statement of financial position.

When you read a club's statement of financial position, you must remember that it reflects the club's financial position only at a single point in time—generally, the last day of the accounting period. This is considered a limitation of the statement of financial position.

Another limitation of this statement is that the value of most of the club's assets is based on historical cost—that is, the cost of assets, especially property and equipment, less accumulated depreciation. If a club's facilities are maintained in excellent condition, they may well be increasing in value and should generally be insured at their replacement cost rather than any lesser net book value. For example, a club's building might have cost $2 million in 1950 but today it might be worth $5 million. In the meantime, the building may have been depreciated down to $500,000 (its net book value). The value shown on the statement of financial position is $500,000, even though the building is worth $5 million and should be insured for that amount. Thus in this hypothetical case the statement of financial position fails to reflect a realistic value.

Finally, the club's employees are a major "asset" of the club. A well-trained work force with high morale will provide quality service to club members, thereby enhancing the value of the club, yet this human asset is not reflected on the statement of financial position.

Despite these limitations, the statement of financial position is useful because it reveals, as of a particular date:

- The amount of the club's total debt

- The resources currently available to pay debt coming due—that is, the current assets that are available to pay current liabilities

- The amount of club assets, broken down into the five categories mentioned earlier: current assets; noncurrent receivables, net of current portion; designated funds; property and equipment; and other assets

- The amount of members' equity in the club

Exhibit 1   Sample Club Statement of Financial Position

		STATEMENT OF FINANCIAL POSITION Assets		Exhibit A (Page 1)
			Date	
		19X1		19X2
Current Assets				
Cash and cash equivalents		$		$
Investments				
Receivables				
Accounts receivable—members				
Notes and deferred initiation fees receivable				
Other				
Total		_____		_____
Less allowance for doubtful accounts		_____		_____
Inventories				
Food				
Beverages				
Other				
Prepaid expenses				
Insurance				
Licenses and taxes				
Real-estate taxes				
Other				
Other current assets				
Total current assets		_____		_____
Noncurrent Receivables, Net of Current Portion		_____		_____
Designated Funds				
Cash				
Investments		_____		_____
Property and Equipment				
Land				
Buildings				
Leasehold and leasehold improvements				
Construction in progress				
Furniture, fixtures and equipment				
Total		_____		_____
Less accumulated depreciation and amortization		_____		_____
Other Assets		_____		_____
Deferred charges				
Security deposits				
Other		_____		_____
Total Assets		$ _____		$ _____

Exhibit 1   *(continued)*

	STATEMENT OF FINANCIAL POSITION Liabilities and Members' Equity (Net Assets)	Exhibit A (Page 2)	
		Date	
		19X1	19X2
Current Liabilities			
Notes payable		$	$
Accounts payable			
Taxes payable and accrued			
Accrued expenses			
Salaries and wages			
Interest			
Other			
Current portion of long-term debt			
Unearned income			
Other current liabilities		____	____
Total current liabilities		____	____
Long-Term Debt, Net of Current Portion			
Notes payable			
Mortgage or other long-term debt		____	____
Total long-term debt		____	____
Other Noncurrent Liabilities			
Deferred income taxes			
Refundable member deposits		____	____
Total liabilities		____	____
Members' Equity (Net Assets)			
Membership certificates (or capital stock)			
Designated equity			
Undesignated equity		____	____
Total members' equity		____	____
Total Liabilities and Members' Equity		$ ____	$ ____

Source: Club Managers Association of America, *Uniform System of Financial Reporting for Clubs* (Dubuque, Iowa: Kendall/Hunt, 1996), pp. 6–7.

Financial analysis of the statement of financial position will be covered in more detail in the ratio analysis section of this chapter. However, two ratios provide special insight into the statement of financial position and should be mentioned here. The current ratio, determined by dividing current assets by current liabilities, is a general indicator of the club's ability to pay its bills in the short run. The debt-equity ratio compares the amount of total debt to the total members' equity. The larger this ratio, the greater the financial risk to a club's creditors and members.

Exhibit 2   The 1995 Country Club Income Dollar

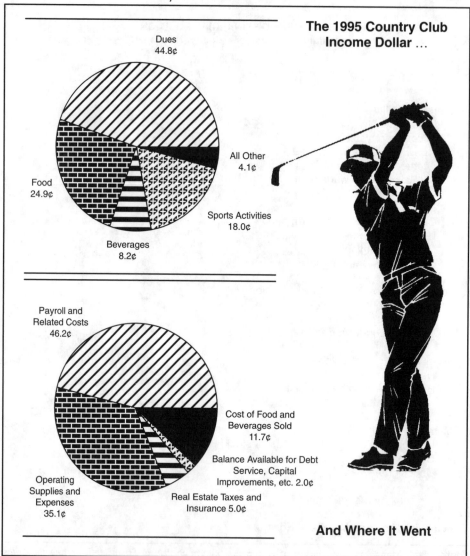

The 1995 Country Club Income Dollar ...

Dues
44.8¢

Food
24.9¢

All Other
4.1¢

Sports Activities
18.0¢

Beverages
8.2¢

Payroll and
Related Costs
46.2¢

Cost of Food and
Beverages Sold
11.7¢

Balance Available for Debt
Service, Capital
Improvements, etc. 2.0¢

Operating
Supplies and
Expenses
35.1¢

Real Estate Taxes and
Insurance 5.0¢

And Where It Went

Source: *Clubs in Town & Country 1995* (Houston, Texas: Pannell Kerr Forster Worldwide, 1996), p. 9.

Statement of Activities

The statement of activities reflects the operating results of the club for a period of time. In particular, it shows income (also referred to as sales or revenues) and expenses. The accounting firm of Pannell Kerr Forster Worldwide annually conducts a survey of both city and country clubs and publishes the results. Exhibit 2 reveals the major sources of the 1995 country club income dollar and where it went. It is interesting to note that 44.8% of the average club's total income came from dues, followed next by 24.9% from food sales. By far the largest expenditures, at 46.2%, were for payroll and related costs.

The USFRC provides two sample statements of activities for country clubs— one for club members (see Exhibit 3) and one for club managers (see Exhibit 4). The statement for club members is a summary statement only, because club members typically don't want or need a lot of detail; managers receive a detailed statement that includes all of the supplemental schedules because they are responsible for the club's operations.

First let's look at Exhibit 3, the statement of activities for country club members. As you can see, the statement is divided into five sections:

1. *Income.* Income includes membership dues, initiation fees, and various revenues such as overnight rooms, food, and beverage revenue.

2. *Operating expenses.* Some operating expenses are listed by department (rooms, food, beverage), while others are listed under more general terms such as "golf operations," "other sports activities," and "entertainment." Operating expenses include salaries, wages, payroll taxes, employee benefits, cost of food sold, and cost of beverage sold.

3. *Fixed expenses.* Fixed expenses include real-estate taxes, insurance, interest, and depreciation.

4. *Provision for income taxes.* Provision for income taxes is the estimated amount of taxes for the period. The "results of operations" line is the difference between income and expenses.

5. *Other support.* This section follows the results of operations and is called "other support" because the items listed here support the club financially, but they represent support "other than" the support (revenue) generated by the club's operations.

   This section includes initiation fees, capital assessments, proceeds from the sale of membership certificates, and disbursements for redemption of membership certificates. The initiation fees listed in this section are initiation fees that were designated for capital improvements to the club or for other non-operational activities; the initiation fees listed in the "Income" section at the top of the statement are initiation fees used for normal club operations. "Membership certificates" are what members receive in return for refundable deposits they make to the club; these certificates entitle the members to vote for the governing board of the club. (Owning member certificates is somewhat similar to owning capital stock in a for-profit corporation.)

   The bottom line of the statement of activities is "increase (decrease) in members' equity."

The phrase "see notes to financial statements" at the bottom of the statement of activities refers readers—in this case, club members—to supporting documentation. Notes to financial statements often consist of several pages of explanation to help members interpret the numbers on the financial statements. Notes to financial statements typically include such information as the club's accounting policies and information on the club's leases, long-term debt, and membership certificates.

Exhibit 3   Sample Statement of Activities for Members—Country Club

<table>
<tr><td colspan="2" align="center">**COUNTRY CLUB**
Statement of Activities</td><td>**Exhibit B-2**</td></tr>
<tr><td></td><td></td><td>Period
Ended</td></tr>
<tr><td colspan="3">Income</td></tr>
<tr><td colspan="3">   Membership dues</td></tr>
<tr><td colspan="3">   Initiation fees</td></tr>
<tr><td colspan="3">   Overnight rooms revenue</td></tr>
<tr><td colspan="3">   Unused food and beverage minimum (See page 8)</td></tr>
<tr><td colspan="3">   Food revenue</td></tr>
<tr><td colspan="3">   Beverage revenue</td></tr>
<tr><td colspan="3">   Golf operations</td></tr>
<tr><td colspan="3">   Tennis operations</td></tr>
<tr><td colspan="3">   Other sports activities</td></tr>
<tr><td colspan="3">   Other operating departments</td></tr>
<tr><td colspan="3">   Other income</td></tr>
<tr><td colspan="2">   Total income</td><td>_____</td></tr>
<tr><td colspan="3">Operating Expenses</td></tr>
<tr><td colspan="3">   Rooms</td></tr>
<tr><td colspan="3">   Food</td></tr>
<tr><td colspan="3">   Beverage</td></tr>
<tr><td colspan="3">   Golf operations</td></tr>
<tr><td colspan="3">   Tennis operations</td></tr>
<tr><td colspan="3">   Other sports activities</td></tr>
<tr><td colspan="3">   Other operating departments</td></tr>
<tr><td colspan="3">   Clubhouse</td></tr>
<tr><td colspan="3">   Entertainment</td></tr>
<tr><td colspan="3">   Administrative and general</td></tr>
<tr><td colspan="3">   Energy costs</td></tr>
<tr><td colspan="2">   Total expenses</td><td>_____</td></tr>
<tr><td colspan="2">   Income before fixed expenses</td><td>_____</td></tr>
<tr><td colspan="3">Fixed Expenses</td></tr>
<tr><td colspan="3">   Real-estate taxes</td></tr>
<tr><td colspan="3">   Insurance</td></tr>
<tr><td colspan="3">   Interest</td></tr>
<tr><td colspan="3">   Depreciation and amortization (See page 8)</td></tr>
<tr><td colspan="2">   Total fixed expenses</td><td>_____</td></tr>
<tr><td colspan="2">   Income (loss) before income taxes</td><td>_____</td></tr>
<tr><td colspan="2">Provision for Income Taxes</td><td>_____</td></tr>
<tr><td colspan="2">   Results of operations</td><td>_____</td></tr>
<tr><td colspan="3">Other Support</td></tr>
<tr><td colspan="3">   Initiation fees</td></tr>
<tr><td colspan="3">   Capital assessments</td></tr>
<tr><td colspan="3">   Proceeds from sale of membership certificates</td></tr>
<tr><td colspan="3">   Disbursements for redemption of membership certificates</td></tr>
<tr><td colspan="2">   Increase (decrease) in members' equity</td><td>$ _____</td></tr>
<tr><td colspan="3">*See notes to financial statements*</td></tr>
</table>

Source: Club Managers Association of America, *Uniform System of Financial Reporting for Clubs* (Dubuque, Iowa: Kendall/Hunt, 1996), p. 10.

Exhibit 4   Sample Statement of Activities for Managers—Country Club

BLANK COUNTRY CLUB **Statement of Activities** **(In Departmental Form)**			**Exhibit E-2**
	Schedule	Period Ended	
Membership Income		$	$
Membership dues			
Initiation fees			
Unused food and beverage minimum		_____	_____
Total membership income		_____	_____
Cost of Sports Activities			
Golf operations income (loss)	1-C		
Less golf course maintenance	3-A		
Net golf profit (expense)			
Racquet sports	2-B		
Swimming pool	2-C		
Health and fitness	2-D		
Other sports			
Net cost of sports activities		_____	
Dues available for clubhouse operation and fixed expenses		_____	
Clubhouse Operating Income (Loss)			
Food	1-A		
Beverage	1-B		
Overnight rooms	2-A		
Minor departments			
Rentals and miscellaneous income	2-E	_____	
Total clubhouse operating income (loss)		_____	_____
Undistributed Operating Expenses			
Clubhouse	3-C		
Locker rooms			
Administrative and general	3-B		
Energy costs	4-A	_____	_____
Total undistributed operating expenses		_____	_____
Net cost and expenses and clubhouse operations		_____	
Income before fixed expenses		_____	_____
Fixed Expenses	4-D		
Real-estate taxes			
Insurance			
Interest			
Depreciation and amortization		_____	_____
Total fixed expenses		_____	_____
Income (loss) before income taxes		_____	_____
Provision for Income Taxes	4-D		
Results of operations		$_____	$_____

Source: Club Managers Association of America, *Uniform System of Financial Reporting for Clubs* (Dubuque, Iowa: Kendall/Hunt, 1996), p. 19.

These notes are provided with the financial statements that are issued to *external* users of the statements. All of this information and much more is always available to *internal* users, and so these notes are not normally included with financial statements generated for internal users only.

The statement of activities for country club managers (see Exhibit 4) is divided into the following sections:

1. *Membership income.* This section includes membership dues, initiation fees, and unused food and beverage minimums.

2. *Cost of sports activities.* This section covers the sports activities of country clubs, and this is the first section that refers readers (in this case, country club managers) to supplemental schedules. Because USFRC's sample statements of activities for both city and country clubs are based on responsibility accounting, each club department must give a detailed report of its revenues and expenses on supplemental schedules. With these detailed numbers, it's easier to hold each department head responsible for the results of his or her department's operations. For example, supplemental schedule 1-C details the income and expenses for the club's golf operation (excluding golf course maintenance, which is under a separate manager and is given its own supplemental schedule, 3-A). The other items in this section are racquet sports, swimming pool, health and fitness, and other sports income and expenses. The difference between membership income and the net cost of sports activities is called "dues available for clubhouse operation and fixed expenses."

3. *Clubhouse operating income (loss).* This section reflects clubhouse operating income (or loss). Included in this section are the club's operating results in the food, beverage, overnight rooms, minor departments, and rentals and miscellaneous income areas. Reference is made to the supplemental schedule for each department. For example, the supplemental schedule for the food department is 1-A (see Exhibit 5). This schedule includes food and related income such as service charges and dining room rental. In addition, the food schedule shows all the related direct expenses of the food department, including payroll and related expenses and such "other expenses" as contract cleaning, equipment rental, linen, and so on. The supplemental schedule for "rentals and miscellaneous income" includes all income not included elsewhere. Examples of other income include rentals of space to members, concessions, commissions, dividends, interest income, and salvage revenue.

4. *Undistributed operating expenses.* Undistributed operating expenses is the next section on the statement of activities for country clubs (Exhibit 4). A supplemental schedule is included for three of the four items listed in this section. These operating expenses increase or decrease as operating income increases or decreases; they are described as "undistributed" because they are not allocated to the various profit centers of the club.

5. *Fixed expenses.* The fifth section of the statement, fixed expenses, shows expenses related to the club's physical facilities. The real-estate taxes are based on the assessed value of the club's land and building(s). The insurance expense

Exhibit 5   Sample Supplemental Schedule—Food Department

CITY OR COUNTRY CLUB **Food**	**Schedule 1-A**
Food Sales (List Revenue by Location)	$ _____
Cost of Food Sold	
Cost of food consumed	
Less credit for employees' meals	_____
Cost of food sold	_____
Gross profit on food sales	_____
Other Income	
Unused minimum	
Service charge	
Dining room rental	_____
Total other income	_____
Total gross profit and other income	_____
Departmental Expenses	
Payroll and related expenses	
Salaries and wages	
Payroll taxes and employee benefits	
Employees' meals	_____
Total payroll and related expenses	
Other expenses	
China, glassware, and silver	
Contract cleaning	
Equipment rental	
Kitchen fuel	
Laundry and dry cleaning	
Licenses and permits	
Linen	
Music and entertainment	
Operating supplies	
Other operating expenses	
Printing and stationery	
Refuse removal	
Repairs and maintenance	
Uniforms	_____
Total other expenses	
Total departmental expenses	_____
Departmental Net Income (Loss)	$ _____

Source: Club Managers Association of America, *Uniform System of Financial Reporting for Clubs* (Dubuque, Iowa: Kendall/Hunt, 1996), p. 24.

relates to the cost of insuring the club's physical facilities and their furnishings. Interest expense, for the most part, is based on the debt incurred to finance the club's facilities and equipment, while depreciation is the periodic write-off of the club's facilities and equipment as expense.

"Total fixed expenses" is the sum of real-estate taxes, insurance fees, interest fees, and depreciation expenses. "Income (loss) before income taxes" is the income or loss the club experienced for the accounting period; this number is arrived at by subtracting the total fixed expenses from income before fixed expenses.

6. *Provision for income taxes.* For clubs subject to income taxes, provision for income taxes is shown just prior to the bottom line, called "results of operations." Membership income, minus the cost of sports activities, plus (or minus) clubhouse operating income, minus undistributed operating expenses, minus fixed expenses, minus provision for income taxes equals results of operations.

The major focus of a club's general manager is on operations. Therefore, referring to the statement of activities in Exhibit 4, a country club's general manager is focused on, and has authority to control, all those revenues and expenses shown on the statement, down to the "income before fixed expenses" line. Working with the department heads of each profit and expense center, the general manager will attempt to maximize the club's profits while maintaining the quality of service desired by club members. The general manager will hold the club's department heads responsible for the departments they manage, just as the club's board will hold the general manager responsible for how well he or she manages the club.

Although each club manager should focus primarily on his or her area of responsibility, a club's managers must also function as a team and support one another. For that reason, department heads need to understand the supplemental schedules of other departments as well as their own. Each department head should feel free to make recommendations for improving operations in any area of the club, and these recommendations should be welcomed by the other members of the management team.

The fixed expenses of the club, as shown in the "fixed expenses" section of the statement of activities, are outside the general manager's control and relate to decisions made by the club's board. For example, the amount of interest expense relates primarily to the financing of the club's facilities and equipment; the more the club goes into debt to purchase facilities and equipment, the greater the interest expense. A club's board and finance committee have prime responsibility for this area. The results of their decisions regarding financing are directly reflected in this portion of the statement of activities.

For the sake of comparison, Exhibit 6 is the USFRC's sample statement of activities for city club managers. Note that the major difference between this city club statement and the country club statement shown in Exhibit 4 is that the city club statement does not have a section for sports activities. However, if a city club does have some sports activities, it can modify Exhibit 4 for its own use.

Depreciation. Throughout this section on the statement of activities, we have referred to depreciation. Since depreciation is a major club expense that is sometimes misunderstood, we should take a brief look at depreciation before we move on.

The expenditure of cash for most expenses shown on a club's statement of activities occurs in the year, and often in the same month, the expense is recorded; however, capital expenditures, which include payments for the club's facilities and

Exhibit 6   Statement of Activities for Managers—City Club

BLANK CITY CLUB Statement of Activities (In Departmental Form)		Exhibit E-1
	Schedule	Period Ended
Membership Income	$	$
Membership dues		
Initiation fees		
Unused food and beverage minimum		
Total membership income		
Clubhouse Operating Income (Loss)		
Overnight rooms	2-A	
Food	1-A	
Beverage	1-B	
Minor operated departments		
Rentals and miscellaneous income	2-E	
Total clubhouse operating income (loss)		
Deduct Undistributed Operating Expenses		
Clubhouse	3-C	
Administrative and general	3-B	
Energy costs	4-A	
Total undistributed operating expenses		
Clubhouse net (loss)		
Income before Fixed Expenses		
Fixed Expenses	4-D	
Real-estate taxes		
Insurance		
Interest		
Depreciation and amortization		
Total fixed expenses		
Provision for Income Taxes	4-D	
Results of operations	$	$

Source: Club Managers Association of America, *Uniform System of Financial Reporting for Clubs* (Dubuque, Iowa: Kendall/Hunt, 1996), p. 18.

their furnishings, are initially recorded as property and equipment and shown on the statement of financial position. The expensing of these capital costs over time is referred to as depreciation expense. Depreciation is simply the allocation of capital costs to expense for the periods of time the facilities and furnishings are used to generate income. The allocation can be achieved by a number of methods. The simplest depreciation method is straight-line. This method results in an equal allocation of cost annually over the useful life of the asset. For example, assume that a club purchases a van for $27,000. Further, assume that the van is expected to have a useful life of five years, after which it is expected to be sold for $2,000, its estimated salvage value. The van's annual depreciation, based on the straight-line method, is determined as follows:

$$\frac{\text{Annual}}{\text{Depreciation}} = \frac{\text{Cost} - \text{Salvage Value}}{\text{Years of Useful Life}}$$

$$\frac{\text{Annual}}{\text{Depreciation}} = \frac{27{,}000 - 2{,}000}{5} = \$5{,}000$$

Statement of Cash Flows

The third major financial statement is the statement of cash flows (SCF). Like the statement of activities, the SCF is a dynamic statement in the sense that it covers activity for a period of time. The SCF reflects sources and uses of cash by area of activity.

Exhibit 7 is the sample SCF from the *Uniform System of Financial Reporting for Clubs.* This statement is divided into two major categories—cash flows from operating activities, and cash flows from non-operating activities (investing and financing).

Cash Flows from Operating Activities. The cash flows from operating activities reveal the amount of cash generated by the club's operations for the accounting period. This section starts with the bottom line from the statement of activities for club members, which is "increase (decrease) in members' equity." The next line, "Adjustments to reconcile increase (decrease) in members' equity to net cash provided (used) by operating activities" is simply a descriptive line to identify what the following lines—"depreciation and amortization," "deferred income taxes," "(gains) losses on sales of investments," "(increase) decrease in assets," and "increase (decrease) in liabilities"—represent: adjustments to the "increase (decrease) in members' equity" to reflect the cash provided by the club's operations.

Depreciation expense is always added at this point. Depreciation is simply a bookkeeper's number; it does not represent a cash disbursement. However, depreciation expense was subtracted in determining the bottom line of the statement of activities ("increase [decrease] in members' equity"), which is what we are adjusting to arrive at cash flow from operations, so it must now be added back.

Other adjustments listed in this section are the changes in the current asset and current liability accounts. Increases in current asset accounts between statement of financial position dates covered by the accounting period are subtracted, while decreases are added. For example, if accounts receivables increase from $250,000 at the beginning of the period to $300,000 at the end of the period, then the difference—$50,000—is subtracted because, in effect, the increase in accounts receivable during the accounting period took cash, because the club's members did not pay their accounts. Changes in current liability accounts related to operations are also shown as adjustments to determine the cash flows from operations. For example, if the accounts payable increases during the accounting period, then the increase is

Exhibit 7   Sample Statement of Cash Flows

STATEMENT OF CASH FLOWS	Exhibit C
Cash Flows from Operating Activities	$
Increase (decrease) in members' equity	
Adjustments to reconcile increase (decrease) in members' equity to	
net cash provided (used) by operating activities	
Depreciation and amortization	
Deferred income taxes	
(Gains) losses on sales of investments	
(Increase) decrease in assets	
Accounts receivables	
Inventories	
Prepaid expenses	
Other current assets	
Security deposits	
Increase (decrease) in liabilities	
Accounts payable	
Taxes payable and accrued	
Accrued expenses	
Unearned income	
Other current liabilities	
Net cash provided (used) by operating activities	_____
Cash Flows from Investing Activities	
Deposits to designated funds	
Withdrawals from designated funds	
Expenditures for property and equipment	
Purchases of investments	
Redemption of investments	_____
Net cash provided (used) by investing activities	_____
Cash Flows from Financing Activities	
Proceeds of debt	
Repayment of debt	
Membership certificates sold	
Membership certificates redeemed	_____
Net cash provided (used) by financing activities	_____
Increase (decrease) in cash and cash equivalents	
Cash and Cash Equivalents, Beginning of Period	_____
Cash and Cash Equivalents, End of Period	$ _____
Supplemental Disclosure of Cash Flow Information	
Interest paid during the year	$
Income taxes paid during the year	$
See notes to financial statements	

Source: Club Managers Association of America, *Uniform System of Financial Reporting for Clubs* (Dubuque, Iowa: Kendall/Hunt, 1996), p. 13.

reflected as an increase in this section. In essence, an increase in payables results in more cash, as more credit has been extended to the club by suppliers.

Cash Flows from Non-Operating Activities. The second section of the SCF reflects non-operating financial activities of the club. These activities consist of the club's investing and financing activities. The cash flows from investing activities reflect cash activities related to designated funds, property and equipment, and investments. For example, a club's purchase of undeveloped land for possible future expansion would be shown as a disbursement of cash in this section (under "expenditures for property and equipment"); a sale of an investment would be shown as receipt of cash from a redemption of an investment. The purchase of the land would be shown as a negative number, since it reduces cash, while the sale of the investment would be shown as a positive number, since cash is increased.

The "cash flows from financing activities" section relates to debt and membership-certificate activities. Borrowing money and selling membership certificates result in increases in cash, while repaying debt and redeeming membership certificates result in the reduction of cash.

The "increase (decrease) in cash and cash equivalents" line is the sum of the net cash flows from the three major activities—operating, investing, and financing. This sum is equal to the change in cash for the period. For example, if the cash balance at the beginning of the month is $50,000 and it is $60,000 at the end of the month, then there has been an increase of $10,000 in cash. The sum of cash from operating and non-operating activities as shown on the SCF for this period in this example must equal $10,000.

The "supplemental disclosure of cash flow information" section simply reveals the amount of cash disbursed during the accounting period for interest expense and income taxes.

The major focus of a club is its operations. Therefore, the club's board and its management team generally are most interested in the club being able to generate positive cash flows from operations. If a club's operations are using or decreasing cash flows rather than providing cash flows, then other sources of funds must be sought to provide sufficient cash flows to operate the club.

Analyzing Financial Statements

Financial statements are often presented on a comparative basis—that is, statements of financial position are shown for the end of two successive years, or the statement of activities for two years are shown. Comparing the two successive sets of numbers by computing the dollar change and the percentage change is called **horizontal analysis.** Exhibit 8 shows the current asset section of a comparative statement of financial position. Note that the amount of cash and other current assets are shown for each statement of financial position. The dollar difference is simply the difference between the two years, with increases shown as positive and decreases shown as negative. The dollar change of an item divided by the statement-of-financial-position number from the earliest year results in the percentage change. The value of this analysis is that it makes it easier for users of the financial statement to focus on significant changes. A wise general manager will analyze any significant differences and provide the club's

Exhibit 8   Sample Club Comparative Statement of Financial Position (Current Assets Only)

COMPARATIVE STATEMENT OF FINANCIAL POSITION (CURRENT ASSETS ONLY) December 31, 19X1 and 19X2				
	19X1	19X2	Dollar Change	Percentage Change
Current Assets:				
Cash	$ 30,000	$ 35,000	$ 5,000	16.67%
Accounts Receivable	350,000	385,000	35,000	10.00%
Inventory	20,000	18,000	<2,000>	<10.00%>
Prepaid Expenses	$ 12,000	$ 12,000	–0–	–0–
Total	$412,000	$450,000	$ 38,000	9.22%

board and appropriate committees with succinct explanations. The key for the manager is to anticipate and be prepared for board- and committee-member questions.

A second analytical approach is referred to as **vertical analysis**. In a vertical analysis, the financial-statement numbers are reduced to percentages. These statements are generally called common-size statements. For a common-size statement of financial position, "assets and liabilities" and "owners' equity" are set equal to 100% and all subelements are shown as a percentage of those totals. Vertical analysis is often used for analyzing departmental operating statements. On a department statement, net revenue is set equal to 100% and each expense is shown as a percentage of net revenue. The percentages then can be compared to the prior period's percentages and/or the budgeted percentages to determine the department's efficiency.

A third approach to analyzing financial statements is the calculation of financial ratios. Simply calculating a ratio does not reveal very much; ratios are most meaningful when they are compared to a standard. The standard for club managers is usually the current budget, although ratios can also be compared to the club's past performance. The same ratios calculated at intervals over a period of time can alert club managers to meaningful trends.

There are five major classes of financial ratios:

- *Liquidity ratios*—ratios designed to indicate a club's ability to pay its bills in the short run.

- *Solvency ratios*—ratios designed to indicate a club's long-term financial viability.

- *Activity ratios*—ratios designed to indicate management's effectiveness in using the club's resources.

- *Profitability ratios*—ratios designed to indicate the club's degree of profitability.

- *Operating ratios*—ratios designed to measure the club's operating efficiency.

Different users of financial statements tend to be interested in different classes of ratios. Owners of clubs, especially nonequity (profit-oriented) clubs, are generally most interested in profitability ratios. Creditors (lenders and suppliers) use profitability and solvency ratios to evaluate the solvency of clubs and determine the risk involved in granting loans or extending credit. Club general managers use ratios to monitor the club's operating performance and evaluate their success in meeting a variety of goals. Department heads tend to focus on their own areas of responsibility and generally are most interested in operating ratios related to their departments. Since general managers must work with owners, creditors, and department managers, they must have an interest in all classes of ratios.

There are literally hundreds of ratios; however, our discussion will be limited to just a few examples of the ratios within each ratio class. Each ratio presented will be briefly described and the formula for its calculation provided.

Liquidity Ratios

The three liquidity ratios discussed in this section are the current ratio, the accounts receivable turnover ratio, and the operating cash flows to current liabilities ratio.

The current ratio is determined as follows:

$$\text{Current Ratio} = \frac{\text{Current Assets}}{\text{Current Liabilities}}$$

The current-assets number and current-liabilities number come from the statement of financial position.

The current ratio compares current assets, which include cash and assets to be converted to cash or used in the club's operations within a year, to current obligations that must be paid within a year. The higher this ratio, the greater the capability of the club to pay its bills as they become due.

The accounts receivable turnover ratio is determined as follows:

$$\text{Accounts Receivable Turnover} = \frac{\text{Revenues}}{\text{Average Accounts Receivable}}$$

Revenues are recorded on the statement of activities, while the average accounts receivable is determined by dividing by two the sum of the beginning and ending accounts receivables shown on the beginning- and end-of-the-year statements of financial position.

Since most clubs have relatively large amounts of accounts receivables, it is imperative that this ratio be calculated to determine the overall condition of accounts receivable. A goal of club managers is to turn accounts receivable into cash in a timely fashion. The accounts receivable turnover ratio gives club managers a quick reading of how well the club is achieving this goal. If the ratio does not meet the club's target ratio, then club managers need to look into the reasons.

Finally, the operating cash flows to current liabilities ratio is computed as follows:

$$\frac{\text{Operating Cash Flows to}}{\text{Current Liabilities Ratio}} = \frac{\text{Operating Cash Flows}}{\text{Average Current Liabilities}}$$

The operating cash flow figure is taken from the SCF, while the average current liabilities figure is based on statement-of-financial-position numbers. Since a club's bills are paid with cash, a useful comparison would be between operating cash flows for an accounting period and the average liabilities due over the same period.

Solvency Ratios

The two solvency ratios discussed here are the debt-equity ratio and the number of times interest earned ratio. The debt-equity ratio views solvency from a statement-of-financial-position perspective, while the number of times interest earned ratio looks at the club's financial viability from an income perspective.

The debt-equity ratio is computed as follows:

$$\text{Debt-Equity Ratio} = \frac{\text{Total Liabilities}}{\text{Total Members' Equity}}$$

This ratio uses two numbers from the statement of financial position to compare the club's total debt to its total members' equity.

The debt-equity ratio is especially useful to auditors. Club managers can calculate it and compare it to targeted or historical figures to determine whether the ratio is too high. The higher the ratio, the greater the reliance on debt and the greater the financial risk the club is taking. If the ratio is too high, a club might not be able to make its debt payment and it might be on its way to insolvency.

The number of times interest earned ratio is determined as follows:

$$\text{Number of Times Interest Earned} = \frac{\text{Earnings before Interest and Taxes}}{\text{Interest Expense}}$$

The numerator of this ratio consists of the club's earnings prior to the payment of income taxes and interest expense. This number is then divided by interest expense.

This ratio is especially useful to auditors because they grant credit to clubs. It can be compared to the targeted ratio or historical ratios to determine whether the ratio is too low. The higher this ratio, the greater the club's perceived ability to pay its long-term bills. If it is too low, insolvency and even bankruptcy could be in the near future.

Activity Ratios

The activity ratios presented in this section are inventory turnover, asset turnover, and paid occupancy percentage.

The inventory turnover is calculated as follows:

$$\text{Inventory Turnover} = \frac{\text{Cost of Goods Used}}{\text{Average Inventory}}$$

The word "goods" is used in a generic sense. This ratio should be calculated for food, beverages, and other "goods" sold at the club.

Club department managers should calculate the inventory turnover ratio for each type of inventory. At most clubs this will include a separate calculation for food and beverages. The results indicate the number of inventory turns for the time period. A very low turnover suggests too much inventory. Excessive inventory items are likely to be wasted, especially when inventory items have a short shelf-life. On the other hand, a very high turnover might indicate that the club frequently runs out of some of its inventory items and thus is sometimes unable to meet member expectations.

The asset turnover ratio reflects the relationship between a club's total revenue and its average total assets. It suggests the general manager's ability to generate revenues with the use of the assets he or she has been entrusted with. The asset turnover ratio is calculated as follows:

$$\text{Asset Turnover Ratio} \quad = \quad \frac{\text{Total Revenues}}{\text{Average Total Assets}}$$

Paid occupancy percentage is a useful ratio for clubs with overnight rooms. This ratio is determined as follows:

$$\text{Paid Occupancy \%} \quad = \quad \frac{\text{Rooms Sold}}{\text{Rooms Available}}$$

The "rooms sold" number comes from adding the number of rooms sold for each day of the accounting period (the daily report of operations would generally include the number of rooms sold); the "rooms available" number is the total number of overnight rooms available for sale at the club.

Rooms are the "inventory" of the rooms department; the potential revenue from a room not sold is lost forever. The paid occupancy percentage reveals the percentage of available overnight rooms that were sold during the period. The higher the percentage, the better. This percentage is generally regarded as the single most useful ratio for revealing how successful the club's rooms department has been.

Profitability Ratios

There are a multitude of profitability ratios. However, this section will be limited to profit margin, operating efficiency ratio, and return on members' equity.

Profit margin is calculated as follows:

$$\text{Profit Margin} \quad = \quad \frac{\text{Results of Operations}}{\text{Total Revenues}}$$

The numbers used in this and other profitability ratios are virtually all found in the operating results shown on the statement of activities and the related department schedules.

The profit margin ratio reveals the percentage of revenue that "drops" to the operating bottom line as "profits." For example, a profit margin of 5% means that for every $1 of revenues the club takes in, it makes $.05. Though profitability per se is generally not a major objective of equity (nonprofit) clubs, the profit margin ratio is still useful, because it reflects how efficiently the club managers are managing the club. Board members are often very interested in this ratio, because if the profit margin falls too low for too long, the club might experience difficulty in covering its fixed expenses and membership dues might have to be increased.

The operating efficiency ratio is determined as follows:

$$\text{Operating Efficiency Ratio} \quad = \quad \frac{\text{Income before Fixed Expenses}}{\text{Total Revenues}}$$

The operating efficiency ratio is designed to measure the general manager's overall success in managing the club. Generally, the general manager has the authority to control operating expenses—those expenses above the "income before fixed expenses" line on the statement of activities (see Exhibit 4). (As mentioned earlier, the "fixed expenses" section shown on the statement of activities relates primarily to board decisions rather than to those of the general manager.) Thus, the operating efficiency ratio is generally considered to be a key measure of the general manager's performance. A club's general manager should calculate this ratio to make sure he or she is in line with the targeted ratio.

Finally, the return on members' equity compares the earnings of the club to the equity of its members. It is calculated as follows:

$$\text{Return on Members' Equity} \quad = \quad \frac{\text{Results of Operations}}{\text{Average Members' Equity}}$$

The return on members' equity ratio is typically calculated by a club's general manager and/or chief financial officer. It reveals the results of operations for the year as a percentage of the average members' equity. The average members' equity is determined by dividing the sum of the members' equity from the statements of financial position at the beginning and end of the year by two. In general, the higher the return on the members' equity, the greater the profitability of the club. This ratio is considered extremely valuable for clubs whose goal is to make profits for its owners/members.

Operating Ratios

The final category of ratios is referred to as operating ratios. Generally, club department heads and the general manager are most interested in these ratios, since they reflect the operating success of individual club departments. A club's board generally views department activities as the primary responsibility of the club's management team and prefers that the general manager deal with these issues. Only a few key operating ratios are presented in this section: average food service check, cost of food sold percentage, and cost of labor percentage.

For the club's food and beverage outlets and other profit centers, the average check should be calculated. For a food operation, the average check is determined as follows:

$$\text{Average Food Service Check} \quad = \quad \frac{\text{Food Revenue}}{\text{Covers Served}}$$

The "food revenue" number comes from the statement of activities; the "covers served" number comes from the daily report of operations.

The department manager should compute the average food service check by meal period for each food outlet. The results can then be compared to budget targets to determine the club's success in achieving its desired average food service check. Similar ratios should be computed for the club's other profit centers, such as bars, overnight rooms, the golf course, and so on.

A major ingredient of a sale is the cost of the product sold. Therefore, the cost of products as a percentage of profit-center revenue should be calculated. For a club's food service operation, the cost of food sold percentage is calculated as follows:

$$\text{Cost of Food Sold Percentage} \quad = \quad \frac{\text{Cost of Food Sold}}{\text{Food Sales}}$$

The "cost of food sold" number and "food sales" number come from the food department schedule.

Generally, only a single cost of food sold percentage is determined for food service operations; therefore, this usually cannot be calculated by outlet or meal period.

The cost of food sold percentage is compared to budget targets or historical numbers. If the percentage differs significantly from the target, this suggests to the club's food and beverage managers that the club's operating standards in the food department are not being met. Further investigation must be undertaken to determine the problem or problems (waste, failure to follow standard recipes, theft, and so on).

The cost of food sold percentage is useful in controlling product costs and should be modified and used by the managers of other profit centers in the club, such as the golf shop, tennis shop, beverage department, and so on.

For most club operations, labor costs are the major expense, often averaging more than 50% of the operation's revenues. As an overall means to determine whether labor costs are within desirable boundaries, department managers should calculate the cost of labor percentage for their departments and the general manager should calculate it for the club as a whole. The cost of labor percentage for a department is calculated as follows:

$$\text{Cost of Labor Percentage} \quad = \quad \frac{\text{Cost of Labor}}{\text{Department Revenue}}$$

The "cost of labor" and "department revenue" numbers come from department schedules. Remember, the cost of labor includes wages and salaries and related payroll costs, including fringe benefits and payroll taxes.

Budgeting

A club uses at least three different budgets as guidelines for managing its financial affairs: an operations budget, a capital budget, and a cash budget.

The operations budget is developed as a guideline for the club's managers. This budget includes projected revenues and expenses. The capital budget includes the club's plan for acquiring property and equipment. Two major models useful for cost-justifying or rejecting proposed capital projects will be presented later in the chapter. The third budget is the cash budget. This budget projects the club's future cash receipts and disbursements. This budget is extremely useful for the club's general manager and board because it gives them estimates of the availability of cash in the future. Generally, a cash budget is prepared along with each operations budget.

For example, if a club prepares operations budgets for five years into the future, cash budgets should be prepared for the same five years.

Operations Budget

At most clubs, the general manager is responsible for preparing the club's operations budget. Of course, the general manager also uses the talents of the club's management team to prepare it. Often the club's controller will coordinate the budget's preparation by working with the department heads. The controller provides department heads with the past operational history of their various profit and service centers. The department heads then prepare their forecasts of revenue and expenses, which are submitted to the controller. These are compiled as the initial draft of the club's operations budget. During the preparation process, various club committees often work closely with the department heads. For example, the finance committee would provide input for the budget and review it prior to its finalization. An operations budget usually is reworked a few times before it is presented to the club's board for approval.

Club managers benefit from preparing an operations budget in at least four ways:

- Budgeting requires club managers to examine alternatives before selecting a particular course of action. For example, when deciding how membership dues will be structured for the budget year, managers must think about how any proposed dues changes might affect membership levels.

- Budgeting provides a standard of comparison. At the end of an accounting period (generally monthly), the club's management team is able to compare actual operating results to the budget plan. Significant differences between budgeted and actual results should be analyzed to determine the probable cause(s). These causes might require additional investigation and corrective management action.

- Budgeting compels the club's management team to look forward, especially when strategic planning is involved. Managers spend a lot of their time either solving current problems or reviewing the past. Budgeting requires managers to anticipate the future.

- Finally, when participative budgeting is practiced, the budget process involves the entire management team. This involvement helps motivate lower-level managers, because they get real input into the process rather than being forced to adhere to budget numbers imposed on them.

The Budget Process. Putting an operations budget together involves several major steps:

- Establishing financial objectives
- Forecasting revenues
- Forecasting expenses
- Forecasting results of operations
- Presenting the budget

Establishing financial objectives. Before the club's management team prepares the operations budget, the club's board should establish the club's financial objectives for the upcoming year. A major objective established by many clubs is a targeted results-of-operations figure. In addition, nonfinancial objectives that impact the operations budget should be established up front. For example, a country club may aspire to have the most challenging golf course in the area. This objective may take several course enhancements that require cash expenditures. The management team must be informed of this objective in order to plan for the expenditures necessary to realize it.

Forecasting revenues. Forecasting revenues is the second major step in preparing the operations budget. To forecast revenue for their departments, the club's department managers must be provided with information regarding the economic environment, the club's marketing plans, the club's capital budgeting, and detailed historical financial results of their departments.

Historical financial information often serves as the foundation on which department managers build their revenue forecasts. Two basic approaches are used by managers. First, some department managers base their revenue forecasts on prior actual results plus an overall expected-percentage of increase. For example, assume the dues for January for a hypothetical club were $70,000 the prior year and that over the past three years dues in January had increased by 5% a year. Using this approach, the estimated dues for January of the budget year would be determined as follows:

$$70,000 \times 105\% \quad = \quad \underline{\underline{\$73,500}}$$

An alternative approach would be to base the dues forecast on the expected number of members and the monthly dues. For example, if the forecasted number of members is 1,000 and the average dues is $73.50, then the forecasted dues for January of the budget year would be $73,500.

Both approaches yield the same forecast; however, using the second approach might make it easier to find the cause(s) for differences between budgeted and actual amounts.

Similar scenarios could be shown for club profit centers such as the food department and the golf shop. Since the focus is on meeting members' needs and wants, budgeting approaches that focus on the number of members are more likely to be useful for comparing budgeted and actual results.

Forecasting expenses. After forecasting revenues, the management team forecasts expenses. Department managers forecast their expenses based on historical experience, forecasted revenues, and other factors affecting their costs, such as increases in the minimum wage.

Departmental expenses can often be segregated into two major categories, fixed and variable. Fixed expenses remain relatively constant month after month, while variable expenses change directly with departmental revenues. A department's fixed expenses would generally include the department manager's salary. If the department manager receives monthly compensation of $3,500, then the monthly budget for this department would reflect this amount. Variable expenses can be calculated as either a percentage of sales or as X number of dollars per unit sales. For example, assume that the cost of food sold percentage is 35% and that on average the cost of food sold is $3.50 per cover. If the food sales budget for the period consists of 10,000 covers at $10 per cover, the cost of food sold forecast would be $35,000, based on either of the following approaches:

$$\text{Forecasted Sales} \times \text{Food Cost \%} = \text{Forecasted Cost of Food Sold}$$
$$\$100,000 \times 35\% = \underline{\$35,000}$$

$$\text{Forecasted Covers} \times \begin{array}{c}\text{Estimated Food}\\ \text{Cost per Cover}\end{array} = \text{Forecasted Cost of Food Sold}$$
$$10,000 \times \$3.50 = \underline{\$35,000}$$

If food sales are expected to increase to $120,000 for the second month, then, using the "percentage of sales" approach, the forecasted cost of food sold would be $42,000, determined as follows:

$$\$120,000 \times 35\% = \underline{\$42,000}$$

Overhead expenses, including service-center costs and fixed expenses, are forecasted by members of the club's management team other than the profit-center managers. ("Service centers" are club departments that incur only costs, such as the accounting department; "profit centers," as indicated earlier, are club departments that generate revenue, such as the food department.) The head of each service center will estimate the center's expenses using historical expenses and projected increases. As mentioned earlier, the coordinator of the budget-preparation process is often the club's controller—he or she is the person who forecasts the fixed expenses. The controller has the fixed-expenses numbers readily available or can fairly easily forecast amounts for inclusion in the budget.

Forecasting results of operations. The next step in the budget-preparation process is the results-of-operations forecast. This part of the process is simply mathematical: revenues less expenses equals results of operations. However, part of the process is determining that the forecasted results of operations meets the financial objective set by the board in step one of the budget process. Often the initial draft of the budget fails to meet the board's objective, so the initial forecasts must be reviewed and revised until a budget acceptable to the board is prepared.

Presenting the budget. Finally, the operations budget must be "sold" to the club's board and committees. The presentation of the operating budget to the board is the general manager's opportunity to convince the board that the operations budget is the club's best plan of action for the upcoming year.

Capital Budget

A club's capital budget relates to the club's building and equipment acquisition plan. By its nature it is part of a club's strategic plan. Usually, management proposes capital acquisitions and presents them to the board for approval, since they impact the club over several years and often require large cash outlays or the borrowing of funds on a long-term basis.

Virtually all capital projects should be *cost-justified* prior to approval. Possible exceptions would include capital expenditures required by law, such as changes

Percentage of Clubs Using Specific Financing Methods for Recent Capital Projects				
Project Area	**Cash**	**Assessment**	**Debt Financing**	**Combination**
Golf Course Renovations/Improvements	43%	19%	15%	9%
Clubhouse Improvements/Minor Renovations	63%	10%	9%	7%
Dining Room Improvements	53%	8%	19%	7%
Locker Room Renovations/ Improvements	65%	17%	5%	2%
Pool Renovations/Improvements	36%	28%	18%	8%
New Exercise Facility	53%	10%	20%	0%
Tennis Facilities Renovations/ Improvements	51%	9%	17%	7%
Kitchen Renovations	62%	6%	14%	4%
Major Clubhouse Renovations and Additions (Including New Clubhouse)	9%	20%	27%	30%
New Parking Lots	46%	21%	18%	8%
Golf Facilities Improvements (Including Pro Shop, Cart Sheds, Bag Storage, etc.)	58%	7%	8%	6%
New Maintenance Building	51%	9%	17%	9%

mandated by the Americans with Disabilities Act, or perhaps expenditures for replacement of equipment. Even these expenditures can be cost-justified, but since they are "forced," some clubs choose to simply do the projects without undertaking rigorous cost justification.

The critical numbers in capital budgeting are cash flows. There is the initial cost of the project, then there are future cash outflows and often cash inflows related to the capital project. In order for a proposed capital project to be cost-justified, the future savings or incremental cash inflows must outweigh the cash outflow necessary to complete the project.

The two capital-budgeting approaches presented in the following sections are the payback approach and the net present value approach.

Payback Approach. The payback approach is considered simpler than the net present value approach and is used to determine how many years it will take for a capital project to pay for itself. The calculation of the payback period is as follows:

$$\text{Payback Period} = \frac{\text{Project Cost}}{\text{Annual Cash Flow}}$$

A project is considered acceptable if the payback period of the proposed project is equal to or less than the payback objective established by the club's board.

To illustrate the payback approach, assume that club managers want to purchase a new computer system at a cost of $20,000. Further assume that future cash expenditures related to this system total $5,000 per year, and that the proposed system's value to the club is worth $15,000 per year. Further, assume this computer system is deemed to have a useful life of five years, after which it is considered to be worthless due to expected technological advancements. The payback period for the proposed computer system is calculated as follows:

$$\text{Payback Period:} \quad \frac{\$20{,}000^*}{\$10{,}000^{**}} \quad = \quad \underline{\underline{2 \text{ years}}}$$

* Cost of computer system.
** Annual increased cash inflow less annual increased cash outflow from the project: $15,000 − $5,000 = $10,000.

If the club's board sets a payback objective of two years or less, this proposed capital project would be acceptable.

Net Present Value Approach. An alternative and more sophisticated capital-budgeting model is called net present value (NPV). The NPV approach also considers project cash flows.

Prior to discussing the NPV approach, we need to consider how future cash flows are discounted. This "time value of money" concept can best be explained by using a couple of simple examples. First, consider whether you would rather receive $100 today or $100 one year from today. A wise person would quickly take the $100 today. Why? When invested at 10% annual interest, the $100 would earn $10 in a year, so the $100 today would be worth $110 one year from now and the person would be $10 ahead.

The second example focuses on present value. We must determine what amount today (present value) will yield a future amount, given X% as the annual interest rate. To illustrate this process, assume that you would like to have $100 a year from today. What amount would you have to invest today in order to receive $100 a year from now?

The formula for determining present value is as follows:

$$P = F\left(\frac{1}{1+i}\right)$$

Where: "P" stands for present value, "F" stands for future value, and "i" stands for annual interest rate

Using this formula, the present value today of $100 a year from now, given an annual interest rate of 10%, is $90.91, determined as follows:

$$P = \$100\left(\frac{1}{1.10}\right)$$

$$P = \underline{\underline{\$90.91}}$$

Exhibit 9   Net Present Value Approach

	NET PRESENT VALUE APPROACH		
Year	Net Cash Inflow	Discount Factors*	Present Value
1	$10,000	.9091	$9,091
2	10,000	.8264	8,264
3	10,000	.7513	7,513
4	10,000	.6830	6,830
5	10,000	.6209	6,209
	Present Value of Cash Inflows		$37,907
	Less: Cost of Computer System		20,000
	Net Present Value		$17,907

* The discount factors can be taken from a standard discount-factor table. Alternatively, they could be computed based on the formula $1/(1+ i)^n$ where i = interest rate and n = year of cash flows.

To verify this present-value calculation, simply multiply the present value by the interest rate to determine the interest earned. The present value plus the interest earned must equal the future value. For our present example, this is determined as follows:

$$\$90.91 + \$90.91 \,(.10) \;=\; \underline{\$100}$$

Now back to the net present value approach. To determine the NPV of a proposed capital project, we compare the present value of future cash flows from the project to the initial cost of the project. If the difference between the cost of the project and the present value of future cash inflows or cash savings is zero or positive, then the proposed project should be accepted. Remember, future cash flows are discounted at the interest rate the club would have to pay if it had to finance the proposed capital project.

To illustrate the NPV approach, let's go back to the example used earlier to illustrate the payback approach—the purchase of a new computer system for $20,000:

Facts:

Cost of proposed computer system	$20,000
Future net annual cash inflows	$10,000
Relevant interest rate	10%
Expected life of project	5 years

Exhibit 9 contains the computations to yield the net present value of $17,907. Since the net present value is positive, the proposed project should be accepted.

The general managers of most clubs will find their financial experts knowledgeable about these capital-budgeting models. Since many club board members have a financial background and understand these models, a general manager may be most convincing when cost-justifying proposed projects for the club using these fairly sophisticated capital-budgeting approaches.

Financing Capital Projects. Many options exist for financing capital projects. The best approach for a particular club depends on the club's resources and the desires of its members. In other words, the best approach will differ from club to club.

An ideal way to finance capital projects is to invest excess funds generated by the club's operations until the desired funds are realized to purchase the proposed project for cash. This method means funds will not have to be borrowed nor members be assessed for the desired funds. This approach is reasonable for many clubs when the capital projects are relatively small. However, very few clubs are able to finance large projects this way, because they simply are unable to set aside sufficient funds over an extended period of time.

A second approach is to fund the capital project by borrowing the funds from a financial institution. Generally, a financial institution will only finance a percentage of the project; the remainder must be funded by the club. Debt financing is generally easy if the club has maintained a very good to excellent credit rating. The major drawback is that the funds must be repaid with interest on a periodic basis. This cash flow requirement must be considered when the club prepares its cash budget. The amount it borrows often depends on its ability to repay the loan. For clubs that are profit-oriented from a tax perspective, the interest paid on borrowed funds is deductible for tax purposes, so the real cost of borrowing is reduced by the related tax savings.

A third approach is to raise the required funds through a capital assessment drive. This approach involves billing club members for the capital assessment. This process can be facilitated by billing members a capital improvement assessment each month along with the monthly dues billing. The assessments are invested in a capital improvement fund to finance the capital project approved by the club's board. The benefit of this approach is that, unlike the borrowing option, it does *not* require repayment, and, when planned over a long period of time, it may be "painless" to the members, because the monthly assessments may be fairly small.

A combination of the above approaches is often used for major projects, unless the club has an extremely future-oriented board that plans far in advance and has planned for capital projects through capital assessment drives or internally generated funds.

Cash Budget

Statements of cash flows, discussed earlier in the chapter, are financial statements that report a club's historical receipt and disbursement of cash. Cash budgets, on the other hand, are *forecasts* of cash receipts and disbursements. The major purpose of preparing a cash budget is to enable the club's general manager to effectively manage the club's cash flow. A properly prepared cash budget will alert managers to times when they will need to borrow funds and times when they will have excess funds to invest.

Exhibit 10   Sample Cash Budget for the Fictional Greenwood Country Club

CASH BUDGET Greenwood Country Club For the month of June 19X1		
Estimated Cash at June 1, 19X1		$ 15,500
Estimated Cash Receipts:		
Cash sales	$ 4,000	
Collection of accounts receivable	158,000	
Proceeds from sale of equipment	2,000	164,000
Estimated Available Cash		179,500
Estimated Cash Disbursements:		
Labor expenses	65,000	
Fringe benefit expenses	10,000	
Payroll taxes	10,000	
Cost of food and beverages	23,000	
Golf course supplies	15,000	
Energy costs	6,000	
Mortgage payment	7,000	
Insurance premium	2,000	
Property taxes	4,000	
Other	15,000	157,000
Estimated Cash at June 30, 10X1		22,500
Minimum Cash Balance		15,000
Cash Overage		$ 7,500

Exhibit 10 is a simplified sample cash budget. This budget was prepared for a single month; however, realistically, cash budgets should be prepared for several months and possibly years in the future. The first element shown on the sample cash budget is estimated cash at the beginning of the month. The "estimated cash receipts" section reflects the club's major sources of cash—in this case, cash sales, collection of accounts receivable, and proceeds from the sale of equipment. The sum of estimated cash at the beginning of the month and forecasted cash receipts equals estimated available cash.

"Estimated cash disbursements" includes a detailed list of cash outflows. The amount of detail should be based on the desires of the user. A given general manager or controller may desire only 10 to 12 lines of expenditures, while others may desire much more detailed reporting.

The sum of estimated cash disbursements is subtracted from the estimated available cash to equal the estimated cash balance at the end of the month. A minimum cash balance (this is simply a target set by the general manager) follows the estimated cash balance and acts as a buffer in case there is a cash shortfall for the period. The difference between the estimated cash balance and the minimum cash balance is either a cash shortage or a cash overage. If a cash shortage is forecasted, plans must be made to cover the shortfall. A projected cash overage is a short-term investment opportunity.

Federal Income Taxes and Clubs ————————————————

A club's general manager is generally charged by the board with ensuring that the club complies with federal income tax laws. Nonprofit clubs are exempt from federal income taxes if they meet five provisions from the Internal Revenue Code, section 501(c)(7), as follows:

1. The organization is a club.

2. The club is organized for pleasure, recreation, or other nonprofit purposes.

3. Virtually all club activities must be for purposes described in provision 2.

4. No part of the club's profits may benefit the members or any private shareholder.

5. At no time during the tax year can the club's charter, bylaws, or other governing instrument contain a provision that discriminates against any person on the basis of race, color, or religion.

A nonprofit club must file an annual information Form 990 with the Internal Revenue Service.

Income unrelated to the purpose constituting the basis for the club's federal income tax exemption is referred to as "unrelated business income." This income is taxable at regular corporate tax rates. Unrelated business income of a tax-exempt club includes all gross unrelated business income, less all allowable deductions directly related to producing the gross income for unrelated purposes of the club. For example, assume a club allows a nonmember to use the club for a party. The nonmember is charged $5,000 and related expenses are $3,000. In this example the unrelated business income is $2,000 and the club is taxed on $2,000, not $5,000.

The determination of related expenses is often not so simple. If club facilities or personnel serve to produce both exempt and unrelated business income, then expenses, including depreciation, must be reasonably allocated between the two uses. The allocation approaches acceptable to the Internal Revenue Service are beyond the scope of this book, but often-tried allocation approaches based on gross incomes of exempt and unrelated business have generally *not* been accepted by the IRS.

Nonmembers who use the club's facilities may be assumed to be guests of members in certain circumstances, and thus income earned from these individuals is not subject to federal income taxes. The IRS guidelines provide that when a group of eight or fewer people, including at least one person who is a club member, uses club facilities, the nonmembers are considered to be guests of the member. This rule applies only if the member or the member's employer pays the club directly for such use. In addition, if 75% or more of a group exceeding eight people using club facilities are members, and the members or their employers pay the bill directly to the club, then all nonmembers in the group are considered to be guests of the members. The club must maintain adequate records to substantiate that nonmembers are treated as guests of members in the two situations just described.

Insider Insights

Kevin Reilly, CPA
Pannell Kerr Forster Worldwide
Alexandria, Virginia

A club's tax-exempt status is a lot different from the status of other tax-exempt entities, such as hospitals or charitable organizations. One big difference is how income is defined or categorized. For a hospital, for example, all income qualifies as "good" income (exempt from taxes) unless the Internal Revenue Service code specifically says it doesn't. For a tax-exempt club, it's the opposite: all income is "bad" (not exempt from taxes) unless the code says it's good. If you want to remain a tax-exempt club, you have to make sure the lion's share of your income falls into the good category.

Generally speaking, good or tax-exempt income for clubs is made up of:

- Dues, fees, charges, or other similar payments by club members as consideration for providing such members (or their dependents or guests) with goods, facilities, or services

- Gifts to the club by a member or nonmember

- Interest charged to members for late payments of assessments or for installment payments

- Transfer fees (such as revenue paid to the club upon the resale of a club member's membership interest)

- Income set aside for charitable purposes, as specified in IRS code 170(c)(4)

Unrelated business income (UBI) is (1) nonmember income from "outside" business such as banquets booked at the club by nonmembers, and (2) investment income such as interest and dividends that are generated by the club's investments. A tax-exempt-club's nonmember income is limited to 15 percent of gross receipts (initiation fees or special assessments are not included in the gross receipts). The difficulty is that many clubs now are aggressively going after outside business because it helps them survive, and when they get outside business, they generate UBI. Clubs should keep a close watch on the amount of nonmember income they're bringing in to make sure they don't go over the 15-percent limit. The penalty for going over the limit can be as severe as losing your tax-exempt status. That's a hefty penalty that you don't want to fall into unknowingly.

We tell club managers that the amount of money the 15 percent represents can go up if they can increase member business. The more member business clubs have, the more money they can fit within the 15-percent limit. So, along with trying to increase nonmember business, most tax-exempt clubs should also be trying to increase their member business. One way to do that is for club managers to look more closely at banquets, parties, and other special events being held at the club to make sure they are properly classified. A fuller understanding of the law might enable club managers to move more of these activities into the member-business category.

(continued)

Insider Insights *(continued)*

The IRS has a lot of recordkeeping requirements for tax-exempt clubs. One of the problems tax-exempt clubs have is getting members and staff members to keep all of the records they're supposed to keep. The person directly responsible for this is usually in the accounting area, but the club's general manager also must stay on top of this. A club can make sure all the bases are covered by using a member-function questionnaire that asks all the questions the IRS says you have to ask to make sure a special event is a member function. We recommend to clubs that they give the questionnaire to the food and beverage department. The catering manager can then give it to members when they are booking a special event at the club.

The question of traditional versus nontraditional activities is becoming more important for clubs. Today's clubs are increasing the amount and variety of services they offer, because the entertainment dollar—the amount of money the average club member is willing to spend on entertainment—is staying steady, not increasing. That means if clubs want more income, they have to work harder to get a bigger percentage of that dollar. One of the ways clubs are going after more of this dollar is by providing takeout food to members and providing catering services. The problem is that the IRS defines this income as nontraditional (nonmember) income. The IRS's position is that, by definition, a tax-exempt club is a place where members come together for social purposes; therefore, if a club is providing takeout or catering services, members aren't eating and socializing at the club and so the money the club makes is coming from a nontraditional club service. The IRS used to be intolerant of nontraditional income, saying that if a club had any income from nontraditional services, it (the IRS) might pull the club's tax-exempt status. When the IRS actually pulled the tax-exempt status of some clubs that only had 5 percent of their gross receipts as nontraditional income, a number of club groups complained to the IRS and asked for some relief. The IRS unofficially said okay, it would let clubs have up to 5 percent of their gross receipts as nontraditional income, but the 5 percent would be counted as part of the 15 percent UBI. A lot of clubs don't agree with that. Most clubs don't think the money they make selling takeout Easter hams or Thanksgiving turkeys to members is nontraditional or nonmember income, but that is the IRS position. Unfortunately, no formal guidance has been issued, so it is tough to rely on the IRS position.

Many clubs are seriously wondering whether they want to remain tax-exempt. They are saying they can't survive without increasing their UBI or nonmember income, which may mean giving up their tax-exempt status. If they become taxable entities, they're not limited in the amount of outside business they can bring in. Each club will have to evaluate the ramifications to see whether trading more outside business for their tax-exempt status is worthwhile for them.

Key Terms

activity ratio—A ratio designed to indicate management's effectiveness in using the club's resources.

horizontal analysis—Comparing financial statements for two or more accounting periods in terms of both absolute and relative variances for each line item.

liquidity ratio—A ratio designed to indicate a club's ability to pay its bills in the short run.

operating ratio—A ratio designed to measure the club's operating efficiency.

profitability ratio—A ratio designed to indicate the club's degree of profitability.

solvency ratio—A ratio designed to indicate a club's long-term financial viability.

vertical analysis—Analyzing individual financial statements by reducing financial information to percentages of a whole; for example, expressing statement-of-financial-position assets as percentages of total assets.

 Review Questions

1. What are the major financial statements clubs use?

2. What are some limitations of the statement of financial position?

3. What are the major sections of a country club's statement of activities?

4. The statement of cash flows is divided into which two major sections?

5. What is a horizontal analysis? a vertical analysis?

6. What are some of the major financial ratios used by clubs to analyze operations?

7. How does preparing an operations budget benefit club managers?

8. How is an operations budget typically prepared at a club?

9. What are two approaches to capital budgeting?

10. How can clubs finance capital projects?

11. Why are cash budgets useful to club managers?

12. What provisions must nonprofit clubs meet to be exempt from federal income taxes?

 Additional Reading

Schmidgall, Raymond S. *Hospitality Industry Managerial Accounting,* Fourth Edition. East Lansing, Mich.: Educational Institute of the American Hotel & Motel Association, 1997.

 Internet Sites

For more information, visit the following Internet sites. Remember that Internet addresses can change without notice. If the site is no longer there, use a browser to look for additional sites.

Hospitality Accounting Organizations

Hospitality Industry Technology
Exposition and Conference
http://www.hitecshow.org

International Association of Hospitality
Accountants
http://www.iaha.org/

Hotel Property Management Systems with Accounting Applications

CLS Software
http://www.hospitalitynet.nl/cls

CMS Hospitality
http://www.cmshosp.com.au

Execu/Tech Systems, Incorporated
http://www.execu-tech.com

Fidelio
http://www.micros.com

HOST Group
http://www.hostgroup.com

Lodging Touch International
http://www.lodgingtouch.com

Resort Systems Incorporated
http://www.resortsystems.ca

Western Hospitality Systems—InnSure
http://www.lodgingsystems.com

Food and Beverage Systems with Accounting Applications

CLS Software
http://www.hospitalitynet.nl.cls

CMS Hospitality
http://www.cmshosp.com.au

Comtrex Systems Corporation
http://www.comtrex.com

Comus Restaurant Systems
http://www.comus.com

Eatec Corporation
http://www.eatec.com

Geac Computer Corporation Limited
http://www.geac.com

Instill Corporation
http://www.instill.com

Integrated Restaurant Software
http://www.rmstouch.com

Micros Systems, Inc.
http://www.micros.com

Sulcus Computer Corporation
http://www.sulcus.com

System Concepts, Inc.
http://www.foodtrak.com

⌐**Case Study**

Jason Terwiliger is a new member of the finance committee of the Windshore Country Club, a 1,200-member club on the outskirts of a city of about 400,000. Jason is also the owner of a successful upscale restaurant in the city. After looking at the club's budget for next year and examining last year's financial figures from the club's food and beverage outlets, Jason approached Steve Buell, the general manager of the club.

"Steve, as you know, the finance committee has been looking at various areas of the club, trying to find ways to improve our bottom line," Jason began. "Because of my restaurant background, I concentrated on our food and beverage outlets. I have to tell you I was a little disappointed at what I found."

"I'm always looking for ideas to improve our operations, Mr. Terwiliger," Steve said. "Have you ever been through our kitchen and storeroom area? There's a lot that goes into running the club's food and beverage outlets that may be different from what you're used to at your restaurant. We can talk about your concerns as we walk."

"Sounds good," Jason said. "I want to learn as much as possible before I make any recommendations to the committee."

The two men started toward the kitchen. As they walked, Steve nodded to the food and beverage outlets they passed. "I'm sure you're familiar with the club's F&B outlets. Each one caters to a different audience and has a different theme. One is our upscale main dining room, another is for family dining, the third is fast food, and the last is a grill. But," Steve smiled, "you may not have known that the food for all four outlets comes from the same kitchen."

Jason shook his head as they entered the kitchen. "That's a big difference between the club and my restaurant. We both have one kitchen, but at my place there's only one outlet and one theme."

Steve nodded. "We have different customer bases, different market sizes, different operating philosophies, too."

"I think that's part of the problem—all the differences," Jason said. "For example, the food costs at the club are running at 42 percent; I'm running 28 percent at my restaurant. That's a huge difference!"

"I agree," Steve said. He introduced Jason to Pierre Robichaud, the club's chef. Chef Robichaud gave each of them a sample of a new dessert he was preparing. They chatted with the chef for a few minutes and looked over the kitchen's new layout, designed to streamline the food-preparation process. After thanking Chef Robichaud, they moved on to look at the club's food-storage areas before returning to Steve's office.

"What other concerns do you have about our F&B operations, besides the food costs?" Steve sat at his desk and took out a pen and paper to take notes.

"Well, there are a number of things I think we could change to make the operations more profitable," Jason said as he sat down. "For example, what about that duck entrée Chef Robichaud told us about? It takes all day to prepare it, so he starts in the morning and prepares six ducks every day, just in case he gets orders for them. But he usually has to throw away at least some if not all of them. It's an expensive waste."

Steve wrote down "food waste on specialty dishes" to start his list. "That's certainly a problem," Steve said aloud.

"Also," Jason continued, "the club only uses fresh ingredients. I'm in favor of using fresh ingredients, too, but some frozen items provide almost the same quality and can save the club quite a bit, especially if we buy in bulk."

Steve added "quality and quantity of ingredients" to the list.

"And speaking of ingredients," Jason said, "I noticed that we keep a huge variety of ingredients in stock, which is costly. For example, on our tour I saw that we still keep the ingredients for Veal Picante on hand, even though Veal Picante isn't on the menu anymore. That's what happens when we let members order items that aren't on the menu. And there are items listed on the menu that are rarely, if ever, ordered. The club's F&B sales volumes fluctuate wildly, too. The numbers fluctuated from a low of $33,000 per month to a high of $135,000 last year. The sales volumes at my restaurant are much more consistent. Maybe the club should raise prices to offset some of the losses and look for ways to make sales volumes more consistent."

"Mr. Terwiliger, you bring up a lot of valid points," Steve said.

Discussion Questions

1. What are Jason Terwiliger's main concerns?

2. How should Steve respond to Jason's concerns?

The following industry experts helped develop this case: Cathy Gustafson, CCM, University of South Carolina, Columbia, South Carolina; Kurt D. Kuebler, CCM, Vice President, General Manager, The Desert Highlands Association, Scottsdale, Arizona; and William A. Schulz, MCM, General Manager, Houston Country Club, Houston, Texas.

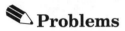 **Problems** ⎯⎯⎯⎯⎯⎯⎯⎯⎯⎯⎯⎯⎯⎯⎯⎯⎯⎯⎯⎯⎯

Problem 1

The Spartan Club provides selected information to you as follows:

Current assets	$250,000
Property and equipment	$1,500,000
Total sales	$2,000,000
Profit margin	5%
Current ratio	1.5 to 1
Return on members' equity	10%
Accounts receivable turnover	20 times

Assume the following:

1. The accounts receivable turnover is based on total sales.

2. Total assets are equal to current assets plus property and equipment.

3. The balances of statement-of-financial-position accounts at the beginning of the year are the same as at the end of the year.

Required:

Determine the following:

1. Total current liabilities

2. Results of operations

3. Total members' equity

4. Long-term debt

5. Accounts receivable at end of the year

6. Debt-equity ratio

Problem 2

Golden Ridge Golf Course has decided to erect a fence to keep intruders off its golf course. The estimated cost of the fence is $30,000, and annual maintenance is expected to be $2,000. The fence is expected to have a useful life of 20 years. The value of the benefits is expected to be as follows:

- Eliminating vandalism to the course, which is costing an estimated $6,000 annually.

- Increased play. It is estimated that several partial rounds are played by golfers playing on the back nine without paying. The estimated annual benefit, net of any increased costs, related to more rounds of golf is $4,000.

Required:

Determine the payback of this project.

Solutions to Problems

Solution to Problem 1

1. **Total current liabilities**

$$Current\ Ratio = \frac{Current\ Assets}{Current\ Liabilities}$$

$$1.5 = \frac{\$250,000}{Current\ Liabilities}$$

Current Liabilities = $166,667

2. **Results of operations**

    Results of operations = profit margin (total sales)
    Results of operations = .05 (2,000,000)
    Results of operations = $100,000

3. **Total members' equity**

$$Return\ on\ members'\ equity = \frac{Results\ of\ operations}{Average\ members'\ equity*}$$

*Balance of this account is the same at the beginning and end of year (Assumption #3)

$$10\% = \frac{\$100,000}{Average\ members'\ equity}$$

Total members' equity = $1,000,000

4. **Long-term debt**

$$A = L + E$$

$$CA + P\&E = CL + LTD + E$$

$$250,000 + 1,500,000 = \$166,667 + LTD = 1,000,000$$

$$LTD = \underline{\$538,333}$$

Key: A = Assets; L = Liabilities; E = Equity; CA = Current Assets; P&E = Property & Equipment; CL = Current Liabilities; LTD = Long-Term Debt

5. **Accounts Receivable End-of-Year**

$$AR\ Turnover = \frac{Total\ Sales}{Average\ AR}$$

$$20 \ = \ \frac{2,000,000}{\text{Average AR}}$$

$$\text{Average AR} \ = \ \underline{\underline{\$100,000}}$$

AR at EOY = \$100,000, since balances on the statement of financial position are the same at the beginning and end of year

Key: AR = Accounts Receivable; EOY = End of Year

6. **Debt-Equity Ratio**

$$\text{Debt-equity ratio} \ = \ \frac{\text{Liabilities}}{\text{Members' Equity}}$$

$$\text{Debt-equity ratio} \ = \ \frac{750,000}{1,000,000}$$

$$\text{Debt-equity ratio} \ = \ \underline{\underline{75\%}}$$

Solution to Problem 2

$$\text{Payback period} \ = \ \frac{\text{Cost of Project}}{\text{Annual Cash Savings}}$$

$$\text{Payback period} \ = \ \frac{\$30,000}{\$8,000^*} \ = \ \underline{\underline{3\,{}^{1}\!/_{2}\,\text{years}}}$$

*Annual Cash Savings and Cash Inflows

Annual savings from eliminated vandalism	\$6,000
Annual maintenance	(2,000)
Annual benefit of increased play	\$4,000
Annual cash savings	\$8,000

REVIEW QUIZ

When you feel you have covered all of the material in this chapter, answer these questions. Choose the *best* answer.

1. Which of the following is a major financial statement used by clubs?

    a. statement of financial position
    b. statement of activities
    c. statement of cash flows
    d. all of the above

2. Which of the following statements is a "snapshot" that reflects a club's assets, liabilities, and members' equity on a particular day?

    a. statement of financial position
    b. statement of activities
    c. statement of cash flows
    d. none of the above

3. A club's total liabilities divided by its total members' equity is called the _____ ratio.

    a. current
    b. debt-equity
    c. solvency
    d. asset turnover

4. What is a cash budget?

    a. A record of a club's receipt and disbursement of cash for some time period in the past (the previous month or year, for example).
    b. A budget that estimates how much cash the average club member has available to spend on club products and services.
    c. A forecast of cash receipts and disbursements (for next month or next year, for example).
    d. A budget that outlines how a club could turn its assets into cash should an emergency arise that requires such action.

Answer Key: 1-d-C1, 2-a-C2, 3-b-C3, 4-c-C5

Each question is linked to a competency. Competencies are listed on the first page of the chapter. An answer reading 3-b-C4 translates to:

    3:   the question number
    b: the correct answer
    C4: the competency number

Chapter 11 Outline

Competencies

1. Outline the benefits of an automated information system for clubs. (pp. 379–381)

2. Identify the hardware components of a computer system and describe typical hardware configurations. (pp. 381–384)

3. Describe club applications for generic software programs. (pp. 384–388)

4. Identify features and functions of a computerized club accounting system. (pp. 388–390)

5. Describe the automation challenges associated with point-of-sale systems. (pp. 390–392)

6. Identify the features and functions of event management software. (pp. 392–393)

7. Identify the features and functions of golf course management software. (pp. 393–394)

8. Describe the steps club managers can take to ensure the successful purchase or upgrade of a club computer system. (pp. 394–398)

9. Explain the fundamental features and functions of email and the World Wide Web and describe Internet applications for clubs. (pp. 399–406)

11

Club Computer Systems

This chapter was written and contributed by Michael L. Kasavana,
Professor, *The* School of Hospitality Business,
Michigan State University, East Lansing, Michigan.

DURING THE PAST DECADE, computers have dramatically changed the information systems club managers use to plan, coordinate, control, and evaluate club operations. Every business collects and analyzes data about its operations. While all businesses use some type of information system, a computerized information system enables managers to achieve their goals more easily. A computer system streamlines the process of collecting and recording data and expands the ways in which information can be organized and reported. In addition, a computer system speeds up the process by which useful information is made available to decision-makers. With a computerized information system, the club's general manager, the management team, the board of directors, and club committees can obtain timely information formatted in reports tailored to their specific needs.

While the degree of automation varies tremendously across the club industry, software programs exist for virtually every area of club operations. Basic accounting functions and point-of-sale systems in food and beverage outlets were the first areas within clubs to benefit from computer systems. Today, catering and special-event programs help club managers with each step in planning and executing banquets, weddings, and other celebrations. Generic and customized database management and spreadsheet programs assist in managing recreational activities. Specialized software for golf operations not only schedules tee times but also tracks member usage and provides daily reports that golf course managers can use to evaluate and improve operations. The appendix at the end of the chapter contains tables that indicate how computers are used at clubs.

From the moment prospective members contact a club, to their eventual participation in club activities, a computerized information system records, monitors, and charts significant member/club transactions. The key to success for club operations is the degree to which the computerized information system is transparent to club members. Members expect to benefit from their investment in a club's automation; they don't want nuisances and annoyances from cumbersome procedures that sacrifice personal service. For example, a club's management team might analyze incoming calls and consider purchasing a touch-tone voice-mail system as a cost-effective alternative to live telephone-attendant service. While automating this telephone function may reduce operating costs, it fails the transparency test:

> *"Hello. Thank you for calling the Country Club. For hours of operation, press one; for dining room reservations, press two; for the pro shop, press three; for membership account information, press four; for new-member information, press five. For all other requests, please stay on the line and your call will be answered in the order it was received."*

Instead of a warm, friendly greeting, every caller experiences the same monotonous drone of high-tech "reception." While cost savings and increased operational efficiencies are always important considerations in any automation effort, whether or not club managers have successfully computerized functions within their club is always measured by member acceptance and satisfaction.

Computer Basics

In order to use a computer, club managers do not need to learn about silicon chips or the intricacies of electronic circuitry; they only need to learn the commands necessary to instruct the computer to carry out desired functions. However, if club managers also have some basic knowledge about the essential operations of a computer system, they will be better equipped to use a computer as an effective tool in managing the information needs of their clubs. A basic understanding of the way computer systems operate also enables club managers to select computer systems that best meet the information needs of their operations, or to wisely expand the data-processing functions of their current computer systems. This section defines basic principles of electronic data processing, focusing on the advantages of a computerized information system for clubs. The section ends with a description of the fundamental hardware components of a computer system and the types of hardware configurations found in clubs.

Electronic Data Processing

Every day, club managers are bombarded with facts and figures about the results of club operations. However, these individual pieces of data are relatively meaningless until they undergo a process that organizes or manipulates them into useful information. **Data processing** involves transforming raw facts and isolated figures as input (data) into timely, accurate, and useful output (information).

Information, the result of data processing, is clearly one of the most valuable management resources. Information can increase a club manager's knowledge regarding membership, services, labor, finance, and other areas of concern. For example, the results of a member dining survey can provide managers with important information about how satisfied members are with the club's food and beverage outlets; such information may help managers develop better food and beverage operations.

Information is the key to effective decision-making. Relevant, timely, and accurate information enables club managers not only to do things right, but also to know if they are doing the right things. An efficiently designed electronic data-processing system provides club managers with rapid access to the information they need in order to make timely and effective decisions. In addition, after a decision is made, information processed via computers can provide club managers with feedback on the appropriateness and member acceptance of the decision and may even indicate new areas of concern that call for corrective action.

The speed, accuracy, and efficiency required for an information system to be ideally effective are best achieved through the electronic data processing performed by computers. A computer is a managerial tool capable of processing large quantities of data much more quickly and accurately than any other data-processing method. Computers can perform arithmetic operations such as addition, subtraction, multiplication, and division and can perform logical functions as well, such as assembling, ranking, and sorting data. In addition, computers are capable of storing and retrieving tremendous amounts of information and thereby allow managers to exercise control over procedures that might otherwise be overlooked.

An electronic data-processing system also brings efficiency to daily operations, enabling club employees to respond quickly to management and member needs. For example, club members calling to validate their current account balances can be served during their calls by an accounting employee who uses a computer to access the information electronically from club members' files. In this way, computer systems minimize **throughput**—the processing time it takes from data input to information output. Well-designed systems also streamline information output, generating only those reports that are requested by those who actually use the information.

Another advantage of an electronic data-processing system is that it reduces the number of times that the same piece of data is handled. Consider the difference between a manual accounting process and a computer-based system. In a manual process, invoice amounts must first be recorded in a journal; the amounts are then carried over to a ledger; and amounts recorded in the ledger are then used to prepare financial statements. During each of these steps, it is possible for an accounting employee to make any number of mistakes, such as transposing digits, calculating a total incorrectly, overlooking an entry, and so on. In a computerized data-processing system, the invoice amount is entered only once. The amount can then be accessed by the programs designed to prepare the journal, ledger, and financial statements. If an amount is entered incorrectly, but the mistake is identified and corrected, the correction flows automatically from the journal to the financial statements.

Computer Hardware

The physical equipment of a computer system is called **hardware**. Computer hardware is visible, movable, and easy to identify. Regardless of type, every computer system must have three hardware components: an input/output unit, a central processing unit, and an external storage device.

An input/output (I/O) unit allows the user to interact with the computer system. The user can input data by using a keyboard or mouse and receive output on a monitor (display screen) or on paper through a printer. The most common I/O unit in the club industry is the cathode-ray tube (CRT) unit (a television-like video screen or monitor) with a keyboard that is similar to a typewriter keyboard. Data entered through the keyboard can be displayed on the monitor. The user edits and verifies the on-screen input before sending it for processing. Other types of club I/O equipment include electronic cash registers and various types of printers.

The most common input/output unit in the club industry is the CRT unit (a television-like video screen or monitor) with a keyboard.

The electronic form of information displayed on a monitor is referred to as "soft copy" because it cannot be handled by the user or removed from the computer. Printers are used to generate "hard copy"—a paper copy of the output. Many systems are designed so that they can produce both types of output. For example, a club's computer will have a monitor that an accounting employee can use to view a soft copy of a member's electronic files that show an account statement between billing dates. However, at billing time, a hard copy of the up-to-date statement is printed and sent to the member.

The **central processing unit (CPU)** is the control center of the computer system. Inside are the circuits and mechanisms that process data, store information, and send instructions to the other components of the system. All input entering the computer system from an input device (such as a keyboard or mouse) is processed by the CPU before it is sent to either the internal memory, an output device, or an external storage device.

An external storage device retains data and computer programs that can be accessed by the CPU. Such devices include magnetic tapes, disks, and hard disks (also known as "hard drives"). In a personal computer, the hard disk is inside the casing of the computer. Exhibit 1 diagrams the hardware components of a personal computer system.

Hardware Configurations. A computer system's hardware components and their design and layout throughout a club are referred to as a **hardware configuration.**

Exhibit 1   PC Hardware Components

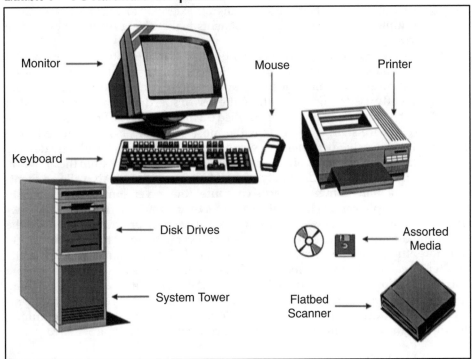

The club's size and the number of departments needing access to the computer system are significant factors club managers should keep in mind when selecting an appropriate configuration of hardware components. A very small club may find that a single workstation with a personal computer (PC) is sufficient to meet the needs of its limited number of users. This workstation would be a complete computer system with input/output units, a single CPU, and external storage capability. Other clubs may have a number of user groups from different departments that need access to the computer system. These clubs can avoid spending unnecessary funds on computer equipment by selecting the particular configuration of hardware components that best meets their needs. In many cases, it is possible for users to share output devices (such as printers) as well as the internal memory and processing capability of a central processing unit.

The major differences among the various hardware configurations are speed and cost. The CPU is the most expensive component in a computer system; the more CPUs a configuration requires, the greater its cost will be. The tradeoff in configuring a number of CPUs, however, is that the closer the CPU is to the I/O devices, and the fewer I/O devices making demands on the CPU, the faster the computer system will operate.

A stand-alone hardware configuration creates self-sufficient workstations, each with a complete set of hardware components. The presence of many individual stand-alone computers at various locations limits the communication between computers; data can only be shared by exchanging external storage devices, such as disks. The duplication of hardware components makes this a relatively expensive hardware configuration.

A **local area network (LAN)** is a configuration of workstations that enables users to share data, programs, and output devices (such as printers). Data-sharing facilitates system-wide communications, and program-sharing enables users to access infrequently used programs without the loss of speed or memory capacity that would result if those programs were installed on their machines. From an economic perspective, device-sharing is perhaps the most important benefit derived from networking. Expensive peripheral devices, such as high-capacity storage devices and color laser printers, are available to all workstations cabled within the network.

While there are many different types of LANs, one type of LAN, called a client-server network, links a single powerful computer (the server, sometimes referred to as a file server) to several (a handful, dozens, or even hundreds) of other, less powerful computers (the clients). Clients access a variety of programs loaded in the server and draw upon the server's processing power to perform tasks more quickly and more efficiently than if they operated in a stand-alone fashion. For example, the transfer of sales data from a food and beverage point-of-sale (POS) system to a club's LAN allows for detailed analysis of the data without affecting the ongoing operation and speed of the POS system. Timely management reports can be processed without disrupting the speed and quality of service to members dining throughout the club. Exhibit 2 diagrams the components of a typical LAN.

Generic Software

The hardware of a computer system does nothing by itself. In order for hardware components to operate, they must have a set of instructions to follow. Instructions that command a computer system to perform useful tasks are called computer programs or **software.**

Application software is a term for computer programs designed for specific uses, such as word processing, electronic spreadsheet analysis, and database management. Many of these types of applications are purchased separately from the hardware components of a computer system and are usually available at retail computer outlets or from vendors of club computer systems. Such software is usually called generic software.

When a club plans to computerize its information system, application software must be selected before the club chooses computer hardware components. Club managers must determine what functions or tasks they want the computerized information system to perform, then identify which application software will best meet those needs. This will in turn determine the hardware requirements.

Some software programs perform very specific applications, while others can be used to perform a variety of tasks. For example, a club manager can purchase a software program designed specifically for menu engineering. This type of software performs all of the necessary calculations involved in menu analysis and prints a series of reports. Because this software has one specific purpose, it is designed so that it requires no programming by the user. The user simply inputs the

Exhibit 2   Local Area Network (LAN) Diagram

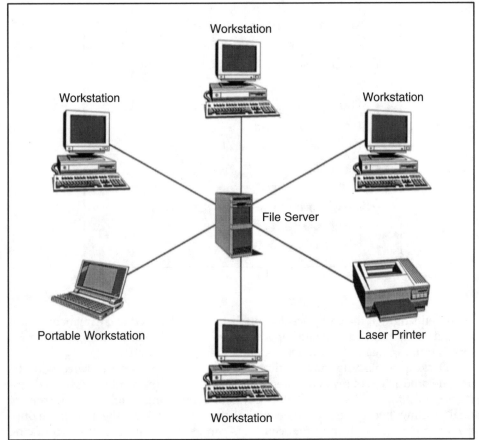

appropriate data and the program does the rest. Other types of application software are less task-specific. For example, off-the-shelf spreadsheet programs found in most retail outlets can be used for a number of applications, but the user must create the appropriate spreadsheets that will accomplish the various tasks.

Word-Processing and Desktop-Publishing Software

Word-processing software offers an electronic means of writing, editing, storing, and printing textual material. Special-function keys and combinations of keys permit the user to move words, phrases, paragraphs, or even entire pages of textual material from one point in the document to another. Many word-processing packages include special features that allow the user to tailor a document's appearance to meet specific needs. Increasingly, word-processing software offers desktop-publishing capabilities, including graphics and design applications. Using today's sophisticated, off-the-shelf word-processing programs for desktop publishing enables club staff members to create, design, edit, and print an assortment of club

Exhibit 3   Desktop Publishing Applications for Clubs

- Menu layout design and printing
- Tabletop displays
- Advertisement copy
- Newsletters
- Fliers for special events and promotions
- Discount coupons
- Employee training materials
- Internal reports
- Posters and signs
- Member mailings
- Event calendars and charts
- Custom forms

documents right at the club. Desktop publishing can be used to create menus, promotional materials, advertising copy, employment applications and other business forms, training manuals, newsletters, and other printed matter.

Desktop publishing can significantly reduce the expenses associated with the outside production of printed materials. Perhaps one of the most important advantages of desktop publishing is that it allows for copy changes right up to the time of final printing. Because there are no outside vendors involved, the time of the publishing cycle is significantly reduced. This can be especially useful in producing club newsletters. In-house staff can create professional-quality newsletters at a reasonable cost and within a production timetable that meets the club's needs rather than the schedule of outside printing firms.

Another popular use of desktop-publishing software in the club industry is the design, layout, and printing of food service menus. Menu content can be changed daily, offering club managers the ability to present a perfect menu that reflects current market prices, daily specials, or new and experimental menu items. The menu flexibility offered by in-house menu production is especially useful in the design of special-event menus and promotions for private parties, banquets, and holiday service. Typical desktop-publishing applications for clubs are listed in Exhibit 3.

Electronic-Spreadsheet Software

One of the greatest advantages of a computerized accounting system is that figures need to be entered only once into the accounting records. These figures can then be accessed by electronic-spreadsheet software: programs that prepare mathematically correct journals, ledgers, and financial statements. An electronic-spreadsheet program allows a user to input a model of the accountant's traditional worksheet in the computer system and view it on a monitor. The electronic model is essentially a blank page of a worksheet, divided into rows and columns that intersect to form cells. Cells can hold several types of data: alpha data (words), such as titles for the columns and rows; numeric data, such as dollar amounts or figures; and formulas, which instruct the computer to carry out specific calculations, such as adding all the numbers in a certain range of cells.

Electronic-spreadsheet software is not limited to bookkeeping functions; it is capable of performing many tasks that may be extremely useful to club managers. For example, the recalculation feature of an electronic-spreadsheet program offers club managers opportunities to explore "what if" possibilities. An electronic spreadsheet could be created to indicate trends in food and beverage preferences of members, pro-shop activity, golf-course traffic, and patterns within other areas of club operations. Information that would take hours to calculate manually takes only seconds when calculated electronically. Additionally, the data processed by electronic-spreadsheet programs can be quickly output in easily interpreted visual forms such as bar charts, line graphs, and pie charts. The speed and ease of obtaining financial information increases a club manager's ability to make timely and informed operational decisions.

Database-Management Software

Database-management software allows club managers to catalog and store information about their clubs for future use. A database is a collection of related facts and figures designed to serve a specific purpose. The structure of the database provides a means of organizing related facts and figures and arranging them in ways that facilitate searching for data, updating data, and generating accurate, timely, and useful reports for managers. Database management refers to the design and organization of databases, as well as to how data are handled within the computer system.

Think of a database-management system as an electronic file cabinet. The way information is organized within a file cabinet will depend on the kind of information stored and the particular needs of the user. File cabinets have separate file drawers. Each file drawer contains separate file folders. The folders within each drawer contain similar records of related information. Each record within a folder contains specific facts or figures. Exhibit 4 diagrams the similarity between a typical office file cabinet and a database-management system. In the language of database-management software, the file cabinet is called the database, the drawers of the cabinet are called database files, the folders within the drawers are called database records, and the detailed facts and figures within the records are called database fields.

Club managers could use a generic database program to track membership participation in special events held at the club, or track member participation in regularly offered recreational activities. Searches through several databases could reveal patterns and preferences of individual members that could be useful in promoting future events or in filling enrollments for future recreational activities. The value of a database-management system can be enormous. Not only does it save physical storage space, but, more importantly, it limits the number of times that

Exhibit 4   Database Files, Records, and Fields

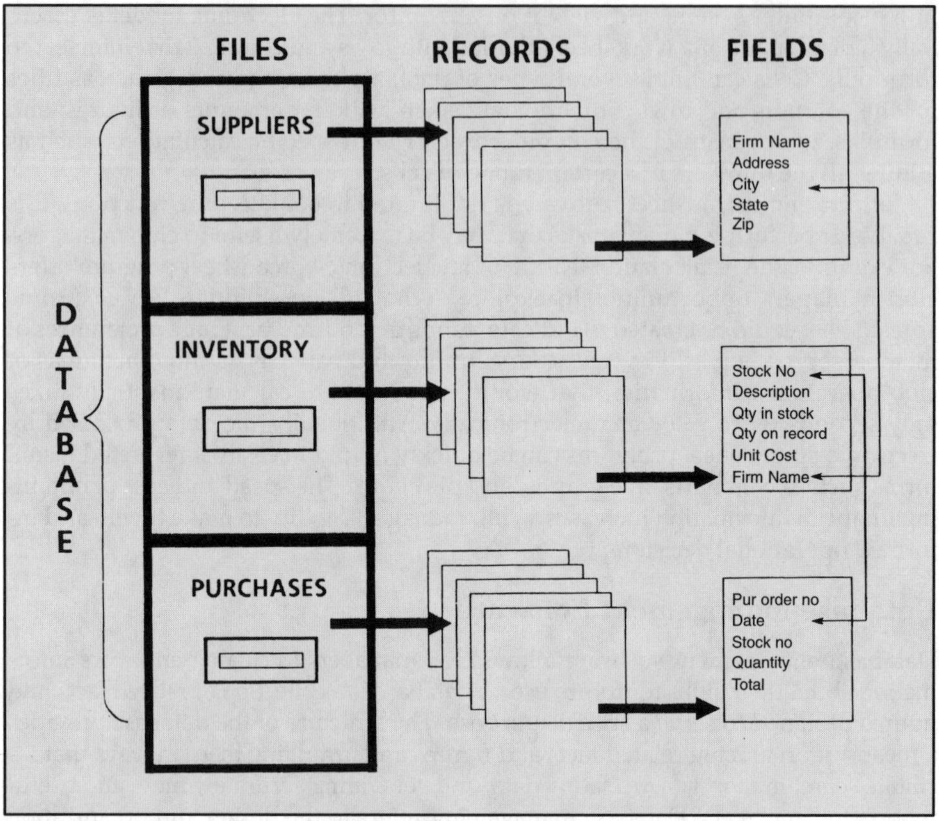

data must be handled and ensures that everyone using the database is working with the same information.

Computerized Accounting Systems

Club accounting is a systematic process of collecting and reporting financial information to help club managers make decisions and plans. Club accounting software should be both modular and integrated. **Modular software** is a group of related computer programs that can be purchased individually based on need. Buying based on need can reduce the overall purchase price for a computerized accounting system. The separation of accounting software into modules—such as accounts payable, accounts receivable, and payroll—also simplifies the division of labor associated with these functions. The user responsible for accounts payable, for example, need only learn the accounts-payable program rather than a program designed to encompass an entire accounting system. Exhibit 5 lists typical club accounting modules. **Integrated software** is a package of compatible programs designed to work together. Such software allows for data- and information-sharing,

Exhibit 5   Typical Club Accounting Modules

Accounts Receivable Module

Functions: Maintains account balances
Processes billings
Monitors collection activities
Produces audit report listing all accounts receivable transactions

Major Files: Member master file
Accounts aging file

Accounts Payable Module

Functions: Posts vendor invoices
Monitors vendor payment discount periods
Determines amounts due
Produces checks for payment
Facilitates reconciliation of cleared checks
Generates management reports

Major Files: Vendor master file
Invoice register file
Check register file

Payroll Module

Functions: Calculates gross and net pay for salaried and hourly employees
Prints paychecks
Produces payroll tax registers and reports
Prepares labor cost reports for management

Major Files: Employee master file
Payroll register file
Paycheck register file

---

which minimizes the time-consuming manual transfer of figures from one program to another and reduces the possibility for error associated with this process. With an integrated software package of accounting programs, posting a vendor invoice within the accounts payable program produces a simultaneous posting in the general-ledger program, eliminating the need for an additional manual entry. Similarly, a payroll program would automatically transfer data to the general-ledger and financial-statement programs.

An automated club accounting system has two primary objectives: to provide effective internal control and to produce accurate financial reports. The internal control provided by an automated accounting system includes protecting the club against omissions in documentation, inaccuracies within the accounting process, and dishonest employees. The accounting system must be capable of detecting these problems and, as much as possible, their source.

Financial statements are among a club manager's most important sources of information. A club accounting system must be designed to generate accurate reports in a minimal amount of time for both internal and external use. Outdated or inaccurate financial reports serve little purpose and are in fact dangerous, as they misinform users and can lead them to make poor decisions.

Point-of-Sale (POS) Systems

The primary objectives of a point-of-sale (POS) system are to improve member service, enhance staff productivity, and provide managers with better information and increased control over revenue centers throughout the club. A POS system should also be relatively easy to operate. New POS systems have been designed with these important objectives in mind.

Until recently, electronic-cash-register (ECR) and POS technology involved the purchase of proprietary vendor systems, which usually included specialty hardware, unique operating systems, and licensed software. Purchasers typically had to commit to an expensive service contract and depend on a single source for replacement parts or program enhancements. The current ECR/POS generation, however, is characterized by nonproprietary (industry-standard), PC-based hardware and numerous third-party software providers. What does all this mean? It means that clubs are now able to purchase software independently of hardware suppliers and can create a POS system that more appropriately meets their individual needs.

After PC-based hardware became an industry-standard platform for POS systems, software developers were able to focus on increasing the user-friendliness of their programs. Club managers now have more software options and fewer compatibility problems than ever before. The same technology used to monitor and control POS transactions is capable of direct, seamless integration with accounting, inventory-control, desktop-publishing, and electronic-settlement software. This can be especially appealing for clubs that transfer member charges to accounts-receivable files for deferred billing.

Despite the significant technological advancements, there are still challenges associated with POS systems. These challenges include coordinating kitchen production and dining-room service, ensuring data integrity, designing I/O units for operational efficiency, and securing timely vendor support.

Production and Service Coordination

The coordination of kitchen production and dining-room service is often cited as a major obstacle to effective POS operations. POS terminals and remote workstation units (printers and displays) do not solve coordination problems by themselves. For example, when servers enter a hot and a cold entrée at a POS terminal for a table of two, they are confident that the orders will be relayed to the proper preparation areas in the kitchen. However, the servers cannot know the current workloads of each preparation area. Hot food may be left cooling due to delays in the cold-food production area, or cold foods may be held too long waiting for hot items to be prepared.

Some food-service operations overcome such problems by having employees work as dispatchers, expediters, and runners. Dispatchers work in the kitchen and orchestrate food production by identifying preparation lags, distributing orders in an efficient time sequence, and maintaining overall production continuity. Expediters set up tables prior to service and tray food items during service. Runners deliver complete orders to the appropriate serving station for server presentation to members. In many clubs, a single employee may function as a dispatcher, expediter, and runner.

Remote-service bar terminals are another source of concern with POS systems. The bar-menu keyboard on the POS terminal may not offer sufficient space for all drink items available or have enough modifier keys for entering precise drink orders.

Data Integrity

In order to ensure data integrity within a POS system (and thereby ensure the reliability of the information the system provides), club managers must establish operating procedures and insist that they be consistently followed.

Data integrity is often affected by order-entry problems that arise because a POS system does not support server-editing functions at the time of input. Many systems do not print all keystrokes or provide on-screen text review of orders as they are entered into POS terminals. This makes it difficult for servers to correct input errors until after the system processes their orders and outputs the entered menu items or, in some cases, the entire order.

Without properly established procedures, servers often create their own unique order-entry techniques, which only serve to confuse kitchen personnel and invalidate many system reports. A classic example is the way different servers handle large parties requesting separate checks. One server may choose to first enter all orders onto a single check and later transfer items to separate checks through the use of a void key. Problems may arise in the kitchen because some systems relay voids to remote workstation printers, and a busy kitchen employee who fails to notice the word "void" printed below the ordered item may mistakenly produce another serving. Another server may choose to enter each order separately but input the number in the party as the number of members at the table (rather than "1"), hoping that kitchen personnel will recognize that the number-in-the-party figure indicates a multiple order that must be served at the same time. Again, busy kitchen personnel may fail to interpret the order correctly. In addition, the number-in-a-party is information that affects a number of operating statistics generated by the POS system. A single entrée attributed to a party of two or more will produce misleading average-check figures and member counts for the dining period.

I/O Units

While the hard copy provided by POS printing devices is a tremendous improvement over handwritten documentation, it can also pose problems. The same is true for the soft copy displayed by service and kitchen monitors. The design of dining-room service areas may not allow for all system terminals to be equipped with identical printers. Stations serving as order-entry locations may require only a receipt (flimsy paper tape) printer for internal-control purposes. Devices located furthest from a central processor typically require more maintenance. Workstation printers should be capable of transmitting complete information, thereby reducing or eliminating nonproductive server travel. Placing an order through a dining-room terminal should allow the server to remain in his or her assigned service area while production occurs. Club operations not employing a runner will find that servers will be distracted by service monitors and/or frequent trips to the kitchen to determine the status of their orders. Silent paging devices can be used to reduce traffic flow.

To many club staff members, the most critical success factor in a POS system is keyboard/screen design. The number and nature of the keys (preset keys, price-look-up [PLU] keys, modifier keys [price and nonprice], settlement keys, and so on) are the crucial elements. How many hard keys (dedicated) and how many soft keys (user-determined) does the keyboard/screen contain? The keyboard/screen should be laid out in a logical framework, with similar items grouped together, in order to enhance employee productivity and reduce search time. An efficient keyboard/screen design will enhance employee and system performance and improve operational control. Recent developments in POS I/O units include hand-held terminals and other wireless devices, and color touch-screen terminals.

Vendor Support

The documentation (user's manual) provided by the vendor of a POS system can be an enormous help in coordinating service and production communications and establishing efficient and consistent order-entry procedures. Too often, however, user's manuals are outdated and fail to correspond with current system screens, parameters, protocols, prompts, keys, and commands. Poor documentation can be fatal to system operations.

A vendor's commitment to continuing research and development in the area of POS systems is another important factor that may extend a system's useful life and operational capabilities. Club managers cannot be expected to keep abreast of technological advances, software breakthroughs, and other computer-related developments. Vendors with a history of updating the systems they offer are likely to provide the kind of enhancements that will keep a club's POS system current.

Computerized Event Management

Given the number of private parties and catered events serviced by clubs, event-management software can be a helpful tool. Most event-management software programs are designed primarily for hotel and independent catering operations. However, many of these programs are just as useful for club event-management purposes, and some may be customized for a better fit with club-specific needs.

Event-management programs monitor and control the activities associated with each stage of a catered event. Typical files within an event-management software package include:

- Ingredient file

- Recipe file

- Menu-item file

- Proposal/contract file

- Inventory file

- General-accounting files

While ingredient, recipe, and menu-item files are similar to those typically used in programs for restaurant operations, these files are expanded to include the nonfood "ingredients" related to the planning and execution of an entire catered event. Ingredients include not only food items but also function rooms, banquet space, and other public space within the club, as well as labor, serving utensils, production equipment, rental equipment, disposable items, decorations, provisions for supplemental recreational activities, and entertainment options.

For example, tables and chairs would be listed within the ingredient file. A recipe file would help combine the ingredients for a particular event. A club with eight-top tables (tables that can accommodate eight people), for example, could input this as a nonfood ingredient. When an event is planned for 240 persons, the table-and-chairs recipe accesses the ingredient file and lists 30 tables and 240 chairs as required "ingredients" for the event. In addition, the recipe file generally accesses cost data contained in the ingredient file and generates the cost of supplying tables and chairs for an event. The table-and-chairs recipe would be used as a subrecipe within a larger recipe for the entire event.

Any number of subrecipes can be chained together to produce a "menu" for a single event. The menu-item file stores the recipes used to create an event and can be accessed when managers plan similar functions in the future. The proposal/contract file accesses data contained in the menu-item file, develops prices, and maintains a record of commitments. The inventory file and general-accounting files perform functions similar to traditional food-service-inventory and back-office-accounting applications.

The usefulness of event-management software will depend on the degree to which the programs integrate with the club's existing computer system. If the ingredient, recipe, menu item, and inventory files cannot easily transfer data to and from software programs used in the food and beverage areas of the club, data will have to be re-input. This "double input" of data is usually tedious, cumbersome, and error-prone. Similarly, the proposal/contract and general-accounting files should be compatible with the other computer programs used at the club in order to be ideally effective.

Computerized Golf Course Management

Golf course management software automates the reservation function of a club's golf facility and may monitor member usage, update individual-member statistics (handicaps), facilitate golf-lesson and tournament planning, and track golf revenue and related revenue. In addition, some programs generate daily reports that evaluate key areas of golf-facility management. For example, after the club has input the standard time it takes a foursome to play a round of golf, a program might generate starting-time sequences for maximizing course usage and generate daily reports that compare actual course usage against the maximum or ideal course usage.

From a member's perspective, computer-based reservations may be the greatest service enhancement offered by golf course management software. With many manual scheduling practices, control concerns and limited access to up-to-date reservation sheets force some clubs to designate one staff person per shift to respond to tee-time requests from members. This often results in slow response times, telephone bottlenecks, and anxious, impatient callers. A computer-based reservation network enhances service by allowing several reservationists to access a shared, real-time database of open tee-times. If a club has several golf courses, reservationists can handle requests for specific courses and, if the desired course is unavailable for the tee-time requested, they can immediately tell members about the open times available at the other courses.

Some computerized golf-reservation systems allow members to reserve their tee times directly, without going through a reservationist or other club staff member. Members simply dial the reservation number and use the telephone's touch-tone keypad to respond to a series of system prompts. Typically, system-prompts lead the member to key-in his or her member-identification number, preferred play date, number in party, desired start time, and course specification (if the club has more than one golf course). The system then provides the member with a confirmation number. If the requested tee-time is not available, the system offers alternative times, dates, or courses. In addition to booking reservations, some systems allow members to enter their scores after their rounds of golf. The computer system can also be used to update tournament-play information and such member statistics as handicaps.

Touch-tone reservation systems can be programmed to prompt callers to enter the member-identification numbers of all players in their groups. This feature helps club employees learn who is scheduled to play each day and also reduces the problem of double bookings. Some telephone-based reservation systems can be programmed to restrict advance bookings, based on the type of membership the member has. For example, a member with full golf privileges may have a status code that permits tee-time bookings up to ten days in advance, while a nonresident member may have access to tee times only two days in advance. While not all members may choose to use a touch-tone reservation system, many might appreciate the system's 24-hour accessibility. Reservations can be made at the member's convenience, instead of only during those hours that are convenient to club operations.

Purchasing or Upgrading Computer Systems

The process of purchasing a start-up computer system or upgrading a current system can be complex and time consuming. Club managers should begin the process by putting a project team together. This team will be responsible for identifying the club's information needs, requesting proposals from vendors, scheduling site visits by vendors, evaluating vendor proposals, scheduling product presentations by vendors, negotiating with the selected vendor (or vendors), and purchasing the

---

Steps in Purchasing a Computer System

1. Appoint a project team.

2. Identify the club's information needs.

3. Establish computer-system requirements.

4. Request vendor proposals.

5. Schedule site surveys by vendors.

6. Evaluate vendor proposals.

7. Schedule product demonstrations by selected vendor(s).

8. Negotiate with selected vendor(s).

9. Purchase a system.

---

selected system. By adhering to this sequence of steps, the team is better able to ensure that the system eventually purchased will meet the rigorous demands of club operations, conform to budgetary constraints, produce cost savings, and enhance service to members.

Appoint a Project Team

As just mentioned, when selecting a computer system, the first step a club should take is to appoint a computer-system project team. The team leader should have overall responsibility for purchasing the computer system. This person is also responsible for determining a schedule for the purchasing process and monitoring the team's progress.

Throughout the purchasing process, the team should keep in mind two important guidelines:

1. Involve as many of the club's staff members as possible when defining the club's information needs and application specifications. The more input the team receives about data-processing needs, the better the chances of selecting a good system that will be well received by the staff responsible for operating it.

2. Make sure that, during system demonstrations, the same data is processed by competing vendors. Differences in processing techniques become more obvious when applied to the same set of data.

Identify the Club's Information Needs

The team should identify the types of information that the club's various levels of management use in the course of operating the club. This can be accomplished by compiling samples of reports presently prepared for managers and supervisors throughout the club. The reports should be analyzed with respect to such variables as purpose, content, use, and frequency of preparation.

While this analysis identifies the types of information currently used by management, it does not necessarily reveal all of a club's current information needs. Therefore, the team should also survey managers to evaluate the effectiveness of the format and content of the reports that are currently in use. The results of this survey will reveal the improvements club managers want to make to the current information system.

Establish Computer-System Requirements

The next step in the purchasing process is to establish computer-system requirements. This does not mean that club managers must become experts in computer-system design. Managers do not need to know the mechanics and details of electronic circuitry, but they must be able to make general determinations about what data to process, how that data is to be processed, and the formats in which processed data will be output as information.

Determining what data to process involves identifying the information tasks that can best be performed by a computer system. Determining how data is to be processed is a matter of making sure that any proposed computer system uses management-approved formulas when performing such calculations as food-cost percentages. Determining the formats in which processed data will be output as information involves decisions that may change the structure and style of current business forms, guest checks, management reports, and other printed materials.

Request Vendor Proposals

After translating the club's information needs into computer-system requirements, the project team is ready to request proposals from vendors. A request for proposal (RFP) is typically made up of three major sections: the first section introduces the vendor to the club and its operations, the second section establishes bidding requirements for vendor proposals, and the third and most important section deals specifically with the club's computer-application requirements.

A property profile is a useful way to tell vendors about the information needs of the club. The property profile should include information such as business volume (total revenues, number of employees, number of members served), physical-plant description (square footage, number of food and beverage and other retail outlets), operating statistics (average check, number of covers, average inventory turnover, food costs), and similar types of information. This information goes into the first section of the RFP.

After creating a property profile, the computer-system project team can collect sales literature on a variety of computer systems that seem to meet the general information needs of the club. Effective ways to collect relevant product literature include inquiries to state and national trade associations, attendance at industry trade shows, and visits to local computer-system vendors. This information will help the team standardize the second section of the RFP. Establishing bidding requirements for vendor proposals prevents vendors from using their own bid formats. A standardized bid form makes it easier for the team to compare the prices and system-performance specs of the various vendors. Vendors should also be required to include a statement of their financial stability.

The RFP should ask vendors to include as much information as possible about the systems and support services they are proposing to sell to the club, including such details as:

- Hardware configurations

- Software descriptions

- Maintenance and support services

- Installation and training programs

- Guarantees and warranties

- Payment options

- System expansion plans, if any

Once created, the RFP should be distributed to selected vendors.

Schedule Site Surveys

After receiving an RFP, conscientious vendors typically schedule a visit to the club in order to conduct a **site survey.** The purpose of a site survey is to identify important factors about the club's operation that may affect computer-system design. For example, the physical parameters of the club are key factors in determining hardware configurations. During a site survey, a vendor may analyze other characteristics specific to operations that are critical to overall computer-system planning. Many details regarding the club's internal organization, policies and procedures, and daily operations directly affect a vendor's computer-system proposal.

In order to secure all of the information necessary to complete their proposals, vendors may require a great deal of information from various club departments. To facilitate vendor access to information and key club staff members, the club's general manager or the project-team leader may designate a management representative to coordinate the flow of information to vendors; this can help keep disruptions to the club's daily operations to a minimum. This representative may also provide the team with valuable information on how efficiently the various vendors conducted their site surveys; this may provide a clue as to which vendor is right for the club.

After conducting site surveys, vendors complete and submit their proposals.

Evaluate Vendor Proposals

While there are many ways to evaluate a set of vendor proposals, a multiple-rating system can be an efficient method. A multiple-rating system uses the same criteria to judge the worth of each vendor's proposal. Generally, the criteria consist of several key issues that the club's managers consider to be of critical concern in computerizing the club. The issues are ranked in the order of their importance and assigned a percentage value that denotes their relative importance within the overall evaluation scheme. The ratings that each vendor receives for each issue are multiplied by their appropriate percentage values and then totaled to yield an overall score for each vendor's computer-system proposal. The proposal receiving the highest overall score identifies the vendor with whom the project team should seriously consider negotiating a contract. Sometimes two or three vendors receive similarly high scores; in that case, the team may wish to schedule product demonstrations with more than one vendor.

Schedule Product Demonstrations

Scripted product demonstrations, or "scripted demos" for short, prevent vendor product demonstrations from becoming unfocused presentations of "neat system tricks." The project team should provide each vendor with a script indicating what it wants the vendor to demonstrate, thereby ensuring that (1) the demo covers features relevant to the club, and (2) that every vendor demonstration covers the same ground.

There are several steps in developing a script for vendor product demonstrations:

1. Determine which system capabilities are most important to the club and request that vendors demonstrate them.

2. Script scenarios that as closely as possible mimic what really happens at the club. Have club staff members propose typical member behaviors and preferences and also describe unusual patterns of business that will have to be monitored by the system.

3. Arrange scenarios in a logical order, but stagger transactional information to simulate actual business conditions. For example, in the case of food and beverage areas, ask visiting vendors to enter food orders into their systems in a way that closely simulates actual member orders, modifications, and settlement activities. This will test the system's ability to perform a variety of transactions in a random fashion. Advise the vendor of the importance of strict adherence to the scenarios as written.

4. Identify future events that may be relevant to the system, such as physical-plant expansion, changes in staff size, use of online credit-card authorization, satellite-system interfacing, electronic mail, online communication to purveyors, and so on.

5. Limit the vendor's demonstration time. This directs the vendor to address features and functions that the club is most interested in seeing rather than what the vendor is most interested in showing. A 90-minute presentation period should be sufficient.

In addition to requiring a scripted demo, the project team should require vendors to use the actual hardware components and application software included within their proposals to the club.

Vendors should be informed that those who successfully pass the scripted-demo stage will be invited back for a second visit. At that time, vendors may demonstrate any additional system features that the scenarios failed to illustrate.

After the team has had a chance to see all of the computer-system demonstrations by vendors, all that remains is to negotiate with the vendor and purchase the system. For some final words of caution, see Exhibit 6 for a list of ten "nevers" club managers should keep in mind if they plan to purchase or upgrade a computer system.

Exhibit 6   The Ten Nevers of Computer-System Purchasing

1. **Never purchase hardware before software.**

   A club should select software first, then identify the hardware it requires.

2. **Never make a purchase decision based solely on cost.**

   Too often, economic factors are given a disproportionate weight in the decision process.

3. **Never lose control of the purchasing process.**

   A process that isn't under control could have disastrous results. Develop request for proposal (RFP) documents, script on-site vendor demonstrations, and apply uniform criteria when evaluating vendor proposals.

4. **Never rely on enhancement promises.**

   A system feature that is advertised but not yet available for sale may not actually become available for months. Don't be fooled by "vaporware"—promised capabilities that evaporate after you purchase the system and are never delivered.

5. **Never be the first system user.**

   New systems have no operational history and therefore are difficult to evaluate. Remember: club members are investing in enhanced club operations; they are not investing in the product-development process of a computer-system vendor.

6. **Never select a proprietary system.**

   Avoid selecting a nonstandard computer system or platform. Proprietary systems can result in heavy dependence on a single vendor and severely limit the enhancement or expansion capabilities of the system purchased.

7. **Never allow the system to dictate operations.**

   Changing club operations to fit the demands of the system is a case of the tail wagging the dog and can get the club into trouble. Streamlining data-processing procedures may be important, but don't let it adversely affect the service goals of the club.

8. **Never be the largest system user.**

   Pushing the envelope of a system's processing speed, file parameters, memory capabilities, and other system functions may lead to a series of problems that the vendor may not be able to solve in a timely fashion.

9. **Never be the last system user.**

   Being the last user implies that the vendor is no longer in business. System maintenance, on-going technical support, enhancements, and the like may be difficult or impossible to obtain.

10. **Never allow a vendor to rewrite your computer-system requirements.**

    A computer system that meets vendor specifications may not meet the club's needs. Provide the vendor with an RFP and stand firm on computer-system requirements.

The Internet and Clubs

The Internet has created a communications and information explosion that has the potential to impact virtually every aspect of daily life. Likened to a network of interstate roads, the Internet is a network of computer networks, connecting an ever-growing number of regional sites to an international superhighway of communications and information.

As discussed earlier, in an office environment, most local area networks (LANs) connect individual PCs to a separate computer, called a server or file server. The file server controls the flow of information along the network. This file server can also be used to establish a gateway to other computer networks beyond the office environment. The Internet takes the concept of networks to its fullest application by connecting large numbers of very complex networks. The **Internet** is an affiliation of tens of thousands of private, commercial, educational, and government-supported computer networks around the world. When a user connects to the Internet, messages and information can be shared with millions of other users.

A full discussion of the Internet is beyond the scope of this chapter; the focus of the following sections will be on the two most common ways club managers use the Internet: sending email and surfing the Web for information.

Sending Email

Electronic mail or email enables Internet users to communicate with people down the hall, across town, or around the world. After arranging for Internet access, new Internet users typically find immediate applications for email communications. The only requirement is that the sender know the intended receiver's **email address.** The alphanumeric format of an email address is generally based on the name of the intended receiver, coupled with the name of the email system being used and the host computer network. For example, the most commonly used format for an email address is *localname@domain*. "Localname" refers to the Internet name of the intended receiver. The domain portion of the address identifies the host computer system on which the intended receiver has an email account. The address on either side of the "@" symbol can be extended, allowing for a more precise identification of an individual or host computer system. Exhibit 7 diagrams the email communications process.

A club equipped with email not only enables the internal staff to communicate from their individual work areas, but also allows managers at the club to communicate with managers from other clubs who have email capability. In addition, for some clubs, email opens a convenient communications link with members. Email systems enable club managers to create their own electronic mailing lists and distribute messages to targeted audiences. If one of these lists contains the email addresses of club members, messages can be easily and inexpensively distributed to that portion of the membership. Similarly, communications involving club committees and board members can be sent using the appropriate email mailing lists. Additional mailing lists can be developed for special-interest groups within the membership. Members could sign up (that is, release their email addresses to the club) to receive communications on specific club functions and activities—gourmet dining, bridge, swimming, bingo, golf, and more. One of the greatest advantages of email over regular mail, or what some computer users call "snail mail," is not just the speed of the communication but the convenience of the communication. Email can be sent and received at any time, day or night. This advantage also brings with

Exhibit 7   Email Communications

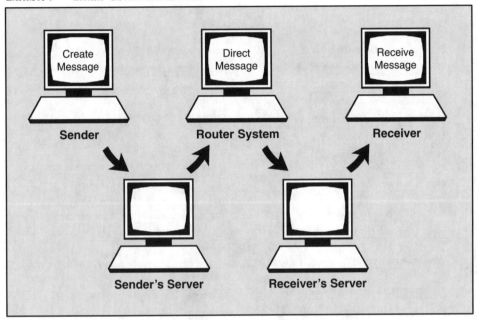

it greater responsibility in terms of responding to email messages and requests. Club managers should check their email often and prepare timely responses to the inquiries and messages they receive.

As with many aspects of the Internet, it's easiest to learn by doing. Once you are on the Internet and clicking your way through menus and screens, you will find resources to help you get started. Perhaps the most-used resource today to learn about the Internet is the Internet itself. Exhibit 8 is from one of many email tutorials that can be accessed free by those on the World Wide Web. The user simply clicks on any of the questions and the screen jumps to the answer, which may be several pages into the document. After reading an answer, the user can simply click on the "back to top" link and the screen jumps back to the main menu of frequently asked questions about email.

Surfing the World Wide Web

The World Wide Web is only one of the many parts of the Internet. It is the best-known part because its user-friendly features have attracted millions of people, from grade-school children to business executives. Unlike text-only sites found on much of the Internet, the World Wide Web offers an incredibly rich combination of text, images, sound, animation, and video. The visual options of the World Wide Web and the surging numbers of "surfers" have enticed thousands of businesses, organizations, educational institutions, government agencies, and individuals to create their own Web pages and participate in the dissemination of information along the Web.

Exhibit 8   Email Tutorial on the World Wide Web

FAQ—E-MAIL

> How do I get setup with e-mail?

> Which e-mail package should I buy?

> How do I retrieve my e-mail?

> What is my e-mail address?

> Now that I have e-mail, what can I do?

> How do I send a message?

> How do I send a message if I don't know someone's address?

> How fast does my message get to its recipient?

> How do I reply to a message?

> How do I know if my message was received?

> What can I do if a message is returned to me?

> How do I know if I have new e-mail?

> Do I have to manually check my mail?

> Can I save messages?

> How do I delete messages?

> How do I keep track of people's addresses?

> Is there a way to file my mail?

> Can I forward mail?

> Can I forward mail to myself at another address?

> How do I attach a file?

> Is attaching a text file different from attaching a multimedia file?

> How will I know if I have an attachment?

> Can I send a fax through e-mail?

> How do I get my e-mail when I'm on vacation or away from my computer?

> Is there a way to let people know I'm on vacation?

> Can I access Internet e-mail when I'm not connected?

> How can I create a signature?

> Can I give my messages priority?

> Do I have any control over the messages that people send me?

> How can I avoid viruses, harassment, and forgery?

Source: http://www.netguide.com/server-java/NGPage/KnowhowNetcoachEmail

Much of the user-friendly nature of the World Wide Web stems from the *HyperText Transfer Protocol* (**http**) that structures information on the Web. This protocol is a specialized set of file download commands embedded within the hypertext markup language (html) used to place text, graphics, video, and other information displays on the Web. The "http" indicates that the Web page can handle nonsequential links to other hypertext pages—a trait characteristic of all Web pages.

A **uniform resource locator (URL)** designates the Internet address of a site, usually the site's homepage. A site's **homepage** is the first screen or Web page presented when you reach a site. URLs are usually built into the hypertext of a Web document, enabling users to jump from site to site along the Web. The URL or Internet address for an organization, club, or individual consists of a series of letters and punctuation marks that may seem confusing, even intimidating, to a first-time Web user. Each grouping of letters represents a section of the path that leads to a desired site. Reading an Internet address from left to right moves from the general to the more specific location of information. For example, consider the following fictional Internet address:

http://www.doublebogey.com

---

net.slang/net.speak

Here are translations of some of the terms and abbreviations frequently found on the Internet.

net.slang

Cybermall—commercial domains on the Internet
Cybersquabbles—online chat sessions
Flame Mail—inflammatory comments
Mouse Potato—a net junkie surfer
Netizen—long-time Internet user
Netiquette—proper use of the Internet
Netnotized—"All that on the net is good."
Newbie—inexperienced Internet user
Wirehead—experienced, expert Internet user

net.speak

BOF—birds of a feather
BTW—by the way
FAQ—frequently asked questions
IMO—in my opinion
RFC—request for comments
RFD—request for discussion
YAA—yet another acronym

Inputting this address would take a user directly to the Web homepage of the Double Bogey Country Club. The suffix "com" (for "commercial") is used for businesses, "org" for organizations, "edu" for educational institutions, and "gov" for government agencies. Extending the address to:

http://www.doublebogey.com/proshop.html

would take a user past the club's homepage and directly to those Web pages devoted to the golf pro shop. Extending the address even further to:

http://www.doublebogey.com/proshop/gloves.html

would take the user immediately to information about golf gloves that are available through the pro shop at the Double Bogey Country Club.

Keeping track of Internet addresses is one of the functions performed by a Web browser. The term **Web browser** refers to software that coordinates and organizes information on the Internet. The most popular Web browsers are by Netscape (Navigator) and Microsoft (Internet Explorer). Web browsers tend to have similar

Insider Insights

Bill Caldwell, CCM, General Manager
Cosmos Club, Washington, D.C.

We have an internal system for email that we use all the time. It's a wonderful tool because it's reduced the number of meetings we have. We can communicate via email instead.

We also just installed a system that scans every source coming in from the Internet. It automatically picks up all of our email from CompuServe, America On-Line, ClubNet, and any other service and dumps it into our local email service. It makes everything available as soon as we turn on our computers. It's very convenient.

We use first names with our email addresses, so it's easy for our members to access us and remember our addresses. Soon we'll be sending out a bookmark to our members—we're an academic club and our members will use bookmarks—and these bookmarks will contain all of our direct dial-in numbers for club areas such as reservations, catering, the front desk, etc. We're also going to put all of our personal email addresses on it.

I look at email as being a great tool. Anyone in a large club who doesn't have it is really missing out. I can take follow-up information from a meeting and immediately send it out to everyone involved. When there is a catering event, I can send details to the catering manager, who can then reply to me with an email. We then attach a hard copy of the email to the function sheets. We also use email to inform employees of events that they should know about. We have about 30 people on email, and they can spread news on to their employees. We still have operations meetings every two weeks, but the email system really reduces the amount of time spent in meetings. The staff is now in constant communication.

The club also has a communications room that acts as a business center for our overnight guests. We have a copier in there and a Pentium computer. We also have a club computer newsgroup that our club computer group runs. This group puts information up on the newsgroup/bulletin board for all club members. Club members can dial up from home, log on, and get into the system.

Every year the club produces the Cosmos Club Journal, and that is now published on the Internet. The journal contains emerging issues from club members.

It really helps to have a business manager who is computer savvy. Being able to write computer programs has given me access to all sorts of tools. I can get information about how we're doing and correct problems before it's too late.

designs and operating procedures. They generally feature a tool bar along the top of the screen with pull-down menus, icons for accessing utility programs, and a directory for saving (bookmarking) Internet addresses of sites frequently visited by the user. **Bookmarking** a favorite site on the Web logs or saves the path used to direct the browser to the site, enabling the user to go back to the site quickly without having to remember and input a long Internet address. (Think of bookmarking as similar to the redial feature of a touch-tone phone.) It's not a good idea to randomly bookmark every site you like, because the individual addresses will get lost in a long miscellaneous list of favorites. To alleviate this problem, many browsers allow you to organize bookmarked sites into specific categories and store them in labeled folders.

When you don't know the appropriate addresses, the best way to find information on the Web is to use one of the many Web search engines easily accessed through a menu option provided by most Web browsers. Commonly used search engines include:

Yahoo	www.yahoo.com
Netscape	www.netscape.com
Web Crawler	www.webcrawler.com
Net Guide	www.netguide.com
Lycos	www.lycos.com
Excite	www.excite.com
Altavista	www.altavista.digital.com

A **search engine** is a software program that reads indexed Web sites and creates lists and links to sites that match with a user's inquiry. Most search engines provide tips on how to efficiently search for information. Generally, the more specific your query, the more relevant will be the list of sites your query generates. However, even if the resulting list is long, you can usually scroll or page through the list and decide which sites are worth a look. Then it's simply a matter of clicking on the link or URL/address to go directly to the Web document.

Internet Applications for Clubs. ClubNet (http://www.cmaa.org) is the online member-service of the Club Managers Association of America (CMAA), linking club managers around the world. Exhibit 9 shows CMAA's homepage. Keep in mind that change is the only constant characteristic of the Internet. Tomorrow's Web site may look very different from the one you access today. Web pages are continually updated with new information, new services, and new links to new sites.

Fundamental features of ClubNet enable club managers to:

- Send and receive email to CMAA members, including CMAA's board of directors, chapter officers, and the national staff

- View, print, or download CMAA publications

- View, print, or download the Mid-Management Career Opportunities list

- Access information about professional-development opportunities and register for seminars and workshops

- Review their education-credit history

- Access information about the annual CMAA conference and register for meetings

- Access legislative updates

Exhibit 9   ClubNet Homepage

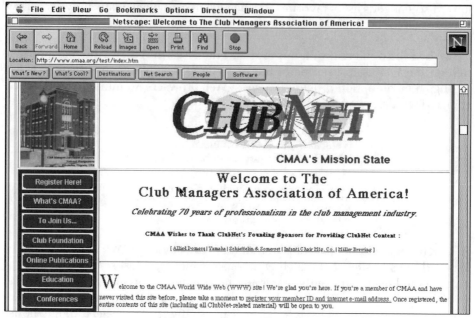

ClubNet also provides links to the Web sites of individual clubs and to the home-pages of some club-industry suppliers and vendors. The Club Foundation, CMAA's educational fund-raising arm, is also on the Web (http://www.clubfoundation.org).

Many private clubs have developed their own Web sites. Since anyone with access to the Internet can visit a club's Web site, the information posted on a club's Web pages should be selected with care. Many clubs use their Web sites to market themselves to potential members and promote club activities and events to their current membership. Commonly found information on club Web sites include a history of the club, a list of facilities and services, membership information, sections of the club's newsletter, photographs of recent club activities, and descriptions of upcoming events.

Dedicating several of the club's computers as Internet-access terminals for members capitalizes on the information and entertainment value of the World Wide Web. A "cyberzone" or "cybercafe" within a club could provide Web-savvy members with the opportunity to explore sites that they may never think to visit through their normal surfing routines. For example, club managers could encourage members to pursue their individual interests by bookmarking sites related to recreational activities at the club—golf, tennis, swimming, bridge, and so on. For members new to the electronic superhighway, clubs could offer instructional classes that focus on the fun and entertainment value of the World Wide Web. Internet applications for clubs are limited only by the creative imaginations of club managers searching for new ways to delight members and exceed their expectations.

Insider Insights

Ron Comfort, Director of Information and Technology Systems
Club Managers Association of America
Alexandria, Virginia

CMAA started ClubNet in October 1994 as a completely private dial-up network. ClubNet allowed club managers to access, via computer, information in CMAA's databases that the managers previously had to call in and ask for. From its initial debut to managers worldwide in August 1995 until its close in November 1996, the network was accessed more than 750,000 times. The private network had many advantages, of which the most notable was tight security; the biggest disadvantage was the cost—there was a per-minute online charge associated with the service.

By the summer of 1996, it became clear that the World Wide Web offered a chance for ClubNet to extend services to CMAA members and non-members alike. Unlike private networks, there are no fees associated with access to the Web, and the Web offers the potential to reach millions of people worldwide. Once it was moved onto the Web, ClubNet became even more popular. As of May 1997, ClubNet was averaging 4,511 accesses per day.

Although ClubNet is now a Web site much like any other, we still offer private sections that only CMAA members can access. We also have the ability to limit access to any section of ClubNet on a per-person basis. For example, recently a report was placed on ClubNet for access by CMAA chapter officers only. In order to view the report, you had to meet two requirements: you had to be a CMAA member and be designated in the database as a chapter officer. This additional security allows us to offer most of the secure services the private network offered, but with the much broader appeal of the Web.

Every department at CMAA is represented in some fashion on ClubNet. Our Executive Career Services Department, including employment listings, is found there. The Club Foundation scholarship program found on ClubNet has generated numerous email messages from students. Our printed newsletters, which on ClubNet are called "Online Publications," are there, along with archived issues. CMAA's Bookmart offers industry publications with ClubNet-only specials. The Education Department is particularly well represented, with the complete education calendar, including all of CMAA's seminars, Business Management Institutes, and other educational opportunities listed. The education calendar, while printed each month in our newsletters, can be continually updated on the Web—something that just can't happen with a printed calendar. There's a section on ClubNet dedicated to our student members, with links to student-chapter Web pages. Club managers can use these listings to contact students directly.

Our online Global Membership Directory is by far the most popular section of ClubNet. While the online directory bears a striking resemblance to the printed membership directory in the CMAA Yearbook, the Web allows us to continually update members' listings. In addition, we assign all CMAA members an email address that ends in "cmaa.org"; this instantly identifies them worldwide as CMAA members. With this address, CMAA members can send each other messages without having to know the receiver's private email address or which

(continued)

Insider Insights *(continued)*

online service the receiver uses; ClubNet acts as an interpreter of all the various email addresses and online services. A CMAA member simply sends the message to the CMAA email address and the message is passed through to the receiver's private email box.

It's even possible to send a manager email before that manager ever visits ClubNet, since every manager, online or not, is listed. This can result in a new online member receiving a backlog of CMAA mail just after he or she visits ClubNet for the first time. In one particular instance, a member received 117 email messages the day after he visited ClubNet for the first time, since many other managers had been sending mail to him.

The "Industry Links" section of ClubNet is the second most popular. Here, you find all of the member-managed clubs that have a Web site, all of the CMAA chapters that are online, and our allied associations and organizations. Managers building Web sites for their clubs can visit clubs that already have a Web presence to get ideas for the layout of their sites.

Ordinarily, Web "surfers" seek out Web sites and decide which information to view. This process, called "pulling" information out of the Web, has one big disadvantage: how do you keep people informed of changes to the material made after they've viewed it the first time? With the new "push" model of information transfer, a Web surfer, when initially visiting ClubNet, checks a box indicating he or she would like to automatically receive the updates we make to a particular section of ClubNet. From then on, an actual visit to ClubNet is no longer required—updates are sent to the person via email.

ClubNet can't turn you into a great club manager, but it can help you be a better one. It's almost like having all other members of CMAA and CMAA's staff available 24 hours a day, 7 days a week. You can send an email question to a manager halfway around the world and not have to worry about the time zone difference. There are more than 13,700 links to information helpful to you in your day-to-day career via ClubNet. Electronic communication and commerce are tools, just like other tools club managers use to perform their jobs, and more club managers are embracing them.

Key Terms

bookmarking—A feature of Web browsers that logs/saves the path to favorite Internet sites, enabling the user to arrive quickly at a site without inputting a long Internet address.

central processing unit (CPU)—The control center of a computer system.

ClubNet—The online member-service of the Club Managers Association of America, linking club managers around the world.

data processing—The transformation of raw facts and isolated figures as input (data) into timely, accurate, and useful output (information).

database-management software—Allows users to catalog and store information about their businesses for future use.

email address—An alphanumeric format generally based on the name of the intended receiver, coupled with the name of the email system and the host computer network. The most commonly used format for an email address is *localname@domain*.

hardware—The physical equipment of a computer system, consisting of input/output (I/O) units, a central processing unit, and external storage devices (disks, hard disks, magnetic tapes, and so on).

hardware configuration—The design and layout of the physical components of a computer system.

homepage—The first screen or Web page presented when you reach a site.

HyperText Transfer Protocol (http)—A specialized set of file download commands embedded within the hypertext markup language (html) used to place text, graphics, video, and other information displays on the Web.

integrated software—Separate but compatible computer programs designed to work together, sharing data and information across programs.

Internet—An affiliation of tens of thousands of private, commercial, educational, and government-supported computer networks around the world.

local area network (LAN)—A local (within one office, for example) configuration of workstations that enables users to share data, programs, and output devices (such as printers).

modular software—A group of related programs that can be purchased separately.

scripted product demonstration—A product demonstration by a vendor that is directed by a script prepared by club managers; the script ensures that the demonstration covers areas relevant to club operations and that each vendor covers the same ground.

search engine—A software program that reads indexed Web sites and creates lists and links to sites that match with a user's inquiry.

site survey—A visit from a computer-system vendor to identify important factors about club operations that may affect computer-system design and implementation.

software—Programs that instruct or control the operation of the hardware components of a computer system; software programs tell the computer what to do, how to do it, and when to do it.

throughput—The processing time it takes from data input to information output.

uniform resource locator (URL)—Designates the Internet address of a site, usually its homepage.

Web browser—Software that coordinates and organizes information on the Internet.

Review Questions

1. What are some of the advantages of electronic data processing?

2. What three hardware components must every computer system have?

3. What are some examples of generic software?

4. What are some of the challenges clubs face with point-of-sale (POS) systems?

5. What do event-management and golf-course-management software programs enable clubs to do?

6. What steps should clubs follow when purchasing or upgrading their computer system?

7. How can club managers use email on the Internet?

8. How can club managers make use of the World Wide Web?

 Additional Reading

Dern, D. P. *The Internet Guide for New Users.* New York: McGraw-Hill, 1994.

Ellsworth, J. H., and M. V. Ellsworth. *The Internet Business Book.* New York: Wiley, 1994.

Internet World Magazine. Westport, Conn.: Meckler Media Corporation.

Kasavana, Michael L., and John J. Cahill. *Managing Computers in the Hospitality Industry,* Third Edition. East Lansing, Mich.: Educational Institute of the American Hotel & Motel Association, 1997.

PC Computing Magazine. New York: Ziff-Davis.

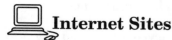 **Internet Sites**

For more information, visit the following Internet sites. Remember that Internet addresses can change without notice. If the site is no longer there, use a browser to look for additional sites.

Computer Systems Hardware

Apple Computer, Incorporated
http://www.apple.com

Compaq Computer Corporation
http://www.compaq.com

Dell Computer Corporation
http://www.dell.com

Digital Equipment Corporation
http://www.digital.com

Elo TouchSystems
http://www.elotouch.com

Gateway 2000 Incorporated
http://www.gw2k.com

Intel Corporation
http://www.intel.com

International Business Machines, Inc.
http://www.us.pc.ibm.com

NEC Corporation
http://www.nec.com

Sony Electronics, Incorporated
http://www.sony.com

Word-Processing Software

Corel Corporation—WordPerfect
http://www.wordperfect.com

hSoft Inc.
http://www.hsft.com

Microsoft Corporation—Word,
Publisher, PowerPoint
http://www.microsoft.com/msword
http://www.microsoft.com/
publisher/
http://www.microsoft.com/
powerpoint/

Electronic-Spreadsheet Software

Lotus Development Corporation—
Lotus 1-2-3
http://www2.lotus.com/123.nsf

Microsoft Corporation—Excel
http://www.microsoft.com/excel

Spreadsheet User Group
http://www.sheet.com

Point-of-Sale Systems

InfoGenesis
http://www.infogenesis.com

NCR Corporation
http://www.ncr.com

Remanco International Inc.
http://www.remanco.com

Squirrel Companies Inc.
http://www.squirrel-rms.com

System Concepts Inc.
http://www.foodtrak.com

Internet and World Wide Web

FoxWeb
http://www.foxweb.com

Guide to Internet
http://netscape.yahoo.com/guide/
technology.html

Microsoft Corporation—Internet
Explorer
http://www.microsoft.com/ie/
default.asp

Netscape—Navigator
http://home.netscape.com

Chapter Appendix

The following tables indicate how computers are used in clubs today. These statistics, based on a survey of 709 clubs, were found in *Club Operations and Financial Data Report*, a 1996 publication of the Club Managers Association of America.

Day-to-Day Use of Computers By Departments	
Department	**Percentage**
General Manager	56%
Golf Pro Shop	63%
Tennis Pro Shop	17%
Dining	56%

Computer Equipment Used by Clubs	
Computer Item	**Percent Using**
A 386 or Faster PC	90%
3 1/2" Floppy Disk Drive	87%
At Least 4 Megabytes of RAM	88%
Color Monitor	86%
Windows 3.1 or Higher	84%
9600 Baud or Faster Modem	68%
Dedicated Phone/Fax Line	87%
Computer at GM's Desk	62%
E-Mail Address	21%
Networked Computers	71%

Percent of Clubs Using Computers for Specific Automated Operations	
Operation	**Percent Using Computers**
Accounting	91%
Fitness Testing/Monitoring	2%
Golf Handicap Records	59%
Inventory	59%
Membership Database	77%
Desktop Publishing	50%
Spreadsheets	78%
Electronic Timekeeping	31%
Word Processing	81%
Point of Sale	54%

Word Processing Software Used By Clubs	
Percentage of Clubs That Use Computer for Word Processing Functions	81%
Software	**Percent Using**
WordPerfect	63%
Microsoft Word	26%
Microsoft Works	3%

Desktop Publishing Software Used By Clubs	
Percentage of Clubs That Use Computer for Desktop Publishing	50%
Software	**Percent Using**
Aldus Pagemaker	20%
Microsoft Publisher	11%
WordPerfect	8%
Word	6%
Microsoft Office	4%
Print Shop	4%

Spreadsheet Software Used By Clubs	
Percentage of Clubs That Use Computer for Spreadsheet Functions	78%
Software	**Percent Using**
Lotus 123	45%
Excel	27%
Quattro Pro	6%

Membership Database Software Used By Clubs	
Percentage of Clubs That Use Computer for Membership Database	77%
Software	**Percent Using**
Country Club Systems	17%
Diamond Management Systems	10%
Flex Screen	6%
Aces	4%
Custom Software	3%
MSI	3%
Clubware	2%
MAI Basic 4	2%
Club Data	1%
Watson & Steach	1%

Inventory Software Used By Clubs	
Percentage of Clubs That Use Computer for Inventory Functions	59%
Software	**Percent Using**
Lotus 123	16%
Country Club Systems	11%
Excel	8%
Diamond Management System	6%
Food Trak	2%
MSI	2%

Accounting Software Used By Clubs	
Percentage of Clubs That Use Computer for Accounting Functions	91%
Software	**Percent Using**
Country Club Systems	18%
Diamond Management Systems	11%
Flex Screen	5%
Aces	4%
MAI Basic 4	3%
MSI	3%
Custom Software	2%
Club Data	2%
Clubware	2%

Point of Sale Software Used By Clubs	
Percentage of Clubs That Use Computer for Point of Sale Functions	54%
Software	**Percent Using**
Micros	15%
Country Club Systems	10%
Diamond Management Systems	7%
Digital Dining	7%
Squirrel	5%
Positouch	3%
FlexScreen	2%

Golf Handicap Software Used By Clubs	
Percentage of Clubs That Use Computer for Golf Handicap Records	59%
Software	**Percent Using**
GHIN	20%
Handicomp	7%
USGA	7%
Summner	5%
Country Club Systems	3%
MGA	3%
SCGA	3%
CDGA	2%
NCGA	2%
Golf Net	2%

REVIEW QUIZ

When you feel you have covered all of the material in this chapter, answer these questions. Choose the *best* answer.

1. Which of the following computer terms relates to the transformation of raw facts and isolated figures as input (data) into timely, accurate, and useful output (information)?

   a. data processing
   b. data integration
   c. data configuration
   d. data streamlining

2. Two years ago, the Hollow Haven Club computerized some of its accounting functions by purchasing modular software. The resulting savings and increased efficiencies prompted the management team to consider computerizing the club's payroll system. Which of the following would be the most important issue in purchasing a payroll module if the management team expects to generate complete financial statements from the computer system it purchases?

   a. hardware configuration
   b. software integration
   c. throughput
   d. streamlined output

3. Which of the following statements about software applications for clubs is *true?*

   a. Purchasing industry-standard hardware commits a club to a single source for software enhancements.
   b. The usefulness of event management software will depend on the degree to which the programs integrate with the club's existing computer system.
   c. Workstation printers of a POS system eliminate food production errors in the kitchen.
   d. POS systems eliminate the need for dispatchers, expediters, and runners.

4. Which of the following would be the best electronic tool a club could use to communicate with special-interest groups made up of its own club members?

   a. email
   b. Internet
   c. World Wide Web
   d. ClubNet

Answer Key: 1-a-C1, 2-b-C4, 3-b-C6, 4-a-C9

Each question is linked to a competency. Competencies are listed on the first page of the chapter. An answer reading 3-b-C4 translates to:

   3: the question number
   b: the correct answer
   C4: the competency number

Chapter 12 Outline

Competencies

1. List and describe golf facilities typically found at clubs. (pp. 421–427)

2. Describe handicap systems, club tournaments, golf instructional programs at clubs, caddie programs at clubs, and golf-car issues at clubs. (pp. 427–435)

3. List typical golf staff positions, summarize the duties and responsibilities of golf staff positions, and list and briefly describe major golf associations that can assist clubs. (pp. 435–441)

12

Golf Operations in Clubs

This chapter was written and contributed by Raymond R. Ferreira, Assistant Professor, Cecil B. Day School of Hospitality Administration, Georgia State University, Atlanta, Georgia.

IN THIS CHAPTER we will take a look at typical golf facilities at a private club and golf programs and services commonly offered to club members. We will also look at the golf staff members who are not involved in golf course maintenance: the golf director, assistant golf professionals, and other staff members such as pro shop and practice range employees. The chapter concludes with a section on golf organizations.

Golf Facilities

The golf facilities at a private club account for approximately 10 percent of a club's income.[1] Club golf facilities typically include a golf course (or several golf courses), a practice range, a pro shop, a golf-bag room or bag-storage area, and a golf car barn.

Golf Course

Golf courses at private clubs are usually 9 or 18 holes in length, with 18 holes being the most common. Each hole on a golf course has a tee box (the starting or tee-off area), a fairway (the strip of mowed grass between the tee box and green), the rough (tall grass, weeds, trees, etc. on either side of the fairway), and a green (a putting surface with a cup). Some holes have obstacles to challenge the golfer, such as bunkers (sand traps) and water hazards.

The golf courses at private clubs are used in a variety of ways by club members. Some members prefer to play golf just a few times a month for recreational purposes. Others enjoy the competitive nature of the sport and participate in the club's tournaments and other structured golf activities. Parents may enroll their children for golf lessons. Members may also play rounds of golf with business associates. The average club golf course supports 30,000 rounds of golf per year.[2]

The first tee times of the day will be at least one hour after sunrise at most clubs. On some days the starting times may be pushed back to allow the grounds crew to complete its regular maintenance duties. The crew needs time to cut the tee boxes, fairways, and greens; rake the bunkers; and perform other maintenance duties before members play. The crew can usually stay ahead of the players if it is given time to complete maintenance on the first three or four holes before the first players are allowed to start. Many clubs do not allow play on Mondays so that the grounds crew can perform major maintenance duties. If play is allowed on a Monday, normally play doesn't begin until the afternoon.

From the Fairways ...

by Mike Plummer
Golf Course Superintendent

When you, as a member, come to the club to enjoy a fine meal, the dining room staff has already set up the table properly prior to you being seated. I'm sure that you wouldn't want your meal to be served and then have your fork brought to the table and your napkin brought out near the end of the meal. You probably wouldn't enjoy your meal very much if that occurred. Likewise, when you come to the club to play golf and step up to the first tee, you want everything ready for play. I know it would be distracting if one of the grounds crew mowed the putting green or raked a green-side bunker while you were putting. Obviously, just like the dining room staff needs time to set up the table prior to you being seated, our grounds staff needs time to set up the golf course.

To get the course set up properly during the prime golfing season, our mechanics and assistant golf course superintendent report for work at 5:30 A.M. to get the equipment and job assignments ready for the rest of the grounds staff. The staff starts setting up the golf course at 6:00 A.M. By starting well ahead of play, staff members can stay in front of play and accomplish their jobs much quicker than if they were working around play.

Even with good planning and training, there are times when we are delayed with the set up and have to work right along with play, due to weather delays, equipment breakdowns, and so on. When this happens, the grounds staff understands that the member comes first. During the day, you will still see many maintenance tasks being performed, but most do not affect play as much as the set up of the tees, bunkers, and greens. So, please understand that it takes time to set up the course prior to you stepping up to the first tee.

In his monthly newsletter column, this club's golf course superintendent asked members to be patient with the grounds crew and its efforts to get the golf course ready for play each day.

Source: Adapted from *The Lakewooder: Lakewood Country Club News*, Dallas, Texas: Lakewood Country Club.

Clubs usually restrict the times that guests of members can play golf, limit the number of times guests can play per month or per year, and stipulate who is to be considered an out-of-town or in-town guest when golf course usage is restricted to in-town guests. At the time of check-in at the pro shop, members should register their guests and sign the charge slip for the guest fee.

Some clubs restrict play to men-members only during the busiest time periods (Friday afternoon, Saturday morning, and holidays). The argument for this policy is that the men-members work all week and typically can play only at those times. Clubs who accept women as members are having a difficult time maintaining this policy because many of the women-members work all week just like the men-members and the women are demanding equal access to the golf course. Another argument some club members make for restricting the golf course to men only during certain busy times is that women tend to slow the pace of play. Ensuring that all members are educated on the regulations of the course and the importance of timely play will combat this problem, however.

Speed of Play

A sign at the Old Course at St. Andrews in Scotland, the birthplace of golf, states most succinctly: "Your position on the golf course is immediately behind the group in front of you—not immediately in front of the group behind you." In the interest of all, players should play without delay. Under normal circumstances, no round should take more than four hours to complete. In order to speed up play, please observe the following:

- Be ready to play your shot when it is your turn.

- Pick up if you are out of contention for the hole.

- When possible, park golf cars beyond the green to avoid delays upon completion of the hole.

- When the play of a hole is completed, leave the putting green immediately. Do not compile your score on the putting green.

- If there is a possibility of a ball being lost or out of bounds, play a provisional ball.

- If you are out of contention for the hole or feel that you may be holding up your group, it is considered a sporting gesture to pick up and move to the next hole so that your group may keep its proper place on the course.

Source: Adapted from the Baltimore Country Club's "Five Farms Rules and Etiquette," pp. 2–3.

During the week, many clubs designate time periods when the course is open for play only to organized club groups (see Exhibit 1). For example, the club's women golfers may hold an event on a weekday morning or evening, or the juniors may have an organized activity on a weekday right after school.

Practice Range

The **practice range** or driving range is an area designated for members to practice hitting a variety of shots. The practice range should be located near the first tee so that it is easy for members to move to the golf course after practicing. The practice range should be situated so that no stray balls are hit onto the golf course or into other areas where members and guests may be. The club should install protective netting if there is a possibility of an errant shot striking someone. A club may have a practice green and bunker near the practice range for members to practice their putting and sand game.

The practice range staff should set up all practice equipment at the beginning of the day and store it at the end. Collecting and washing the practice range balls should be performed at the end of the day or during the day when there is heavy usage. A quantity of practice range balls should be bagged or bucketed ahead of time so that members do not have to wait for them. Practice range balls should be replaced often. Clubs may be able to have their practice range balls paid for by corporations who want the advertising exposure: the corporation buying the range balls might print its logo on them, for example. The practice range may have mats made of AstroTurf or some other synthetic material for members to tee off from during inclement weather. Permanent bag stands in the practice range area allow members to stand their bags up while practicing. Benches allow members to rest while waiting for partners or their turns on the range.

Exhibit 1   Sample Golf Course Schedules for a Club with Two Golf Courses

— EAST COURSE —

	MONDAY	TUESDAY	WEDNESDAY	THURSDAY	FRIDAY	SATURDAY	SUNDAY
7:30 a.m.	OPEN PLAY	Ladies 9-H on 27 Holes — Limited Times Available on Alternate Nine to Gentlemen & Ladies	Ladies 18-H on 36 Holes — Limited Times may be Available for Gentlemen & Other Ladies	OPEN PLAY	OPEN PLAY	Gentlemen's Play Starting Times Required, Out-of-Town Guests after 10:00 a.m.	Gentlemen's Play Starting Times Required, Out-of-Town Guests after 10:00 a.m.
	One Course Closed for Maintenance on Alternate Mondays.	11:00 a.m. Gentlemen's Play, with Guests after 1:00 p.m. 2:00 p.m.				12:00 Noon OPEN PLAY	12:00 Noon OPEN PLAY
		2:00 p.m. OPEN PLAY	2:00 p.m. OPEN PLAY	OPEN PLAY		Starting Time Required	Starting Time Required
DUSK	Juniors Before 11:00 a.m. or After 3:00 p.m.	Juniors After 3:00 p.m.	Juniors After 3:00 p.m.	Juniors After 3:00 p.m.	Juniors Before 11:00 a.m. or After 3:00 p.m.	Juniors After 3:00 p.m.	Juniors After 4:00 p.m.

— WEST COURSE —

	MONDAY	TUESDAY	WEDNESDAY	THURSDAY	FRIDAY	SATURDAY	SUNDAY
7:30 a.m.	OPEN PLAY	Ladies 9-H on 27 Holes — Limited Times Available on Alternate Nine to Gentlemen & Ladies	Ladies 18-H on 36 Holes — Limited Times may be Available for Gentlemen & Other Ladies	OPEN PLAY	OPEN PLAY	Gentlemen's Play Starting Times Required, Out-of-Town Guests after 10:00 a.m.	Gentlemen's Play Starting Times Required
	One Course Closed for Maintenance on Alternate Mondays.	11:00 a.m. Gentlemen's Play, with Guests after 1:00 p.m. 1:00 p.m.				11:00 a.m. OPEN PLAY	9:00 a.m. Out-of-Town Guests After 10:00 a.m. OPEN PLAY
		1:00 p.m. OPEN PLAY	1:00 p.m. OPEN PLAY			Starting Time Required	Starting Time Required
DUSK	Juniors Before 11:00 a.m. or After 3:00 p.m.	Juniors After 3:00 p.m.	Juniors After 3:00 p.m.	Juniors After 3:00 p.m.	Juniors Before 11:00 a.m. or After 3:00 p.m.	Juniors After 3:00 p.m.	Juniors After 4:00 p.m.

Courtesy of the Baltimore Country Club, Baltimore, Maryland

Pro Shop

The merchandise in the golf pro shop can be owned by the golf director or the club; there are almost as many arrangements and contractual agreements as there are private clubs. In many clubs, the golf director owns the merchandise and pays rent for the shop space. In some clubs, instead of rent, the director pays the club a percentage

Members can find golf apparel and chat with the club's golf pro in the club's pro shop.
(Courtesy of the Congressional Country Club, Bethesda, Maryland)

of the profits from the pro shop. In a small number of cases, the pro shop may be leased out to a third party in return for rent or a percentage of total sales or net income. This lease arrangement may be managed by the golf director or the club.

Golf directors who own their merchandise usually must secure credit to purchase their inventory, fixtures, and displays. When the director owns the pro shop merchandise, the club should require the director to carry liability and property insurance.

Golf products typically offered in pro shops include golf clubs and head covers, golf bags, golf balls, golf gloves, assorted apparel (men's, women's, and junior), golf shoes and hats, and miscellaneous golf-related items (videos, books, glassware and other souvenirs with a golfing theme, and so on). Exhibit 2 lists golf-apparel guidelines provided by the Professional Golfers' Association of America (PGA). Golf-related services include repairing, regripping, reshafting, and refinishing golf clubs.

The golf items carried in a club's pro shop should be of higher quality than the items sold in local sporting-goods stores and golf retail shops. Because the pro shop deals with a relatively unchanging clientele, displays should be changed regularly (as often as every two to four weeks).

Some pro shops have a **cost-plus program,** whereby a member pays a fee to join the program and then pays only the pro shop's cost for merchandise plus a set percentage. One example of a cost-plus program is referred to as the Mill River

Exhibit 2   Recommended Percentage of Golf Apparel in the Pro Shop

Men		Women		Junior	
Shirts	43%	Blouses	31%	Shirts	65%
Sweaters	25%	Sweaters	25%	Shorts	20%
Slacks and shorts	20%	Slacks, shorts,		Sweaters	15%
Socks	5%	and skirts	20%		
Outerwear	5%	Accessories	10%		
Miscellaneous	2%	Outerwear	3%		
		Socks or PEDS	2%		

Plan; under this plan, a member can purchase merchandise at cost plus 10 percent after paying a once-a-year fee of $100.[3]

Instead of receiving prizes or trophies in tournaments, winning golfers can receive a line of credit at the pro shop. This helps to move merchandise and increase sales. Other ways to increase sales include having a strong **club-demo program** (in which members can try out golf clubs before buying them) and making sure that the golf professionals use only club models that are carried in the pro shop while playing at the club. Custom-fitting golf clubs is a special service that the pro shop can provide to members that will also help increase sales.

A good source for information on merchandising items in golf pro shops is the *PGA Merchandising Manual*. This manual covers sales analysis, merchandise-buying programs, inventory-control procedures, and sales techniques.

Bag Room

Members typically have the option of storing their golf bags at the club. The bag room, where the golf bags are stored, is usually located close to both the pro shop and the area where members pick up their golf cars. Members who store their bags at the club should have their bags placed on golf cars approximately one hour before their scheduled tee times. The bag room staff should notify the pro shop concerning which car each member's bag was placed on. Golf staff members (usually bag room attendants or caddies) should monitor the bag pickup area near the parking lot so that when members who do not store their clubs arrive or when their guests arrive with clubs, staff members can carry the golf bags from the automobiles to the club.

After members finish play, staff members should take the golf bags to the members' cars or to the bag-storage room if the bags are stored at the club. If a member's bag is stored at the club, bag room attendants should clean and dry the bag, club heads, grips, and shafts before returning the bag to its storage area. All bags should be tagged with the member's name and identification number. If the staff member cleaning a member's clubs notices that a repair is needed, a note should be left on the club or bag recommending the repair and advising that the pro shop can perform it for the member. All bags should be entered into an inventory system. The club's general insurance policy should be checked to ensure that it covers any damage to or loss of member items stored in the bag room.

Golf Car Barn

The golf car barn is where the club's golf cars are stored and recharged (if they are battery-operated) or refueled (if they are gas-operated). For battery-powered cars, the car barn should have a fan installed at the highest point in the ceiling; the fan must be capable of changing the air in the building at least five times per hour. This is a safety issue; recharging batteries produce hydrogen gas, which can become explosive if it is allowed to accumulate in concentrations of more than two percent. Hydrogen gas is lighter than air and will rise to the highest point in a building. The golf car barn's wiring should be sufficient to handle the peak power requirements when all of the chargers are being used. Every charger should have an individual circuit breaker or fuse of at least 15 to 20 amperes.

Clubs that use gasoline-powered cars should make sure that their gasoline storage meets all Occupational Safety and Health Administration standards and local building and fire codes. Gasoline must be stored in an approved storage tank that is ventilated properly and located at a safe distance from the car barn.

The car barn, just like the club's other buildings, should have an alarm system to protect it and its contents from vandals and thieves.

Maintenance of Golf Facilities

The practice range area, golf car storage area, and grounds around the golf pro shop should be as clean and tasteful as the rest of the club's facilities. These areas are often maintained by the golf course grounds crew or the club's gardeners. The golf director should work cooperatively with these individuals to maintain the grass, flowers, plants, trees, benches, chairs, trash cans, and so on in these areas.

Decorating and cleaning the inside of the pro shop usually is the responsibility of the golf staff. Repairs and other large maintenance items are the responsibility of the club's maintenance staff.

Golf Programs and Services

The most common types of golf programs offered at private clubs are activities organized for the club's men and women golfers, member-guest tournaments, junior golf events, and club championships. The biggest concern in conducting any organized event on the golf course is that the entire course or portions of it will be unavailable for use by the general membership. The golf committee and golf director must ensure that the dates, times, and number of holes used for an organized event is in the best interest of the general membership. If possible, a few tee times should always be open during an organized event for members who are not participating in the event.

The golf programs and services discussed in the following sections are handicap systems, tournaments, instructional programs, caddie programs, and golf car rentals.

Handicap Systems

A **handicap system** allows club members with different abilities to play golf together and compete on an equal basis. Members must play regularly and report their scores after each round so that accurate handicaps can be determined.

Exhibit 3   Golf Handicap Software Used by Clubs

Percentage of Clubs That Use Computers for Golf Handicap Records	59%
Software	**Percent Using**
GHIN	20%
Handicomp	7%
USGA	7%
Summner	5%
Country Club Systems	3%
MGA	3%
SCGA	3%
CDGA	2%
NCGA	2%
Golf Net	2%

Source: Club Managers Association of America, *Club Operations and Financial Data Report* (Alexandria, Virginia: CMAA, 1996), p. 68.

Handicaps should be updated regularly and posted on a bulletin board. Clubs can implement a computerized handicapping system by purchasing the software themselves, paying a fee to another club to process their handicaps for them, or forming a group of clubs to purchase the software and share it. Exhibit 3 shows the percentage of clubs that use computers to keep handicap records, and the types of software programs they use.

Tournaments

Most private clubs conduct a regular schedule of golf tournaments each season that includes a club championship, invitational tournaments, events for the club's men golfers, events for the club's women golfers, member-guest tournaments, men-women events, junior events, and so on. For clubs seeking more members, the main purpose of **member-guest events** is to introduce prospective members to the club and its services.

A club should promote every golf event in order to foster interest and participation. Signs should be posted throughout the club and notices placed in the club newsletter informing members of when the golf course will not be available because of scheduled events. A few weeks prior to an event, telephone calls should be

This notice in a club newsletter invites members to sign up for the club's member-guest tournaments.
Source: *The Lakewooder: Lakewood Country Club News,* Dallas, Texas: Lakewood Country Club.

made to those who have signed up to remind them of the event. Members who regularly participate but have not signed up should be called to fill up any open spots in a tournament. The fees members and others pay for an event should cover the direct costs of the event: food and beverages served, prizes, pro shop certificates, and so on. When scheduling an event, the organizer should make sure that it does not conflict with other club events. Each major golf tournament held at the club should have a tournament chair who assists the golf course staff in planning, promoting, and conducting the event.

Each golf event can be made more special by putting player names on the golf cars' sign holders, providing entry gifts, preparing scorecards with player names typed on them, and so on. Golf directors should dress up the course by placing yardage markers along the holes, marking all out-of-bounds areas, and placing attractive signs at holes that have special activities or contests associated with them: closest-to-the-pin contests, longest-drive contests, prizes for a hole in one, and so on. Tournament results should be posted on a scoreboard near the pro shop in an outside area that gives players enough room to socialize. The results should be announced and prizes awarded as soon as possible after the event or during the post-event banquet (if one is planned). There are many golf event formats, some of which have unique titles such as Bingle-Bangle-Bungle, Crier's Tourney, and so on. Some basic golf-event formats are listed in Exhibit 4.

Exhibit 4   Basic Golf Event Formats at Private Clubs

NAME	DESCRIPTION
Best Ball	The lowest score among partners or team members on each hole is used to calculate the team's score for 18 holes.
Bingle-Bangle-Bungle	Each hole counts three points. One point goes to the player whose ball first comes to rest on the surface of the green; a second point goes to the player whose ball is nearest the cup after all the players are on the green; the third point goes to the player who first sinks a putt. The winner is the player with the most points at the end of the round.
Crier's Tourney	Each player gets to pick out his two (or three) worst holes and revert his or her score on these back to par.
Four Ball	There are two partners on a team, each partner playing his or her own ball. The low ball of each team counts on each hole, and the team with the lowest score wins the hole. The winning team is the team with more holes won than there are holes left to play.
Foursomes	Players use one ball, with partners stroking alternately between the tee box and the green.
Handicap Stroke Play	Players play 18 holes, adjusting their score at each hole for their handicap.
Match Play	Lowest score wins the hole; the winning individual has more holes won than there are holes left to play.
Nassau	Winners for an 18-hole round of golf are determined in three ways: best score for the first 9 holes, best score for the second 9 holes, and best score for all 18 holes.
Scramble	All teammates tee off. The best shot among the teammates is selected and all teammates hit their second shot from that location. After all have hit their second shot, they again decide which shot is best and all hit their third shot from that location. This is continued until the ball is in the cup.
Shotgun	Eighteen teams of foursomes all start play at the same time. A team is assigned to begin at each hole on the golf course and all teams start at the sound of a gun or horn. For example, players starting at the 17th hole will play the 18th hole second, the 1st hole third, and so on.

Outside Golf Tournaments. Outside golf tournaments are conducted at many private clubs. An **outside tournament** is a tournament that is not organized primarily for members and invited guests. Some clubs do not allow any outside tournaments, others only allow a few outside tournaments a year, and clubs that are seeking additional revenues may aggressively pursue tournaments. An outside tournament may be organized by a company or organization that wants to host a golf tournament and banquet for a special event, such as a charity fund-raiser or a corporate outing. Clubs usually host these events on Mondays so as not to inconvenience members (most country clubs are closed on Mondays). Organizers of outside events usually

Exhibit 5   Outside Golf Events per Club

Region	Average Number	Average Revenue
Northeast	13	$41,878
Mid-Atlantic	13	$15,838
Southeast	10	$7,657
North Central	8	$22,086
South Central	9	$13,806
West	15	$31,988

Source: Club Managers Association of America, *Club Operations and Financial Data Report* (Alexandria, Virginia: CMAA, 1996), p. 60.

must pay a greens fee for each participant, rent the club's golf cars, pay a set fee for use of the practice range, host a lunch or dinner at the club, and pay for the food and beverages consumed on the golf course. Outside tournaments are usually sponsored by a club member. Exhibit 5 shows, by region, the average number of outside golf events a club schedules and the average revenue realized by the club.

Typically, food and beverage service is provided for outside tournaments. Although clubs prefer to cater these events themselves, some organizations may want to bring their own food and beverages. Club managers should check with the local liquor commission before allowing anyone to bring alcohol onto club property (such an action might be in violation of the club's liquor license).

Instructional Programs

Golf instruction is the foundation of a private club's overall golf program. Instruction is a key to getting members to use the golf course and to visit the club more often. The club's instructional programs are good feeders into other golf activities at the club. Instructional programs are not just for beginners; clubs offer programs to teach intermediate and advanced golf skills, too.

Members usually pay an additional fee for golf lessons. Golf lessons can be in the form of private lessons, group lessons, or clinics. The group lessons or clinics are usually organized by age group (adult or junior), gender, skill level, and topic (rules, stroke improvement, playing strategy, and so on). Private lessons give members the individual attention that some desire, but at a high cost. Group lessons and clinics are less expensive and allow members to socialize with other members while improving their skills. A club should never allow the entire practice range and other practice areas to be used solely for lessons, especially during peak hours.

The golf professionals who give lessons may receive all of the instruction fees or a certain percentage of them; payment policies are set annually by the club's golf committee or board of directors, with input from the golf director and the general manager. Often the golf director receives a percentage of the revenues from lessons taught by the assistant golf professionals, based on the experience of the assistant; the more experienced the assistant, the smaller the percentage received by the director.

Junior Golf Program. A club's **junior golf program** typically consists of group lessons, tournaments, clinics, regular or modified golf games, and supervision of juniors on the golf course. At some clubs, there is a junior subcommittee within the golf committee that assists the committee in planning, promoting, and implementing the junior golf program. The junior program should promote its activities through phone calls, personal contacts, and notices on the club bulletin board and in the club newsletter. Educational activities for juniors include instruction on the rules of golf, proper etiquette, the club's course rules, and the history of the game. Other types of junior golf programs are junior member-guest events and parent-child events. For junior programs to be successful, all junior events should combine fun, instruction, and social interaction.

During the summer, many clubs have golf clinics and camps for children. During the school year, programs can be run immediately after school for juniors. Children should be grouped together based on age and ability. The pro shop should carry junior-size clubs; the right equipment will increase the success of any junior program.

Caddie Programs 球僮

Fewer and fewer clubs are offering caddie services to members. In 1995, just 35 percent of country clubs had caddie programs.[4] The two biggest reasons are that a declining number of members want to walk when they play golf, and it is difficult for a club to keep a trained caddie work force. However, some clubs that traditionally have had strong caddie programs have implemented policies to keep these programs going.

A **caddie master** is essential to having a trained and competent caddie work force. The caddie master recruits caddies from a number of sources, including high-school golf players, applicants referred by current employees, children of current employees, and caddies who have worked at the club in prior years. Clubs use various incentives to recruit and retain caddies: caddie scholarships, bonuses for not missing days of work, a comfortable caddie waiting area, free meals, attractive uniforms, and so on. The caddie master trains the caddies each season to ensure that they conduct themselves properly on the golf course and possess adequate skills.

The duties of a caddie include retrieving the player's bag and proceeding to the first hole, standing to the side or slightly behind the player and being still and quiet during the player's shot, watching where the ball lands on each shot, collecting the club from the player after each shot and cleaning the club head, and walking to where the ball landed with the player's bag and waiting for the player. (See the chapter appendix for a list of duties performed by caddies.) The caddie whose player lands his or her golf ball on the green first should tend the flag; another caddie should take this caddie's bag along with his or her own over to the next tee area. When the landing area for a tee shot is difficult to see, one of the caddies should move down the fairway and stand in the rough to see where the tee shots land. Additional duties include helping other caddies find their players' golf balls if necessary, never placing the bag on the green, never touching the ball until the player has holed out, raking out sand traps the player enters, replacing all divots, repairing green marks, and periodically washing the player's golf ball. The average caddie fee is around $20.[5]

Golf Car Rentals

Almost all clubs rent golf cars for member usage. Some clubs allow members to use golf cars that they (the members) personally own. Usually a usage fee or trail fee is charged to members who use their own cars; the average trail fee for 18 holes is $13.[6] This is collected to help pay for maintenance and repairs to the golf car paths. At a small number of clubs, members are also allowed to store their golf cars at the club for a fee. The trend for most clubs that currently allow members to use privately owned golf cars is to slowly phase these cars out by not allowing any member who uses a private car to replace that car with a new one, and not allowing other members to start using a privately owned car. Clubs that allow privately owned cars should specify their color and size so that there are no "eyesores" at the club. Passengers on privately owned cars often have to pay the club's single-rider rental rate. Clubs that allow members to use their own cars should make sure that the members have adequate liability insurance to cover accidents involving their vehicles and that the club is named on their insurance policies as an additional insured.

Golf car rentals are administered through the golf pro shop. When a member registers to tee off and requests a car, a key for the assigned car is issued to the member and he or she is notified of the car's number and location. If the member stores his or her bag at the club, often the staff will have the member's bag already on the back of the car, if the car was reserved ahead of time. There should be a designated area to which members can conveniently return cars after a round of golf.

It's common for clubs to have a policy requiring golf cars to be used during peak golf course usage times, such as Saturday mornings. This increases club revenues through rentals and promotes faster play. Compulsory car usage is strongly opposed by avid walkers, however. These individuals either prefer to walk for the exercise or believe that golf cars damage the course.

The car rental fee can be based on many factors, including a set price for 18 holes or 9 holes played, weekday and weekend rates, and prices for one rider versus two riders. Some clubs have one pricing structure, others include combinations of these factors to determine price. Golf car rental fees average $18 for 18 holes and $10 for 9 holes.[7]

Discount programs can increase golf car usage. Examples of such programs include books of coupons for car rentals that are sold at a reduced price; frequent rider programs, where members get a free rental after renting golf cars for a certain number of times; unlimited monthly golf car rentals at a set fee; and so on.

The number of golf cars a club should have is based on the demand for car rentals. Some clubs estimate that number by calculating one golf car for every eight playing members. The fleet size is considered adequate if only 75 percent of the cars are rented on an average day. The club should have 25 percent more golf cars than its daily average rental to handle peak-demand periods and allow for cars taken out of service for repairs.[8] According to the Club Managers Association of America, the average number of golf cars for clubs with 9 holes of golf is 30, for clubs with 18 holes of golf is 56, for clubs with 36 holes of golf is 88, and for clubs with more than 36 holes of golf is 175.[9]

The club should have an insurance package to cover its fleet of golf cars. The policy should provide for both liability and property damage.

Golf Car Maintenance. The head mechanic or car-maintenance supervisor should keep all golf cars in proper working order and service them according to the manufacturer's specifications. Golf cars should be cleaned and serviced after every use. Few things are worse in a member's eyes than a golf car that is dirty, runs poorly, or stops running in the middle of a round of golf. The PGA's *Golf Car Fleet Maintenance Handbook* is a good resource for information on how to maintain a golf car fleet.

Golf car batteries should be checked for complete charges or gas tanks checked to make sure they have adequate fuel before the cars are delivered to the pickup area. Service should include checking the battery charge levels, battery terminals, battery water level, tire pressure, brake operation, steering action, cleanliness, and so on. At the end of the day, the staff should clean the interior of the car, replace pencils and scorecards, and wash the exterior. The car should be parked in the golf car barn. If the golf car is electric, the charger should be plugged in and turned on; if the car is gasoline-powered, the tank should be refilled. Before leaving at the end of the day, the staff should secure the golf car barn and make sure that the fan is turned on. A rotation system should be in place so that the same cars are not used day in and day out when play is slow and all cars are not used. All daily, weekly, monthly, and seasonal maintenance as well as repairs should be recorded and the records stored in an easily accessible place for all staff members.

Clubs should replace their golf cars every three to five years. (According to the Club Managers Association of America, the typical golf car is replaced every four years.[10]) A fleet of cars can be replaced entirely at one time or a portion at a time. Clubs with concerns about their cash flow may replace a quarter or a third of their golf cars every year.

Leasing versus Purchasing Golf Cars. The question of whether a club should lease or purchase its fleet of golf cars has been bantered around for years. Approximately 55 percent of clubs own their golf cars; approximately 40 percent lease their cars. (At the rest of the clubs, the golf pro owns or leases the cars.)[11]

Many variables affect a club's decision. Proponents of ownership argue that non-equity (for-profit) clubs that are well capitalized, have a healthy debt-equity ratio, and have the staff to properly service the golf cars will benefit from the depreciation expenses that they can deduct if they own the cars, whereas an equity (nonprofit) club will not benefit from the depreciation factor.

Advantages of leasing are that no large cash outlay is required and the club's maintenance responsibilities are less than if it owned the golf cars. On the other hand, club-owned cars tend to be treated better than leased cars. Disadvantages of purchasing golf cars include the large cash outlay, high maintenance responsibilities, and low return on investment.[12]

Electric versus Gasoline-Powered Golf Cars. Another common question asked about golf cars is whether to buy electric-powered or gasoline-powered cars. According to the Club Managers Association of America, the vast majority of clubs (approximately 80 percent) use electric golf cars.[13]

Electric golf cars require less maintenance than gasoline-powered cars; they create less noise and don't produce fumes or smoke. They are also less expensive than gasoline-powered cars. Disadvantages of electric-powered golf cars include the fact that electricity is more expensive than gasoline, golf car batteries must be replaced every two to three years, the cars are only good for two to four rounds of golf per charge, and electric golf cars are heavier and harder on the turf than gasoline-powered cars.

Gasoline-powered golf cars do not need expensive charging equipment and have unlimited turnarounds; they can be used all day. However, they require more day-to-day maintenance than electric golf cars and create more noise, fumes, and smoke. As alluded to earlier, gasoline-powered golf cars cost more per car than electric-powered cars.[14]

Golf Staff

If the club is small, all of the duties involved in the golf program (except for golf course maintenance)—teaching, pro shop management, golf car rental and maintenance, and practice range administration—may be performed by the golf director and the assistant golf professionals. Larger clubs may have additional staff members working in the pro shop to handle tee times and sign-up for organized functions, sell products, and carry out other duties. If a club's golf program has many participants, the golf staff will include additional employees to maintain the golf cars, store golf bags, and administer the practice range. These employees will also perform the daily, weekly, and monthly non-golf-course maintenance that is necessary. The golf operation may also have starters and marshals during peak periods on the course to control the flow of golfers and maintain an appropriate speed of play.

All golf staff members should be well dressed and groomed. The pro shop staff and golf professionals should be encouraged to wear pro shop apparel to promote its sale. This can be done by offering staff members a discount or by issuing apparel for them to wear while on duty.

Golf Professionals

The golf professionals at a club are the golf director and assistant golf professionals.

Golf Director. The golf director, referred to at some clubs as the golf pro or director of golf, should be a member of the Professional Golfers' Association of America (PGA) and should have years of experience as an assistant golf professional and golf instructor. The director should also have good administrative and supervisory skills. The chapter appendix has a sample job description for a golf director.

The golf director is responsible for promoting and administering the club's complete golf program. This involves organizing golf tournaments, administering lessons and clinics, reserving tee times, collecting guest fees, enforcing guest policies, and administering the practice range. In addition, the director is responsible for pro shop sales (merchandising, inventory ordering, and control procedures) and for golf car administrative activities (reservation, rental-fee collection, maintenance, and storage). The golf director prepares and monitors golf department budgets and is responsible for the fiscal soundness of the golf program. The

PGA's Golf-Professional Classifications

The PGA of America has several classes of membership. The following descriptions of each of the classifications of PGA members and apprentices should assist club managers in determining the current status of the PGA professionals that apply for work at the club.

Master Professional

The Master Professional classification recognizes PGA members who have successfully completed advanced professional training. The Board of Directors establishes the requirements for members to be classified as Master Professional, including the requirement that such members shall have served in the capacities of Class "A" Head Golf Professional and/or Director of Golf at PGA-Recognized Golf Courses for a minimum of six years.

Class "A" Head Professional

PGA members employed as Head Golf Professionals at Recognized Golf Courses (A-1), PGA-Recognized Golf Ranges (A-2), or at a facility under construction (A-7).

Class "A" Tour Players

PGA members who are exempt players on the PGA Tour, Senior PGA Tour, Nike Tour, or LPGA (A-3).

Class "A" Golf Director

PGA members who are Directors of Golf at one or more PGA-Recognized Golf Courses (A-4).

Class "A" Golf Instructors

PGA members employed at PGA-Recognized Golf Facilities or PGA-Recognized Golf Schools as either golf instructors or supervisors of golf instructors. If employed at a PGA-Recognized Golf Facility, the facility must employ a PGA member or apprentice as a Head Golf Professional (A-6).

Class "A" Assistant Golf Professionals

PGA members who are employed as Assistant Golf Professionals to a Class "A" Head Golf Professional, Master Professional, or Class "A" LPGA member (A-8).

Class "A" Professional Positions

PGA members who are employed in professional positions in management, development, ownership, operation, and/or financing of golf facilities (A-9).

Class "A" Golf Clinician

PGA members who are employed as golf clinicians (A-10).

Golf Administrator

PGA members who are employed by the Association, a PGA Section, or the PGA Tour in an administrative capacity; and PGA members who are employed full-time as employees of golf associations recognized by the PGA Board of Directors.

(continued)

PGA's Golf-Professional Classifications *(continued)*

Golf Coaches

PGA members who are employed as golf coaches at accredited colleges, universities, and junior colleges.

Class "F" Professionals

Members who fail to meet the requirements of the Professional Development Program.

Life Members

Members who are not eligible for classification as active members and have held active classification for at least 20 years (whether continuous or not).

Inactive

Members who are not eligible for classification as active or life members.

Apprentices

A nonmember professional registered in the PGA training program leading to membership. Has not completed one or more of the following: schooling requirements, time requirements, playing ability test, and membership interview.

Source: Adapted from Professional Golfers' Association of America, *How to Hire a Golf Professional* (Palm Beach Gardens, Florida: PGA, 1991), p. 41.

director hires, supervises, trains, and evaluates golf staff members. The director must work in close cooperation with the golf course superintendent so that appropriate decisions can be made on when the course is in playable condition and when golf cars can be allowed on the course or should be limited to the golf car paths only.

The assistant golf professionals and other golf staff members report to the golf director. When the golf director is not at the club, the senior assistant golf professional assumes the director's responsibilities. The golf director reports to the club's general manager. The golf director also communicates with the chairperson of the golf committee and other golf committee members. The general manager should be informed of any official communication between the golf director and golf committee members.

The golf director receives a salary, plus all or some of the following in compensation, depending on his or her contract with the club:

- Ownership rights to the pro shop merchandise or a percentage of the gross sales or net profit

- Income from lessons

- Percentage of the income from the practice range

- Percentage of golf car rental income

- Percentage of guest fees for rounds of golf

- Percentage of the profits from tournaments (or a set fee)
- Percentage of the income from bag storage
- Income from regripping and repairing clubs
- A benefits package (insurance, vacation, sick days, retirement, and so on)
- Bonuses on meeting operational goals
- Professional expenses such as dues, subscriptions, and tuition
- Club privileges and meals
- Housing or automobile allowance

Although the club will not pay this portion, the golf director (and other golf professionals) also should be given the opportunity to win prize money in local golf tournaments.

Employee or independent contractor? While the courts have yet to determine clearly whether golf directors (and other golf professionals) working at a private club are truly independent contractors, it appears most likely that a golf director is *not* an independent contractor if one or more of the following conditions apply at the club:

- The golf director has signed an employment agreement with the club.
- The hours the golf director works are specified by the club.
- The club provides the golf director with pro shop space, utilities, telephone service, and meals at no charge.
- The club bills members, collects from members, and pays the revenue due to the golf director.

These items have been clearly interpreted by the Internal Revenue Service to demonstrate that the club has an employer relationship with its golf director. Should any wage disputes arise involving the golf director or assistant golf professionals, it's likely that the U.S. Department of Labor will consider these professionals to be employees of the club.

Assistant Golf Professionals. Qualifications for assistant golf professionals include PGA membership or registration in the PGA Apprentice Program (or the expectation to register), good golf skills, some competitive golf experience, and preferably some teaching and work experience at a golf facility. Assistant golf professionals should be good communicators and be patient, friendly, and outgoing. See the chapter appendix for a sample job description for an assistant golf professional.

Other Golf Staff Positions

Pro Shop Employees. The employees who work in the pro shop should be knowledgeable about golf. They should also be trustworthy and organized, possess good phone-etiquette skills, be good communicators, and be friendly and outgoing. See the chapter appendix for a sample job description for a pro shop salesperson.

Although specific duties vary from club to club, pro shop employees sell pro shop merchandise and usually book lessons, keep track of tee-time reservations, sign members up for tournaments, and keep track of member handicaps, under supervision of the golf professionals. Pro shop employees at some clubs use computers to perform these duties; at other clubs, employees perform them manually.

As part of the golf director's negotiated contract, the salaries of the pro shop staff may be paid partially or in full by the club. This is because part of their duties are club-related—taking tee-time reservations, answering the pro shop telephone, registering members for organized golf events, and so on.

Bag Room and Practice Range Staff. Bag room and practice range staff members should also have a knowledge of golf and should have the dexterity and strength to perform the manual tasks required to maintain the bags, clubs, buckets, and practice balls (that is, lift heavy golf bags, operate machinery, and so on). See the chapter appendix for a sample job description for a bag room attendant.

Starters and Marshals. Starters and marshals should be experienced golfers who are familiar with the rules of golf and with the club's policies and regulations. The starter and marshals work at tournaments to promote efficient play among the members and guests. The number of starters and marshals that a club employs depends on the number of golf rounds members and guests play at the club and the degree of concern the club has over speed of play and violations of golf course regulations.

The **starter** is stationed near the first tee to ensure an orderly flow of play based on reserved tee times. If players are late, the starter will ask a group that is ready to play to tee off, so as to stay on schedule. The starter will place players with no partners into groups or will match twosomes together. The starter will cover tournament and club rules and remind players of commonly committed errors to avoid. The starter should record the names of members and guests and the exact times they begin, in addition to issuing scorecards and pencils to players who do not have them. Other duties that starters at some clubs may perform are listed in the chapter appendix.

The main task of a **marshal** is to monitor the pace of play on the golf course. A marshal will ask slow groups to allow faster players behind them to play through. If the group in front of the slow group is more than one hole ahead, a marshal may ask the slow group to pick up their golf balls and immediately move ahead to the next hole to tee off. Other duties performed by marshals at some clubs are listed in the chapter appendix.

Head Mechanic. Clubs with a large fleet of golf cars should have a head mechanic to maintain the cars and car barn. The mechanic should have experience in maintaining golf cars and performing a variety of mechanical repairs. This individual will also supervise any staff members who are assigned to the golf car barn to assist in the maintenance and servicing of the cars.

Golf Associations

Exhibit 6 lists some of the major golf trade and professional associations. The three largest golf organizations that can assist private clubs are the Professional Golfers'

Exhibit 6   Golf Trade and Professional Associations

American Junior Golf Association (AJGA) 2415 Steeplechase Lane Roswell, GA 30076	**National Sporting Goods Association (NSGA)** Lake Center Plaza Building 1699 Wall Street Mount Prospect, IL 60056
Hook a Kid on Golf 2611 Old Okeechobee Road West Palm Beach, FL 33409	**Professional Golfers' Association of America (PGA)** 100 Avenue of Champions Palm Beach Gardens, FL 33418
Ladies Professional Golf Association (LPGA) 2570 Volusia Avenue, Suite B Daytona, FL 32114	**PGA Tour** 112 TPC Blvd. Ponte Verdra, FL 32082
National Golf Foundation (NGF) 1150 S. U.S. Highway 1 Jupiter, FL 33477	**Sporting Goods Manufacturers Association (SGMA)** 200 Castlewood Drive North Palm Beach, FL 33408
National Retail Merchants Association (NRMA) 100 West 31st Street New York, NY 10001	**United States Golf Association (USGA)** P.O. Box 708 Far Hills, NJ 07931

Association of America (PGA), United States Golf Association (USGA), and the National Golf Foundation (NGF). The PGA Tour is the association for the top male touring professionals and is part of the PGA. The Ladies Professional Golf Association is the association for the top female golf players who play on the professional circuit.

The PGA is the primary association for golf professionals who teach golf. A primary focus of the PGA is to educate golf professionals through an apprentice program and by offering PGA Business School I and II (week-long training programs), seminars, workshops, clinics, and publications. The PGA also offers a certification program to ensure that certified golf professionals are skilled players who are educated on the basics of running a successful golf operation. Assistant or head golf professionals must complete an apprentice program before becoming PGA members. There is also the PGA Master Professional certification, which is achieved by golf professionals with outstanding credentials.

The USGA is the governing body of golf in the United States. This organization develops and modifies most of the rules and regulations that govern golf play and golf tournaments in the United States. It also serves as a major sponsor of turf-grass and golf-course-maintenance research. The NGF provides golf-industry research data for both private clubs and public golf courses.

The National Sporting Goods Association and Sporting Goods Manufacturers Association specialize in the merchandising and manufacturing of sporting goods. Both organizations carry a great deal of information on golf products. A new golf organization is Hook a Kid on Golf. The goal of this organization is to provide information and products to help people educate children about golf and encourage them to participate in the game.

Endnotes

1. Club Managers Association of America, *Club Operations and Financial Data Report* (Alexandria, Virginia: CMAA, 1996), p. 35.

2. *Club Operations and Financial Data Report*, pp. 1–3.

3. *Club Operations and Financial Data Report*, p. 59.

4. *Club Operations and Financial Data Report*, p. 57.

5. *Club Operations and Financial Data Report*, p. 58.

6. *Club Operations and Financial Data Report*, p. 57.

7. *Club Operations and Financial Data Report*, p. 55.

8. *Golf Car Fleet Management Handbook* (Palm Beach Gardens, Florida: PGA, 1989).

9. *Club Operations and Financial Data Report*, p. 55.

10. *Club Operations and Financial Data Report*, p. 55.

11. *Club Operations and Financial Data Report*, p. 54.

12. Advantages and disadvantages of electric-powered cars adapted from *Golf Car Fleet Management Handbook* (Palm Beach Gardens, Florida: PGA, 1989).

13. *Club Operations and Financial Data Report*, p. 54.

14. Advantages and disadvantages of gasoline-powered cars adapted from *Golf Car Fleet Management Handbook* (Palm Beach Gardens, Florida: PGA, 1989).

Key Terms

caddie master—An experienced caddie who recruits, trains, and supervises other caddies.

club-demo program—A pro shop program designed to increase sales, in which members can try out golf clubs before buying them.

cost-plus program—A pro shop program in which club members pay a fee and are then able to purchase pro shop merchandise at cost plus a fixed percentage (typically ten percent).

handicap system—A system in which a golfer is either awarded strokes or has strokes taken away, based on his or her ability to make par; this system allows golfers with different playing abilities to play golf together and compete on an equal basis.

junior golf program—A number of organized golf activities—lessons, tournaments, clinics, camps, modified golf games, and so on—designed for the children of club members.

marshal—An individual who monitors the pace of play on the golf course and enforces club rules.

member-guest event—An organized golf event at a club in which guests are allowed to participate with members; such an event is often used by clubs to recruit new members.

outside tournament—A golf tournament held at the club that is not organized primarily for members and invited guests.

practice range—An area designated for members to practice hitting a variety of golf shots. Also called a driving range.

starter—An individual who is stationed near the first tee to ensure an orderly flow of play based on reserved tee times.

Review Questions

1. What are some of the golf facilities commonly found at clubs?

2. What is a handicap system?

3. What are some of the golf instructional programs typically offered at clubs, and why are they important to clubs?

4. What are some typical golf-car-rental policies at clubs?

5. How is a golf director compensated at a club?

6. What are the duties of an assistant golf professional?

7. What are a starter's responsibilities on the golf course? a marshal's?

8. What are some of the major golf associations?

Additional Reading

Beard, J. B. *Turf Management for Golf Courses.* New York: MacMillan, 1982.

Cayce, K. *PGA Book of Golf Shop Policies and Procedures.* Palm Beach Gardens, Florida: PGA, 1984.

Gammon & Grange, P.C. "Will the Real Independent Contractor Please Stand Up?" *Club Director,* August 1992.

Golf Course Superintendents Association of America, "Selecting a Professional Superintendent." Lawrence, Kansas: Golf Course Superintendents Association of America, no date.

"The Greening of a Great Committee Chair." *Club Director,* October 1994.

Jobbe, F. W., L. A. Yocum, R. E. Mottram, and M. M. Pink. *Exercise to Better Golf.* Champaign, Ill.: Human Kinetics, 1995.

Lowes, R. "The Successful Tournament." *Club Management,* January 1992.

Professional Golfers' Association of America. *Golf Car Fleet Maintenance Handbook.* Palm Beach Gardens, Florida: PGA, 1982.

———. *Golf Car Fleet Management Handbook.* Palm Beach Gardens, Florida: PGA, 1989.

———. *How to Hire a Golf Professional.* Palm Beach Gardens, Florida: PGA, 1991.

———. *Marketing the Public Golf Course.* Palm Beach Gardens, Florida: PGA, 1990.

———. *The PGA Merchandising Manual.* Palm Beach Gardens, Florida: PGA, 1991.

White, T. E., and L. C. Gerstner. *Club Operations and Management,* Second Edition. New York: VNR, 1991.

Wiren, G. *The PGA Manual of Golf: The Professional's Way to Play Better Golf.* New York: MacMillan, 1991.

Internet Sites

For more information, visit the following Internet sites. Remember that Internet addresses can change without notice. If the site is no longer there, use a browser to look for additional sites.

Golf Course Builders Association of America
http://www.gcbaa.org/

Golf Course Superintendents Association of America
http://www.gcsaa.org/

Ladies Professional Golf Association
http://www.lpga.com/

National Golf Course Owners Association
http://www.golf.com/tour/assoc/ngcoa/

PGA Tour
http://www.pgatour.com/

Professional Golfers' Association of America
http://www.pga.com/

United States Golf Association
http://www.usga.org/

Case Study

Comfortville Country Club is celebrating its 40th anniversary this year. The club was the first private club in the region and it has a lot of traditions. The club has approximately 450 members, 300 of which have golfing memberships. Many of the members own houses with backyards on the golf course.

The club has allowed members to use privately owned golf cars for years. Approximately 50 members presently use their own golf cars at the club. Members with private cars pay $25 per month as a trail fee. The club also rents golf cars. Its fleet size of 50 is adequate for its current usage on most days except for the busiest Saturdays and holidays. The club is leasing the fleet of electric-powered cars; the fleet is about two years old. Car-rental fees for 18 holes are $20 for two riders and

$10 for one rider. Feedback on member surveys indicate that members are happy with the club's golf cars. They like their quality, the way they are maintained, and the prices charged for their use.

However, there were a number of written comments on the survey about the club's policy of allowing privately owned golf cars on the course. Some of the members complained about the color and appearance of some of the private cars. Others said that some of the members who owned their own golf cars were entering the course at the hole nearest their home without checking in with the starter.

At the last board of directors meeting, there was much discussion about these comments on the survey, some of it heated. At one point a motion was made to ban private golf car usage, but it was withdrawn. The board appointed a special committee to investigate the problems associated with private golf car usage at the club and make recommendations for action at the next board meeting.

Discussion Question

1. What are the different potential courses of action? What are some of the impacts these actions might have?

Chapter Appendix

The following are sample job descriptions for golf operations personnel from the Club Managers Association of America's *Job Descriptions in the Private Club Industry*, Fourth Edition, published by Kendall/Hunt. These job descriptions will give you an idea of the typical duties, responsibilities, and reporting relationships of the positions listed, although it is important to note that these will vary from club to club.

Position: Golf Director

Job Summary: Manages all golf and golf-related activities and business.

Job Tasks (Duties):

1. Designs, promotes, and directs all golf activities.
2. Prepares annual and monthly budgets for golf operations.
3. Orders merchandise for the golf pro shop.
4. Orders supplies associated with golf activities.
5. Maintains an attractive, orderly appearance in the pro shop.
6. Supervises the maintenance of golf cars and maintenance personnel.
7. Supervises pro shop personnel.
8. Provides golf lessons to members and guests.
9. Plays golf with members of all skill levels to encourage enthusiasm.
10. Designs and conducts golf clinics.
11. Supervises assistant golf professionals.
12. Designs and conducts junior golf clinics and training programs.
13. Supervises locker room staff.
14. Supervises practice range staff.
15. Supervises golf bag and club storage facilities and staff.
16. Supervises on-course personnel.
17. Collects charges and fees for all golf-related activities.
18. Organizes and conducts club tournaments.
19. Interprets and enforces golf rules and regulations.
20. Interprets and enforces club policies, rules, and regulations.

Reports to: General Manager

Supervises: Assistant golf professional(s)

Position: Assistant Golf Professional

Job Summary: Executes essential functions of golf-professional responsibilities when on duty.

Job Tasks (Duties):

1. Assists golf director in instructing, merchandising, on-course, golf car, and personnel-management responsibilities.
2. Maintains pro shop inventory-control system.
3. Assists members by providing and interpreting golf policies, rules, and regulations.
4. Conducts golf clinics.
5. Maintains handicap records.
6. Operates pro shop in absence of the golf director.

Reports to: Golf Director

Supervises: Golf shop salespeople; starters; marshals; caddies; golf car maintenance mechanic(s)

Position: Starter

Job Summary: Helps control the pace of play on the golf course by directing players to the first tee at appropriate times.

Job Tasks (Duties):

1. Provides information regarding the golf course, play time, and other golf-related issues.
2. Verifies that all revenues have been properly recorded by inspecting receipts for all players before they depart to the golf course, practice tee, or practice range.
3. Dispenses range balls in accordance with club policies.
4. Keeps the assistant golf professional informed regarding rate of course play.
5. Determines rate of course play.
6. Maintains a clean and orderly starter's booth at all times.
7. Arranges players in proper starting order and assigns appropriate tees.
8. Assigns golf cars.
9. Starter may also perform the following duties:

    • Ensure that members' and guests' bags are appropriately placed in golf cars.

    • Assign caddies.

- Train and instruct caddies in duties and proper etiquette.
- Assist the golf director in running tournaments, clinics, and other special events.

10. Supplies players with scorecards, pencils, and rules of play.
11. Advises players and caddies of course conditions.

Reports to: Assistant Golf Professional

Supervises: No supervisory duties are included in this position

Position: Marshal

Job Summary: Ensures a smooth pace of play on the golf course.

Job Tasks (Duties):

1. Observes the pace of play.
2. Requests slow-playing groups to speed up the pace, if appropriate.
3. Requests slow-playing groups to allow others to play through, if appropriate.
4. Escorts unauthorized people from the course.
5. Ensures that divots and ball marks are repaired.
6. Reports all infractions to the starter.
7. Ensures that sand traps are raked.
8. Carries and provides clean towels and water for ball washers.
9. Replaces the ball-washer towels.
10. Replenishes water in the ball washers.
11. Assists the starter at the first tee during heavy demand periods.

Reports to: Assistant Golf Professional

Supervises: No supervisory duties are included in this position

Position: Caddie

Job Summary: Carries golf bags for members and guests.

Job Tasks (Duties):

1. Is courteous and polite to members and guests at all times.
2. Keeps the caddie area clean and neat.
3. Counts clubs in the bag before starting every round and maintains the count throughout the round.
4. Protects the player's clubs from damage.

5. Advises players regarding the course or conditions, as requested.

6. Cleans golf balls and clubs as needed during play.

7. Rakes bunkers.

8. Replaces all divots taken by the player.

9. Repairs ball marks.

Reports to: Assistant Golf Professional

Supervises: No supervisory duties are included in this position

Position: Bag Room Attendant

Job Summary: Provides bag, golf car, and practice-range services to members and guests.

Job Tasks (Duties):

1. Brings golf cars from the car barn to the car-staging area outside the golf shop.

2. Removes bags from the bag storage room and loads them onto golf cars.

3. Transports practice range golf balls to each end of the range and fills appropriate containers.

4. Places baskets of golf balls at evenly spaced intervals on the range.

5. Operates a tractor and ball-picker on the practice range to retrieve golf balls.

6. Washes all practice range golf balls daily.

7. Removes bags from golf cars and returns each bag to its assigned rack in the bag storage room.

8. Returns golf cars to the golf car barn; removes towels, pencils, scorecards, tees, drink cans, and so on from the cars and saves reusable items; washes cars with a pressure cleaner; parks cars in the car barn and connects the charger cables.

Reports to: Assistant Golf Professional

Supervises: No supervisory duties are included in this position

Position: Golf Shop Salesperson

Job Summary: Sells merchandise in the golf shop.

Job Tasks (Duties):

1. Advises members and guests about attire, golf clubs and supplies, etc.

2. Arranges and displays pro shop inventory.

3. Records all sales transactions.

4. Collects and records greens fees and golf car rental fees.

5. Issues receipts for greens fees and golf car rentals.
6. Takes messages for members who may be on the golf course.
7. Assists in packing and unpacking inventory.
8. Recruits tournament participants.
9. Assists in special orders.

Reports to: Assistant Golf Professional

Supervises: No supervisory duties are included in this position

REVIEW QUIZ

When you feel you have covered all of the material in this chapter, answer these questions. Choose the *best* answer.

1. Which of the following statements about a club's golf pro shop is *false?*

   a. The merchandise in the pro shop can be owned either by the club or the golf director.
   b. A pro shop's cost-plus program is designed to enable the golf director to buy merchandise at below-wholesale prices.
   c. Pro shop displays should be changed frequently.
   d. Custom-fitting golf clubs is a special pro shop service that can help increase sales.

2. An outside tournament is a club golf tournament that:

   a. is held outside or away from the club.
   b. does not abide by PGA rules (play is allowed "outside" the rules).
   c. is not organized primarily for club members and invited guests.
   d. rewards players for hitting their golf balls "outside" the fairways (that is, hitting their balls in the rough).

3. A golf director is responsible for:

   a. promoting the club's golf program to members.
   b. organizing golf tournaments.
   c. administering the practice range.
   d. all of the above.

4. The primary golf association for golf professionals who teach golf is the:

   a. Professional Golfers' Association of America.
   b. United States Golf Association.
   c. National Golf Foundation.
   d. National Golf Teachers Association.

Answer Key: 1-b-C1, 2-c-C2, 3-d-C3, 4-a-C3

Each question is linked to a competency. Competencies are listed on the first page of the chapter. An answer reading 3-b-C4 translates to:

   3: the question number
   b: the correct answer
   C4: the competency number

Chapter 13 Outline

Fitness Operations
    Fitness Center
        Fitness Floor
        Exercise Classroom
        Sports Areas
        Spa Areas
    Fitness Center Staff
    Fitness Programs
    Risk Management and Liability Issues
    Payment Policies
    Fitness Associations
Aquatics Operations
    Aquatics Programs
        Swim Teams
    Special Events
    Aquatics Staff
        Staff Duties
    Safety Policies
    Pool Operation and Maintenance
    Aquatics Associations
Tennis Operations
    Tennis Programs
        Competitions
        Lessons
        Junior Programs
    Tennis Staff
    Pro Shop
    Maintenance
    Tennis Associations

Competencies

1. Identify and describe the major areas and pieces of equipment in a typical club fitness center, and summarize how members use them. (pp. 453–460)

2. Identify fitness center staff positions and describe their qualifications and duties. (pp. 460–461)

3. List typical club fitness programs, summarize fitness-center risk management and liability issues, describe typical payment policies for club fitness centers, and list fitness associations. (pp. 462–466)

4. Describe typical club aquatics programs and special events, and summarize the qualifications and duties of aquatics staff positions. (pp. 466–472)

5. List aquatics safety policies, describe pool operation and maintenance activities, and list aquatics associations. (pp. 472–475)

6. Describe typical tennis programs offered at clubs, and summarize the qualifications and duties of tennis staff positions. (pp. 475–484)

7. Explain club pro-shop policies, describe tennis-operation maintenance issues, and list tennis associations. (pp. 484–488)

Club Fitness, Aquatics, and Tennis Operations

This chapter was written and contributed by Raymond R. Ferreira, Assistant Professor, Cecil B. Day School of Hospitality Administration, Georgia State University, Atlanta, Georgia.

CLUB MEMBERS USE fitness facilities for a variety of reasons—to improve personal fitness and health, engage in social and family activities, entertain business clients, and so on. Because of the importance of fitness programs to a large portion of the membership, club managers should ensure that their clubs have fitness and athletic programs and facilities that will satisfy members and therefore help keep membership levels high.

Clubs with exercise and fitness facilities may offer membership categories that offer members various combinations of privileges. Typically, a club's full or regular membership category (that with the highest initiation fee and dues) allows members access to all facilities and services at the club, including the fitness programs. Some country clubs offer athletic memberships that allow members access to everything (fitness and tennis facilities, aquatics areas, and food and beverage outlets) except the golf course. Fitness memberships generally limit members to the fitness facilities and programs. There are many such membership categories used at clubs throughout the country; each club determines its membership categories based on the specific needs and demands of its members. (Offering memberships with limited privileges at prices below those of a full membership is often referred to as "unbundling" club services.)

A club's fitness and athletic operations can be divided into three major areas: fitness, aquatics, and tennis. The directors of these athletic areas communicate with the appropriate club committees—the fitness director with the fitness/exercise committee, the aquatics director with the aquatics (or swim) committee, and the tennis director with the tennis committee. Some clubs do not have a separate committee for each area. For example, in some clubs the aquatics committee is responsible for the fitness center as well as the club's swimming areas and programs, so the fitness director and aquatics director both work with the aquatics committee. In some clubs, the fitness, aquatics, and tennis directors may report to a club athletic director.

We will discuss club fitness, aquatics, and tennis operations in the following sections. Golf usually is not considered part of a club's fitness and athletic operations; it plays such an important role in many private clubs that it is a subject unto itself and will not be discussed in this chapter.

Fitness Operations

In this section we will discuss fitness centers, club staff members who work in fitness centers, fitness programs, risk management and liability issues, payment policies, and fitness associations.

Fitness Center

A club's fitness operations are conducted in an area commonly called a **fitness center.** Fitness centers in clubs are diverse in both size and offerings. While a few clubs have separate fitness areas for men and women, most now have coed fitness centers, because the baby boomers—who constitute the majority of fitness center users—prefer coed facilities.

A club's fitness center generally comprises the following areas:

- Fitness floor

- Exercise classroom

- Sports areas

- Spa areas

Fitness Floor. The **fitness floor** is where most of a club's fitness equipment is located. The fitness floor usually includes stretching, cardiovascular, and weight-training areas. These areas allow for warm-up activities, flexibility and stretching exercises, aerobic or cardiovascular conditioning, strength and endurance training, and cool-down activities. The fitness floor is usually the most heavily used area within a club's fitness center.

The American College of Sports Medicine (ACSM) recommends having at least one instructor or leader for every 30 individuals using a fitness floor. The optimal size for the fitness floor is 20 to 25 square feet of space for each person expected during peak times. The ACSM also recommends that 20 to 40 square feet of space be allocated for each piece of exercise equipment.

Stretching area. The fitness floor's stretching area is where members warm up and stretch before and after exercise to minimize the chance of injury. This area is extremely important, but it is often overlooked when club managers plan a fitness center. The stretching area should contain four to six nonabsorbent mats that members can lie on to stretch. The area should be carpeted with antistatic carpet treated with antifungal and antibacterial agents. While the stretching area need not be in a room separate from the other parts of the fitness floor, it should be designated as the stretching area and not used for other purposes.

Cardiovascular area. The equipment found in the cardiovascular area generally includes treadmills, stationary bicycles (both upright and reclining), stepping or stair-climbing machines, rowing machines, cross-country simulators, and upper-body ergometers. Cardiovascular conditioning strengthens the cardiovascular system by working large muscle groups and elevating the heart rate.

Member preferences and usage patterns will dictate how many pieces of each type of equipment a club should have. Members should not have to wait a long time to use a piece of equipment, even when the fitness floor is at its busiest. If there is

Some clubs place television monitors in their cardiovascular areas to help keep members from becoming bored while exercising. (Courtesy of Cherokee Town & Country Club, Atlanta, Georgia)

high demand for a certain piece of equipment, a time limit—10 or 15 minutes, perhaps—should be instituted during peak usage times. A sign-up sheet with a clipboard can be attached to the equipment or placed nearby.

Many members will use a single piece of cardiovascular equipment for ten minutes or more during their daily workout. In order to help alleviate boredom, many clubs install televisions, stereos, and reading racks in the cardiovascular area. Multiple television monitors may be placed on the fitness floor, with some attached to videotape players. Using headsets, members can select the frequency of the monitor they are watching in order to hear the audio element of the program. Clubs with stereo units allow members to listen to their favorite compact discs or cassettes; the members put a compact disk or cassette in a stereo and select the frequency on their headset that matches that of the stereo unit they are using. Many fitness center users bring their own portable stereo units ("Walkmans" and other personal stereos) to listen to while exercising. Reading racks attached to treadmills, bicycles, stepping or stair-climbing machines, and cross-country simulators allow participants to read while using the equipment. Many reading racks are made with additional compartment space for headphone receivers, drinking bottles, or cups. Frequent exercisers often expect these additional features.

Weight-training area. A club's weight-training area generally has two types of equipment: progressive-resistance training equipment and free weights.

Progressive-resistance training equipment is designed to optimally position an individual to train a specific muscle group. Such equipment is also designed to minimize injuries caused by lifting weight incorrectly. The machine progressively increases resistance as the muscle group moves through its full range of motion;

Dumbbells and other types of free weights are popular in club weight-training areas. Notice the weight-lifting belt hanging between the two dumbbell racks.
(Courtesy of Cherokee Town & Country Club, Atlanta, Georgia)

since a muscle is weakest at the start of the movement range and strongest at the end of the range, such progressive resistance makes the muscle group work hard throughout the exercise.

A group of progressive-resistance training machines that together work all of the body's major muscle groups is known as a **circuit.** A circuit usually comprises about 12 machines. A fitness floor should have at least one complete circuit, and the machines should be arranged in an order that encourages users to train the largest muscle groups first. Most manufacturers of progressive-resistance training equipment provide signs with directions and diagrams showing not only the proper use of each piece of equipment but also the recommended progression from one piece of equipment to the other. These signs should be installed on the equipment.

Free weights have gained in popularity during the last few years. A basic set of free-weight equipment typically includes a supine bench-press, an incline bench-press, an adjustable incline bench, a cable-crossover system, adjustable abdominal benches, paired dumbbells in a wide range of weights, Olympic bars and clamps, and assorted plates of various weights.

Weight-lifting belts of various sizes should be available for members who wish to use them. Mirrors on the walls in the free-weight area help members use correct form as they lift. The free-weight area should be closely supervised to ensure that members use spotters when needed.

Exercise Classroom. The fitness center's exercise classroom is used to hold classes in low- and high-impact aerobics, step or bench aerobics, slide aerobics, guided stretching, social dance (ballroom, country line, and so on), martial arts, and other activities. It is usually in a room separate from the fitness floor. The exercise classroom should provide at least 40 to 45 square feet of space per participant at peak periods. Classes should have a maximum of 30 participants. The room should have mirrors on at least two of the four walls so that members can check to make sure they are using correct form.

Proper flooring in this room is critical. Wood or a comparable flooring material is recommended to minimize drag, tripping, and the chance of ankle or knee injuries. The subfloor should allow the floor to flex at least a half inch; this will help members avoid many common impact injuries that are associated with certain types of exercise. The subfloor may consist of springs, rubber pads or disks, wooden furring strips, or a combination of these.

The exercise classroom should have a sound system for music and a public address system for the instructor. Other equipment typically found in an exercise classroom includes exercise mats, benches or steps, slide mats and booties, and small hand-weights. Ideally, a variety of classes should be scheduled and promoted to members, with class schedules posted near the entrance to the room and throughout the fitness center. Members should be informed of the risks, limitations, and benefits of each class.

Before they participate in an exercise class, members should be encouraged to have a fitness center staff person create individualized exercise prescriptions for them. An **exercise prescription** is an exercise program of recommended exercises and intensity levels developed for an individual by a trained fitness professional. An exercise prescription is usually developed for a member after the staff person gives the member an overall health-risk appraisal, which includes assessing the member's strength, endurance, flexibility, cardiovascular health, and percent of body fat.

Sports Areas. In addition to a fitness floor and exercise classroom, many clubs will have sports areas in their fitness center. Common sports areas are gymnasiums and indoor courts.

Gymnasiums. A club's gymnasium is a large multipurpose area where a variety of sports can be played, such as basketball, volleyball, badminton, indoor soccer, and children's sports. In addition to having gym time set aside for classes, leagues, tournaments, and sports camps, the club should have open gym time for members to play "pickup" games or otherwise use the area at their convenience. A schedule of activities should be posted near the gym's entrance and promoted to members.

Basketball is a particularly popular activity among many young club members. The walls behind the backboards, and any other walls or obstacles that a player might run into, should be padded. Backboards made of glass should have breakaway rims to reduce the chance of shattering the backboard.

All gymnasium equipment should be placed in storage areas when not in use. If equipment such as volleyball stands or gymnastic equipment must be stored on the gymnasium floor, it should be wrapped in padding. All equipment should be cleaned, inspected, and maintained on a regular basis. Defective equipment should be removed from service until it can be repaired or replaced.

Indoor-court areas. Common indoor-court sports in club fitness centers include racquetball, squash, handball, and walleyball. (Walleyball is an adaptation of

Clubs should post signs in indoor court areas to remind members of the club's court policies. (Courtesy of Atlanta Athletic Club, Duluth, Georgia)

volleyball played on a racquetball or handball court with a net stretched across the middle.) In addition to scheduled classes, leagues, and tournaments, a club's indoor courts should have unscheduled times available so that members can book the courts. The schedule of indoor-court activities should be posted near the courts and promoted to members. Leagues and tournaments are typically organized by skill or experience level (novice to advanced), gender (men only, women only, mixed, or open), number of participants (singles, doubles, etc.), and age range (youth, teens, adults, over 40, seniors, and so on).

Protective eyewear and appropriate footwear should be required of all members playing on indoor courts. A sign indicating these requirements can be posted on each court door. All door windows and court walls made of glass should be shatterproof. Court doors should open out from the court, and the inside handles and hinges should be recessed to minimize injuries and "bad" ball deflections. Court floors are typically made of a cushioned hardwood; court walls are constructed of either

Exhibit 1   Court Dimensions for Court Sports

Court Sports	Dimensions
Racquetball/Handball/Walleyball	20' W × 40' L × 20' H
Squash (Singles American)	18'6" W × 32' L × 16' H
Squash Singles International	21' W × 32' L × 16' H
Squash (Doubles)	25' W × 45' L × 16' H

laminated, composition panels or plaster/concrete. Many clubs have a glass back wall or side wall on one or more indoor courts for spectator viewing.

Exhibit 1 indicates the court dimensions recommended by the national governing organization for each indoor-court sport. Avid squash players prefer courts built according to the singles-international dimensions, and many of these players are demanding that their clubs convert their older singles-American squash courts to these dimensions.

Spa Areas. Spas in clubs are usually housed in the locker room area. A typical club spa has a massage room, sauna, steam room, and whirlpool (Jacuzzi). These amenities are designed to complement the members' physical activities in the fitness center with soothing, relaxing experiences.

Massage room. The massage room should be located in or near the locker rooms and should be private, with a quiet, restful atmosphere. It should be furnished with massage tables, which are adjustable in height and have a face cradle and double-padding. Massage-table sheets should be changed after each massage. The room's lighting should be adjustable so that it can provide high illumination before and after a massage, low illumination during. The room should also have a sink to allow the masseur or masseuse to wash up after a massage.

There are various types of massage—Swedish, sports, reflexology, executive, and so on. Obviously, a club should offer the types of massage its members want.

The club's massage therapist should have a degree from a school accredited by the American Massage Therapy Association. Many states require massage therapists to be licensed; club managers should check with their local departments of public health for the applicable regulations. If the massage therapist is considered an independent contractor, he or she must have professional liability insurance.

The wet areas. The spa's wet areas—sauna, steam room, and whirlpool—are high-risk areas because of their extreme heat and humidity. The intense heat in these areas may pose a health risk to members who have cardiovascular disease, high blood pressure, or diabetes, as well as to members who are taking certain medications, are under the influence of alcohol, are pregnant, or are dehydrated by exercise. The humid environment of these areas is a haven for infectious diseases. The club must safeguard its members by posting warning signs and following local health-board sanitation guidelines. Some localities may require that a whirlpool be supervised by a staff member who is a certified pool operator.

Exhibit 2   General Wet-Area Guidelines

Acceptable Water-Chemistry Ranges

Water Chemistry	Acceptable Range
pH Level	7.2–7.8
Free Chlorine/Bromine Level	0.5–2.0 parts per million
Total Alkalinity Level	50–150 parts per million
Calcium Hardness Level	100–400 parts per million (depends on the total alkalinity and pH levels)

Appropriate Temperature and Humidity Levels for the Wet Areas

Wet Area	Temperature	Humidity
Sauna	170–180 degrees F.	5% relative humidity
Steam Room	100–110 degrees F.	100% relative humidity
Whirlpool	102–105 degrees F.	

Signs in wet areas should clearly outline the risks associated with using these areas and explain the club's policies on using them. The information on the signs is often dictated by local health boards. Clocks in the wet areas help members monitor their usage and stay within recommended time limits. Thermometers should be installed in each of the areas and checked regularly by staff members. The wet areas should be cleaned and disinfected according to local health codes.

Whirlpool chemical levels should be monitored and recorded every few hours, or more frequently if local regulations require it. Exhibit 2 indicates acceptable water-chemistry ranges and appropriate temperature and humidity levels for the wet areas. (These are general guidelines only; clubs should follow the specific guidelines dictated by their local health boards.)

Fitness Center Staff

Typical fitness center staff positions include fitness director, assistant fitness director, fitness instructor, personal trainer, floor leader, and such support staff positions as locker room attendant and front desk staff member. The fitness director usually reports to the general manager or clubhouse manager. Fitness directors and assistant fitness directors are responsible for managing the fitness center and staff. Fitness instructors typically offer workout suggestions to members and teach them how to use fitness equipment safely. **Personal trainers** provide one-on-one training sessions. Floor leaders help members use fitness facilities and equipment and monitor member usage. Support staff attend to administrative and maintenance tasks in the fitness center—for example, cleaning locker rooms, taking court reservations, and so on.

The size and composition of the fitness center staff will depend on the size of the club. Also, in some clubs, some fitness center positions are combined with other club athletic positions. For example, in some clubs the same person handles the fitness director's duties and the aquatics director's duties.

Many of the staff positions in the fitness center require special qualifications and certifications. The club's fitness director and assistant fitness director should each have an undergraduate degree in a health-, fitness-, or recreation-related field. These individuals should have experience and knowledge in fitness operations, fitness-program development, supervision, and exercise physiology. They should have current certifications in cardiopulmonary resuscitation (CPR) and first aid as well as advanced fitness/exercise certifications from nationally recognized organizations in the health and fitness industry, such as the American College of Sports Medicine (ACSM) or YMCA. Chapter Appendix A outlines three levels of ACSM's health and fitness certification program; Exhibit 3 is a sample job description for a fitness director at a club (note that, in this job description, the fitness director's duties and the aquatics director's duties are combined into one position).

The fitness instructors, personal trainers, and floor leaders who work directly with members should each have or be working toward an undergraduate degree in a health-, fitness-, or recreation-related field, and should possess experience and knowledge in fitness and exercise programs. They should have basic fitness/exercise certifications from nationally recognized organizations in the health and fitness industry, along with current certifications in CPR. The fitness center's support staff should be certified in CPR as well.

Contractors hired to teach classes in the fitness center (in nutrition, stress management, and so on) should have appropriate certifications or degrees. Racquetball, squash, and handball instructors should have teaching experience and be ranked players in their sport's local organization.

Although many fitness instructors and personal trainers consider themselves independent contractors, some may not be. The Internal Revenue Service (IRS) has taken strong measures to reduce the number of individuals who are incorrectly classifying themselves as independent contractors. Exhibit 4 lists criteria that the IRS uses to determine whether an individual is an employee or an independent contractor. The criteria identify the extent of the employer's control over the individual and his or her work. The more control an employer has, the more likely the IRS is to classify the individual as an employee. If the answer is yes for a majority of the criteria listed in Exhibit 4, the individual should be considered an employee. If a club misclassifies an employee as an independent contractor, the club might be liable for the amount of taxes not withheld, FUTA taxes, both the employer's and the employee's share of FICA tax, and interest and penalties.

Exhibit 3   Sample Job Description: Fitness and Aquatics Director

Job Summary: Responsible for coordinating, implementing, and directing all activities and personnel associated with the fitness center, locker rooms, and pools.

Duties:

1. Hire, fire, and manage personnel associated with the fitness center, locker rooms, and pool departments.

2. Construct and adhere to an operational budget in accordance with the fitness and aquatics committee.

3. Construct and implement a capital budget and capital projects in accordance with the fitness and aquatics committee.

4. Oversee the overall operation and maintenance of the fitness center, locker rooms, and pool departments.

5. Coordinate and promote programs associated with the fitness center and pool departments. Submit, on a monthly basis, articles for the club newsletter.

6. Report to the general manager.

Special Qualifications:

- Education: A bachelor of science degree or higher in a field related to physical fitness (i.e., physical education, exercise science, or exercise physiology).

- Certifications from the American College of Sports Medicine, AFAA, IDEA, Red Cross, and American Heart Association as appropriate.

- Good management skills and related work experience required.

Reports to: General Manager

Supervises: Assistant Aquatics Director and all other personnel associated with the fitness center and club pools.

Fitness Programs

Instructional fitness programs may include individual lessons, group lessons, and clinics. One-on-one personal trainers are very popular. Club members usually pay an extra fee for all types of fitness instruction, and the percentage received by the instructor is negotiated with the club.

Exercise or sports camps at clubs are popular with children during the summer and on weekends during the school year. These camps usually include instructional sports programs, recreational activities, and food and beverages, and may even include instruction in a cognitive learning area such as computers or a foreign language.

A club may also offer **wellness programs** to its members, since individuals who are interested in exercise are often concerned about their health in general. Program topics might include weight management, nutrition, stress management, and smoking cessation. These classes can meet in a private meeting room or in a section of a

Exhibit 4   IRS Criteria for Independent Contractors

20 Factors to Consider—Answer Yes or No

The worker:

1. complies with the employer's instructions about the work.
2. receives training from, or at the direction of, the employer.
3. provides services that are integrated into the business.
4. provides services that must be rendered personally.
5. hires, supervises, and pays assistants for the employer.
6. has a continuing working relationship with the employer.
7. must follow set work hours.
8. works full-time for the employer.
9. performs work on the employer's premises.
10. performs work in a sequence set by the employer.
11. must submit regular reports to the employer.
12. receives payments of regular amounts at set intervals.
13. receives payments for business or traveling expenses.
14. relies on the employer to furnish tools and materials.
15. lacks a major investment in equipment, tools, or facilities used to perform services.
16. cannot make a profit or suffer a loss from services.
17. performs work for only one employer at a time.
18. can be fired by the employer.
19. does not offer services to the general public.
20. may quit work at any time without incurring liability.

Source: Gammon & Grange, P.C. (703-761-5000), "Will the Real Independent Contractor Please Stand Up?" *Nonprofit Alert Memorandum 9110-2,* 1994, pp. 1–5.

large dining room. Nutrition and weight management programs can be coordinated with the club's food and beverage department, which might offer "heart-healthy" menu items or weekly specials prepared specifically to coordinate with program goals. Experts in each subject can be hired as contractors to offer these classes.

Risk Management and Liability Issues

When individuals are exercising, they are at a higher risk for a cardiovascular incident or death than when they are not exercising. For this reason, clubs should screen members to detect coronary or other medical risk factors. There are numerous

Exhibit 5   Typical Fitness Assessment Components

- Blood analyses for cholesterol and high- and low-density lipoprotein
- Blood pressure while resting and while exercising
- Flexibility testing for the upper and lower body
- Muscular strength and endurance measurements
- Body composition through skin-fold measurements, hydrostatic weighing, etc.
- Submaximal cardiovascular fitness test for aerobic fitness level and target heart-range (treadmill, bicycle ergometer, or step test)

screening instruments a club can use. The *PAR-Q and You,* produced by the British Columbia Ministry of Health, and the *Health History Questionnaire,* produced by Fitcorp Healthcare and Koeberle, are two commonly used instruments. If a fitness center staff person identifies a member as high-risk, the staff person should advise the member to see a doctor before beginning an exercise program.

Members also should undergo a **fitness assessment** at the club before beginning an exercise program (see Exhibit 5); such an assessment identifies each member's fitness level so that the fitness staff can recommend an exercise intensity level that will minimize injuries and maximize results. The fitness assessment should follow the protocols established by the American College of Sports Medicine.

Members who participate in an organized exercise activity for which they register should be required to sign an **informed consent form.** This form lists all of the risks associated with the activity, advises members that their participation is voluntary, and states that, by signing the form, they assume the risks identified. In addition, the club should have signs posted to inform members of fitness center safety policies and procedures; these signs are usually required by local health and safety codes.

The club should have a written emergency plan and evacuation plan for the fitness center. The fitness center's control desk should be the control center during an emergency or evacuation. The control desk and the other areas in the fitness center, such as the locker room and fitness floor, should each have a first aid kit. The fitness center's staff should undergo regular training and drills on dealing with emergencies and evacuations.

The emergency plan should indicate who is responsible for treating an injured person, who will notify the club manager on duty, who will call the emergency medical service (and what number should be called—usually 911), who will meet the emergency medical team at the club's entrance, and who will complete the appropriate report.

The club's fitness director should make sure that the following documentation is kept at the fitness center: emergency and evacuation plans, accident and injury reports on both members and staff, copies of the staff members' certifications, reports on the emergency training and drill sessions the staff participates in, and verification of the restocking and updating of first aid kits.

Insider Insights

Albert Armstrong, CCM, General Manager
University Club of Washington, Washington, D.C.

One of the things that makes the University Club of Washington unique is the quality of its athletic facilities. Six years ago the club underwent a major capital-improvement project and converted a formerly men-only fitness facility focused on bowling into a coed, state-of-the-art, world-class fitness center.

The bowling lanes were only used by about a dozen people on Friday nights. The new fitness center is packed all the time. Our members don't bowl anymore, but they sure do work out. We have all the right equipment—mats for stretching, Stairmasters, weight machines, free weights, and so on. That's all great, but everyone's got that. What makes us unique is personal service. Our members are fairly wealthy, but they're time-bankrupt. When they come in for an hour of fitness training, they want to make that hour count. We have trainers at the club all the time to make sure members get the most out of their workouts.

Before the trainers set members up with fitness programs, they give them complete personal fitness assessments: What's their lifestyle history? How fit are they now? How fit do they want to be? Some members want to be Olympic athletes. Some want to lose 20 pounds. Some want to run a marathon. Tell us where you want to be, tell us where you are now, and we'll develop a fitness program to bridge that gap—that's essentially what our trainers do. We think personal fitness assessments are so important that we provide them free to anyone who joins the club.

As great as the expansion of our fitness facility was, it was shortsighted. We underestimated the number of women-members who would want to use the new fitness center. Initially, we built a women's locker room with 60 lockers. Since women didn't use the old fitness center, going from 0 to 60 lockers seemed like more than enough. Two years later, the athletic director and I had to put in 60 more, even though the locker room really wasn't designed for 120 lockers. A big discussion point over the last two years has been, How do we expand the women's locker facilities even more? Do we grow upstairs? Downstairs? Do we look at alternate-site facilities? How do we meet the needs of our women-members as we grow as a club?

We run a fitness competition among our members called the Swimathon. The Swimathon is 5,000 laps of the pool, or 113 miles. Members will come in and do 20 laps, perhaps, and we'll write it down. We monitor members' progress throughout the year and chart it on the wall. The first person to go all the way across the chart—put in 5,000 laps—becomes the Swimathon winner. Winners get their names placed on the club's champion board. One member, Blake Clark, wins a lot, which is amazing when you consider that he's 87 years old. A few years ago we renamed the Swimathon Award the Blake Clark Award to give Blake some recognition and give the award a unique identity more personal and meaningful to club members.

We do a lot of internal tournaments at the club. We have a member here named Frank Gould. Frank was a naval commander in World War II. When the Korean conflict began, he went back into the service. He was the Maryland state squash champion and was squash champion of the Maryland Club in Baltimore before he went off to fight in Korea. When he came back in 1953, he became a member of the

(continued)

Insider Insights *(continued)*

University Club and moved into one of our guestrooms until he could find an apartment. He hasn't found one yet. He became the squash champion at our club. When my good friend Ed Urbin took over the Maryland Club, I called him up and suggested we do a squash tournament between our two clubs and name it after Frank Gould, because he's been a member of both clubs and has been the squash champion at both clubs. He's almost 90 years old now. He traveled the globe competing in squash into his early 80s, becoming the world's oldest squash competitor. So every year now, we have a tournament. One year we have it at the Maryland Club, the next year we have it here. Again, naming the tournament after Frank is a way of recognizing a club member and making the tournament more meaningful to the rest of our members. In the real-estate business, the key to success is "location, location, location." In the club business, it's "recognition, recognition, recognition."

Payment Policies

A club must decide which fitness activities will require members to pay a **user fee.** Members are generally not charged a user fee for participation in unorganized activities in the fitness center. Most clubs charge user fees for the following fitness center activities and services:

- Massages—hourly and half-hourly rates

- Indoor-court usage during peak hours—hourly rate

- Personal trainers—hourly rates

- Lessons (group or individual)—hourly and half-hourly rates

- Sports camps, classes, leagues, or tournaments—fee for the series of sessions

- Screening and fitness evaluations—fee for the service

Fitness Associations

Fitness associations can assist club managers in creating exercise programs and determining staff qualifications. Some of these associations also offer training programs, certification, and continuing education for staff members, as well as information on trends within the fitness and exercise industry. Exhibit 6 lists some of the major fitness associations.

Aquatics Operations

Aquatics facilities at a club usually consist of a main pool and a separate, smaller "baby pool" just for infants and toddlers. Some clubs may have another separate pool for adults or for lap swimming; there may also be a separate pool just for diving, or a diving well in the main pool, separated from the rest of the pool by a cord

Exhibit 6   Fitness Associations

American Alliance for Health, Physical Education, Recreation and Dance (AAHPERD)
1900 Association Drive
Reston, VA 22091

American Amateur Racquetball Association
1685 W. Uintah
Colorado Springs, CO 80904–2921

American College of Sports Medicine
P.O. Box 1440
Indianapolis, IN 46206–1440

American Council on Exercise
5820 Oberlin Drive, #102
San Diego, CA 92121

American Heart Association
7320 Greenville Avenue
Dallas, TX 75231

American Massage Therapy Association
1130 West North Shore Avenue
Chicago, IL 60626

International Dance Exercise Association (IDEA)
6190 Cornerstone Court East, Suite 204
San Diego, CA 92121

International Health, Racquet, and Sportsclub Association
263 Summer Street
Boston, MA 02210

National Health Club Association
12596 W. Bayaud Ave., 1st Fl.
Denver, CO 80228

National Strength and Conditioning Association
P.O. Box 38909
Colorado Springs, CO 80937

National Wellness Association
1045 Clark Street, Suite 210
Stevens Point, WI 54481–0827

President's Council on Physical Fitness and Sports
701 Pennsylvania Avenue, NW, Suite 250
Washington, DC 20004–2608

U.S. Squash Rackets Association
P.O. Box 1216
Bala-Cynwyd, PA 19004

Wellness Councils of America
1701 Newport Avenue, Suite 311
Omaha, NE 68152–2175

with buoys. When children and adults share the main pool, 10 or 15 minutes of every hour is sometimes designated as adults-only. (Some clubs allow children in the pool during the adult swim period if a parent or guardian is in the water with them and within close proximity.) Members who use the aquatics facilities for physical conditioning may require such equipment as kickboards, pull buoys, leg floats, hand paddles, fins, pace clocks, drag devices, underwater benches, buoyancy jackets, swim bars, and weights.

In this section we will take a look at club aquatics programs, special events held in the pool area, the aquatics staff, safety policies, pool operation and maintenance, and aquatics associations.

Aquatics Programs

Clubs typically offer a wide variety of aquatics programs so that they can meet the needs and desires of many members. Club members with children are especially

Exhibit 7   American Red Cross Instruction Programs in Aquatics

- Infant and preschool aquatics
- Learn to swim (levels I to VII)
- Basic water safety
- Emergency water safety
- Basic lifeguarding
- Lifeguard training
- Water safety instructor aid
- Water safety instructor

interested in the aquatics area because of the instructional programs offered for children. Swim lessons at clubs are very popular during the summer months when children are not in school. Instruction can include private lessons, group classes, and clinics. **Clinics** offer advanced instruction in specific areas such as competitive starts, turns, and so on. Instruction levels range from infant to adult and are often distinguished by catchy names like "tadpoles," "guppies," "dolphins," and "sharks."

The American Red Cross and the YMCA pioneered swim instruction in the United States. Both organizations offer detailed guidelines on implementing swim instruction programs. Exhibit 7 lists the Red Cross's aquatic instruction programs.

Adult exercise classes in the pool include "swimnastics" or water exercises, water walking (walking in water with a buoyancy jacket), and adult swim-stroke improvement. In addition, other classes such as skin diving, snorkeling, scuba diving, canoeing, and kayaking are popular with adults and can be offered in the pool. Staff members running summer camps for children usually use the aquatics facilities for a number of their instructional and recreational activities.

Members normally pay a user fee for swim lessons. The swim instructors receive a percentage of the fees, which are established at the beginning of the swim season by the club's general manager, aquatics director, and aquatics committee. Because he or she supervises the instructional program, the aquatics director may receive a percentage of fees for all swim lessons.

Swim Teams. Many clubs organize swim teams, usually composed of children under the age of 18. Swim team competition is divided into different age-groups, typically children under 10, 11 to 12, 13 to 14, 15 to 16, and 17 to 18. Races are held for specific swim strokes such as freestyle, butterfly, breaststroke, and backstroke. Swim team events include single strokes, a medley or combination of strokes, relays, and (in some cases) diving events.

Club swim teams are usually closely supervised by the club's aquatics committee, which may consist of members who have children on a swim team or who have a strong interest in the aquatics area. As with other club committees, a member of the board of directors usually serves on the aquatics committee in order to keep the board abreast of aquatics activities. Along with the swim team coach, the aquatics committee is usually responsible for recruiting swim team parents to perform tasks associated with swim team management. Typical volunteer activities include transporting team members to off-premises meets and serving as timers, judges, and event organizers. These volunteers should be trained in their responsibilities and scheduled much like employees.

Swim team practice sessions are usually held early in the morning or late in the afternoon, five days per week. Clubs with very competitive swim team programs may have two practice sessions a day. Many cities have a swim team league comprising teams from several clubs. If a league does not exist, a club's swim teams usually can find comparable club or public swim teams to compete with.

Promoting the club's swim teams is done primarily by word of mouth. Having a swim team bulletin board near the aquatics facilities helps promote swim team events, keeps club members informed of swim team activities, and alerts swimmers as to when the pool will be used for team practices or home swim meets. A swim team newsletter or a special section in the club newsletter can promote the club's teams and praise individual participants.

Special Events

Clubs should offer special aquatics events based on member interest. Events that involve member families and friends are popular, especially on holidays. Many clubs host special events at their aquatics facilities on the major summer holidays: Memorial Day, Independence Day, and Labor Day.

Special aquatics events include water volleyball tournaments, coin searches in the pool, team relay races involving rafts or inner tubes, water polo matches, innertube water polo, and underwater hockey. Outdoor events in the evening around the pool are also popular; casual parties such as barbecues or Hawaiian luaus lend themselves to swimming and outdoor dining. Teen nights at poolside with music and casual dining are also very popular. Night swimming should only be allowed if the club's pool has adequate underwater and deck lighting. Any evening activity at the pool should be closely monitored by club lifeguards because of the decreased visibility and—at adult parties—because alcoholic beverages are often served. As during the day, no glass or china should be allowed in the immediate pool area.

Aquatics Staff

Typical aquatics staff positions include aquatics director, assistant aquatics director, swim instructor, swim team coach, and lifeguard. Some of these positions might overlap—for example, swim instructors might also serve as lifeguards; or the aquatics director, the assistant aquatics director, or a swim instructor might also serve as the swim team coach. At some clubs, the aquatics director is considered the assistant fitness director and performs the responsibilities of both positions.

The positions in the aquatics area require special qualifications and certifications. A club's aquatics director should have lifeguard certification, CPR certification, standard or advanced first-aid certification, water-safety-instructor certification, and pool-operator certification (both national and local or state certification, if required by the local board of health). The aquatics director should also have experience as an

Exhibit 8   Sample Job Description: Aquatics Director (and Assistant Fitness Director)

Job Summary: Responsible for management of club pools during the summer season and maintenance during the off-season, including but not limited to day-to-day operations, maintenance, and supervision of pool staff and summer programs. Responsible for day-to-day operations of the fitness center, including but not limited to exercise program setup, equipment maintenance, and implementation of fitness incentive programs.

Duties:

1. Manage club aquatics personnel and summer programs.

2. Maintain club pools during the summer season and off-season.

3. Implement fitness incentive programs and assist in the development of these programs, using flyers and bulletin boards at the club.

4. Supervise the club's "on-call" massage program.

5. Create personalized programs and conduct fitness assessments for members. Must take an active role in the follow-ups to track progress and keep member retention high.

6. Clean and maintain exercise equipment in the weight room and provide a safe atmosphere that enhances exercise participation at the club.

7. Report to the fitness director.

Special Qualifications:

• Education: Possess or currently be working toward a bachelor of science degree or higher in a field related to physical fitness.

• Must be knowledgeable of all types of weight-training programs and machinery.

• Certifications from the American College of Sports Medicine, AFAA, IDEA, Red Cross, and American Heart Association as appropriate.

Reports to: Fitness Director

Supervises: Aquatics personnel at the club.

assistant aquatics director, swim instructor, and lifeguard, and possess administrative and supervisory skills. Exhibit 8 is a sample job description for an aquatics director (note that, in this job description, the duties of aquatics director and assistant fitness director are combined into one position).

An assistant aquatics director should have the same certifications as the aquatics director. An assistant aquatics director typically has less on-the-job experience than an aquatics director. Prior experience as a swim instructor and lifeguard is highly recommended for assistant aquatics directors.

Qualifications for a swim instructor include lifeguard certification, CPR certification, standard first-aid certification, and water-safety-instructor certification. A swim instructor should also have good communication skills and be patient, friendly, and outgoing.

The qualifications for a swim team coach are usually the same as those for a swim instructor, with the addition of the following: American Red Cross certification in safety training for swim coaches, experience as a swim team competitor, experience as an assistant coach with a variety of age-groups, an understanding of the biomechanics of competitive swim strokes, and group organizational skills. Often, the swim team coach is the aquatics director or assistant aquatics director, or at least has some additional responsibilities in the aquatics program.

Lifeguards should have lifeguard certification, CPR certification, and standard first-aid certification.

The lifeguards, swim instructors, swim coach, and assistant aquatics director report to the aquatics director. When the aquatics director is not at the club, the assistant aquatics director or head lifeguard assumes the director's responsibilities. The aquatics director at a club normally reports to the general manager or clubhouse manager. The aquatics director will also communicate with the chairperson of the aquatics committee, as well as with other aquatics committee members, about aquatics programs and facilities. The general or clubhouse manager should be informed of any official communication between aquatics committee members and the aquatics director.

Generally, lifeguards are paid on an hourly basis, while swim instructors receive a percentage of the fees generated from lessons. The aquatics director, assistant director, and swim coach typically receive salaries. The aquatics director may also receive fees from lessons and classes that he or she teaches directly, a percentage of the fees from all aquatics lessons and classes, a percentage from summer camp fees or fees from special swim activities that generate revenue, and the proceeds or a percentage of the proceeds from the sale of aquatic products—depending on whether the inventory is owned by the director or the club.

Staff Duties. Typical lifeguard duties include conducting surveillance of the pool and pool-deck area; enforcing swimming pool rules and regulations; performing rescue, safety, and emergency procedures when needed; testing the swimming pool water at regular intervals and adding chemicals as instructed by the aquatics director; setting up aquatics and rescue equipment; and performing daily opening, closing, preventive maintenance, and trash collection duties in the pool area. Lifeguards should be dressed in a standard lifeguard swimsuit and shirt so as to be easily identifiable.

Swim instructors meet with students in classes, private lessons, and clinics when scheduled. They should wear swim attire so that they can enter the water for demonstrations. Swim instructors generally take attendance in their classes and are responsible for making sure that the appropriate paperwork is completed so that billing information is correct and the proper certification cards are issued to participants at a course's completion.

The swim coach is responsible for all the components of swim team organization, which include recruiting team members, leading team practices, organizing swim team competitions, interacting with the swim team committee (this committee may be a separate club committee or a subcommittee of the aquatics committee), and planning social events for team participants. The swim team coach needs to be a motivator as well as a teacher and administrator. Keeping kids motivated to attend practices and compete throughout the swim season are major goals. The swim coach also needs to work well with the swim team children's parents, who typically are asked to volunteer in a number of capacities: transport children to "away" swim meets; serve as officials, timers, and judges at swim meets; help in planning parties and award ceremonies for the team; and so on. There is more to being a swim coach than just knowing proper stroke techniques.

The aquatics director and assistant aquatics director perform all administrative, supervisory, and training functions for the aquatics facilities. Administrative duties include purchasing equipment, supplies, and chemicals; hiring aquatics staff; organizing and completing all reports (covering accidents, chemicals added to the pool, inventory, maintenance activities, and so on); developing rules, operating manuals, and emergency and evacuation procedures for the aquatics area; ensuring that signs are appropriately placed in the aquatics area; and completing payroll forms and submitting them to accounting.

Supervisory duties include evaluating lifeguard surveillance techniques, enforcing the staff dress code, and evaluating the performance of staff members. Staff training includes conducting emergency and evacuation drills as well as reviewing aquatics-area policies and procedures. Aquatics directors also monitor instructional programs and sometimes teach classes themselves.

Aquatics directors interact with local boards of health to ensure that their clubs' aquatics facilities meet all requirements. They also interact with and support the club's swim teams and coach (if they are not themselves the coach). Directors promote aquatics activities by posting notices of upcoming activities, writing articles for the club newsletter, and calling members about upcoming events.

Many club pools are open only part of the year. Aquatics directors may perform seasonal opening and closing activities or may supervise the club's maintenance staff. Aquatics directors may also have the responsibility of monitoring and maintaining the pool during the off-season. Some clubs contract with a pool management company to operate and maintain the pool year-round.

Safety Policies

Because of the potentially life-threatening situations that can occur in relationship to the pool or pool activities, members of the aquatics staff must have the authority and the personality to deal forcefully with both members and guests when dangerous or emergency situations occur. The aquatics staff should also have a plan that covers emergencies that might arise. As with the club's fitness center staff members, all aquatics staff members should know who is responsible for treating injured parties, who makes sure the emergency or accident scene is safe, who monitors the pool during the emergency, who calls the emergency medical service (EMS) if the problem is life-threatening (and what number should be called—usually 911), who meets the EMS personnel at the club's entrance, who notifies the club manager on duty, and who completes the accident report.

Lifeguards on duty should constantly monitor the pool and surrounding deck for swimmers who need assistance or who may be engaging in dangerous activities. Lifeguards should sit in elevated chairs to maximize their range of vision.

These chairs should be equipped with umbrellas and appropriate lifesaving equipment. When in a chair, a lifeguard should not be talking to members or staff or performing any other activity. Lifeguards should rotate their positions or duties at least every 20 minutes to combat fatigue and boredom.

The following safety equipment should be available at the pool: rescue tubes, ring buoys and lifelines, throw bags, shepherd's crooks or reaching poles, a backboard and collars, resuscitation and oxygen equipment, a first aid kit, and a cot and blankets.

Members should not be allowed to run near the pool. Glass and other breakables should not be allowed in the pool area. Water depths should be clearly indicated around the pool, and deep-water areas should be separated from shallow areas by a buoyed line. If the bottom of the pool is not visible, or if testing indicates the water chemistry is not within acceptable limits, the pool should be closed. In fact, if the safety of the facility is questionable for any reason, the pool should be closed.

Diving should not be allowed from the deck into water less than five feet deep or from diving boards into water less than nine feet deep. The American Red Cross recommends that such areas be clearly marked with "No Diving" or "Shallow Water" signs. Diving or jumping from the pool's diving board should be allowed only off the front of the board, not the sides. Divers should not run off the board or try to dive out a long distance from the board, and no more than one bounce should be allowed. Only one person should be on the diving board at a time. After diving, the diver should immediately proceed to the nearest exit ladder and be near or on the ladder before the next diver is allowed to dive.

Pool Operation and Maintenance

The swimming pool consists of the structure holding the water, a filtration system, and sanitation devices. Water is removed from the pool for filtration through the main drain at the bottom of the pool and the skimmers or gutters at the water's surface. A pump draws the water through these openings to the filter system. A strainer in front of the pump collects debris, hair, and other large particles, preventing the serious damage that could result if these items collected in the pump's impeller. The strainer should be cleaned on a daily basis.

Pool water is pumped through the filter or filters. Three common pool-filtering materials are sand, diatomaceous earth, and paper cartridges. After filtration, the water is returned to the pool via return lines that are usually spaced evenly around the pool wall a few feet below the water's surface. Chemical feeders typically are attached to the main return line; there may be one chemical feeder or a number of feeders that add a variety of chemicals. The pool may have an automated system that tests the water and adds the appropriate chemicals. If there is no automated system, staff members must periodically check the water chemistry and either turn on the chemical feeders or add chemicals manually. Exhibit 9 indicates acceptable pool-water chemistry and the chemicals used to maintain it.

Because of its low cost, chlorine is the most common form of sanitizer used in swimming pools. Chlorine comes in three forms: gas, liquid (sodium hypochlorite), and powder (calcium hypochlorite). While chlorine gas is the most economical, it is also the most dangerous: its vapors can cause lung damage or even death. Liquid chlorine can also be harmful if it comes in contact with the skin and is not rinsed off immediately. Powdered chlorine is the safest form of chlorine, but it too can be a

Exhibit 9   General Pool-Water Guidelines

Acceptable Water-Chemistry Ranges

Water Chemistry	Acceptable Range
pH Level	7.2–7.8
Free Chlorine/Bromine Level	0.5–2.0 parts per million
Total Alkalinity Level	50–150 parts per million
Calcium Hardness Level	100–400 parts per million (depends on the total alkalinity and pH levels)

Chemicals for Maintaining Swimming Pools

Action Desired	Chemical
Sanitize	Chlorine or Bromine
Increase pH Level	Soda Ash/Sodium Carbonate
Decrease pH Level and Alkalinity	Muriatic Acid/Sodium Bisulfate
Increase Alkalinity	Sodium Bicarbonate
Increase Calcium Hardness	Calcium Chloride
Increase Stabilizer	Cyanuric Acid

hazard if water or other liquids get into the storage canister and the lid is then closed; the powder and liquid mixture causes the release of chlorine gas, creating the potential for an explosion. Bromine, which is more expensive than chlorine, is often used as a whirlpool sanitizer because it is more stable than chlorine at high temperatures.

The swimming pool's surface should be skimmed of debris and its deep-end-well vacuumed on a daily basis. The entire pool generally needs to be vacuumed at least once a week—more often if there are trees around the pool, if the pool is heavily used, or if there is a great deal of air pollution in the area.

The pool's filter system must be backwashed when too much debris accumulates on the filters; this is usually indicated by pressure gauges on the influent (incoming) lines to the filters and the effluent (outgoing) lines. As the filters get dirty, the water coming into the filters will slow down, causing an increase in the influent pressure, and the water returning to the pool will slow down, causing a decrease in the effluent pressure. To backwash the filters, the pump is turned off, the valves are

Water from the swimming pools is circulated through the two large sand filters (behind the pipes) via an assortment of influent and effluent lines. (Courtesy of Cherokee Town & Country Club, Atlanta, Georgia)

adjusted to reverse the water flow through the filters, and the dirty water is diverted to the sewer. Five to ten minutes of backwashing is usually sufficient to clean the filters.

Aquatics Associations

There are a number of aquatics associations that offer certification programs, operating pamphlets, and other services to clubs (see Exhibit 10). The National Swimming Pool Foundation and the National Spa and Pool Institute offer a national certification program for pool operators that covers the basics of pool filtration systems, water sanitation, and aquatics safety. The American Red Cross certifies individuals in a number of skills, including standard first aid, CPR, lifeguarding, water safety instruction, and safety training for swim coaches; it also certifies individuals in such aquatics activities as canoeing, sailing, and kayaking. The United States Water Fitness Association and the Aquatic Exercise Association offer certification in water fitness instruction. The YMCA certifies individuals as lifeguards and swim instructors. The National Safety Council and the National Recreation and Park Association endorse the Ellis & Associates' National Pool and Waterpark Lifeguard Training license and the Learn-to-Swim Instructor certification.

Tennis Operations

Club members who are interested in tennis vary in their expectations of their club's tennis operations. Some may play tennis only for recreational purposes and may want to play just a few times per month; others may enjoy the competitive nature

Exhibit 10   Aquatics Associations

American Red Cross Health and Safety
17th & D Streets, NW
Washington, DC 20006

American Swimming Coaches Association
1 Hall of Fame Drive
Fort Lauderdale, FL 33316

Aquatic Exercise Association
P.O. Box 1609
Nokomis, FL 34274–1609

Council for National Cooperation in Aquatics
901 West New York Street
Indianapolis, IN 46202

National Recreation and Park Association (Aquatics Section)
2775 South Quincy Street, Suite 300
Alexandria, VA 22206

National Safety Council
444 North Michigan Avenue
Chicago, IL 60611

National Spa and Pool Institute
2111 Eisenhower Avenue
Alexandria, VA 22314

National Swimming Pool Foundation
10803 Gulfdale, Suite 300
San Antonio, TX 78216

United States Lifesaving Association
425 East McFetridge Drive
Chicago, IL 60605

United States Masters Swimming
2 Peter Avenue
Rutland, MA 01543

United States Synchronized Swimming, Inc.
201 South Capitol Avenue, Suite 510
Indianapolis, IN 46225

United States Water Fitness Association
P.O. Box 3279
Boynton Beach, FL 33424–3279

United States Water Polo, Inc.
201 S. Capitol Avenue, Suite 520
Indianapolis, IN 46225

YMCA of the USA
101 N. Wacker Drive
Chicago, IL 60606

YWCA of the USA
726 Broadway
New York, NY 10003

of the sport and may want to play more often in leagues and tournaments. Parents may want the club to have instructional tennis programs for their children. Businesspeople may want to have "business tennis matches" at the club with clients who enjoy tennis. Offering a variety of tennis programs to meet these and other member needs will help make the club's tennis operations successful.

In this section we will cover tennis programs, tennis staff, pro shops, maintenance of tennis areas, and tennis associations.

Tennis Programs

Competitions. Some of the most common tennis programs at clubs are competitions—ladders or pyramids, round-robin mixers, leagues, and other tournaments. The biggest concern in conducting any organized event on the tennis courts is the number of courts that will be used and therefore unavailable to the general membership. If possible, a few courts should always be left open for free play.

A **ladder** or **pyramid** is an ongoing competition among club members. In this competition, the names of participating club members are arranged in a ladder or pyramid and then posted. At first the members are placed in the ladder or pyramid randomly; the order changes as the members play each other and their standing within the group changes. Players challenge others who are above them; the ultimate goal is to get to the top of the ladder or pyramid. If the challenger wins, he or she moves up the ladder, while the loser moves down to the challenger's position (or one position down). The players schedule their own matches and report the results to the tennis staff. There are many variations on the ladder or pyramid concept. Changing the format from time to time will keep the event exciting.

Round-robin mixers allow members to play tennis with a large number of other members with similar abilities. Round-robin mixers are competitions that are normally played on one day, over a weekend, or over the course of a week. The number of matches scheduled should never exceed the number of courts; this will ensure that members will not have to wait for an open court. If there are many participants, they can be organized into groups, or **flights**, that are scheduled to play at different times. If the round-robin is to be played in a single day or weekend, each match may consist of only one set or have a time limit (say, 30 minutes). Shortened matches allow participants to play a larger number of individuals without getting tired or losing interest. As with ladder competitions, there are many variations of the round-robin mixer, and variety will ensure continuing member interest and enjoyment. A good guide to conducting round-robin mixers is *Easy On—Easy Off*, published by the United States Tennis Association.

There are many types of club tennis leagues. A club may have a tennis team in a competitive league, playing other club or city teams in both home and away matches. There are also less competitive, more "fun-oriented" leagues, with matches played only among a club's own teams. Leagues are usually structured by skill level, gender, and type of play (singles, doubles, or mixed doubles). Club teams should have enough players to make up for no-shows at scheduled matches. League competitions usually last a number of weeks.

A club may provide food and beverage service (for a fee) for league matches at the club, although members or their opponents may provide their own refreshments at some clubs. The club's general manager should check with the local alcohol and beverage authority before allowing anyone to bring alcohol onto club property, since this usually is a violation of the club's liquor license.

The overall club tennis team comprises a number of teams: men's teams, women's teams, and teams for various age-groups among the junior participants. The tennis director or one of the assistant tennis professionals often assumes the responsibility of tennis-team coach. Club members may act as team captains to assist in recruiting players, purchasing team attire, assigning players to teams and positions (first singles, second singles, and so on), and organizing practice sessions, matches, and transportation. The team captains are often members of the club's tennis committee.

Insider Insights

Steve Fiske, Director of Athletics
Belle Haven Country Club, Alexandria, Virginia

I've been at the Belle Haven Country Club for 21 years. I came here originally as a tennis professional, but my job description has expanded with the club's athletic facilities. Now I'm director of athletics. We employ two teaching tennis professionals and a pro shop manager. We also have a part-time staff to work evenings and weekends. In addition to that, in the fitness area we have an aerobics instructor and two personal trainers who see members by appointment. We also employ interns—students from colleges that offer degrees in professional sports management.

My athletic background is tennis; my degree is in psychology. After college I played tennis professionally for about two years. I played all the big tournaments. I was what I would call a "peripheral player"; I wasn't going to be the world champion by a long shot. At the end of your playing career you have to decide what direction the rest of your life is going to take. I chose to be a club tennis professional. Historically, the pro tennis world has been the source of most club tennis professionals.

At Belle Haven Country Club we have a fairly large tennis program. As head tennis professional, I'm in charge of designing and implementing programs for the club's tennis players. For example, I help with the administration of the tennis teams that we field to play other clubs. I direct all of the club's tennis events: tournaments, round-robins, and social functions. The tennis pros and I do quite a bit of teaching as well, about 20 hours a week each. The rest of our time is spent administering our tennis programs. As the head pro, my duties are extremely varied. It's the diversity of job functions that is the really rewarding part of my job.

You shouldn't take a job like this if a lot of time on the job is a problem for you. This is not a 9-to-5, Monday-through-Friday job. Lots of members come out to use the club on weekends, so you have to be here on weekends. A tennis pro, in order to do the job properly, has to put in at least 60 hours a week. For example, we have an early-morning tennis clinic that starts at 7 A.M., designed for members to get a lesson in before work, and we have tennis programs in the evening. And I have to be here for all of them. My family is very patient with me, very understanding. But I have three children and I don't think any of them have their hearts set on being a tennis pro. Actually, it's a wonderful life for my family. I say that I don't see them much, but I do. They come over to the club. My children learned to play tennis here, and my wife plays here. I try to play once or twice a week to stay in shape.

The tennis staff usually meets once a week. We recommend to the tennis committee what we think would be popular tennis programs, based on what we've heard from members. There also might be maintenance issues or requests for large expenditures that we must bring to the tennis committee for its consideration. I regard the tennis committee as an advisory group representing the members of the club who play tennis. There are eight people on the committee. The committee's chairpersons try to populate the committee with people from the various segments of the club's tennis-playing population, which numbers about 200.

I own the pro shop. When the tennis pro owns the pro shop, there's obviously more incentive for the pro to listen to members and care more about issues like

(continued)

Insider Insights *(continued)*

overstocking. If pros don't personally own their shops, they don't have as much at risk and there's not as much incentive to really listen to members. I try to tune in to what the members want. There might be a piece of tennis merchandise that I think is absolutely terrific, but I can look at my inventory controls and see that it's not selling, and I have to adjust accordingly. I may think it's great, but the members don't.

Today's tennis pros seem to be taking a more businesslike approach than pros did 10 or 20 years ago. I didn't take a lot of business classes in school. I've learned by going through the school of hard knocks and reading a lot on how to merchandise correctly and do inventory control and all that. People with a business background are more prepared for modern clubs than people who don't have that background.

The USPTA has a very good continuing-education program. It offers seminars in pro shop management, business administration, marketing, and so on. It requires that you take a certain number of courses periodically. I would highly recommend the USPTA to people who want to be tennis professionals, because when you've received your college degree, your education has just begun.

Most clubs conduct at least a few tennis tournaments each season, as well as a club championship tournament or a member-guest tournament. A standard tournament allows participants to lose only once or twice before they are eliminated; the major types of competition are single elimination (one loss means you are out of the tournament), double elimination (two losses allowed), and consolation (losers play in a separate single-elimination tournament). As in league play, tournament participants usually are divided into groups based on skill level, gender, and type of play.

One of the primary purposes of a **member-guest tournament** is to introduce prospective members to the club and its services. The tennis director should be sure to interact with guests and members to show guests the type of personal services that members receive.

Food and beverages should be served at organized tennis tournaments. There should be ample promotion of each tournament to foster member interest and participation. Notices in the club newsletter and posted signs should alert members to limited court availability during organized tournaments. Tournament fees should cover direct costs: food and beverage service, prizes, pro shop certificates, balls, etc. When scheduling a tournament, the organizer must make sure that it does not conflict with other club events.

Lessons. Tennis instruction is the foundation of a club's overall tennis program. Instruction is the key to getting members to use the tennis courts and visit the club more often. Moreover, the instructional program increases participation in other tennis activities such as leagues, round-robin mixers, and tournaments. Instructional programs should cover beginning, intermediate, and advanced skill levels.

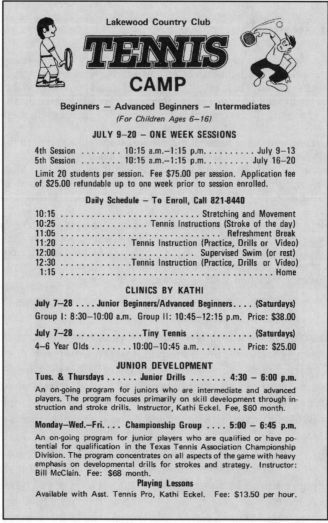

Lakewood Country Club

TENNIS

CAMP

Beginners — Advanced Beginners — Intermediates
(For Children Ages 6–16)

JULY 9–20 — ONE WEEK SESSIONS

4th Session .... 10:15 a.m.–1:15 p.m. .... July 9–13
5th Session .... 10:15 a.m.–1:15 p.m. .... July 16–20

Limit 20 students per session. Fee $75.00 per session. Application fee of $25.00 refundable up to one week prior to session enrolled.

Daily Schedule — To Enroll, Call 821-8440

10:15 .... Stretching and Movement
10:25 .... Tennis Instructions (Stroke of the day)
11:05 .... Refreshment Break
11:20 .... Tennis Instruction (Practice, Drills or Video)
12:00 .... Supervised Swim (or rest)
12:30 ....Tennis Instruction (Practice, Drills or Video)
1:15 .... Home

CLINICS BY KATHI

July 7–28 .... Junior Beginners/Advanced Beginners.... (Saturdays)
Group I: 8:30–10:00 a.m. Group II: 10:45–12:15 p.m. Price: $38.00

July 7–28 ....Tiny Tennis .... (Saturdays)
4–6 Year Olds .... 10:00–10:45 a.m. .... Price: $25.00

JUNIOR DEVELOPMENT

Tues. & Thursdays ...... Junior Drills .... 4:30 – 6:00 p.m.
An on-going program for juniors who are intermediate and advanced players. The program focuses primarily on skill development through instruction and stroke drills. Instructor, Kathi Eckel. Fee, $60 month.

Monday–Wed.–Fri. .... Championship Group .... 5:00 – 6:45 p.m.
An on-going program for junior players who are qualified or have potential for qualification in the Texas Tennis Association Championship Division. The program concentrates on all aspects of the game with heavy emphasis on developmental drills for strokes and strategy. Instructor: Bill McClain. Fee: $68 month.

Playing Lessons
Available with Asst. Tennis Pro, Kathi Eckel. Fee: $13.50 per hour.

Many clubs offer tennis camps for children during the summer months. (Courtesy of Lakewood Country Club, Dallas, Texas)

The key to keeping members enrolled in tennis lessons is to make them interesting, challenging, and—most of all—*fun.*

Tennis lessons can be in the form of private lessons, group lessons, or clinics. Group lessons and clinics are divided by age-group (adult and junior), gender, skill level, and topic (stroke improvement, strategy, conditioning, and so on). Offering a variety of lessons will attract the most participants. Private lessons allow members to receive individual attention; group lessons and clinics allow members to interact with other members while improving their skills. Group lessons use court time more efficiently, which may be important if facilities are limited. The club should never allow all of the courts to be used at the same time for lessons, especially during peak hours (after work and early on weekends).

Club members generally pay a fee for lessons. Tennis instructors—the tennis director and assistant tennis professionals—may keep all of the fee or a certain percentage. Fee policies are established annually by the club's board, with input from the tennis committee, the club manager, and the tennis director. Often, the tennis director receives a percentage of the revenue from lessons taught by assistant tennis professionals. The percentage, which may be as high as 50 percent, is usually based on the experience of the assistant tennis professional—the more experienced he or she is, the smaller the percentage received by the director.

Some clubs offer a new member or new player one free private lesson. This can help the staff assess the member's skills and place him or her in the correct level for group lessons or league or tournament play.

Junior Programs. Tennis clinics and camps for children are popular during the summer when children are out of school; the club usually has plenty of courts available during the day on weekdays. During the school year, junior programs can be scheduled immediately after school, before the peak after-work hours for adults. Junior programs may include group lessons, clinics, round-robins, tournaments, group games, member-guest events, and parent-child events. Junior tennis players should be grouped by age and ability for each event. The pro shop should carry junior-size rackets to accommodate program participants. Successful tennis events for juniors combine fun, instruction, and social interaction.

Tennis Staff

Typical tennis staff positions include tennis director, assistant tennis professional, tennis instructor, pro shop employee, and maintenance staff member. In a small club, all of the duties involved in the tennis program—teaching, pro shop management, and maintenance—may be performed by the tennis director and assistant tennis professionals. Larger clubs may have additional staff members working to sell products from the pro shop, handle court reservations and sign-ups for organized tennis events, and carry out other duties. Large clubs may also employ someone to perform daily and weekly court maintenance.

The tennis director (sometimes called the head tennis professional) is responsible for administering the overall tennis program. This involves organizing tennis programs; administering lessons, exhibitions, and court reservations; collecting guest fees and enforcing the club's guest policies; overseeing the club's tennis teams; and overseeing court maintenance. The tennis director is also in charge of the pro shop's administration—sales, merchandising, purchasing, and control procedures—and the ball machines—reservations, rental fee collection, and machine maintenance and storage. The tennis director is responsible for the fiscal soundness of the tennis program and the preparation and maintenance of its budget. The director hires, supervises, trains, and evaluates the tennis staff.

The tennis director may receive any of the following as part of a compensation package: a salary; ownership rights to the pro shop merchandise or a percentage of the sales; income from lessons; income from ball machine rentals; a benefits package that includes insurance, vacation time, and a retirement plan; a bonus for meeting operational goals; reimbursement for professional expenses such as association dues and continuing education; comp time to play in tennis tournaments; and club usage privileges and free meals, according to terms agreed upon between the club and the director.

The assistant tennis professionals and pro shop staff report to the tennis director. When the director is not at the club, the senior assistant tennis professional assumes the director's responsibilities. The tennis director normally reports to the club's general manager. The director also communicates with the chairperson of the tennis committee, as well as with other tennis committee members, about tennis programs and facilities. The general manager should be informed of any official communication between tennis committee members and the director. Exhibit 11 is a sample job description for a tennis director. (See Chapter Appendix B for a sample job description and sample employment agreement for a tennis director that were created by the United States Professional Tennis Association.)

Qualifications for a tennis director, an assistant tennis professional, or a tennis instructor include United States Professional Tennis Association or United States Professional Tennis Registry tennis-professional certification or Associate Member status; competitive tennis experience and skill; and preferably some teaching and work experience at a tennis facility. He or she should be a good communicator; be patient, friendly, and outgoing; and have a sense of humor. Tennis directors should also have good administrative and supervisory skills.

Tennis professionals should be highly visible to club members; they should be seen both teaching and playing on the club's courts. They must be careful, however, to avoid playing only with a few members. A frequent complaint among club members is that some tennis professionals "play favorites" when choosing members to play tennis with. Tennis professionals should also be given opportunities to win prize money in local tennis tournaments.

While courts of law have yet to determine clearly whether tennis professionals working at a club are truly independent contractors, a tennis pro is likely to be considered a club employee if one or more of the following conditions apply under normal circumstances:

- The tennis professional has signed an employment agreement with the club.

- The tennis facility's hours of operation are specified by the club.

- The club provides the professional with pro shop space, utilities, telephone service, and meals at no charge.

- The club bills members for tennis services, collects revenue from members, and pays the revenue due to the professional.

These conditions (which exist at many clubs) have been interpreted by the IRS to demonstrate employer control over a tennis professional. The IRS criteria listed in Exhibit 4 provide additional guidelines as to whether a tennis pro is an employee or an independent contractor. In the event of a wage dispute, the Department of Labor will likely consider all tennis staff members, including the director and assistant professionals, to be employees of the club.

Exhibit 11   Sample Job Description: Tennis Director

Job Summary: Responsible for planning and directing all tennis activities; supervising and coordinating the work of assistant professionals, pro shop employees, and court maintenance staff; implementing and administering tennis committee directives and policies; and reporting violations of tennis policies and club rules to the chairperson of the tennis committee.

Managerial Duties:

1. Establish all operational procedures for assistant pros, maintenance, and reservation desk personnel.
2. Establish the yearly operating budget with the tennis committee.
3. Establish the yearly capital needs with the tennis committee.
4. Formulate the instruction program and the events program.
5. Formulate the yearly calendar of events with the tennis committee.
6. Attend tennis committee meetings and give direction in establishing short- and long-term tennis plans.
7. Hold meetings with member associations to guide them in their goals and plans.
8. Hire, train, promote, and fire all tennis employees as necessary.
9. Set employee salaries and approve all salary changes.
10. Hold staff meetings to examine safety measures, procedure improvements, and personnel morale.
11. Approve all personnel disciplinary action.
12. Originate labor distribution, accident reports, and work and vacation schedules. Sign the time cards.
13. Formulate the annual master plan for the pro shop.

Supervisory Duties:

1. Observe all work of tennis employees to ascertain that the work conforms to department standards.
2. Supervise the administration of ongoing tennis programs and special events.
3. Observe all work performed by outside contractors to ascertain that the work conforms to contractual agreements.
4. Inspect equipment and tools to ensure that they are in proper condition.
5. Make a daily inspection of the physical facility to ensure that it is in good condition.

Technical and Administrative Duties:

1. Conduct individual and group tennis instruction.
2. Coordinate with other department heads for jobs performed in conjunction with other departments.

(continued)

Exhibit 11   *(continued)*

---

3. Originate and sign materials requisitions for supplies, tools, and parts.

4. Contract outside contractors and deal with them when outside work is to be performed.

Equipment Used: Tennis racquet, racquet stringer, ball machine, computer, court maintenance equipment and tools.

Special Qualifications: Must be a certified USPTA professional, should be a college graduate, should have extensive teaching experience, must have outstanding people skills, and should have at least ten years' experience in similar positions. Extensive playing experience is desirable.

Reports to: General Manager

Supervises: Assistant tennis professionals, program director, pro shop manager, and all other tennis staff.

Pro shop employees should be knowledgeable about tennis and possess the same social and communication skills as the other members of the tennis staff. Although some of their duties are related to the tennis director's revenue operation—selling merchandise, stringing rackets, scheduling lessons, and so on—pro shop staff members are usually paid by the club, either in part or in full. This is because some of their duties are club-related, such as taking court reservations and registering club members for organized tennis activities.

Tennis maintenance employees should have a knowledge of tennis along with the dexterity and strength to perform the manual tasks required to maintain the courts, such as operating machinery and lifting large bags of chemicals. Clubs with soft-surface tennis courts should employ a technician or head maintenance person with experience in maintaining soft-surface courts. In some clubs, the tennis maintenance employees may be part of the golf course grounds crew, performing tennis court maintenance guided by the tennis director.

All tennis staff members should be appropriately dressed and groomed. Tennis pros and pro shop staff members should be encouraged to wear pro shop apparel to promote its sale. This can be done by offering a staff discount or by providing pro shop apparel for them to wear while on duty. Name tags give a professional finish to their attire.

Pro Shop

Products and services offered for sale in a typical tennis pro shop include rackets (including demonstration models), balls, apparel, shoes, and racquet stringing and regripping. The pro shop's merchandise should be of high quality and include items that are not available in local sporting-goods stores and retail tennis shops.

Moreover, because the pro shop deals with a limited clientele (club members and guests), displays should be changed frequently.

The pro shop usually offers a discount on uniforms and supplies to members in a tennis league. The pro shop may sell to club members via a **cost-plus program:** members pay a fee to join the program and then can purchase merchandise for cost plus a set percentage (usually ten percent). The club may award credit at the pro shop as a tournament prize, which helps to move merchandise and increase sales. A racquet "demo" program, whereby members can try out rackets before buying them, will increase racquet sales, as will requiring the club's tennis professionals to use only rackets that are carried in the pro shop.

The merchandise in the tennis pro shop may be owned by the tennis director or by the club; there are almost as many arrangements and contractual agreements as there are clubs. For example, some tennis directors may negotiate only for the pro shop's racquet-stringing operation, as this is a very profitable enterprise. Tennis directors who own the pro shop's merchandise usually must secure their own credit to purchase inventory, fixtures, and displays. In many clubs, the tennis director owns the pro shop's merchandise but does not pay rent for the space. In some clubs, the club receives a percentage of the profits from the pro shop in lieu of rent. In a small number of cases, the pro shop may be leased out to a third party in return for rent or a percentage of total sales or net income; this lease arrangement may be managed either by the tennis director or the club. The club should require the tennis director to carry liability insurance and property insurance if the director owns the pro shop merchandise and operation.

Maintenance

The tennis courts, pro shop, and grounds in the tennis area should be as clean and as aesthetically pleasing as the rest of the club's facilities. The grounds around the tennis courts, including grass areas, landscaped terrain, and sitting areas, often are maintained by the club's grounds crew or gardeners. The tennis director should work cooperatively with these individuals to help them maintain the tennis area's grass, flowers, plants, trees, benches, chairs, tables, trash cans, water fountains, and windscreens.

Decorating and cleaning the pro shop usually falls to pro shop employees, while repairs and other major pro-shop maintenance are generally the responsibility of the club's maintenance staff.

Hard-surface tennis courts are relatively easy to maintain. They should be dried with a squeegee if play is to resume immediately after it rains. If leaves, debris, or dirt are on the courts after a storm, the courts should be swept or cleaned with an air blower after the items have dried. As hard courts age, small cracks begin to develop. Filling in these cracks and resurfacing the courts on an annual basis will increase the life of the courts.

Soft-surface courts, such as those made of red clay or synthetic clay (Har-Tru, Rubico, Fast-Dri, Teniko), are harder to maintain than hard-surface courts. (Exhibit 12 lists periodic maintenance activities for synthetic-clay tennis courts.) There are very few soft-surface courts in the United States with grass or red clay surfaces; the majority of soft-surface courts are synthetic clay. Most tennis players, especially older players, prefer soft-surface courts over hard courts because they

Exhibit 12   Maintenance Activities for Synthetic-Clay Tennis Courts

Period	Maintenance
Spring—Open	Scrape off clumps, debris, and old clay material. Add new material to the court surface. Clean old tape lines or replace, if applicable. Check sprinkler system for operation, if applicable. Repair or replace windscreens.
Monthly	Fill in low spots with clay material. Apply calcium chloride during the hot season to retain moisture.
Weekly	Roll courts two or three times per week to ensure proper hardness and compaction. Rake out divots.
Daily	Ensure that courts receive the appropriate amount of water during hot stretches; water at night and during the midday. Sweep the tape lines or relime the court lines. Roll the courts if needed. Brush the courts.
Fall—Close	Blow out the sprinklers if freeze conditions are possible. Remove the tape lines if it is desirable to try to save the lines for another year of use.

Source: United States Professional Tennis Association, Inc., *The USPTA Guide to Country Club Tennis Operations* (Houston, Texas: USPTA, 1989), pp. 97–98.

Exhibit 13   Tennis Associations

Lawn Tennis Association
The Queens Club, West Kensington
London, ENGLAND W14 9EG

National Sporting Goods Association
1699 Wall Street
Mt. Prospect, IL 60056

Sporting Goods Manufacturers Association
200 Castlewood Drive
North Palm Beach, FL 33408

Tennis Industry Association
200 Castlewood Drive
North Palm Beach, FL 33408

United States Professional Tennis Association
1 USPTA Centre, 3535 Briarpark Drive
Houston, TX 77042

United States Professional Tennis Registry
P.O. Box 4739
Hilton Head, SC 29938

United States Racquet Stringers Association
P.O. Box 40
Del Mar, CA 92014

United States Tennis Association
70 W. Red Oak Lane
White Plains, NY 10604

To maintain their soft-surface courts, some clubs use a golf car or small tractor specially equipped with a sweeper and roller. (Courtesy of Atlanta Athletic Club, Duluth, Georgia)

are easier on the lower body; the feet slide or give on the soft surfaces much more than on hard surfaces. In addition, the ball travels slower on soft surfaces, which helps players return more shots.

Tennis Associations

Exhibit 13 lists major tennis associations. The two largest U.S. tennis associations that assist clubs are the United States Professional Tennis Association (USPTA) and the United States Tennis Association (USTA). The Association of Tennis Professionals (ATP) is the association for the nation's top male professional tennis players; the Women's Tennis Association (WTA) is the corresponding association for female professional players. The ATP has recently instituted an instructional program that prepares retiring tennis players to teach.

The USPTA is the primary association for tennis professionals who teach. It offers a variety of services and programs, with the focus on educating tennis professionals through classes, conferences, seminars, and publications. It also offers a certification program to ensure that certified tennis professionals are educated on the basics of running a successful tennis operation and are skilled players. The USPTA offers three standard levels of certification—Professional 1 (the highest rating), Professional 2, and Professional 3—based on certification test scores. The USPTA's Master Professional certification is awarded to tennis professionals with outstanding credentials. New USPTA members who are working toward certification are designated as Associate Members. Chapter Appendix C outlines the USPTA's tennis professional classifications.

The USTA is the governing body of tennis in the United States. This organization develops and modifies most of the rules that govern U.S. tennis play and tournaments. The USTA is a member of the International Tennis Federation, the worldwide tennis governing board.

The Tennis Industry Association specializes in the merchandising of tennis products and is an arm of the Sporting Goods Manufacturers Association. The United States Professional Tennis Registry is a new tennis association. Its goals are similar to those of the USPTA (education and certification of teaching tennis professionals).

Key Terms

circuit—A group of progressive-resistance training machines that together work all of the body's major muscle groups.

clinic—Advanced instruction in a specific area of a sport, such as competitive starts in swimming or competition strategy in tennis.

cost-plus program—A pro shop program in which club members pay a fee and are then able to purchase pro shop merchandise at cost plus a fixed percentage (typically ten percent).

exercise prescription—An exercise program of recommended exercises and intensity levels, developed for an individual by a trained fitness professional.

fitness assessment—An assessment of an individual's overall level of fitness; fitness assessments are often used by clubs to determine appropriate exercise programs and intensity levels for members.

fitness center—The area of a club devoted to physical fitness, usually comprising a fitness floor, an exercise classroom, sports areas, and spa areas.

fitness floor—The part of a club where most of the fitness equipment is located, comprising stretching, cardiovascular, and weight-training areas.

flight—A group of competitors in a tournament; tournament participants are divided into flights for scheduling purposes.

informed consent form—A form for club members that lists all of the risks associated with a physical activity, advises members that their participation is voluntary, and states that a member, by signing the form, assumes the risks identified.

ladder (pyramid)—An ongoing tennis, racquetball, squash, or other racquet-sport competition among a group of club members in which the participants challenge each other to matches in order to improve their standing within the group.

member-guest event—An organized athletic event at a club in which guests are allowed to participate with members; such an event is often used by clubs to recruit new members.

personal trainer—A fitness center staff member who provides club members with one-on-one instruction, advice, and motivation—usually in cardiovascular or weight-training exercises.

round-robin mixer—A club tournament, normally played in a short amount of time (a day, weekend, or week), during which members play many opponents of similar ability.

user fee—A fee charged to club members for certain fitness activities.

wellness program—An instructional program in a health-related area such as nutrition or stress management.

 Review Questions ⎯⎯⎯⎯⎯⎯⎯⎯⎯⎯⎯⎯⎯⎯⎯⎯⎯⎯

1. What are the major areas of a typical club fitness center?

2. How can a club help alleviate boredom for members participating in cardiovascular exercise?

3. A club spa's wet areas present what types of special risks/concerns?

4. What qualifications and characteristics should a fitness director possess? an aquatics director? a tennis director?

5. What are the duties of a club's fitness director? aquatics director? tennis director?

6. What types of instructional programs might a club offer in fitness/exercise, aquatics, and tennis?

7. What are some IRS guidelines a club can use to determine whether a fitness or tennis staff member is an employee or an independent contractor?

8. What types of special events can a club host at its aquatics facilities?

9. What is the difference between filtration and sanitation in swimming pools?

10. What are some typical tennis programs offered at clubs?

 Additional Reading ⎯⎯⎯⎯⎯⎯⎯⎯⎯⎯⎯⎯⎯⎯⎯⎯⎯⎯

American College of Sports Medicine. *ACSM's Guidelines for Exercise Testing and Prescription*, 4th ed.

Battersby, M. E. "Lease, Buy or Rent." *Fitness Management*, July 1994.

Chu, D. A. *Power Tennis Training*. Champaign, Ill.: Human Kinetics Publishers, 1995.

Clayton, R. D., and D. G. Thomas. *Professional Aquatic Management*, 2d ed. Champaign, Ill.: Human Kinetics Publishers, 1989.

Colwin, C. M. *Swimming into the Twenty-First Century*. Champaign, Ill.: Human Kinetics Publishers, 1992.

Gabrielsen, M. A. *Swimming Pools: A Guide to Their Planning, Design, and Operation*. Champaign, Ill.: Human Kinetics Publishers, 1987.

Gammon & Grange, P.C. "Will the Real Independent Contractor Please Stand Up?" *Nonprofit Alert Memorandum 9110-2*, 1994.

Golding, L. A., C. R. Myers, and W. E. Sinning (Eds.). *The Y's Way to Physical Fitness: A Guide Book for Instructors*, 3d ed. Chicago: YMCA of the USA, 1989.

International Dance Exercise Association. *How to Choose a Quality Aerobic Fitness Instructor.* San Diego, Calif.: IDEA, 1992.

———. *How to Choose a Quality Personal Trainer.* San Diego, Calif.: IDEA, 1992.

Lustigman, A. "Reviving Racquet Sports." *Club Industry,* October 1994.

Mood, D., F. F. Musker, and J. E. Rink. *Sports and Recreational Activities for Men and Women,* 9th ed. St. Louis, Mo.: Times Mirror/Mosby, 1987.

National Spa and Pool Institute. *American National Standard for Public Swimming Pools.* Alexandria, Va.: NSPA, 1991.

National Swimming Pool Foundation. *Pool-Spa Operators Handbook.* San Antonio, Texas: NSPF, 1989.

Patton, R. W., W. C. Grantham, R. F. Gerson, and L. R. Gettman. *Developing and Managing Health/Fitness Facilities.* Champaign, Ill.: Human Kinetics Publishers, 1989.

"Pool Chemistry Primer." *Club Industry,* December 1990.

Sol, N., and C. Foster. *American College of Sports Medicine's Health/Fitness Facility Standards and Guidelines.* Champaign, Ill.: Human Kinetics Publishers, 1992.

United States Professional Tennis Association, Inc. *How to Hire a Tennis Professional.* Houston, Texas: USPTA, 1993.

———. *Tennis: A Professional Guide: Official Handbook of the USPTA.* Houston, Texas: USPTA, 1993.

———. *The USPTA Guide to Country Club Tennis Operations.* Houston, Texas: USPTA, 1993.

———. *The USPTA Tennis Professional's Business Manual.* Houston, Texas: USPTA, 1993.

United States Tennis Association. *Coaching Tennis Successfully.* Champaign, Ill.: Human Kinetics Publishers, 1995.

Van Rossen, D. *Aquatic Managers Handbook.* Springfield, Ore.: Aquatic Resources and Programs, 1992.

White, M. *Water Exercise.* Champaign, Ill.: Human Kinetics Publishers, 1995.

Williams, K. *The Aquatic Facility Operator Manual.* Hoffman Estates, Ill.: National Recreation & Park Association, National Aquatic Section, 1992.

YMCA of the USA. *On the Guard II: The YMCA Lifeguard Manual,* 2d ed. Chicago: YMCA of the USA, 1994.

———. *YMCA Exercise Instructor Manual.* Chicago: YMCA of the USA, 1995.

———. *YMCA Pool Operations Manual,* 2d ed. Chicago: YMCA of the USA, 1994.

Case Study

The Pleasantville Country Club has decided to add a fitness center, based on numerous member requests, feedback on annual member surveys, and the recommendation of the long-range planning committee. The club's membership has approved the addition of the fitness center and the financing of it through an assessment over the next three years. The club's board of directors, membership, and management are excited about the addition of the fitness center.

The club's aquatics committee would be responsible for managing the fitness center. The committee chairperson has been the driving force behind the development of the plan to add the fitness center and has been instrumental in gaining the approval of the board and the membership. This individual has been a club member for ten years and a board member for four years; he has two more years to serve on the board and has expressed an interest in running for board president next year.

The chairperson has given a lot of credit for his ideas on the fitness center to a friend of his who is an avid exerciser, a former star-athlete in high school and college, and a former semiprofessional baseball player. The friend has a degree in business and is a salesperson at a local sporting-goods store. He has never worked in a club or at a fitness center. The chairperson has indicated to the club's general manager that his friend would be an ideal candidate for the new fitness director position at the club. The chairperson is aggressively promoting this idea to other board members and the club's staff.

Discussion Question

1. Should the club's general manager hire the chairperson's friend as the fitness director for the club's new fitness center? Why or why not?

Chapter Appendix A

American College of Sports Medicine (ACSM) Certification Requirements: Health and Fitness Track

The ACSM certification program includes six professional certifications: three in the clinical track and three in the health and fitness track. The association's goal with its certification program is to increase the competence of individuals involved in preventive and rehabilitative exercise programs and increase the public's acceptance of the criteria required for professional competence in exercise and fitness.

ACSM certification is earned by professionals who have met specific prerequisites and successfully passed both a written examination testing knowledge and a practical exam measuring skill mastery. Each certified person is reviewed every four years and must provide evidence of continuing education to ensure his or her ongoing competence.

The three Health and Fitness Track Certifications acknowledge progressive levels of competence in working with apparently healthy individuals who have no histories of disease or have controlled diseases. They include:

- ACSM Health/Fitness Director

- ACSM Health/Fitness Instructor

- ACSM Exercise Leader

ACSM Health/Fitness Director. The Health/Fitness Director is the highest level of certification for professionals working in a health/fitness program for apparently healthy individuals who have no histories of disease or have controlled diseases. A successful candidate for Health/Fitness Director must demonstrate administrative, supervisory, practical, and theoretical competence for developing and managing preventive exercise and health enhancement programs. In addition, a Health/Fitness Director must successfully meet the following criteria:

- Documentation of a minimum of 800 hours of supervisory experience in a health/fitness program for apparently healthy individuals

- Successful completion of the written and practical examinations for the ACSM Health/Fitness Instructor, ACSM Program Director, or ACSM Exercise Specialist

- A post-baccalaureate degree in an allied health field, or the equivalent

- Current cardiopulmonary resuscitation (CPR) certification

ACSM Health/Fitness Instructor. The Health/Fitness Instructor certification recognizes professionals who have demonstrated the knowledge, skills, and competence required to lead exercise and health enhancement programs for apparently healthy individuals. In addition, a Health/Fitness Instructor must meet the following criteria:

- Demonstration of an adequate knowledge of health-appraisal techniques, risk-factor identification, submaximal exercise testing results, or field physical performance to properly recommend an exercise program

- A baccalaureate degree in an allied health field, or the equivalent
- A demonstrated understanding of appropriate techniques for promoting lifestyle changes, including motivation, counseling, teaching, and behavior modification.
- A knowledge of basic exercise science, including exercise physiology, kinesiology, functional anatomy, nutrition, and cardiorespiratory fitness
- Current cardiopulmonary resuscitation (CPR) certification

ACSM Exercise Leader. The Exercise Leader certification recognizes experienced professionals who have demonstrated the knowledge and performance-competence necessary to lead safe, effective, and enjoyable exercise programs. An ACSM Exercise Leader must meet the following criteria:

- A high level of knowledge and competence in proper leadership of safe, effective exercise programs
- A basic knowledge of exercise science, including kinesiology, functional anatomy, exercise physiology, nutrition, health appraisal techniques, and injury prevention
- Current cardiopulmonary resuscitation (CPR) certification

Source: ACSM's pamphlet on certifications and guidelines.

Chapter Appendix B

Sample USPTA Job Description: Club Tennis Director

General Duties

1. Supervise all tennis play, as directed by the tennis committee.

2. Supervise proper charging of court fees and other privilege fees.

3. Supervise the rental of club/facility equipment and the maintenance thereof.

4. Provide competent tennis instruction for all groups and levels of players.

5. Supervise the operation of a player-rating system such as the National Tennis Rating Program (NTRP), as directed by the tennis committee.

6. Supervise personnel such as assistant professionals, shop personnel, maintenance staff, etc., in the performance of their duties. The division of the employment of such personnel will be determined in the contractual arrangement.

7. Enforce all the club's rules and regulations governing the use of the club/facility, its equipment, and other property.

8. Operate and maintain a reputable pro shop staffed with competent personnel and featuring quality merchandise and services.

9. Maintain close relationships with the other club professionals (golf, swimming, etc.).

10. Devote a reasonable number of hours to playing tennis with members regardless of their tennis excellence; such play is not considered a playing lesson.

11. Plan tennis evenings to promote tennis and fellowship in the club/facility. Prepare tennis clinics, films, fun playing events or tennis education programs, etc., for such evenings. Enthusiastically promote tennis.

12. Represent the club/facility in professional tennis activities, including meetings of the national and/or local division of USPTA and in tournaments such as Pro-Ams with members, as well as state or national tennis events as time permits, but only with the approval of the club's/facility's tennis committee.

Specific Duties (Where Applicable)

Tournaments:

1. Meet with the tournament committee chairperson and event chairperson for the purpose of preparing and planning the details of tennis events in writing.

2. Secure adequate support personnel for various aspects of tournament events (publicity, umpires, etc.).

3. Coordinate match schedules with the referee and/or activities director.

4. Ensure all facilities are ready for events.

5. Secure draw sheets, scorecards, and other such items necessary for tournaments.

6. Prepare and distribute event information sheets (entry blanks) to participants.

7. Coordinate with the club/facility on the use of other departmental amenities by participants (food, etc.).

8. Be available for rules, decisions, and other necessary coordination throughout the event.

9. Prepare post-tournament reports with all the details of the events for the tennis committee.

Programs:

1. Ensure programs are in place at the club/facility to service the entire membership (Juniors, Adults, Seniors, etc.).

2. Organize periodic special events at the club/facility in an effort to attract/hold members' tennis interests.

3. Provide beginning through advanced instruction to enhance broad-based member participation.

4. Provide educational opportunities for the entire membership so they can understand and enjoy tennis more.

5. Provide guidance to the tennis committee for the proper programming of the club/facility based on the number of courts, personnel, and funds necessary for operational management.

6. Help in the preparation of an annual calendar of tennis activities for the club/facility.

7. If required, assist club/facility officials with the preparation of an annual budget for the responsible operation of the tennis facilities.

Maintenance:

1. Inspect the courts/facilities on a daily basis prior to the start of play and ascertain that all necessary maintenance has been performed.

2. Be certain that personnel necessary for the maintenance of the club/facility are hired and knowledgeable.

3. Make certain that the equipment necessary for the maintenance of the club/facility is on hand and properly maintained.

4. Keep the tennis committee informed on the status of the club/facility and equipment for the purpose of budgeting for replacement items and repair services.

5. Ascertain that all areas of the tennis club/facility are neat and clean at all times.

Tennis Pro Shop Operations:

1. Maintain the pro shop in a clean and presentable condition.

2. Maintain the hours of operation of the pro shop agreed upon by management and the tennis committee.

3. Maintain tennis merchandise at a reasonable level commensurate with members' needs.

4. Provide necessary coordination with the club/facility accounting system to assure a smooth billing operation.

Source: United States Professional Tennis Association, *How to Hire a Tennis Professional* (Houston, Texas: USPTA, 1993), pp. 12–13.

Sample USPTA Employment Agreement: Club Tennis Director

THIS AGREEMENT, entered into at _____ this _____ day of _____, 19____, by and between _____ hereinafter referred to as "CLUB," and _____ hereinafter referred to as "PROFESSIONAL."

    WHEREAS, the CLUB is desirous of engaging the services of the PROFESSIONAL, and,

    WHEREAS, the PROFESSIONAL is desirous of undertaking the duties of the Professional of the CLUB,

    NOW, THEREFORE, the parties, in consideration of the mutual covenants and agreements herein contained, agree as follows:

I. Term

The CLUB hereby engages the services of the PROFESSIONAL as its CLUB Professional for the tennis facility operated by it at _____ for a term of _____ years, commencing _____, 19____, and ending _____, 19____, which shall be the term of this agreement.

    (Once the Club is clearly satisfied that it has the right person, a multiple-year contract (3–5 years) should be offered. This provides the Professional with the confidence and security to appropriately stock the tennis shop and make longer-term program plans.)

II. Duties of the Professional

A. The PROFESSIONAL shall devote his/her time, attention, and energies to the performance of duties as Tennis Professional at the CLUB during the term of this Agreement. He/she shall conduct him- or herself at all times and in all matters in accordance with the standards accepted for Tennis Professionals and established by USPTA.

B. In cooperation with the Chairperson of the Tennis Committee, the PROFESSIONAL shall conduct all tennis tournaments and shall initiate and promote tennis activities for members and guests.

C. The PROFESSIONAL shall cooperate with members of the CLUB, guests, and the Chairperson of the Tennis Committee, and render professional advice, opinions, assistance, and services as required.

D. The PROFESSIONAL shall maintain a credit rating with suppliers and manufacturers and others so as not to discredit the reputation or name of the CLUB.

E. The PROFESSIONAL shall supervise, direct, and train a staff of employees, including Assistant Professionals, so as to perform duties and meet requirements for sales, rentals, and services that are, in the opinion of the CLUB and the PROFESSIONAL, necessary.

F. The PROFESSIONAL shall operate and maintain a tennis shop for repairs, handling, storage, sales, and services related to tennis equipment/accessories.

G. The PROFESSIONAL will cooperate and work closely with the CLUB Manager and other CLUB Professionals.

H. The PROFESSIONAL agrees to be available to attend the regular and special meetings of the Board of Directors/Tennis Committee and to discuss areas both within the realm of the PROFESSIONAL'S duties and those for the benefit of the CLUB.

(USPTA recommends that the Tennis Professional sit as a member of the Professional Management Team in all Board/Committee meetings where operations of the Club or facility are discussed.)

III. Duties of the Club

The CLUB agrees:

A. To act as an agent for the PROFESSIONAL in collecting and distributing to the PROFESSIONAL all charges made by him/her to members and guests and others, in all relating matters set forth herein, including sales, services, rentals, and concessions. Said charges shall be paid to the PROFESSIONAL not later than the 10th of the month following submission of charges by the PROFESSIONAL to the CLUB, and payment of said amount to be guaranteed by the CLUB.

B. To be responsible for the salaries of the tennis shop personnel, maintenance staff, and others employed by the CLUB and supervised and directed by the PROFESSIONAL.

    (It is important that the contract delineate which employees are paid by the Club and which by the Professional. To determine this, it may be helpful to establish whom they are primarily serving, the Professional or the Club.)

C. To encourage all tournament administrators, CLUB members, and CLUB committees to purchase prize requirements from the Tennis Pro Shop.

D. To pay annual membership dues to USPTA on behalf of the PROFESSIONAL.

E. To provide hospitalization coverage for the PROFESSIONAL.

F. To provide life-insurance coverage for the PROFESSIONAL.

G. To include the PROFESSIONAL in any pension plan or similar plans for CLUB employees.

H. To provide meals for the PROFESSIONAL and assistants during all hours that they are required by their employment to be on the CLUB premises.

I. To provide membership privileges for the PROFESSIONAL and his/her family.

J. To name the PROFESSIONAL as an additional insured on the CLUB'S liability policies.

K. To furnish the PROFESSIONAL for his/her use and sole occupancy all necessary facilities, properly maintained, for the operation of his/her business as set forth herein, including but not limited to areas on the CLUB premises for the tennis shop operation, tennis club services, business office, all including proper furnishings, fixtures, floor coverings, and utilities.

L. To furnish facilities to store, house, and maintain all tennis equipment necessary to the facility.

M. To furnish and maintain both a practice court and teaching courts as necessary for the PROFESSIONAL to conduct his/her lessons as well as those of his/her assistant teachers.

IV. Compensation

In addition to other remuneration herein indicated to be received by the PROFESSIONAL, under Paragraph V., Concessions, the PROFESSIONAL shall be paid for his/her services the sum of _____ Dollars ($_____) for each annual period payable in 12 equal monthly installments commencing the _____ day of _____, 19_____. In each succeeding year of this Agreement this sum will be adjusted to reflect the change in the cost of living based upon the previous year's index. During the term of this Agreement, the PROFESSIONAL shall be under the supervision of and directly responsible to (title) _____.

If the relationship between the CLUB and the PROFESSIONAL with respect to the employment referred to in this Section shall be that of employer and employee, the CLUB shall pay all Social Security Benefits and Unemployment Compensation Taxes, both Federal and State, which are required of the employer with respect to such employment.

(A salary or retainer is the Club's payment to the Professional for his/her expertise in tennis, the development of a program of events, promotion of the Club and the game, and management of a total tennis operation. It should be representative of his/her ability and the importance of his/her duties. Once the initial figure is established, it should take into consideration, on an annual basis, the cost of living and any changes in his/her responsibilities. Traditionally, the Professional reports directly to his/her Tennis Chairperson. In cases where the Professional serves as the Pro/Manager or General Manager, he/she would report to the Board or Club President. The most important consideration is that the lines of reporting and communication are clearly defined.)

V. Concessions

In addition to performing the duties required under Paragraph II herein, the PROFESSIONAL shall perform the following duties, and shall retain all receipts for such services:

A. Sale of Merchandise. The PROFESSIONAL shall have the exclusive right to sell merchandise on the CLUB'S property with the obligation upon the PROFESSIONAL to maintain a proper stock to adequately serve the members. The

PROFESSIONAL shall set and post business hours for the Tennis Shop according to the season.

(Club officials should strongly encourage members to purchase their tennis equipment from their Professional—providing he/she has earned that loyalty. Club regulations generally limit the Professional from advertising for outside business to expand his/her market. If the tennis shop is a service to the members, they should support it.)

B. Tennis Instruction. The PROFESSIONAL and his/her staff shall have the exclusive right to give tennis lessons at the location of the CLUB. Charges for such lessons shall be fixed by the PROFESSIONAL.

(The established charge should reflect the Professional's reputation and experience plus a comparison of hourly charges for services in similar professions.)

C. Other.

1. The PROFESSIONAL shall have the exclusive right to have a Ball Machine Service for the practice enjoyment of the members and their guests. Said Ball Machines shall be provided by the PROFESSIONAL, and all revenues realized from their rental shall be returned to the PROFESSIONAL.

2. The PROFESSIONAL shall supervise all tennis activities in connection with outside parties and shall provide the guests with adequate services, including rental rackets, etc., as may be required. The PROFESSIONAL shall be compensated by each guest for his/her time and expense at normal rates.

D. Annual Review. It is agreed that during the term of this contract all concessions, rates, and percentages are subject to an annual review.

VI. Vacations

Provided the PROFESSIONAL is not employed on a seasonal basis, he/she shall be entitled to time off during each week, exclusive of any tennis events. In addition, the PROFESSIONAL, if employed on a 12-month basis, shall receive three (3) weeks vacation during each annual period, for which compensation under Paragraph IV. shall be paid in full.

VII. Tournament Play and Meetings

The PROFESSIONAL shall have the right and is expected to represent the CLUB in various tennis competitions. He/she shall submit his/her tournament schedule (exclusive of events on his/her day off or during vacation) for approval by the Tennis Chairperson or Board of Directors. In the event that he/she qualifies, he/she shall have the right to play in the U.S. Open (or any other Grand Slam Championship), any USPTA National Championship event, or any Circuit event held locally. The PROFESSIONAL will also have reasonable time off, with compensation under Paragraph IV., to attend USPTA regional meetings and the USPTA National Convention.

VIII. Termination

This Agreement will terminate upon the happening of any of the following events:

A. Upon its normal termination if not renewed.

B. Upon the death of the PROFESSIONAL.

C. Upon the physical disability of the PROFESSIONAL. Said disability shall be such as will incapacitate the PROFESSIONAL for an aggregate of six months during the working period of this Agreement. After such period, the CLUB can elect to terminate this Agreement within 60 days after notice is delivered to the PROFESSIONAL.

D. Upon written notice by the CLUB of termination for good cause and sufficient cause. Such good and sufficient cause shall include, but not be limited to, the following:

   1. Dishonesty detrimental to the best interests of the CLUB.

   2. Continuing inattention to or negligence of duties.

   3. Suspension from USPTA for more than 30 days.

   4. Serious illegal or immoral conduct.

In the event of termination of this Agreement, the PROFESSIONAL shall be paid his/her compensation to and including the month of death or, in the event of disability, shall be paid to the last day of a month in which termination occurs.

In the event of the termination of this Agreement by death, disability, or by the CLUB other than for good and sufficient cause prior to the normal termination date, the PROFESSIONAL or his/her representative may elect to have the CLUB purchase all merchandise at the PROFESSIONAL'S cost less depreciation, as set forth under standard accounting practices, and to pay the same to the PROFESSIONAL or his/her representative within 30 days of the date of the notice of such election.

The PROFESSIONAL or his/her representative shall be responsible for all outstanding debts of the PROFESSIONAL.

IX. Breach

A. In the event that either party claims that the other is guilty of a substantial breach of any of the provisions of this Agreement, a conference will be called between the parties and every reasonable effort shall be made to reach an amicable solution. At said conference, either party shall be entitled to have representatives present.

B. Either party shall have 30 days within which to correct any activity or conduct claimed by the other to have constituted a substantial breach of the Agreement.

C. In the event that either party notifies the other in writing within said 30-day period of their denial of said substantial breach, then in such event the dispute shall be submitted for arbitration under and pursuant to the rules of the American Arbitration Association.

D. In the event that either party shall, within said 30-day period, fail to correct the activity claimed to constitute a substantial breach of this Agreement, or to notify the other party in writing of their denial of said substantial breach of this Agreement, then in such event this Agreement shall cease and terminate as of the expiration of said 30-day period.

X. Arbitration

Any controversy or claim arising out of or relating to this Agreement shall be settled by arbitration in accordance with the rules of the American Arbitration Association, and judgment upon the award rendered in such arbitration may be entered in any court having jurisdiction thereof; however, arbitrators shall not determine damages where liquidated damages under Paragraph XVII are applicable.

XI. Notice

Any notice required or permitted to be given under this Agreement shall be sufficient if in writing and sent by registered or certified mail, in the case of the PROFESSIONAL to his/her residence, and in the case of the CLUB to its principal office.

XII. Construction

This agreement shall be controlled by the laws of the state in which it is drawn.

XIII. Severability

The invalidity or unenforceability of any provision hereof shall in no way affect the validity or enforceability of any other provision.

XIV. Waiver

Failure to insist upon strict compliance with any terms, covenants, or conditions of the Agreement shall not be deemed a waiver of such, nor shall any waiver or relinquishment of such right or power at any time be taken to be a waiver of any other breach.

XV. Waiver or Modification

Any waiver, alteration, or modification of any of the provisions of the Agreement, or cancellation or replacement of this Agreement, shall not be valid unless in writing and signed by the parties.

XVI. Benefit and Assignment

This agreement shall inure to the benefit of and bind the parties hereto and their respective legal representatives, successors, heirs, personal representatives, and assigns.

XVII. Liquidated Damages

In the event the PROFESSIONAL is discharged prior to the normal expiration of this Agreement for reasons other than death, disability, or for good and sufficient cause, the CLUB shall pay the PROFESSIONAL the salary for the remainder of the term, plus an amount to cover anticipated profits to be derived from all other sources contemplated in this Agreement and arrived at as follows:

A. Using the PROFESSIONAL'S latest Federal Income Tax Return, a total of net income from all other sources will be divided by 12 and multiplied by the number of months remaining in the term.

B. The amount arrived at shall be construed as liquidated damages and shall be paid by the CLUB to the PROFESSIONAL within 30 days of the termination of employment.

C. Payment and acceptance of this amount shall be in lieu of any other claim the parties may have against the other.

XVIII. Relationship Between Parties

The PROFESSIONAL is retained and employed by the CLUB only for the purpose and to the extent set forth in this Agreement. He/she shall be free to dispose of such other portion of his/her time, energy, and skill as does not interfere with his/her obligation to the CLUB.

XIX. Non-Breach

Termination of the Agreement as herein set forth by reason of death or disability of the PROFESSIONAL, or termination without good and sufficient cause, shall not be deemed a breach of this Agreement by the PROFESSIONAL.

XX. Renewal

This Agreement will automatically renew itself for the same period as referred to herein unless written notice to the contrary is given by either of the parties hereto at least 90 days prior to the termination date of the Agreement. Renegotiation should commence 180 days prior to normal termination.

XXI. Entire Agreement

This Agreement contains the entire agreement between the parties.

IN WITNESS WHEREOF, the parties hereto have executed this Agreement on the date first above written.

(CLUB)	(DATE)

(PROFESSIONAL)	(DATE)

Chapter Appendix C

USPTA's Tennis Professional Classifications

There are certain rights and privileges that go with USPTA membership. Some of these rights and privileges are limited to specific classifications. When considering hiring a USPTA professional, it is important to be aware of his/her member classification.

Based on successful completion of USPTA's extensive certification examination, applicants are placed in one of three classifications. These classifications—*Professional 1, Professional 2,* and *Professional 3*—represent overall performance on the certification examination. These are the primary classifications for teachers in the Association and should not be confused with other categories of membership in which a certification exam was not necessary.

In addition to the three teaching categories above, there is one elite teaching category—the *Master Professional.* Master Professionals must previously have been Professional 1 certified and have performed considerable industry service in order to earn this distinguished membership level.

The basic requirements for each USPTA membership classification are:

Master Professional—A USPTA Master Professional has completed all qualifications required of the highest teaching category—Professional 1—for at least ten years, in addition to fulfilling a broad spectrum of industry service requirements. In addition, Master Professionals are required to fulfill a certain number of specialty courses to maintain their status in this category.

Professional 1—A Professional 1 must be at least 22 years of age, must have three full years or five summers of teaching experience, and must pass the on-court and written tests for the Professional 1 rating. In addition, a Professional 1 is required to submit a sequence of references—personal, employment, and financial—prior to being certified.

Professional 2—A Professional 2 must be at least 18 years of age, must demonstrate teaching ability through either an apprenticeship or previous experience, and must pass the on-court and written tests for a Professional 2 rating. Professional 2s must also submit the required personal, employment, and financial references prior to being certified.

Professional 3—A Professional 3 must be at least 18 years of age, must pass the on-court and written tests for a Professional 3 rating, and must upgrade their certification within 36 months. Failure to do so results in the individual being placed in the inactive membership category. Professional 3-rated members are not required to submit credit references or employment references.

Affiliate Member—The Affiliate Membership category provides for companies or persons who do not teach tennis, but who have a full-time commitment to tennis in an executive, administrative, or commercial capacity, to be associated with USPTA. Affiliate members are entitled to most privileges and obligations of active membership but may not vote, hold office, or play in USPTA National Tournaments and are not covered by USPTA's on-court liability insurance policy.

Club Member—The Club Membership category is open to all public and private tennis facilities. Member Clubs are entitled to most privileges and obligations of active membership but may not vote or hold office, nor are they enrolled in USPTA's on-court liability insurance program. Club Members must be listed in the club's name only and membership is not transferable.

Honorary Member—The Honorary Membership category is open only to persons who, as voted on by the USPTA Executive Committee, have made an outstanding national or international contribution to the sport of tennis or to USPTA. Honorary Members who were previously active members are entitled to all privileges and obligations of active membership (except they do not pay yearly dues).

Inactive Member—A provisional category for teaching members who have failed to meet continuing certification or education requirements. Upon fulfillment of all ongoing requirements, the inactive member will be reinstated as active.

Retired Member—A retired member must be 65 and must no longer teach on a full- or part-time basis. These members are exempt from the continuing education requirements and are charged one-half the usual dues.

Source: United States Professional Tennis Association, *How to Hire a Tennis Professional* (Houston, Texas: USPTA, 1993), p. 35.

REVIEW QUIZ

When you feel you have covered all of the material in this chapter, answer these questions. Choose the *best* answer.

1. A fitness floor, exercise classrooms, sports areas, and spa areas are found in a club's:

   a. weight-training area.
   b. aquatics area.
   c. fitness center.
   d. tennis facility.

2. Clubs typically charge their members a user fee for which of the following fitness-center activities or services?

   a. massages
   b. personal trainers
   c. sports camps
   d. all of the above

3. The sanitizer that most clubs use for their swimming pools is:

   a. chlorine.
   b. calcium.
   c. cyanuric acid.
   d. oxygenated sodium.

4. Which of the following statements about tennis courts and tennis-court maintenance is *true?*

   a. Most soft-surface tennis courts in the United States are grass courts, not clay.
   b. Hard-surface courts are preferred by most tennis players.
   c. Soft-surface tennis courts are more difficult to maintain than hard-surface tennis courts.
   d. a and c.

Answer Key: 1-c-C1, 2-d-C3, 3-a-C5, 4-c-C7

Each question is linked to a competency. Competencies are listed on the first page of the chapter. An answer reading 3-b-C4 translates to:

3: the question number
b: the correct answer
C4: the competency number

Appendix
Club Entertainment

This appendix was written and contributed by Rhonda J. Montgomery, Associate Professor, and Kathy Nelson, Lecturer, William F. Harrah College of Hotel Administration, University of Nevada-Las Vegas, Las Vegas, Nevada.

PRIVATE CLUBS are places where club members gather for social and recreational purposes. Therefore, the entertainment of members, whether it be through sporting activities, parties, or educational opportunities, is of primary concern to club general managers and their staffs. In fact, it could be said that a general manager and his or her staff are the entertainment brokers for their club's membership. They provide not only the facilities but also the professional staff and expertise to meet a variety of entertainment needs.

Providing outstanding entertainment opportunities for members should be at the heart of a private club's mission, because a successful entertainment program will:

- Increase member participation in the club

- Increase member satisfaction with the club

- Add perceived value to a club membership

- Improve the financial position of the club (if the entertainment is budgeted and managed correctly)

The following types of entertainment are typically planned at a club:

- Sports-related entertainment, such as golf or tennis tournaments, and parties associated with sporting events (victory banquets, for example) that are usually planned by a club's golf or tennis pro and the club's sports committees.

- Parties and other social events planned by the club's general manager and entertainment committee. (At clubs that do not have an entertainment committee, entertainment duties are carried out by the club's social or house committee.) These events are placed on the club's yearly entertainment calendar and include holiday parties, dances, and so on.

- Parties planned by club members to celebrate personal occasions such as birthdays, anniversaries, or retirements.

In this appendix, we will focus on the parties and other events that are part of the club's entertainment calendar and are planned by the club's general manager and entertainment committee; more specifically, we will discuss how to look for and book entertainers for special events held at the club.

Club special events are often built around holidays.
Source: *The Lakewooder: Lakewood Country Club News,* Dallas, Texas.

Determining the Entertainment Needs of Club Members

A club's general manager should make an effort to find out what club members really want in the way of entertainment. If a club is already using member-needs assessment tools such as comment cards, surveys, and focus group questionnaires, the manager can add a section about entertainment to these already existing tools and gather feedback about what types of entertainment members want.

The club's entertainment committee can also help the general manager understand the entertainment needs of members. Members of the entertainment committee represent the general membership and are often creative, resourceful, and hard-working. They bring to the committee their own ideas about what types of entertainment would be well-received at the club, but they also listen to ideas and suggestions from other club members. While the entertainment committee can be

This country club planned a theme party around the television broadcast of the Academy Awards ceremony. (Courtesy of Sally Burns Rambo, CCM, and the Lakewood Country Club, Dallas, Texas)

one of the most challenging club committees to serve on, it also has great potential for providing committee members with a strong sense of fulfillment. Few things are as satisfying as throwing good parties for friends, and that is essentially what a club's entertainment committee does (or helps others at the club do).

Special Event Entertainment

Club special events are opportunities for members to come to their club and have fun. The goal of most clubs is to have a number of special events throughout the year that will entice members to come to the club more often than they might otherwise. Increased member attendance usually translates into increased club revenues, and increased revenues help a club attain its financial goals.

Special events that typically are part of a private club's entertainment calendar include the following:

- Holiday parties (New Year's, Memorial Day, Fourth of July, Labor Day, Halloween, and Christmas)
- Easter egg hunts and other parties for the children of members
- Parties planned around special days—St. Patrick's Day, Valentine's Day, etc.
- Nostalgia parties—examples include Big Band Era, Fabulous Fifties, Return to the Sixties, and Disco Daze (1970s)
- Theme parties

Theme parties can provide club members with some of their most treasured club memories. A theme party is simply a party planned around a central theme or

Clubs often put on special events with a nostalgic theme.
Source: *The Lakewooder: Lakewood Country Club News*, Dallas, Texas.

idea. A theme party could be built around Hollywood's annual Academy Awards ceremony, for example. Or, theme parties might be inspired by a club's geographic location. For example, clubs in the Southwest might have theme parties for Cinco de Mayo (the celebration of Mexico's victory over the French on May 5, 1861); clubs in Kentucky might have "Derby Days" parties planned around the Kentucky Derby. Theme parties can inspire the club's staff to pull out all the stops and really be creative. They are excellent opportunities for the club's general manager to engage all of the club's staff in the planning process. Some clubs award prizes (money, days off, gifts from the pro shop, and so on) to employees who contribute good theme party ideas.

Funds for special events are set aside in the annual budgets of most clubs. The amount of money earmarked for special events may be a recommendation of the club's entertainment committee as part of the normal budgeting process at the club. Club general managers must be sure that the budgets for special events include all applicable expenses, ranging from entertainment to decorations to publicity.

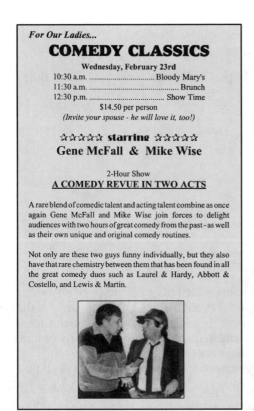

For Our Ladies...

COMEDY CLASSICS

Wednesday, February 23rd

10:30 a.m. .... Bloody Mary's
11:30 a.m. .... Brunch
12:30 p.m. .... Show Time

$14.50 per person
(Invite your spouse - he will love it, too!)

☆☆☆☆☆ **starring** ☆☆☆☆☆

Gene McFall & Mike Wise

2-Hour Show
A COMEDY REVUE IN TWO ACTS

A rare blend of comedic talent and acting talent combine as once again Gene McFall and Mike Wise join forces to delight audiences with two hours of great comedy from the past - as well as their own unique and original comedy routines.

Not only are these two guys funny individually, but they also have that rare chemistry between them that has been found in all the great comedy duos such as Laurel & Hardy, Abbott & Costello, and Lewis & Martin.

Children's Christmas Party Entertainment

Best Texas Entertainer for Families:

TIE: Eddie Coker and Barney.
Eddie Coker now has two albums of kid's music to his credit and is now tied for best Texas entertainer with last year's winner, Barney. How do you tell the two apart, since both are from the Dallas area, both sing and both inspire great loyalty in their fans? Easy! Barney is the prehistoric purple-and-green dinosaur. Runners-up: Joe Scruggs, Mr. Peppermint. *And: Gifts for all Children!*

Eddie Coker

Also...

A Puppet Show

Stringbini   **Old Santa**

And

Gifts for all Children!

Singers and bands are not the only types of entertainers who perform at clubs.
Source: *The Lakewooder: Lakewood Country Club News,* Dallas, Texas.

Types of Entertainers for Special Events

Entertainers who perform at club special events include singers (from opera to rap), bands (rock, country-western, easy-listening, big-band-era, oldies, and so on), comics, fortune tellers, dancers (from belly to ballet), acrobats, escape artists, magicians, mimes, hypnotists, clowns, illusionists, marching bands, puppeteers, ventriloquists—the list could go on and on.

Selecting the Right Entertainment

Sometimes the entertainment committee will know what entertainer it wants for a particular special event. Sometimes it is a club tradition to have a certain entertainer perform at a certain event (a popular local band might always play at the President's Ball, for example). However, at other times the committee might only have a general idea of what type of entertainment it wants, or may not even have it narrowed down that far. At such times the committee looks to the club's general manager for guidance and suggestions.

If it is up to the club's general manager to suggest an entertainer or entertainment act for a special event, the manager should first have answers to the following questions:

1. What is the purpose of the event?

2. Who are the participants? The answer to this question should include:

   - The ages of the participants (all ages? children included? teens only? seniors only? etc.)

   - Participants' general backgrounds

   - Gender (all men? all women? mixed?)

   - Musical likes and dislikes

   - Reasons for attending

3. What is the date of the event?

4. How long will the entertainers be needed? (An hour? two hours? all evening?)

5. How much space is available?

6. Are there any other activities included in the special event?

General managers should develop a standard list of questions to be answered when selecting entertainment for a club special event. Although the majority of the questions will be the same for each event, there should also be a section on the questionnaire to allow the general manager to write in questions addressing any unique elements or requirements a particular special event might have.

When selecting special event entertainment, club general managers should keep the following guidelines in mind:

1. Never buy only according to your personal taste. Many club members might enjoy an entertainer or type of entertainment you don't care for, and vice versa.

2. Choose musicians who play music that fits the demographics of the expected attendees of the event.

3. Choose entertainers or entertainment acts with an image that fits your club.

4. Consider booking "event bands"; they may be more expensive, but they can get things going and create a fun environment for your members.

5. Choose acts that will work with you—in other words, acts that are flexible regarding set-up, volume, size of equipment, and so on.

6. Choose "self-contained" acts (that is, acts that take care of everything—set-up, break down, and so on); they are usually a better value.

7. When you purchase entertainment, keep in mind that it is the entertainment value you should be buying, not the number of bodies on stage. In other words, club members probably will be more impressed and happy with a small act featuring two people who are truly entertaining than an extravaganza featuring 50 people who aren't.

Talent Agencies. One of the things a club general manager must decide when looking for special event entertainment is whether to look for entertainment on his or her own or use a talent agency.

Insider Insights

Cathy Gustafson, CCM
Professor, University of South Carolina
Former General Manager of The Faculty House of Carolina,
Columbia, South Carolina

"Entertainment" can be defined as anything over and above what a club member comes to expect. It might be giving roses to women who come to the club on Valentine's Day, for example. Entertainment covers a wide range of activities. Entertainment can be interactive for members, such as a gaming night, or passive, such as listening to live music during dinner.

Most clubs have a house committee that oversees club entertainment as part of its duties; some large clubs have an entertainment or social committee set up just for entertainment. Whichever committee is in charge of entertainment, it is the committee's job to create member enthusiasm and be the driving force behind the special events held at the club. Committee members should represent a cross-section of the membership. Ideally, you should have some older, some younger, some retired, and some professional members on the committee. The committee either generates or (more typically) approves the general manager's ideas for special events. Especially at clubs where the general manager has been employed for many years, the committee usually merely reviews and approves a detailed calendar of club special events that the general manager puts together. Over time, the manager learns what types of events the members enjoy and support.

As a club manager, you want your members to feel that their club membership is a valuable asset. Special events are very visible ways a club can demonstrate to members that their membership is valuable. They couldn't participate in these events if they were not a member. It builds a cohesive group.

A significant amount of a club's budget is set aside to offset the costs of special events. Members usually pay something to attend, but such fees rarely cover the event's cost. A special-event fee is usually well below market value, sometimes half the cost. In addition, there are usually a few special events that are completely complimentary to members.

Special events encourage members to visit the club. It's been shown that once you get members accustomed to using the club, they'll choose to use it more often. If you can't get them to use it, they won't form the habit and eventually they'll cease to see the value of their membership.

As alluded to earlier, a club's general manager is usually the one who comes up with ideas for special events and develops a special-events calendar. He or she sets criteria for the event, determines how formal or elaborate it will be, and what time the event will be held. A seasoned general manager usually will map everything out so that all the committee has to do is approve the plans. When there's a new general manager, the committee will take more leadership in planning special events.

Once an event's theme is developed, the manager should book the event's entertainment. General managers should never book entertainers until they've seen them perform; this is true whether the entertainment is a band, a musician, a

(continued)

Insider Insights *(continued)*

strolling artist, Santa in costume, a balloon artist, whomever. The entertainer's brochures and glossy photos can't tell you whether the entertainer is a good fit for your membership. If you have a conservative membership, an entertainer can't be too casual or tell inappropriate jokes.

The amount of time entertainers need to set up and break down their equipment, props, and so on should be stated in their contract with the club. A general manager must know this information in order to properly schedule an event. The manager also needs to know the entertainer's equipment and electrical needs; these needs may exceed what's available at the club.

It's great if clubs can appeal to both children and adults at the same special event. Clowns, face painters, and balloon-animal makers are usually hits with children. If you can keep the kids happy, you keep the parents happy, too. Some special events are planned especially for a single age group. For example, some clubs have teen nights in which teens can come to the club unchaperoned.

There's a fun element to planning entertainment. One club had a fifties prom night for parents on the night of the high school prom. There was a classic fifties car out front, all sorts of fifties memorabilia, and members came dressed in poodle skirts, leather jackets, and other appropriate fifties attire.

Where do general managers get ideas for special events? Talking to other club managers is one of the best ways. Also, the Club Managers Association of America's annual Idea Fair has a special-event/theme-party section that many clubs submit entries to. There are many unique ideas there that club managers can take back to their clubs.

Talent agencies seek jobs for entertainers. The booking or talent agents who work at these agencies are brokers between entertainment buyers (in this case, a club) and sellers (the entertainers or "talent"). Successful booking agents earn the respect and confidence of buyers and sellers alike.

There are two types of talent agencies. Regional talent agencies represent talent within a relatively small geographic area. National talent agencies such as William Morris represent talent from across the country. (National agencies may have regional offices to better serve local buyers.) Agencies earn their money by collecting commissions from the entertainers or acts they book. For example, the standard commission for booking bands that perform in clubs on a weekly basis is 15 percent. When an entertainer or entertainment act signs an exclusive agreement with an agency, the entertainer or act must pay the agency a commission on any job worked. Talent agencies are regulated by state laws.

The following are some of the advantages of working with a talent agency:

- The agency acts as a liaison between the club and the entertainer.

- One source can provide the club with many performers.

- The agency will have promotional materials on its entertainers (video- and audiotapes, biographies, press write-ups, publicity pictures, and so on) available for review.

Standards/Suggested Rules for Bands and Other Music Performers

Performance time—The standard in the entertainment industry is for a band to perform for 45 minutes and then take a break.

Break time—The standard break time in the entertainment industry is 15 minutes; for every 45 minutes of playing time, the band is entitled to a 15-minute break. A band sitting on stage playing "chaser music" (providing music while speakers are placed on or removed from the stage, for example) is still considered to be working.

Set-up time—Insist that the band set up at a time that is convenient for the club. However, make sure you have arranged the special event's production schedule to allow for the band to set up at the agreed-upon time.

Beverages—Clubs can set guidelines for beverages consumed by musicians while performing. For example, a club can stipulate that no alcoholic beverages be consumed. But the club must provide beverages of some type for the performers (coffee, tea, sodas, juices, and so on) and should clearly define the methods by which the band members receive the beverages, to prevent misunderstandings or abuses.

Food—Clubs should provide food for the band. Generally, clubs provide a cheese and sandwich tray or similar food items backstage.

Smoking—Band members should follow the club's smoking guidelines.

Crew—Crew members should remain in the backstage area when not performing duties. Crew members must adhere to all rules set for the band.

Entourage—Depending on the club's rules, a band's entourage may or may not be permitted to accompany band members to the club. If members of an entourage are permitted, the club should ask that they remain in the backstage area and adhere to all rules set for the band.

Security—Make sure the club's security department has been alerted about the band. Give security a copy of the special event's production schedule and a list of all band and crew members.

Parking—Advise parking attendants and band members where the band's vehicles should be parked.

Loading/unloading—Advise security, parking attendants, and band members where to park band vehicles for loading or unloading.

- The agency will be familiar with the acts it represents and should be able to help general managers select only those acts that are appropriate for their clubs.

- If an entertainer becomes ill prior to an event, the agency should be able to provide a replacement.

- If an act is on tour, the agency may be able to offer the club a reduced price if the club can book the act while it is in the club's area. (This only works if the club can be flexible about dates.)

The biggest disadvantage of booking entertainment through a talent agency is that an agency can only sell the acts contractually bound to it. This limits the club's entertainment choices.

Event Producers. Club managers may also use an event producer to book entertainment. An event producer is an individual or company that provides everything needed for an event except food, beverages, and service staff. For example, if a private club wanted to do a theme party centered on Broadway shows, the event producer would provide the staging, lights, sound, costumes, and decor as well as the star impersonators, comics, and dancers needed to transform a club's ballroom into a Broadway production stage. (See Exhibit 1 for a sample contract between an event producer and a talent agency.)

There are many advantages to using an event producer. Event producers:

- Provide one-stop shopping for all event needs.

- Can produce custom shows to suit specific themes.

- Do not represent specific entertainers and therefore can shop around for the best entertainers for an event.

- Usually carry $1 million worth of liability insurance.

The biggest disadvantage to using event producers is that they can be costly.

Besides talent agencies and event producers, other sources for special event music and entertainment for clubs include the following:

- American Federation of Musicians (a union for musicians)

- Bars, nightclubs, restaurants, and taverns

- Club members (as entertainers or as leads to find entertainers)

- Fraternal organizations

- Local theater groups

- Local colleges and universities

- Local churches

- Local dance conservatories

- Ads in special events magazines

Auditioning and Interviewing. Unless a club general manager already knows about the entertainer (either because the entertainer is well-known or is a local entertainer whom the general manager has seen perform before), a general manager should audition (either in person or by videotape) or at least interview an entertainer before booking him or her. There is too much at stake to take a chance on an unknown quantity. The manager should always request to see the entertainer's promotional packet as well. A promotional packet usually includes some or all of the following:

- Photos

- Biography

- Press write-ups

- Videotapes

- Audiotapes

- Letters of recommendation

Exhibit 1   Sample Contract Between an Event Producer and a Talent Agency

CAA
COUNTRY ARTISTS AGENCY, INC.
NASHVILLE, TN
(555) 123-4567

AGREEMENT made this _____ day of __[month], [year]__ between __"Name" Country Artist__ hereinafter referred to as "PRODUCER," and Dan Nelson Productions hereinafter referred to as "PURCHASER."

It is mutually agreed upon between the parties as follows: The PURCHASER hereby engages the PRODUCER and the PRODUCER hereby agrees to furnish the entertainment presentation hereinafter described, upon all the terms and conditions herein set forth:

1. Name and Address of Place of Engagement: Old Fashioned Hoedown at the ABC Club

2. Date(s), Starting and Finishing Time of Engagement: Thursday, August 20, 19XX—Show starts at 6:30 p.m. and ends at 9:00 p.m.—Artist to perform one complete show.

3. Type of Engagement: Open Air Concert—No Admission Fee

4. Additional Provisions: Artist to receive 100% Top Headline Billing and close show. Purchaser to provide and pay for first class sound and lights per Artist specifications. Purchaser to provide and pay for support talent, subject to Artist's approval. Artist to be paid in full in event of inclement weather. Purchaser to pay and provide for backline equipment, local ground transportation, and 12 hotel rooms for 2 days.

5. Compensation Agreed Upon: $20,000.00 FLAT GUARANTEE.

6. Purchaser Will Make Payments As Follows: All payments shall be paid by Certified Check, Money Order, Bank Draft, or Cash.
   DEPOSITS: $10,000.00 shall be paid by PURCHASER to COUNTRY ARTISTS AGENCY, INC., as agents, not later than July 20, 19XX.
   BALANCE of Guarantee to be paid in United States Currency by Purchaser to Artist not later than End of the performance, evening of engagement.
   All payments shall be made in full without any deductions whatsoever.

7. Riders Attached Hereto Are Hereby Made a Part Hereof.

8. If Artist is Headlining this Engagement: "All Support Talent is Subject to Artist's Approval."

9. If Artist is Supporting this Engagement: "Artist's Performance is Subject to the Appearance and Approval of The Headliner."

10. No performance on the engagement shall be recorded, reproduced, or transmitted from the place of performance, in any manner or by any means whatsoever, in the absence of a specific written agreement.

11. The agreement of the musicians to perform is subject to proven detention by sickness, accidents, riots, strikes, epidemics, acts of God, or any other legitimate conditions beyond their control.

"Name" Artist _____ (PRODUCER)
By
Dan Nelson Productions _____ (PURCHASER)
By
Address: 1234 Street Name
          City, State 12345
Phone: (555) 987-6543

Source: Dan Nelson Productions, Las Vegas, Nevada.

Down Sally's Alley

My, my, where has the year gone? It's Christmas time again—what a wonderful time of year! For the past few years we have won an award for the best decorated building in East Dallas. Members come and bring guests just to show off the club. If you haven't done this, you should; it is always beautiful. We start decorating right after Thanksgiving and the decorations are complete by December 1st for you to enjoy. I love Christmas. It's a fun time of year.

The Halloween puppet show was a big success and so was the haunted house. I had lots of phone calls thanking us for the party.

We are doing something very special for New Year's Eve! All you "achy-breaky hearts," bring yourselves to Lakewood for a country-western Christmas party in the Men's Card Room—we are turning the Card Room into a big barn dance with country Christmas decorations, a big dance floor, and a great band called "Broken Spoke." This will be a kicker!

In the Ladies' Card Room we will have a piano bar where you can sing Christmas carols, eat, drink, and make merry. Larry Armer will play. Last year some members stayed till 3:30 A.M. in this room.

Then, in the big ballroom we will have Jack Melick and his Big Band playing ballroom music as only he can play.

We will have country hors d'oeuvres in the Men's Card Room, snacks in the Ladies' Card Room, and hors d'oeuvres in the Garden Room. You can mix and mingle all over the club and share in all the fun!

The 55-Senior party was the best ever. Everyone seemed to enjoy Ed Burnett and the Levee Singers. That was my surprise for them. The Quintet Band from Paris is always great. We had a dancing bunch. Even the weather did not dampen the fun for the 220 who attended.

I sure hope the Lakewood Golf Association members turn out big for their Christmas dance on December 9th. Where else can you go for such a small price? We should have at least 200. Last year we had only 91. The food and music are always great. Make your reservations early so we will know how to plan. I am going to plan on a big crowd.

Be sure to call in your child's reservation for the Christmas party. It is going to be very special this year. We must have your reservation by Wednesday, December 14th, in order for your child to receive a gift. The gifts are expensive and I try to buy just what we need, but I do not want any child to leave without one. So please call.

This new year brings increases in taxes and insurance, so we are going to need your support more than ever before. We, the staff, try to make your every visit to the club a pleasant one. We all put a lot into each party to ensure its success. We also like to have activities that please all age groups. But to be able to do that, you, the members, must participate.

I want to thank all the employees who helped make this a better club this year. They care about you, the members, and I appreciate that.

Keep well.

Sally

The general manager devoted her letter in this month's club newsletter to discussing and promoting special events at the club.
Source: Adapted from *The Lakewooder: Lakewood Country Club News*, Dallas, Texas.

Once an entertainer is booked, his or her photos, biography, and press write-ups might be used in the club's promotional pieces for the special event.

General managers considering booking an entertainer should see him or her actually perform in front of an audience whenever possible, ideally in a club setting. General managers should also ask entertainers for references from other clubs where they have performed and should call the managers of those clubs to get their impressions. A general manager should ask these managers not only how entertaining the performers were, but also about the performers' set-up and break-down practices and their treatment of club facilities. For example, did they respect club property or did they "trash" their dressing rooms?

Entertainment Contract Negotiations. Once an entertainer is chosen, the club must sign a contract with him or her. If the general manager doesn't know much about contracts, he or she should ask the club's legal counsel to review all entertainment contracts before anyone signs them.

The following basic information should be covered in any entertainment contract:

- Club's name and address
- Name of the entertainer or entertainment act
- Number of performers
- Type of act: band, magician, dancers, etc.
- Transportation and lodging expenses (if the entertainer or act is from out of town)
- Room name where the entertainment will take place (if applicable); for example, in the club's Trophy Room
- Performance time (date, time, and length of performance—for example, "on June 10, 19XX, from 8:00 P.M. to 11:00 P.M."
- Set-up time
- Pre-event rehearsal time on-site (if applicable)
- Payment procedures and overtime policies
- Deposits (a 50 percent deposit is usually required to book an entertainer)
- Balance due at the end of the performance
- Cancellation clause
- Indemnification clause (ideally, the entertainer or act should carry at least $1 million liability insurance; many independent acts don't have this but event producers usually do)
- Hold-harmless clause
- Rider requirements
- Set-up specifications

Clubs that book "name" entertainment (any entertainer or act that is well-known) should pay very close attention to the rider attached to the contract. A rider is an attachment to the main contract agreement that lists additional terms and conditions. A rider usually includes support elements that are important to the entertainer, such as sound, stage, and lighting requirements. It also includes all backstage amenities for the entertainer. These can get very specific and somewhat strange. For example, one rock band insists that its backstage M&M candy be free of brown M&Ms; another entertainer requires at least one World Wrestling Federation

Well-known entertainers often perform at clubs. The cover of this club's newsletter promotes a special event using a photo from the entertainer's promotional packet.
Source: *The Lakewooder: Lakewood Country Club News*, Dallas, Texas.

action figure in his dressing room. Entertainers say that they include these types of requests in their riders as an easy way for them to make sure that the purchaser has read every line of the contract.

It is important to note that an act's rider requirements can sometimes cost more than the performance fee itself. Club general managers must keep this in mind when selecting entertainment, especially name entertainment. When a booking agent quotes a price for name entertainment, it is a "performance price" and does not include the cost of the rider requirements. Therefore, a club should have the booking agent or entertainer (if independent) fax over a copy of the rider, and someone at the club should cost out the rider requirements before the club makes a formal offer.

When negotiating the contract fee, clubs may be able to barter something in exchange for part of the fee, depending on the club's facilities (and the club's bylaws and rules). Entertainers may be willing to reduce their fees in exchange for golf, tennis, or dining privileges at the club, for example. Entertainers may also be willing to perform for a reduced rate if the club books them for multiple events or refers them to club members and others who are planning special events.

Although musician unions used to be a fairly important part of negotiating an entertainment contract, they are no longer a consideration in most parts of the country. The musicians who are most likely to use American Federation of Musicians (AFM) contracts are musicians who play for symphony orchestras. To be on the safe side, however, club managers should check on the strength of the AFM in their area before booking musicians.

Clubs should also be careful about the set-up specifications of an entertainment contract. If a club has a "tight turn" in a room (not much time between the end of one event and the start of the next), it will run into trouble if the entertainer it booked for the first event takes a long time to tear down, or the entertainer it booked for the second event takes a long time to set up. Club general managers should be sure to have the entertainer provide a production schedule, in chronological order, in the contract. (See Exhibit 2 for a sample production schedule drawn up by an event producer.)

Payment Procedures. As mentioned earlier, entertainers usually require a 50 percent deposit when their contracts are signed. If a club books a band or an entertainer frequently, the deposit may be smaller or waived entirely. The balance of the contract fee should be paid on the night of the event. Traveling entertainers, even name performers, usually want the balance paid in cash.

Licensing

Clubs must be careful about licensing issues when using music. Copyrighted music should not be performed or broadcast in public without the permission of the copyright owner. A "public performance of music" is defined as music played for third parties by almost any means, including compact discs, cassettes, records, videos, live musicians, telephone music-on-hold, jukeboxes, and radio or television music played over a commercial system.

Under U.S. copyright law, protected material can be used only after permission is obtained from the copyright owner. In the case of copyrighted music, the permission is customarily given by the granting of a license. Music licensing agencies such as the American Society of Composers, Authors & Publishers (ASCAP) and Broadcast Music, Inc. (BMI) collect performance royalties from people who use music in a public setting, then pass the royalties on to the composers, songwriters, lyricists, and music publishers of the songs that are used. ASCAP and BMI also distribute awards, lobby Congress, sue infringers, and promote music scholarships. As businesses that often have recorded or live music for special events, clubs should obtain license agreements with music licensing agencies. Clubs can contact ASCAP at One

Exhibit 2   Sample Production Schedule

Dan Nelson Productions
Production Schedule
Downtown Hoedown

Date	Start	Activity/Venue	Persons	Stop	Notes
8/20	7:00 A.M.	Hay Bales Delivered	Kevin Gibbs	7:30 A.M.	Horse n' Around Contact: Jean 555-1859
	7:15 A.M.	Power Drops from Golden Nugget Horseshoe Las Vegas Club	Terry Cornett	9:00 A.M.	
	7:30 A.M.	Pick-Up Fire Extinguishers	Kristy Hadden	7:45 A.M.	Contact: Robin 555-1546
	9:00 A.M.	Pick Up RV	Bob Naugle	10:00 A.M.	Sahara RV Contact: Felicia 555-7039
	10:00 A.M.	Sound Load In Both Stages	Terry Cornett Kevin Gibbs	12:00 P.M.	Enterprise West Contact: Chris 555-2632
	12:30 A.M.	Blue Roan Load In Stage 2	Terry Cornett Kevin Gibbs	1:30 P.M.	Contact: Jason Lugo
	1:45 P.M.	"Name" Country Artist Load In Stage 2	Terry Cornett 4 Labor Crew	3:00 P.M.	Contact: Tee Sands
	1:45 P.M.	Celia Lawley Load In Stage 1	Kevin Gibbs	2:30 P.M.	Contact: Celia Lawley
	2:30 P.M.	Sound Check Celia Lawley Stage 1	Kevin Gibbs	3:00 P.M.	Contact: Celia Lawley
	3:00 P.M.	Sound Check "Name" Artist Stage 2	Terry Cornett	4:30 P.M.	Contact: Tee Sands
	3:15 P.M.	Inflatables Load In	Kristy Hadden	4:00 P.M.	Contact: Steph Purdy 555-1221
	4:00 P.M.	Set-Up Concession Area at Barn	Kevin Gibbs	5:00 P.M.	Contact: Esther Carter
	4:30 P.M.	Blue Roan Sound Check	Kristy Hadden	5:00 P.M.	Contact: Jason Lugo
	5:20 P.M.	Channel 8 Live Remote Mark Allen	Kristy Hadden	5:30 P.M.	Contact: Kevin Janison
	5:30 P.M.	Don and Waddie Sound Check	Terry Cornett	6:00 P.M.	Contact: Kathy Edwards
	6:15 P.M.	Places Everyone			
	6:30 P.M.	Event		9:00 P.M.	See Event Schedule
	9:15 P.M.	Tear Down/Load Out	Terry Cornett Kevin Gibbs Kristy Hadden	12:00 A.M.	

Source: Dan Nelson Productions, Las Vegas, Nevada.

Lincoln Plaza, New York, New York 10023 or via the Internet at http://www.ascap.com; BMI's Licensing Department can be contacted at 10 Music Square East, Nashville, Tennessee 37203 or via the Internet at http://www.bmi.com.

The official sponsor or organizer of a special event at the club is the entity or person responsible for obtaining the music license. Even if the general manager or club is not the official sponsor or organizer of a party (for example, in the case of a retirement party at the club put on by a club member), the club's general manager should still check to make sure that the member has a license, or that the club's music license(s) will "cover" the member's party.

Exhibit 3   Sample Member-Event Worksheet

Event:	
Member:	
Telephone:	Date:
Location:	Time:
# of Attendees:	Theme:
Entertainment:	
Lights:	
Sound:	
Decor:	
Insurance:	
Comments:	

Club Members Who Book Their Own Entertainment

When club members want to plan their own club parties and book the entertainment for the parties themselves, the club's general manager can provide them with a member-event worksheet to help them gather basic information helpful in planning the event (see Exhibit 3 for a sample member-event worksheet that clubs can adapt to their needs). A member-event worksheet could also be incorporated into the club's existing banquet event order form.

Club managers should also provide a written set of guidelines to club members planning their own entertainment. Such guidelines might include the following:

- You are welcome to consult with the club's entertainment committee and general manager concerning entertainment acts, booking agents, event producers, and themes that have worked well for the club in the past.

- Feel free to talk with entertainment committee members and the general manager about challenges they have faced when booking entertainment; it may save you time and grief.

- Be sure to *preview* the entertainer or act.

- Have the general manager review the contract you have with your entertainer *before* you sign it.

- Check with the general manager to make sure that the club's liability coverage and music licenses transfer to you.

- Ask the general manager about in-house supplies that you might be able to use at your event, such as centerpieces, lighting systems, sound systems, etc.

- Please clear all props, centerpieces, staging, and so on with the general manager to ensure that they meet all of the club's fire codes and other safety requirements.

Nontraditional Entertainment Options and Services

In an attempt to provide members with the ultimate in club services and amenities, many clubs are pushing the envelope in the area of special events and entertainment. Some of the types of nontraditional entertainment options and services being offered at private clubs include the following:

- *Concierge services.* Some private clubs now provide their members with a service similar to the concierge service offered by hotels—that is, the club will book tickets to shows, plays, sporting events, and other events for members. This allows club members to make all of the arrangements for a special evening with one phone call to the club. For example, a member might call the club, make reservations for dinner at the club on some future date, and request tickets for a play on the same date. When the day arrives, the member and his or her party can have dinner at the club, pick up the tickets after dinner or have them delivered to their table, and go on to the play from the club.

- *Speakers/forums.* More and more clubs are sponsoring speaker or lecture series and training workshops at the club that club members can attend for an additional fee. These entertainment options have been very well-received by club members.

- *Travel/tour groups.* Many clubs now make travel arrangements for their members for club-organized tours or trips. A number of clubs in the Southeast organize trips to New York City to experience Broadway and shopping during the Christmas season, for example, while other clubs have sponsored more exotic trips, such as African safaris.

Index